War and Society in East Central Europe
Vol. VI

Essays on World War I:
Total War and Peacemaking,
A Case Study on Trianon

Béla K. Király, Peter Pastor, and Ivan Sanders,
Editors

Social Science Monographs, Brooklyn College Press
Distributed by Columbia University Press, New York

1982

EAST EUROPEAN MONOGRAPHS, NO. CV

ATLANTIC STUDIES

Brooklyn College Studies on Society in Change
No. 15

A Joint Publication With
Committee For Danubian Research, Inc.

In Memory of
IMRE KOVÁCS
(1913–1980)
Writer and Statesman

Acknowledgement

Brooklyn College Program on Society in Change conducts research, organizes conferences and publishes scholarly books. The Program has been commissioned, encouraged and supported by Dr. Robert L. Hess, the President of Brooklyn College. The National Endowment for the Humanities awarded the Program a research grant for the years of 1978–1981, which was renewed for another three-year term (1981–1984). The Committee for Danubian Research, Inc., Washington, D.C., granted the bulk of the production cost of this volume. The conferences were also partially funded by the Joint Committee on Eastern Europe of the American Council of Learned Societies and the Social Science Research Council and the International Research and Exchanges Board.

The work of Professor Peter Pastor, one of the editors, was greatly facilitated by the release time granted by his institution, Montclair State College of New Jersey.

Professor Batkay of Montclair State College of New Jersey translated from the Hungarian original the essay of Magda Ádám; Dr. Mario Fenyo of New York City translated from the Hungarian original the essays of Maria Ormos, Zsuzsa L. Nagy and Károly Vigh. The maps and chart were prepared by our cartographer, Ida E. Romann.

The preparation of the manuscript for publication was done by Mrs. Dorothy Meyerson and Mr. Jonathan A. Chanis, both on the staff of Brooklyn College Program on Society in Change.

For all these institutions and personalities, I wish to express my most sincere appreciation and thanks.

Highland Lakes, New Jersey, October 23, 1982.

Béla K. Király
Professor of History
Editor-in-Chief

Preface to the Series

The present volume is the sixth of a series which, when completed, hopes to present a comprehensive survey of the many aspects of War and Society in East Central Europe. The chapters of this, the previous, and forthcoming volumes are selected from papers presented at a series of international, interdisciplinary, scholarly conferences. Some were solicited for the sake of comprehension.

These volumes deal with the peoples whose homelands lie between the Germans to the west, the Russians to the east and north, and the Mediterranean and Adriatic seas to the south. They constitute a particular civilization, an integral part of Europe, yet substantially different from the West. Within the area there are intriguing variations in language, religion, and government; so, too, are there differences in concepts of national defense, of the characters of the armed forces, and of the ways of waging war. Study of this complex subject demands a multidisciplinary approach; therefore, we have involved scholars from several disciplines, from universities and other scholarly institutions of the USA, Canada, and Western Europe, as well as the East Central European socialist countries.

Our investigation focuses on a comparative survey of military behavior and organization in these various nations and ethnic groups to see what is peculiar to them, what has been socially and culturally determined, and what in their conduct of war was due to circumstance. Besides making a historical survey, we try to define different patterns of military behavior, including the decision-making processes, the attitudes and actions of diverse social classes, and the restraints or lack of them shown in war.

We endeavor to present considerable material on the effects of social, economic, political, and technological changes, and of changes in the sciences and in international relations on the development of doctrines of national defense and practices in military organization, command, strategy, and tactics. We shall also present data on the social origins and mobility of the officer corps and the rank and file, on the differences between the officer corps of the various services, and above all, on the civil-military relationship and the origins of the East Central European brand of militarism. These studies will, we hope, result in a better understanding of the societies, governments, and politics of East Central Europe, most of whose states are now members of the Warsaw Treaty Organization, although one is a member of NATO and two are neutral.

Our methodology takes into account that in the last three decades the study of war and national defense systems has moved away from narrow concern with battles, campaigns, and leaders and has come to concern itself with the evolution of the entire society. In fact, the interdependence of changes in society and changes in warfare, and the proposition that military institutions closely reflect the character of the society of which they are a part have come to be accepted by historians, political scientists, sociologists, philosophers, and other students of war and national defense. Recognition of this fact constitutes one of the keystones of our approach to the subject.

Works in Western languages adequately cover the diplomatic, political, intellectual, social, and economic histories of these peoples and this area. In contrast, few substantial studies of their national defense systems have yet appeared in Western languages. Similarly, though some substantial, comprehensive accounts of the nonmilitary aspects of the history of the whole region have been published in the West, nothing has yet appeared in any Western language about the national defense systems of the area as a whole. Nor is there any study of the mutual effects of the concepts and practices of national defense in East Central Europe. Thus, this comprehensive study on War and Society in East Central Europe is a pioneering work.

The Editor-in-Chief, of course, has the duty of assuring the comprehensive coverage, cohesion, internal balance, and scholarly standards of the series he has launched. He cheerfully accepts this responsibility and intends this work to be neither a justification nor a condemnation of the policies, attitudes, or activities of any of the nations involved. At the same time, because so many different disciplines, languages, interpretations, and schools of thought are represented, the policy in this and in future volumes was and shall be not to interfere with the contributions of the various participants, but to present them as a sampling of the schools of thought and the standards of scholarship in the many countries to which the contributors belong.

The Editor-in-Chief

Introduction

With the Peace Treaty of Trianon on June 4, 1920, World War I for Hungary was officially over. The Treaty also ushered in a new age for the successor states of the defunct Austro-Hungarian Empire. The changes legitimized by the Trianon treaty were as momentous for the peoples of East Central Europe as were the changes of the Treaty of Versailles for the Western Europeans.

The treaty of Versailles and its consequences have been the subject of innumerable studies in the English language; the effects of the Treaty of Trianon on the other hand have been examined in only one scholarly monograph, Francis Deak's, which was published some forty years ago. We felt there was a genuine gap here, so in 1980, on the sixtieth anniversary of the Treaty, we decided to publish a collection of essays which would deal with the process of peacemaking and with the causes and consequences of this momentous treaty.

Our aim was not to write a new history of the Peace Treaty, but to complement and update the older analyses with new evidence and interpretations which are often based on recently opened archives and/or on recent publications. To facilitate this endeavor, we held a University Symposium on November 12, 1980, where we discussed the most important aspects of the Treaty and solicited additional contributions from experts. Our aim was to make this book as comprehensive as possible, thus a degree of repetitiveness became unavoidable. It was also necessary to give a chance for scholars with opposing viewpoints to treat the same evidence differently. It may even appear, at times, that one contributor's interpretation and conclusion undermine those offered by another. But this is one more reason why we felt that a reexamination of the different aspects of a still controversial subject is more than justified. At no time did we, the editors, attempt to interfere with the contributors' views and interpretations. The contents of the book will, we hope, attest to this. Trianon was a controversial act; present-day evaluations of it are also bound to be that. Calling the readers' attention to these controversies was the fundamental goal of the editors.

Béla K. Király, Peter Pastor, Ivan Sanders

Contents

Acknowledgement v
Preface to the Series vii
Introduction ix

Part I
Overview

R. W. Seton-Watson and the Trianon Settlement 3
 Hugh Seton-Watson
Total War and Peacemaking 15
 Béla K. Király
Hungary's Road to Trianon:
 Peacemaking and Propaganda 23
 Stephen Borsody
The Consequences of World War I:
 The Effects on East Central Europe 39
 Stephen D. Kertész
The Causes and Consequences of Trianon:
 A Re-Examination 59
 Károly Vigh
The Economic Problems of the Danube Region After
 the Breakup of the Austro-Hungarian Monarchy 89
 Iván T. Berend and György Ránki

Part II
Hungary and the Great Powers
in the Process of Peacemaking

Great Britain and the Making of the
 Treaty of Trianon 107
 Thomas L. Sakmyster

The Hungarian Soviet Republic and
   Intervention by the Entente   131
   Mária Ormos
France and Hungary at the Beginning of the 1920's   145
   Magda Ádám
France and Hungary in 1920: Revisionism and Railways   183
   Anne Orde
Italian National Interests and Hungary in 1918–19   201
Zsuzsa L. Nagy
American Peace Plans and the Shaping
   of Hungary's Post-World War I Borders   227
   Sandor Taraszovics

Part III
Hungary and Its Neighbors
in the Process of Peacemaking

Hungarian Territorial Losses During the
   Liberal-Democratic Revolution of 1918–1919   255
   Peter Pastor
The Czechoslovak-Hungarian Dispute   275
   Josef Kalvoda
The Baranya Republic and the Treaty of Trianon   297
   Leslie C. Tihany
The Sopron (Ödenburg) Plebiscite of December 1921
   and the German Nationality Problem   321
   Thomas Spira

Part IV
The Settlement and Its Repercussions

Post-Trianon Searching: The Early Career
   of László Németh   347
   Ivan Sanders
Trianon in Interwar Hungarian Historiography   361
   Stephen Bela Vardy
Trianon and the Emigré Intellectuals   391
   Lee Congdon

CONTENTS

Trianon in Transylvanian Hungarian Literature:
Sándor Reményik's "Végvári Poems"   407
Agnes Huszar Vardy
Trianon and Romania   423
Stephen Fischer-Galati
The Treaty of Trianon and Czechoslovakia:
Reflections   439
Yeshayahu Jelinek
The Impact of Trianon on the Jews of Hungary   457
Thomas Karfunkel
Trianon and the Problem of National Minorities   479
Edward Chaszar
Partition of Hungary and the Origins
of the Refugee Problem   491
István I. Mócsy
Trianon: Cause or Effect—Hungarian Domestic
Politics in the 1920's   509
William Batkay
The Economic Consequences of Trianon   529
Paul Jonas

Part V
Sixty Years After

The Forgotten Legacy of the League of
Nations Minority Protection System   547
Frank Koszorus, Jr.
Hungarian Minorities and Minority Boundary
Maintenance in Burgenland   573
Michael Sozan
The Hungarians of Transylvania   597
Andrew Ludanyi
A Contemporary Analysis of Trianon's Aftermath:
Gyula Illyés' Spirit and Violence   627
Károly Nagy
Trianon Two Generations After   639
George Schöpflin

Biographical Index   647
Gazetteer   667
List of Maps and Charts   671
List of Contributors   677

Part I

Overview

(See maps at the end of the book)

Hugh Seton-Watson

R. W. Seton-Watson and the Trianon Settlement

The following is a provisional estimate of the attitude of R. W. Seton-Watson to the Treaty of Trianon. This is of course a part of his general relationship to Hungary, and it is necessary in this article to refer from time to time to that wider background.

Seton-Watson completed his studies of History in Oxford in 1902, and a year later, on the death of his father, inherited an income which relieved him from any immediate need to enter a regular profession, thus enabling him for some years to devote himself to the study of European history and contemporary politics. After two and a half years in Germany, France and Italy—mainly in Berlin and Paris—he came to Austria-Hungary at the end of 1905.

At that time he was very favorably disposed both to the Monarchy and to Hungary. His view of the Monarchy was based on respect for the Habsburg dynasty and its historical achievement, as well as on sympathy for a European state which had long been Britain's ally, and seemed by its very nature to be committed to the sort of European balance of power which it was then considered to be Britain's interest to support. In the Hungarians he saw a nation which had made great sacrifices for the cause of liberty, and also had traditional links with Britain. Hungarian liberalism, whose parliamentary style seemed to resemble the British, and Hungarian Calvinism, which had much in common with the Presbyterian culture of his native Scotland, attracted him. He arrived in Vienna when the conflict between the Hungarians and the Habsburg dynasty was at its height, and he came to Budapest at the time of the 1906 election which gave a big majority to the nationalist Coalition. Seton-Watson's sympathies were thus divided.

After some weeks in Budapest he travelled for some weeks more in the provinces. It was in Transylvania, where he met first Saxon and then Romanian spokesmen, that he first realized the acuteness of the "nationality question." It became clear to him that there was a three-cornered struggle between Vienna, Budapest and the Nationalities.

He would have liked to see all three reconciled with each other. In particular, he hoped that agreement between Hungarians and Nationalities would make possible pressure on Vienna to institute more liberal government. As it became clear to him that this was not possible—and his second journey to Hungary in 1907, to the Slovak regions, Ruthenia and Budapest, confirmed this belief—then his hopes were placed on the alternative of joint pressure by Vienna and the Nationalities on Budapest. This combination was associated with hopes of reforms by the heir to the throne, Archduke Franz Ferdinand, when he should succeed the old emperor. These hopes were most forcibly expressed to Seton-Watson by Milan Hodža, the Slovak Agrarian, and Alexandru Vaida-Voevod, the Romanian nationalist leader. However, this combination also was disappointed: the Archduke was kept waiting, and Vienna antagonized at least three of the nationalities—Croats, Serbs and Czechs—no less than Budapest antagonized the others. One may in fact argue that the persistent conflict between all three elements—Crown, Hungarian leadership and Nationalities—in the end destroyed the Monarchy.

Seton-Watson's most active period of concern with Hungarian problems was in the years 1906–1908, culminating in the publication of his book *Racial Problems in Hungary* in the latter year. In the remaining years before 1914 he became more and more absorbed by Croatian and Serbian affairs, on which he published *The South Slav Question and the Habsburg Monarchy* in 1911 (enlarged German edition 1913). In these problems the role of Hungary was much smaller than that of Vienna, in which the leaders of the growing Yugoslav Movement saw their principal enemy. In 1910 there was an interlude, when Seton-Watson once more concentrated on Hungarian affairs. This was his study of the Hungarian parliamentary election of that year, which he personally witnessed in Szakolka (Skalice). His short book *Corruption and Reform in Hungary* appeared in 1911.

It is difficult to reconstruct precisely Seton-Watson's political hopes in relation to Hungary on the eve of the Great War. The notion of "Trialism," which would have replaced the Dualism of 1867 by adding a third unit, consisting of all the South Slav provinces,[1] attracted him; but of course it would not have solved the nationality problems of Hungary. He continued to have hopes of Franz Ferdinand. Even after his assassination, in the brief period before the outbreak of war, he believed in the maintenance of the Monarchy.[2]

Probably his hope was that combined pressure from a new emperor and from the Magyar and non-Magyar peoples of Hungary would compel the introduction of universal suffrage in Hungary; and that not only the consequent enormous increase of non-Magyar representation, but also the entry of new democratic and socialist Magyar forces into the Budapest parliament would make possible farreaching reforms. Certainly he had hopes of Oszkár Jászi and of the Hungarian socialists, and in this was encouraged by Hodža, who considered that the land-hungry Magyar peasants were natural friends of the Slovaks.

This is the best estimate I can make. Understandably, as he was concerned with day-to-day problems, as well as with the impending appearance of a new international periodical, to be edited by him, entitled European Review,[3] he had neither time nor inclination to record his overall view of Hungarian political prospects in the summer of 1914. What is certain is that, at this time, he had no expectation, or indeed desire, that either Slovakia or Transylvania would be removed from Hungary. He never referred in his correspondence of this period, to a new Czech-Slovak unit to be formed within the Monarchy; and as for Transylvania, not only did he himself not advocate incorporation into Romania, but he had good reason to believe that statesmen in the Romanian Kingdom, though desiring it in general terms, were opposed in practice because the consequent weakening of Austria-Hungary would strengthen Russia, and make Romania unhealthily dependent on the Russian Empire.[4]

* * *

All this changed when war broke out in Europe, and the Monarchy became the enemy of Britain. Seton-Watson regarded Austria's declaration of war on Serbia as proof that the Monarchy had abandoned its role as a major independent factor in the European balance of power, and had become an instrument of Pan-German expansionism, in which he considered the Hungarian ruling class to be willing accomplices. He therefore assumed that Entente victory must bring large-scale losses of territory to the Monarchy; and later, convinced by T. G. Masaryk's arguments for an independent Bohemia to include the Slovak lands, he became an advocate of the complete dissolution of the Monarchy.

In a letter of 6 August 1914 from London to his wife, we find the

words: "Dalmatia, Bosnia, Croatia, Istria must be united to Serbia
. . . Romania must have all her kinsmen."[5]

During the first half of the war, Seton-Watson had no official
status, but was a sort of unofficial adviser to the British Foreign Office (with which he had had no connection at all until that time). In
1917 and 1918 he was in official employment, first in the Department
of Information Intelligence Bureau (DIIB) under the War Cabinet,
and then in the Enemy Propaganda Department, headed by Lord
Northcliffe. His correspondence and papers show that his main concern was with Yugoslav affairs, affecting policy to both the enemy
state Austria and the allied state Italy, and to a lesser extent with the
Czechoslovak movement headed in exile by Masaryk and Beneš.
Hungarian problems played a smaller part, except in relation to
Romania. The Slovak lands, which were politically quiet in these
years, feature less. His weekly reports to DIIB on Austria-Hungary
mention political events in Hungary, but they are less prominent
than the affairs of the Cisleithanian Slav territories.

Seton-Watson visited Serbia and Romania in January and
February 1915, with the encouragement of Sir Edward Grey. In
Bucharest his main aim was to persuade the Romanians to come to
the aid of Serbia. In an interview with the daily paper *Adeverul* he
declared: "What Prussian militarism is for us, Magyar hegemony is
for you: these are the principal obstacles to European progress. We
together with our French and Russian allies must fight the German
danger; but you with the Serbs must put an end to the brutal and artificial domination of the Magyar race over all its neighbors."

He was thus bitterly hostile to the dominant policies, and the
dominant political leadership, of Hungary. At the same time,
however, he was against excessive expansion by neighboring states
at the expense of Hungary.

On 4 January 1915 he had a long conversation after dinner with
Crown Prince Alexander in his HQ at Kragujevac. Alexander's map
showed the borders which it was hoped to attain, and which included the annexation not only of all Bácska but also of the cities and
districts of Nagykanizsa and Pécs. Seton-Watson argued that "if
there are to be tolerable relations between the new state and the new
Hungary, Serbian claims in Bačka must be very considerably reduced, if not altogether abandoned" and that "Pécs and all its district
are mainly Magyar and German, and must be left to Hungary under
all circumstances."[6]

As regards Romania, Seton-Watson was convinced that Transylvania and most of Banat must be ceded to Romania, but he did not accept the most extravagant claims of the Romanian government at the expense of Hungary. He was in no way involved in the diplomatic negotiations of 1916, but he learned the approximate terms of the treaty that was being prepared. On 21 July 1916 he wrote to his wife: "We seem—to my horror—to be promising them the Theiss frontier for immediate entry. That will put an end for ever to Magyar intrigues. Unhappily it will also make an independent Hungary almost impossible, and so might upset the whole balance further West."

In October 1916 Seton-Watson published the first issue of a weekly periodical, *The New Europe*, which lasted for four years, and in which he himself wrote many articles and small news items. He was allowed to continue this work after he became a government official, on condition that he ceased to be Editor and that his contributions were not signed with his name. At the end of the war, leaving government service, he resumed the formal editorship and signed his main articles again.

In the more than 200 issues of the periodical which appeared before it ceased publication in October 1920, Hungarian affairs are frequently discussed, and there is both general and detailed discussion of possible future frontiers. Seton-Watson assumed that Croatia, Banat, Transylvania, the Slovak and Ruthene provinces would be detached from Hungary, but was much less certain about Bácska. His principle was to make the frontiers coincide as far as possible with the ethnic distribution of the population, though certain cases were noted where injustice was inevitable for geographical reasons, by far the most important being the Székely territory.

*   *   *

Seton-Watson was not a member of the British delegation to the post-war Peace Conference; but he spent several months of the winter of 1918–1919 in Paris as a member of the office of *The Times* in close partnership with that paper's Foreign Editor, his old friend from Vienna and colleague in the Enemy Propaganda Department, Henry Wickham Steed. Seton-Watson and Steed were in constant contact with members of the British, American and, to a lesser extent, also the French delegations, as well as with Czechoslovak,

Romanian and Yugoslav representatives. Seton-Watson was respected as an expert on Austria-Hungary, and probably had a certain amount of influence on the general attitudes of the professional diplomats and specialists; but in the only case in which he and Steed made a strong and sustained effort to propose a solution of a difficult problem—the drawing of the frontier between Yugoslavia and Italy in Istria—they failed.

Seton-Watson detested the political climate of the Peace Conference. He was indignant that decisions were made not on the merits of each case but in accordance with the party interests or even personal whims of the leading Allied politicians. He expressed his feelings in *The New Europe* of 1 January 1920, in a review of the recently published and later widely famed work of John Maynard Keynes, *The Economic Consequences of the Peace*. Fully agreeing with Keynes's description of the atmosphere of the Conference, he wrote: "However long I may live, I hope I shall never breathe such an atmosphere again. The true Paris had been submerged by a wave of fetid intrigue, and a babel of small men in big positions surged round a few big men whom the strain of an unexampled crisis had made small and sterile."

His attitude to Hungary in these months was strongly influenced by the changes in its rulers. The presence of Oszkár Jászi in Michael Károlyi's government briefly awakened hopes of a better Hungary. (At this time, however, he regarded Károlyi himself with suspicion as a great landowner and a pre-1914 nationalist. It was only in the 1920's that he got to know Károlyi personally, and the two men became firm friends). However, the advent to power of Béla Kun aroused his worst fears. Seton-Watson shared the view, widespread at that time though subsequently shown to be unsound, that the Russian Bolsheviks were agents of Germany. He feared a resurgent unholy alliance of German and Hungarian militarism in co-ordination with Bolshevik revolution. The fact that Hungarian former officers supported Kun, in the belief that he would with Russian help maintain Hungary's territory, lent plausibility to these fears. His first visit to the new republic of Czechoslovakia, in May 1919, coincided with the successful Hungarian counter-offensive in Slovakia. After two weeks in Prague and two more in Slovakia, he returned to Paris to urge the allied authorities to give aid to the Czechoslovak forces.

Kun's replacement by the regime of Admiral Horthy gave Seton-Watson no satisfaction at all. As he saw it, the dangerous Bolshevik regime had been replaced by the old political class, and Hungary seemed likely to be a centre of reaction and chauvinism in the future too.

Undoubtedly these events tended to preserve Seton-Watson's effective political hostility. His hopes of democratic forces in Hungary appeared unreal; and though he recognized that there were avoidable injustices in the frontiers which were now proposed by the Peace Conference for Hungary, he felt no inclination to battle on behalf of Horthy's Hungary against his friends in the succession states. In a full discussion of the proposed frontiers in *The New Europe* of 15 January 1920, with population figures for each of the counties of old Hungary (excluding Croatia), he noted that the settlement was "unduly severe to the Magyars," especially in the region of Subotica (Szabadka); in the Grosse Schütt island; and in the region of the frontier with Romania, which "could undoubtedly be pushed further east in such a way as to leave considerable numbers of Magyars in Hungary, without sacrificing more than a few thousand Roumanians." However, it was at least gratifying that "the idea of ceding Miskolcz and the Salgotárján mines to Czechoslovakia, and Pécs (Fünfkirchen) with its no less important mining district to Jugoslavia, would seem to have been abandoned. Both would have been acts of crying and gratuitous injustice." The arguments used by the spokesmen of Horthy's regime, and of their sympathizers in Britain, in order to modify the frontiers, infuriated him. In *The New Europe* of 22 April 1920, he referred to the argument of Count Apponyi that the cultural superiority of the Hungarians over neighbor peoples was proved by their higher level of literacy and the scanty number of non-Magyars with a middle-school training. "Such an argument in such a mouth is nothing less than infamous, for it was Count Apponyi himself who, by his Education Acts of 1907, carried to their utmost limit those methods of Magyarisation of the schools, to which above all the backwardness of Roumanian and Slovak education was due."

*   *   *

Between the world wars, Seton-Watson's attitude to the Trianon settlement was consistent. He continued to be aware of its injustices. Some of these he considered irremovable (above all, the Székely situation). Others could be improved by frontier revision, to which he was not dogmatically opposed. However, he did not believe that the way to improve Hungary's relations with its neighbors was to begin with frontier revision, but rather that political conciliation should be the aim, and that if once the political climate were improved, then revision could be one of the matters to be discussed.

However, he remained profoundly distrustful of the Horthy regime. He was convinced that the Hungarian leader's aim was not mere frontier revision, but a restoration of the old borders, regardless of the national aspirations of the non-Magyars. And indeed the statements of Hungarian leaders were profoundly ambivalent. The fact that revision was supported by Mussolini and by Lord Rothermere made it seem even less desirable to him.

More urgent, he believed, was the effective implementation of the rights of the Hungarian minorities, as provided by the peace treaties. In 1928, in a visit to Slovakia, his main purpose was to study the situation of the Hungarian minority. He met a number of Hungarian representatives, and received a number of written statements from Hungarians, some of which remain in the papers in our possession. After his inquiries, he wrote a long memorandum for President Masaryk, of which a copy also went to Foreign Minister Beneš. There is a copy in the papers, together with a handwritten draft of a letter to Masaryk. There is no record of a reply from either of them; but this may be explained by the likelihood that they discussed it when they met in the following year.

He was also interested in the Hungarian minority in Romania, and on at least one occasion was able to intervene successfully on behalf of a Hungarian journalist. However, his opportunities were limited by the fact that his relations with the Liberal Party governments of the 1920's, dominated by the Brătianu family, were not good. Only when the National Peasants led by Maniu came to power in 1928 was there a better opportunity, and at that time the disputes about the return of King Carol II, and still more the onset of the world economic depression, drove Hungarian minority affairs into the background.

In Yugoslavia he was unable to do anything. In the 1920's the Serb-Croat conflicts absorbed almost all his attention. The dictatorship of King Alexander, introduced on 6 January 1929, developed in such a way that, in Seton-Watson's view, almost the whole population of Yugoslavia became victims of repression. If nothing could be done for the Croats, or even for the Serbs, it was hopeless to think of the Hungarians.

In 1930 Seton-Watson had a conversation in London with Count Stephen Bethlen, of which a few notes have survived in his papers. The most interesting point which emerged was Bethlen's insistence on a high priority for the improvement of relations with Romania. The advent to power of Maniu, for whom Bethlen expressed respect, seemed to hold out hopes. Seton-Watson was impressed by Bethlen's personality. They did not discuss revision of frontiers, on which they simply "agreed to differ."

The economic depression, the rise of Hitler to power, the ascendancy of Gömbös in Hungary, and the retreat of western statesmen before German and Italian claims, made frontier revision seem even less expedient to Seton-Watson. He argued against it in his short book *Treaty Revision and the Hungarian Frontiers*, published in 1934.

The cession of territory by Czechoslovakia to Hungary after the Munich agreement of 1938 was a source of deep disagreement between Seton-Watson and his younger colleague C. A. Macartney. These two had long known, respected and liked each other, and the differences between their views of the past and present of Central Europe were comparatively small. However, Macartney felt that, though Hitler's victory at Munich was bad, at least some good had come of it through the return to Hungary of territories with a mainly Magyar population; whereas Seton-Watson felt that Hitler was a deadly menace to all Europe, that any surrender to him was a disaster, and that any government which accepted favours from him was making itself his satellite and undermining its own national independence. Macartney put his view in an article in *The Times* shortly after Munich, and there followed a painful interchange of private letters between the two men.

During the Second World War Seton-Watson advocated the restoration of Czechoslovakia, Yugoslavia and Romania. In particular, he insisted in 1940 that Transylvania should be part of Romania. This by no means implied that the Romanian-Hungarian frontier of 1940 was sacrosanct in every detail. However, the views of Seton-Watson, Macartney and any other western scholar or politician on desirable future frontiers for Hungary were of absolutely no importance, since the post-1945 frontier settlement was imposed unilaterally, by force, by the dominant Soviet empire.

*   *   *

Looking back over Seton-Watson's relationship to Hungary, and in particular to territorial problems, there can be no question that he was a consistent political opponent. This does not however mean that he hated Hungarians. On the contrary, he had Hungarian friends whom he greatly esteemed, especially Károlyi and Jászi, and did his best, both between the wars and during the Second World War, to help Hungarians who had preferred exile to life in a Hungary increasingly dominated (though not with the consent of all Hungarian political leaders) by Hitler. The tragedy was that those Hungarians whom Seton-Watson respected—the radical liberals, socialists and believers in equal status for nationalities—were never in power in Hungary. When it briefly appeared that they might have some influence, they were summarily dismissed either by the old Right or by the extreme Left obedient to Moscow. Stephen Tisza and Stephen Bethlen, Béla Kun and Mátyás Rákosi, all rejected, though in different degree, the values of Seton-Watson's Hungarian friends.

This summary, which is intended neither to criticize nor to defend but to explain, and which inevitably leaves a good deal still unexplained, is the best that I can do on the basis of the evidence known to me.

Notes

For more than ten years I have been studying—together with my brother Christopher, Fellow of Oriel College, Oxford—the papers of R. W. Seton-Watson in our joint possession, as well as searching for related documents in other archives, in the United Kingdom and abroad. The main result of these labors is a political biography written by us jointly, on the period of his life in which he was most active in political affairs: *The making of a New Europe: R. W. Seton-Watson and the last years of Austria-Hungary.* It was published jointly by Methuens (London) and the University of Washington Press (Seattle) in April 1981. Apart from this, two volumes of correspondence, together with some other miscellaneous documents, relating to Yugoslav matters, were published in Zagreb (Institute of History) and London (British Academy) in 1976. Edited jointly by us and by our Yugoslav colleagues, Ljubo Boban, Mirjana Gross, Bogdan Krizman and Dragovan Šepić, the volumes are entitled *R. W. Seton-Watson and the Yugoslavs:*

Correspondence 1906–1941. Both these books contain much material relating to Hungary. Three further articles by myself, containing excerpts from original documents or full texts, are: "R. W. Seton-Watson and the Romanians" in *Revue roumaine d'histoire*, no. 1 (1971), pp. 25–42; "R. W. Seton-Watson's Einstellung zur Habsburger-Monarchie 1906–1914" in *Österreich in Geschichte und Literatur*, no. 6 (1973), pp. 361–381; and "Anton Štefánek and R. W. Seton-Watson" in *Bohemia* (yearbook of the Collegium Carolinum in Munich) (1977), pp. 226–254. Further documents are contained in *Századok*, no. 4, (1977), pp. 749–774 entitled "Jászi Oszkár és R. W. Seton-Watson levelezése az elsö világháború elötti években," with an excellent introductory essay by Géza Jeszenszky. I am, at present, engaged, with Romanian colleagues, on the publication of a volume, similar to the Yugoslav volume of 1976, of documents relating to Seton-Watson's relations with Romanians. I also hope to produce a substantial study, probably a long article with documentary supplements, on his relations with Hungarians. Colleagues at the Historical Institute in Budapest have long expressed an encouraging interest in such an article, and it is my strong hope that I shall produce it soon. Unfortunately the burdens of life in our increasingly despised, obstructed, and bureaucratised universities (a phenomenon which of course also has its counterpart in the United States), together with the weaknesses to which all flesh is heir, have delayed me. Meanwhile, I am most grateful to Professor Király for giving me the opportunity to offer this provisional, and insufficiently documented, contribution.

References

1. Probably not including Vojvodina, since the incorporation of the Serbs of Bácska and Banat in the South Slav unit would have been extremely difficult. See also below.
2. See his article "The Archduke Francis Ferdinand" in *Contemporry Review*, August 1914. The article was written before outbreak of war.
3. For details, see *The Making of a New Europe*, pp. 98–100. He counted very much on the co-operation of Jászi.
4. See especially the statement to him in June 1909 of Take Ionescu. *Ibid.*, p. 72.
5. *Ibid.*, p. 102.
6. *R. W. Seton-Watson and the Yugoslavs: Correspondence 1906–1941*, Vol. I, no. 117, pp. 192–193. This document is a memorandum written in Nish and dated January 12, 1915, intended for the Foreign Office.

Béla K. Király

Total War and Peacemaking

War, if reason prevails, is waged to obtain a better peace than that
which existed prior to the hostilities. During the 19th and early 20th
century—an era of balance of power and limited wars—the victor
usually attained his goals or at least part of them, through peace
negotiations, which often contained compromises. During the last
war cycle which preceeded World War I, this was still the case. In the
Crimean War Russia lost; consequently she had to give up the
southern part of Bessarabia and demilitarize her Black Sea shores. In
1859, France and its Sardinian ally won. As a result, Austria had to
give up Lombardy, satisfying part of the victor's goal. In 1866
Prussia won; consequently Austria was expelled from Germany and
the German Confederation was dissolved. In 1870 the Germans won,
and France had to give up Alsace and Lorraine and reconcile itself to
the unification of Germany. In 1905 Russia lost, resulting in Japan's
expansion of its possessions in the Pacific area at the expense of
Russia. In the two Balkan wars, the Balkan states won. The consequence was the virtual elimination of the Ottoman Empire from the
Balkans.

In all these wars the belligerents entered the war with a design for
the post-war peace and attained all or part of what they intended to
gain. Thus the resulting peace was, without exception, better for the
victors than what they had enjoyed prior to the wars.

This was not, however, the case in World War I. None of the great
powers started hostilities in 1914 with a definitive design for the
post-war peace.[1] In fact, not one of the belligerents, victors, or vanquished envisaged in 1914 anything which would have been similar
to the consequences of World War I. Except for a small band who
followed Pilsudsky into Russia even before the official declaration of
war in 1914, no one went to war to restitute Poland nor to create a
Yugoslavia. Even the small group of political and military leaders in
Belgrade, who wanted the war more than anyone else, envisaged in a
possible victory only the enlargement of Serbia. Nor did anyone
enter the war to create Czechoslovakia. Even Masaryk went into

exile in the fall of 1914 to propagate the transformation of the Habsburg monarchy from its dualistic into a trialistic form, to achieve for the Czechs rights identical to those that the Hungarians had achieved in 1867. No one went to war to destroy the German, Russian, Ottoman or Habsburg Empires, and most certainly, no one sought to create the first socialistic state—the USSR. Not even Lenin had dreamed of its rise in the near future. Yet these were the wholly unexpected results of World War I.

After the war, considerable scholarship was devoted to substantiating the supposition that the dissolution of the four empires and the inevitable creation or enlargement of various East Central European states were the result of organic historical processes.[2] Inevitability is a questionable assumption in history. While economic, social and other forces certainly dominate historical developments, they do not predetermine them. Among other considerations, the effect of the individual on historical evolution is enormous. Simply consider the course of the French Revolution without Robespierre or Napoleon; 1917 without Lenin; the USSR without Stalin; or, for that matter, German National Socialism without Hitler.

The thesis that the reorganization of East Central Europe after World War I was an inevitable culmination of organic developments, determined by forces accumulated through generations, is questionable. These forces had only a moderate effect on developments, and came to play a role only when the character of war changed to totality. This, in turn, defeated any effort to conclude a rational peace.

Until 1916, excepting a few peace feelers, no meaningful peace proposal was made by belligerent governments. In late 1916 a series of peace proposals were suddenly put forward, all of them without exception advocating compromises. They contained no demands for unconditional surrender or a dictated peace.

On November 14, 1916, Lord Landsdowne,[3] a minister without portfolio in the Asquith cabinet, put forward a memorandum on the need for peace negotiations. The Landsdowne memorandum recommended a serious investigation of the possibility of a peace and advocated that a statement be made by the British government indicating that the destruction of the German Empire was not her goal. He favored a peace on the basis of *status quo ante bellum*. The fall of the Asquith government and the installation of the Lloyd George cabinet on December 16 put an end to Landsdowne's activities,[4] at least temporarily. However, the affair did not die without vitriolic attacks on Landsdowne later.[5] Shortly after the Landsdowne memorandum was drafted, Francis Joseph I died. The date was November 21, 1916. Upon ascending the throne, the new Emperor and King, Karl, declared in a manifesto[6] his desire to do everything in his power to end as soon as possible the horrors and sacrifices of the war. Germany, embarrassed by the statement, felt obliged to issue a memorandum. It proposed that the belligerents bring forward recommendations for a post-World War peace. The Reichstag passed a peace resolution on July 1917.[7] Shortly after the German announcement, President Wilson proposed[8] that as an essential prerequisite to peace negotiations, the belligerents state their war aims. Several other propositions followed, including a papal Encyclical,[9] whose aim was to promote the cause of peace. None of these propositions negated with greater force all the heretofore universally accepted theses—among them the idea of the inevitability of a factual peace arrangement for East Central Europe and the thesis of the inevitability of the dissolution of empires—than did the Sixtus affair.[10] Emperor and King Karl asked his brother-in-law, Prince Sixtus of Bourbon, an officer in the Belgian army, to forward his peace proposals to the British and French governments. The Prince accepted the mission and made several trips to Vienna, Paris and London. As the particulars of the affair are well known, a detailed exposition is unnecessary; only a few points should be emphasized. Above all, the Habsburg Emperor and King was the first among all the belligerent heads of state who offered to give up territories under his own sovereignty for the sake of peace. He proposed the establishment of a South Slavic monarchy that would include Serbia, Montenegro, Albania and the two Austro-Hungarian provinces of Bosnia and Herzegovina. After long and arduous negotiations, in early August 1917, the entente powers' reply was positive. It contained nothing about unconditional surrender or the dissolution of the Habsburg Empire, and recommended that only Trentino should be ceded to Italy. Even Trieste was to remain a free port. Instead of the dissolution of the Austro-Hungarian monarchy, the entente powers proposed the enlargement of the dual state by the addition of Silesia and Bavaria. Even resurrected Poland was to become, within her 1772 borders, a monarchy under a Habsburg king.

During the Sixtus negotiations, a number of new, concrete peace proposals emerged. Prior to the Brest-Litovsk Treaty on February 9, 1918, none of them was anything but a compromise peace proposal. For example, Prime Minister Lloyd George declared in January 1918 that the breakup of Austria-Hungary was Britain's aim. Even according to President Wilson's fourteen points, promulgated on January 18, 1918, the place of Austria-Hungary was to be safeguarded among the nations.[11] Two facts are demonstated here. First, that the entente intention was to negotiate a peace with possible compromises. Second, and more important, the dissolution of Austria-Hungary was not contemplated by the Western powers until early 1918. The question arises: why did a multitude of peace proposals begin to emerge in late 1916, whereas none had been put forward before. One can also question why the original spirit of compromise changed in 1917 to a determination to fight to the bitter end, and to impose a treaty on the vanquished rather than to negotiate with them.

With no intent at oversimplification, it should be emphasized that one of the major causes of this change of attitudes and purposes was the change in the nature of warfare in 1916 and 1917—a period when World War I changed into a total war.

Total war is an armed combat waged with all national resources: human, as well as material. In total war, big batallions are neither more nor less important than energy and financial resources such as farms, factories, mines, transportation systems, research establishments. All these become elements in waging the war and, subsequently, legitimate targets of hostile action. The unrestricted British blockade of the Central Powers and the German reply—unrestricted submarine warfare—are cases in point. Since all citizen soldiers and civilians participate in the war effort in total war, the maintenance of morale, the efforts to increase the population's will to fight and destroy the enemy, became pivotal. Thus, psychological warfare is a basic ingredient of the war effort, and it is not any less important than armed combat and economic warfare.[12]

Whether World War I was a total war is a question that can be resolved by analyzing the events of 1916 and early 1917. Between February 1916 and mid-May of 1917, three battles changed the face of World War I. In the battle of Verdun 522,000 Frenchmen and 434,000 Germans died. In the battle of Somme 615,000 allied soldiers (420,000 British and 195,000 French) and 650,000 Germans died. The Nivelle offensive, which lasted from April 29 to May 20, 1917, and was supposed to break through the German position, resulted in the death of 120,000 Frenchmen in five days. It did not result in mentionable advance in the front.[13] This outcome precipitated widespread mutiny in the French Army.[14] Only the extraordinary discipline of the entente media and the deficiency of German intelligence service prevented the German High Command from learning that the French sectors of the western front were virtually denuded. These battles, with their unprecedented waste of human lives and material, and their remarkable lack of success, revealed that the war was hopelessly stalemated. Rapid industrial development and technological advances prior to and during the war created a formidable fire power. They did not at the same time produce equivalent means of mobility. (This happened only later, in the interwar decades.) The result was a deadlock in the trenches. Statesmen saw but two alternatives: either to start peace negotiations and accept compromises, or to push the war effort to its extreme limits, and dictate peace to the vanquished. This explains the multitude of peace proposals, most of which date from late 1916.

Since all the compromise efforts failed for one reason or another, only the second alternative appeared to remain open. Subsequently, the world was dragged into the continuation of the first total war in modern times. As it was already indicated, a basic ingredient of total war is psychological warfare. Propaganda is a major weapon in this warfare, thus it is not surprising that the role of propaganda grew by leaps and bounds, to the point of madness. In a life and death struggle, propaganda served no other purpose but to strengthen the morale of its own and undermine the enemy's will to fight. In such efforts truth plays no role.[15] War propaganda on both sides fostered the belief that one's own side was without flaw while the enemy was the embodiment of evil. It created a state of mind which tolerated no compromise and which was slow in yielding its distortions. This war propaganda poisoned European minds and created a cancer more harmful and more lasting than the physical losses caused by the war. The failure of compromises led to the intensification of combat in a total war. And total war shaped total victory, and led to a reflex action: dictated peace, a peace that saw no victors. Even though the victorious leaders foresaw that a dictated peace would be the harbinger of future wars (Professor Sakmyster argues this point eloquently below), they seemed to be unwilling or incapable of overcoming its momentum. The statesmen of the victors could have shaped history in harmony with their beliefs. They rather declined that august role. World War I, therefore, became what Raymond Aron has called a "hyperbolic war,"[16] one that created more problems than it resolved. Among the problems created was Trianon.

Notes

1. Kenneth J. Calder, *Britain and the Origins of New Europe*, 1914–1918 (London: 1976), p. 8.

2. Wilfried Fest. *Peace or Partition* (New York: 1978), pp. 7–9. For a brief but excellent summary of the war aims see Gerhard Schulz. *Revolutions and the Peace Treaties*. This book also identifies peace feelers in 1915; first swallows that did not herald the arrival of the spring of peace. On war aims see A.J.P. Taylor "The War Aims of the Allies in the First World War" in R. Pares and A.J.P. Taylor, eds., *Essays presented to Sir Lewis Namier*. (London, 1956). For Hungary's position see Norman Stone "Hungary and the Crisis of July, 1914," in Walter Laquer and George L. Mosse, eds., *1914 The Coming of The First World War* (New York, 1966), pp. 147–64.

3. Sir Charles Petrie, *Diplomatic History, 1713*–1933 (London: 1944), pp. 316, 317, 322. For the increasing interest in peace in 1916, see also Z.A.B. Zeman. *The Gentlemen Negotiators: A Diplomatic History of the First World War* (New York: 1971).

4. Lloyd George, *War Memoirs* (London, 1933–36). W. S. Churchill, *The World Crisis* (London: 1923–31). A.J.P. Taylor, *English History, 1914–45* (New York, 1965), p. 65.

5. Gordon A. Craig, "The Revolution in War and Diplomacy" in Jack J. Roth, ed., *World War I: A Turning Point in Modern History* (New York, 1967), p. 16.

6. Petrie, *Diplomatic History* . . . , p. 317.

7. *Verhandlungen des Deutschen Reichstages (1917)*, July 19, 1917. See also Zeman, *The Gentlemen Negotiators* . . . , p. 116.

8. R. S. Baker, *Woodrow Wilson: Life and Letters* (New York, 1927–39).

9. Pope Benedict XV's Peace Proposal, August 1, 1917. Sidney Z. Ehler and John B. Morall, *Church and State Through The Centuries* (Westminster, Maryland, 1954), pp. 374–377.

10. Robert A. Kann, *Die Sixtus Affare und die geheimen Friedensverhandlunger Österreich Ungarns im ersten Weltkrieg* (Wien, 1966); Fest, pp. 64–76.

11. *Congressional Record*, vol. LVI (1918), part I., pp. 680–81. Richard B. Morris, ed., *Basic Document in American History* (New York, 1956), pp. 153–57.

12. Charles Roetter, *The Art of Psychological Warfare, 1914–1945* (New York: 1974), pp. 27–94.

13. For the place of World War I in the framework of wars since the defeat of Napoleon see J. David Singer and Melvin Small, *The Wages of War 1816-1965; A Statistical Handbook.*

14. Richard M. Watt, *Dare Call It Treason* (New York, 1963).

15. Arthur Ponsonby, M.P., *Falsehood in War Time. Containing an Assortment of Lies Circulated Throughout the Nations during the Great War* (Torrance, Cal., 1980). First published in Britain in 1928.

16. Raymond Aron, *The Century of Total War* (Boston, 1955), pp. 24-31.

Stephen Borsody

Hungary's Road To Trianon:
Peacemaking and Propaganda

To Hungarians, the word "Trianon" is a symbol of a national catastrophe—a rather unlikely connotation for the twin names of two lovely palaces in the gardens of Versailles. In less subjective terms, the Treaty of Trianon, concluded with Hungary after the First World War, belongs to the tortuous history of Europe's reorganization according to the principle of nationality and nation-state. As a controversial act of peacemaking, it is a typical product of European nationalism, hailed by some and cursed by others. And since the ideas of nationalism—more recently in tandem with Marxism—have conquered mankind's mind as a whole, it is proper to place "Trianon" in the context of a world revolution.

Bourgeois nationalism and revolutionary Marxism, two ideas of Western origin, have given modern mankind two world religions which have divided rather than united the nations of the world. It is not surprising, therefore, that both nationalist and Marxist interpretations of the Treaty of Trianon have shared lively controversies.

*   *   *

The negative nationalist interpretation of Trianon from the Hungarian point of view is quite well known, though perhaps not always duly appreciated. Trianon sanctioned not merely the territorial partition of historic Hungary, but the ethnic dismemberment of the Hungarian people as well. In statistical terms: Trianon left only about two-thirds of the Hungarians in territorially radically reduced Hungary, while almost one-third of them ended up under the domination of three neighboring states—newly created or drastically enlarged—Romania, Czechoslovakia and Yugoslavia.[1] The Hungarian nation's dislike for having been cut up into four parts is understandable. Moreover, following the Second World War, as a sequel to Trianon, the Hungarians came to be further divided, now into five parts. Namely, the transfer of the former Subcarpathian

Ruthenia from Czechoslovakia to the Soviet Union placed a good number of Hungarians under Ukrainian rule. Thus, today, while about three-fourths of the Hungarians of the Danube region live in Hungary proper, one out of four Hungarians lives either in Romania, Czechoslovakia, Yugoslavia, or the Soviet Ukraine. The drop of the ratio of Hungarians outside Hungary from one-third after World War I to one-fourth today is due mainly to the fact that, in the adverse minority environment outside Hungary, the Hungarian population is not growing at all, or only at a rate far below that of Hungary's proper—let alone that of the majority populations of Hungary's neighbors. It should be kept in mind that nationalist rivalry in the Danube region is a cutthroat race for both the size of land and the number of people. Trianon only exacerbated this ill-fated race.

Of course, the nationalist interpretation of Trianon among Hungary's neighbors is quite different from the negative Hungarian interpretation. Hungary's neighbors believe that Trianon liberated the Danubian people. To them, the Trianon peacemaking is the epitome of justice and truth. Moreover, the reaffirmation of the provisions of the Treaty of Trianon by the Treaty of Paris after the Second World War is seen by them as a vindication of the Trianon peace settlement following Hitler's destruction of it.

Arguing with nationalist interpretations of peacemaking is a rather hopeless exercise. On more neutral academic grounds, however, attention should be called to the fact that the Western Powers themselves, who drew up the Trianon Treaty, came very close at one time to admitting the shortcomings of their own peacemaking. This happened during the appeasement period of European history—admittedly, a very bad time for clarifying the conditions of a just peace. Repudiation of Munich, along with the events that led up to it, and followed from it, became during the Second World War, as well as during the postwar peacemaking in 1946, a condition, so to speak, of democratic sincerity and allied unity. Thus, as far as the search for a just peace in the Danube region is concerned, the positive effects of the policy of appeasement were discarded along with its negative results—a typical case of throwing out the baby with the bath water. It could not be admitted in 1946, at the time of the Nuremberg Trials of Nazi war criminals, that the drawing of Hungary's boundaries under Hitler's auspices was actually more fair from the point of view of ethnic justice than the Trianon boundaries.[2]

Arguments of ethnic fairness are of no avail against the rigidity of nationalist interpretations. On the other hand, Marxist interpretation of Trianon, the Soviet interpretation, has evaded fairness by indulging in too much flexibility. After the First World War, the Soviets denounced passionately the work of the "bourgeois-imperialist-capitalist" peacemakers of Paris. After the Second World War, however, they endorsed it no less passionately, insisting—against very mild Western objections in a few instances—on a total restoration of the Trianon territorial settlement. Forgotten was the much vaunted superior sense of proletarian international justice. The Soviets acted, not unlike the much maligned capitalist West, in a way that seemed at the moment to serve their own power interests.

A memorable document of the Soviet anti-Trianon interpretation is the so-called "Resolution on the National Question in Central Europe & Balkans," endorsed by the Fifth Congress of the Comintern in 1924. It states in its introduction:

Saint-Germain, Versailles and subsequent treaties dictated by the victorious Entente powers, created a number of new small imperialist states—Poland, Czecho-Slovakia, Yugoslavia, Rumania, Greece—as a means of fighting against the proletarian revolution. These states were formed by the annexation of large territories with foreign populations and have become centres of national oppression and social reaction.[3]

After going on in this vein for several pages, the Comintern resolution embraces "the rights of every nation to self determination, even to the extent of separation," and supports the "political separation of the oppressed peoples from Poland, Rumania, Czecho-Slovakia, Yugoslavia and Greece." More specifically, Point VIII of the Comintern Resolution, on the so-called "Magyar Question," considers it essential to intensify Communist work among the Hungarian populations of the territories annexed by Czechoslovakia, Romania and Yugoslavia. It launches the slogan of "the right of these Magyars to self-determination, even to separation from the States that annexed them." And Point IX of the Comintern Resolution, on the so-called "Transylvania Question," approves the slogan advanced by the Communist Party of Rumania for "the separation of Transylvania from Rumania," and the forming of an "independent region" of Transylvania.[4]

These were, in Marxist terminology, "prerevolutionary" aspects of the Soviet interpretation of Trianon. Today, in the "post-revolutionary" period of the Danube region's history, the Communist parties of all countries in the Soviet orbit of power have radically changed their minds. The most intriguing spectacle in this process is the change in the position of the Hungarian Communist Party. In the name of proletarian internationalism, the Hungarian Party now approves the Trianon settlement reimposed on Hungary after the Second World War. This may make the Communist regime of Hungary popular with Hungary's neighbors, but as far as Hungarian feelings go, the Communist position adds only insult to injury. "Trianon" is surely not only a problem of the past but of the Communist present as well.

*   *   *

In discussing Hungary's road to Trianon, I chose to emphasize the propaganda aspects because it seems to me that the Trianon peacemaking was above all a triumph of propaganda.[5] The victors, persuaded by their own propaganda, believed that the structure of peace designed for the Danube region would be good for that region, as well as for the peace of Europe as a whole. National self-interest and idealism met in perfect harmony in their peace plans. Propaganda won the day.

Since the structure of peace in the Danube region was anti-Hungarian, the victors' propaganda, not surprisingly, had an unusually favorable view of Hungary's victorious neighbors, whereas it had an unusually unfavorable opinion of the defeated Hungarians. This black-and-white propaganda view was well expressed by Harold Nicolson, secretary of the British delegation to the Paris Peace Conference, in his memorable book, *Peacemaking 1919.* Summing up the victors' view of so-called "New Europe," then in the making, he wrote:

> We thought less about our late enemies than about the new countries which had arisen from their tired loins. Our emotions centred less around the old than around the new. . . . It was the thought of the new Serbia, the new Greece, the new Bohemia, the new Poland which made our hearts sing hymns at heaven's gate. This angle of emotional approach is very significant. I believe it was a very general angle. It is one which will not be apparent from the documents in the case. It is

one which presupposes a long and fervent study of 'The New Europe'—a magazine then issued under the auspices of Dr. Ronald Burrows and Dr. Seton-Watson with the doctrines of which I was overwhelmingly imbued. Bias there was, and prejudice. But they proceeded, not from any revengeful desire to subjugate and penalize our late enemies, but from a fervent aspiration to create and fortify the new nations whom we regarded, with maternal instinct, as the justification of our sufferings and of our victory. The Paris Conference will never properly be understood, unless this emotional impulse is emphasized at every stage.[6]

Wise advice, indeed, only it has never been taken to heart. Refusal in fact to understand "this emotional impulse" became one of the main reasons why a rational understanding of the blunders of Danubian peacemaking never penetrated the minds of those living there nor those who, as ultimate arbiters, decided the destinies of that region. Incidentally, a continental counterpart of "The New Europe" magazine was "L'Europe Nouvelle," edited in the same emotional spirit of wartime bias and prejudice.

Recalling the emotional times of New Europe's rise over the ruins of defeated Austria-Hungary, Mr. Nicolson confessed his own emotions on peacemaking as follows:

My attitude towards Austria was a rather saddened reflection as to what would remain of her when the New Europe had once been created. I did not regard her as a living entity: I thought of her only as a pathetic relic. My feelings towards Hungary were less detached. I confess that I regarded, and still regard, that Turanian tribe with acute distaste. Like their cousins the Turks, they had destroyed much and created nothing. Buda Pest was a false city devoid of any autochthonous reality. For centuries the Magyars had oppressed their subject nationalities. The hour of liberation and of retribution was at hand.[7]

How had the Hungarians fallen into such ill repute? Partly it was their own doing. They had been successful in joining the nationalist currents of contemporary European history but had failed to respond with equal enthusiasm to the modern world's democratic currents. More democracy certainly could have lessened the distaste both Hungary's neighbors and foreign observers, such as Harold Nicolson, felt toward the Hungarians. However, it should be emphasized that more democracy would not necessarily have reduced the gravity of what came to be known at the time of the First World War as the great crime of the Hungarians—namely, the oppression of their subject nationalities. For had the policy of so-called Magyarization proceeded hand in hand with democracy—as, for instance, Americanization did in the United States—the assimilation of non-Hungarians would most likely have been even more successful. It is also true, however, Hungary's other great crime, her alliance with Germany in the war, would have blackened her once bright prestige in the West under any circumstances.

Neither assimilation motivated by the ideal of the homogeneous nation state, nor alliances to serve nationalist interests, are uniquely Hungarian phenomena. Hungary's neighbors had committed similar, and sometimes even worse, crimes in the pursuit of nationalist objectives, in particular after the Second World War. What was unique in Hungary's case at the time of the Trianon peacemaking, so rightly emphasized by Mr. Nicolson, was the emotional manner in which Hungary's as well as her neighbors' historical records were evaluated by the peacemakers. The principal fountainhead of that emotionalism was the formidable success of wartime propaganda mounted against Hungary by her rival neighbors. And its most effective agent was the propaganda of Czech exiles under the twin leadership of T. G. Masaryk and Eduard Beneš.

Masaryk distinguished himself mainly by impressing the Western democracies with his attractive analysis of the brave new world to be born with the implementation of the "New Europe" plans. Advocating the partnership of the fair-minded Slavs with the West against the abominable Germans was the crux of Masaryk's propaganda.[8] Beneš, while fully identifying himself with Masaryk's pro-Slav and anti-German ideas, distinguished himself throughout his political career by his singularly vitriolic attacks against the Hungarians. Masaryk, too, was anti-Hungarian, but without Beneš's venom.

*   *   *

Beneš's famous pamphlet, *Détruisez l'Autriche-Hongrie!*, was a particularly successful wartime propaganda weapon in arousing indignation against the crimes of Austria-Hungary, both real and imaginary.[9] It advanced a liberal cause which the Western democracies at that time felt was worth fighting for: the liberation of Europe's small nations. It branded Austria-Hungary as the most dangerous tool of German imperialism—obviously the highest conceivable crime at a time when the Allies were locked in a life and death struggle with the German enemy. But the other enemy pilloried by Beneš, which the Allies knew much less about than they did about the Germans, was the Hungarians—or the Magyars, as wartime propaganda preferred to call them, in order to distinguish them from the non-Magyar half of Hungary. As enemies of European peace, the Magyars in some respect ranked even higher in Beneš's propaganda than the Germans.

Beneš spared no effort to cure the liberal-democratic world of its still lingering sympathies for the Hungarians, earned by their heroism against the Habsburgs in 1848–49, and also by their moderation in the compromise peace with the Austrians in 1867. Beneš described the Magyars as "the most loyal allies" of the Germans, "spiritual kins" of the Germans, "members of the band of Central European oppressors." He also made the Magyars responsible for the outbreak of war in 1914. The Magyars, he argued, were the instigators of the Habsburg Empire's anti-Slav Balkan policy which triggered the war. He also burdened the Magyars with crimes of more ancient origin against the Slavs. They had prevented, he claimed, the union of Serbs and Croats into a Yugoslav nation, as well as the union of Czechs and Slovaks into a Czechoslovak nation.

The nefarious role of the Hungarians in Slav history was originally invented by the 19th century Czech historian, František Palacký. In the anti-Hungarian wartime propaganda, this unattractive role of the "Asiatic" Magyars—an epithet Hungary's rivals were fond of using—sounded even more odious. The wartime propaganda skipped Palacký's recipe for reconcilation, his federalization program of the Habsburg Monarchy, that is. Instead, to undo the historic injustices inflicted by the Hungarians and Germans upon the Slavs, a punitive program was propagated, which allowed no room for reconciliation. Particularly hard hit by the supposedly historic German-Magyar alliance against the Slavs were the Czechs and Slovaks, or Czechoslovaks, as they came to be called during the war. It was nothing short of miraculous, Beneš exclaimed in his *Détruisez l'Autriche-Hongrie!*, that the Czechoslovaks survived the "brutal millenial German and Magyar oppression."

In short, Austria-Hungary was guilty of crimes deserving nothing less than the death penalty. She was an arch-foe of the Slavs, a tool of Germany's bid for European hegemony; she existed in violation of the liberal-democratic ideals and principles the Allies were fighting for. By contrast, the Slavs, democratic and peace-loving, were natural allies of Europe, both East and West, against the central German power, as well as against the Germans' perennial allies, the Magyars. Austria-Hungary's destruction was necessary not in the interest of the Slavs alone but also in the interest of the Allied powers and of Europe as a whole, and, added Beneš for good measure, in the interest of mankind.

*   *   *

History written in the heat of war seldom distinguishes itself by objectivity. Beneš's pamphlet, and the anti-Austro-Hungarian wartime propaganda in general, is no exception to the rule. In times of war, even more so than in times of peace, truth has a hard time prevailing. On the other hand, the accusations leveled against Austria-Hungary were not without foundation. Austria-Hungary's mistakes were numerous. However, her evil role had nothing to do with any "millenial" German-Magyar alliance against the Slavs. What caused the trouble was the result of a relatively recent change in the structure of the Habsburg Empire—the Austro-Hungarian Compromise (or *Ausgleich*) in 1867, the act by which Austria-Hungary was created.

The Dualist Monarchy created by the Compromise of 1867 was a Habsburg surrender to Hungarian nationalism. The Compromise acknowledged Hungarian supremacy in multiethnic Hungary, while it reaffirmed the long established German supremacy over the multiethnic Austrian half of the Monarchy. Propositions for equal rights for the nine other nationalities of the Empire were ignored. The losers were mostly Slavs who made up the ethnic majority of Austria-Hungary.

The Dualist system worked differently in the two halves of the Austro-Hungarian Empire. In the Austrian half, the state remained supranational under Habsburg dynastic rule. In Hungary, on the other hand, the state became national under Hungarian chauvinistic rule. The ancient kingdom of Hungary was being energetically refashioned into a unitary Hungarian nation-state on the Western model. (Parenthetically: I am most critical of the policy of Magyarization and wish the Hungarian political leadership of the Dualist era had had the political wisdom to follow a federalist policy instead of emulating the Western model of a unitary nation-state. However, criticism of the policy of Magyarization without an equally forceful criticism of the nation-state policies of Hungary's neighbor since World War I to the present, it seems to me, perpetuates a widely accepted point of view which condemns the Hungarians for a policy which is either overlooked or treated much less critically in the case of Hungary's neighbors—not to speak of the fact that the Hungarians in their eagerness to achieve nation-state homogeneity in the pre-W.W.I liberal era have never committed acts of brutalities comparable to those committed by Hungary's neighbors in the post-W.W.II totalitarian age.)

A federalist trend in the Austrian half of the Monarchy was trying to deal with the peculiar problems of Danubian multinationalism. But this feeble Austrian federalism fighting against overwhelming odds was unable to slow down the momentum of Hungarian nationalism. And the example of a Hungarian nation-state in the making only whetted the nationalist appetites of the other Habsburg nationalities. Moreover, the rising nationalist temper of contemporary Europe further hindered the efforts of the handful of Danubian federalists, who were anxious to see Dualism replaced by Federalism.

The survival of the Habsburg Monarchy depended above all on a *modus vivendi* with the Slavic majority of the Empire. Around the turn of the century, 60 percent of the population in the Austrian half of the Habsburg Monarchy was Slavic, while in the Hungarian half (with Croatia-Slavonia included) the Slavs accounted for 30 percent of the total population. However, without Croatia-Slavonia, Hungary proper only had a total Slav population of less than 20 percent—largest among them being the Slovaks, about 12 percent. (Hungary's single largest non-Hungarian nationality were the Romanians, about 17 percent, who were not Slavs.) Austria's rulers at least tried to meet the crucial Slav problem by making concessions to the Slavs through a policy of Austro-Slavism. No similar effort was made by Hungary's rulers. "Hungaro-Slavism" was a non-existent concept. And even Austro-Slavism, in the other half of the Monarchy, was ill-thought-of and suspected of hurting Hungarian interests.

The Hungarian-Slav conflict was of relatively recent origin. There was no historical analogy as portrayed by wartime propaganda between Hungarian-Slav hostility and the age-old German-Slav antagonism. The Hungarian-Slav conflict began only when both sides discovered that their modern national aspirations were mutually incompatible. However, the peace of the distant past between Hungarian and Slav was of no help in curing the new-born feelings of hostility. Magyarization convinced the Slavs that the Hungarians were their mortal enemies, while Russian intervention against Hungary in 1849 deepened Hungarian fear of a Slav menace. The bogey of pan-Slavism had so deeply entrenched itself in the Hungarian mind that any kind of Slav demands for national equality during the Dualist era became lumped together with the threat of Russian imperialism.

The sum total of problems undermining the very existence of multiethnic Austria-Hungary was staggering. The "ramshackle" label attached to the old Empire during the War of 1914 was a fitting one. Yet, Austria-Hungary was not on the verge of collapse in 1914—and her internal problems became a threat to world peace only because they were enmeshed with the external conflicts of the Great Powers.

Among the many conflicts that plagued the Habsburg Empire both internally and externally, none was loaded with graver perils to peace than the South Slav problem. Its focus was in the Balkans where the vanishing supremacy of the Ottoman Turks left a power vacuum. Both Russia and Austria-Hungary, the two powers bordering on the Balkans from the North, were looking for a sphere of influence there.

Europe in 1914 would not let Austria-Hungary get away with a military solution to a local crisis in the Balkans—unlike Soviet Russia, which has been getting away, so far, with invading neighboring states in Central and Eastern Europe since the Second World War. The Sarajevo murder tripped off a general war in Europe which became the First World War, instead of adding still another local war—or "little war" in contemporary terminology—to the two Balkan wars of the preceding two years.

*   *   *

More than half a century after Austria-Hungary's demise in the First World War, the debate over the crimes of Austria-Hungary and over the punishment she suffered is far from over. In particular, the debate continues over such matters as whether or not the multinational Habsburg Empire was a viable state, and whether it was doomed to dissolution in the age of national states or destroyed only because of a lost war.

Speculations apart, the facts are clear enough to furnish the answer to a few fundamental questions, both with reference to Hungary and to Austria-Hungary as well. First and foremost, the rulers of Austria-Hungary decided to declare war on Serbia, at the risk of a European war, in order to preserve the status quo. There were no straws in the wind showing strong new directions of change. There were no convincing signs the Danubian Empire was about to fulfill her modern mission as a commonwealth of nations, and thus she forfeited her ancient role in the European balance of power as well. Hungarian national hegemony was unyielding. Austrian supranationalism was disintegrating. The Habsburg Empire was not on a federalist course which could have saved her from nationalist fragmentation. She was not on the road to becoming an "eastern Switzerland." She was not leading mankind away from nationalism to universalism—as many believed that she should and some still believe that she did.[9] In brief, Austria-Hungary went to war in defense of national inequality. She also stood for the preservation of a structure of society which was hostile to democracy.

Germany's backing was a decisive factor in Austria-Hungary's decision to go to war. Reliance on the German alliance filled the rulers of Austria-Hungary with confidence that they could win. They also agreed with the widely held German view that the war was a struggle between Slavs and Teutons for the mastery of Central Europe. On the other hand, Germany's aims in Central Europe—let alone her aims in the world beyond Austria-Hungary's orbit of interest—were not clearly understood either in Vienna or Budapest; perhaps because only during the war did German hegemony fully replace the so-called Central European confederation of Hohenzollerns and Habsburgs conceived by Bismarck. When the governments of Austria-Hungary learned about Berlin's wartime *Mitteleuropa* plans there was no rejoicing either in Vienna or Budapest. Yet, apprehensions and misgivings concerning the war aims of their German ally notwithstanding, Austria-Hungary's rulers certainly preferred a Berlin-dominated *Mitteleuropa* to a Central European new deal with equal rights for all.

The mistakes of Austria-Hungary were grave indeed. The Dualist system had to be dumped in order to liberate the Danubian people from national discrimination. The old regime had to be terminated in the interest of both domestic justice and international peace. In the cruder language of wartime propaganda: Austria-Hungary had to be destroyed. But the war also raised the question of what to put in Austria-Hungary's place? The truth of the matter is that the "New Europe" peace plans of Slav exiles and their Western supporters fell woefully short of providing a satisfactory answer to that vital question.

*   *   *

In declaring my dissatisfaction with the victors' "New Europe" plans, I feel obliged to disclose what would have been, in my opinion, a better peace plan for a truly new Europe in the Danube region, free of the shortcomings of the old. I have expressed my views on this subject many times in many forms. And rather than pretend that these are new ideas, I would prefer to quote from an essay I wrote on the 50th anniversary of the break-up of Austria-Hungary:

> The program that carried the day when Austria-Hungary collapsed was the liberation plan of the Western Allies. "National self-determination"—the lofty principle of that plan, associated with President Wilson's name—unfortunately turned into a policy of territorial punishment and territorial reward. An irreconcilable conflict existed between the territorial demands, supported by the victorious Allies, and the Wilsonian principle of national self-determination. Only a federal reconstruction of the Danube region could resolve the conflict—and the experts knew it. The American Peace Commission's Committee in charge of boundary questions clearly recognized this fact when it reported to Wilson that it was unable to discover a territorial division of Austria-Hungary which would be both just and practical. The Committee's report pointed out that the difficulties could be solved only if the boundaries were to be drawn "with the purpose of separating not independent nations but component portions of a federalized state." . . . An Allied federalist liberation policy, emphasizing the democratic solidarity of the Danubian people, could have perhaps united victors and vanquished. In that case, T. G. Masaryk, Eduard Beneš, Karl Renner, Otto Bauer, Mihály Károlyi, Oszkár Jászi, Milan Hodža, and other liberal Danubians—essentially all of them of the same democratic persuasion—might have joined forces as founders of a Danubian federation, instead of going their separate national ways. In concrete political terms, a federalist liberation policy would have meant a program of preserving the unity of the Habsburg empire without the Habsburgs.[11]

Admittedly, in actual life, policies can be made only with existing forces—and no federalist forces were at hand in the Danube region or anywhere else in Europe at the time of Allied victory over the Central Powers, except among the defeated Austrians and Hungarians. A Danubian peacemaking according to the federalist plans of the defeated Austrian and Hungarian Socialist and liberal democrats, Oszkár Jászi's plans of the United States of Danubia in particular,[12] would certainly have made a better peace than the nation-state plans of Masaryk, Beneš, and other Central and East European victorious nationalists, supported by the "New Europe" well-wishers of the Western democracies.

However, even a nation-state peace, such as the "New Europe" plans of Danubian exiles supported by the Western democracies, could have made a better contribution to peace had propaganda and emotions not triumphed over reason and common sense. For there was no reasonable need whatsoever, from the point of view of European peace, to humiliate the Hungarian people the way Trianon did. Legitimate rights to national independence in the Danube region could have been safely satisfied without placing one-third of the Hungarians under foreign domination of triumphant neighbors. Justice as well as common sense dictated reconciliation. The peace dictated by the Danubian victors to the vanquished Hungarians perpetuated national conflicts. Trianon did the opposite of a true peacemaking.

Instead of encouraging regional union and cooperation, peacemaking in the Danube region after the First World War placed the issue of nation-state boundaries at the top of Danubian politics, thus fanning the flames of rivalry and territorial imperialism. Not unlike the Dualist system of the *Ausgleich*, the post-First World War nation-state system too poisoned the relations among the Danubian peoples; both systems failed to recognize the rule of national equality, the only way to make enduring peace. The inequities of the *Ausgleich* era do not vindicate the inequities of the Trianon settlement—the less so because the Trianon peace was supposed to carry out the Western democratic ideals of national self-determination which the *Ausgleich* never claimed to do.

Thus did the Western democracies, total victors of the first total war, miss a unique opportunity to create out of the ruins of the Habsburg Empire in the Danube region a modern democratic community of self-governing peoples, founded on a mutual recognition of equal rights.

Notes

1. According to the Treaty of Trianon, of the then ca. 10,000,000 Hungarians only about 67% were left in territorially radically reduced Hungary. The rest of them were divided among the territorially enlarged or newly founded neighboring states as follows: Romania got roughly 16% of them, Czechoslovakia 10%, and Yugoslavia 6%. A small number of Hungarians was attached to Austria, a loss which has never been resented the way Hungary's other losses were. The new boundary between Austria and Hungary, moreover, had partly been decided by a plebiscite, keeping the city of Sopron in Hungary.

2. Following the revisions of the Trianon boundaries with Hitler's help, the ratio of ethnical majority and minority in Hungary was not worse, but rather better than in most of the Central and Eastern European countries favored by the territorial settlement of the Paris peacemakers after the First World War. In 1941, the Hungarians held an almost 80% majority in their enlarged country, whereas the majorities in the victor states after the First World War were as follows: around 70% in Czechoslovakia and Poland, 72% in Romania, and 83% in Yugoslavia. Cf. Stephen Borsody, *The Tragedy of Central Europe: Nazi and Soviet Conquest and Aftermath* (New Haven, 1980), p. 97.

3. *The Communist International*, No. 7, December 1924–January 1925 (Moscow), p. 93.

4. *Ibid.*, p. 99.

5. Only after the Second World War did Western scholarship turn its attention to a systematic study of First World War propaganda. Scholars of Czech origin did a pioneer work in this field: Z[byněk]. A. B. Zeman, *The Break-up of the Habsburg Empire, 1914–1918* (London, 1961); Harry Hanak, *Great Britain and Austria-Hungary During the First World War: A Study in the Formation of Public Opinion* (London, 1961); D. Perman [Dagmar Horna-Perman], *The Shaping of the Czechoslovak State: Diplomatic History of the Boundaries of Czechoslovakia, 1914–1920*, (Leiden, 1962).

6. Harold Nicolson, *Peacemaking 1919* (London 1933), pp. 32–33.

7. *Ibid.*, p. 34.

8. Masaryk's wartime memoirs offer a detailed account of his propaganda activities: Dr. Thomas Garrigue Masaryk, *The Making of a State: Memoirs and Observations 1914–1918*; An English Version, Arranged and Prepared with an Introduction by Henry Wickham Steed (London and New York, 1927). However, Masaryk's memoranda which so decisively influenced Allied postwar plans were published only during World War II: R. W.

Seton-Watson, *Masaryk in England* (Cambridge, 1943). Of particular interest in that collection of documents is Masaryk's memorandum, "At the Eleventh Hour," circulated confidentially in 1916 with a Preface by Ronald M. Burrows and R. W. Seton-Watson, later editors of the periodical, *The New Europe*, a public propaganda forum for Masaryk's ideas. The peace program Masaryk advised the Allies to implement was called a "Non-German, Anti-German European Central Europe," made up of an "anti-German barrier" formed by Poland, Czechoslovakia and Yugoslavia, three Slav states. One of the "corollaries" of this plan was "the organization of a *Magyar* as opposed to a *Hungarian* State," a Trianon Hungary, that is, only even smaller in the sketches Masaryk submitted with his memoranda to the Allied Governments. A book-length elaboration of Masaryk's peace plans was his *Nová Evropa: Stanovisko Slovanské* (The New Europe: A Slav Point of View) which appeared only after the war.

9. Beneš's pamphlet is available both in French and English; the phrases quoted in my summary are translated from the French original: Edvard Benes, *Détruisez l'Autriche-Hongrie! Le martyre des Tchéco-Slovaques à travers l'histoire* (Paris, 1916). A less shrill version of the same in English translation: *Bohemia's Case for Independence*. With an Introduction by Henry Wickham Steed (London, 1917). Beneš's wartime memoirs supplement those of Masaryk's on Czech propaganda activities: Dr. Eduard Beneš, *My War Memoirs* (London, 1928). Also of interest on the implementation of Czech plans for the reorganization of Central Europe are the memoranda to the Paris peace conference, composed either by Beneš personally or under his direction. The text of those memoranda was published in the context of German anti-Czech propaganda of the appeasement thirties, itself a fact of interest: Hermann Raschhofer, *Die Tschechslowakischen Denkschriften für die Friedenskonferenz von Paris 1919–1920* (Berlin, 1937).

10. See Adam Wandruszka, *The House of Habsburg: Six Hundred Years of a European Dynasty* (New York, 1965), pp. 155–157.—The flare-up of interest in Habsburg studies both in the United States and in Europe after the Second World War is a phenomenon which transcends the narrow world of scholarship; it reflects the general concern over the political developments in Central Europe since the break-up of the Habsburg Empire. The best source of information on a broad range of topics and views in this area are the volumes of *Austrian History Yearbook*, edited by R. John Rath.

11. Stephen Borsody, *The Break-Up of Austria-Hungary: Fifty Years After*, reprinted under the title "The Empire: An Unrealized Federal Union," in *The Austrian Empire: Abortive Federation?* Edited by Harold J. Gordon, Jr. and Nancy M. Gordon (Lexington, 1974), pp. 151, 153.

12. On the eve of the Habsburg Monarchy's collapse, Oszkár Jászi presented his vision of a federal reorganization of Central and Eastern Europe in his *A monarchia jövője: A dualizmus bukása és a dunai egyesült*

allamok (The Future of the Monarchy: The Fall of Dualism and the Danubian United States) (Budapest, 1918). This pamphlet was translated into German by Stefan V. Hartenstein: Dr. Oskar Jászi, *Der Zusammenbruch des Dualismus and die Zukunft der Donaustaaten* (Vienna, 1918). While Jászi in Hungary was writing his federalist plan, Masaryk, traveling in Russia from Moscow to Vladivostok on his way to the United States, was working on his "The New Europe," projecting the nation-state reorganization of the Danube region. See my essay on "A Story of Two Books" in Hungarian: István Borsody, "Jászi és Masaryk: Két könyv története," *Látóhatár* (Munich) X, 1-2 (1959), pp. 56-61.

Stephen D. Kertész

The Consequences of World War I:
The Effects on East Central Europe

One of the momentous results of the First World War was the dismemberment of the Austrian-Hungarian Monarchy. The peacemakers of 1919, instead of reforming the antiquated political structure of the Danubian Empire on a democratic and federative basis, created small successor states dominated by jingo-nationalism. At the peace table the Allied and Associated Powers, still under the spell of their own wartime propaganda, did not even endeavor to maintain the unity of the Danubian area in one form or another. The subsequent unfortunate situation in this region was only the natural consequence of this territorial dismemberment and of the lip service paid at the peace settlement to some of the principles of President Wilson. This destruction of the Eastern bastion of the European state system not only proved foolhardy for the victors of 1918, but was eventually catastrophic for all the nations of Western civilization.

By virtue of the peace treaties of St. Germain and Trianon, the territory was divided among Austria, Czechoslovakia, Yugoslavia, Italy, Hungary, Poland and Romania. Some of these states inherited much of the complex nationality pattern of the Monarchy, but none of the states possessed the fallen Monarchy's economic advantages. The new settlement opened the door to political and economic nationalism on a scale unheard of before. The roles changed. German and Hungarian supremacy was wiped out and some of the oppressed peoples became the oppressors.

The dismemberment of the Monarchy was a flagrant contradiction to the general trend of world evolution which favored economic integration, a necessary consequence of the growing interdependence of nations. Destruction of the Danubian Empire created a vacuum of power in the Danubian area, thereby flinging open a strategic gateway of Europe.[1] In the light of the political events of the last thirty years, it is commonplace to say that its destruction, without adequate substitution, was probably one of the greatest diplomatic errors in modern history.[2] Winston Churchill was fully justified in calling the complete break-up of the Empire a "cardinal tragedy."[3] Anthony Eden recently expressed the opinion that: "The collapse of the Austro-Hungarian Empire was a calamity for the peace of Europe. If the countries that formed it could one day find some arrangement that would allow them to work together again in a happy association, how welcome this would be."[4] Such statements emanating from outstanding British statesmen are all the more significant since the secret treaties concluded by Great Britain and France during the First World War and the wartime policy and propaganda of the same powers were instrumental, if not decisive, in bringing about the collapse of the Monarchy and the establishment of a small state system in the Danubian area.

Although Oscar Jászi, a distinguished student of the nationality problems of Austria-Hungary, has written that the dissolution of the Monarchy was not a mechanical but an organic process,[5] and although many facts support this view, there are some facts to the contrary.[6] A fundamental reorganization of the Monarchy, along democratic and federative lines, would, in any event, have been necessary.[7] Although in the last period of the war the discontent of the nationalities was stirred up by various means, important cohesive forces still existed. The armies of the Monarchy everywhere stood on foreign soil. With the exception of a considerable part of the Czech army groups, the nationalities of the Monarchy by and large fought well, despite war-weariness, economic hardships, growing Allied propaganda and Allied preponderance.[8] Although composed of many nationalities, the administration and especially the foreign service fulfilled their task loyally until the last.[9]

In the light of these and some other evidences, then, one might say that the collapse of the Monarchy was not entirely self-inflicted. Social and political reforms and federalization probably could have revitalized the Monarchy. Serious discontent existed, and revolutionary movements were encouraged and fomented from outside, but the change of attitude by the victorious Western powers was the decisive factor.[10] The leaders of the various nationalities received encouragement, support, and even instructions from abroad. The chance of being able to switch from the defeated camp to that of the victorious powers had a strong appeal to all nationalities. Under these conditions and prospects the discontented nationalities themselves had no particular reason to remain with the old Monarchy. It is therefore somewhat understandable that most of the nationalities, irrespective of other political considerations, eventually preferred to belong to the victorious Allied nations.[11]

In Hungary the government declared on October 16, 1918, that the dual system with Austria had ended and that only personal union existed between the two countries. Soon revolutionary movements broke out and a National Council formed. King Charles, on October 31, appointed Count Mihály Károlyi as Prime Minister. Károlyi was a rich aristocrat but a staunch left-wing politician with an outspoken pro-Entente and anti-German record. He attempted to bring about a compromise with the nationalities, within a democratic Hungarian state. His minister of nationalities, Oszkár Jászi, advocated the formation of an "Eastern Switzerland" in historic Hungary. In this spirit the new regime tried to persuade the nationalities to live together in a commonwealth.[12] These actions came too late, for the victorious great powers had promised complete independence to them.

The Croat Parliament at Zagreb decided, on October 29, to sever constitutional relations with Hungary and Austria. A National Assembly of the Romanians in Alba Iulia (Gyulafehérvár) decided, on December 1, upon the unification of all Romanians in one state.[13]

King Charles surrendered the reins of government on November 13, 1918, but did not abdicate. Hungary was proclaimed a "People's Republic" on November 16, 1918, and the Hungarian National Council elected Count Mihály Károlyi President of the Republic in January, 1919.

In a recent publication, a British historian has remarked, concerning Károlyi's failure, that "Unfortunately for Hungary and for Central Europe, Károlyi was not Masaryk: he had not carried his peoples with him."[14]

Nevertheless, in the cases of Károlyi and Masaryk, popular support was not the primary or decisive factor. Masaryk enjoyed the full support of the Allied powers, and this Allied support—rather than the opinion of the Czech people—assured Czechoslovakia the status of a victorious nation. Károlyi, however, was openly rebuffed and humiliated by the Entente powers and could not give anything to the Hungarians, or, for that matter, to the other nationalities. The occupation of Hungarian territories by the successor states was authorized by the Supreme Council of the Allied powers in Paris. The Romanian, Yugoslav, and Czech armies violated even these prescriptions by advancing beyond the demarcation lines. This situation foreshadowed the territorial provisions of the Treaty of Trianon, that is, the loss of considerable territories inhabited by Hungarians.

Károlyi frankly admitted that his confidence in the Entente powers and in the principles of President Wilson had been misplaced and, in desperation, he resigned his office of President of the Hungarian Republic. The succeeding Communist regime of Béla Kun (March-July, 1919) created general fear of the spread of Bolshevism all over Europe.[15] In addition, the Communist Republic, to win popular support, lost no time in organizing an army, which overran a substantial part of Slovakia and attacked the Romanians. All these happenings, particularly the Bolshevist rule and subsequent reaction, did not make Hungary popular in Western Europe.[16]

Although at the peace settlement the Monarchy was destroyed in the name of the self-determination of peoples, this principle was grossly violated in practice. None of the nationalities living within the former Monarchy was allowed to express its will through a plebiscite. Only the treaty of St. Germain provided for a plebiscite in a small area of Carinthia. The Slovene majority there decided to join with defeated Austria, instead of with the newly created victorious state of the Serbs, Croats and Slovenes.[17] This case did not justify the principle of nationality solemnly proclaimed at Paris as the principle of the new *status quo*. The Hungarian peace delegation futilely proposed plebiscites in territories to be detached from Hungary by the peace treaty.

In an answer given in the name of the Allies on May 5, 1920, Premier Millerand of France explained that plebiscites were unnecessary because their result would not be substantially different from the condition established by the peacemakers.[18]

Eventually the peace treaties shifted 38,000,000 of the 52,000,000 inhabitants of the Monarchy into countries belonging to the victors. Only small Austria (6,289,380) and Hungary (7,615,117) were considered as defeated states, and treated as such. Winston Churchill characterized the absurd situation as follows: "Two soldiers have served side by side sharing in common cause the perils and hardships of war. The war is ended and they return home to their respective villages. But a frontier line has been drawn between them. One is a guilty wretch, lucky to escape with life the conqueror's vengeance. The other appears to be one of the conquerors himself."[19] The internal political structure of Austria-Hungary was obsolete, but the Empire still held advantages. It was located in the most strategically important region of Europe, and comprised an area greater than that of any European state, save Russia, with a common tariff and currency. Thus the 52,000,000 inhabitants of the Monarchy could trade freely over an area of 267,239 square miles.[20] In the ten years preceding the first World War, the money income in Austria increased by 86 percent and in Hungary by 92 percent: the increase in the real income per head was 63 percent in Austria and 75 percent in Hungary. This rate of increase was much more rapid than in Great Britain or Germany.[21] Despite many adverse political factors, the advantages of the great internal market and the natural division of labor among the different parts of the Empire resulted in a rapid rise in wealth, shared in by all nationalities.

But the nationality struggle in the Danubian Empire was a serious and baffling problem to Western observers. Under the impact of this complicated and often ugly picture, it was rather easy to forget wider horizons, and to overlook the fact that the existence of a Danubian great power was both a benefit to its own people and a necessity for the European state system. In June, 1946, the late Jan Masaryk was to tell Sir Alfred Duff Cooper, then British Ambassador to France, that "Czechoslovakia had never been so happy as when forming part of the Austro-Hungarian Empire." Sir Alfred Duff Cooper thought this a tragic admission on the part of the son of Thomas Masaryk, commenting: "Time has given it proof. It is surely now generally recognized that the disappearance of the Austro-Hungarian Empire has proved to be one of the major calamities of this disastrous century."[22]

From the point of view of the European state system the victorious powers committed a fundamental mistake in failing to compel the new Danubian states to form a federal state not incompatible with the reestablishment of an independent Poland. This would have enabled the Danubian peoples and the Poles, together, later to resist pressure or invasion by outside forces. At that time the potential opponents of such a scheme, the neighboring great states of Germany and Russia, did not exist as power factors. Thus the victorious Western powers had practically a free hand in Eastern Europe. Of course the extreme nationalism of the leaders of the new states still remained an obstacle to any new form of integration. But the peace-makers had the necessary means at their disposal to check the intransigent nationalism of the governments of the new states. It would not have been difficult to make their recognition and support dependent on the maintenance of Danubian unity in one form or another. The lack of foresight of the victorious allies paved the way for Hitler's aggressive policy in Eastern Europe and eventually opened wide the door for Russian penetration.

All the newly created Danubian states, whether victorious or defeated, besides falling into political chauvinism, followed the policy of an exaggerated protectionism. They erected high tariff walls and engaged, from time to time, in economic wars. The general result was a rise in unemployment and the cost of living, and a decline in national income. As Frederick Hertz later pointed out, "progress achieved in one field was as a rule offset by retrogression in another."[23]

There were a few vague endeavors towards integration but these did not prove successful. Certain sections of the Treaty of St. Germain, and of the Treaty of Trianon opened the way for negotiating preferential trade agreements,[24] but in the hostile political atmosphere these negotiations proved fruitless, as did Tardieu's endeavors in 1932, which promised France's financial assistance in the event of preferential trade agreements being concluded between the Danubian States.

Cooperation in the sphere of agriculture, proposed at the Bucharest Conference of 1930 between Yugoslavia, Romania and Hungary; the attempt at economic collaboration by the member states of the Little Entente according to the provisions of an agreement reached in February, 1933; and the Rome Protocols signed by Austria, Hungary and Italy in March, 1934, should all be considered short-lived expedients brought about by momentary exigencies. These agreements could not achieve tangible and lasting success. They could not substitute for true economic collaboration between the Danubian countries. The failure of such endeavors as these made it clear that, without a reasonable settlement of basic political issues, durable cooperation in economic fields could not be established.

Politically, it has often been claimed that Soviet Russia easily conquered and transformed the Danubian area because she found there a vacuum of power. The vacuum of power was created in 1919. The new political system established along the banks of the Danube was a weak superstructure, without solid foundation, and could not fill either the political or the economic place of the Monarchy in the international community. The expectations attached to the creation of small national states in the Danubian Valley did not materialize. The new states could not develop sufficient cohesive force, could not bring about an effective cooperation among themselves, and were swept away.[25]

Though American intervention in the first World War was accompanied by a proclamation of lofty political ideas—"to make the world safe for democracy"—the new Danubian order, sometimes called the Balkanization of the Danubian area, did not help toward establishing political democracies.[26] In some of the successor states retrograde political conditions and corruption reached a point altogether unknown in the Monarchy. In Yugoslavia, for example, the leader of the Croatian opposition party, Stjepan Radič, and two other Croatian deputies, actually were shot while in a session of Parliament in June, 1928. In most of the successor states, political democracy remained meaningless to the masses, which were ruled by pseudo-parliamentary regimes or by outright dictatorships. Only Czechoslovakia was considered in the West as a notable exception in this respect. This country received the lion's share of the Monarchy and considerable financial support from abroad. But while the balanced economic and social conditions, the well-known administrative qualities of the Czechs, and the industrial skill of the Sudeten Germans facilitated the functioning of democratic political institutions, political democracy alone could not assure the independence and survival of Czechoslovakia in the serious crises of 1938 and 1944–48.[27]

Despite the existence of the League of Nations, which was to end alliance-making throughout the world, alliances multiplied in Eastern Europe. France attempted to consolidate the new territorial settlement by her alliance with Poland and by supporting the alliance concluded between Czechoslovakia, Yugoslavia and Romania, known as the Little Entente. Opposition to this alliance resulted in close cooperation among Austria, Hungary, and Italy. The Little Entente, the Balkan Entente and the Hungaro-Italo-Austrian combination, however, could not survive the soon resurgent and overwhelming outside force from Germany and Russia.[28]

The fact that jingo-nationalist, but internally weak and quarrelling, small states would not be able to check the overwhelming outside forces was disregarded by the peacemakers after the First World War. The might of Germany and Russia existed potentially even in the 1920's. Perhaps Austrian and Hungarian statesmanship had made a poor showing in the decades preceding the destruction of the Dual Monarchy, but the peacemakers of 1919 and the leaders of the successor states between the World Wars certainly surpassed them in political shortsightedness. This has been demonstrated *ad oculos* by the outcome of their policies in the Danubian area.

The political structure of the multi-national Empire may have been antiquated, but the new order proved to be less stable and offered less security for the Danubian people and for the whole of Europe. In one man's lifetime the Danubian nations experienced the destruction of three international and domestic orders. *Peccatur intra muros et extra muros.* In the course of these events, almost all nationalities committed errors and mistakes. Although one cannot turn back the wheels of history, the positive and negative teaching of these manifold experiences, if examined with mutual understanding and humility, might suggest some solutions for the future. Probably the advantages of a great political and economic unit combined with the benefits of democratic equality, extended to all nationalities, might open the door for better developments after the ordeal of the present period.

Hungary's status after the first World War was particularly difficult. After the defeat and disintegration of the Red Army of Béla Kun, Romanian troops occupied Budapest and the major part of the country.[29] The occupation was accompanied by extensive looting, which caused damages of almost three billion gold crowns.[30] This was followed by a disastrous peace treaty. As Francesco Nitti put it: "By a stroke of irony the financial and economic clauses inflict the most serious burdens on a country which has lost almost everything: which has lost the greatest number of men proportionately in the war, which since the war has had two revolutions, which for four months suffered the sackings of Bolshevism—led by Béla Kun and the worst elements of revolutionary political crime—and, finally, has suffered a Rumanian occupation, which was worse almost than the revolutions of Bolshevism."[31]

Negotiations with Hungary did not precede the peace settlement; the provisions of the treaty were established by the victorious states. Subsequently the Hungarian peace delegation was merely heard on one occasion. The Treaty of Trianon made Hungary the most dissatisfied of all the Danubian states.[32] The Peace Conference decided the claims of the neighboring states put forward against Hungary, but did not consider the cumulative effect of these claims on the new Hungary itself. As one outstanding chronicler of the Peace Conference, Harold Nicolson, points out, the Conference "approached its problems in terms, not of the enemy Powers, but of the respective 'claims' of the succession and smaller States."[33] Dealing with the problem of the Territorial Committees, Nicolson noted the defects in their proceedings, pointing out that the main task of the Committees was not to recommend a general territorial settlement, but to pronounce on the particular claims of certain states.[34] The adverse effects of such a procedure are obvious.

The American recommendations concerning Hungary's frontiers were more favorable than the final provisions of the Trianon Treaty.[35] A member of the American Peace Commission, Professor Archibald C. Coolidge of Harvard, visited Hungary in January of 1919 and prepared a very objective report on the conditions in Hungary and the repercussions to be expected from the projected peace settlement.[36] And as Lloyd George himself pointed out in a memorandum of March 25, 1919, "There will never be peace in Southeastern Europe if every little state now coming into being is to have a large Magyar irredenta within its borders." Therefore he recommended that the different races should be allocated to their motherlands, and that this criterion "should have precedence over considerations of strategy or economics or communications, which can usually be adjusted by other means."[37]

Such considerations were discarded. The frontiers of the new Hungary were fixed principally according to Romanian, Czechoslovak, and Yugoslav demands, and after consideration of their geographical, strategic, economic and ethnographic arguments. Territories inhabited by Hungarians figured as a sort of "no man's land."[38] A remark attributed to Beneš was characteristic of the general atmosphere of the conference. "I am alarmed," Beneš said to a friend, "when I see that they give me everything that I ask for. It is too much."[39]

The upshot of the matter was that the peace settlement was incomparably more severe for Hungary than for Germany or Bulgaria. True, Austria lost even more than Hungary, but Austria was a frequently changing federation of heterogeneous territories gradually acquired by the House of Habsburg and the Germans formed only a little over one-third of its population. Hungary had existed for centuries as a unitary state which demonstrated a remarkable degree of stability and stamina through the vicissitudes of history. The Treaty of Trianon reduced Hungary proper to less than one-third of her former territory and about two-fifths of her population.[40] Over three million Hungarians were attached, against their wishes, to the neighboring states. The Hungarian peace delegation vainly proposed a plebiscite for the territories in dispute.[41]

As a result of the territorial changes effected under the peace treaty the population of Hungary decreased to a figure considerably less than the actual number of Hungarians residing in Eastern Europe, while the population of Czechoslovakia, Romania and Yugoslavia became, in every case, considerably greater than the actual number of any of their respective national groups. This situation is especially evident in the light of the 1910 and 1920 censuses, but it can also be clearly seen from the 1930 censuses which were least favorable to the Hungarians.[42]

It is generally known that because of the complication of ethnographic conditions in the Danube Valley it was impossible to establish completely satisfactory frontiers. However, about one and a half million Hungarians who lived in compact blocks along the new frontiers were detached from Hungary. This artificial separation could not be justified, even in the eyes of a disinterested observer, let alone to the Hungarian people themselves.

The dissolution of the Monarchy in itself had a very unfavorable effect on the economy of Hungary. The great internal market and balanced economy suddenly ceased to exist. Most of the factories and industrial areas remaining in Hungary were deprived of their markets and were cut off from their sources of raw materials within the neighboring states. In addition, the Trianon frontiers produced a whole series of special economic difficulties. For example, the new frontiers cut in half the areas of twenty-four flood control companies. As a result of the uncooperative attitudes of Czechoslovakia and Romania, Hungary became exposed to grave risk of floods on the lower reaches of her rivers without being able to establish sufficient protection against them. A careless deforestation policy in both countries increased the flood danger to Hungary. The major part of Hungary is a lowland, and nearly one quarter of the productive area of the country consists of land which had been protected against inundations only at an enormous cost in money and labor. In many cases such troubles could have been avoided by minor frontier rectifications or other suitable arrangements, if Hungary's case had been seriously considered and Hungarian experts had been consulted at the peace settlement.

The general economic difficulties created by the peace settlement were increased by the refugee problem. More than 350,000 Hungarians were forced to leave the neighboring states and move to the reduced territory of Hungary. These homeless masses, largely middle-class people, greatly increased Hungary's economic and social difficulties. They also became, as a matter of course, the moving spirits of revisionist movements.

The situation created by the peace treaty would have been unacceptable to any self-respecting people, but the Hungarians were particularly proud of having organized and maintained a state on one of the most dangerous spots of Europe for a thousand years. Their bitterness was made even greater by their conviction that after Hungary had defended the whole of Europe against invasions in the past—a claim asserted by a number of the countries of Eastern Europe—the West had, so to speak, "stabbed them in the back."

The Hungarians looked with great confidence to the United States and especially to the principles promulgated by President Wilson.[43] However, the vindictive peace settlement imposed by the victors in the name of democracy gave that term a rather doubtful meaning to many Hungarians. It seemed to them that, at the peace table, the lofty principles were applied only against them and never in their favor. Trianon had a harmful effect in domestic politics as well. It gave an evil connotation to the term "democracy," and indirectly retarded democratic forces in the country.

Notes

1. According to an American student of international affairs, the sudden disappearance of Austria-Hungary "has been characterized as the most important purely political occurrence since the fall of the Western Roman Empire in 476 A.D." Raymond Leslie Buell, *Europe: A History of Ten Years* (New York, 1928), p. 296.

2. According to the famous Czech historian, Frantisek Palacky, it would have been necessary to create the Habsburg Monarchy, had it not existed. Other outstanding Slav and Romanian statesmen also believed that the polyglot Empire was a necessity to its own people and to Europe. Eduard Beneš stated in one of his books that he did not believe in the dismemberment of Austria. He argued that the historic and economic bonds between the Austrian nations are too powerful to make such a dismemberment

possible. And he predicted that the national struggles would play an important role in Austria for a long time but that they would not be the same as they used to be in the preceding half century. Eduard Beneš, *Le problème Autrichien et la question Tchèque* (Paris, 1908), p. 307.

A Romanian patriot, Aurel C. Popovici, the Austro-Romanian champion of ethnic federalism, correctly pointed out the international aspect of the Austrian problem: "Rumania, based on her urge for self-preservation, has a great interest in the existence of a mighty Austria. This interest excludes *a priori* any dream, any thought of an annexation of Austrian territories inhabited by Romanians. Such annexation would be possible only in the case of an Austrian debacle, and such a debacle with mathematical certainty would in the course of a few decades lead to the ruin of Romania, her destruction in the Russian sea." *Die Vereinigten Staaten von Gross-Oesterreich* (Leipzig, 1906), p. 418. English translation in Robert A. Kann, *op. cit.*, Vol. I, pp. 314–315.

3. Winston S. Churchill, *The Gathering Storm* (Boston, 1948), p. 10.

4. *New York Times*, October 3, 1950.

5. Oscar Jászi, *The Dissolution of the Habsburg Monarchy* (Chicago, 1929). Cf. Macartney, *National States and National Minorities* (Oxford University Press, 1934). R. W. Seton-Watson, *Racial Problems in Hungary* (London, 1908). R. W. Seton-Watson, *Southern Slav Question and the Habsburg Monarchy* (London, 1911). Ferenc Eckhardt, *A Short History of the Hungarian People* (London, 1931). Jules Szekfü, *Etat et Nation* (Paris, 1945). A.J.P. Taylor, *The Habsburg Monarchy 1809–1918* (London, 1948). Dominic G. Koráry, *A History of Hungary* (Cleveland, 1941). Oscar Halecki, *Borderlands of Western Civilization. A History of East Central Europe* (New York, 1952). For the general aspects of modern nationalism, see, Carlton J. H. Hayes, *Essays on Nationalism* (New York, 1926); *The Historical Evolution of Modern Nationalism* (New York, 1931). Hans Kohn, *The Idea of Nationalism* (New York, 1944). Alfred Cobban, *National Self-Determination*, Revised edition (Chicago, 1947).

6. The case of Austria-Hungary has been ably presented by Archduke Otto, the eldest son of Emperor-King Charles, the last Austro-Hungarian ruler. "Danubian Reconstruction," *Foreign Affairs*, 20 (1941–42), 243–252.

7. Count Ottokar Czernin, writing under the impact of the events in 1918, was rather pessimistic and thought that "Austria-Hungary's watch had run down" in any event. "We could have fought against Germany with the Entente on Austro-Hungarian soil, and would doubtless have hastened Germany's collapse; but the wounds which Austria-Hungary would have received in the fray would not have been less serious than those from which she is now suffering; she would have perished in the fight against Germany, as she has as good as perished in her fight allied with Germany." *In the World War* (New York, 1920), pp. 36–37.

8. See *Oesterreich-Ungarns letzter Krieg 1914–1918*, published by the

Austrian Bundesministerium für Heereswesen, editor-in-chief Edmund Glaise-Horstenau, 7 vols. (Vienna, 1931–1938).

9. The Austrian Minister to Great Britain between the world wars made the following statement concerning the foreign service: "Although its personnel consisted of Germans, Hungarians, Poles, Ruthenians, Rumanians, Czechs, Croats, Italians and Serbs from the different parts of the Monarchy, the service was inspired by a single-minded patriotism, and I remember no single case in which an official ever put the interests of his own nationality before those of the Monarchy." Sir George Franckenstein, *Diplomat of Destiny* (New York, 1940), p. 25.

10. In the early stages of the First World War, the Entente Powers did not plan the destruction of Austria-Hungary. With respect to President Wilson, Colonel House noted that "In common with the leading statesmen of western Europe he believed that the political union of Austro-Hungarian peoples was a necessity." Charles Seymour, *The Intimate Papers of Colonel House*, Vol. III (Boston, 1928), pp. 335–336. When President Wilson, in his address of December 4, 1917, proposed to Congress a declaration of war on the Habsburg Monarchy, he emphasized that "We do not wish in any way to impair or to rearrange the Austro-Hungarian Empire. It is no affair of ours what they do with their own life, either industrially or politically. We do not purpose or desire to dictate to them in any way. We only desire to see that their affairs are left in their own hands, in all matters, great or small." *Foreign Relations 1917*, pp. xi–xii. According to point ten of President Wilson's Fourteen Points, "The peoples of Austria-Hungary, whose place among the nations we wish to see safeguarded and assured, should be accorded the freest opportunity of autonomous development." At almost the same time, on January 5, 1918, Prime Minister Lloyd George stated that the British were not fighting to destroy Austria-Hungary and that a break-up of that Empire was no part of their war aims.

Notwithstanding these various declarations of principle, the specific promises made in the course of the war to Italy, to Romania, and later to the other nationalities could not have been fulfilled without the destruction of the Monarchy. Moreover, in the last months of the war the propaganda and diplomatic activity of the Entente powers underwent a fundamental change with regard to the fate of Austria-Hungary. Clemenceau's revelations in April, 1918, concerning Emperor Charles' peace overtures had a decisive impact on the course of events. Some Western statesmen possibly fell under the spell of the wartime propaganda encouraged and supported by themselves, at first perhaps only for military expediency. In this process, Czech political leaders in the western countries played a leading role and the creation of Czechoslovakia was the most decisive blow to the Monarchy. For details see, Eduard Beneš, *My War Memoirs* (Boston, 1922). E. Beneš, *Détruisez l'Autriche-Hongrie* (Paris, 1916), published in English in the following year. T. G. Masaryk, *The Making of a State* (London, 1927). Henry Wickham

Steed, *Through Thirty Years 1892–1922* (Garden City, 1925). R. W. Seton-Watson, *Masaryk in England* (Cambridge, 1943). *War Memoirs of Robert Lansing* (Indianapolis, 1935). Charles Pergler, *America in the Struggle for Czechoslovak Independence* (Philadelphia, 1926). Count Stephen Burian, *Austria in Dissolution* (London, 1925). Heinrich Lammasch, *Europas elfte Stunde* (München, 1919). Mitchell Pirie Briggs, *George D. Herron and the European Settlement* (Stanford, 1932). A.J.P. Taylor, *op. cit.* Victor S. Mametey, "The United States and the Dissolution of Austria-Hungary," *Journal of Central European Affairs,* X (1950), 256–270.

11. The allegation made by Stefan Osuský, one of the founders of Czechoslovakia, that Emperor Charles' irresolution and procrastination caused the downfall of the Monarchy is unsubstantiated by facts and is contrary to the events, especially as explained by Masaryk and Beneš who, since 1915, had been doing successful spade work for the destruction of the Monarchy. Cf. *Freedom and Union* (May 1949), pp. 22–23. Regardless of what Emperor Charles might have offered to the nationalities in 1918, the positions in Paris, London, Rome and Washington were definitively taken against the survival of the Monarchy.

12. For details see, Oscar Jászi, *Revolution and Counter-Revolution in Hungary* (London, 1924). Count Michel Károlyi, *Fighting the World; the Struggle for Peace* (New York, 1925). Gusztáv Gratz, *A forradalmak kora 1918–1920* (Budapest, 1935).

13. For a description of these events, see, C. A. Macartney, *op. cit.*, pp. 275–279, 364–370, 390–395.

14. A.J.P. Taylor, *op. cit.*, 250.

15. Albert Kaas, *Bolshevism in Hungary* (London, 1931). F. Borkenau, *World Communism* (New York, 1939), pp. 108–133. In Soviet Russia itself the establishment of the Hungarian Soviet Republic was considered an event of the greatest importance. Even the cautious Lenin asserted in his speech of April 17 that "the Hungarian Revolution plays a larger role in history than the Russian revolution." Quoted by David T. Cattell, "The Hungarian Revolution of 1919 and the Reorganization of the Comintern in 1920," *Journal of Central European Affairs,* XI (1951), 27–38.

16. Herbert Hoover gave a colorful description of these events in the following: "Hungary in the year 1919 presented a sort of unending, formless procession of tragedies, with occasional comic relief. Across our reconstruction stage there marched liberalism, revolution, socialism, communism, imperialism, terror, wanton executions, murder, suicide, falling ministries, invading armies, looted hospitals, conspirators, soldiers, kings and queens—all with a constant background of starving women and children. . . .The relief organization contributed something to their spiritual recovery. But had there not been a magnificent toughness in the Magyar spirit, the race would have collapsed." *The Memoirs of Herbert Hoover 1874–1920* (New York, 1952), p. 397.

17. Sarah Wambaugh, *Plebiscites Since the World War*, Vol. I (Washington, 1933), pp. 163–205. H.W.V. Temperley, *A History of the Peace Conference of Paris*, Vol. IV (London, 1921), pp. 368–381.

18. "As regards the question of plebiscites the Allied Powers considered them needless, when they perceived with certainty that this consultation, if surrounded with complete guarantees of sincerity, would not give results substantially different from those at which they had arrived after a minute study of the ethnographic conditions and national aspirations." H.W.V. Temperley, *op. cit.*, Vol. IV, p. 422. Concerning the Hungarian peace treaty negotiations see, Francis Deák, *Hungary at the Paris Peace Conference* (New York, 1942).

19. Winston Churchill, *The World Crisis—The Aftermath* (New York, 1929), pp. 231–232.

20. At this time the United States had 92,000,000 inhabitants.

21. Frederick Hertz, *The Economic Problem of the Danubian States* (London, 1947), pp. 24, 38, 49.

22. *Daily Telegraph*, April 18, 1950. In connection with the centenary of Thomas Masaryk's birth an exchange of opinion took place on the break-up of the Austro-Hungarian Empire in April 14, 17, 18, 19, 27 and June 1, 1950 issues of the *Telegraph*.

With regard to the establishment of Czechoslovakia, Samuel Hazzard Cross of Harvard, gave in retrospect the following description of events:

"It is worth remarking that in 1914 Bohemian ambitions had not extended beyond vague hopes of eventual autonomy within a federalized monarchy, while the utopia of independence was conceived mainly in the minds of emigré leaders like Professor Masaryk and Dr. Beneš. It was not until 1917 that the domestic Bohemian attitude became definitely revolutionary, and Slovak sympathy was not finally secured until May, 1918, through the celebrated Treaty of Pittsburg, which guaranteed the Slovaks a degree of autonomy which they never attained until just before the Czechoslovak Republic was dismembered by Hitler. As a matter of fact, the relations between Czechs and Slovaks were never so dove-like as Bohemian statesmen would have had us suppose and at the Armistice, Czech troops had simply marched in and occupied the Slovak section of Hungary." *Slavic Civilization Through the Ages* (Harvard University Press, 1948), p. 182.

23. In the light of statistics, his conclusion was that "all the efforts to foster, by an extreme protectionism, either the rapid increase of agricultural production or that of industrial output had only a very limited success. Increases of production were smaller than the progress under the former conditions of free trade within the Austro-Hungarian Customs Union." Hertz, *op. cit.*, p. 220.

24. See article 222 of the Peace Treaty of St. Germain, and articles 205, 207 and 208 of the Peace Treaty of Trianon.

25. Hugh Seton-Watson has published the best general description of these events. See *Eastern Europe between the Wars 1918–1941* (Cambridge, 1945) and *The East European Revolution* (New York, 1951). Cf. C. A. Macartney, *Hungary and her Successors* (London, 1937).

26. The internal development of two newly created states, Czechoslovakia and Yugoslavia was described by a British historian in the following way: "Czechoslovakia and Yugoslavia, despite their national theory, reproduced the national complications of Austria-Hungary. Constitutional Austria had contained eight nationalities; Czechoslovakia contained seven. Great Hungary had contained seven nationalities; Yugoslavia contained nine. Czechoslovakia became a unitary state, in which the Czechs were 'the people of the state,' as the Germans had been in constitutional Austria. Yugoslavia had a period of sham federalism; then it too became a unitary state, which the Serbs claimed as their national state, after the model of the Magyars in Hungary. . . .

"The Czechs could outplay the Slovaks; they could not satisfy them. Masaryk had hoped that the Czechs and the Slovaks would come together as the English and the Scotch had done; the Slovaks turned out to be the Irish. In the same way, the Serbs could master the Croats; they could not satisfy, nor even, being less skillful politicians, outplay them." A.J.P. Taylor, *op. cit.*, pp. 254–255.

27. In his report of November 1, 1938, Newton, the British Minister to Prague, characterized Czechoslovak democracy in the following way: "There can be little doubt that the democratic system as it has developed in this country during the past twenty years has not been a wholly unmixed blessing, even for the Czechs by whom and for whom it was elaborated. Under it quick and clear decisions were difficult to come by, and party considerations were only too often given pride of place over national. Moreover, it is hardly an exaggeration to say that all public appointments even down to that of crossing sweeper depended upon possession of the necessary party ticket so that each party became almost a State within the State. Today there is a natural tendency to say goodbye to all that, and one of the constant themes in the press is that public life and social services must be cleansed of patronage and the misuse of political influence. Criticism is heard not only of the quality but of the quantity of officials in the civil service. It is said, for example, that there are more officials in the Ministry for Foreign Affairs in Prague than there were in the Ballplatz of Imperial Vienna." *British Documents*, Third Series, Vol. III, Doc. 245.

28. The situation resulting from the peace settlement has been well characterized by the late Professor Cross of Harvard. He writes: "If there is any lesson to be learned from the experience of the last thirty years, it is that setting up a series of economically weak national states solely on the basis of romantic ideals and strategic aims is no guarantee of peace. To bolster up

their weak budgets or to favor local industry, such states erect tariff barriers which prevent the normal flow of commerce and exchange on which their very life depends. If their territories contain linguistic minorities, the latter are discriminated against in business and politics until they seek support from the nearest larger state to which they are akin, and eventually provide that state with a natural pretext for intervention. In order to counterbalance their more powerful neighbors or checkmate some adjacent state with good diplomatic connections, these little states unite in ententes and alliances which become the pawns of international politics, and give statesmen of these minor organisms a chance to assume positions of influence for which they are not qualified by experience or vision." Samuel Hazzard Cross, *op. cit.*, p. 183.

29. Romania concluded a separate peace with the Central Powers in January, 1918 and re-entered the war in the following November.

30. The loot of Hungary and the general behavior of the Romanian army was described in detail by the American member of the Inter-Allied Mission to Hungary. See Maj. Gen. Harry Hill Bandholtz, *An Undiplomatic Diary* (New York, 1933), pp. 18, 50, 92–93. Herbert Hoover explained that the Romanian army occupied Budapest on August 5, 1919, in defiance of direct orders of the 'Big Four,' and "then began a regime equally horrible with Béla Kun's. The Romanian army looted the city in good old medieval style. They even took supplies from the children's hospitals. Many children died. They looted art galleries, private houses, banks, railway rolling stock, machinery, farm animals—in fact, everything movable which Béla Kun had collected." *Op. cit.*, pp. 400–401.

31. Francesco Nitti, *The Wreck of Europe* (Indianapolis, 1922), pp. 170–171.

32. For the peace negotiations the best general sources are: D. H. Miller, *My Diary at the Conference of Paris*, Vol. XXI (New York, 1924). Harold W. V. Temperley, *A History of the Peace Conference at Paris*, Vol. I–VI (London, 1920–24). *Foreign Relations, The Paris Peace Conference*, Vol. I–XIII (Washington, 1942–1947). The foremost study of the diplomatic history of the Treaty of Trianon is Francis Deák's work: *Hungary at the Paris Conference*, which is based mainly on original documents and deals with all the pertinent material. The Hungarian Foreign Ministry published the official Hungarian material in The *Hungarian Peace Negotiations*, Vol. I–III and maps (Budapest, 1920–22). C. A. Macartney condensed comprehensive material in his standard work: *Hungary and Her Successors The Treaty of Trianon and Its Consequences* (London, 1937).

33. Harold Nicolson, *Peacemaking* (London, 1933), p. 117. Cf. Harold Temperley, "How the Hungarian Frontiers Were Drawn," *Foreign Affairs*, 6 (1928), 432–433, and *A History of the Peace Conference* at Paris, Vol. I, p. 258.

34. Nicolson mentioned as an example that the Committee on Romanian claims thought only in terms of Transylvania, and the Committee on Czech claims concentrated upon the southern frontiers of Slovakia. "It was only too late that it was realized that these two entirely separate Committees had between them imposed upon Hungary a loss of territory and population which, when combined, was very serious indeed. Had the work been concentrated in the hands of a Hungarian Committee, not only would a wider area of frontier have been open for the give and take of discussion, but it would have been seen that the total cessions imposed placed more Magyars under alien rule than was consonant with the doctrine of Self-Determination." *Op. cit.*, pp. 127–128. Nicolson's observations were not influenced by any sympathy toward Hungary. He repeatedly explained in his various writings that he disliked the Hungarians. When the Red Army advanced on Budapest he was pleased and detected in himself "stirrings of positive delight." *Spectator*, November 10, 1944.

35. Cf. Deák, *op. cit.*, pp. 27–29.

36. *Ibid.*, pp. 15–23.

37. D. Lloyd George, *Memoirs of the Peace Conference* (New Haven, 1939), p. 266.

38. In the words of an English scholar, "One point after another was conceded; and in the end Roumania was given an area in which the Roumanians formed only 55 per cent of the total population. The Slovaks in Slovakia were 60 per cent, the Ruthenes in Ruthenia 56 per cent, the Serbs in the Voivodina only 28 per cent, or 33 per cent counting all the Yugoslavs together; while the Magyar-speaking persons in each area formed close on one-third of all the inhabitants; over one million in the territory assigned to Czechoslovakia, over 1,650,000 in that given to Roumania, 450,000 in Yugoslavia's portion." C. A. Macartney, *op. cit.*, p. 4. True, these figures were based on the census of 1910 and some aspects of this census were contested. But the overall picture remained the same even according to the censuses carried out by the succession states themselves. For the situation arising from the 1930 censuses, see below, footnote 42.

39. This observation of Beneš was noted by the editor of the *Journal de Genève*, William Martin, *Les Hommes d'Etat pendant la guerre* (Paris, 1929), p. 316. In any case this is an overstatement because not all demands of Beneš were fulfilled. For example, a corridor between Yugoslavia and Czechoslovakia was not established.

40. According to the 1910 census, Hungary proper possessed a population of over 18,000,000 persons, of whom 54.5 percent declared Hungarian to be their mother tongue. Including Croetia-Slavonia the total population was over 20,000,000 of whom 48.1 percent spoke Hungarian as their mother tongue.

41. In reality the Hungarian peace delegation was confronted with a *fait*

accompli. According to Temperley no event affected the frontiers of Hungary more decisively than the Béla Kun regime, which Temperley considered partly a socialist experiment, partly a Hungarian protest against the advance of the Czech and Romanian army. "Béla Kun finally sent forces to attack both Czechoslovaks and Romanians, and it was this action that forced the Big Four to come to a decision. . . . And the *finis Hungariae* . . . was decreed on June 13, 1919." Harold Temperley, "How the Hungarian Frontiers Were Drawn," *Foreign Affairs,* 6 (1928), pp. 434–435.

42. The result of the 1930 censuses disclosed that: with 10.8 million Hungarians in Europe, the new Hungary had a population of 8.7 millions on an area of 93,000 square kilometers; with 13.8 million Romanians in Europe, the new Romania had a population of 18.1 millions and an area of 295,000 square kilometers; with 11.9 million Serbs, Croats and Slovenes in Europe, the new Yugoslavia had a population of 13.9 millions and an area of 249,000 square kilometers; with 10.2 million Czechs and Slovaks in Europe, the new Czechoslovakia had a population of 14.7 millions and an area of 140,000 square kilometers. This means that the Czechs and Slovaks were able to unite 96.6 percent of the Czechs and Slovaks living in Europe in their own country, but despite this, these groups made up only 66.2 percent of the total population of the country. The Romanians assembled 96 percent of their own people within their own frontiers but this group was only 72 percent of the total population. The Yugoslavs had 93 percent of their own nationals within their country, but they were only 79.8 percent of the total population of Yugoslavia. In contrast to this, at this time only 74 percent of the Hungarians lived in their own country but they made up 92 percent of the total population of Hungary.

43. See the report on Hungary by A. C. Coolidge. Quoted by Deák, *op. cit.,* pp. 16–18.

Károly Vigh

Causes and Consequences of Trianon:
A Re-Examination

No country or nation in contemporary history has been struck by a calamity of such lasting impact as Hungary when, on June 4, 1920, as a consequence of the peace treaty of Trianon, she was deprived of her historical boundaries and about two thirds of her territory and population, including 3,400,000 Hungarians attached to the neighboring states. At the same time Germany lost but 13.5 percent of its former lands to her victorious neighbors, and Bulgaria a mere 8 percent. Thus, the greatest injustice in Paris was committed against Hungary, as if that country were mainly to blame for the war and its outbreak.

The attitude of British political circles and the changes in the Foreign Office are particularly instructive and even decisive with regard to Hungary from the turn of the century down to 1918. It should be pointed out right from the start that the British attitude towards Hungary was always a corrolary of its attitude and policies towards the Habsburg Monarchy. Until 1918 these policies were basically shaped by the well-known view of Queen Victoria's Foreign Secretary and Prime Minister, Henry J. T. Palmerston, that Hungary was only part of the Habsburg realm. Palmerston was the person who made practically a dogma of the thesis that British policy towards Central Europe relied on Austria as a great power.

This Palmerstonian thesis lost none of its validity for over 65 years. For this very reason, in the period 1860–67 official England and its press strived to find a solution to the Hungarian question, some kind of agreement between the dynasty and Hungary. There was general agreement in this regard between the conservative and liberal elements of the British establishment. Even in the 1850's, during the climax of Kossuth's popularity, the pro-Hungarian public opinion and the government never reached the point where they would accept Hungarian independence as a necessity, no matter how lasting an impression the leader of the struggle for independence may have made on the English people. After the Compromise of 1867, however, it was the Deák line which got the upper hand in England, and the Tory cabinets disapproved of the Hungarian opposition that aimed at breaking up the Dualist foundations. At the same time British liberals hoped that liberal Hungary would become the focal point of a Monarchy that was in the process of turning into a Danubian empire; and that Hungary would act as the conveyor of civilization to the Balkans.[1]

Although the name of Lajos Kossuth continued to enjoy high respect even after 1867 as a symbol of national liberation, and at the time of his death in 1894 his uncompromising personality was eulogized in lengthy articles, not a word was said about his principles regarding independence, or of his vision of a federation.

The nationalities problem began to assume ever greater importance in the statements of British politicians, diplomats, and journalists concerning the Austro-Hungarian Monarchy from the 1890's on. The opinion of the Foreign Office in this regard was influenced to a large extent by Sir Arthur Nicolson, Consul at Budapest, soon to be named Ambassador to St. Petersburg; in his elaborate dispatches from Budapest he gave an account of the dissatisfaction and complaints of the Croatians and Romanians. He also mentioned in his reports the oppressive measures of the Hungarian government and its attempts to assimilate the nationalities. Nicolson's evaluation found an echo among several of his diplomat colleagues. The Romanian question in particular was publicized in the press, well-known British journalists and scientists calling attention to the relationship between Hungary and Romania.[2]

At the turn of the century the official British estimate of Hungary cannot be said to be unfavorable. For instance, the *Times* wrote in connection with the visit of Kaiser Wilhelm II to Budapest, that the political center of gravity of the Monarchy seems to have shifted to Budapest because, in spite of its many nationalities, Hungary "is a homogeneous political unit compared with Austria proper. The Magyars have always shown a remarkable instinct for constitutional politics and their leadership behind the Leitha, in a kingdom associated with great traditions, is practically unchallenged."[3] The comments on Hungarian politics were likewise positive on the occasion of the Budapest visit of King Carol of Romania.

In general it can be said in this period from the fall of 1897 to the summer of 1898, that the most important British newspapers, the *Times*, the *Economist*, the *Foreign Office Papers*, several monthlies, and the liberal *Fortnightly Review* all wrote favorably about domestic conditions in Hungary and the country's prospects. But it would be a mistake to attribute too much importance to this evidence, because it was only in relation to the deplorable conditions in Austria that the Hungarian political conditions seemed good.

The criticisms of Hungarian politics emanating from Nicolson soon found confirmation in the brutal and undemocratic methods of the Dezső Bánffy regime. The *Times* and other dailies criticized Bánffy not only because of his law on servants and his breaking up the harvest strikes, but also because in 1898 he issued an ordinance regarding the Magyarization of non-Hungarian placenames.[4] (As we know, following his example the Czechoslovakian government changed the names of ancient Hungarian settlements in Slovakia after the Second World War!) One of the prestigious periodicals, the *Quarterly Review*, published an article in a similar vein. It claimed that in no other country is the ruling nationality as tyrannical and impatient as in Hungary, the country of liberalism and liberty.[5]

The first ominous signs of the unfavorable turn in British public opinion vis-à-vis Hungary appeared in its appraisal of the Hungarian political crisis of 1904–06. This was the period when the *Times*, sympathetic to the Hungarian cause ever since the 1850's, and its increasingly well-known correspondent in Vienna, H. W. Steed, struck a more and more critical tone regarding conditions in Hungary. Both the British press and the Foreign Office begin to distrust not only the foreign policy of the Monarchy, but also conditions inside Hungary. British politicians expressed growing disappointment in the political wisdom and common sense of the Hungarian nation, in contrast to their former views. The criticism of the coalition voted into power by the electorate, of the recalcitrance in military matters (commands to be given in Hungarian), of the exacerbation of the separatist mood which could lead to grave international consequences, of the tragi-comedy of "national resistance," of the narrowness of Hungarian chauvinism in general, which was presumptuous enough to confront simultaneously Francis Joseph and his army, the government of Austria, and the nationalities—all of this criticism became markedly sharper. The voices critical of the Hungarian coalition soon embraced all things Hungarian.

To make the picture complete, we should add that the change in the British attitude was caused not simply by the Hungarian political crisis of 1904–06, but by other factors which played a prominent role about this time (the rise of German power, the serious defeat the Russians suffered at the hands of Japan, etc.). Certain circles began to believe that the Monarchy could fulfill its role as a counterpoise to Germany only if its fate were in the hands of more reliably anti-German nationalities.

In the vanguard of those critical of Hungary we find prestigious, competent, respectable journalists such as Wickham Steed, the Vienna correspondent of the *Times*. His debate with the Hungarian press, with Jenő Rákosi, the chauvinist editor-in-chief of the *Budapesti Hirlap*, and with Albert Apponyi, in the columns of the *Times*[6] only enhanced his objections to Hungarian policies. He traveled to Budapest in September 1906, for the new session of parliament, and what he experienced there quickened his disillusionment with political Hungary.

That year Steed had arrived to the rejection of dualism, to the notion of a federalized monarchy.[7] Steed had arrived at the awareness that the ruling classes in Hungary were no longer able to fulfill their former function as the solid foundation on which the power of the Austro-Hungarian Empire was built.

Steed's view of the Hungarians underwent a profound change during the crisis. His knowledge became deeper, most of his illusions dissipated: although he saw Hungary through the prism of anti-German British imperialism, in some ways his views were progressive, hence Hungary appeared to him an increasingly backward, reactionary, and even internationally weak country. His subjective sentiments were undoubtedly affected by the attacks his comments elicited in the Hungarian press. It occurred to him well before the outbreak of the World War that the federalization of the Monarchy and Slav leadership would be the most effective antidote to the German peril. He had not yet arrived at a final opinion; he would come to it only as a result of the pace of events following the outbreak of the war.

In the days when R. W. Steed offered well-founded and almost scientific analyses of conditions in Hungary, and an alternative for its future, there were journalists who were wont to side with Hungary against Vienna. According to an article in the *Scottish Review*, Hungary was justified in struggling for an independent army, for an enhanced sovereignty; the article observed, furthermore, that Hungary had outgrown the framework of the Compromise. It expressed hopes that the Hungarians' effort will be crowned with success. The author of the article was R. W. Seton-Watson.[8]

As we have included in this volume a noteworthy study by Hugh Seton-Watson, there is no reason for me to dwell on Seton-Watson's activities in connection with Trianon here. I will only mention a few essential elements for the sake of continuity.

Seton-Watson was the son of patriotic Scottish parents, and was among those British intellectuals who shared the "conventional admiration," even while young, of the majority towards Lajos Kossuth and his nation. The young Seton-Watson extended this feeling to the Hungarian Independence Party and arrived in Vienna, in November 1905, convinced of the just cause of the Hungarian coalition. Here the skeptical, superior smile of Steed did not change his views; as mentioned above, in the spring of 1906 he still believed in the glory of the "phoenix of nations." He began to have doubts when he reached Budapest in the spring of 1906 and met political leaders such as Apponyi, Ferenc Kossuth, Sándor Esterházy, Lajos Láng, Jenő Rákosi, but also Saxon intelectuals from Transylvania, as well as Romanian politicians and journalists. In spite of this, the work he published in 1907 indicates that he still had faith in the future of the Monarchy.[9] In it, however, he was calling for the federalization of the Monarchy. In a pessimistic vein he believed, though, that foolish Hungarian policy of forceful assimilation would never allow that to come about.[10]

Reporting on the experiences gathered during his travel in the Slovak area in the columns of the *Spectator*, the *Times*, and the *Morning Post*, he criticized the antinationalities aspect of the school laws attributed to Apponyi, as well as the obsolete electoral system, the autonomy of the Church, the coolie life of the servants on the estates, etc. Seton-Watson denounced the oppression of the Slovaks in particular—an oppression confirmed by the bloody incident at Csernova on October 27, 1907, which resulted in the tragic death of 15 victims. (The gendarmes fired into the crowd on the occasion of the consecration of the Catholic Church at Csernova, performed by Father Andrej Hlinka in spite of the objections of the authorities.)

Following the massacre at Csernova, and as a result of the antagonistic articles published by Seton-Watson and others in the British press, the public mood soon turned anti-Hungarian; along with the analyses of W. Steed in the *Times*, this mood was to constitute the basis of the anti-Monarchy propaganda that became widespread among the politicians from the area of the future successor states following the outbreak of the war.

Steed and Seton-Watson, former friends of Austria-Hungary, played a leading role in the propaganda campaign launched against the enemy countries during the World War. They were no longer concerned with internal reform, but strived to sweep away the state which stood in the way of the nationalities within the Monarchy. Steed, as the foreign policy editor of the *Times*, and Seton Watson as the editor of *New Europe* which he founded at his own expense in 1916, used the press as weapons, often arbitrarily and with biased arguments, on behalf of the imperialist objectives of the Entente: the maximum territorial claims of the Slavs and the Romanians.

When the War Cabinet directed by Lloyd George established, in February 1918, the Department of Propaganda in Enemy Countries, he named Steed and Seton-Watson as the co-directors of the Austro-Hungarian section. The latter was also closely associated with the Austro-Hungarian experts in the Political Intelligence Section of the Foreign Office.[12] The articles and secret memoranda which flooded the British press mainly thanks to their efforts, succeeded, in late spring and summer of 1918, in convincing the British political leadership and public opinion to give up the foreign policy principle which it had held for centuries with regard to the Habsburg Monarchy. The exiled politicians from the Monarchy were given the green light to proceed with their plans for dissolving the Habsburg Empire. Steed, Seton-Watson, and the officials and specialists, including journalists, historians, and politicians brought up on their writings contributed a great deal to the process of dissolution, to the fermentation within the Monarchy. The new order in Central Europe, and the new boundaries can be regarded largely as the fruits of their work before and after 1914.

*   *   *

The above-described anti-Hungarian turn in the official policies and public opinion of Great Britain can only be understood in the context of the changes in European politics; Hungarian politics could not have played a decisive role in the formation of the two imperialist blocs immediately preceding the world war. Analyzing the road leding to Trianon and to the dissolution of the Habsburg Empire, including Hungary, we must emphasize two basic trends. Both Kossuth and Deák were aware of the tendency towards the dissolution of multinational Hungary, or its tendency to become part of a larger unit. After the defeat of the Revolution and War of Liberation of 1848–49, both Kossuth and Deák feared these tendencies and strived to avoid them in defining the situation of Hungary. Kossuth sought the guarantee of a more secure future in some kind of compromise solution to the parallel and often conflicting nationalism of the small nations of the Danube, whereas Deák sought compromise with the reality of great power, with the Habsburg Empire.[13]

Since the alternative realized was the one Deák had proposed, the Hungarians became stalwart supporters of the Habsburg dynasty and partners of the Austrians in the consolidation of the Monarchy. In the eyes of the future victorious Entente powers—not to mention the antagonistic propaganda of the representatives of the successor states—this attitude compromised Hungary, which became fatefully involved with the losing imperialist group through the Monarchy and its alliance with the German Kaiser. Since the European events were not conducive to the alternative proposed by Kossuth after the defeat of the War of Liberation, namely, some kind of confederation of the small nations of the Danube basin, the elite which came to political power in Hungary with the Compromise of 1867 had to renounce the traditional, millenary concept of sovereign statehood, and accept responsibility, along with the Austrian ruling class, for the consequences of the mistaken foreign policy and incorrect nationalities policy.

Although during the decade and a half preceding the First World War the outlines of the weakness of the Austro-Hungarian Monarchy had become clearly visible, the oppressed nations and nationalities invariably sought the solution to their problems within the Monarchy. In his work *The Austrian Concept of State*, published in 1865,[14] František Palacký advocated the conversion of the Monarchy into a federal state, on the basis of eight ethnic groups. He was the author of the oft-quoted statement: "If Austria did not exist, it would have to be invented." Only a few years before the outbreak of the World War, T. G. Masaryk, then a university professor in Prague, still professed the views of Palacký and in general espoused only moderately nationalist principles. As late as 1908 he felt the demand for an independent Czech nation-state was utopistic. The Romanian writer from Transylvania, Aurel Popovici, in a work published in Leipzig in 1906, stressed the need for the unification of the small

nations along the Danube in face of the great power ambitions of
Germany and Russia. Much like Palacký, he described the concept
of a "Greater Austrian United States."[15]

Oszkár Jászi, the Hungarian specialist of the nationalities issue,
nurtured on the principles of bourgeois radicalism, would have liked
to transform Hungary into an "Eastern Switzerland."[16]

The outbreak of the World War radicalized the politicians of the
nationalities as it had Steed and Seton-Watson. Already in 1915
Masaryk began to proclaim, in the Entente countries, that one of the
major war aims was the dissolution of the Austro-Hungarian Monarchy. In 1916, his disciple, the young Eduard Beneš, published in
Paris his work titled *Détruisez l'Autriche-Hongrie!* Masaryk and his
circle strived with success to win an ever greater number of French,
British, and American journalists, politicians, and diplomats to their
cause. The same goes for other exiled politicians of the Austro-
Hungarian monarchy. There was no Hungarian counter-propaganda
to speak of.

Mihály Károlyi, an opponent of the war and the leader of the
Károlyi Independence Party, became a key participant in the events
only at the end of the war, at the time of the collapse. When the National Council was formed at the end of October 1918, and the
bourgeois democratic revolution triumphed, Hungary too regained
its national independence in the process of the dissolution of the
Monarchy. The task which awaited Károlyi, now President of the
Republic and its most prestigious personality, was to create the conditions for an independent state and defend the country against the
attacking Czech and Romanian conquerors. But he gave pacifist illusions a free rein, helplessly tolerated the disintegration of the
Hungarian armed forces, and proved incapable of assuming the
leadership of a defensive struggle.

The January 8, 1918, message of President Wilson to both houses
of Congress, in which he summarized the war and post-war objectives of the United States, determined the pacifist attitude of Károlyi.
Among Wilson's Fourteen points, number ten dealt with the
Habsburg Monarchy: "The peoples of Austria-Hungary, whose
place among the nations we wish to see safeguarded and
assured, should be accorded the freest opportunity of autonomous
development."[17]

The Fourteen points, the notion of a peace without victory, the
right of self-determination, etc., had a particularly deep influence on

the nations of the Austro-Hungarian Monarchy. But the leaders of the Entente and of their allies in Central Europe believed already at that time that these beautiful principles applied only to the minority nationalities, and not to the Austrians, let alone the Hungarians. By November 1918 a number of facts indicated that the victorious powers regarded Wilsonianism as a thing of the past.

The amendment of the basic principles and the "updating" of point 10 concerning the Monarchy brought about the following essential modification enunciated in Wilson's speech on Independence Day, followed by his statement on September 27, to the effect that Slovakia was part of the Czechoslovak state, and Transylvania would undoubtedly join Romania.[18] The obsoleteness of the Wilsonian principles was demonstrated later by other episodes involving Hungary: the failure to recognize the armistice signed at Padua, the military convention with Károlyi at Belgrade and its repeated infractions, hence the occupation of substantial portions of historical Hungary.

The National Council under the presidency of Károlyi still harbored illusions, as indicated by its proclamation of October 26. Here we read, in part: "In the spirit of the Wilsonian principles, and imbued with the hope that these principles not only do not threaten the territorial integrity of Hungary, but actually place it on a more secure footing. . . ." The nationalities problem was expected to be solved through the means of "cultural and administrative autonomy."[19]

In vain did the Károlyi government strive to reach an agreement with the nationalities, primarily the Romanians and the Slovaks: their representatives rejected all proposals. At the same time Czech and Romanian troops continued to penetrate into Slovakia and Transylvania. Even the events abroad should have dispelled all hopes based on the Fourteen Points. In the elections of November 5, Wilson's Democratic Party lost its former majority both in the House of Representatives and in the Senate, and the victorious Republicans did not even want to hear of the lofty principles. Yet Mihály Károlyi still outlined his foreign policy at the meeting of Independence Party, on December 30, 1918, in the following terms: "I base our foreign policy on the Wilsonian principles. I am confident that Wilson will triumph not only in America, but in Europe as well. The task awaiting America is to knead over all of Europe, to exterminate all thought of revenge within it, and to bring about a peace which will not leave a bitter taste in the mouth of any nation."[20] Thus Károlyi, typically enough, proclaimed Wilsonianism as the basic principle of his foreign policy at a time when it was completely *dépassé*, anachronistic, when Wilson himself was regarded as a defeated politician; his principles could no longer play a role in the policies of the allies. What is more, as we have seen, Wilson himself had several times modified his points, depriving them of their original, attractive, democratic content.

While the Károlyi government attempted to strengthen its international standing through the Italian and Yugoslav connections, as well as in other ways, the invasion of the imperialist Czech and Romanian forces, and the seriousness of the economic and political situation made the bourgeois democratic regime face insoluble tasks. The Allied directive designating a neutral zone in Hungary implied decisive military measures. Accordingly the Paris Peace Conference authorized the Romanian units to advance to the eastern limit of the neutral zone. This decision—which signified a death sentence for the Károlyi government—was taken in Paris on February 26, but was conveyed only in a note dated March 19. The note itself was handed to Mihály Károlyi on March 20 by Lt. Colonel Fernand Vix, the official representative of the Great Powers in Budapest, accompanied by US Navy Captain Nicholas Roosevelt.[21] Károlyi told Vix on the spot that no government could accept these demands; hence he would be obliged to resign. The following day, on March 21, Vix was handed Károlyi's negative answer.

Thus on March 21 the bankruptcy of the bourgeois democratic regime on the international scene became complete—an inevitable consequence of the policy of the Great Powers. The so-called Vix memorandum was only the climax of the policy with which the victorious Western Entente, giving way to its imperialist greed, forced the pro-entente Károlyi government to resign. True enough, the Károlyi government had internal weaknesses and made diplomatic mistakes, but its blind faith in a no-longer-existent Wilsonian pacifism also contributed to the collapse, to the proclamation of the proletarian dictatorship, to the establishment of the Hungarian Soviet Republic.

The news of the proclamation of the Soviet Republic surprised the Paris Peace Conference, which was now inclined to negotiate. The fiasco of the Vix policy line, the Hungarian revolution, and the insecurity of the surrounding states, made the victorious powers more cautious. Accordingly, the Peace Conference sent General Jan Christian Smuts, member of the British war cabinet and delegate to the conference, to Budapest. At this time the Anglo-American attitude prevailed in Paris, whereas the French tendency was relegated to the background. Thus, Smuts left France on April 1 on a special train and reached Vienna, via Switzerland, on April 3. From there he continued on his journey to Budapest accompanied by Elek Bolgar, the Hungarian Consul in Vienna, and arrived at daybreak on April 4. The general and his escort did not leave the train, and did not accept the lodgings offered to them. Yet he reacted realistically to the conditions in Hungary during his negotiations with Béla Kun. For instance, he accepted Kun's proposal to hold a conference with the participation of the governments of central European states (Hungary, Austria, Germany, Czechoslovakia, Serbia, Romania) and in the presence of the representatives of the Great Powers, especially for the sake of economic cooperation. His proposal regarding the establishment of a neutral zone was more favorable than the one contained in the Vix note, because it would have pushed the line of the Romanian troops about 25 kilometers further East. Furthermore, he made promises regarding the lifting of the economic blockade and the invitation of Hungarian representatives to the Peace Conference. He did not, however, offer a guarantee regarding any of this. In his reply, Béla Kun rejected the revised demands of the Great Powers, and insisted on Allied adherence to the Belgrade Convention. With this reply in his pocket, Smuts left Budapest 48 hours after his arrival.

It was not the counterproposal of Kun that played the decisive role in the interruption of the negotiations, because that note of the Hungarian government was conducive to further negotiations. The unfavorable turn took place in Paris where the aggressive Czechoslovakian and Romanian elements under French guidance busied themselves with projects of armed intervention.[22] The American peace delegation, however, was not at all in agreement with military intervention, and felt that resorting to Czech and Romanian troops was a poor idea. General T. H. Bliss pointed out in no uncertain terms that contact should be maintained with the Council government. What's more, he added: in case the Hungarian government did not accept the line of the neutral zone, and resorted to arms to defend itself against the Romanian troops, the Entente should withdraw its support from Romania because the lines of the neutral zone were absolutely unjust, therefore the Allies must not continue to carry out an unusually unjust decision.[23]

While the Romanian and Czechoslovakian governments supported the most aggressive elements of the Entente (Marshal Foch and Winston Churchill) intent on the project of immediate military intervention, finally the Great Powers did not opt for open intervention. They were eager to maintain the appearance of not interfering in the affairs of the Republic of Councils. They intended to force the hand of Hungary by relatively "peaceful" means, such as the economic blockade.[24] Such a policy, however, gave the Council breathing space and the opportunity to organize its military forces and fight in order to repel the Romanian and Czech imperialist forces which had penetrated deep into its territory. It succeeded in averting danger along the northern front by throwing the Czech forces back a considerable distance.

As a consequence of the successful northern campaign the Peace Conference insisted by its *note verbale* of June 7 that the Hungarian Red Army halt its advance, and promised in return that the representatives of the Council would be received in Paris—which would have signified the *de facto* recognition of the Republic of Councils.[25] In reality it was a matter of substituting diplomatic war for military intervention, and the Czech bayonets which had failed, while preserving the same objectives. In the words of Harold Nicolson: "They have decided to get rid of Béla Kun . . ."[26]

Of course, the Council rejected this note, the plain purpose of which was to stop the Red Army. In Paris, on June 9 and 10, the Council of the Four debated the Hungarian reply amidst mutual reproaches. The British general, Wilson, pointed out that the attack was initiated by the Czechoslovak army, provoking the Hungarian counterattack. Lloyd George underlined the responsibility of the Romanian government and army, since their repeated infraction of the demarcation line, the army's attack and advance, brought about a situation which, as he stated, made even the officer class of the old army side with Kun.[27] The telegrams sent by the Council of Four on June 13 to Hungary, Czechoslovakia, and Romania were not couched in the same terms. The telegrams demanded of Hungary that it withdraw its troops from Slovakia, and hinted at the possibility of withdrawing the Romanian forces from the Tisza in exchange. While the Council in Hungary received no guarantee to that effect, it nevertheless accepted the ultimatum proposed by Clemenceau, acting as the chairman of the Peace Conference. The consequences are well known: the Hungarian Red Army evacuated Slovakia, whereas the Romanian troops did not retreat. What's more, a critical situation developed along the Tisza eventually leading to the defeat of the Red Army, its complete disintegration, and the fall of the Republic of Councils.

*   *   *

A number of essays in this volume deal with the Paris Peace Conference and those of its episodes relating to Hungary. A number of monographs have been published recently in Hungary dealing with the topic.[28] Some of these essays also deal with the propaganda activities of the successor states, first of all with Eduard Beneš. I would merely like to cite and stress those factors which had a decisive impact on the peace conditions imposed on Hungary.

First, the matter of responsibility for the war. The war guilt of Hungary is mentioned even in the famous Millerand letter of which only a portion is usually quoted. This letter states:

> The belated measures of the Hungarian government with which it intended to satisfy the nationalities yearning for autonomy, will not delude anyone; they do not alter in any way the historical fact that during long years Hungary dedicated all its efforts to repress the voice of the minorities.[29]

It is worth noting, in this connection, that the Committee in charge of war responsibility of the Paris Peace Conference, in its report of March 29, 1919 to the Peace Conference, does not include the above-mentioned statement of responsibility.[30] Even the Serbian government did not accuse Hungary of responsibility for the war in its report to the Committee. On the other hand, Beneš, in one of his works published in London in 1917[31] wrote: "The war against Serbia was brought about more by Hungary, with over four million Serbo-Croats, than by Austria, who commanded only one million." As if these statistics were the criteria for determining guilt!

The question of war guilt has its own historiography. We selected some data characteristic of the Hungarian aspect of the issue.

The declaration of Balfour, the British Foreign Secretary, on August 9, 1918, signals the clear victory of the policy aimed at the dissolution of the Monarchy. Balfour stated that the United Kingdom considered the Czechoslovak nation as an ally, the Czechoslovak legions as an allied army, and the Czechoslovak National Council as the trustee of the future Czechoslovak government. This declaration was followed by that of the American Secretary of State, Lansing, on September 3, 1918, which recognized the Czechoslovak National Council as a *de facto* government. Finally Wilson's statement of October 19, which included a reply to Austria-Hungary's peace proposal, spells out clearly that *the United States has changed its concept regarding Austria-Hungary and its relationship to the United States;* the United States can no longer be satisfied with the autonomy of the nations constituting the Monarchy and such autonomy cannot form the basis of a peace treaty.[32] Thus, the dissolution of Austria-Hungary was already decided in theory before the Peace Conference set upon determining the new boundaries at the beginning of 1919, under the chairmanship of Wilson.

The records of the Council of the Ambassadors have not been made public, in accordance with an international agreement to that effect. Thus our picture of the debates among the allies regarding the Hungarian peace treaty is not complete to this day. Mária Ormos succeeded in giving us a clearer picture through her research in the French archives. Thus she observes, in the manuscript of her dissertation, that "the possibility of the meaningful modification of the original text was considered."[33]

At the London conference of the Supreme Council the Hungarian peace treaty was discussed on March 8, 1920. Speaking for the absent Italian Prime Minister Nitti, Foreign Minister Scioloja demanded a thorough investigation and modification of the treaty which was opposed by British Foreign Secretary Curzon, as well as the French delegation. Decision was in the hands of Lloyd George; if he were to speak against his own Foreign Secretary and for the Italian side, the treaty project would go down in defeat. He said that in his heart, he agreed with Nitti. Having studied the documents, however, he noted that the frontiers had been accepted in Paris and he came to conclusion that the only solution was compliance.[34]

The American observations were conveyed by the American ambassador in Paris, Wallace, *post facto*, avoiding the publicity of the Conference in the course of diplomatic contacts. His stand was transmitted to London on March 30 by the new French secretary, Maurice Paléologue. According to Wallace, says the telegram by

Paléologue, "the American government accepts, against its better judgment, the decision not to announce a plebiscite in the matter of the final drafting of frontiers. He believes that *in many respects the frontiers do not correspond to the ethnic requisite,* nor to economic necessity, and that significant modifications would be in order, particularly in the Ruthenian area." Later on Wallace submitted for the consideration of the Great Powers proposals with regard to a restoration of the economic unity of the Danubian states. The American initiative, however, came too late . . . The only thing left was the Millerand cover letter, which did not oblige anyone to do anything!

The Hungarian peace delegation signed the peace treaty consisting of 14 points at the so-called Great Trianon palace, near Paris, on June 4, 1920. Hungary's fate was determined for an unforeseeable future by the second part of the treaty which defined the new borders. According to this section Hungary's area (without Croatia) would be reduced from 282,000 km^2 to 93,000 km^2, whereas its population decreased from 18 million to 7.6 million. This meant that Hungary lost two thirds of its territory, whereas Germany lost but 10 percent and Bulgaria but 8 percent to the benefit of their victorious neighbors.

As regards population, Hungry lost more than 60 percent of its inhabitants as opposed to the 10 percent lost by Germany. In the lands taken away from Hungary there lived approximately 10 million persons. Persons of Hungarian nationality constituted 3,424,000 in the areas taken away from Hungary. Of these 1,084,000 were attached to Czechoslovakia, 1,705,000 to Romania, 564,000 to Yugoslavia, and 65,000 to Austria. Thus 33.5 percent of all Hungarians came under foreign rule, i.e., every third Hungarian. For the sake of comparison: while the treaties of Versailles and Neuilly placed only one German or one Bulgarian out of every twenty under foreign rule, the Trianon treaty placed seven out of twenty Hungarians in the same position.

Furthermore about one half of the Hungarian minority attached to the neighboring states was ethnically directly next to the main body of Hungarians on the other side of the borders. Had the peace treaties signed in the Paris suburbs really tried to bring about, however incidentally, nation-states, then it would have had to leave at least 1½ to 2 million more Hungarians inside Hungary. In contrast the 42 million inhabitants of the successor states there were about 16 million minorities, as a consequence of which Czechoslovakia, Romania, and Yugoslavia became multinational states much like the Austro-Hungarian Monarchy had been. What is more, according to the census of 1910 the percentage of Hungarians in Hungary had reached 54.4 percent, whereas in the nations that came about as a result of the peace treaties, in Czechoslovakia and Yugoslavia, the leading Czech and Serbian elements constituted but a minority as compared to the other ethnic groups.

The Treaty of Trianon was a great blow to Hungary in economic terms as well. Hungary was deprived of 62.2 percent of its railroad network, 73.8 percent of its public roads, 64.6 percent of its canals, 88 percent of its forests, 83 percent of its iron ore mines and of all its salt mines.

At the Peace Conference the Entente powers, in order to satisfy the imperialist greed of their allies in central Europe, cut across roads, canals, railroad lines, split cities and villages in two, deprived mines of their entrances, etc.

There was but one modification of the frontier: thanks to Italian intercession and the stand taken by patriotic forces in Western Hungary, a plebiscite was obtained in Sopron and its environs. At the plebiscite of December 4, 1921, 65 percent of the population opted for Hungary.[35]

The perceived injustices of the Treaty of Trianon gave rise to a special body of literature. Statesmen, diplomats, journalists, and the crown witnesses at Versailles, Neuilly, and Trianon spoke out in the period between the wars, and often revealed the behind-the-scenes secrets about the preparation of the treaties.

French Prime Minister and Foreign Minister Aristide Briand, for example, openly admitted to his critics during the July 11, 1921, session of the National Assembly:

> It was impossible to draw those just boundary lines which you demanded a moment ago, hence the decisions were necessarily prejudicial to someone or other. Between Hungary and Romania I prefer that it not be Romania that should suffer injustice.[36]

At the same session, the socialist labor leader Paul-Boncour evaluated the Treaty of Trianon in the following terms:

> A glance at the map which indicates what the treaties of Trianon and Saint Germain have done to the territories of Austria and Hungary

would probably reveal that none of the countries born of this partition could exist solely within its own borders. Hungary did exist independently and its economic organization was in accordance with this situation. And now she has been carved to pieces, dissolved.

To which Briand responded: "This is the terrible contradiction between the principle of nationality and economic interest!"[37]

One of the curious aspects of the Treaty of Trianon is that it was signed neither by the United States, nor by the young Soviet Union. The American delegation took its leave from the allies in Paris as early as December 9, 1919, since Congress had definitely rejected the ratification of the peace achievements.[38] Washington signed a separate peace with the defeated states. Thus peace was concluded between the United States and Hungary on August 29, 1921, a treaty written in the books of the League of Nations (1921, XLVIII). The text of the treaty makes no mention of the boundaries designated at Trianon.[39]

The Millerand cover letter constituted the legal basis of the Hungarian revisionist propaganda between the wars. Millerand, the Chairman of the Conference of Ambassadors, attached a letter to the peace treaty which stated, in order to preempt any further discussion regarding territory, that the eventual modification of the designated boundaries would be referred to the boundary committees "in accordance with the same conditions." The Hungarian governments between the wars tried to use this letter to arouse false hopes regarding revision of the treaty. The truth is that this document did not place any obligation whatever on the victors.

The successor states, supported by their western allies, did not even want to hear of any restitution of territory. The only exception was Czechoslovakia whose leaders, Masaryk and Beneš, felt that with certain modificaion of the boundary line they might achieve peace and stability along their southern borders. The Hungarian-Czechoslovak negotiations took place in March of 1921 at Brück-ander-Leitha. The participants included, on the Hungarian side, Prime Minister Count Pál Teleki and Foreign Minister Gusztáv Grátz, on the Czechoslovak side Foreign Minister Beneš. The Hungarians engaged in the negotiations on the condition that territorial matters would also be discussed. Beneš, inasmuch as the Czechoslovak government was indeed interested in normalizing relations, was not adamant. But the Czechoslovak delegation relegated territorial issues to the background. The Hungarian consul at Prague, László Tahy, reported that Beneš "would not preclude the discussion of territorial questions." In spite of this, no agreement could be reached in this matter because the negotiations were interrupted by the first coup engineered by Charles Habsburg. They were adjourned until June, but no significant agreement was ever reached even in other areas (financial, economic, transportation).[40] Information leaked out that the Hungarian delegation insisted on the restitution of southern Slovakia before agreeing to any economic or financial settlement. Since Beneš rejected this claim the meeting ended in complete failure.[41]

Hungary became less isolated and her international position improved somewhat when she was admitted to the League of Nations on September 18, 1923. Yet she had to wait for years longer for any significant diplomatic achievement. It was only in 1927, with the signing of the Italian-Hungarian treaty of "eternal friendship," that the Bethlen government could claim that Hungary overcame its isolation imposed by Trianon.

By the same token, this new treaty meant the beginnings of revisionist propaganda, promoted to a large extent by the so-called Rothermere initiative. Not long after signing the treaty, Mussolini met with Lord Rothermere, the conservative magnate of the press, and the owner of the British *Daily Mail;* the latter agreed to launch a campaign, in his paper, on behalf of the revision of the Treaty of Trianon. Rothermere even met with Bethlen and, as a consequence, on June 21, 1927, published his controversial article, "Hungary's Place under the Sun." In this article he emhasized that security in Central Europe can only be achieved by changing the Trianon boundaries, and took a stand in favor of restituting an area inhabited by about two million Hungarians. These areas lay along the Trianon frontiers in Czechoslovakia, Romania, and Yugoslavia.[42]

The Rothermere initiative had wide international repercussions and elicited an intensive counterpropaganda in the countries of the Little Entente as well as in France. Nor did the British government look favorably upon the initiative, and dissociated itself from it. Nevertheless, the Revision League was founded that same year, on the initiative of Rothermere, under the chairmanship of the writer Ferenc Herczeg. Its objective was to influence international public opinion to support revision by propaganda and other means.[43] It soon became clear, however, that there was no adequate international support for Hungarian revisionist claims. Even the Rothermere initiative proved to be but an ephemeral will-o'-the-wisp. While the Hungarian governments strived to keep the cause of revision of the peace treaties on the agendas of the League of Nations and of other international bodies, revision did not receive serious consideration until the time of Munich. But the decisions taken in the shadows of Hitlerian aggression could bring no lasting solution to benefit Hungary.

The stand taken by the Hungarian and international Communist movement in the matter of revision, between the wars, is worth discussing, because of its lasting theoretical and practical implications to this day.

The Communist Party of Hungary confronted this issue already at its first reorganizing Congress in Vienna. On August 18, 1925, it formulated the problem in the debate on the international situation as follows: how should Hungarian Communists react to the Trianon Peace Treaty and to the irrredentist propaganda having currency in Hungary at the moment? The Communist International had condemned Versailles and other peace treaties from the beginning, harshly criticizing their imperialist nature. The Hungarian Communist leaders (Alpári, Kun) nevertheless got around the essence of the problem, even though the Hungarian Communists could have expected a clear stand from Béla Kun, who was then at the head of the Agitation and Propaganda Section of the International.

Instead, Kun expressed incredible views, to the effect that the Western powers were disillusioned with the Versailles policy! Talking about the right of self-determination of the Hungarians living in neighboring countries, he declared that it was the duty of the Communist parties in the successor states to fight for it. The participants could not have been satisfied with such general observations. The specialist of the topic, Ágnes Szabó, is justified in pointing out:

> In theory the Congress did condemn the Versailles peace . . . , but it did not provide guidance to the party on how to struggle against the unjust imperialist peace in its daily propaganda work.[44]

Béla Kun himself felt that his arguments had been weak, explaining that the Communist International had no detailed program concerning this matter. Thus in a letter to the Executive Committee of the International he wrote:

On the basis of our experiences we must state that the Fifth Congress [of the Comintern] and its decision in the matter of nationalities are not specific enough to allow that a specific stand be taken under present circumstances in the matter. We have experienced in the course of our work that *the nationalities policy of some of the Communist Parties in Southeastern Europe had created the impression among its conscious masses that this policy is not sufficiently internationalist.*[45]

József Révai, one of the leading theoreticians of the party, formulated the stand of the Communist movement much more clearly in the review *Uj Március*, the organ of the Hungarian Communist emigration, published in Moscow:

The Trianon peace treaty was the dictate of the imperialist powers which defined the boundaries not on the basis of the self-determination of nations, or that of the 'will' or 'sympathy' of the people, but rather on the basis of the interests of the ruling classes among the Romanians, Czechs, Serbs in alliance with the victorious great powers.

Thus the struggle against Trianon is one of the fronts of the struggle of the international working class against the order established by the Versailles robber peace. The Communist parties in the successor states, especially since the Fifth Congress of the Communist International, have come up with the slogan of the right of self-determination of the oppressed nationalities against the Serbian, Romanian, and Czech bourgeoisie, *including the right of secession. The Fifth Congress has particularly stressed that the Communist Parties in the successor states must also struggle for the right of secession of the oppressed Hungarian nationalities.*

Révai continues by criticizing the Bethlen government, because "it began to sound the program of 'peaceful coexistence' with the successor states. After establishment of the Little Entente, Bethlen soon surrendered in the matter of the foreign policy directed against Trianon." The article also criticized Bethlen because once Hungary's financial situation became stabilized, the policy that seemed to prevail was one of complete acquiescense, as a way of reaching a rapprochement with France and indirectly the Little Entente countries. We should note, regarding Révai's criticism of the Bethlen regime, that it was entirely without foundation. His evaluation of Bethlen's diplomatic steps towards internal political and economic consolidation was incorrect. As we have seen above, the Bethlen government did not discard the policy of revision of Trianon. In any case, it is noteworthy that Révai spoke out in favor of revision in such determined, radical terms, referring even to the right of secession of the Hungarian minorities.

Further in the article Révai deals with the contradictions in foreign policy among the Little Entente countries and East Europe in general; he establishes a connection between the liberation of Bessarabia and that of Transylvania.

> This fact was noted not only by the boyars of Romania, not only by the Rumanian Communist Party, but the Hungarian bourgeoisie of Transylvania as well. Even the Hungarian bourgeois press of Transylvania considered the Soviet Union as the defender of the right of self-determination for Hungarians. Soviet Russia has officially declared, by way of comrade Rakovsky, its ambassador in London, that it is demanding the right of national self-determination not only for the oppressed of Bessarabia, but for those of Transylvania as well.

In this connection Révai points out that Hungarian foreign policy, instead of recognizing the community of Soviet and Hungarian interests, "has conformed to the campaign against Russia," even though "the only possible national foreign policy for Hungary would lead to an alliance with Soviet Russia."

In connection with the parallel between Bessarabia and Transylvania we must refer to the year 1940, when Soviet and Hungarian interests once again found a common ground, and the Soviet government even made a gesture towards Hungary proposing that they make their claims good against Romania jointly. At that time the Hungarian government would not hear of it, and preferred to accept the consequences of the Second Vienna Decision.

The final conclusion of Révai's article was:

> The solution of the Hungarian national question, the shattering of Trianon, can only be accomplished by the Hungarian proletarian revolution in conjunction with the working-class of the successor states, under the banner of the Communist International.[46]

Even if we do find many doctrinal aspects to Révai's arguments, it remains a fact that in the mid-twenties, in the matter of the peace treaties, including Trianon, the Communist movement had adopted a completely internationalist stand. At the same time the bourgeois and Social Democratic exiles, in their struggle against Horthyite reaction, and because of the weakness and errors of the bourgeois democratic forces at home, placed their hopes increasingly in the democratic forces in the successor states and the policies of their governments directed against official Hungary. The concept of Jászi and his circle, and the hope of Social Democrat Hungarian exiles, could not be realized because of the consolidation under Bethlen.[47]

Between February 27, 1930, and March 15, 1930, the Hungarian Communist exiles, at their second Congress held in the Soviet Union, also dealt with the matter of the revision of Trianon. The newly elected secretary of the party, Sándor Serényi, who became a member of the Politburo of the ruling party in Hungary only after 1956, in an article signed with his name in the movement, "Sas" (eagle), appraised the meaning of the Congress and criticized those left-wing manifestations which came up with the slogan "down with revision." The party Congress itself disapproved of this stand, which would have meant for all practical purposes "a surrender of the struggle gainst the imperialist peace treaties." His article summarizes the stand of the Party in the following terms: "The Congress declared that since such views might isolate the party from the broad masses we must carry on an intense struggle against them and specify that the *Party is indeed determined to struggle against the imperialist peace of Trianon* for the sake of the right of self-determination of the Hungarian nation," alongside the "Soviet Union, the international proletariat, first of all with the working class of the successor states."[48]

An important theoretical article which appeared in the paper of the Hungarian Communist Party that same year confirms the stand taken by the Party Congress with regard to revision. In its lead article titled "The United Block for Revision" it contrasts the diplomatic alliance of the Bethlen regime with the block of the revolutionary workers. It stresses that the program of the Party "cannot be complete without the revolutionary struggle against the Trianon peace treaty." Then it continues: "The Communist Party must combine the domestic program of the proletarian revolution with the revolutionary struggle against the imperialist peace treaties. Following the example of our German brother party we must let the Hungarian workers know about the program of the Communists against the Trianon peace of plunder." The lead article ends with the following rather illusionary conclusion: "We intend to shatter the imperialist chains of Trianon with the help of the workers of Rumania, Czechoslovakia, and Yugoslavia."[40]

It seems that even after the takeover by Hitler and the aggressive National Socialist regime the Hungarian Communist Party did not change its own revisionist line. During the debate of the so-called Blum theses in Moscow (this was the title György Lukács used for his presentation of ideological matters pertaining to the movement, which was rejected) the Party issued its slogan regarding the "democratic revision of Trianon."[50] The term "democratic" is quite important here because, in contrast to the stand taken in the twenties, this implied that the concept of revision within the framework of the counter-revolutionary Horthy regime was unacceptable.

The Party's approach to Trianon was further modified at the time of the Munich Pact. While Hitler forced the revision of the Versailles Treaty but was jeopardizing peace in Europe in so doing, the Communist parties, including the Hungarian Party, advocated the preservation of the status quo and urged, within the framework of the Popular Front, the alliance of all democratic forces on an international scale against the Fascist prospect of war. By the same token this meant that from 1938 the Party was definitely opposed to the revision of Trianon which could only come about with Hitler's help.

The series of articles published by József Révai in the *Szabad Szó* of Paris in the fall of 1938 accurately reflect the views of the Hungarian Communists. This important statement begins with the following theoretical observation:

> The specific execution, form, method, means, aspects, and timing of revision has to be subordinated to the higher requirements of Hungarian national independence and the universal interests of the nation. Today, however, the situation is that the territorial revisions carried out thanks to Hitler in the long run makes Hungary into his vassal state—both nationally and internationally.

Further, on the article contrasts the Hungarian Soviet Republic with counterrevolutionary Hungary: the Soviets waged a war of liberation for the return of lands belonging to Hungary and the nationalities, as well as for the social liberation of nations; in contrast, the Trianon treaty signed by the Horthy regime gave up lands inhabited exclusively by Magyars to the benefit of Romania, Czechoslovakia, and Yugoslavia. He continues:

Trianon, like all imperialist peace treaties, was unjust. It replaced old injustices by new ones. Everyone had the right to raise this issue except the Hungarian ruling class which shares with the victorious and defeated imperialist powers the responsibility for this national calamity which struck primarily the people, those who remained in the fatherland, and those who were torn away against their will.

In a later article in the series Révai continues to advocate the need for the revision of the treaty, but ties it to certain conditions:

Yes, there should be revision, if the revision outside is accompanied by revision inside; if the returning Hungarians can not only avoid deprivation of rights but can find, beyond that, a country where conditions are freer, more democratic economically and politically. Today the situation is just the opposite.

Then he compares conditions under the bourgeois democratic regime in Czechoslovakia with the Hungary of the three million beggars, where the large landholders and the aristocracy have maintained power through the local overseers (ispáns) and judges already notorious from the period of the Dualism.

The program of the Party in the matter of revision at the time of the aggression against Yugoslavia in April 1941 changed to the extent that it tied the defense of independence to the rejection of territorial revision. It pointed out that revision would signify not only the continued fascization of the country, its drift into the war, the surrender of its independence, but would also be a stab in the back of the international anti-Fascist forces.[52]

Hungary's entry into the Second World War, its complicity in the aggression gainst Yugoslavia, its acceptance of the role of satellite on the side of Hitlerian Germany in the campaign against the Soviet Union, then the declaration of war against Great Britain and the United States did not merely constitute a crude mockery of the revision of the peace of Trianon, but also jeopardized Hungary's fate and future.

The Hungarian political opposition, from the legitimists all the way to the Communists, did not prove sufficiently strong to divert the establishment, and Hungary, from their fateful path. In the critical years of the war a few outstanding representatives of the democratic opposition attempted, in several written works, to answer the big question: how did Hungary once again find itself among the losers, on the side of the German imperialists? Among them Endre Bajcsy-Zsilinszky, the foreign policy spokesman and martyr of the largest opposition party, the Independent Smallholders, felt that it was about mid-way into the Dualist period (i.e., the time of the turn of the century) that the Hungarian nation strayed from the "ancestral road" giving up completely its concept of independence. He gave this part of his work the title "The Lost Rider" sowing his historic political views deep into the furrows of the symbolist poetry of Endre Ady, the great Hungarian poet-prophet.[53] Another prestigious figure of the democratic opposition in Hungary, the history professor Gyula Szekfü sought the answer to this problem in a series of articles titled "We lost our way somewhere."[54] Reaching back into the first half of 19th century, into the Reform period, he analyzes in detail the program of the centralists such as Antal Csengery, Móric Lukács, László Szalay, József Eötvös. In his opinion it was a great tragedy in Hungarian history that it was not this centralist group within the reform generation that prevailed in 1848; the Kossuth road led first to the dethronement of the Habsburgs, then to the surrender at Világos, then, in 1867, thanks to the triumph of the Deák wing, to the compromise with the Habsburgs, that is to say, the surrender of independent Hungarian policy. The Hungarian nation and the historical state were not able to sail between Scylla and Charybdis.

Nevertheless during the war it seemed that Hungary's position in Central Europe was better than that of Romania, where an openly Fascist regime came to power under the leadership of General Antonescu, or in Slovakia, where Fascism had also triumphed with German help. It was only in the southern region that the developments were unfavorable to Hungary—in spite of the Croatian puppet state—because of the unfortunate incident at Novi Sad.

The fate of Hungary was sealed, however, by the German occupation on March 19, 1944, which met with no resistance, the Fascist measures having been carried out by the Sztójay puppet government. The cruel deportation to Auschwitz of the provincial Jewry followed, as well as the unsuccessful attempt to bail out on October 15, 1944, and finally the Fascist takeover by Szálasi with all its monstrous consequences.

One part of the peace treaties concluding the Second World War, including the Hungarian one, was once again worded in Paris. Knowing the precedents, democratic Hungary did not have much to look forward to in signing the treaty. Twenty-seven years after the dictate of Trianon, in February of 1947, not only were the Trianon boundaries restored at Paris, but three additional Hungarian villages (Oroszvár, Horvátujfalu, Dunacsún) in the vicinity of Bratislava were attached to Czechoslovakia.

*   *   *

More than sixty years have passed since the treaty of Trianon and 34 years since the peace treaty signed in Paris. Between the two wars the Hungarian masses, including the millions who had become a minority, could reasonably expect a revision of the treaty. But after the Second World War the principle and practice which prevailed was the one Sir Winston Churchill proclaimed in the British Parliament on December 15, 1944, that the expulsion of the national minorities seems to be the most satisfactory and purposeful solution.[55] The fate of the Hungarians of Slovakia during the years "without a country" is a sad demonstration of this principle.

Neither at the United Nations nor at the peace negotiations were the rights of minorities guaranteed in any way. The view which regarded the nationalities as the so-called fifth column of Fascist attempts at revenge, as the *casus belli*, actually confused the true reason for aggression with the propaganda gimmick resorted to as a justification.[56] The representatives of the Allies at the Paris peace negotiations curtly rejected the claims of the minorities which the Hungarian delegation, among others, brought up. As Walter Bedell Smith stated in 1946: "It is difficult for a citizen of the United States to understand the desire to perpetuate racial minorities rather than absorb them." This view was confirmed by his British colleague, Lord Hood: "Our aim should be to assimilate racial minorities in the countries where they live rather than perpetuate them."[57]

It was only in the 1970's that the U.N. began to notice that some 600 million people in the world live without any minority rights. Thus, at Ohrid in 1974 at the Seminar on Minorities of one of the special agencies of the United Nations, a unanimous decision was taken regarding the defense and support of minority rights.[58] This decision, however, had no force of legal compulsion, hence the U.N. still does not provide for the legal defense of the minorities. Professor Imre Szabó, condemning this shortcoming of the United Nations, notes: ". . . the problem of the minorities cannot be solved by the guarantee of human rights. The positive counterpart of this negative thesis is that the international defense of minorities requires special international provisions and guarantees."[59] Even among the socialist countries of Europe the rights of minorities is mentioned only in one international document: the Polish-Czechoslovakian friendship and assistance treaty of 1947.

In the socialist countries of Eastern Europe, not counting the Soviet Union, there are ten nations (German, Polish, Czech, Slovak, Hungarian, Romanian, Bulgarian, Serbian, Croatian, Slovene) with close to 50 national minorities. The Hungarians constitute but 2 percent of the population of Europe (not counting the Soviet Union), and 10 percent of its 40 million minorities! After the Albanians the Hungarians provide the largest numbers of minorities in Europe. About two thirds of them live along the Hungarian borders in the five neighboring countries.

The recent historical events including the defeated revolutions, lost wars, humiliating peace treaties, various retaliatory measures, the negative, harmful or spontaneous assimilating factors in economic, social, and cultural areas, have all decimated the Hungarian minorities living in neighboring lands. A historical balance sheet on the occasion of the sixtieth anniversary of the Trianon peace treaty, therefore must also come to grips with the phenomena threatening the future—the survival of that part of the nation which lives in neighboring states.

Notes

1. The English language sources of this process are analyzed by Géza Jeszenszky's doctoral dissertation, "Magyarország megítélése Nagybrittán-niábañ" [Hungary's appraisal in Great Britain] (Budapest, 1979), 129-31.

2. *Ibid.*, 143-45.

3. *The Times*, September 23, 1897.

4. *The Times*, May 31, 1898.

5. *The Quarterly Review*, October 1901, 389.

6. Jeszenszky, 190-94.

7. *Ibid.*, 206.

8. *Scottish Review*, March 12, 1906, quoted in Jeszenszky, 109.

9. Scotus Viator, *The Future of Austria-Hungary and the Attitude of the Great Powers* (London, 1907).

10. Jeszenszky, 237.

11. R. W. Seton-Watson, *Political Persecution in Hungary. An Appeal to British Public Opinion* (London, 1908); *The Southern Slav Question and the Habsburg Monarchy* (London, 1911).

12. Sir Campbell Sturt, *Secrets of Crewe House* (London, 1920); V. H. Rothwell, *British War Aims and Peace Diplomacy 1914-1918* (Oxford, 1971), 207-208, 216.

13. Péter Hanák, *Magyarország a Monarchiában* [Hungary within the Monarchy] (Budapest, 1975), 445.

14. František Palacky, *Oesterreichs Staatsidee* (Prague, 1866).

15. Aurel Popovici, *Die Vereinigten Staaten von Gross Osterreich* (Leipzig, 1906).

16. Oszkár Jászi, *A nemzetiségi kérdés és Magyarország jövője* [The nationalities problem and Hungary's future] (Budapest, 1911); *Magyarország jövője és a Dunai Egyesült Államok* [Hungary's future and the United States of the Danube] (Budapest, 1918).

17. *Papers*, vol. I (Washington, 1933), 15.

18. *Ibid.*, 270, 319; *Papers PPC*, I (Washington, 1942), 359; III, 333 ff.

19. *Népszava*, October 26, 1918.

20. Mihály Károlyi's speech at the December 30, 1918, meeting of the Independence and 1948 Party, *Pesti Hirlap*, December 31, 1918.

21. *Papers PPC*, XII, 413-416; Tibor Hajdu, *Március huszonegyedike* [The twenty-first of March] (Budapest); Akadémiai Kiadó (1959), 51 ff.

22. Zsuzsa L. Nagy, "Smuts tábornok Budapesti küldetése 1919 áprilisában" [The Budapest mission of General Smuts in April 1919], *Történelmi Szemle* (1963), no. 6, 195-214 and her *A párizsi békekonferencia és Magyarország, 1918-1919* [The Paris Peace Conference and Hungary] (Budapest, 1965), 101-115.

23. *Papers PPC*, XI, 134-135.

24. L. Nagy, *A párizsi békekonferencia*, 95.

25. *Papers PPC*, VI, 246-247.

26. H. Nicolson, *Peacemaking 1919* (London, 1934), 358.

27. L. Nagy, *A párizsi békekonferencia*, 158-159.

28. L. Nagy and Mária Ormos, "Saint-Germain és Trianon. Franciaország politikája Ausztriával és Magyarországgal szemben, 1918-1920" [The policy of France towards Austria and Hungary]. Dissertation draft.

29. Jenö Horváth, *Felelösség a világháboruért és a békeszerzödésért* [Responsibility for the world war and for the Peace Treaty].

30. Horváth, *Ibid.*, 4-5.

31. E. Benesch, *Bohemia's Case for Independence* (London, 1917), p. 43.

32. Gusztáv Gratz, *A forradalmak kora* [The age of revolutions] (Budapest, 1935), 287-288.

33. Mária Ormos, 600.

34. *Ibid.*, 604.

35. Yves de Daruvár, *A feldarabolt Magyarország* [Carved up Hungary] (Luzern, 1976), 286.

36. Antal Ullein-Revitzky, *A trianoni szerződés területi rendelkezéseinek jogi természete* [The legal nature of the territorial provisions of the Treaty of Trianon] (Pécs, 1943), 174.

37. *Ibid.*, 175.

38. *PPC*, IX, 547.

39. Jenö Horváth, 230.

40. Ferenc Boros, *Magyar-csehszlovák kapcsolatok 1918-1921* [Hungarian-Czechoslovakian relations in 1918-1921](Budapest, 1970), 284-285; Beneš, *Problémy nové Evropy a zahraničný politika československská* (Prague, 1956), 287.

41. István Borsody, *Magyar-szlovák kiegyezés* [Hungarian Slovakian agreement] (Budapest, no date), 71.

42. Regarding the Rothermere initiative see Dezsö Nemes, *A Bethlen kormány külpolitikája 1927-1931 ben* [The foreign policy of the Bethlen regime in 1927-31] (Budapest, 1964), 167-182.

43. Gyula Juhász, *Magyarország külpolikája, 1919-1945* [Hungary's foreign policy] (Budapest, 1969), 115.

44. György Borsányi, *Kun Béla* (Budapest, 1979), 286-287; Ágnes Szabó, *A KMP ujjászervezése* [The reorganization of the Hungarian Communist Party] 1919-1925 (1970), 197.

45. Borsányi, 287.

46. József Révai, "Trianon-Genf-Moszkva" [Trianon-Geneva-Moscow], *Uj Március* (1925), nos. 1-2, 31-36. In one of his notes Révai remarks "The Fifth Congress issued the slogan of Transylvanian autonomy as a new approach to resolving the Hungarian national issue."

47. The members of the Károlyi circle in exile, the so-called Octobrists, wrote mainly for the *Magyar Ujság* in Vienna and the *Reggel* published in Bratislava.

48. *Uj Március* (1930), nos. 1-3.

49. "Reviziós blokk" [The revisionist bloc], *Uj Március* (October-November 1930), 427.

50. Intervention by Dezsö Nemes in the debate of the so-called Blum theses which took place between June 20 and 30, 1956. *Párttörténeti Közlemények* (1956), no. 3.

51. Endre Rozgonyi, "A trianoni revizió kérdése" [The issue of the revision of Trianon], *Szabad Szó* (Paris), November 5, 12, 19, and 26, 1938.

52. István Pintér, *A magyar antifasiszta Hitler-ellenes ellenállás történetéhez* [Contribution to the history of the anti-Hitlerian anti-Fascist resistance in Hungary] (Budapest, 1976), 117.

53. Endre Bajcsy-Zsilinszky, *Helyünk és sorsunk Európában* [Our place and fate in Europe] (Budapest, 1941), 5.

54. *Magyar Nemzet*, December 1943 to January 1944.

55. Lajos Für, "Kisebbség, nemzetiség, tudomány" [Minority nationality, and science] (Budapest 1980), 7, typescript.

56. Rudolf Jóo, "Az Egyesült Nemzetek tervezete és a nemzeti kisebbségek védelme" [The projected United Nations and the defense of the minorities], *Külpolitika* (1976), no. 4, 61.

57. Inis L. Claude, *National Minorities: An International Problem* (Cambridge, 1955), 141.

58. László Kővágó, *Kisebbség-nemzetiség* [Minorities and ethnic groups] (Budapest, 1977), 198.

59. Imre Szabó, *A kisebbségek és az emberi jogok* [Minorities and human rights], *Valóság* (1979), no. 1, 7.

Iván T. Berend and György Ránki

The Economic Problems of the Danube Region After the Breakup of the Austro-Hungarian Monarchy

In October 1918, the Austro-Hungarian Monarchy collapsed. The Monarchy had previously provided a broad framework within which a number of nations had undergone social transformation, and modern capitalist economies had come into being. The strains and tensions engendered by the internal economic contradictions characteristic of the twentieth century, and which were reflected in the level of economic development as compared with more advanced powers, were no doubt a contributory factor in the breakup of the Monarchy, but its main causes should rather be sought in the political and social contradictions of the time and their reflection in public consciousness.

After the 1914–18 war, the political map of Europe was completely transformed. The decay of the Austro-Hungarian Monarchy had significantly contributed to this. Instead of large areas, each uniform in colour, smaller units appeared, each of a different hue. These small countries with populations ranging from seven to fifteen millions, entered on the struggle for an independent existence. On the territory of the former Monarchy, three successor states emerged—the Austrian republic, the Czechoslovak republic, and Hungary. Other important sections of it were incorporated into neighbouring states: newly resurrected Poland, an enlarged Serbia (now Yugoslavia), and Romania. The enormous extent of this redistribution of territories and populations denoted in itself a radical transformation of economic conditions.

The changes in territory and population did not, of course, account completely for the changes in the economic situation of the countries concerned. The economic potential inherited by the successor states bore no relation to their inheritance of land and people.

Czechoslovakia, for example, came into possession of a dispropor-tionately large share of the Monarchy's industrial potential. From the statistical calculations (which differ in some respects), we can conclude that 70 percent of the entire industrial capacity of Cisleithania was concentrated in the new Czechoslovak state: 75 per-cent of the coal mines, 63 percent of the lignite, 60 percent of the iron industry, 75 percent of the chemical industry, 75–80 percent of the textile and shoe industries. With its 13.6 million inhabitants—hardly more than a quarter of the population of the defunct Monar-chy—Czechoslovakia disposed of an economy on a western Euro-pean level, and of a powerful industry producing a large surplus for export.[1]

Similarly, the economic structure of Hungary, which lost the regions inhabited largely by the national minorities, underwent con-siderable change. It gained in industrial strength, for within its new boundaries, which enclosed about a third of its former territory, there remained about 55 percent of its industry, and 41 percent of its population. There was, however, a marked disproportion between its sources of raw materials and its manufacturing capacity; in other ways, too, the internal economic balance had been seriously upset: for instance, only 11 percent of the iron ore and 15 percent of the timber was left within the new boundaries, while it retained 80–90 percent of the engineering and printing plants. Thus, even from the territorial standpoint alone, the postwar economies of the states of central, eastern, and southeastern Europe were not just continua-tions of the prewar economic setup.[2]

The creation of independent states in the place of great empires, the dissolution of large territorial and economic units, the contrac-tion of some countries to a third of their former area and the expan-sion of others to twice or even three times their former size in land and population, the economic condition of countries pieced together out of territories at different stages of economic development and taken from different states—all these circumstances created a radically new situation. Even under normal circumstances, a con-siderable period of time, in fact an entire historical era, would have been required to complete the adjustment to new conditions, the in-tegration into a unified economic whole, the opening up of new development possibilities and the attainment of a steady and sus-tained rate of economic growth. But history did not allow the prob-lem to be presented in this fashion. The needs of the new order became apparent at a moment when the problems of the transition

TABLE I. Area and Population before and after the War

Country	Area in sq. km. 1914	Area in sq. km. 1921	Population in 100,000 1914	Population in 100,000 1921
Austria-Hungary	676,443*	—	51,390*	—
Austria	—	85,533	—	6,536
Hungary**	325,000	92,607	20,900	7,800
Czechoslovakia	—	140,394	—	3,613
Bulgaria	111,800	103,146	4,753	4,910
Romania	137,903	304,244	7,516	17,594
Yugoslavia (Serbia)	87,300	248,987	4,548	12,017
Poland	—	388,279	—	27,184

*Including Bosnia and Herzegovina
**Hungarian Kingdom in the Austro-Hungarian Empire

from a war to a peace economy were being added to the already dif-difficult problems faced by an economy crippled by war, and all clamoured for immediate solution. The simultaneous appearance on the scene of all these problems brought about complete economic chaos, almost inextricable confusion, and a state of utter hope-lessness.

The most difficult conditions were to be found in the countries which had suffered the worst upheavals, Austria, Hungary, and Poland. By 1917, it was already plain that the Monarchy's Austrian territories were at the end of their economic tether. In the summer of 1918, the economic experts were unanimously of the opinion that Austria could not face another winter of war. Agricultural produc-tion had sunk to about 50 percent of its prewar level, and at their best the Austrian territories were far from self-sufficient; they had always been dependent on imports, especially from Hungary. Hungary, however, could not come to the rescue, for she was not even in a position to satisfy her own requirements.

In many industries, production fell because of the shortage of raw materials, and even those branches of industry—such as coal and iron—which were essential for the prosecution of the war did not reach prewar production levels. Hence the young republic of Austria, created in the autumn of 1918, found itself in a catastrophic economic situation. To add to these difficulties, food supplies in the country were at a dangerously low level. The bread and flour rations were—to quote Schuschnigg—too big to die on, but too small to live on. At the beginning of 1919, the consumption of milk in Vienna was only 7 percent of the prewar figure. The supplementary foodstuffs sent in aid secured, at the best, a condition of bare existence; agricultural output even by 1920 did not exceed 50 percent of what it had been before the war. For lack of coal, the railways had, for the most part, been brought to a halt. Furnaces could not be fired. In the summer of 1919, 200,000 factory workers were unemployed. Inflation had started long before as a result of the enormous war expenditure. By the end of 1918, the value of the crown, eroded by numerous war loans, had fallen by two-thirds. In 1919, the situation continued to deteriorate, for the country had been bled white and was now to all intents and purposes cut off from the other parts of the former empire. In these circumstances, economic decline could not be arrested; on the contrary, it grew worse: industrial production was hardly more than one-third of the 1913 figure.

Conditions in Hungary were similar. Here, agriculture was the main source of the national income, and because of labour shortages, the requisitioning of horses by the army, and the fall in the number of cattle, it had suffered a sharp decline. The production of grain fell from 142 million cwt. in 1913 to 84 million cwt. in 1918, maize from 96 million to 48 million. There was a comparable industrial decline. In 1918, many consumer goods industries, long deprived of raw materials and fuel supplies by the war industries, showed a fall in production of 60–70 percent. Even coal-mining, essential to the prosecution of the war, showed as early as 1917 a decline in production of about 17 percent, and by 1918 the output of iron and steel had fallen by a half.

By 1918, the decline had reached such a nadir that the needs of the army could no longer be satisfied and the civilian population had to endure severe deprivations. Expenditure on the war swallowed up 40–50 percent of the national income and was financed largely by the issue of paper money. Inflation had become as rampant as in Austria.

The short-lived success of the revolution had, naturally, hardly any effect on the economic difficulties, and after the counterrevolution had gained the upper hand in the autumn of 1919, conditions became even more chaotic. The Romanian forces in the country which had helped to overthrow the Hungarian Republic of Councils contributed to this situation by dismantling and carrying off a not inconsiderable quantity of machinery and rolling stock. By 1919, Hungary's agricultural output had fallen to about a third, and by

1920, to about 50–60 percent of the prewar figure. In the autumn of 1919, industrial production was only 15–20 percent of the peacetime level, and by 1920, it had risen to only 35–40 percent.

Even Czechoslovakia, which started on its way in more favourable circumstances than any of the other states in the area, could not avoid a temporary recession. The utter exhaustion and the inflation which in 1917–18 were characteristic of the monarchy in its death throes, had, of course, also involved the Czech and Slovak regions of the empire. At the end of 1918, in the months following the creation of the Czechoslovak republic, industrial production was only half the prewar figure, and even in 1920 it rose only to about 70 percent. (Of the more important products, steel production was around 78 percent, iron about 72 percent, and cement about 85 percent.) Owing to its greater strength and its more favourable situation on the side of the victors, the Czechoslovak economy had access to quicker and better possibilities of rehabilitation. By 1921, when Austria and Hungary were just beginning to emerge from their critical economic condition, Czech industry was already reaching 75–80 percent of its prewar output, and on this foundation the republic could successfully tackle the currency depreciation.[4]

The whole production situation of the immediate postwar years, more especially the ubiquitous and steep decline in agriculture, dealt a heavy blow to the export possibilities of those countries in the region which were particularly dependent on foreign trade. Hungary furnishes a characteristic example: compared to prewar figures, it exported only 0.1 percent of wheat, 0.3 percent of flour, 2.1 percent of cattle, and 2.5 percent of meat. (By 1921, the figures were respectively 7.4, 33, 20, and 78.) Only the export of wine and feathers reached or exceeded the prewar volume. By 1920, the total export of agricultural produce reached 21 percent, and in the following year 41 percent of the prewar level. Given Hungary's economic structure, this enormous setback could not be compensated for by the export of manufactured goods; and in any case, industrial exports had also declined. In 1920, they scarcely exceeded 40 percent, and in 1921 reached only 57 percent of the prewar totals. A vicious circle hindered the development of the export trade. For the economy to function and for industry to be put on its feet, foreign currency and raw materials were essential, but these could be secured only by the export of agricultural produce, a thing then impossible; the place of these missing agricultural products could have been taken by competitively-priced manufactured goods, but to produce these was impossible without importing raw materials.[5]

In the nations of East Central Europe, the crippling of foreign trade created a catastrophic situation, for they had emerged from the breakup of the Monarchy with a so-called export-import sensitive economy. When Austria, Bohemia, and Hungary were parts of the old empire they did not have to cope with export problems, for a considerable proportion of Austrian and Czech industrial products—for instance, three-quarters of their textile manufactures—were marketed in the agricultural regions of the Monarchy, and the same in reverse applied to agricultural produce. For example, 80 percent of Hungarian agricultural exports (primarily grain and flour) had been marketed in the Austrian and Czech areas.

Thus, foreign trade—that is, exports to countries outside the Monarchy—had played a relatively subordinate role, given the variety of possibilities within the empire itself. In the new situation, the successor states disposed of one-sided, unbalanced productive capacities. Some of them had inherited relatively too much industry, others too little. But in both cases, within the new frontiers, only part of the commodities required to operate the national economy was present. Without these essential prerequisites, these economies could not function satisfactorily within the restricted national markets. For Czechoslovakia and Austria, this implied the export of manufactured goods and the import of agricultural products and many industrial raw materials; Hungary, on the other hand, had to export agricultural produce and import industrial raw materials and capital goods. Thus, for the successor states foreign trade became vitally important; all of them became to a large extent dependent on it.

The foreign trade problem in its turn posed in a new form the question of capital accumulation. The very importance of trade, the restricted outlets for exports, the unavoidable need for imports were in themselves enough to increase the need for capital to finance trade. But capital accumulation, which had always been small, sank even lower because of the decline in production and the rapidly spreading currency depreciation. The fall in internal capital accumulation was particularly marked in the case of Austria, which had formerly been a relatively big exporter of capital and had played a leading role in supplying the capital needs of the more backward regions of the Monarchy. Inflation, always a corollary of economic exhaustion, had wiped out a large part of its monetary capital. In

1913, the deposits in the leading Viennese banks and in the savings banks of the capital and the countryside, came to 2.2 billion crowns. In 1923, this figure—converted to its gold value—had sunk to 8.7 million. The extraordinarily slow pace of recovery is demonstrated by the fact that even by the summer of 1925, average deposits stood only at 11 percent of prewar levels. All this was an inseparable part of the new problems of financing, and forced Austria as well as Hungary to seek large injections of capital from abroad. Their only means of recovery from the economic chaos of the postwar years was to tap foreign sources. Currency stabilization, based on credits from western countries and the loans which followed, became one of the most important factors in the consolidation of their economies. The situation in Yugoslavia, Romania, and Poland was very similar. Only Czechoslovakia, by its own unaided efforts, managed to extricate itself from the postwar confusion and to embark on a programme of independent development.[6]

However, the results of the breakup of the Austro-Hungarian Monarchy stretched much further than the short-term manifestations of economic chaos, or the troubles and convulsions caused by adjustment to new conditions. The confusion, which lasted for several years, was such as could lead both to great progress and to a state of permanent regression. When the Monarchy broke up, it was by no means clear which of these two possibilities would be realized, for conditions in the Monarchy had influenced the economic development of its constituent peoples in very diverse ways. Living together within a large area had brought both advantages and disadvantages. It had, for instance, been advantageous to Austrian and Czech industrialization, to the development of Hungary's agriculture and agricultural industries; it had been unfavourable to Austrian and Czech agriculture and to Hungary's consumer goods industry. In addition to these reciprocal advantages and disadvantages, the Monarchy had embodied a system based on the inequality of its constituent parts, as reflected in the division of labour. The economic unity of the empire had rested on the integration of backward agrarian regions with others which had attained a standard of industrial development comparable to that of Western Europe. Apart from the splitting up of an economic community which had endured for half a century, and of the capitalist development which had held it together, the end of the Monarchy denoted for the newly emerging states a release from both the favourable and the unfavourable aspects of the system through which the division of labour had been carried out. Thus, the longer-term developments in one or other of the successor states were not merely the result of the empire's disintegration, or of the economic potential which had been inherited, but were largely dependent on the path followed after the breakup and on the success of the economic strategy that was planned and pursued. Therefore, attention should be focused above all on the economic strategy of the various countries of the Danube Basin between the two World Wars.

In the economic chaos of the postwar period, the first efforts of the new states were directed towards making a clean break with their old economic ties and towards attaining, as far as possible, complete economic independence. They regarded it as their main task to eliminate the last traces of the division of labour prevailing in the former empire, and to make themselves independent of even those regions which had up till then been their natural market for some goods and their main source of supply for others. The value of the goods exported by Austria and Czechoslovakia to Hungary in 1924—even taking postwar territorial changes into consideration—sank to 60 percent of the 1913 figure.

The newly independent states quickly walled themselves in with import prohibitions and high protective tariffs. For in the twenties, the European states—especially in Central and Eastern Europe—vied with each other in setting up the highest possible customs barriers. At the turn of the century, Hungary had already raised the cry for its own tariff system, and she could now turn this slogan into a practical economic policy. Although, by the conditions of the peace treaty, the customs duties of the erstwhile Austro-Hungarian Monarchy as set forth in Law no. 53 of 1907 were still obligatory for Hungary, Law no. 21 of 1920 gave the government the power to impose by decree new regulations for foreign trade. From July 1921 onwards, one decree after another was issued, placing ever larger numbers of commodities which had formerly been freely imported onto the list of prohibited goods. This applied above all to products of the textile, iron, leather, and engineering industries. Compared with the prewar 10–20 percent duty on consumer goods, the duty from 1925 onwards averaged 50 percent *ad valorem* and thus kept the principal imports of former days out of the Hungarian market.[7]

Of course, the Central and East European states intended these barriers around their national economies to act as a protection against all their trading partners equally. In practice, however, protection did not work in a uniform way; its impact was most marked on the neighbouring states. This was a natural outcome, for both in agriculture and industry these countries used less up-to-date techniques than did the more advanced nations; consequently, their goods were dearer and could not compete successfully on the world market. Thus, although at the Austrian and Czechoslovak frontiers the same duties were imposed on grain and flour irrespective of origin, these proved to be much more effective against Hungarian than against American produce, in spite of the higher transport costs of the latter. While the customs tariffs of the Balkan states imposed a heavy burden on imported machinery, they affected Austrian products much more than, for example, English and Belgian.

Thus, the barriers which had been erected to promote self-sufficiency unquestionably divided the Central and East European states more deeply from each other than from those of Western Europe. It is significant that between the wars, Yugoslavia's trade with its Balkan neighbours was quite small, exports and imports ranging between 5 and 9 percent of the total foreign trade turnover. Although immediately after the war Czechoslovakia, maintaining its old economic associations, still sold more than half of its exports to the Danubian states, by about the middle twenties the percentage had fallen to little more than a third. This process was reciprocal: parallel with this radical fall in exports to the Danubian states, Czechoslovakia, at the end of the decade (and partly for political reasons) was importing more than half its flour from overseas and not from its agrarian neighbours. The same situation developed in Austria, which was already buying a third of its wheat requirements in America, and during the same period was unable to sell the products of its engineering industry to its agrarian neighbours. Midway through the twenties, the Balkan states were buying French and English machine tools and equipment for textile factories, at a time when Austria's engineering industry was producing hardly more than a third of its prewar output. In spite of geographical closeness, of historical tradition, and the existence of natural markets near at hand, trade between the eastern and southeastern European states shrank to a minimum: to about 10–15 percent of their total trade. An additional reason for this was that they all consistently and rigidly excluded the Soviet Union from their economic life. A large part of what was now Poland had formerly been part of the Russian Empire, and the greater part of its market lay, so to speak, on Russian soil; yet only 1.5 percent of Poland's export trade was carried on with the Soviet Union. Conditions were similar in Czechoslovakia; while in the other East European states, not even this figure was reached. Exports from East Central Europe were directed largely to Western Europe which, by the Second World War, took 75–80 percent of their exports and supplied 70–80 percent of their imports.[8]

The economic policies pursued were naturally accompanied by the growth of autarkic tendencies. Austria and Czechoslovakia, for instance, made great efforts to increase their output of agricultural produce and livestock which they had formerly obtained from the agrarian districts of the Monarchy. In Austria, by 1934, the stock of pigs was almost double that of the postwar reconstruction period. About the middle of the twenties, home-grown wheat could hardly satisfy one-third of the domestic requirements, but ten years later, it was already covering more than half. In the middle of the postwar decade, Czechoslovakia's production of wheat came to about 20 million hundredweight; ten years later, it had reached 34 million. In a particularly favourable year, Czechoslovakia, ordinarily an importer of wheat, showed a surplus on its own harvest.

It is, therefore, not surprising that the markets which the Danubian countries could have offered each other shrank more and more as, following the 1929–33 overproduction crisis, still greater efforts were made to achieve self-sufficiency. After 1918, Hungary still sold a fifth or a sixth of its exports to Czechoslovakia; but by the middle thirties, this had fallen to 5 percent. On the other hand, it used as much of its available capital as possible to develop those consumer goods industries which it had formerly lacked.

In comparison with prewar standards, production in the Hungarian textile industry had doubled by 1925, trebled by 1929, and by the end of the thirties, had reached four times the prewar figure; the import of textiles, which in 1913 accounted for 70 percent of total home consumption, now covered only 2–3 percent. The most striking example of this severance of the associations based on the earlier division of labour can be found in the way Austria and Czechoslovakia developed their own industries. In the Monarchy, most of the spinning for the textile industry was done in Austria, while the weaving was concentrated in Bohemia. Each country wanted its textile industry to become independent of the other, so Austria began to enlarge its weaving industry, and by 1925 had already set up 5,000 looms, while Czechoslovakia, for its part, built spinning mills. Those Balkan states which had enjoyed independence before the war now also strove to consolidate their economic independence, but they were so backward industrially that international economic ties were not of paramount importance. Their efforts were in many ways successful, helping to correct the one-sidedness of their economies and to promote industrialization.[9]

Unfortunately, these methods of encouraging development were by no means the most efficacious. As the states—dazzled by national pride and driven by nationalist passion—began the all-round development of their economies, they paid no heed to the narrow and restricted basis of their economic potentialities as compared to those of the economic cooperation formerly practised with the neighbouring Danubian states. Thus, their venture proved to be not only extremely costly, but also led to much overlapping of effort and superfluous parallel capacity. As a consequence, much of the economic capacity created earlier, both agricultural and industrial, was wasted. By the time Hungary's textile industry was built up, or Austria expanded its weaving, and Czechoslovakia its spinning mills, the old Austrian and Czech textile industries had lost a considerable part of their markets and had fallen into a critical condition. The same thing happened to Hungarian agriculture and flour milling which, deprived of a large part of their share of the Austrian and Czech markets, had also sunk into a state of chronic crisis. Austria tried to promote the cultivation of cereal crops and to develop its own milling industry. It introduced state subsidies, and in 1930 created a special fund by levying taxes on sugar, beer, and alcohol. Hungary's milling industry had supplied the total requirements of the Monarchy, but between the wars it could never, even in boom periods, produce more than three-quarters of its former output. The giant Hungarian mills, which had formerly worked for the export trade, closed down one after the other; their assets were disposed of, their empty premises were sold for conversion into textile factories, or were simply razed. Thus, apparently insurmountable difficulties in selling their products was one of the most obvious consequences of the developments in the agrarian countries of Central and Eastern Europe after the First World War. The developed and even the less well developed countries soon discovered that part of their industrial capacity was superfluous.

This, together with the endeavour of each country to develop industries which already existed in neighbouring states at a level high enough to produce export surpluses hindered, indeed rendered impossible, the creation of national economies based on the newest technological achievements, or the development of modern industries capable of competing on the world market. In other words, the effort to achieve agricultural self-sufficiency in the more industrialized states and the industrial ambitions of the agrarian states had indeed contributed to their own economic development, but had, at the same time, aggravated the new contradictions in the economic development of the entire area.

True, the more backward countries, through state aid and protective tariffs, succeeded in reducing imports, and thus laid the foundations for the relatively rapid development of consumer goods industries. Throughout most of these East Central European states it was the textile and other light industries which showed the most substantial progress. In Hungary, as already mentioned, the textile industry was in a position to cover practically all domestic requirements, compared to the only one-third of former days. In Yugoslavia also, it was the textile industry which between the two World Wars showed the fastest development. In the first half of the twenties, textiles had accounted for almost a third of all imports; in the second half of the thirties, for no more than 10 percent. On the other hand, the import of machines and factory equipment doubled. In Romania, before the Second World War, textiles represented more than a fifth of the value of the total industrial output.[10]

This rapid advance in the production of textiles and other consumer goods undoubtedly gave a great impetus to the industrial development of Eastern Europe; but it served also to conceal the discrepancy between the obsolete manufacturing processes and the industrial needs of the age. For during the first half of the twentieth century, the textile industry, indeed, consumer goods industries as a whole, were, in the more developed countries of Western Europe, already entering a relative decline. For example, during the years immediately preceding the Second World War, the output of the textile industry in England sank from 19 percent to 11 percent of the total industrial production; and in continental Europe, from 18 to 11 percent. On the other hand, the share of the iron, steel, metal-working and chemical industries rose in England from 32 to 44 percent, and on the continent from 41 to 50 percent.[11]

After the First World War, industry underwent a radical transformation. Through the use of new techniques, it became possible to provide electricity much more cheaply; industry, therefore, used it on a steadily expanding scale, and electrical power entered on its triumphant course. The multi-purpose electric motor forged ahead in competition with the clumsier steam engine. At the same time, the second great factor in the transformation of industry was making itself felt: the internal combusion engine, the invention of which led to completely new methods of industrial mass production. The modern assembly line was used first of all in the automobile industry; it opened the path to modern factory organization and management techniques, and to new ways of increasing output. It is no coincidence that these new mass production methods quickly spread to other industries, first to the manufacture of machine tools, with a marked effect on costs of production. All these processes naturally caused changes in the whole structure of industry, and in the more advanced capitalist countries, heavy industry advanced by leaps and bounds. In Western Europe, its share of the total output rose from 25–30 to around 50 percent.

The majority of the Central and Eastern European states could not keep pace with this development; it was only the light industries which managed to increase production, while the potentially dynamic heavy industries, where the new technology could and should have bgeen adopted, stagnated. In this part of Europe, there was practically no country which could adapt its engineering industries for modern mass production; with their small and restricted markets, they were unable to take advantage of the new developments in industrial technology. If we measure the advance of modern industry by the per capita consumption of steel, the increase in England and Sweden between 1913 and 1938 was between 50 and 100 percent; whereas even in Czechoslovakia and Poland, there was virtual stagnation.[12]

The exclusion of certain types of commodities and the effort of each country to produce goods which had formerly been imported meant that the advantages following from the intense efforts to increase production in certain branches of industry were counterbalanced by the recession in others for the lack of markets. The example of Hungary is typical and highly instructive: while textile production quadrupled, heavy industry made no progress, and the food processing industries showed a substantial decline; as a result, total industrial production rose very slowly indeed, by not quite 30 percent over a period of twenty years. Owing to the stagnation in agriculture, the annual rate of increase of the national income was only about 1.5 percent. In Austria, the rate of growth was similar, while Poland, which had regained its longed-for independence, was, between the two World Wars, quite unable to reach even that minimal economic growth. One important reason for Central and Eastern Europe's slow economic development was that these countries—though foreign sources of capital were less plentiful than before—still persisted in attempting to make themselves independent economically, and thus dissipated even the restricted opportunities of development open to them. Their exertions to promote economic development and industrialization were, therefore, bound to have only limited success.

In all the countries of the region, the problem of employment was the gravest. It was quite impossible to eliminate chronic unemployment; in Poland, Romania, Yugoslavia, and Bulgaria a fifth to a third of the rural population could find no work, and industry was in no position to absorb them.

Given the slow pace of economic development and the serious internal contradictions, there was, of course, no possibility of attaining the much desired economic independence, and in the end, little had been done to overcome the general backwardness. Before the outbreak of the Second World War, 75–80 percent of the population of Albania, Bulgaria, Yugoslavia, and Romania still earned their living on the land. Even in Poland, the rural population had only fallen from the 64 percent after the First World War to 61 percent. In Hungary, about half the country's population worded on the land.[13]

As a result of the policy of exclusion and autarky, of the consequent restriction of markets, and of the slow pace of industrial development and its consequences for capital accumulation, the economies of the Danubian countries remained extremely vulnerable and unstable. During the second half of the twenties, generous foreign credits and relatively favourable world market prices had enabled them to consolidate their economies; they even enjoyed a moderate prosperity. But when the temporary boom broke and the economic crisis of 1929–33 struck the world, all the economic problems flared up again more fiercely than ever before. Czechoslovakia, which had developed well during the twenties and appeared genuinely industrial; Austria, industrialized but stagnating after the First World War; Hungary, stuck in its old agrarian-industrial pattern;

and the Balkan states, no longer facing competition from the Monarchy and longing for swifter industrialization—all fell into the most severe social and economic crisis, which, in its turn, brought to the fore the basic problem of their existence and progress. The dead-end reached in the thirties left only the choice between continuing as they were, or adapting themselves to be the *Lebensraum* of the new and frightening Germany of Hitler. The defencelessness of the Danube-Basin countries in the face of economic crisis did, indeed, prove fertile soil for the determined advance of the Germans. The rapid growth of German influence and her economic domination prepared the ground for the *Anschluss*, for the subjection of Czechoslovakia, and finally, for the Second World War. The incompetence and helplessness of the states of the Danube Basin on the eve of the war reflected the fiasco of the political pretensions, of the nationalist economic policies and of the plans for industrial development which they had clung to for twenty years. The economic problems created by the breakup of the Monarchy remained unsolved between the two World Wars.

Notes

1. Alice Teichova, *An Economic Background to Munich International Business and Czechoslovakia 1918-1938* (Cambridge, 1978); R. Olsovsky, V. Prucha, et al., *Prehled gospodursveho vývoje Československa v letech 1918-1945* [Survey of the economic development of Czechoslovakia] (Prague, 1961).

2. Ivan Berend and György Ránki, *Magyarország gazdasága 1919-1929* [Hungary's economy] (Budapest, 1965).

3. G. Gratz and R. Schuller, *Die Wirtschaftliche Zusammenbruch Oesterreich Ungarns* (Vienna, 1930); K. Rotschild, *Austria's Economic Development Between the Two Wars* (London, 1946).

4. T. Faltus, *Povojnová hospodárska kriza v rokoch 1912-1923 v Československu* [Postwar Depression in Czechoslovakia] (Bratislava, 1966).

5. Iván Berend and György Ránki, *Hungary, Hundred Years of Economic Development* (London, 1974).

6. N. Layton and Ch. Rist, *The Economic Situation of Austria* (Geneva, 1923).

7. H. Liepmann, *Tariff Levels and the Economic Unity of Europe* (London, 1938).

8. A. Basch, *European Economic Nationalism* (Washington, 1943); L. Pasvolsky, *Economic Nationalism of the Danubian States* (New York, 1929).

9. W. Weber, *Oesterreich Wirtschaftsstruktur gestern-heute-morgen* (Berlin, 1962); *Die Wirtschaft der Tschechoslovakei 1918–1928* (Prague, 1928).

10. V. Madgearu, *Evolutia economiei românești dupa razboi mondial* [Evolution of the Romanian Economy after World War I] (Bucharest, 1940); M. Mirković, *Ekonomska Historija Yugoslavija* [The economic history of Yugoslavia] (Belgrade, 1962).

11. A. Lewis, *Economic Survey 1919–1939* (London, 1932); A. Maisels, *Industrial Growth and World Trade* (Cambridge, 1974).

12. I. Svennilson, *Growth and Stagnation in the European Economy* (Geneva, 1954).

13. League of Nations, *Industrialisation and Foreign Trade* (Geneva, 1945).

14. Iván Berend and G. Ránki, *Economic Development of East Central Europe* (New York, 1974).

Part II

Hungary and the Great Powers
in the Process of Peacemaking

(See maps at the end of the book)

Thomas L. Sakmyster

Great Britain and the Making
of The Treaty of Trianon

Great Britain's role in the making of the peace treaty with Hungary after World War I presents a perplexing anomaly. In early 1920, when the text of the Treaty of Trianon had been made public but the treaty had not yet been signed by Hungary, strong and influential voices were raised in Britain calling for a reexamination of what seemed to be unduly severe and unfair peace terms. In its preparation for the peace conference, the British Foreign Office in late 1918 had established a fundamental principle: the peace settlement should be just and permanent so that all concerned parties, including the Germans and the Hungarians, would feel "that on the part of the British nation there has been an honest attempt to carry through a disinterested policy which has sought the best interest of all."[1] In early 1920, however, many members of Parliament and British representatives in East Central Europe questioned whether the Treaty of Trianon, which left some 2 1/2 million Hungarians outside a Hungary greatly reduced in size, was indeed a just treaty. Most significant was the attitude of the British Prime Minister, David Lloyd George. Warning that the creation of large Hungarian irredentas constituted an apparent injustice that could create a very unstable situation in Danubian Europe, he urged his counterparts on the Allied Supreme Council to study the peace terms with a view to making possible concessions to Hungary.[2]

Yet despite this surge of sympathy for Hungary from several quarters of British opinion, the Treaty of Trianon remained unaltered. An examination of Britain's role in the making of the treaty with Hungary provides an explanation of this curious circumstance and demonstrates the great influence which a handful of East European specialists in the British Foreign Office had on the shaping of policy in Danubian Europe after the Great War. It should be noted that neither Britain nor her allies was primarily responsible for the collapse of the Habsburg Empire and the dismemberment of

Hungary.[3] Yet British policy certainly gave impetus to this process, and the Foreign Office played a critical role in determining the precise frontiers of the new Hungarian state.

Despite the harsh terms of the Treaty of Trianon, which was signed on June 14, 1920, the dismemberment of Hungary had by no means been a British war aim at the start of the Great War. Indeed, Britain had gone to war against Austria-Hungary somewhat reluctantly, and almost to the very last months of the conflict the idea of luring the Dual Monarchy away from the true enemy, Germany, by negotiations for a separate peace was never completely abandoned.[4]

At the outbreak of the war the image of Hungary in Great Britain was on the whole quite favorable. For some time the Hungarians had been the best known and most admired of the ethnic groups in the Habsburg lands.[5] From about 1905, however, the image had become slightly tarnished, and during the war years many politically conscious Britons came to the conclusion that Hungary's intolerant policies toward her minorities had been a major cause of the war. Hungary's stature in British wartime public opinion seemed to decline in direct proportion to the rise of acceptance of the principle of national self-determination. Moreover, whereas during the war few Britons were willing to stand up and speak in defense of Hungary, an enemy state, proponents of what has been called "liberal nationalism" were increasingly bold in propagating their political theories.

A major tenet of the "liberal nationalists" was that thwarted nationalism in Eastern Europe had been, even more than Prussian militarism, the fundamental cause of the Great War.[6] The principal spokesmen for these views, Henry Wickham Steed and Robert Seton-Watson, thus emerged early in the war as the most important and persistent critics of the Habsburg Empire in general and of Hungary in particular.

In the decade before the war, Henry Wickham Steed, the political correspondent for *The Times* who dealt with the affairs of East Central Europe, had come to the conclusion that the Hungarians (or "Judaeo-Magyars" as he often called them) were at the heart of the problems of the Habsburg Empire. By persisting in their oppressive policies toward the minority groups who represented more than 50 percent of the population of Hungary, the Hungarian ruling class was creating conditions that would lead to disaster. Once the war broke out, Steed, now head of the foreign department of *The Times*, worked assiduously to enlighten British public opinion about the necessity of breaking up the Austro-Hungarian Empire.

In this crusade Steed found Robert Seton-Watson to be a most congenial collaborator. A scholar of independent means and an accomplished linguist, Seton-Watson had earlier in his career been something of a Hungarophile. A trip to Hungary in 1905, however, had caused him great disillusionment. Feeling that he had been deceived by the Hungarians, who had tried to conceal from him the true nature of their oppressive rule, he embarked on a career of scholarship and polemics aimed at exposing the "racial problems in Hungary" and championing the South Slavs, Romanians, Czechs, and Slovaks.[7] As early as December, 1914, he published a pamphlet calling for the dismemberment of Austria-Hungary and the liberation of the subject nationalities. To bolster his arguments Seton-Watson strove in particular to inform the British public about Hungary's "systematic oppression" of the Slovaks, "one of the greatest infamies of the last fifty years."[8]

As a forum for his ideas, Seton-Watson founded and edited a journal appropriately called *The New Europe*. In addition to condemnations of the Germans and Hungarians, the articles of *The New Europe* were designed to acquaint intellectual circles in Britain and North America with the leaders, culture, and political ideals of the small Slavic nations and the Romanians. Readers were assured that the "Successor States" that would arise from the ruins of the Habsburg Empire would be stable, democratic, and mature. In contrast to the Hungarian and German ruling classes, the new leaders would be tolerant toward any remaining minority groups. Moreover, the new states would represent a formidable barrier to any future German *Drang nach Osten*, and would be natural allies of Britain.[9]

There is no doubt that *The New Europe* and the articles in *The Times* inspired by Steed had a profound impact on politically conscious Britons, particularly in the academic world and in the lower and middle echelons of the Foreign Office. However, the key leaders of the British government in the last years of the war, Prime Minister David Lloyd George and Foreign Secretary Arthur Balfour, were not easy converts to the banner of national self-determination. Aside from the dangerous implications that that principle might have for

Ireland and British possessions overseas, the British leadership preferred to base its policy toward Austria-Hungary on strategic needs. If sponsoring the cause of the Slavs and Romanians was essential to winning the war, that policy would be undertaken and few would mourn the demise of the Habsburg Empire. But if prospects for victory could be enhanced by a separate peace which left Austria-Hungary intact, that policy would be pursued.

The first major initiative taken on the basis of this pragmatic policy occurred in 1915 and 1916, when Italy and Romania were persuaded to enter the war on the side of the Entente. In the secret Treaty of Bucharest an extravagant offer of territory was made to Romania, including all of Transylvania and eastern Hungary up to the river Tisza. The implications of this treaty were quickly seen by Henry Wickham Steed, who privately declared that the treaty "signs the death warrant of Hungary" and "foreshadows the reconstruction of Europe on the basis of ethnically complete states."[10]

Yet there were some in the British Foreign Office who felt uneasy about the willingness of the government to commit itself to such radical changes in the map of East Central Europe. One of the Balkan experts in the Foreign Office, Harold Nicolson, who at the peace conference was to be a stalwart and enthusiastic supporter of the Successor States, warned in 1915 of the danger of promising to grant exhorbitant claims. "We cannot," he asserted, "blot Austria and Hungary out of the map and convert them into larger Switzerlands with no sea access. Promises hastily made now for an immediate object will be most embarrassing to realize when peace terms come to be discussed."[11] Referring specifically to Hungary, Nicolson later declared that if, after a prolonged war, Hungary was "so crushed as to submit to any terms, we should be sowing the seeds of future conflicts."[12]

The precedent set by the Treaty of Bucharest nonetheless made an impression on those officials of the Foreign Office entrusted with framing British policy in East Central Europe. In the fall of 1916, William Tyrrell and Robert Paget composed a memorandum in which they suggested that if at war's end the Allies were in a position to determine the future of Eastern Europe, Austria-Hungary would have to be destroyed, in accordance with "the principle of giving free play to nationalities." Hungary, the authors believed, would be formed of the purely Magyar portions of the country, though it was acknowledged that if an independent Hungary was to be viable, it would be unwise to "deprive it of territory beyond that which is necessary in order to conform to the principle of nationality." Tyrrell and Paget envisioned a Hungary shorn of Croatia and the Romanian portions of Transylvania. However, Baranya, Bácska, and the Bánát would remain with Hungary, as would Slovakia and Ruthenia.[13] Implicit in this important tentative statement of British war aims was support for an enlarged Romania, an enlarged Serbia (or new South Slav state), and a reduced Hungary that still retained a large number of non-Hungarians. The idea of creating a Czecho-Slovak state had clearly not yet taken strong roots in the Foreign Office.

In 1917, however, British policy toward Austria-Hungary seemed to take an abrupt turn. Prospects for an Entente victory were dimmed by the failure of the Romanian offensive and the outbreak of revolution in Russia. In these circumstances the British government endeavored to find some accommodation with the Dual Monarchy. There seems little doubt that if Vienna and Budapest had been amenable to a separate peace, the British would have abandoned any plans for a major diminution of Austria or Hungary. Significantly, British leaders no longer felt bound by the Treaty of Bucharest.[14]

By early 1918, however, it was clear that Austria-Hungary was not interested in, or was incapable of, negotiating a separate peace. Once this was realized, London hesitantly adopted the strategy of undermining the Habsburg Empire by exploiting national discontent. Although no firm decision to destroy Austria-Hungary was subsequently made by the Cabinet or Prime Minister, an inexorable step-by-step process was initiated that led to this result.

An important milestone was the creation in the spring of 1918 of the Political Intelligence Department of the Foreign Office (P.I.D.). Its director, William Tyrrell, recruited a staff that read like a roster of contributors to *The New Europe*, including Allen Leeper, Lewis Namier, and Arnold Toynbee. Seton-Watson, however, had been appointed as co-director of the Austro-Hungarian section of the newly established Department of Enemy Propaganda (Crewe House), the government agency responsible for propaganda aimed at enemy states.

The result was the creation of a powerful government lobby in support of a strong British commitment to national self-determination in Eastern Europe. Throughout 1918 the Political

Intelligence Department circulated reports and recommendations concerning Austria-Hungary. Whenever questions about Eastern Europe arose in the Foreign Office, the experts in P.I.D. or Seton-Watson at Crewe House were consulted. By the autumn of 1918, as one historian has suggested, Crewe House and the Political Intelligence Department were really in charge of British policy in East Central Europe.[15] The culmination of the efforts of these advocates of a "New Europe" came in August, 1918, when the British government granted recognition of the Czechoslovaks as an allied nation. From this point there could be no turning back: the imminent collapse of the Habsburg Empire had already been sanctioned by Great Britain.

The unexpectedly rapid collapse of the Central Powers on both the eastern and western fronts in November, 1918, required that the British government move quickly to articulate the policy it would pursue at the peace conference. Since no detailed sketch of war aims in Eastern Europe had been made since the now outdated 1916 memorandum of Tyrrell and Paget, and since no directives on the subject were now issued by the War Cabinet, British policy was set out in a series of new position papers produced by the Foreign Office in November and December. In the major memoranda devoted to British aims in Europe, it was now firmly stated that national self-determination would be the guideline for the peace settlement:

> Our object is to establish national States. This is a great gain, for there is every reason to hope that States based on the conscious existence of a common nationality will be more durable and afford a firmer support against aggression than the older form of State, which was often a merely accidental congeries of territories without internal cohesion, necessary economic unity, or clearly defined geographical frontiers.[16]

Yet even as the Habsburg Empire was in the process of dissolution, there were still those in the British government who warned of the possible pitfalls of too rigid an application of national self-determination. Several authoritative figures in the Foreign Office thought that some sort of federation in East Central Europe would be a better arrangement than independent states. Lord Curzon reflected this sentiment when he asserted that "unless we can induce the small states we are setting up to federate with one another, the last state of Europe may well be worse than the first."[17] Some had their doubts about the nature of the new states that were appearing. Robert Cecil,

Undersecretary of State for Foreign Affairs, even ventured to ask whether "a new Europe with two or three additional Slav states will really be more peaceful than the old Europe."[18]

As an expression of the concern of those skeptical of the magical powers of national self-determination and of the virtues of the Successor States, the point was clearly made in the position papers of the Foreign Office that the peace would have to be a just one that left "no avoidable cause for future friction." Germans and Hungarians would have to be treated "on exactly the same principles as the Czechs and the Roumanians."[19] The traditional British sense of fair play was to be honored as well: "Our object should be that when the whole transaction is concluded, all these nations, Czecho-Slovaks, Jugo-Slavs, Poles—we may perhaps add even Bulgarians, Magyars, and Germans—will feel that on the part of the British nation there has been an honest attempt to carry through a disinterested policy which has sought the best interests of all."[20]

These noble principles were consciously modeled on the words of Woodrow Wilson, who suggested that "we should be just towards those to whom we should wish not to be just." Yet an examination of British policy toward Hungary at the Paris peace conference suggests that to a great extent the Hungarians were not treated "by the same principles as the Czechs and Roumanians," and that the Foreign Office was far from disinterested in its contribution to the making of the Treaty of Trianon. Two circumstances help explain this development. In the general confusion prevailing in the time between the armistice and the opening of the peace conference, no clearly defined British policy toward East Central Europe was articulated by the prime minister or Cabinet. At the same time those individuals in the Foreign Office least infatuated with the prospect of a reconstruction of East Central Europe based on the principle of nationality were turning their attention to other pressing matters, thus leaving both the formulation of British policy and the actual drawing of the new frontiers in the hands of a small group of East European specialists, including Allen Leeper, Harold Nicolson, and Sir Eyre Crowe (with Robert Seton-Watson in an advisory capacity). These men had already demonstrated their warm sympathy for and emotional ties to the Czechoslovaks, Romanians, and South Slavs. None of them could be said to have been neutral in his attitude toward Hungary; indeed, several of them were strongly hostile to and mistrustful of the Hungarians.

The anti-Hungarian sentiments of Seton-Watson have already been described. Allen Leeper, who had been honorary secretary of the Anglo-Romanian Society during the war, harbored a deep distrust of all Hungarians and a corresponding admiration for and confidence in the Romanians. During 1919 and 1920 he emerged as the staunchest defender of the Trianon Treaty against its British critics. The sentiments of Harold Nicolson were candidly recorded in his memoir of the peace conference:

> My feelings toward Hungary were less detached. I confess that I regarded, and still regard, that Turanian tribe with acute distaste. Like their cousins the Turks, they had destroyed much and created nothing. . . . For centuries the Magyars had oppressed their subject nationalities. The hour of liberation and retribution was at hand.[21]

"Bias and prejudice there was," Nicolson later admitted of the British peace conference delegation.[22] As they embarked on this exciting venture, Nicolson and his colleagues preferred to dwell not on how the Kingdom of Hungary should be dismantled, but on how the promising new states should be constructed. For Nicolson it was "the thought of the new Serbia, the new Greece, the new Bohemia, the new Poland which made our hearts sing hymns at heaven's gate."[23] In determining the borders of the Successor States, these Foreign Office officials felt obliged to give the new states "unity, independence, and strength."[24] What this meant in practice was a British willingness to ignore ethnic frontiers in cases where economic, strategic, or geographical factors were deemed to be paramount. In theory, given the Foreign Office commitment to a policy of disinterested mediation, this would have meant that the economic and strategic needs of Hungary as well as the Successor States would be taken into account. But for active partisans like Crowe, Leeper, Nicolson, and Seton-Watson such a level of impartiality was not easy to attain.

In the Foreign Office the task of drafting the key position paper on Hungary's frontiers for use by the British delegation was entrusted to Robert Seton-Watson. Not surprisingly, Seton-Watson suggested that the Hungary that should emerge in the peace settlement was "roughly, that portion of the former kingdom of Hungary which is inhabited by compact Magyar minorities."[25] In light of later developments, however, Seton-Watson's advice on how this goal should be achieved was relatively moderate in tone and prescient in pointing out the problems to be confronted.

Seton-Watson divided the Kingdom of Hungary into three categories: a) areas incontestably Slovak, Romanian, or South Slav in character, which would be automatically assigned to the appropriate Successor State; b) areas incontestably Magyar, which would go to the new Hungary; and c) "grey zones," areas in which both Hungary and her neighbors might have legitimate claims. Pointing out that it was precisely in these "grey zones" that national fervor might lead to exaggerated propaganda, intrigue, and incidents, Seton-Watson suggested that these areas by placed under international control until boundary commissions of the peace conference could make on-the-spot investigations.[26]

Since Seton-Watson was skeptical of the validity of the Hungarian census of 1910, he regarded certain regions and cities that the Hungarians were to claim (such as Nyitra, Kassa, and Temesvár) as incontestably non-Hungarian. Yet he placed into the "grey zones" many areas which the new Yugoslav, Czechoslovak, and Romanian governments regarded as vital to the well being of their countries. In the north of the old Hungary, this included the Grosse Schütt[27] and several areas along the frontier that stretched northeastward. The "grey zone" between Romania and Hungary extended along the whole frontier and included the counties of Szatmár, Bihar, and Arad. On the Hungarian-Yugoslav frontier the "grey zone" included Bácska and portions of the Baranya and Bánát.

On the basis of Seton-Watson's memorandum the suggested frontiers of Hungary and her neighbors were sketched on a map of Southeastern Europe,[28] the frontiers drawn so as to divide the "grey zones" equally among Hungary and the Successor States. In this way several important areas claimed by Czechoslovakia, Romania, and Yugoslavia were tentatively assigned to Hungary.

As the Foreign Office labored to prepare for the peace conference, a decision that would have enormous importance for Danubian Europe was taken by the War Cabinet. At the time of the signing of the armistice with Austria-Hungary, French units in the Balkans were the only Entente troops that could quickly be assigned to occupation duty in Hungary. However, when the French suggested that Britain join France in sending troops to occupy Budapest and Vienna, the British rejected the idea. Not only did Arthur Balfour, the Foreign Secretary, see no reason for British troops to "act as police in the Austrian capitals," but the military leadership throught the commitment of troops had already reached "appalling dimensions," what with units in Baku, Batum, Archangel, Mesopotamia, and elsewhere.[29]

This decision meant that a highly unstable situation would prevail in East Central Europe for many months thereafter. Seton-Watson's idea of internationally supervised " grey zones" could not easily be implemented. Moreover, because of France's desire to serve as patron of the Successor States, who were regarded as valuable future allies, the French army in Danubian Europe, far from maintaining strict order, actually facilitated occupation of Hungarian territory by the Successor States.[30] In addition, the absence of British and American forces and the delay in opening the peace conference were exploited by the new states, who, as one historian has described it, "were hurriedly and avidly endeavoring to fill in the white spots on the political map of Europe."[31] Thus, when the peace conference finally assembled in Paris in January, 1919, it was faced with a fait accompli in the form of a Hungary already severely dismembered.

These events seriously undermined the new government of Hungary, a republic under Mihály Károlyi. Repeated attempts were made by Károlyi to enlist British support for an end to the military advances of the Romanians, Czechs, and Yugoslavs.[32] But the Foreign Office regarded Károlyi, who hoped by an enlightened minorities policy to maintain the territorial integrity of most of historic Hungary, with contempt.[33] A positive response to Hungary's call for assistance, Lewis Namier argued, would be tantamount to preventing the "natural disintegration of Hungary."[34] Thus, all of the numerous Hungarian approaches to the British government in late 1918 and into 1919 were rebuffed, and the arguments of all individuals (both Hungarian and non-Hungarian) who pleaded for a fairer treatment of Hungary were abruptly dismissed as "pure propaganda." As a result of this attitude and the generally chaotic state of communication in Europe, the Hungarian viewpoint rarely penetrated the phalanx of Leeper, Namier, and Nicolson to other segments of the British government.

When the peace conference finally convened in Paris in January, 1919, it was recognized by the Allied heads of state that swift action had to be taken to determine the new political frontiers of East Central Europe. The obvious complexity of the issues, however, led to the decision to seek the guidance of East Central European specialists on two commissions, one dealing with Czechoslovak affairs, the other with Romanian and Yugoslav affairs. Before the territorial commissions began their work, the British experts (Crowe, Leeper, and Nicolson) consulted with their American counterparts, and were delighted to discover, in the words of Nicolson, "a remarkable unanimity" with respect to "the whole frontiers of Jugo-Slavia, Czecho-Slovakia, Rumania, Austria and Hungary."[35] In broad terms this was doubtless an accurate assessment of the situation. Both delegations were prepared to reject the more extreme demands and proposals of the Successor States, such as Romanian claims based on the Treaty of Bucharest and Beneš's proposal for a "Slav Corridor" separating Hungary and Austria. Moreover, an American map of proposed borders for Hungary was remarkably similar to the British map based on Seton-Watson's memorandum. On both maps, for example, the Grosse Schütt is assigned to Hungary and the Romanian-Hungarian frontier is further to the east than the final Trianon frontier.[36]

In the workings of the territorial commissions, however, the "remarkable unanimity" between the American and British positions proved to be an illusion. The American delegation did not deviate from the principle that in drawing the new frontiers greater consideration should be given to the ethnic composition of an area than to economic or strategic factors. The French delegates, of course, stressing the need to make the new states "viable," supported Czechoslovak, Romanian, and South Slav claims unreservedly and quite adeptly.[37] On most points in which the French and American positions differed, however, the French point prevailed, largely because of British support.

In addition to Sir Eyre Crowe, who sat on both territorial commissions, the British delegation on the Czechoslovak Commission consisted of Harold Nicolson and Sir Joseph Cook, the Australian Minister of the Navy. This was an unhappy choice. Nicolson was perplexed to find himself selected, for he had not prepared to work on Czechoslovak affairs and did not consider himself an expert on that area. Cook spoke no French and was ignorant of East Central European affairs, yet this did not prevent his taking an active role in the proceedings. It seems unlikely that he had read the position papers prepared for the British delegation, for he inexplicably supported the French position on almost all issues, including the award of the Grosse Schütt to Czechoslovakia. Cook's attitude, as explained to an American delegate, was to let "our friends the Czechs have what they want."[38] Since Crowe apparently shared this sentiment, and Nicolson did not choose to take a firm stand in support of the previous British position,[39] the Commission adopted frontiers between Czechoslovakia and Hungary that left to Czechoslovakia virtually all of the "grey zones" Seton-Watson had identified.

A similar outcome occurred in the Territorial Commission on Yugoslav and Romanian Affairs. Here the two British delegates, Crowe and Leeper, made no pretense of agreeing with the American position. Crowe stated the British point of view quite clearly when he suggested that when the commission was confronted with difficult frontier decisions in which it was impossible to do justice to both parties, "it was only natural to favor our ally Romania over our enemy Hungary."[40] Leeper exemplified this attitude when, in justifying the awarding of Hungarian territory near Szatmár Németi to Romania, he recognized the possible danger to Romania of incorporating a large Hungarian population, but insisted that considerations of economics and transportation "ought to prevail over this inconvenience."[41] Again, the decisions of the Commission resulted in almost all of Seton-Watson's "grey zones" being assigned to Romania and Yugoslavia.

The reports of the two territorial commissions were completed by early April and submitted separately to the Council of Foreign Ministers and Council of Four in May. The examination of these reports was rather perfunctory, and at no time were the cumulative effects of these decisions on Hungary directly addressed. Robert Lansing, the American Secretary of State, did express some concerns about the large number of Hungarians to be transferred to the new states, but his arguments were successfully met by Arthur Balfour, who pointed out that the trusted Eastern European experts of the four Great Powers had come to unanimous agreement on the justice of the proposed frontiers.[42]

So hasty was the approval of the Hungarian frontiers by the Council of Four that David Lloyd George would later claim that he could not recall having passed judgment on the territorial provisions of Trianon. Of course, the minds of Lloyd George and his colleagues were preoccupied with weightier matters at that time, including the most difficult task of fashioning an Allied policy toward the Soviet regime of Béla Kun, the establishment of which in late March had sent political tremors across Europe. Yet despite the furor caused by the appearance of a Communist government in East Central Europe, the Treaty of Trianon was not affected. The territorial provisions approved in May, 1919, were to appear virtually unchanged in the treaty signed and ratified in 1920.

Thus, the British Foreign Office in late spring of 1919 considered the task of drawing the new frontiers of Danubian Europe to be completed. The British Prime Minister, however, did not concur in this judgment. Quite early in the Paris deliberations Lloyd George had become uneasy about what he regarded as unduly severe peace terms that the Allies wished to inflict on Germany. In an important memorandum that he drew up at Fontainebleau on March 25, 1919, he argued that a harsh and humiliating peace would create serious instability in Central Europe and facilitate the spread of Bolshevism. To buttress his arguments, Lloyd George referred also to Hungary:

> What I have said about the Germans is equally true of the Magyars. There will never be peace in South Eastern Europe if every little state now coming into being is to have a large Magyar Irredenta within its borders. I would therefore take as a guiding principle of the peace that as far as is humanly possible the different races should be allocated to their motherlands, and that this human criterion should have precedence over considerations of strategy or economics or communications which can usually be adjusted by other means.[43]

It is difficult to determine what specifically sparked Lloyd George's interest in the Hungarian problem.[44] During the war he had paid little attention to Hungary,[45] and in the swirl of events in the post-war period many other critical issues were accorded a higher priority. Moreover, the "New Europe" group in the Foreign Office, perhaps sensing that the prime minister might not fully approve the policy they were pursuing in East Central Europe, tried to ensure that no reports on Hungarian conditions that might be misinterpreted would reach Lloyd George. Thus, when William Beveridge, the British member of an economic mission sent to Budapest early in 1919, returned with increased sympathy for Hungary and a proposal for establishment of political ties between Britain and Hungary and for positive help in reconstruction, Nicolson and his collegues tried to discredit him in Lloyd George's eyes.[46]

It is quite possible that Beveridge's proposals strengthened a growing suspicion in Lloyd George's mind that something was amiss in

Britain's policies in Danubian Europe. Though the "New Europe" group had erected a barrier that nearly eliminated communication between the Hungarian and British governments, one important appeal stating the Hungarian case did manage to reach the prime minister: a letter from Archduke Joseph of Hungary to his distant cousin, King George V.[47] Similar to numerous other messages that prominent Hungarians were trying to send to influential British intermediaries, Archduke Joseph's letter desperately implored Great Britain to give a hearing to Hungary and not just to the Successor States, the "ruthless conquerors who—naturally enough—have explained everything to the Entente from the point of view of their own interests." The archduke asked King George to raise his "mighty voice to demand that the invaders . . . shall be ordered to retire beyond the sacred frontiers of our land." The letter concluded with the suggestion of a political and economic alliance between Hungary and Great Britain, since "every serious minded man in this country today rests his every hope in Great Britain."

This letter, which evoked no interest when a copy reached the Foreign Office,[48] seems to have touched Lloyd George quite deeply. At a session of the Council of Four in Paris he described it as a "moving document,"[49] and from this point on Lloyd George began to emerge as a spokesman, albeit not an uncritical one, for the Hungarians at the peace conference. At a meeting of the Council of Ten on March 11, 1919, when reports of the tentative proposals of the territorial commissions may have reached the Allied leaders, Lloyd George thought it timely to re-emphasize a point that had been strongly stressed in the Foreign Office pre-conference memoranda. Great care should be taken, he asserted, "to show fairness to all parties. The new map of Europe must not be so drawn as to leave cause for disputation which would eventually drag Europe into a new war."[50] Later he was to urge that the Allies try to establish relations with the Hungarians, just as they had done with the Croats and Slovenes. "The Magyars have never been enemies of France or England," he asserted. They are a "proud people with a great military tradition," and should be treated on the same basis as their neighbors.[51]

The appearance of a Soviet Republic in Hungary in late March confirmed Lloyd George's suspicion that Bolshevism would thrive in political instability and national discontent. Béla Kun had succeeded, he believed, because his countrymen feared that "large numbers of Magyars are to be handed over to the control of others."[52] When in early summer Czechoslovakia and Romania, citing the Bolshevik menace in Hungary, began military advances further into Hungarian territory, Lloyd George defended the Hungarians and launched a tirade against the new states. The latter he called "little robber nations" who were out to steal more territory whenever they could.[53] Thus the Hungarians, even though under Communist leaders, were justified in driving "the invader out of what is acknowledged even by him to be Magyar territory."[54]

The most remarkable thing about Lloyd George's forceful intervention on the side of the Hungarians is that it provoked no change whatsoever in British policy in Danubian Europe. His warnings about the creation of large Hungarian irredentas and his similar utterances on the Supreme Council seemed to make no impression in the Foreign Office. Indeed, a historian can sift through the voluminous Foreign Office files of the period and never suspect that the prime minister did not approve of Britain's policies toward Hungary and her neighbors. The explanation of this apparent lack of coordination seems to lie in the uneasy, often strained relationship between Lloyd George and the Foreign Office. Distrusting professional dipomats, Lloyd George often preferred to deal personally with major foreign policy questions. At the same time, he was apparently reluctant to set policy guidelines to which the Foreign Office could refer.[55] Thus, as the peace conference opened, Harold Nicolson and his colleagues were surprised that no instructions about British peace aims and their implementation were received from the prime minister or the Cabinet. They thus assumed they were on their own.

In light of Lloyd George's tendencies in this regard, it appears that in the spring of 1919 he failed to make it clear to Balfour and others in the Foreign Office that he wanted peace terms toward Hungary to be mitigated. This negligence could perhaps be explained by the prime minister's preoccupation with a myriad of other crucial matters, including a successful effort to refashion the report of the Commission on Polish Affairs to make the Polish-German frontier line more palatable to the Germans. Whatever the reason, Nicolson and Leeper (apparently with Balfour's support) made no effort to modify the Treaty of Trianon to meet the objections of Lloyd George.

The territorial provisions of the treaty were thus unchanged when they were finally presented to the Hungarian delegation in January, 1920. By this time, however, the number of British officials who shared Lloyd George's concerns about the peace settlement with Hungary had greatly increased. The British were very well represented on the various Allied commissions sent to Hungary after the fall of Béla Kun in August, 1919. Admiral E. T. Troubridge was commander of the Allied flotilla on the Danube; Sir William Goode was Director of Relief Missions; and Sir George Clerk headed a special Allied political mission sent to facilitate the establishment of a stable government in Hungary. Each of these men became sympathetic to the Hungarians and drew similar conclusions about the situation in Danubian Europe: Hungary had been treated unfairly and her new neighbors, especially Romania, had acted in an uncivilized, despicable manner. In his final report to the Supreme Council, Clerk was sharp in his condemnation of the Successor States. Their "abuses and outrage" on Hungarian territory he characterized as an example of "a higher civilization hopelessly manhandled by those who are still learners in the art of Government."[56]

Similar sentiments were expressed by the first British diplomatic representative in Hungary after the war, Sir Thomas Hohler, in a dispatch sent to London on 1 February, 1920. Hohler directly raised the question of a revision of the territorial terms of the Trianon Treaty. Claiming that his conclusions were shared unanimously by the "various representatives of the Allied and Associated Powers" stationed in Hungary, he argued that the proposed peace terms appeared to be "faulty and incapable of standing the test of time." The treaty violated the principles of nationality and national self-determination, and as a consequence was "an immediate menace to the peace of Europe, and therefore to the interests of His Majesty's Government."[57]

When a flurry of pro-Hungarian activity developed in Parliament at about the same time,[58] the Foreign Office felt constrained to make some response in defense of the Treaty of Trianon. Arthur Balfour, now Lord President of the Council, officially responded to the questions raised in the House of Lords and Commons. His reply, succinctly stated, was that the critics of the Trianon Treaty were "wholly wrong" in their facts. The frontiers of Danubian Europe had been drawn by the finest experts available and were doubtless the best that could be found.[59]

The main burden of mounting the counterattack against the critics of the Trianon Treaty was placed on Allen Leeper, who remained steadfast in his commitment to the peace settlement he had done so much to shape. Leeper composed a memorandum that was intended to rebut specifically the points that Sir Thomas Hohler had made in his dispatch from Budapest.[60] In the memorandum, which was skillfully but also somewhat tendentiously written, Leeper suggested that the Territorial Commissions at Paris had drawn the new frontiers "mainly, if not entirely on ethnic considerations," and had even used Hungarian census figures as their bases. Violations of the strict ethnic line had been approved only when "absolutely demanded in order to make it possible for Czecho-Slovakia and Transilvania to live (not in comfort, but at all)."[61] In any case, Leeper concluded, what the Hungarian government was really after was reannexation of Slovakia and Transylvania and a restoration of the Kingdom of Hungary. This, of course, the Great Powers would not tolerate, for the new frontiers of Hungary had been approved unanimously by the Allied heads of state on the Supreme Council.

Characteristically, Leeper made no mention of the strong reservations that Lloyd George had expressed about the Treaty of Trianon. Perhaps he thought that the prime minister had lost interest in the matter, but such was not the case. The last opportunity for the Supreme Council to consider the treaty with Hungary came in late February and March of 1920, when the Council met in London to consider the response the Hungarians had made to the proposed treaty. The French representatives were of the firm opinion that territorial changes could not be made in the treaty at that late date, since such modifications would involve "endless difficulties" with Hungary's neighbors. But Lloyd George, with the support of Francesco Nitti, Italy's premier, insisted that the Council was bound to consider the Hungarian arguments "fairly and impartially," just as they had done in the case of the Versailles Treaty. Moreover, just as certain concessions had been made to Germany on the Polish frontiers, so, too, such concessions could not in fairness be excluded in the case of the treaty with Hungary.[62]

The most important session of the Supreme Council dealing with the Hungarian treaty occurred on 3 March. The Allied leaders had had time to marshall their evidence, and Lloyd George, who again received vigorous support from Nitti, dominated the discussion with an impassioned plea for a revision of the proposed territorial clauses. The ethnographic information on hand, he suggested, showed that a total of 2,750,000 Magyars were to be transferred to other countries.

Such a proposal would "not be easy to defend," and he urged that if, after additional study, some of the Hungarian claims were found to be justified, the appropriate concessions should be made, even if this upset Romania, Czechoslovakia, and Yugoslavia. Could there ever be peace in Central Europe, he asked, "if it were discovered afterwards that the claims of Hungary were sound, and that a whole community of Magyars had been handed over like cattle" to the Successor States? Referring specifically to Czechoslovakia, Lloyd George warned that with so many minorities that state "would (as it were) suffer from violent appendicitis, and sooner or later an operation would become necessary, under which Czechoslovakia might very well collapse."[63]

Despite objections from the French to Lloyd George's proposal, it was decided to submit the matter to the foreign ministers of the three Council members for a "fair and conscientious examination," with the understanding that territorial revisions not be excluded from consideration. When the Council reconvened on 8 March, however, it was clear that Lloyd George had finally abandoned what perhaps had been a chimerical struggle for change in the Trianon Treaty.[64] The British prime minister was not even present at the meeting, though he had attended a session of the Council earlier in the day. Instead, Britain was represented by Lord Curzon, who did not share Lloyd George's views on Hungary and the peace settlement in Danubian Europe. Armed with another comprehensive memorandum by Leeper,[65] Curzon now proposed that the treaty not be tampered with. As an apparent concession to Lloyd George, however, and as a reflection of the "general feeling that in certain areas of the frontier districts injustice might have been committed," Curzon suggested that if the boundary commissions in the course of their work on the spot were to discover that injustices had indeed been done, they could report their conclusions to the League of Nations. This compromise the French accepted with alacrity, for they correctly inferred that this process would result in only minor, if any, frontier modifications.[66]

What prompted Lloyd George to lose interest in this issue? There is no evidence to document his thinking, but it seems likely that strong opposition to his policy from the Foreign Office (in the form of Leeper's memorandum and perhaps Curzon's recommendation) convinced him that a further effort on his part would be fruitless.[67] Thus, he made no further comment on the issue, and the Treaty of Trianon was duly signed and ratified later in 1920.

In an analysis of Britain's role in the making of the Treaty of

Trianon, the words of an eminent Hungarian historian, Henrik Marczali, writing in 1919, are instructive: "From England we [the Hungarians] have always been able to count on platonic sympathy, but effective support only when it corresponded to her interests."[68] Even after a terrible war, there was, indeed, great sympathy for Hungary in British society, particularly among the aristocrats, financial experts, and professional diplomats in the field. Because these individuals believed that common sense and traditional standards of "fair play" were violated by the treaty with Hungary, their concern was often expressed in passionate terms. Nonetheless, this sympathy did remain platonic, for no action was taken on it by the British government, despite the promptings of David Lloyd George.

The reason for this, as has been seen, was that British national interests, as defined by those individuals in the Foreign Office who fashioned British policy in Danubian Europe, were regarded as best served by creating new national states that had to be given strategic and economic security, even if this meant the creation of large Hungarian irredentas. Clearly, however, the triumph of the ideas of the "New Europe" group was not a reflection of overwhelming support by British policymakers for such a policy. It was instead a byproduct of a relative lack of British interest in East Central Europe. When the critical issue arose of dispatching British military units to occupy Budapest, the War Cabinet was opposed, citing the higher priority to be given to other parts of the globe. When Lloyd George raised objections to the proposed treaty with Hungary, the Foreign Office simply ignored him, correctly assuming that the prime minister would be so occupied with other matters that his advocacy of Hungary would be abandoned.

In light of these observations, perhaps the most revealing contemporary comment was that of William Beveridge, who told Mihály Károlyi early in 1919 that "the Entente Governments had many more important things to worry about than the fate of ten million people in Hungary."[69] Indeed, the only people in Britain who had the time to concern themselves with the fate of Hungary were Allen Leeper and his colleagues, and the imprint of their Hungarophobia was to be found on the Treaty of Trianon.

Notes

1 Unsigned Foreign Office memo Dec. 13, 1918, *Public Record Office* (hereafter cited as *PRO*), Cab 29/2, no. 52.

2. *Documents on British Foreign Policy, 1919–1939,* first series, vol. 7, no. 46, edited by E. L. Woodward and Rohan Butler. (Cited hereafter as *DBFP.*)

3. On this see the perceptive essay of Victor S. Mamatey, "Legalizing the Collapse of Austria-Hungary at the Paris Peace Conference," *Austrian History Yearbook,* vol. 3, pt. 3 (1967), pp. 206–37.

4. V. H. Rothwell, *British War Aims and Peace Diplomacy, 1914–1918* (Oxford: Clarendon Press, 1971), pp. 76–77.

5. Harry Hanak, *Great Britain and Austria-Hungary during the First World War. A Study in the Formation of Public Opinion* (London: Oxford U.P., 1962), p. 2.

6. Kenneth J. Calder, *Britain and the Origin of the New Europe, 1914–1918* (Cambridge: Cambridge U.P., 1976), pp. 18–19.

7. Hanak, p. 22. One of Seton-Watson's most influential books was entitled, *Racial Problems in Hungary.*

8. Robert Seton-Watson et al., *The War and Democracy* (London: Macmillan, 1915), p. 274.

9. Wilfried Fest, *Peace or Partition. The Habsburg Monarchy and British Policy, 1914–1918* (New York: St. Martin's 1978), p. 16; and Arthur J. May, *The Passing of the Hapsburg Monarchy, 1914–1918,* 2 vols. (Philadelphia: University of Pennsylvania Press, 1966), vol. 1, p. 243.

10. Fest, p. 37.

11. Nicolson's minute of 25 April, 1915, PRO, F0371/2244/49484.

12. Nicolson's minute of 2 May, 1915, PRO, F0371/2244/53126. See also Nagy Zsuzsa, "Magyar határviták a békekonferencián 1919-ben" (Debate over Hungarian Frontiers at the Peace Conference of 1919), *Történelmi Szemle,* vol. 21, no. 3–4 (1978), pp. 442–43.

13. Foreign Office memo of Oct., 1916, PRO, Cab 29/1/5.

14. Rothwell, pp. 79–87.

15. Fest, p. 10.

16. Unsigned Foreign Office memo of 13 Dec., 1918, on "Europe," Committee of Imperial Defence, Peace Series, Cab 29/2, no. 52. In a similar vein another Foreign Office memo described Britain's overall goal as the attainment of "a just and permanent settlement based on the principles of nationality, self-determination, security, and free economic opportunity." Unsigned memo on "South-Eastern Europe and the Balkans," Cab 29/2, no. 66.

17. Lord Curzon's minute on PRO, F0371/3136/177223.

18. Fest, p. 247. An excellent analysis of the haphazard debate in the Foreign Office over future British policy in Danubian Europe is found in Marie-Luise Recker, *England und der Donauraum 1919–1929. Probleme einer europäischen Nachkriegsordnung* (Stuttgart: Ernst Klett, 1976), pp. 13–14, 35–36.

19. Cab 29/2, no. 66; Cab 29/2, no. 52.

20. Cab 29/2, no. 52.

21. Harold Nicolson, *Peacemaking 1919* (Boston: Grosset & Dunlap, 1965), p. 34.

22. Nicolson, p. 33.

23. Nicolson, p. 33.

24. Cab 29/2, no. 66. This attitude was reflected in the treatment of Czechoslovakia in the same memo. Since the Czechs "had been throughout the war our most devoted and most efficient Allies" in Eastern Europe and "have proved themselves a nation capable of carrying on an orderly government," we must provide "necessary conditions for organizing a national State of their own." Thus, no plebescites should be held, for "the Czechs might lose districts essential to their national existence."

25. "Hungary," Cab 29/2, no. 66. This memo is undated, but it seems to have been drafted in late November or early December, 1918.

26. Thinking along similar lines, Lewis Namier proposed the dispatch of a commission of experts to Danubian Europe "to supervise the movement of our minor Allies in the districts where zeal may obscure their judgement." Minute (Nov. 11, 1918), PRO, F0371/3134/188553.

27. The Grosse Schütt was an island formed by two channels of the Danube just east of Pozsony (Bratislava). Its population was overwhelmingly Magyar.

28. This map is found as MPI 397 in the PRO map room.

29. War Cabinet meeting (Nov. 22, 1918), CAB 23/8/506. See also Lajos Arday, "Angol-magyar viszony a polgári demokratikus forradalom idején az angol levéltári források tükrében (1918 oktober- 1919 marcius) (English-Hungarian Relations in the Time of the Bourgeois Democratic Revolution as Reflected in English Archival Sources), *Történelmi Szemle*, no. 2-3 (1975), pp. 246-47.

30. For this see the valuable study of Peter Pastor, *Hungary between Wilson and Lenin: The Hungarian Revolution of 1918-1919 and the Big Three* (Boulder: East European Quarterly, 1976), pp. 88-89, 148.

31. D.[agmar] Perman, *The Shaping of the Czechoslovak State: Diplomatic History of the Boundaries of Czechoslovakia, 1914-1920* (Leiden: E. J. Brill, 1962), p. 70.

32. Arday, pp. 249-54.

33. A characteristic statement was that of Sir Eyre Crowe in February, 1919: "We should have no truck with the Hungarians. Count Károlyi has, as it is, no reputation to lose." PRO, F0608/12/2969.

34. Namier did concede, however, that it would be useful to warn the Successor States "that forcible seizure dos not establish a valid title, and that all these territorial questions will be considered at the Peace Congress." Namier's minute (Nov. 11, 1918), PRO, F0371/3134/188553.

35. Nicolson, pp. 106-07. See also PRO, F0608/5/1645.

36. For the American map, see Francis Deák, *Hungary at the Paris Peace Conference. The Diplomatic History of the Treaty of Trianon* (New

York: Columbia U.P., 1942), appendix, map 2. The final Foreign Office memo stating the British position on territorial matters was drawn up by Crowe, Nicolson, and Leeper on February 8. It was substantially similar to Seton-Watson's map, and specifically called for assignment of the Grosse Schütt to Hungary. PRO, F0608/5/1645.

37. Piotr S. Wandycz, *France and her Eastern Allies, 1919-1926* (Minneapolis: University of Minnesota Press, 1962), p. 54; Perman, pp. 94-96.

38. Cook argued that the Grosse Schütt in Hungarian hands would be a "strategic menace" to Czechoslovakia. Minutes of the Commission on Czechoslovak Affairs (in French), PRO, F0374/6, p. 6. See also Charles Seymour, "Czechoslovak Frontiers," *Yale Review*, vol. 28 (1938-39), p. 277.

39. Nicolson apparently professed concern privately about the assignment of too many Magyars and Germans to the new Czechoslovak state (Nicolson, p. 279), but the minutes of the Commission on Czechoslovak Affairs reveal that he did not take a stand before the Commission.

40. Meeting (Feb. 13, 1919), Commision on Romanian and Yugoslav Affairs (in French), PRO, F0374/9.

41. *Ibid.*

42. Deák, pp. 67-71.

43. The Fontainebleau memorandum is found in Martin Gilbert, *The Roots of Appeasement* (New York: New American Libary, 1966), appendix 1, p. 190.

44. In the Lloyd George papers (House of Lords Archives, London) there is no pertinent evidence on his attitude and policy toward Hungary in this period.

45. Before 1918 Lloyd George had only a hazy conception of the geography of Eastern Europe, and in fact could not identify the Slovaks or Ruthenians. Calder, p. 101.

46. Nicolson's diary entry for 16 January: "He [William Beveridge] is very pro-Magyar and ignorant of actualities, which is a pity as he is going to see Lloyd George." Nicolson, p. 240. See also Pastor, pp. 98-100.

47. The letter, dated 21 December, 1918, was transmitted by the War Office to the king, who sent a copy to Lloyd George. PRO, F0371/3514/36995.

48. It was filed away without the usual minutes that items of importance attracted.

49. Paul Mantoux, *Paris Peace Conference, 1919. Proceedings of the Council of Four (March 24–April 18)* (Geneva: Librairie Droz, 1964), p. 72.

50. United States Department of State, *Papers Relating to the Foreign Relations of the United States. The Paris Peace Conference, 1919*, 13 vols. (Washington, D.C.: U.S. Government Printing Office, 1942-47), vol. 4, p. 317. (Cited hereafter as *PPC*).

51. Mantoux, p. 55. Also Paul Mantoux, *Les délibérations du Conseil des Quatre, 24 mars–28 juin 1919*, 2 vols. (Paris: Editions du Centre National de

la Recherche Scientifique, 1955), vol. 2, p. 351.

52. Gilbert, p. 192.

54. Memo of Lloyd George to Balfour (July 13, 1919), PRO, Cab 21/150.

55. Gordon A. Craig, "The British Foreign Office from Grey to Austen Chamberlain," in *The Diplomats, 1919–1939,* 2 vols. (Princeton: Princeton U.P., 1953), vol. 1, pp. 25–32; and Kenneth O. Morgan, *Consensus and Unity. The Lloyd George Coalition Government, 1918–1922* (Oxford: Clarendon Press, 1979), p. 112.

56. Clerk's report to Supreme Council, 29 Nov., 1919, *DBFP,* first series, vol. 2, no. 33, appendix A.

57. *DBFP,* first series, vol. 13, no. 78, pp. 106–09.

58. Among the members of parliament who called for a tempering of the terms of the treaty with Hungary and excoriated the Successor States were Lord Bryce, Lord Newton, Sir Samuel Hoare, and Lord Montagu. For details of the debates, see Deák, pp. 242–45. In a minute (March 7), William Tyrrell remarked on the "complete ignorance of Hungarian history and policy" of people like Lord Newton, which made them "easy dupes" of the "Hungarian gospel according to Magyar magnates." PRO, F0371/3519/180251.

59. Deák, p. 243.

60. Leeper's minute (Feb. 11), 1920, PRO, F0371/3518/176995. A summary is given in *DBFP,* first series, vol. 12, p. 108, fn. 5.

61. Leeper proceeded to make a thorough survey of the specific territorial problems encountered in drawing Hungary's borders, though for some reason he failed to mention the most controversial issue, the Grosse Schütt.

62. *DBFP,* first series, vol. 7, no. 25.

63. *DBFP,* first series, vol. 7, no. 46.

64. Minutes of this meeting are in *DBFP,* first series, vol. 7, no. 54.

65. *DBFP,* first series, vol. 7, pp. 440–44. Leeper's arguments here paralleled those in his earlier memo, and his strong recommendation was that none of the Hungarian requests for territorial concessions be granted.

66. This is the origin of the so-called "covering letter" of the Treaty of Trianon, which became known later as the "Millerand letter," though it is now clear that the impetus came from Lord Curzon.

67. In his memoirs Lloyd George passes quickly over this episode, suggesting only that the Hungarians might have been more persuasive if they had focused on "specific instances of injustice." David Lloyd George, *The Truth about the Peace Treaties,* 2 vols. (London: Victor Gollanz Ltd., 1938), vol. 2, p. 970.

68. Henrik Marczali, "Az angol-magyar érdekközösségről a múltban" (The English-Hungarian Community of Interest in the Past), *Századok,* vol. 53, no. 3–10 (1919), p. 123.

69. Lord Beveridge, *Power and Influence* (New York: Beechhurst Press, 1955), p. 156.

Mária Ormos

The Hungarian Soviet Republic
and Intervention by the Entente

In this paper I would like to shed light on the question of the intervention against the Hungarian Soviet Republic as it appeared to the French government and the French General Staff and reflected in their own records.[1]

Until now assumptions regarding French politics were usually based on the actual events, on the debates at the Peace Conference, or on records in the archives of other countries. Of course, these sources reflect the reality of the situation, but do so with certain adjustments, not to say distortions. The materials in the French archives now make it possible to see certain aspects of the intervention in a new light. This applies particularly to the French plans themselves, and to the motives underlying the changes in these plans. Since I intend to deal with these changes, certain introductory remarks seem to be in order.

A perennial problem in historiography has been the question of alternatives, the "What would have happened if?" syndrome. How to deal with those political or military plans which were never fully carried out and which, with the benefit of hindsight, now appear to have been unrealizable, exaggerated, irrational? And how to deal with contingencies which did not arise under the circumstances but are simply reconstructions after the fact, on the basis of rationalizations which for some reason or other could not have occurred to the participants at the time. . . . In fact, these did not even constitute true alternatives. Hence, perhaps a word of explanation is in order: Why should we bother with, or give significance to, plans which either were never carried out, or which were realized only in a modified form? I believe it is necessary to draw a sharp distinction between the two kinds of alternatives, the actual contingency plan, and the one based on ulterior construction. A plan that has been formulated is a real alternative; an elaborated military or political project becomes a conditioning factor even if it is modified, even if it proves mistaken and is discarded. The elaboration of the plan and its adoption exclude other plans, exclude alternative courses of action, hence influences the situation fundamentally.

Such was the entire plan of intervention designed by the French General Staff and the French government, including intervention plans against the Soviet Union. This plan was never carried out in its entirety, while those aspects of the plan which applied to Hungary were carried out only after considerable modification. Nevertheless, it undeniably affected the climate in Europe, including Central Europe, in a powerful and lasting way.

One aspect of the project of intervention revealed by the French records was its constant dichotomy, as opposed to what was formerly perceived as an undulating line, a sinusoid. More specifically, the constant of economic coercion was accompanied first by military force, then by political promises, then by waiting, then again by military compulsion, and finally by political manipulation. The French documents indicate, however, that the French government and General Staff never abandoned either the military or the political options as parallel expedients. Military intervention and political negotiations do not figure as alternatives in these plans, but were present together all along, and the occasional changes were merely on the surface, in appearance.

The first French project which dealt with the Hungarian Soviet Republic, in addition to the Soviet Russia issue, was dated March 24, 1919. It focused on the danger presented by the spread of Russian Bolshevism and the complementary Hungarian one, including the threat to Poland and Romania. The General Staff noted that the means of compulsion applied or contemplated had not proven effective with regard to Hungary, and came to the conclusion that military force should be considered. It proposed three anti-Bolshevik fronts; one of these was already in existence in southern Russia, centered around Odessa, the second was to be set up with Romanian assistance along the Dniester, starting in Bessarabia, and the third would come into being on Hungarian territory. For the execution of a march on Budapest the project counted on three Serbian infantry and one cavalry divisions, four Romanian infantry divisions, as well as the two French divisions and cavalry brigade stationed in the Balkans.[2]

The project presumed a considerable multiplication of the forces actually available. It was based, first, on the assumption that the bridgehead at Odessa could be maintained until fresh and more significant forces could be dispatched; and this implied, in turn, nothing less than the guaranteed resupply by sea of the units encircled by the Bolsheviks there. A second precondition would have been a fully equipped Romanian army which was then only in the process of formation. Yet another assumption was the consent of the Yugoslav government to significant participation in the intervention against Hungary. This last condition appeared important to the French General Staff as it did not see its way clear to including the Czech army, in its present state, in its calculations; in addition to its lack of training and equipment, there was the problem of the leadership of the Czech army—an issue, however, which the plan did not discuss.

The French project of March 24 was defeated at the meeting of the Supreme Council of the Peace Conference the following day; or, to be more exact, the plan was altered. The Council created the basis for the organization of two fronts rather than three. Indeed, it decided on the evacuation of the bridgehead at Odessa. While the Council made no mention of the other two fronts, the one along the Dniester and the one in Hungary, it did provide for their establishment. It accomplished this by rerouting the important British convoy reserved for General Denikin, which included materials and clothing for 100,000 soldiers, to the Romanian port. It thus created the basis for the active participation of the Romanian army at the Dniester and on Hungarian territory. This decision was probably a matter of priorities, and the Supreme Council opted to bolster the Romanian interests because they seemed more urgent. (I should add, parenthetically, that it soon became evident that this choice was not final, for the British had the capacity to arm the counter-revolutionary forces in Hungary as well. The objective of the maneuver, therefore, was rather to justify the withdrawal of the Entente troops, as well as to cut down on the enormous expense which the supply of Odessa would have warranted.)

Because of the weight given to Romanian interests, this choice implied that the main concern of the Entente forces was Hungary. A simple fact may explain this concern; while the Romanian government was "satisfied" with defending the boundary of Bessarabia against Soviet-Russian forces, its ambitions were to acquire further territories at the expense of Hungary. To be more exact, Romania meant to secure the boundary line it was promised under the secret Bucharest Treaty of 1916: this line led from near Vásárosnamény south of the Tisza River, passed five kilometers east of Debrecen, and reached the confluence of the Tisza and Maros Rivers once again near Szeged. The French General Staff harbored no doubts about the operation: it could always count on Romanian participation in this area, whereas Romanian participation in the anti-Soviet action could not be taken for granted.

On March 27 Marshall Foch, before ordering the execution of the resolution of March 25 taken by the Supreme Council, again tried to convince the Supreme Council to grant an increase of the forces available for intervention, and to obtain in some manner the material contributions of the United States. The attempt of March 27, however, failed completely. Another difficulty had to arise before Clemenceau would order, on March 29, the complete evacuation of the Odessa zone.

The negotiations conducted by Franchet d'Esperey about the forces available for intervention ran into difficulties in Belgrade. Although the Yugoslav government gave no definite reply, its extreme reluctance to participate in the intervention was obvious enough. Prince Regent Alexander let it be known that since the Great Powers had not authorized the conversion of the Serbian army into a Yugoslav army, that is, it did not authorize an increase in its effectives through the addition of military units conscripted in the newly acquired territories of Croatia, Slovenia, and elsewhere, he was "unfortunately" not in a position to order intervention against Hungarian Bolshevism at the moment.

The French had to reckon with these factors—i.e., with the impossibility of securing American financial aid and the refusal of the Yugoslavs—as early as March 29, when the Supreme Council undertook to discuss Béla Kun's offer to take up negotiations. A closer look at the situation revealed that the Romanian army would have to bear the main burden of the attack along both fronts, an undertaking which, in the opinion of the French General Staff, would have exceeded its capacities. Clemenceau based his next moves on this opinion. On the one hand, after four days of delays and hesitation, he ordered the evacuation of the Odessa zone; but, rather than recall the troops, he redirected them towards the Dniester.[4] Thus he decided that France would take part in the defense of Romania's eastern frontier while facilitating the movements of the Romanian army in the West. At the same time, he gave up the Odessa front once and for all. On the other hand, at the Conference table Clemenceau agreed to the Budapest mission of General Smuts; he did not hesitate in reaching that decision, since in any case the conditions necessary for a military intervention had not materialized for the time being because of the reluctance of the Yugoslavs.

Thus political manipulation rather than military offensive became the order of the day. But while Clemenceau temporarily barred an offensive in accordance with the spirit of the decision at the Conference, at the same time he instructed Francet d'Esperey to proceed with the negotiations for the organization of the attack. While Smuts was negotiating in Budapest, Franchet d'Esperey was trying to convince the Yugoslav officials in Belgrade of the absolute necessity of Serbian participation. But since this attempt did not work out, the plan for an open, concentric military action under French command had to be dropped for the time being.

This was when the first significant modification of the French plan took place. It was not a matter of political moves replacing military ones outright; rather, instead of a concentric attack, the modified plan contemplated a limited offensive utilizing the forces of the Romanian army.

I wish to emphasize once more that one of the conditions for such an attack was the transfer of forces from Odessa to the Dniester, initiated shortly thereafter, on April 6. The modification in the French plan was revealed, for the first time, in a telegram from Clemenceau to the commander-in-chief in the Balkans, dated April 14. In this telegram, Clemenceau, who was both Prime-Minister and Minister of War, reacted to a worried report sent by Franchet d'Esperey regarding the contemplated Romanian offensive. The latter had requested Paris to dissuade the Romanian Chief of the General Staff from taking the offensive as it might have disastrous consequences. For the benefit of the general, the Prime Minister summarized the French views in the following terms: "First: If the Hungarians attack the Romanians, the latter are fully justified in retaliating. Second: Since the decision taken by the Peace Conference of February 26 was

not further modified, the Romanians have likewise the right to occupy the area allocated to them, up to the eastern border of the
neutral zone."[5] As we know, the eastern border of the neutral zone
corresponded essentially with what was to become the national
boundary line.

Such was the theoretical framework within which the Romanians
launched their offensive on the night of April 15–16. Clemenceau's
stand was easy enough to defend at the Conference table since it
derived from decisions the Conference itself had reached earlier. But
the Romanians reached the line of demarcation they could legally
claim already by April 25, and then a new justification had to be
found. The Romanian General Coanda, who represented his government in Paris on a number of issues, called on General Alby, the
French Chief of the General Staff, on April 26. He informed Alby
that the Romanian General Staff had decided to cross the demarcation line designated in the Vix memorandum. The Romanian forces
intended to advance as far as the Tisza River, and were ready to
build bridgeheads on the right bank of the river as well. The French
Chief of the General Staff relayed this information without any comment to the pertinent section chief of the Ministry of Foreign Affairs.
In other words, the French General Staff acquiesced in the plan.[6]

This definite and explicit change in view was occasioned by the
Romanian military success. On the day the Romanian army reached
the Tisza, the French General Staff put its views on paper. The gist of
the newly elaborated plan was: "The Romanian advance, brilliantly
executed, without intervention on the part of French forces concentrated in the Szeged area (two infantry divisions and a cavalry
brigade), entitle us to believe that there will be no need to resort to
these forces even if it does become necessary to compel Hungary to
carry out the peace decisions by military force. The concentric action
of the powers directly interested (Romania, Czechoslovakia, and
Serbia), will be amply sufficient for the purpose."[7]

According to the new French military plan, the French forces at
Szeged could be pulled out and transferred to Bulgaria. By so doing,
argued the General Staff, France could exert pressure on Bulgaria to
sign the peace treaty and, at the same time, relieve the Romanian
army of another burden by pinning down the Bulgarian forces.

The execution of this plan, however, became highly problematic as
a consequence of the formation of the Soviet front at the end of April
and the beginning of May. The Soviet Russian government sent an

ultimatum to Romania and gathered significant forces along the Dniester. Under the circumstances, Paris did not venture to give its blessing to the most recent Romanian request, namely that the Romanian army be authorized to continue its advance and march into Budapest. On the contrary: the French authorities insisted that the army be halted along the Tisza and that part of it be transferred to Bessarabia. Even the Romanian Chief of the General Staff felt the situation was serious enough to warrant rescinding the May 4 resolution of the Romanian cabinet regarding the action against Budapest. General Prešan emphasized that Romania did not have territorial claims against Hungary beyond the Tisza, hence the military effort was unwarranted; moreover, the army would not find a better line of defense than the Tisza, hence the action would entail certain military risks as well, while the situation along the Dniester was deteriorating. On May 5 the Romanian government resolved to stabilize the front along the Tisza in Hungary, and to retrieve three divisions for transfer to the Dniester.[8]

This transfer gave rise to bitter reproaches on the part of the Czechoslovakian government. The temporary stabilization of the Romanian front made it possible for the Hungarian Red Army to concentrate its efforts on one front in Slovakia and to attain significant successes against the Czechoslovak forces. As mentioned, as a result of these successes the president of the Conference, Clemenceau, personally decided in favor of a political solution, and he himself persuaded the Supreme Council to endorse his message to Béla Kun. Thus, it was a military dead end that led to this message, but at the moment it was sent the French Prime Minister attributed no greater importance to it than would have been warranted by a well-chosen excuse or alibi; for it was expected that Budapest would reject the proposal.

Such an interpretation is justified by the text of the message itself, which demanded Hungarian withdrawal but gave not even a hint as to how far the Hungarian troops were expected to retreat. It is also made obvious by other measures Clemenceau adopted on the same day. While he persuaded the Supreme Council to endorse the so-called Clemenceau letter, he sent the Hungarian-Romanian file to General Belin and instructed him to work out plans for military measures in case the Hungarians rejected the letter as expected. Belin did not require much time to carry out the instructions. The General Staff was practically ready with the plan, and was able to relay

Clemenceau's instructions to Franchet d'Esperey that very day. The essence of the plan was to concentrate the Romanian forces in the northern sector in order to relieve the Czechoslovak forces and, once this was accomplished, to advance towards Budapest. In the meantime the Serbian units would have to advance directly towards Budapest, while the two French divisions would operate between the two armies and ensure coordination.

The function of the message of June 8 as an alibi is confirmed, moreover, by the exchange of telegrams between the French Ambassador in Prague and the Ministry of Foreign Affairs. Clément-Simon reminded the Ministry that it should require the Hungarians to withdraw to a specific line; Pichon replied that the ambassador should make inquiries regarding the French plans from General Pellé, stationed in Prague.[9] In plain words, this meant that a line of demarcation no longer had any relevance, since the whole country would be occupied. Furthermore, the above interpretation of French intentions is confirmed by the fact that after almost two weeks spent on preparations for the intervention, the excuse considered necessary for the launching of the action did not materialize: the Hungarian government decided to comply with the French demand, and the Conference immediately began the search for a new excuse.

It became clear at this time, as the Hungarian troops were evacuating Slovakia, that Clemenceau, unlike the Parisian representative of the British government, and unlike the British and French military strategists, ceased to insist on military intervention against Hungary. As of July there no longer was a strict parallel between the French military and political plans. While the General Staff did not discard the military plan, its practical value and significance diminished because of Clemenceau's attitude. To find the motive behind the change in the attitude of the French Prime Minister, we must look for the factors revealed by the French documents.

Clemenceau's disillusioned remarks at the Conference in the second half of July cannot be attributed to a single factor. First of all, he was prompted by the circumstance that while France was advocating a policy of intervention, her allies, although constantly harping on intervention, were unwilling to share the military and financial burdens, or even the responsibility for the act. Clemenceau was also swayed by the failures for which the French military and political leadership were ultimately responsible. He was influenced by the fact that he did not have useful, adequate, sufficient military power at his disposal. Moreover, he was reluctant to assume the responsibility for the ill-fated policy of intervention in face of French public opinion, emanating primarily from the left.

In addition to these factors, which are discussed by other historians in far greater detail than my thumbnail sketch can hope to do, there was yet another factor which played a role in Clemenceau's stance, one we had little knowledge of until now. This factor was the French appraisal of the attitudes of the small countries adjacent to Hungary. We have mentioned that the French views changed, in the course of April, expecting the neighboring small states to overthrow the Hungarian regime and make Hungary bow to the resolutions of the Peace Conference even without French contributions.

During the subsequent months, however, it became clear that these countries were far from being completely prepared to achieve these ends and, what's more, they expected a reward for their anti-Bolshevik intervention. As regards the former, the problem was still mainly Yugoslavia. The French exerted themselves considerably to interest Yugoslavia, but the Yugoslav government did not budge from its neutral position. The Entente powers finally recognized the existence of Yugoslavia at the insistence of the French, and tried to whet the appetite of the Yugoslav government with promises of greater or lesser territorial change. None of these efforts, however, was crowned with success. Belgrade never promised the French General Staff to furnish the troops it expected. We need not discuss the reasons for the Yugoslav attitude here.

The prospect of Czechoslovakian participation and the substitution of the Serbian force with a Czech force remained problematic for the French General Staff. This alternative was raised by Franchet d'Esperey as early as the end of March and the beginning of April, whereas General Pellé was constantly urging Paris to give its consent to a Czechoslovak operation that would take place simultaneously with the Romanian operation, but there is no trace of French authorization to that effect in this period.

On the contrary; during the month of April Clemenceau reiterated several times that neither the southern, i.e., the French, nor the northern front should move. The March 20 resolution of the Czechoslovak government, taken before the proclamation of the Hungarian Soviet Republic, to extend its line of occupation, had to be suspended; and because of the veto from Paris, the Czech government hesitated to initiate military action until April 26. The time for the final decision and for the launching of an attack came on April 27 when, because of the Romanian offensive, the Czechoslovak government felt its own interests jeopardized in Ruthenia and certain other areas.

To be sure, in the days immediately preceding, Pellé kept insisting that Paris finally hand down a verdict, but I have found no trace of any such decision in writing. It is possible that the Czechoslovak government did receive some kind of encouragement, but the French authorities did not wish to assume responsibility for this military operation.

Thus military inadequacy remained an obstacle to intervention. There remained yet another obstacle which, in fact, became increasingly decisive, namely the territorial claims of the neighboring states vis-à-vis Hungary; more exactly, those claims which exceeded French expectations regarding the peace terms as well as the frontiers designated at the Conference.

During the period of the Hungarian Soviet Republic the French government did take the initiative to rectify the demarcation line in one area, the southern frontier of Hungary, and part of its proposals were actually adopted. Two factors were involved: one of the reasons for the initiative must have been that the most important role in the intervention—as attested by several French documents—was assigned to the Serbian army. The other was a technical circumstance: namely, that along this front line, because of the confusion of the Austrian and Italian intrigues, no final decision had been reached as yet, while the pertinent territorial committees did sanction the new Hungarian frontiers in the north and in the east even before the proclamation of the Soviet Republic. There is no evidence that any of the Entente powers, including the French government, subsequently intended to change these lines at the expense of Hungary. Both the so-called Territorial Committee and the Supreme Council stuck to their decision regarding these frontiers during the Council's regime.

Neither the Czechoslovak nor the Romanian government was satisfied with these decisions. In fact, it would be more accurate to say that they were intensely dissatisfied. Czechoslovakia launched an active propaganda campaign against the plan at the beginning of March. Its method at this time was to raise a lot of dust about a supposed Hungarian-Austrian-German conspiracy which the three republican governments were to organize with the dismemberment of Czechoslovakia in mind. Since the Conference gave no credence to the Czechoslovak accusations, the Prague government began to claim rectification of the borders for economic and even military reasons, and reached a decision regarding military action to that effect on March 20. Beneš succeeded in obtaining the assent of Marshal Foch for the operation, but after the proclamation of the Soviet Republic, this proposal was voted down by the Czechoslovak committee at the Conference on March 24. This was done at the suggestion of Paul Cambon, the French chairman of that committee.[10] Later on, the Czechoslovak government restricted its participation in the intervention on the grounds that it would occupy only those areas to which it lay claim, regardless of the nature of the Hungarian regime. President of the Republic Masarýk and some members of his cabinet explained on several occasions that Czechoslovakia's internal difficulties prevented it from marching into the Hungarian capital or from participating in the overthrow of the regime. On the other hand, it was quite willing to occupy Miskolc, Sátoraljaújhely, the coal basin at Salgotarján, the foothills of Tokaj, as well as the entire left bank of the Danube down to the level of Vác, in addition to Ruthenia. All this convinced the French government, as the French ambassador in Prague was wont to remark, that the "imperialism" of the Czechs knew no bounds, yet they were not prepared to make sacrifices for the sake of invention, even if their claims were to be satisfied.

It was even more obvious that the measures undertaken by the Romanian government were based on the already mentioned boundary line decided by the secret treaty of 1916. The decisions of the pertinent Romanian authorities, military as well as civilian, made this clear.

Because of the victories of the Hungarian Red Army, and for the sake of the stabilization of the Czechoslovak situation, the decision of the Conference to inform the Czech and the Romanian governments about the irrevocability of the already approved boundaries assumes its full significance. This took place in Paris on June 11. Following this, and particularly in July, the French organization of intervention encountered serious obstacles. When the British Foreign Secretary Arthur Balfour was urging intervention, Clemenceau mentioned several times, among his counterarguments, that the small states involved were demanding compensation. The problem was so obvious that even the French General Staff made allowances for it. It pointed out that should the time for a concentric attack against Hungary finally come, it will become necessary to clarify the French conditions, considering that the interested parties have come up with excessive demands for compensation.[11] If we might conclude from such a formulation of the problem that the General Staff was inclined to give in to these "excessive demands," the French documents and the minutes of the meetings of the Council tend to indicate that Clemenceau was not inclined to undertake the satisfaction of new claims beyond those the Conference had already granted.

Hungarian historiography has often and emphatically pointed out the gap between the measures undertaken at the Paris Peace Conference and the principles it represented and advocated, particularly in the application of the national ethnic principle. Let us add the following: in the name of another proclaimed principle, that of anti-Bolshevism and the defense of democracy, small-state nationalist imperialism forced the Conference to depart in even greater measure from the ethnic principle. Considering that, all in all their claims were substantial, it behooves us to point out that, in spite of its determination to defeat Hungarian Bolshevism, the Conference did not satisfy these claims. While the Republic of Councils elicited this determination by its very existence, it played on the other hand the role of a stabilizing force thanks to its successful military ventures.

As far as Clémenceau's attitude in the matter is concerned, we must not interpret it as mercy towards the Hungarian regime. The French Prime Minister was guided by entirely different considerations. In truth, he had confidence that the relations of power in central Europe would sooner or later, in one way or another, grind the Republic of Councils to bits, and from this he derived the conclusion that there was no need to commit the French government, and especially no need to let himself be blackmailed by his own minor allies. He felt the Republic of Councils was near its demise, for the economic conditions surrounding it would not let it survive long. He also hoped that either the Hungarian or the Romanian government would lose its patience, that the momentary cease-fire would be replaced by renewed hostilities in which the Hungarian side, presumably, would fall as victim. If this be the case then, once again, the issue would be resolved without the French having to intervene. Finally, when news was received concerning the negotiations between Vilmos Böhm and the leaders of the British and Italian missions in Vienna, Clemenceau could also expect that the leaders of the Republic of Councils would, without further ado, draw the logical conclusion regarding the hopelessness of their predicament, and would simply depart from the scene for some kind of coalition government.

Thus, the French Prime Minister adopted a wait-and-see attitude, and expressed at the same time certain basic principles of the French government. One of these was the preservation of the Conference and of the integrity of the decisions taken by the great powers vis-à-vis the small allies. (Indeed, it would be difficult to understand Clemenceau's politics unless we considered France as a great power, a power that would not allow its decisions to become the subject of open bargaining between France and the "states with particularist demands.") Another and equally important principle concerned the reorganization of Central Europe along French lines; this required that some kind of harmony prevail in this area in spite of the transitory antagonisms and troubles aroused by the Hungarian proletarian state.

All things considered, while Paris retained all the means for action against Hungary in its hands to the very end, its plans alternated as the situation warranted. The plan for military intervention, overt and concentric with French participation, or covert and without the French, or even disjointed in appearance; furthermore, the economic blockade and twisting the arms of the Hungarian regime, or the excuses for further steps or delays—all these contemplated measures had two inseparable objectives: the overthrow of the Communist regime and the acceptance of the decisions and conditions of the Peace Conference by all parties concerned. The Entente achieved both these objectives.

The peace delegation finally sent by the Horthy regime did not succeed in obtaining better conditions along the two most debated boundary lines, the northern and the eastern. Nor did the conditions become worse than those which the Conference had elaborated during the Károlyi regime, and which it maintained during the Republic of Councils, thanks in part to the efforts of the latter.

Notes

1. The limits of this article do not allow for the usual scholarly apparatus. As a matter of general information I would add that this summary is based on historical studies and documentary publications, as well as on materials

found in the following French archives: *Archives diplomatiques: Paix 1914-1920; Conférence de la Paix* (mostly the minutes of the Czechoslovakian and Yugoslav-Romanian committees); *Europe Z., Autriche, Hongrie, Roumanie, Tchécoslovaquie, Yougoslavie 1918-1919; Armée de Terre, service historique; Conseil Supérieur de Guerre; Ministère de la Guerre; l'Etat-Major; Armée Française d'Orient; Armée du Danube.*

    2. "Note sur la situation en Orient," March 24, 1919, *Service historique,* 4, n. 53, doss. 1.

    3. Concerning the Yugoslav stance: *Archives diplomatiques, Europe Z, Y,* vol. 45, 40–41, note for March 29, 1919; 10–11, 12–13 and 14, telegrams from Fontenay dated March 29 to April 1, 1919.

    4. Clemenceau, March 29, 1919, *Service historique,* 4 n. 53, doss. 1.

    5. Franchet d'Esperey, April 12, 1919 and 86, Clemenceau, April 14, 1919, *Archives diplomatiques, Europe Z, R,* vol. 47, 83–84.

    6. *Ibid.,* 95. Notes concerning the report of General Alby, dated April 26, 1919.

    7. "Etude sur la situation militaire en Hongrie et en Bulgarie et sur l'emploi des Forces Françaises d'Orient," April 30, 1919, *Service historique,* S.N. 53, doss. 1.

    8. Graziani, May 3, 5, and 6, 1919, *ibid.,* 5, n 202 Roumanie; memorandum of the Rumanian government, May 5, 1919, *Archives diplomatiques, R,* vol. 47, 102–104; 122–124, military attaché Pétain, May 5, 1919.

    9. *Service historique,* 4, n 51, doss. 1. Clemenceau to Belin, June 7, 1919; Clemenceau to Franchet d'Esperey; *Archives diplomatiques, Europe Z., T.,* vol. 44, 62–63, Clemenceau to General Pellé, June 7, 1919; Clement-Simon, June 8, 1919, 70–71; June 9, Pichon to Clément-Simon, June 8, 1919, 70–71; June 9, Pichon to Clément-Simon, 72.

    10. Memorandum of the Czechoslovak committee, session of March 24, 1919, *Archives diplomatiques, Conférence de la Paix.*

    11. "Note sur le conflit entre Tchéco-Slovaquie et Hongrie" summary from the second half of June, *Service historique,* 6, n 75.

Magda Ádám

France and Hungary at the Beginning of the 1920's

The present study discusses the Franco-Hungarian rapprochement. Its aim is to trace the turnabout that occurred in France's Danubian policy, examine its background and aims, and introduce the Franco-Hungarian negotiations, or rather, agreement. The essay attempts to map those European and local forces that separately and together opposed the French endeavors and that were ultimately victorious.[1]

There were many precipitants of the turnabout that occurred in French Danubian policy. At all events those political changes that followed the January 1920 French presidential elections played a significant role in it. Deshanel and Millerand replaced Poincaré and Clemenceau. The new president and prime minister, but mainly the permanent secretary for foreign affairs, Paléologue, began seriously to consider a plan whereby they would create on the territory of the Monarchy a trustworthy, economically unified Danubian power under French influence, which might be a prop for both its German and its Russian policy. That is to say, they felt that this power might thwart Germany's eastward expansion, and at the same time counterbalance the so-called Bolshevik danger coming from the east. Their goal, therefore—as we shall see—remained unchanged: their predecessors—Poincaré and Clemenceau—had also struggled to achieve the same end, first with weapons and then through diplomacy; in taking military steps, as well as in imposing the peace terms, they kept this goal uppermost in their minds. The change manifested itself in the means through which the goal was implemented, for it should be noted that from the outset serious conflicts arose in French political circles concerning the "hows" of the process. Here—just as in international life in general—two tendencies contended with each other. One faction wanted to achieve its goal by imposing severe peace terms, by weakening the enemy to the greatest extent possible, and by strengthening their eastern allies. The devotees of the other tendency—the so-called reconciliationists—regarded as insufficient a security policy resting on the victorious successor states and limited only to that. They did not regard an economically and politically dismembered, "Balkanized" Eastern Europe as a suitable counter-weight to the German and so-called Russian danger. The new leaders at the Quai d'Orsay wanted to unify the small successor states—regardless of whether they were victors or vanquished—either within the framework of a Danubian confederation, or with the aid of a Habsburg restoration. The two ideas were conceived at one time, and existed parallel with each other. In the beginning they experimented with the former; later—when it became evident that every Danubian state was turning against this French plan—with the latter.

Millerand started from the position that previous French policy, which relied only on the victorious successor states, was not suitable for securing East Europe for France. This previous policy pitted two states—Austria and Hungary, countries that were quite important from an economic, geographic, and strategic point of view—against France, which could have resulted in strengthening the influence of England and Italy on these territories, and in the long run driving them both into the arms of Germany. This latter possibility had an especially alarming effect on the leaders of French diplomacy.

Why did Hungary become the central link in French Danubian policy; why did Millerand and Paléologue wish to unite the Danubian states around Budapest—in brief, why did their choice fall on precisely that country with which until then they had the most antagonistic of relations?

The reasons are multi-faceted. From the viewpoint of the building up of a Danubian economic bloc, it seemed most practicable to make Vienna or Budapest the center, since they had at one time played a leading role. Geographic, economic, and transportation considerations argued in favor of this move. It is not accidental, therefore, that the English and Italian conceptions of economic federation also had the same starting point. Nor is it accidental that both, but chiefly the English, decided, as did the French, in favor of Hungary.

What advantage did Budapest have over Vienna?

Above all, while in Austria an uncertain, anarchic state of affairs prevailed, i.e., a left-wing government was in power that could not master the situation and a further shift to the left was to be feared, in Hungary a conservative counter-revolutionary system had come to power that seemed capable of "consolidating" its domestic politics. And from the standpoint of investment of Western capital, this was extraordinarily important, for both England and Italy, as well as France, wished to implement their plans with the assistance of their private enterprises, and these, in the last analysis, were not willing to take risks.[2] Besides its domestic political situation, the geographic position of Hungary also represented an advantage over Austria.[3]

The choice also fell on Hungary because it was a secure point in the assistance to be extended to Poland[4]—this fact played a very important role with Millerand, the chief organizer of the third intervention—and further because France's ideas were received more sympathetically in Budapest than in Vienna, and the Hungarians were prepared for greater economic sacrifices. For Hungary, cooperation with the French was the sole way out of a catastrophic economic situation. For Austria—although at the beginning of 1920 it had already begun to orient itself towards France—*Anschluss* always figured as a realistic possibility, a possibility that might cure the economic ills of the country.

And last but not least, Millerand and Paléologue wanted to pacify Hungary, the most unsettled state in the Danube basin, which was not willing to acknowledge the changes that had occurred, and refused to sign the peace treaty, or rather, stalled the longest. This, naturally, was no accident. The peace terms were the most severe in the case of Hungary. The Hungarian government justified its refusal to sign the peace treaty not only by referring to the territorial losses, but also by bringing up the economic non-viability of the country within the given frontiers. The Millerand faction wished to disarm this opposition by the prospect of economic and political support.[5] For it was obvious that without Hungary the economic and political consolidation of the Danube basin was inconceivable.

Who initiated the Franco-Hungarian negotiations? What did they involve and on what did the parties to the discussions agree?

In February of 1920—shortly after Millerand came to power—a turnabout occurred in the relations between France and Hungary. The new leaders at the Quai d'Orsay recognized Hungary's importance for their East European plans,[6] while in Hungary a foreign policy conception that saw the happiness of the country in a French orientation gained the upper hand. This change naturally was not independent of the one that occurred in France. Already much earlier, before and after the peace negotiations, the Francophile faction was in touch with those French circles that were preparing to assume power. Behind the continual delay in sending the Hungarian peace delegation,[7] and the total rejection of the peace terms, there lay the desire to mark time until the January elections, to which they attached great hopes. And when after the French elections a changing of the guard took place, and it was obvious that the hopes were being vindicated, the leaders in Budapest were prepared for an unambiguous French orientation.[8] They were all the more prepared for this because they had to acknowledge with disappointment that in the foreign policy of Great Britain the Foreign Office line had prevailed, which from the start had disapproved of the pro-Hungarian policy of Lloyd George and the House of Lords, and defended the interests of the victorious successor states.

Under the impact of the above-noted changes in France and Britain, more and more Hungarian politicians became pro-French. The main representatives of the French line were Pál Teleki, Imre Csáky, and Károly Halmos. It was due to their activity that the English-oriented Miklós Horthy finally, if slowly, accepted their ideas, and supported a Franco-Hungarian rapprochement. Later the hitherto anti-French-minded Albert Apponyi also followed suit. This line was especially strengthened with Pál Teleki's assumption of the foreign minister's seat (April 1920). Following this the rapprochement of the two states also started on the governmental level. The Franco-Hungarian negotiations proceeded on a parallel course in Paris and Budapest.

The first Franco-Hungarian conversation took place on March 17, 1920, on the initiative of the Hungarian side. Károly Halmos, on the instructions of his government, sought out Paléologue, and submitted the following proposals to him: France should change its policy vis-à-vis Hungary; it should support the plan for Franco-Hungarian cooperation; it should foster negotiations between Hungary and the neighboring states and lend its support behind the settlement of economic and political questions.[9] Paléologue received the Hungarian initiative sympathetically, for the proposals submitted to him fit in wonderfully with his idea concerning the Danube basin. Having discussed the proposals with Millerand, he made contact with the members of the Hungarian peace delegation who had remained in Paris, namely: Imre Csáky, Pál Teleki, and Boldizsár Láng. As is well known, Apponyi, the president of the peace delegation, refused to sign the peace terms and returned to Hungary, but numerous members of the delegation remained in Paris. At these initial exploratory conversations, the Hungarian side outlined the economic and political situation of Hungary as well as a plan for its economic reconstruction, which they wished to carry out with external assistance. They did not fail to mention the interest of Great Britain and Italy in this undertaking and informed the French side of the Hungarian government's decision to give preference to France in its search for a solution to the problem. For his part, the French permanent foreign secretary acquainted them, in broad outline, with the plan concerning a unified Danubian bloc, and the intended role of Hungary in it. He sketched out the economic ideas of the French government, according to which French capitalist groups would extend assistance in the economic reconstruction of Hungary. The beneficiaries on the French side of the economic agreement, to be created with the assistance of the French government, would be the firm of Schneider-Creusot. The question of territorial revision was bruited already at these first discussions in Paris. Although he emphasized that this would be the most difficult question,[10] Paléologue was ready to discuss the reannexation of purely Hungarian border territories.[11]

Following this, the Hungarian delegation returned to Budapest to inform the government of the results of this first conversation, and to seek guidance for future ones. After their arrival home they met with Horthy. The regent was sympathetic to the plan concerning Franco-Hungarian cooperation.[12] He called a conference of the members of the government as well as the members of the peace delegation staying in Budapest, at which they debated the general situation, the possibility of the new orientation, and the economic and political plan of the French government. The participants at the conference decided in favor of accepting the French proposals. They decided to suspend the English economic negotiations then in progress, recalling at the last moment the Hungarian delegation that was to leave for London to conclude the Danube shipping agreement. They urged the earliest possible start of Franco-Hungarian economic negotiations, which was to deal, *inter alia*, with the construction of a commercial harbor in Budapest. They decided further on a halt to anti-French press attacks, the introduction of censorship aimed at this, as well as on the formation of a government capable of carrying out these grandiose plans.[13]

However, the turn to the new foreign policy orientation did not prove an easy task. Both in political circles and in public opinion a strong anti-French mood predominated; they attributed the hated peace treaty to France, and the high commissioners of Great Britain and Italy in Budapest—Hohler and Cerrutti—also deliberately inflamed this mood.

In the reports he sent to the Quai d'Orsay, Fouchet, the French high commissioner in Budapest, gave a detailed account of the Franco-phobia existing in the country, of the role played in this by his English and Italian colleagues, of their efforts to draw Hungary under British and Italian influence, respectively. Already as a chargé d'affaires, Fouchet was busily engaged in improving Franco-Hungarian relations. On the basis of instructions from the Quai d'Orsay he did his utmost to prepare the ground for the prospective agreement. He endeavored to quiet the Franco-phobia, which manifested itself ever more openly and virulently in government circles, in the press, as well as in public opinion.[14] He established close contacts with the Hungarian aristocracy, above all with Archduke Joseph, whom he wished at all costs to place on the Hungarian throne,[15] as well as with Albert Apponyi, the president of the peace delegation, whom he had to win over for the French plans and for the peace treaty. He established close relations with several responsible politicians, among them Horthy himself. In the first week of April he met on two occasions with the Regent.[16] He conferred with Prime Minister Simonyi-Semadam, Foreign Minister Teleki, and Permanent Foreign Secretary Kánya. The formerly noncommittal politicians all of a sudden became accommodating and friendly. All of them expressed their agreement with the French orientation of Hungary. During these discussions the question of territorial revision came up, naturally; Apponyi sought radical revision, while the prime minister sought a plebiscite in the northern counties, with the aim of bringing into existence a Hungarian-Polish border (which he regarded as a joint Franco-Hungarian interest), from which he anticipated the re-annexation of Carpatho-Ukraine and Eastern Slovakia.[17]

Simonyi-Semadam recommended to Millerand consideration of his position, cautioning the French Prime Minister, according to Fouchet's report, that "if France wants to acquire those unprecedented economic benefits that present themselves in Hungary, it has to make those not very significant political concessions. A gesture on the part of France would at this moment be quite useful."[18] At this time the French representative in Budapest sent several reports to the Quai d'Orsay. He reported on the efforts of the

Hungarian government on behalf of the new political orientation, on the tangible results of the efforts, on the complete cessation of press attacks against France (articles and publications were, on the orders of the press chief, shown to him before they appeared) on the appearance in *Pester Lloyd* of a pro-French article written by István Bethlen, who took an open stand in favor of the Franco-Hungarian rapprochement,[19] and finally, on the serious preparations made for the formation of a pro-French government. Adherents of an English orientation would be excluded from the new government, Fouchet reported, above all Finance Minister Korányi, who had already committed himself to the English with promises and agreements. The government would be headed by Apponyi or Teleki, the foreign ministry by Csáky.

In the following weeks Fouchet regarded support for the formation of a pro-French government as his first priority, because—in his words—"the implementation of great decisions depends on this."[20]

Meanwhile in Paris, too, which was the second site of the Franco-Hungarian negotiations, an important advance occurred. On April 12 Halmos returned to the French capital with maps, plans, proposals, as well as a personal message from Horthy. The next day he called on Paléologue and conveyed the Regent's message to the French government. According to the message Horthy accepted and supported Hungary's pro-French policy, was ready to support with his full authority the political program that had been embarked upon and was prepared to use all his influence to help support this policy. He hoped that in a short time a 500,000-man unified army composed of courageous and loyal soldiers could be created within the framework of a Franco-Hungarian agreement.[21] Halmos mentioned in addition that Horthy viewed the creation of a pro-French government as one of his top-priority tasks. For the office of prime minister they had picked Apponyi, who would accept it on the condition that France had confidence in him. Moreover, he also broached the question of territorial revision, raising the question in a peculiar way, indeed, departing from the instructions he received in Budapest. That is, he was not seeking border rectifications from France, only its support for a solution to the problem that would be arrived at by the interested parties themselves. Finally, he transmitted the Hungarian government's proposal concerning economic cooperation.[22]

Paléologue received Horthy's message and the economic program sympathetically. Moreover, he didn't raise any objection to

Apponyi's appointment. He noted that he would be glad to see Teleki in the foreign minister's seat.[23] On April 15, at Paléologue's request, Halmos called on Count Saint-Sauveur, the director of the Schneider-Creusot firm, and discussed the economic program with him. They agreed in principle on every question.[24]

On April 16 Millerand received Halmos. The conversation took place in a friendly atmosphere. They discussed the details of the planned economic agreement, the signing of which they set for the end of April. The French prime minister promised that they would postpone the transmittal of the final peace terms.[25]

During his one-week sojourn in Paris, Halmos achieved significant results. He had in essence arrived at an agreement with the Schneider-Creusot firm, and succeeded in bridging differences of a political character and in gaining the support of the French side for definite frontier adjustments. The time for the signing of the preliminary agreement had arrived. Halmos requested that the people designated to attend be sent to Paris.[26] The signing that was planned for the end of April, however, did not take place. The Franco-Hungarian negotiations came to a sudden standstill. The French side began postponing the signing, pushing back the date. Because of "work pressures" Millerand did not receive Bethlen and Csáky, who meanwhile arrived in Paris. Paléologue—alluding to a series of questions that still needed to be clarified—kept delaying further negotiations.

Why did the Quai d'Orsay pull up short? What suddenly made Millerand so preoccupied, and what disturbed Paléologue's clear-sightedness? Primarily the Hungarian government's memorandum of April 23. The memorandum and appended map, which the Hungarian government had delivered to the French foreign ministry through Bethlen, requested the reannexation of territories, in exchange for a French orientation, economic concessions, and an agreement or even a modus vivendi, with the neighboring states. The territories were as follows: Pozsony and environs, Eastern Slovakia, the Csallóköz, Carpathian Ukraine, the Hungarian Kisalföld, those parts of Nógrád and Hont counties that were indispensible to the strategic security of Budapest, the northern part of the Bácska up to the Franz Joseph canal, the disputed corner of the Bácska, and the German part of the Bánát. In addition, they sought territorial autonomy for the Transylvanian Hungarians and Saxons and the right to a plebiscite for the population of Western Hungary and the Bánát, to determine whether they wanted to become citizens of Austria, Hungary, Yugoslavia, or Romania. And, finally, they requested a modification of the military aspects of the peace terms.[27]

The content of the memorandum clearly proves that the Hungarian government was not, even in the fall of 1920, capable of rational compromise, that Apponyi's unrealistic aspirations continued to determine the foreign policy of Hungary, the irrationality of which is also pointed out by Lloyd George in his memoirs. He states that the Hungarian delegation would have achieved much better results if, instead of totally rejecting the territorial changes that had in any case been already implemented in practice, it had concentrated its efforts on individual border questions, as did the other delegations, in which case it could have achieved definite border rectifications.[28]

The demands laid down in the April 23 memorandum were unacceptable to the French government.

Another reason for the standstill in the Franco-Hungarian negotiations was the vacillation of the Schneider-Creusot firm. Although the firm's director, Count Saint-Sauveur, agreed in principle with Halmos, still he began to waver at the end of April. He studiously weighed the possibilities of the Hungarian ideas.[29] His vacillation was in all probability related to the April 23 memorandum of the Hungarian government and to the impact that that had on the Quai d'Orsay. The thing came full circle: the Hungarian-French negotiations reached a dead end. The French government did not accept the memorandum even as a basis for discussion.

Halmos, who did not agree with the content of the memorandum in question, sent new notes to Paléologue on April 23, without the approval of Budapest; in these he summarized the results of the negotiations to date and set forth the territorial demands. According to these he requested the reannexation of exclusively Hungarian-inhabited territories, and a plebiscite for the Carpathian Ukraine. Paléologue accepted the Halmos memorandum as a basis for discussion. Subsequently, however, the Hungarian government attempted on several occasions to supplement the memorandum.[30] Bethlen and Csáky, too, tried to do just this when they arrived in Paris on April 28 with the aim of concluding the negotiations on the basis of the April 23 memorandum and of signing the agreement. Their efforts, however, were without result. The note prepared by them,[31] which sought to correct, or rather, supplement, the Halmos note, was acknowledged by Paléologue only as a point of information.

The discussions were scheduled to continue on May 4. In the morning the members of the Hungarian delegation held a conversation with the director of the Schneider-Creusot firm, with whom they reached an agreement on the question of leasing the Hungarian railways, while in the afternoon they debated the political part of the agreement with Paléologue. The French permanent secretary for foreign affairs informed the members of the Hungarian delegation confidentially of the latest note of the French government, which was a response to the Halmos memorandum. According to this, France would support Hungary in correcting the economic or ethnic injustices inherent in the peace treaty, and in creating a treaty that would promote an agreement between Hungary and her neighbors. It was presumed that all this would be done without touching the basic structure of the peace. During the discussions Paléologue stressed on several occasions that France had firmly resolved to rely on Hungary in the execution of its East European policy. For a long time it had wavered between Austria and Hungary, but after serious consideration had decided in favor of the Hungarians. Accordingly it wished, within the given possibilities, to strengthen Hungary economically and politically. In exchange, the Hungarian government would commit itself to a pro-French policy, as well as to reaching an agreement with the neighboring states. This latter question received an especially great emphasis in succeeding discussions; it may be said that it comprised a decisive element. The permanent secretary for foreign affairs stressed that it was the conviction of the French government that peace in East Europe could only be consolidated if the interested nations came to a mutual agreement and reached an understanding on rational and reasonable border adjustments. Csáky and Bethlen, in accordance with instructions from Budapest, attempted to get clarification on how and by what means the French government wished to support the demands of the Hungarians vis-à-vis their neighbors. How could it force them to accept Hungarian claims? Paléologue, however, did his utmost to avoid giving a direct answer. He referred to certain economic means which they wished to employ to this end.[32] The French permanent secretary for foreign affairs was therefore quite aware that they did not possess such means, nor did he himself trust in the efficacy of the economic pressure he referred to. At the end of the discussions Paléologue informed Bethlen and Csáky that the final peace terms would be transmitted the next day to Praznovszky, Hungary's representative in Paris. In the attached covering letter there even appeared a reference to the possibility of a revision of the peace.[33] This letter was made to appear as the work of the French government. The letter was signed, in the name of the Council of Ambassadors, by Millerand, the then-president. For this reason, the Hungarian government, contemporaries, as well as historians have ascribed the document primarily to the French prime minister. Our research does not support this. Quite the contrary, it proves that in opposition to common belief, the letter with the disclosure of Paléologue was not the work of Millerand. At the Conference of Ambassadors the French did not at first agree with the English, American, and Italian proposal concerning the question referred to.[34]

The question has come up: Why did the French government take a position opposed to the Entente proposal, which in essence embodied Millerand's aspirations as well. Probably because the French feared that their allies, who had already advocated milder peace terms at the peace negotiations, wished in this way to implement their ideas—that is, to bring the peace treaty into being on the basis of these conditions. The Millerand faction, however, was opposed to any more significant alteration of the peace terms, especially if it were to occur with the aid of England or Italy. They assented to certain modifications, but they wished to effectuate these themselves; they wanted them to be linked to their name alone, and for this reason—as we have seen—they demanded heavy reparations.

What was the aim of the Millerand *lettre d'envoi?* It was to correct smaller, blatant local injustices, and by holding out the prospect of a revision of the treaty, to get the Hungarian government to sign the peace.[35] In this way it wanted to break the Hungarian opposition, and make the Peace of Trianon final. By this means it wished to promote the consolidation of the Danube basin, which—especially because of the configuration of the Polish-Soviet War—was extraordinarily important and urgent. Not a single Great Power considered more serious territorial modifications—France did not as yet and England and Italy—especially the former—didn't any longer. Each was aware that the victorious successor states would never agree to the reannexation of territories already in their possession. With force they did not want to compel them; with fine words they could not do so. In fact, they could not even get them to vacate territory awarded to Hungary by the peace treaty.

In the period under review, every great power had, naturally, already come to the realization that the peace had been spoiled, that it had grave political and economic consequences, but still it was made, it existed, and three states (four, if we include Austria) defended its inviolability most decisively. Changing it therefore would have led to very serious conflict, which they wanted to avoid at all cost. On May 6, 1920, Millerand delivered the final peace terms to Praznovszky, the permanent secretary of the Hungarian peace delegation. In no way whatsoever did these take the wishes of the Hungarian government into consideration. The original peace terms therefore remained unaltered. The only difference was that now the cover letter referred to the possibility of a revision of the peace.[36]

The peace terms caused great disappointment in Hungarian government circles. Foreign Minister Teleki immediately called on Fouchet, and reported to him on the session of the Council of Ministers and the bewilderment reigning there. The French plenipotentiary emphasized the significance of the Millerand cover letter and of the Franco-Hungarian negotiations and the prospects these held out. For his part, he recommended acceptance of the peace terms. These were the instructions of the Quai d'Orsay.[37]

Paris had shown foresight, and its ideas were vindicated. The prospective revision of the peace and the promised economic support made their impact. The Hungarian government decided in favor of accepting the peace terms. What is more, satisfying a request of the French government, it endeavored to check the press attacks and demonstrations resulting from the official acceptance.[38]

Apponyi, the president of the Hungarian peace delegation, did not agree with his government's position. He did not trust the promises in the letter. The promises, he claimed, were general, while the peace conditions were concrete—they rejected the requested plebiscite. He again refused to sign the peace treaty and submitted his resignation to Horthy. The regent designated Foreign Minister Teleki to be the signatory.[39] The Millerand faction, however, did not regard Horthy's decision as rational. They did not wish to weaken the position of the pro-French Teleki, who had been named to the post of prime minister, and immediately charged with such an unpopular task. Fouchet expressed his misgivings concerning this, whereupon

Horthy designated Ágoston Benárd, the labor minister, for the signing of the peace treaty, which was scheduled for June 4.[40]

After the delivery of the peace conditions, or rather, their acceptance, the pace of the Franco-Hungarian negotiations speeded up. It was important for the Hungarian government that they make their concrete territorial demands known to the French as soon as possible. Inasmuch as the Halmos memorandum, which served as the basis of discussions up until then, set forth these conditions only incompletely, and furthermore did not refer to the inseparability of economic and political questions, Teleki immediately instructed Csáky to hand Paléologue a new memorandum based on the original instructions. This occurred on May 12. The permanent secretary for foreign affairs accepted the new note only as information. He continued to regard the Halmos memorandum as the basis for discussion.[41]

As a consequence, the Hungarian government made efforts to synchronize the economic and political negotiations, and then to subordinate the former to the latter. In economic questions, in other words, it was not prepared to proceed further until it had gained the desired political concessions. The first stage of the economic negotiations therefore come to an end. On May 4 complete understanding was reached with the Schneider-Creusot firm, and this was set forth in a general agreement.[42] The next step would have been the transmittal of a letter concerning the option. The government, however, was prepared to do this only in return for concrete political concessions.

In this situation Paléologue thought it expedient to send Halmos—the man he regarded as the most open and fervent devotee of Franco-Hungarian rapprochement—to Budapest, to inquire about the effect a verbal French declaration would produce in his homeland. If he judged such a declaration necessary, he was asked to report it to Fouchet.

The next day, May 13, Halmos traveled to Budapest. Paléologue on the very same day instructed France's high commissioner in Budapest to read to the Regent the declaration appended to the instructions if Halmos so requested.[43]

Immediately after his arrival in Budapest, Halmos informed Teleki of Paléologue's ideas, then on May 16 called on Fouchet, and requested that he make the planned declaration. The next day Fouchet visited Teleki and showed him the declaration in writing.

The Hungarian foreign minister was satisfied. He emphasized that the declaration would render a great service to the pro-French policy, which, for the sake of national unity, he, too, had adopted.[44]

On the afternoon of May 18, at 5 o'clock, Miklós Horthy ceremoniously received Fouchet, the representative of France. Besides the Regent, Foreign Minister Teleki, Prime Minister Simonyi Semadam, Finance Minister Korányi, Minister of Agriculture Rubinek, Apponyi, Andrássy, Bethlen, Csáky, and Halmos were also present. For domestic political reasons Horthy and Teleki regarded the presence of these people at this important event as expedient, for many among them received the French orientation with reservations or with open hostility. The declaration, which summarized the main guiding principles of France's policy concerning Hungary, marked a significant advance in the Franco-Hungarian negotiations, which had been in progress since March. The first official move was on the part of the French, who implicitly recognized Hungary's territorial claims, and promised support for their attempts to satisfy them. The declaration emphasized that the peace and prosperity of East Europe could be assured only through the cooperation of the interested states. Therefore France was ready to support every effort that would promote this, including discussions between Hungary and the neighboring states, Romania, Czechoslovakia, and Yugoslavia; it would advocate a review of the unjust decisions in the peace terms and the amplification, or rather, revision, of the rights guaranteed to minorities in the peace treaty. After the declaration was read, Fouchet emphasized that his government wanted to bring a strong Hungary into existence, and was therefore ready to support that goal economically and financially. Everyone received the declaration with great satisfaction. Horthy warmly praised its significance.[45] Let us note, however, that the text of the declaration that was read and the one sent to Fouchet by Paléologue were not identical. Stylistic variations masked substantial differences in content. Who changed the text—Fouchet, or the Hungarians responsible for putting it into writing? We can only conjecture.[46]

The declaration, at all events, had its effect. Immediately after it was made, Horthy informed Fouchet that he agreed to the signing of the economic agreement. He requested that in order to negotiate the details he contact the interested Hungarian ministers, who had already received the necessary instructions.[47]

On May 29 the Hungarian government sent two letters to Saint-

Sauveur, the director of the Schneider-Creusot firm. In one it offered the take-over of the Hungarian railways as well as the Budapest and Diósgyőr factories. (An appendix indicated exactly the state of the factories and the length of the railways.) The other offered an option of the construction of a commercial harbor in Budapest.[48] Count Saint-Sauveur accepted both offers, and was ready to sign an agreement immediately. Upon the intervention of the French government, however, he was forced to forgo this.[49] For the Quai d'Orsay now no longer regarded the above economic concessions as sufficient to new economic concessions—the granting of an option on the Credit Bank. Only in return for this was it prepared to make political concessions—that is, to hand over in writing the verbally delivered declaration, with the aim of making it public. Paléologue on several occasions stressed that the option on the Credit Bank was the *sine qua non* of the written declaration requested by the Hungarians.[50]

A diplomatic wrangle of several weeks' duration developed over this question. The Hungarian government did not wish, or rather, was unable, to meet this new request of Paléologue's, while the French permanent secretary for foreign affairs clung determinedly to his position. In the middle of June it seemed that the conflicts that had arisen brought the Franco-Hungarian negotiations to a complete halt. But what was really at issue here? Why was obtaining an option concerning the Hungarian Credit Bank so important to France, and why was the Hungarian government unable to fulfill its request?

From writings to date it has come to light that a race had begun between the Allied Great Powers—above all between England and France—to acquire Hungary's economic assets. It seemed that in the spring of 1920 the French government succeeded in out-distancing even England, which held the best assets. It was the French, who obtained—or were, rather, in the best position to obtain—the option for the construction of the railways, the most significant factories, and the harbor, and not the English, who also made serious efforts in this direction.[51] In order to control the economic life of Hungary, it was important to obtain the option on the Credit Bank as well, or at least to prevent it from coming into English hands. Two hundred thirty Hungarian enterprises were under the control of the bank. In the Anglo-French rivalry that develped in the spring of 1920, the scales tipped in favor of the former. The president of the bank, Baron Adolf Ullmann, was not willing, even at the request of the government, to call off the negotiations then in progress with English capitalists, and continued to give preference to the English. On April 12, 1920, right in the middle of the Franco-Hungarian economic negotiations in fact, Barons György and Adolf Ullmann traveled to London at the invitation of Lord Furness.[52] And this fact caused no small consternation at the Quai d'Orsay. Halmos's reports, according to which the Ullmanns had received instructions from the government to make only evasive statements and to undertake no obligations whatsoever,[53] not even a moral one, did not assuage French fears in this regard. Paléologue was aware that the Ullmanns were hardly paying attention to the wishes of the government. Teleki, on his own, apprised Fouchet of this development.[54] The directors of French diplomacy therefore increased pressure on the Hungarian government in the matter of the Credit Bank. They insisted on the option, and doing it, Paléologue explained to Csáky, for the sake of the Hungarians, for by controlling the interests of the Credit Bank in the ceded territories they claimed they could exert pressure on the neighboring states. Fouchet himself talked with Ullmann, and tried to obtain his agreement on the issue.[55] Ullmann ultimately yielded to the multi-sided pressure. On June 12, after he had received the requested written guarantee from the prime minister, Bethlen, and Apponyi (according to the guarantee the option was an interest not of the Credit Bank, but of the government) he agreed to the deal. He personally traveled to Paris to complete the arrangements.[56]

The Hungarian government, however, kept putting off delivery of the option letters. It did not regard the French written declaration as an adequate recompense for the economic sacrifices: ". . . the declaration [that the French would support negotiations to be carried on with neighboring states—Magda Ádám], of however great value in principle, cannot be viewed as sufficient compensation for the option," stressed Teleki in the briefing he gave to the delegation about to depart for Paris.[57] He instructed Csáky and Bethlen to inform the French government of this, and to point out that ratification of the option by Parliament and defense of the French orientation against its opponents was only possible if, in exchange, they could point to political concessions that were commensurate with respecting economic sacrifices.[58] On June 9 and June 12 similar memoranda were handed to Fouchet and Paléologue by Teleki and Bethlen who was acting on Horthy's instructions. Millerand and Paléologue acknowledged the latest Hungarian notes only under the heading of information.[59] The French permanent secretary for foreign affairs stressed that he would try his utmost, but could not make definite promises until Hungary had clarified the possibility of negotiations with her neighbors. He mentioned that they had been sounding out Prague, Belgrade, Bucharest, and Vienna for a long time, and the results were fairly satisfactory.[60] He again outlined his plan concerning the economic and political unification of the Danubian states and his idea of making Budapest the center of this grouping. Finally, however, he put it explicitly on record that France did not intend to reestablish the Empire of Saint Stephen, but wished only to assist in solving the problems of South-East Europe.[61]

During his conversation with Csáky, Montielle, Paléologue's *chef de cabinet*, pointed out the difficult situation which his government had gotten into on account of its policy concerning Hungary. It could not compel its allies to overturn the peace, the signing of which France itself had been demanding for some time. He expressed his conviction, however, that the time would come when they could tear up the treaty—and in this they could count on the full support of France.[62]

Millerand submitted a note to the Conference of Ambassadors, and recommended the correction of the unjust decisions affecting Hungary and to this end called for direct discussions between the boundary commissions as well as between the interested states.[63]

The confidential instructions issued by the Conference of Ambassadors on July 22, 1922, to the commissions appointed to fix the boundaries disregarded the above request of Millerand's. On the contrary, the instructions narrowed down and sharply circumscribed the activity of the commissions. They set as the top-priority task the fixing of the boundaries determined in the peace treaty.[64] Supplementary instructions given to the commission handling the Hungarian boundaries pointedly underlined that the boundaries were to be drawn on the territory decided in the peace treaty. There could be no question of any modification that would make doubtful the base line designated in the peace treaty.[65] While formerly England, Italy, and the USA had advocated correction of the unjust decisions of the peace treaty and, having broken French opposition, had carried through the formulation of this possibility in a cover letter, the situation was now reversed. They rejected Millerand's proposal, which had originally been their idea. How is this change to be explained? Above all, by the turnabout that occurred in French foreign policy conception, and by the information they obtained—information that exaggerated the actual stiuation—about the secret Franco-Hungarian negotiations. They wished not to promote, but to block, France's economic and political efforts concerning Hungary. When in the middle of June it became evident that the French government was not willing to discuss concrete territorial revisions involving the neighboring states, and had replaced its earlier commitment with general promises, the Hungarian government made an attempt, before transferring the options, to assure France's support for the execution of its plan for Western Hungary, for the reorganization of the army, and for extracting guarantees regarding the rights of Hungarians living in the ceded territory. Teleki presented a request concerning this to Fouchet, as did Csáky to Paléologue.[66]

The French government was ready to discuss these questions with the Hungarians, but at a later time. It feared—with reason—that further discussion would again delay the conclusion of the Franco-Hungarian negotiations, thus causing them to fail. France's allies—above all, England—embarked on vigorous diplomatic activity to thwart the agreement. They protested in notes against the negotiations which, they claimed, ran counter to the peace treaty. (We shall return to these in detail later.) In response to these notes, the Hungarian government became uncertain. Within days, Teleki—according to Fouchet—looked a different man: he had become irresolute and circumspect.[67]

The domestic political situation in France made the rapid conclusion of the negotiations urgent. The Millerand faction's policy concerning Hungary was being attacked in the Chamber of Deputies and in the Senate. Their opponents questioned them, requesting information about the Franco-Hungarian negotiations.[68]

Since speed was necessary, Paléologue was ready to fall into line with Hungarian ideas relative to the concluding of the agreement, although there were significant differences still outstanding.[69] On June 21 the documents were exchanged. Csáky, Bethlen, Halmos, and Kállay delivered the letters of option approved by the Hungarian government to the Schneider-Creusot firm. Following this Paléologue handed over the declaration to the Hungarian delegates,[70] the original copy of which Fouchet delivered to Teleki in Budapest.[71] At the time of the exchange of documents the French permanent secretary for foreign affairs confidentially informed the departing Hungarian delegation that he had already initiated political action in the neighboring states.[72]

What was the substance of the agreement between the Hungarian government and the Schneider-Creusot firm? The option included the takeover of the operations of the state railways, construction of a commercial and industrial harbor in Budapest, a hydro-electric plant, a harbor in Csepel, a Danube-Tisza canal, the regulation of the Danube, and the transfer into French hands of significant shares of the Credit Bank.[73] A further agreement provided that after the ratification of the options by the Hungarian parliament, the French government would provide Hungary with a 260-million-franc loan, would regard the political declaration as being in force, and would see to its implementation.

The French declaration that was delivered in writing was essentially identical to the declaration sent to Fouchet on May 13 by Paléologue, and consequently differed from the text read verbally to Horthy on May 18. We have already referred to the nature and causes of the divergence. The difference was significant on two points: 1. There was a new paragraph in the written declaration, according to which the declaration would come into force only when the Hungarian Parliament had ratified the economic concessions.[74] Through this addition the French government wanted to assure the possibility of withdrawal, should the opposition defeat the agreement in Parliament. Paris saw clearly there was very little probability that Parliament would approve the options. 2. Left out of the declaration, however, was a very important sentence, which emphasized that the ethnic and economic injustices must be remedied without touching the basic structure of the peace.[75]

On June 22, 1920, Paléologue sent instructions to the heads of the French foreign missions: they were to inform their respective governments about the Franco-Hungarian agreement. In the communication the French permanent secretary for foreign affairs outlined only the economic agreements. He did not, however, mention that those were functions of the appended declaration, nor did he mention the fact that he had also sent information on the agreement to the commission charged with fixing the Hungarian boundaries.

The communication dwelt at length on the reasons that had induced the French government to draw close to Hungary. It alluded, *inter alia*, to the interdependence of the East European states, which made cooperation necessary, and to the dangers that isolated, economically ruined small states were heir to. It pointed out that this situation might have serious consequences. Hungary might seek supporters against her neighbors, and thus put the general peace in jeopardy. For this reason, therefore, France regarded as important the consolidation of the economic situation of Hungary and reconciliation with the other successor states. The communiqué stressed that the economic and political prospect held in view decisively contributed to Budapest's decision to sign the peace.

It is worth noting how someone like Paléologue interpreted the political declaration. Its purpose, he emphasized, was to foster cooperation among the states that had come into being on the territory of the Austrian Monarchy, and to help bring about the normalization of relations between Hungary and her neighbors.[76] The strictly confidential part of the instruction referred to one of the most essential incentives for the Franco-Hungarian negotiations—that is, it emphasized that "[i]t was necessary to act quickly, because our allies wanted the business for themselves, and endeavored to ruin us."[77] The English attacks at first induced the French government not to withdraw, but to do the opposite: move quicker; they wanted to obtain the options as soon as possible, and with these in their possession they wished to oppose British demands from a more favorable position.[78] Before we turn to a concrete survey of this question, we must briefly speak about the position of the French government toward the latest Hungarian demands. We have already mentioned that Paléologue kept postponing their discussion. At the time of the exchange of documents Csáky again asked the French government to support Hungary 1. in having the military clauses of the Trianon peace reviewed; 2. in holding on to the Western Hungarian territories; 3. in defending the interests of the Hungarian minority; 4. in locating the seat of the Danube commission and the Reparations Commission in Budapest; and 5. in bringing about the immediate reannexation of the territories, now held under occupation by Yugoslavia and Romania, that had been awarded to Hungary by the Trianon peace. The French permanent secretary for foreign affairs received the Hungarian ideas concerning this sympathetically, but promised a final answer only after they had been thoroughly studied. He therefore asked that they be put into writing. Csáky fulfilled his request on June 23.[79]

The next day Paléologue, through his *chef de cabinet*, Montielle, sent a message to the Hungarian delegation: on first reading he found nothing in the request with which the French government could not in principle agree! He would inform them later, after the qualified officials had thoroughly studied the memorandum,[80] of the form in which he wished to support the requests. But why did Paléologue feel it was necessary—or better yet, possible—to invite the experts at the Quai d'Orsay, above all, Laroche, to join the discussion of the questions, when they had up to this time been almost excluded from the Franco-Hungarian negotiations? The answer is simple. In the conversations to date territorial revision directed against the victorious neighboring states had been at issue. With this, however, many at the Quai d'Orsay—for example, Peretti, Cambon, Bertholot, Laroche—did not agree—indeed, they opposed it most vigorously. However, as we have seen, the latest Hungarian request, besides many other requests, related to adjustments of the boundaries of a defeated state, Austria, to the advantage of Hungary. And this fell under a different judgement. With this the French politicians in general agreed. They started from the position that if it were possible to conciliate the Hungarians at somebody's expense, then let it be only Austria's—the other defeated state's. This, moreover, could be accomplished: from a moral point of view it would be easier to decide against a defeated state, and to carry out the decision, by armed force if necessary, than against allies, whose opposition and regrouping were to be feared. But they also pursued this line of thought because—and for the French this was a very significant consideration—they wanted to weaken an Austria that was heading leftward and striving toward *Anschluss.*

Paléologue invited Laroche to join in the discussion of the latest Hungarian memorandum, and the latter informed Csáky on June 24 of the French position on this matter. It appeared from Laroche's communications and from the telegrams sent by Millerand to Fouchet that despite Paléologue's message cited above, the French government had a series of objections to the matters taken up in the memorandum.[81] Thus, for example, they regarded as untimely the request for a change in the military clauses, because—as they emphasized—Germany would regard this as a precedent. This question could only be raised officially after the complete disarmament of Germany and only with Great Britain's prior approval.[82] Laroche, furthermore, declared the proposal relating to Western Hungary unacceptable.[83] He justified this with the argument that France could not openly make a declaration whose aim and intent was a radical modification of the peace, that is, it could not take a position in favor of Hungary in the manner requested. It would, however, reject any proposal, regardless of its source, that would want to force Hungary to evacuate these territories. In addition, it also regarded as unfulfillable the request for protection of Hungarian minorities, and deemed unacceptable the demand for a Yugoslav evacuation as well. The French government accepted in its entirety only that part of the memorandum which asked for the creation of the two commissions, but it promised concrete support for this. In Budapest they acknowledged with disappointment that the negotiators have not succeeded in getting even the smallest political demands accepted by the French.[84]

The French government made the Franco-Hungarian negotiations appear as being purely economic in character. Thus it is understandable that Hungary's neighbors received them sympathetically at the outset. They began with the assumption that France's Hungarian policy would restrain the ambitions of Italy and England in their region, and it would thwart these two nations' plans for a Danubian confederation. A Hungary under French influence, moreover, would represent a smaller danger to the given status quo than if it were to fall within the Italian or British sphere of interest.[85] French diplomats emphasized this to the Prague, Bucharest, and Belgrade governments. When, at the beginning of June, the French government turned to the Prague, Belgrade, and Bucharest governments with a proposal that they begin direct negotiations with Hungary under the sponsorship of France, all three states responded positively. According to a report made by Paléologue's *chef de cabinet*, Montielle, to Praznovszky, Beneš and Vesnić were enthusiastic about the proposal. Although Take Ionescu was not enthusiastic, he also accepted the French proposal. He felt it necessary to emphasize that "hopefully France will not take part in these negotiations as Hungary's ally."[86] It was at this point that Beneš first proposed the start of negotiations to the Hungarian government.

At almost the same time Yugoslavia and Romania also expressed their willingness to start negotiations. The Romanian government, through Stircea, its representative in Budapest, offered to establish diplomatic relations with Hungary. Unlike Czechoslovakia and Yugoslavia, it was ready to do this even before the ratification of the Trianon peace. It requested help from the French government toward this end.[87] Paléologue supported the Romanian idea. His position, which he made known to Budapest on several occasions, was that Hungary had to come to an agreement above all with Romania. He perceived that negotiations with Romania had to be started. It was the opinion of those in charge of French diplomacy that the Hungarian government should not at the outset bring up the political and territorial demands, because "a premature insistence on these would in all probability knock the Romanian government off a track that was favorable to us—one onto which it had already turned, mainly in response to French pressure—and would drive it completely into the arms of the Serbs and the Czechs, in which case we would find the ring around us completely closed." In the given situation, read Praznovszky's report, Hungary's first-priority foreign policy task was to break this developing ring. This could be accomplished by means of an agreement with the Romanians.[88]

Under the impact of the events of July, the readiness of Czechoslovakia, Yugoslavia, and Romania to negotiate with Hungary disappeared. What were those events?

On June 22, Count Saint-Sauveur arrived in Budapest at the head of a French delegation. He was given a spectacular reception; even Horthy received him at Gödöllő. He had discussions with Apponyi and members of the Hungarian government. Saint-Sauveur prepared a detailed account of his observations in Budapest, in which he analyzed Hungary's political and economic situation. He stated that Hungary could not exist within its new boundaries without an economic agreement with the neighboring states.[89]

During his stay in Budapest the count gathered information, spoke with various people, and made recommendations. He did not, however, conclude an agreement. Still, after his departure the news spread rapidly that at Gödöllő he had indeed signed an agreement. Renner bought the text of this agreement from one of the civil servants in the Hungarian Ministry of Finance for 100,000 crowns.[90] The Austrian chancellor passed the alleged secret agreement to Beneš, who forwarded it immediately to Paris, together with a note of protest. The 11-page document, which had allegedly been signed in Horthy's presence at Gödöllő on the evening of the 19th, listed in the most minute detail the territories that Hungary was to get back. The aim of the alleged agreement was therefore a radical alteration of the Trianon and Saint Germain peace.[91]

The document could have been either a forgery, or one of the dozens of Hungarian plans that were drawn up at that time. Beneš and Renner used this alleged agreement to launch sharp attacks against a Franco-Hungarian rapprochement and in this they were supported by Germany, Yugoslavia, Romania, England, Italy, and in part by the USA as well, giving credence to their propaganda, making it that much easier to attack the French government.[92] When, however, the uproar surrounding the Franco-Hungarian agreement reached its highest pitch, the moves toward rapprochement between the two states had already lost much of its old intensity. Both sides—but mainly the Hungarian—were considering pulling back.

In analyzing the question, it is scarcely possible to ignore the domestic political factors—e.g., the ever-intensifying attacks of the domestic opposition—that demanded a more cautious policy on the part of both sides. The question was nonetheless decided primarily by external factors—international power relations. We must mention above all the policy of Great Britain. We have already noted that from the outset the Foreign Office opposed Millerand's Danubian plans, and attacked his policy concerning Hungary. In the first week of May—and thus at the very start of Franco-Hungarian negotiations—Hohler, the English high commissioner, on the instruction of his government, initiated a counter-action. He attempted to turn Horthy, with whom he maintained close relations, against France. He called the Regent's attention to the fact that France herself was also in an extraordinarily difficult economic and financial situation—it was compelled to rely on the assistance of the USA and England—and therefore Hungary could hardly hope for assistance from her.[93] But on May 27 he presented a written request, a démarche, to the Regent, in which he protested against the Franco-Hungarian economic plans, and at the same time offered to strengthen Anglo-Hungarian economic relations.[94] On June 4 England sent a note to the Hungarian government, in which she protested against the leasing of the Hungarian railways because—the note emphasized—this would be contrary to the provision of the Trianon peace regarding reparations. The chargé d'affaires mentioned that his government was also protesting against this development in Paris: simultaneously with the Budapest protest, Derby, the English ambassador in Paris, had delivered Curzon's letter to Millerand, which protested against the Franco-Hungarian combinations.[95] After the energetic intervention of the English, Teleki began to waver considerably. He did finally agree to the signing of the June 22 agreement, since Paléologue, the French permanent secretary for foreign affairs, characterized the protest of the English in Budapest as insignificant,while he denied the one lodged in Paris. He did this both in his conversation with Halmos (on Teleki's instruction Halmos had asked him about English interventions) and in a telegram that he sent to Fouchet.[96] But what ultimately restored Teleki's confidence was that Paléologue confidentially informed Halmos that there was agreement between England and France on the Hungarian question. Fouchet, however, informed Teleki that Paléologue had discussed the question with Derby, the English ambassador in Paris, and the matter was settled.[97] In his June 10 report Csáky again touched on this question. He set forth his impressions and information concerning the matter. According to these there existed an Anglo-French agreement, according to which Hungary was to fall within France's sphere of interest.

After the signing of the options, the Anglo-French competition for Hungary's favors only intensified. The French at this time were not yet ready to withdraw. On the contrary, they intensified their diplomatic activity for the final acquisition of the options, and wanted to negotiate with Great Britain only afterwards. They wished to use the options as a trump card at the planned Millerand-Lloyd George meeting, where they were also going to put the Hungarian question on the agenda. There is a note to be found in the French foreign ministry that refers to this, noting that the option was important in that it could be used to oppose other English demands.[98] Only later, at the end of July or the beginning of August, that is, after the Anglo-French meeting, did the French begin to pull back.

Italy also played a role in the Hungarian-French estrangement. From the outset Rome was persistently engaged in thwarting France's plans relating to Hungary. It is understandable, therefore, that it did not look kindly on a Franco-Hungarian rapprochement. It did not wish France to lay hands on Hungary, and attempted to block this at all costs. After it became obvious that it could not do this by itself, it joined forces with England, and supported the latter's action. The alignment was therefore the same as at the peace conference: Anglo-Italian collaboration against France.

On June 28 Cerruti protested in the name of his government against the Hungarian-French rapprochement. He reiterated this on July 3. The Italian high commissioner emphasized that Franco-Hungarian collaboration had created bad feeling in both England and Italy. He reminded Kánya that Prime Minister Huszár and

Foreign Minister Count Somssich had personally declared to him in February that Hungary wished to base its foreign policy on cooperation with Italy, inasmuch as it was necessary for Hungarians and Italians to defend themselves jointly against the pan-Slav danger. Beyond this first initiative the Hungarian side had done nothing at all really to further a Budapest-Rome rapprochement. Kánya, the Foreign Minister's trusted permanent deputy, pinned the blame for the standstill in Italian-Hungarian relations on the Italian government. He argued that Italy's policy concerning Romania, which disregarded Hungarian interests, was thwarting the Hungarian government's implementation of its original plan. Cerruti pointed out Romania's importance for the planned Central European stabilizing bloc. In order to achieve this stabilization, Hungary had to normalize its relations with the Romanian government, even at the cost of temporarily accepting the Romanian conditions, that is, of acknowledging the extant situation in this area. This did not mean that later on this situation would not be modified. He trusted that Transylvanian autonomy could now be effectuated.[99]

France's "advice" concerning Romania, as we have seen, did not impede a Franco-Hungarian rapprochement. Here therefore is another factor to be considered: namely that Italy's potential for carrying through a revision was insignificant. Budapest wished to give preference to the power that was capable of securing alternate compensations for certain concessions. In the period under consideration it regarded France as such a power. In the present study we will not touch on the behavior of the United States in connection with the Hungarian-French rapprochement as its attitude in the matter was quite indifferent.[100]

The policy of England and Italy, sketched out above, had an effect not only on Hungary but on her neighbors as well. As we have seen, it induced the former to retreat, and provoked the latter to attack, and take decisive measures. Beneš stood in the forefront of the struggle. The Czechoslovak foreign minister wished to make the most of the possibilities offered by the situation: he wanted to put into execution his old plan concerning a Little Entente. Until the Paris peace conference, collaboration among the three states had been occasional and bi-lateral. Unified action was first taken at the Trianon peace conference. Following this they again went on their separate ways. Both Yugoslavia and Romania rejected Beneš' alliance proposal, and they adhered to their position until the summer of 1920.[101]

The Franco-Hungarian secret agreement, however, nudged the three states toward each other, and played a catalytic role, as it were, in the configuration of their relationship. The director of Czechoslovak diplomacy immediately recognized the possibilities offered by the given atmosphere. Yugoslavia and Romania were in a panic; they were aware that Hungarian revisionist aspirations, along with France's support, represented a potential danger, and that Beneš' present message—"Hungary is no longer our enemy, but our rival"[102] summed up the actual situation. From the end of July communications between Belgrade, Bucharest, and Prague grew more lively. Ninčič traveled to Prague and discussed the new situation with Beneš, and the two foreign ministers agreed on the signing of a treaty. Beneš prepared for the signing of the agreement in Belgrade. Before his departure he informed Renner that the Hungarian revisionist efforts, supported by the French, had made the formation of the Little Entente necessary.[103]

The French government followed Beneš' every move closely—and with great dissatisfaction.

The directors of French diplomacy opposed most vigorously the organization of the Little Entente, and even tried to block it with the means at their disposal. It was obvious to them that this alliance would thwart their plan for a Danubian confederation, whose aim was to obtain the cooperation of every Danubian state, first economically, and then politically. The Little Entente would divide this area into victors and vanquished, and inevitably drive the latter among them into the arms of Germany. Their position found precise expression in Millerand's August 24 circular telegram, addressed to 11 embassies. In the telegram the prime minister mentioned those negotiations that aimed at the creation of an alliance whose member states would be Czechoslovakia, Yugoslavia, Romania, and perhaps Poland and Greece. He referred to the already-extant Czechoslovak-Yugoslav agreement, and then continued thus:

> Such a policy may be accompanied by the serious problem of the isolation of the Hungarian government which then may inevitably attempt to side with Germany, and find support there. Our daily concern, however—quite to the contrary—is to avoid conflicts, and to seek the elements of rapprochement and understanding among the different states of Central Europe. In order to achieve this goal more effectively, I also fostered an economic rapprochement between French and Hungarian enterprises. The strengthening of French influence in

Budapest, therefore, seemed suitable for serving the cause of peace, for this would offer to each of our Central European allies a sure guarantee that will prevent a renewal of Hungary's policy of conquest. Under such conditions the affiliation of Poland or Greece with the planned combination may bring with it the threat that it will promote the break-up of Central Europe into two camps, which would increase the danger of conflict. It is not in our interest, therefore, that the government to which you are accredited enter into a grouping with such an orientation. I request that you, using your judgment and discretion, call the attention of the government to the grave consequences of this policy, which masks the danger of a conjunction of Hungarian and German interests, and makes difficult the development of natural relations among the Central European states.[104]

This, therefore, was the official position of France regarding the formation of the Little Entente. This serious document, possessing the value of a source, gives witness in itself to the fact that Paris not only did not promote the formation of the alliance, but also condemned the Czechoslovak-Yugoslav agreement, and even tried to keep the other states from joining. Under France's determined intervention the Romanian government began to waver, and at the time of Beneš' Romanian negotiations the French Marshall Joffre arrived in Bucharest unexpectedly. Diplomatic circles followed developments with rapt attention, and waited to see who would be the victor, Beneš or Joffre.

The victor turned out to be Joffre. Romania did not adhere to the Little Entente; it was only prepared to make a verbal agreement. It signed the Little Entente agreement only a year later, when the Hungarian danger—as a result of ex-King Charles IV's attempted putsch—again became acute, when a new turnabout occurred in France's Danube basin policy, and when despite its wishes it sided with the established Little Entente. By the fall of 1920 Paléologue's Hungarian-oriented policy had fallen through. After the establishment of the Czechoslovak-Yugoslav agreement the French opposition intensified its attack against the Millerand-Paléologue foreign policy line. In Paris they suddenly realized that the building of a new order in Central Europe had started not only without them, but expressly against them. Consequently, Millerand found it better to repudiate his plans concerning Hungary, and to appease his critics, he made Paléologue, the man who had openly taken up Hungary's cause, the scapegoat.

Notes

1. For a long time historiography evinced considerable vagueness on this question. The documentary material now available from the Quai d'Orsay makes possible a fuller and more accurate description of events.

2. It can be observed in the case of all three Great Powers that private enterprises, supported by the government, got their hands on economic assets of the Danubian states.

3. On this point see France, Ministère des Affaires Étrangères, *Archives Diplomatiques*, Serie Europe 1918-1929 (hereafter *AD*); *Hongrie* (hereafter *H*), vol. 58, f. 4-9, "the Hungarian opening and French interests."

4. Czechoslovakia, Austria, and Yugoslavia declared neutrality in the Polish-Soviet war. Romania, although it did not make a declaration of neutrality, was still not willing to send its army to the Polish front. It wished to utilize it to guard the Hungarian border.

5. *AD*, Europe 1918-29; *H*, vol. 58, f. 197.

6. Another memorandum of the French foreign ministry contains the following line: "La puissance qui dominera la Hongrie possedera la clef venté de l'Europe Centrale." Fouchet, Memorandum, December 11, 1920, *AD*, Europe 1918-29, *H*, vol. 60, f. 140-49.

7. The Hungarian government sent the peace delegation to Paris only after repeated invitations.

8. Before this Hungary had no definite foreign policy. It leaned toward several countries: England, Austria, and Romania, though Great Britain stood in first place.

9. Francis Deák and Dezso Ujváry, *Papers and Documents Relating to the Foreign Relations of Hungary, vol. I* (Budapest, 1939) (hereafter *PDH*); Memorandum on the conversation of Paléologue and Halmos (April 13, 1920), *AD*, Europe 1918-29; *H*, vol. 58, f. 78-79.

10. *PDH*, pp. 243-44; doc. 236.

11. This was signified by the acceptance of Halmos's April 23 memorandum as a basis for discussion.

12. Telegram from Fouchet to Millerand (April 1920), *AD.*, Europe 1918-29; *H*, vol. 58, f. 61-62.

13. *Ibid.*

14. *Ibid.*; Report from Fouchet to Millerand (April 28, 1920), *AD*, Europe 1918-29; *H*, vol. 58, f. 67-71. Having a pro-Hungarian reputation, Fouchet regarded an agreement with Hungary as important, even at the cost of significant concessions. Already at the end of April he reported to Millerand with satisfaction on the decrease in the anti-French mood. Report from Fouchet to Millerand (April 23, 1920), *AD*, Europe 1918-29, f. 101-06.

15. In contrast to the official position of France, Fouchet supported Archduke Joseph in the multi-directional activity in which he was engaged to

obtain the Hungarian throne. Archduke Joseph wished, with French help, to forestall his cousin, Charles IV, and occupy the throne as soon as possible. He discussed this with French contacts on several occasions. Report from Fouchet to Millerand (November 6, 1920), *AD*, Europe 1918–29; *H*, vol. 60, f. 90–97.

16. Telegram from Fouchet to Millerand (April 23, 1920), *AD*, Europe 1918–29; *H*, vol. 58, f. 101–06; Telegram from Fouchet to Millerand (April 10, 1920), *ibid.*, f. 72–73.

17. Report from Fouchet to Millerand (April 28, 1920), *AD*, Europe 1918–29; *H*, vol. 58, f. 67–71; Telegram from Fouchet to Millerand (April 10, 1920), *AD*, Europe 1918–29; *H*, vol. 58, f. 72–73.

18. *Ibid.*

19. The article appeared on April 20, 1920, and produced great surprise. However, as a result of governmental intervention, it did not precipitate a press debate.

20. Telegram from Fouchet to Millerand (April 10, 1920), *AD*, Europe 1918–29; *H*, vol. 58, f. 72–73. The government formed in June conformed to French ideas. Pál Teleki became prime minister, Imre Csáky foreign minister.

21. Note of the conversation between Paléologue and Halmos (April 13, 1920), *AD*, Europe 1918–29; *H*, vol. 58, f. 178–79.

22. *Ibid.*

23. *PDH*, doc. 218, p. 230. Halmos reported on this as follows: "Conversation with Paléologue took place in a cordial and encouraging atmosphere. I outlined the political and economic situation. He seemed satisfied and stated that we can count on the goodwill of the French." Halmos met with Paléologue again on April 17; see *PDH*, doc. 236, pp. 243–44.

24. *PDH*, doc. 224, p. 234.

25. *PDH*, doc. 227, p. 238.

26. *PDH*, doc. 239, p. 249; doc. 249, p. 238.

27. *PDH*, doc. 242, 242/a, pp. 250–54.

28. Lloyd George, *The Truth about the Peace Treaties*, vol. II (London, 1938), p. 172.

29. Saint-Sauveur called a conference for April 28 to clarify anew the questions already decided upon. *PDH*, doc. 225, pp. 268–75.

30. *PDH*, doc. 255/b, pp. 273–74; *ibid.*, doc. 259, pp. 270–84.

31. Having arrived in Paris, Bethlen and Csáky endeavored to curb Halmos's activity. They did not regard it as consonant with Hungarian objectives or with radical revision. They did not agree with his April 23 memorandum.

32. *PDH*, doc. 259, pp. 279–84.

33. Lettre d'envoi from Millerand (May 6, 1920), *AD*, Europe 1918–29; *H*, vol., 58, f. 112–13.

34. On this point see: Telegram from Millerand to the French ambassador

in London (June 26, 1920), *AD*, Europe 1918–29; *H*, vol. 59, f. 61; Memorandum from the French foreign ministry (DEcember 25, 1920), vol. 58, f. 245; *Documents on British Foreign Policy* (hereafter *DBFP*), First Series, vol. XII, doc. 244, pp. 286–89; vol. VII, doc. 54, p. 449.

35. The representatives of the Allied Powers spoke openly about this among themselves.

36. The peace terms remained unchanged. They referred to eventual concessions only as possibilities. "To counter our arguments, the prior treaty obligations of the Allied Powers are repeatedly invoked and eventual concessions are mentioned only as possibilities," Praznovszky reported on May 6. *PDH*, doc. 264, pp. 286–87; Lettre d'envoi from Millerand (May 6, 1920), *AD*, Europe 1918–29; *H*, vol. 58, f. 112–13.

37. Telegram from Fouchet to Millerand (May 8, 1920), *AD*, Europe 1918–29; *H*, vol. 58, f. 118–21; Report from Fouchet to Millerand (May 1920), *ibid.*, f. 138–42. Millerand's instructions to the French high commissioner in Budapest read as follows: "Vous devez ne rien négliger pour accepter ces conditions et à lui assurer l'exécution." Communiqué from Millerand to Doulcet (March 6, 1920), *AD*, Europe 1918–29; *H*, vol. 58, f. 14–17.

38. Although Teleki informed Praznovszky on May 7 that favorable comment on the "lettre d'envoi" in the Hungarian press did not seem feasible (*PDH.*, doc. 268, pp. 292–93), measures by the Hungarian government in this direction were successful. Fouchet reported on this with satisfaction to Millerand. Report from Fouchet to Millerand (May 23, 1920), *AD*, Europe 1918–29' *H*, vol. 59, f. 128.

39. Teleki had Fouchet informed of the above. He communicated to him that with this his political career was in fact over. Telegram from Fouchet to Millerand (May 23, 1920), *AD*, Europe 1918–29; *H*, vol. 58, f. 202.

40. The Trianon peace was signed on June 4, 1920, by Ágoston Benárd, Minister of Labor and Welfare, and Alfréd Drasche-Lázár, Envoy Extraordinary and Minister Plenipotentiary.

41. *PDH*, doc. 266, p. 291; doc. 292, pp. 296–97; doc. 276, pp. 299–301; Note from Halmos to Paléologue (May 12, 1920), *AD*, Europe 1918–29; *H*, vol. 58, f. 122–24. After Paléologue indicated to Csáky that he would not acknowledge the latest demands [*PDH*, doc. 283, p. 304], the newly-delivered memorandum laid down the Hungarian desiderata only in general terms.

42. *PDH*, doc. 259, pp. 279–84; see also: Letter from Halmos to Paléologue (April 23, 1920), *AD*, Europe 1918–29, *H*, vol. 58, f. 95–100.

43. Telegram from Paléologue to Fouchet (May 13, 1920), *AD*, Europe 1918–29; *H*, vol. 58, f. 123.

44. Report from Fouchet to Millerand (May 23, 1920), *AD*, Europe 1918–29; *H*, vol. 58, f. 138–42. Fouchet reported as follows: "Le Comte Teleki m'a témoigné sa très vive satisfaction la politique francophile qu'il a

cru devoir adopter au profit de son pays était trop bien, service par la texte que j'étais autorisé à lui communiquer verbalement, pour que son impression puit être différente."

45. Telegram from Fouchet to Millerand (June 10, 1920), *AD*, Europe 1918–29; *H*, vol. 59, f. 203–12; Telegram from Millerand to Fouchet (June 12, 1920), *ibid.*, vol. 58, f. 239–41; Telegram from Paléologue to Fouchet (May 13, 1920), *ibid.,*; *PDH*, doc. 292, pp. 310–11.

46. The supposition, however, is that Fouchet, who generally adapted the received instructions to the ideas of the Hungarian government, altered the text of the Paléologue declaration. The text verbally delivered by him—which the Hungarian foreign ministry published in 1939—held out the prospect of France's support for the correction of economic and ethnic injustices in the peace treaty, and for the revision and amplification of the minority decisions. Telegram from Paléologue to Fouchet (May 13, 1920), *AD*, Europe 1918–29; *H*, vol. 58, f. 128–29. There are still other—not substantial—stylistic variations between the two declarations. The declaration delivered in writing on June 22 went through further modifications at the hands of Paléologue himself. We will refer to this later.

47. Telegram from Fouchet to Millerand (June 19, 1920), *AD*, Europe 1918–29; *H*, vol. 59, f. 18–20.

48. Letter from the Hungarian government to the Schneider-Creusot firm (June 1, 1920), *AD*, Europe 1918–29; *H*, vol. 58, f. 233–37; Telegram from Fouchet to Millerand (June 10, 1920), *ibid.*, f. 208–11.

49. *PDH*, doc. 323, pp. 335–36.

50. *PDH*, doc. 323, pp. 335–36; doc. 325, p. 337; doc. 341, p. 348; doc. 358, pp. 362–63.

51. Serious competition was under way among Hungarian firms supported by the English and French governments for the aquisition of the key economic assets in Hungary. On this point see: Memorandum from the French foreign ministry (June 9, 1920), *AD*, Europe 1918–29; *H*, vol. 58, f. 204–5.

52. Lord Furness was the president of the English capitalist group that wanted to penetrate the economic life of Hungary.

53. Halmos's memorandum read: "Ces Monsieurs [Barons Adolf and György Ullmann—M.Á.] ont reçu l'instruction de ne faire que des déclarations dilatoires et de ne prendre aucun engagement même morale." Halmos recommended to the French permanent secretary for foreign affairs that he arrange for the Ullmanns to stop in Paris on their way home from London. This in fact took place. Memorandum from Halmos to Paléologue (April 13, 1920), *AD*, Europe 1918–29; *H*, vol. 58, f. 76.

54. Report from Fouchet to Millerand (June 10, 1920), *AD*, Europe 1918–29; *H*, vol. 58, f. 208.

55. Telegram from Fouchet to Millerand (June 1920), *AD*, Europe 1918-29; *H*, vol. 58, f. 208. Ullmann made clear that public opinion was against the leasing of the railways, regarding this as anti-national. The railway and Credit Bank options were interrelated, and as a result the hostile mood also turned against the Credit Bank.

56. Teleki's communique to Csáky read: "C'est grace à une forte pression du gouvernement hongrois que la direction de la Kreditbank, qui a attaché une grande importance au maintien de ses rapports établis depuis longtemps avec d'autres groupes étrangères, donna son consentement à la remise de l'option." *PDH*, doc. 361, pp. 366-68. Teleki to Fouchet: "Le Gouvernement hongrois a enfin réussi à vaincre la résistance du baron Ullmann." *PDH*, doc. 366, pp. 370-71. "He conditioned his approval on a written guarantee to this effect. This was given in the form of a letter to him from the Prime Minister stating that the granting of the Credit Bank option is in the interest of the Hungarian government and not of the Bank. Count Apponyi, Count Bethlen and Popovics have made similar statements in another letter written to Ullmann." *PDH*, doc., 361, pp. 366-68.

57. *PDH*, doc. 301, pp. 318-19.

58. *Ibid.*; Letter from Horthy to Teleki (June 9, 1920), *AD*, Europe 1918-29; *H*, vol. 59, f. 21; *PDH*, doc. 351, p. 355.

59. "Paléologue mentioned today Regent's letter to Your Excellency and remarked that this official document referred, among other things, to the memorandum which Count Bethlen gave him some time ago and which he accepted à titre privé and only as matter of information." *PDH*, doc. 351, p. 355.

60. *PDH*, doc. 349, pp. 353-54.

61. *Ibid.*

62. Csáky reported on this as follows: ". . . he [Montielle—M. Á.] said we may rest assured that we could tear this treaty to pieces whenever we felt sufficiently strong to do so and that when that time came, we could rely on the wholehearted support of France." *PDH*, doc. 368, pp. 371-72.

63. *PDH*, doc. 374, p. 375.

64. Les Commissions de délimitation ont pour mission de fixer sur le terrain: (a) D'abord les frontières décrites dans les Traités de paix; (b) Ultérieurement les frontières qui seron fixées après l'exécution des divers plébiscites prescrites par les dits Traités. League of Nations, *Archives de la Societé des Nations* (Geneva), Instructions relatives aux Commissions de délimitation, 19902/19584. I obtained the document from French historian H. Bagdan, for which I owe him my thanks.

65. "En principe, la frontière devra être tracée sur le terrain telle qu'elle est définie dans le Traité de paix. En aucun cas, les modifications de frontière envisagées plus loin ne devront être de nature à remettre en question les bases mêmes de ligne décrite dans le Traité." *Ibid.*

66. Report from Fouchet to Millerand (June 17, 1920), *AD*, Europe 1918-29; *H*, vol. 59, f. 5-9; *PDH*, doc. 361, pp. 365-68; doc. 324, pp. 336-37.

67. Report from Fouchet to Millerand (June 1920), *AD*, Europe 1918-29; *H*, vol. 58, f. 208.

68. After being informed of the attack directed against Millerand, Csáky pointed out that the Hungarian government's remaining in power depended on the Hungarian question. *PDH*, doc. 309, pp. 323-24; *ibid.*, doc. 578, pp. 576-77.

69. A long discussion ensued over who should sign the declaration. (Horthy, citing the constitution, refused.) Should it be published, and where? To whom should a copy of the declaration be sent? *PDH*, doc. 331, p. 340; doc. 344, p. 350; doc. 353, p. 357; doc. 346, p. 346; doc. 324, pp. 336-37.

70. *PDH*, doc. 384, p. 384; doc. 386, p. 385; Communication from Paléologue to the Hungarian delegation (June 21, 1920), *AD*, Europe 1918-29; *H*, vol. 59, f. 31-32; *PDH*, doc. 384, p. 384.

71. Telegram from Millerand to Fouchet (June 22, 1920), *AD*, Europe 1918-29; *H*, vol. 59, f. 37; *PDH*, doc. 386, p. 385; doc. 393, pp. 381-82. At the time of the delivery of the declaration Paléologue emphasized its significance: ". . . cet déclaration tien grand compte des considérations politiques et économiques dont vous vous êtes faits les interprètes auprès de moi: elle atteste que le Gouvernement français est vivement désireux de voir l'Europe Centrale renaître à l'ordre, au travail et à la prospérité." Letter from Paléologue to Csáky and Halmos (June 21, 1920), *AD*, Europe 1918-29; *H*, vol. 59, f. 31.

72. *PDH*, doc. 378, p. 378.

73. Circular telegram from Paléologue to the French embassy (June 22, 1920), *AD*, Europe 1918-29; *H*, vol. 59, f. 35. It was planned that the Schneider-Rothschild combine come in for a share of 250 million crowns. Memorandum from the commercial department of the French foreign ministry to Paléologue (June 22, 1920), *ibid.*, f. 40-43.

74. *PDH*, doc. 378, p. 378.

75. Paléologue, who did not know that this sentence did not figure even in the verbal declaration of May 18 [we have noted that Fouchet did not read this sentence of the declaration to Horthy], informed Csáky on June 20, in other words two days before the signing of the agreement, that compared to the old declaration there was a change favorable to the Hungarians in the present one: it left out the sentence in question. This meant, continued the permanent foreign secretary, that the French wanted to review the basic structure of the peace in favor of Hungary. PDH., doc. 378, p. 378. Paléologue was not speaking of that modification—i.e., of the insertion of that half-sentence—which to a certain degree compensated for the sentence left out. The new declaration, therefore, emphasized only that revision, under conditions established in the covering letter—"dans les conditions

indiquées par la dite lettre d'envoi"—could be carried out. *PDH*, doc. 393, pp. 391–92. Yet a further significant variation between the two declarations is that while the first, verbal declaration promised support for the redress of ethnic and economic injustices, the second, written, one supported negotiations between Hungary and her neighbors, the aim of which was the elimination of conflicts. The June 22 declaration reads as follows: ". . . [the French government] est disposé à prêter ses bons offices à toute tentative d'accord à l'aimables entre la Hongrie et ses voisins en vue de faire disparaître toute cause d'hostilité entre les parties interessees qui receviaient une satisfaction commun." Circular telegram from Paléologue (June 22, 1920), *AD*, Europe 1918–29; *H*, vol. 59, f. 37; *PDH*, doc. 393, pp. 391–92.

76. Circular telegram from Paléologue (June 22, 1920), *AD*, Europe 1918–29, *H*, vol. 59, f. 37.

77. *Ibid.*

78. Memorandum from the French foreign ministry (June 9, 1920); this viewpoint is vigorously stressed in *AD*, Europe 1918–29; *H*, vol. 58, f. 205–6.

79. Memorandum from Csáky and Halmos to Paléologue (June 23, 1920), *AD*, Europe 1918–29; *H*, vol. 59, f. 44–45; *PDH*, doc. 405, pp. 404–8.

80. *PDH*, doc. 405, pp. 404–8.

81. Telegram from Millerand to Fouchet (June 26, 1920), *AD*, Europe 1918–29; *H*, vol. 59, f. 63–65; Memorandum from Laroche on the conversation he held with Csáky and Halmos (June 24, 1920), *ibid.*, f. 50–152. According to Laroche's memorandùm, Paléologue agreed to the observations connected with the memorandum. *Ibid.*

82. The Hungarian government requested France to further the revision of the military clauses of the Trianon peace, and the establishment of a conscript army in place of the prescribed mercenary army, because they maintained that the latter was unsuitable in the case of Hungary for the maintenance of public order and public security, as it made the economic reconstruction of the country impossible. *Ibid.*; *PDH*, doc. 405a, p. 408; Memorandum from Csáky and Halmos to Paléologue (June 23, 1920), *AD*, Europe 1918–29; *H*, vol. 59, f. 44–45.

83. The proposal was that the French government support Hungary in the retention of the Western Hungarian territories. In this way it could solidify its French political orientation, and prevent Austria, which sooner or later would join Germany anyway, from increasing its territory. *Ibid.* The Hungarian government's idea was—and Csáky informed Paléologue of this—that Teleki would report in parliament in response to an interpellation that Hungary did not intend to withdraw its troops from the Western territories, and Millerand would acknowledge this in some sort of declaration. *PDH*, doc. 361, pp. 365–68.

84. The request concerning the Hungarian minority was that the French government instruct the military missions in the neighboring states to

represent the interests of the Hungarians there. Memorandum from Csáky and Halmos to Paléologue (June 23, 1920), *AD*, Europe 1918–29; *H*, vol. 59, f. 44–45.

85. *AD*, Europe 1918–29, *H*, vol. 59.

86. "Montielle informed me today that both Vesnic and Beneš were enthusiastic about the idea of direct negotiations with Hungary under French auspices." *PDH*, doc. 418, p. 426. Montielle informed Praznovsky that ". . . the Rumanians were also pleased with the suggestion of French mediation, though their attitude was more reserved than that of the other. The Rumanians emphasized their hope that France will not take part in the negotiations as an ally of Hungry." *PDH*, doc. 455, pp. 458–59.

87. Memorandum from Praznovszky to the French foreign ministry (August 4, 1920), *AD*, Europe 1918–29; *Roumanie* (hereafter *R.*), vol. 50, f. 97–98; Report from Saint-Aulaire to Millerand (August 12, 1920), *ibid.*, f. 109; Circular telegram from Paléologue (August 17, 1920), *ibid.*, f. 118.

88. Telegram from Praznovszky to Teleki (August 23, 1920), Hungary, Országos Levéltár, Külügyminisztérium (hereafter *O. K. KÜM*), K. 74-1920, Paris, Incoming cipher telegrams.

89. ". . . la situation est très grave. La Hongrie dans ses nouvelles frontières et sans accords économiques avec ses voisins ne peut vivre." Report of Count Saint-Sauveur (August 4, 1920), *AD*, Europe 1918–29; *H*, vol. 55, f. 169–77.

90. Saint-Sauveur's signature also figures on the document. The count arrived in Budapest on July 24. The agreement, however, was supposedly signed on the night of the 19th.

91. The Franco-Hungarian secret agreement, *AD*, Europe 1918–29, *H*, vol. 59, f. 181–92. This agreement does not figure among the documents published by the Hungarian foreign ministry. If one had existed, then the Hungarian government would have made it public in 1939. Today we know more about the true story of the Franco-Hungarian negotiations and see their background and aim more clearly; we see that, beyond promises and assurances, how far the directors of French diplomacy wanted to go on the question of revision, and we also have more precise information on the conditions they set. France concluded neither a political nor a military agreement with Hungary, but gave only a declaration of a political character, which implicitly included the possibility of territorial revision. Further, we know that Millerand stood essentially on the basis of the given status quo, and considered only minor border corrections. Paléologue, on the other hand, went further than this in the revision of the peace treaty: he regarded even more far-reaching border adjustments as permissible. He even expressed this verbally on several occasions to the members of the Hungarian delegation. Thus, he informed Csáky on June 20, 1920, why he had left out of the written declaration the earlier phrase protecting the basic structure of

the peace. Csáky's report reads: "Paléologue intimated that the omission of the phrase signifies the willingness of the French Government to overlook in our favour, if necessary, the general structure of the treaty." *PDH*, doc. 378, p. 378. This is also demonstrated by Paléologue's acceptance of Halmos's April 23 memorandum as basis for discussion. After Paléologue's fall they often spoke openly in the house of representatives about the efforts of the former permanent secretary of foreign affairs in this direction; see Paul-Boncour's remarks: Chambre des deputes, 1-re séance du mardi, 7. juin, 1921.

92. On this point see: Report of the French ambassador to Prague (August 9, 1920), *AD*, Europe 1918–29; *H*, vol. 59, f. 180; Report of the French ambassador to Prague (August 11, 1920), *ibid.*, f. 193l; Telegram from Pontalis, French ambassador to Vienna (August 13, 1920), *ibid.*, f. 196; Telegram from Charles Roux, French ambassador to Romania (August 30, 1920), *ibid.*, f. 208–9; Telegram from Fouchet, French high commissioner in Budapest (August 18, 1920), *ibid.*, f. 200; Telegram from Marcilly, France's representative in Berlin, to Millerand (June 4 and June 6, 1920), *ibid.*, vol. 58, f. 175–76, 189; Italy, *ASMAE*, SEria politica 1920–30, Ungheria 1920, pacco 1741, Telegrammi i portenza.

93. Report from Fouchet to Millerand (May 12, 1920), *AD*, Europe 1918–29, *H*, vol. 58, f. 154–62.

94. "La situation est très émouvante depuis le commencement de la semaine à cause des démarches et parait-it de l'arrogance de mon collegue anglais, qui a porté avant hier matin au Regent des offres de Londres." Report from Fouchet to Millerand (May 27, 1920), *AD*, Europe 1918–29; *H*, vol. 58, f. 146.

95. Telegram from Fouchet to Millerand (June 8, 1920), *AD*, Europe 1918–29; *H*, vol. 58, f. 198; *PDH*, doc. 315, p. 328. According to this paragraph of the peace treaty it would impound the state property of the country as security for reparations. The French government was aware that in reality the planned option conflicted with the decisions of the peace treaty concerning reparations. This is witnessed by a note to be found in the French foreign ministry, which contains the position of the legal expert. Note of June 9, 1920, *ibid.*, f. 204–'.

96. *PDH*, doc. 327, p. 328; Memorandum on Halmos's visit (June 9, 1920), *AD*, Europe 1918–29; *H*, vol. 58, f. 204; *PDH*, doc. 342, p. 349.

97. Telegram from Paléologue to Fouchet, *AD*, Europe 1918–29, *H*, vol. 58, f.

98. Note of June 8, 1920, *AD*, Europe 1918–29; *H*, vol. 58, f. 205.

99. *PDH*, doc. 415, pp. 421–23; Telegram from Martin to Sforza, July 14, 1920, Italy, *ASMAE*, Serie politica, Roumania 1920, pacco 1520, fasc. 6670.

100. The diplomats of the United States followed events closely, and filed reports on the negotiations. They did not protest officially against the

Franco-Hungarian combination. The American press, however, giving credence to the rumors of a secret agreement, attacked the French government, against which the Millerand faction protested.

101. Report of Joung, English ambassador to Belgrade, to Curzon (March 2, 1920), *DBFP*, doc. 120, pp. 149–54. We do not touch here on events connected with the formation of the Little Entente; on this see: Magda Adám, *Magyarország és a kisantant* (Budapest, 1968), pp. 9–40.

102. Telegram from Beneš (July 30, 1920), Czechoslovakia, *AMZV*, *PZ*, teleg. odesle.

103. Telegram from Torretta, Italian ambassador to Vienna (August 15, 1920), Italy, *ASMAE*, Serie Politica 1920–30, Cecoslovachia 1920, pacco 934, fasc.

104. Circular telegram from Millerand (August 24, 1920), *AD,*Europe 1918–29; *H*, vol. 47, f. 71–72. Osusky, Czechoslovak ambassador to Paris, gave an account in his reports of the attacks directed against Paléologue. The French permanent secretary for foreign affairs warned him that his government was following a dangerous path. Report of Osuský to Beneš, *PZ.*, Paris 1920, Aug. 20. In the Prague archives may be found several reports from the Czechoslovak ambassador to Paris, which reflect the French position concerning the developing Little Entente; see: Report from Osusky to Beneš (September 1, 5, 6, 7, 10, 1920), Czechoslovakia, *AMZV.*, *PZ.*, Paris, 1920.

Anne Orde

France and Hungary in 1920:
Revisionism and Railways

French policy in central Europe immediately after the peace conference has never been fully elucidated. It is generally accepted that
for a time the Prime Minister, Alexandre Millerand, and particularly
the Secretary-General of the Ministry of Foreign Affairs, Maurice
Paléologue, favoured making Hungary its pivot, that France did not
at first approve of the Little Entente formed to contain Magyar revisionism, and that things changed after Paléologue left the Quai d'Orsay in September 1920. But, confident statements by some writers
notwithstanding, a number of questions remain unresolved: for example whether the Hungarian policy formed part of a grand design
to recast the peace settlement, and whether Hungarian expectations
of help were based on real French promises.

Until fairly recently most of the documentation available was
Hungarian and obviously partisan.[2] Piotr S. Wandycz's authoritative *France and Her Eastern Allies*[3] was written before the French archives were opened. These throw a great deal more light on the subject, but still leave certain gaps due to inadequacies of recording. It is
the purpose of this article to explore French relations with Hungary
in the context of central Europe as a whole. Whilst the nature of
Paléologue's involvement remains rather obscure, it will be suggested that Hungarian expectations were much exaggerated, that the
change of course in the autumn of 1920 was neither an about-turn
nor due solely to Paléologue's resignation, and that French policy in
east central Europe lacked coordination.

During the war French governing and official circles had not been
anxious to break up the Habsburg Empire. In the end the French led
the way in recognizing the Czechoslovak National Council, but they
did not bring to the peace conference a plan for the settlement in

central Europe. French conservatives thought of a new Danubian union and criticized the settlement as it emerged from the conference; but the French delegation supported Czechoslovak claims against Hungary.[4] As the Italians, who were strongly opposed to anything like a revival of the Empire, were suspicious of French talk of a confederation while the French were opposed to a union between the new Austrian republic and Germany, the possibility of a bargain arose: France would not support a Danubian union if Italy would oppose an *Anschluss*.[5] It does not seem that there was ever an actual agreement to this effect, but there is evidence of a tacit understanding. Hungary seems to have been largely ignored by the French until after the fall of Bela Kun's communist régime, but in the winter of 1919 they began to think about it as a component in a barrier against Germany, a field of economic opportunity, and a source of trouble if not brought under French influence. French representatives in the region feared that Britain had got there first and was favouring the reactionaries. The author of a memorandum of early January 1920, advocating a French initiative, did so at least in part on the ground that French influence in Hungary would mean democracy.[6]

Britain was indeed at this time thought of as the special guardian of Hungary. The Allied flotilla on the Danube was commanded by a British admiral; an Englishman, Sir George Clerk, had been sent to Hungary by the Supreme Council in September 1919 to disentangle the political situation after the fall of Béla Kun; the Austrian section of the Reparation Commission (which at this time covered Hungary) was headed by another Englishman. Admiral Troubridge was accused of supporting the candidacy for the Hungarian throne of Archduke Joseph, head of a branch of the Habsburg family long settled in Hungary; and the British High Commissioner, T. B. Hohler, who arrived in Budapest early in 1920, was an old friend of Admiral Horthy, the Governor and alter Regent.[7] British firms were among the many active in central Europe hoping to buy up assets cheaply and take over from German interests. For example a group which included the shipowner and Minister of Munitions, Lord Inverforth, was seeking a controlling interest in Danube shipping, and early in 1920 asked (in vain) for British government guarantees of fiscal privilege in Austria.[8] All in all, although the Foreign Office did not pay much attention to Hungary, the French fears were not without colour.

The new Hungarian frontiers were adopted by the Supreme Council in the summer of 1919, but it was not until January 1920 that a Hungarian delegation arrived in Paris to be handed the peace terms. A group of businessmen arrived at about the same time: they had economic openings to offer and hoped that France would support improvements in the treaty. At this time, as was clear at the Allied conference in London in February and March, both the British and the Italians were more willing than the French to consider revising the territorial provisions: the suggestion eventually embodied in the Allied note of 6 May, that the commissions entrusted with frontier demarcation could suggest minor modifications, came from the British.[9] About the middle of March, however, there began intensive negotiations for economic concessions to a group headed by Schneider-Creusot, in return for which, the Hungarians hoped, the French Government would take the lead in securing extensive territorial revisions. The initiative seems to have been taken by Dr. Charles Halmos, a lawyer and member of the Hungarian business group, who evidently fancied himself as a political intermediary. The Hungarian version of events is that Halmos obtained from Paléologue a promise to encourage negotiations with Hungary's neighbours and a forecast that if the economic concessions were granted, Hungary would be made the centre of a new combination in central Europe. After visiting Budapest Halmos gave Paléologue a list of the Hungarian desiderata: territory including the Grosse Schütt island, Bratislava and southern Slovakia, Ruthenia or at least a plebiscite there, parts of Transylvania, the Baczka and southern Baranya; also autonomy for minorities in Rumania, plebiscites in west Hungary and the Banat, and economic facilities. In reply Paléologue is said to have given Halmos a note, dated 15 April, setting out the bases for a Hungarian-Rumanian agreement meeting most of the wishes that concerned Rumania, stating that there would be a Franco-Hungarian military and economic convention, and promising that the French Government would declare willingness to intervene in favour of Hungary and would carry out the plan when the note had been ratified by the Hungarian National Assembly.[10]

This document, which Deák treats as genuine despite the fact that its authenticity was denied, in 1927, by Halmos as well as by Paléologue, reads much more like a Hungarian than a French note. Even according to the Hungarians, Paléologue on all other occasions gave only general assurances and said the *rapprochement* would be a long-term affair; and no explanation is offered as to why, if this document is genuine, he should suddenly have committed himself so far. There is no copy of the note in the French archives, but they contain a letter from Halmos of 22 March with a memorandum on the bases for a Hungarian-Rumanian agreement which are identical with those of the supposed Paléologue note. In another letter Halmos summarized a conversation on 17 March in which Paléologue apparently offered help in bringing Hungary and her neighbours together but held out no hope of territorial changes. Paléologue gave Halmos an introduction to the French High Commissioner in Budapest, Maurice Fouchet, and told the Romanian Minister in Paris of the proposals. Fouchet reported that France was regarded as the chief author of the peace terms but the government was considering a *rapprochement* and he thought some gesture would be useful to secure the economic advantages.[11] Halmos, according to his own note, told Paléologue on 12 April that he could give complete satisfaction on economic matters and was charged by Horthy to convey approval of the orientation of Hungarian policy towards France and the political programme outlined so far, and pointed out that the Hungarian army would be available as soon as agreement was reached. On 14 April Halmos sent the Comte de Saint-Sauveur, a director of Schneider-Creusot, a note on the openings available to French groups: they included the state railways, state factories, construction of a Danube-Theiss canal, port works at Budapest, and privately-owned utilities. At a luncheon next day Paléologue listed concessions in which French firms might be interested, and agreed that the Schneider group would examine them at once. As for the political side, Halmos on 23 April sent Paléologue a note of what he, describing himself as Horthy's representative, proposed: a secret agreement that France would facilitate conversations between Hungary and her neighbours on frontier modifications, autonomy for minorities in Romania, plebiscites in several border areas, and economic advantages; and Hungary would put her economic and military forces at France's disposal, would be prepared to make alliances with states designated by France, and would give guarantees that arms supplied to her would not be used against France or France's allies. The agreement would come into force as soon as the French group took up the options under negotiation.[12]

Thus far it is clear from the French evidence that Paléologue was promoting the economic negotiations and had held out a prospect of Hungary playing a part in the new central european order. But that he had made specific offers or approved Hungarian territorial claims seems most unlikely, and this is indirectly confirmed by instructions given to Hungarian officials who were now sent to Paris. The Foreign Minister, Count Teleki, stated that the negotiations must be on the basis of reciprocal advantage, the concessions must all come into force together, and France must give some indication of how Hungary's neighbours were to be made to surrender territory. But the most important thing was to secure France's good will. The officials, Count Bethlen, Count Csáky and the director of the state railways, M. Tolnay, thought that Halmos had gone rather too far with Paléologue, especially in describing himself as Horthy's representative, and recommended that the options to be given to Schneider-Creusot should be made conditional on some definite political assurance from the French government. On 4 May agreement was reached on the French group taking over the Hungarian railways; but on the political side Csáky and Bethlen got no more from Paléologue than an assurance that the French government would express willingness to promote agreements between Hungary and her neighbours.[13]

The final peace terms, little altered from those of January, were handed to the Hungarian delegation on 6 May. They caused great agitation in Budapest, but the government attached much weight to the promise in the Allied covering letter, that the frontier demarcation commissions would be able to suggest minor adjustments. The fact that the letter was signed by Millerand enabled the Hungarians to regard it as evidence of French good will. More concretely, the French undertook that if the peace treaty was signed and the economic deals concluded, they would declare that France was ready to facilitate conversations between Hungary and her neighbours, and to lend her good offices to any agreements which, without affecting the general structure of the treaty, would correct minor injustices.[14] Fouchet read the draft declaration to Horthy and his ministers on 18 May, with encouraging effect; and the peace treaty was signed on 4 June.

By this time the negotiations had become public knowledge and Teleki was subjected, according to Fouchet, to public anger and British efforts to discredit France. Rumours had begun to reach the British in Budapest in the middle of April but the ambassador in Paris, Lord Derby, whilst prepared to believe that French officials had used language that might have encouraged the Hungarians, could see no sign of French efforts to alleviate the peace terms.[15] The reports multiplied and became increasingly circumstantial, until finally the Hungarian Prime Minister confirmed to Hohler on 26 May that negotiations were taking place and said that he supposed the Allies had come to some arrangement. The Foreign Office did not take very seriously the alleged French offer to obtain territorial revisions, but Hohler was instructed to tell the Hungarians that there was no Anglo-French understanding and the reported offers were contrary to the terms of the peace treaty.[16] As for the public, according to Teleki 'responsible circles' in Budapest were saying that even a guarantee of territorial integrity—in other words, restoration of the whole of the old kingdom of Hungary—would not compensate for loss of control over the railways. The Hungarian Government therefore redoubled its efforts to pin the French down to a precise commitment, while the French demanded written confirmation that Horthy approved the business deals. Eventually on 21 June options were handed over, for the lease of the state railways and locomotive works, for the construction of a port at Budapest, and for control of the General Credit Bank. Next day Fouchet conveyed the French declaration, which spoke in general terms of the government's conviction that prosperity and peace in central Europe depended on the collaboration of all the states concerned, of its readiness to facilitate conversations between Hungary and her neighbours and to lend its good offices to any friendly agreement to correct minor injustices in accordance with the Allied letter of 6 May, and especially its willingness to facilitate discussions about restoring communications. The declaration would come into force when the economic agreements had been ratified. Paléologue refused to make any more definite promises, but Fouchet thought it important to give the Hungarians something quickly. He reported their immediate wishes as permission to recruit the army by conscription, delay (at least) in handing over the western counties allotted to Austria, speedy Romanian and Yugoslav evacuation of occupied territory, early examination of minorities questions, and making Budapest the headquarters of the International Commission on the Danube.[17]

These requests, and one for a separate Hungarian section of the Reparation Commission, were repeated formally after the options were handed over. Paléologue approved the comment of Quai d'Orsay officials, that France was not responsible for imposing the system of voluntary recruitment for the armies of the defeated countries but believed that the same system must apply to all of them. She must not take the initiative but could agree to examine the question provided a modification did not endanger any other country. No promise could be given on the western counties nor any initiative taken on the evacuation of occupied territory. France could not intervene on behalf of Magyar minorities as such but could try to rectify injustices both in occupied territory and, for Allied subjects, in Hungary itself. There was no objection to the International Commission having its seat at Budapest, and a separate section of the Reparation Commission could be welcomed. On 24 June Laroche, the assistant Political Director, tried to explain to Csáky and Halmos what could and could not be done. Eventually they accepted his assurance that Hungary would be treated impartially, but said that if the options were to be ratified Hungarian opinion must be given something to show that a pro-French orientation was worth-while. Laroche conceded this, but said that the French Government could not make statements that would be interpreted as a change of policy and abandonment of France's allies.[18]

Where, as in the case of this conversation, it is possible to compare Hungarian and French accounts directly, it becomes obvious that the Hungarians put the most favourable possible construction on French statements. A striking feature of the whole story is indeed the Hungarians' wishful thinking. Sir George Clerk had commented in the previous November on their delusion that the Allies needed peace more than they did.[19] Now it was not just Halmos, politically inexperienced and self-important, who seems to have believed it possible to get the peace terms changed or ignored. Teleki evidently shared the illusion: his attempts to get a statement as to how the desired promises were to be carried out betray some doubt about French ability to control the countries concerned—doubt which was certainly justified in view of the difficulty the Supreme Council had had in controlling the Romanian advance in the autumn of 1919—but not enough doubt as to whether the promises were within the French Government's power to make. The explanation is presumably that the Hungarian political class was both desperate and ignorant. It had not yet met the new Europe; it was devoted to the unitary kingdom of St. Stephen; the economy was in a state of collapse; and so it overcame its hesitations about the concessions and clutched at any hope of outside aid. As for what the French promised, there is no reason to think that it was anything specific. That general assurances of good will were given is not in question. From the French point of view there was no ground for lasting hostility to Hungary. Even if the idea of a confederation had been abandoned, including her in a new regional system made good sense, and geographically Budapest was a suitable centre. But if the Hungarians believed that meant French help in overturning the peace settlement, they were victims of their own desires more than of changes in French diplomacy. Their boasting of French support helped to create the coalition of their enemies; but Paléologue was far too experienced to make rash promises, and even before his departure, the support the Hungarians actually received was small.

On the economic side Schneider-Creusot and French banks were building an empire in central Europe. The Schneider group's most important undertakings, however, were in Czechoslovakia, and they were not able ultimately to exploit all the available openings.[20] Hungarian assets were on offer to the highest bidder. When in July British representatives tried to explain that France had no power to promise to alter the territorial provisions of the treaty, and alienation of state assets seemed incompatible with the reparation clauses, the Hungarians simply asked for British counter-offers.[21]

The French Government informed other countries in the region about the economic agreements and the declaration of 22 June. Csáky, who saw the instructions, told his government that they were extensive, which was hardly true; but the Polish Foreign Minister regarded the *rapprochement* as important. The Hungarians in Paris also reported that the Czechoslovak and Yugoslav Governments were keen to negotiate under French auspices, and the Romanians willing.[22] Although Benes, the Czechoslovak Foreign Minister, was ready to discuss restoring communications, his enthusiasm for negotiations may be doubted, as also his professed unconcern at the Franco-Hungarian agreements; for the declaration, although general, was benevolent, and the Czechs had reason to feel alarm at Hungarian attempts to profit from the Soviet-Polish war. The Hungarians had for some time thought of Poland as a possible ally. Early in May Halmos told the Polish Foreign Minister that Hungary could offer military help against the Bolsheviks, a share in the French business options, and support against Czechoslovakia, in return for Polish support in her negotiations and help in equipping the army. The Poles, although cautious, apparently promised to help with arms; and they extolled to the French Minister in Warsaw the advantages of a Polish-Romanian-Hungarian entente.[23]

The Russian counter-offensive against Poland, which began in June, stimulated Hungarian offers of help. The French were well aware that the chief motive was a hope of recovering Ruthenia and at least part of Slovakia, but some, like Fouchet, thought that Hungary offered a better barrier against both Bolshevism and Germany than did Czechoslovakia. Whilst not taking up the Hungarian offers, the French Government used them to press Benes to ensure the defence of the Carpathians.[24] As the Russian advance continued, Czechoslovakia on 7 August declared neutrality and prevented the transport of arms to Poland. The Hungarian Government asked for arms and sent Halmos to Paris with the chief of Horthy's military cabinet, Baron Lang. Millerand and Paléologue were not anxious to see them but Lang was allowed to talk to General Desticker, Foch's chief of staff. He was at first encouraging and, according to Csáky, said that the Czechs would be dropped if necessary. But after the Polish victory outside Warsaw the tone changed, and at the end of August all that Desticker—mindful of French armament interests—would promise was help in equipping the Hungarian army to the extent allowed by the peace treaty.[25]

Hungarian activity during the Polish crisis precipitated the Czechoslovak-Yugoslav alliance, the first stage of the Little Entente. The idea of close co-operation between the successor states of the Austro-Hungarian Monarchy was not new: Czechoslovakia, Romania and Yugoslavia collaborated at the peace conference, and by May 1920 there was talk of an agreement between them. In the last week of July a Czechoslovak-Yugoslav alliance was said to be imminent. However Benes went first to Austria where the Chancellor, the Social Democrat Karl Renner, gave him copies of two purported Franco-Hungarian secret treaties, said to have been signed at Gödöllö on 23 July. One leased the Hungarian state railways and provided for military collaboration; the other gave France the oversight of Hungarian domestic affairs and abandoned sovereignty over the railways in return for French agreement to extensive frontier revision. Beneš told the French Minister in Prague, Couget, that he knew enough about the real Franco-Hungarian agreements not to be worried; but Renner was very much alarmed, and despite an official French denial of the treaty's authenticity he allowed them to be published in his party's newspaper, justifying his action by the continual Hungarian threats and boasts of French support.[26]

In Belgrade on 14 August Benes signed a defensive alliance naming

Hungary as a possible aggressor. But for the time being his Romanian opposite number, Take Ionesco, would agree only to a protocol
on neutrality in the Russo-Polish war and an oral promise of mutual
assistance in case of Hungarian attack. Even though Romania was
not fully committed, and it was not certain that other countries
would not join, the system that quickly became known as the Little
Entente was effectively born; and it was almost immediately said to
be directed against French patronage of Hungary.[27] Although Benes
presented it as something constructive, the step was unwelcome in
Paris and was thought to cut across French policy. The Ministers in
Warsaw and Athens were instructed to advise the Polish and Greek
Governments not to join, because the system isolated Hungary; the
Minister in Vienna, Lefèvre-Pontalis, assumed that it was fundamen-
tally anti-French; and Fouchet considered that Benes had not served
French interests. French representatives in Czechoslovakia,
however, were surprised at the expressions of disapproval. General
Pellé, the head of the military mission, wrote that he had explained
Czech intentions when he had been in Paris in July, and Millerand
had not only not objected but had suggested extending the agree-
ment. Couget thought that its timing had given the agreement a pro-
Bolshevik appearance which the authors never intended.[28]

One of the objections voiced in France was that the Little Entente
cut across efforts to build an anti-Bolshevik combination of Poland,
Romania and Hungary in which Poland and Romania would col-
laborate with the last White forces in Russia (those of General
Wrangel, whom France had just recognized), and even
Czechoslovakia and Yugoslavia would join.[29] But such ideas were
far-fetched. Millerand was indeed more interested in Russia than in
Poland, but the Poles had no desire to co-operate with Wrangel and
were now inclined to make peace with the Soviet Government; the
Romanians had no desire to fight; Czechoslovakia was afraid of
Polish adventurism; Poland was resentful of Czech behaviour over
the war with Russia and about Teschen. It cannot be said that it was
the formation of the Little Entente that frustrated French aims.
Another suggestion was that the Little Entente was a product of, or
at least supported by, Italian intrigue. In their hostility to anything
resembling a Danubian confederation the Italians were suspicious of
all attempts to encourage co-operation in the region. By 1920 the
French Government had realized that there was no chance of the successor states agreeing to a confederation, but it favoured economic

co-operation and said so when occasion offered, while the Italians were accused of stirring up the Danubian states against each other. There was talk in Vienna and Budapest of Italy having been behind Benes's meeting with Renner: the Italian press expressed satisfaction at French disapproval of the Little Entente.[30]

Partly for this reason some French representatives thought it a mistake to betray hostility and to overdo the Hungarian policy. The chargé d'affaires in Rome, Charles-Roux, considered that friction with Italy in the Danubian area was inevitable, despite any tacit bargain over a confederation and Austrian independence, because Italy wanted a dominant position in the region and would be upset whenever she found France in the way.[31] To the Foreign Office it seemed that the Little Entente might be an obstacle to both French and Italian intrigue, and they were prepared to approve it so long as it was purely defensive and was based on the maintenance of the peace treaties. Lloyd George, however, warned Take Ionesco against admitting Poland, which he regarded as a source of trouble. Having earlier in the summer not taken very seriously the reports of Franco-Hungarian agreements, the Foreign Office was prompted by the stories of a secret treaty to make an official enquiry in Paris. The French replied that there was no treaty, no political promises had been given to Hungary, and there was no intention of breaching the Treaty of Trianon.[32]

On 25 September, following Millerand's election as President of the Republic, Paléologue resigned from the Quai d'Orsay. By this time Wrangel's forces were isolated in the Crimea, and shortly afterwards the Polish-Russian preliminaries of peace were signed. There were soon signs of a shift in French policy. The new Secretary-General, Philippe Berthelot, was regarded as pro-Czech. The press began to write more favourably of the Little Entente, and at the beginning of October the Polish Foreign Minister was startled to be told that France did not oppose Poland's making peace with Russia and joining the Little Entente. The obstacles to the latter were too great; but the French encouraged the Polish-Romanian agreement which Take Ionesco hoped would form part of a combination between all the victors in central and eastern Europe.[33] There was no French intention of dropping Hungary, but greater caution was shown over semi-official dealings. When Fouchet reported at the end of September that Halmos was coming to Paris again to talk about army recruitment, he was told that there could be no such discussions when Hungary had not ratified the peace treaty. The Ambassadors' Conference had recently taken up this matter, but at first neither the French nor the Italians pressed the Hungarians very hard, and the latter made great efforts to secure prior concessions and assurances, especially over the army, the frontier commissions, and a separate section of the Reparation Commission. Athelstan-Johnson, the British chargé d'affaires in Budapest, commented that in view of its earlier assertions that changes in the peace terms would be secured, the Hungarian Government badly needed something to show to public opinion. Fouchet thought that it would be very useful if any concessions could be seen to come from France; and the Hungarian representative in Paris pointed out that the economic concessions depended on the political programme.[34] The Allies refused to allow changes in the army: Laroche told Halmos that while France was not responsible for imposing voluntary recruitment, it could not be changed now. He also said that the demarcation commissions could not be appointed until the treaty came into force; but the names of the French members might be announced when Hungary ratified. Baron Lang had to be content with a statement that France did not refuse to supply equipment within the treaty limits. Finally the Hungarians asked the Ambassadors' Conference for assurances that the successor states were being asked to treat former Hungarian subjects with moderation, and that steps were being taken to implement the promise in the Allied letter of 6 May. These assurances were given, and on 13 November the Hungarian National Assembly assented to ratification.[35]

Although Fouchet still worked for French influence, the Schneider-Creusot options expired in the middle of November without being taken up: the affair which had caused so much excitement seemed to have vanished like smoke. The group's resources were not large enough for all the contemplated enterprises, and the Ministry of Finance refused to provide government money.[36] When Briand took office in France in January 1921 French policy was clarified. The Quai d'Orsay admitted that a fear that France was helping Hungary had probably contributed to the formation of the Little Entente. This had been a misunderstanding, spread by the Hungarians themselves: the French Government had never admitted the exaggerated expectations which the Hungarians had nurtured about the declaration of 22 June. Earlier suspicions had now been dispelled: France was above all loyal to the treaties and favoured her allies; but she wished to help

Hungary and Austria in order to prevent economic collapse and establish general pacification. Briand expressed to Benes "special sympathy" for the Little Entente; and after Halmos had turned up again with roposals for French intervention in Hungarian affairs and financial help, Fouchet was sent instructions on the attitude he was to adopt. He must avoid any appearance of favouring the monarchists, for the Allies would not accept any Habsburg and understanding between them in central Europe, based on respect for the peace treaties, was improving. The ex-enemy states had to be convinced that the treaties must be carried out. There might one day be some agreed improvements to Hungary's frontiers but she must first earn the Allies' confidence by showing her intention to fulfil her obligations. France would encourage economic co-operation but would not be drawn into a policy of treaty revision, and Fouchet must be on his guard against attempts to misrepresent French intentions.[37]

The Hungarians, however, did not give up lightly. At the time of the ex-Emperor Charles's attempt, in March, to return to Hungary, it was rumoured that he had been encouraged by Briand.[38] Afterwards the Hungarian Government sent first Halmos and then Teleki to Paris to ask for help in avoiding execution of the peace treaty. But Teleki was given no hope that France could do more than encourage conversations with Hungary's neighbours about practical matters; and Loucheur, the Minister for Liberated Territories who had connections in French heavy industry, was discouraged from seeing Halmos.[39] The story of the supposed secret treaty took some years to die.[40] Hungary fared no better with Poland. In the second half of 1921 Polish-Czechoslovak relations improved: as Panafieu commented, the idea of a Polish-Hungarian-Romanian bloc was now admitted to be a chimera; and although the *rapprochement* did not last, Poland's attitude was more favourable to the Little Entente than to Hungary during the crisis in October over the ex-Emperor's second return.[41] The only remaining possible friend was Italy, and she seemed uncertain whether leadership in central Europe could best be achieved by blocking reconstruction, courting the Little Entente, or supporting Hungary in mediating over the frontier with Austria.[42]

The handling of the ex-Emperor's second venture put some strain on relations between the major Allies and the Little Entente. It also confirmed that group's cohesion and its weight in the Danubian area. A couple of months later Benes remarked to Couget that he would like in future to concert on such problems in advance. He hoped France would be disposed to support the Little Entente: sentiment apart, it was in her interest to consolidate the new order created by the peace treaties.[43] Having signed with Austria an agreement on recognition of territories and mutual support, Benes believed he had included that country in the Little Entente orbit. Hungary's isolation seemed complete, apart perhaps from Italy. French policy now settled into the pattern of the eastern alliances, although French representatives in Budapest continued to think that Italian patronage was not welcomed there, and that Hungary could, given some good will, be reconciled to her neighbours.[44]

It is difficult to see much evidence of a French grand design in central Europe in 1919–20. Rhetoric about creating a United States of Eastern Europe under French aegis or 'the continental hegemony which victory ought to assure us'[45] was not lacking, but it had little foundation. Was this due to lack of planning or to lack of means? The answer would seem to be both. Between about March and September 1920, the effort put into gaining influence in Hungary was considerable, and greater than the country's own economic importance warranted. On the other hand the effort put into co-ordinating the region was small. If Millerand and Paléologue had a scheme, they did not develop it even within their own ministry: Hungary remained virtually a case apart. But if the French had tried to promote a new Danubian system centred on Budapest they would certainly have failed. The other countries concerned were in no mood to give up any of their new territory or independence, and none of the great powers had the means to compel them. Hungary was largely responsible for her own isolation: as long as the Hungarians intransigently rejected the Treaty of Trianon so long, as Benes warned Couget, would patronage of Hungary alienate the other successor states. France was never able to overcome the mutual distrust of her two eastern allies: she would have been no more able to impose a plan on central Europe.

Notes

1. My thanks are due to the British Academy and the University of Durham for grants which facilitated the research on which this article is based.

2. Hungary, Ministry of Foreign Affairs, *Papers and Documents relating to the Foreign Relations of Hungary*, Vol. I, 1919–1920, eds. Francis Deák and Dezső Ujváry (Budapest 1939), henceforth cited as *FRH*; also Francis Deák, *Hungary at the Paris Peace Conference* (New York 1942).

3. Minneapolis 1962.

4. See Wandycz, *France and her Eastern Allies*, 3-26, 62-74; and a recent study of British policy, Wilfried Fest, *Peace or Partition* (London 1978).

5. See France, Archives of the Ministère des Affaires Étrangères, series Europe 1919–1929, Autriche Vols. 3, 61-2; series Paix, Vols. 99–100; and Barrère (Rome) to Paris, 2 June 1919, series Europe, Italie Vol. 89, Hongrie Vol. 55; Paris to Barrère, 17 June, Hongrie Vol. 55. Documents in the series Europe 1919–1929 are henceforth identified as MAE, with country and volume number.

6. Reports from Vienna, Bucharest, Budapest and Prague, October–December 1919, in MAE, Hongrie Vol. 46, Autriche Vol. 62; memorandum, 5 January 1920, Hongrie Vol. 58.

7. See *Documents on British Foreign Policy 1919–1939*, eds. E. L. Woodward and R. D'O. Butler, and others (London 1947 ff.), Series I, henceforth cited as *DBFP*, Vol. VI, ch. 1; Vol. XII, No. 120.

8. See Public Record Office, London, FO 371/3550, file 168474/3, 1920 (documents in the Public Record Office are henceforth identified by file number, class and volume number); *DBFP*, Vol. VI, Nos. 50, 166, 299; Vol. XII, Nos. 70, 109, 161, 185, 189.

9. Discussion on Hungary at the conference of London, *DBFP*, Vol. VII, Nos. 26, 46, 54, 63, 65.

10. *FRH*, Political diary of the peace delegation, and Nos. 218, 224, 226, 242.

11. Halmos to Paléologue, 18 and 22 March 1920; minutes by Paléologue, 23 and 24 March; Paléologue to Fouchet (Budapest), 30 March; Fouchet to Paris, 5, 9, and 10 April, MAE, Hongrie Vol. 58.

12. Halmos to Paléologue, 13 April 1920; Halmos to Saint-Sauveur, 14 April; minute, 15 April; Halmos to Paléologue, 23 April, MAE, Hongrie Vol. 58; *FRH*, No. 255 enclosure.

13. *FRH*, Nos. 240, 242, 245, 247, 255, 259.

14. Fouchet to Paris, 8 May 1920; Halmos to Paléologue, 12 May; Paris to Fouchet, 13 May; Fouchet to Paris, 19 May; Paris to Fouchet, 28 and 30 May, MAE, Hongrie Vol. 58; *FRH*, Nos. 265–301; Allied covering letter in Deák, *Hungary at the Paris Peace Conference*, 551-54.

15. Fouchet to Paris, 30 May and 2 June 1920, MAE, Hongrie Vol. 58; 191329, 192091, 193530, 194177/7067/39, FO 371/4268.

16. Correspondence, 3 May-6 June 1920, file 196614/3, FO 371/3560; 197112, 198639/7067/39, FO 371/4269.

17. Correspondence, 2-17 June 1920, MAE, Hongrie Vols. 58-9; *FRH* Nos. 308-93.

18. Correspondence, 23-24 June 1920, MAE, Hongrie Vol. 59; *FRH*, No. 405.

19. *DBFP*, Vol. VI, No. 291 and n. 2.

20. For French investment in east central Europe see F. Gregory Campbell, 'The struggle for Upper Silesia 1919-22,' *Journal of Modern Hstory*, 42 (1970); Georges Soutou, 'La politique économique de la France en Pologne 1920-24,' *Revue historique*, 251 (1974): Alice Teichova, *An Economic Background to Munich. International Business and Czechoslovakia 1918-1938* (London 1974).

21. Correspondence, 18 June-6 August 1920, in file 196614/3, FO 371/4855-6; *DBFP*, Vol. XII, Nos. 184-86, 192; Fouchet to Paris, 30 June and 3 July, MAE, Hongrie Vol. 59; *FRH*, Nos. 344, 420, 433. British interests had been credited with plans for a port at Budapest earlier in the year: see *DBFP*, Vol. XII, No. 120.

22. Circular telegram, 22 June 1920, MAE, Hongrie Vol. 59; *FRH*, Nos. 387, 418, 455; Wandycz, *France and her Eastern Allies*, 190.

23. Note by Halmos, 8 May 1920, MAE, Hongrie Vol. 58; Panafieu (Warsaw) to Paris, 16 June, POlogne Vol. 71; Wandycz, op. cit., 191-92.

24. Correspondence, 19-29 July 1920, in MAE, Hongrie Vol. 47, Russie Vol. 290, Tchécoslovaquie Vol. 65; *FRH*, Nos. 451, 471, 492, 501, 523. The allocation of most of the Teschen area to Czechoslovakia was announced on 27 July: Wandycz, op. cit., 157-60.

25. Correspondence, 4-11 August 1920, in MAE, Hongrie Vol. 47, Roumanie Vol. 50; *DBFP*, Vol. XII, Nos. 198, 208, 217; *FRH*, Nos. 550-615 passim.

26. Correspondence, 20 July-17 August 1920, in MAE, Tchécoslovaquie Vol. 65, Hongrie Vol. 59, Autriche Vol. 63; C 3910/3910/12, FO 371/4722. For the origins of the Little Entente see also the Czechoslovak White Book *Documents diplomatiques relatifs aux conventions d'alliance conclues par la République Tchécoslovaque avec le Royaume des Serbes, Croates et Slovènes et le Royaume de Roumanie, décembre 1919-août 1921* (Prague 1922); Albert Mousset, *La Petite Entente* (Paris 1923), 17-21; Robert Machray, *The Little Entente* (London 1929), 118-26; Eduard Benes, *Five Years of Czechoslovak Foreign Policy* (Prague 1924), 12-13; Felix Vondracek, *The Foreign Policy of Czechoslovakia 1918*-1935 (New York, 1937), 104-05.

27. Wandycz, op. cit., 193-94; Fontenay (Belgrade) to Paris, 15 August 1920; Pellé to Paris, 23 August, MAE, Tchécoslovaquie Vol. 65; *DBFP*, Vol. XII, No. 215; C 5064/4025/19, FO 371/4700.

28. Correspondence, 24 August-25 September 1920, in MAE, Tchécoslovaquie Vol. 65.

29. Correspondence, 28 August-28 September 1920, in MAE, Russie Vol. 295, Roumainie Vol. 35, Tchécoslovaquie Vol. 65.

30. Correspondence, 5 January-30 August 1920, in MAE, Hongrie Vols. 45, 58–59, Autriche Vol. 63, Italie Vol. 79, Tchécoslovaquie Vol. 65.

31. Correspondence, 4–20 September 1920, in MAE, Tchécoslovaquie Vol. 65, Hongrie Vols. 48, 60, Italie Vol. 79; *DBFP*, Vol. XII, No. 221.

32. *DBFP*, Vol. VII, No. 92; Vol. XII, Nos. 242, 244; C 5737, 7593, 8479, 8515, 8791, 8858/137/21, FO 371/4865. For Lloyd George's attitude to Poland see Norman Davies, 'Lloyd George and Poland 1919–20,' *Journal of Contemporary History*, 6, 3 (1971).

33. Paris to Panafieu, 1 October 1920, MAE, Russie Vol. 296; Panafieu to Paris, 4 October, Tchécoslovaquie Vol. 65. Correspondence on Polish-Rumanian negotiations, November 1920-February 1921 in Pologne Vols. 71–72; Wandycz, op. cit., 201–07.

34. Correspondence, 25 September-25 October 1920, in MAE, Hongrie Vol. 60; *DBFP*, Vol. XII, Nos. 216, 224, 232, 238; *FRH*, Nos. 601, 726.

35. Memoranda by Praznovsky, 25 October 1920; memorandum by Laroche, 27 October, MAE, Hongrie Vol. 60; *DBFP*, Vol. XII, Nos. 237, 245, 247, 259, 261, 275; *FRH*, Nos. 727–819, passim.

36. Fouchet to Paris, 30 October 1920, MAE, Roumanie Vol. 50; Fouchet to Paris, 6, 7, and 15 November, Hongrie Vol. 60. The Schneider group later got a contract for a smaller harbour scheme at Budapest, and the Union Parisienne kept an interest in the General Credit Bank.

37. Quai d'Orsay memorandum, 15 January 1921; Paris to Fouchet, 18 February, MAE, Hongrie Vol. 60; Wandycz, op. cit., 207. In addition to an agreement on frontiers and Fiume, Italy and Yugoslavia signed in November 1920 an undertaking to watch over the maintenance of the peace treaties and to take measures in common to prevent a Habsburg restoration in Austria or Hungary. The convention was made binding as between Italy and Czechoslovakia when it was ratified at the beginning of February 1921. The Franco-Polish alliance was signed on 19 February.

38. C 6800, 6821, 7409, 8422/180/21, FO 371/6102; Wandycz, op. cit., 240–01. Briand was known to be pro-Habsburg but the Foreign Office did not believe that he had been involved.

39. Correspondence, 16 April-27 June 1921, MAE, Hongrie Vols. 49, 61.

40. See for example Fouchet to Paris, 3 May 1921; De Monicault (Bucharest) to Paris, 21 July, MAE, Hongrie Vol. 61. In the autumn of 1927 an extreme right-wing Hungarian newspaper published the supposed note of 15 April 1920 and said it was signed by Paléologue and an unidentifiable Sir Francis Barker. The authenticity of the document was denied all round, even by Halmos. The Hungarian Government then published the French declaration of 22 June. See Hongrie Vol. 62; file C 5327/21, FO 371/12586.

41. Panafieu to Paris, 10 August 1921, MAE, Pologne Vol. 72; Wandycz, op. cit., 207 n. 108, 240–53.

42. Correspondence in MAE, Italie Vol. 79, Tchécoslovaquie Vol. 66, Autriche Vol. 85, Hongrie Vol. 56. The British also found Italian policy in the area dubious. For the Burgenland settlement see C. A. Macartney, *Hungary and her Successors* (London, 1937), 54–60.

43. Couget to Paris, 18 January 1922, MAE, Tchécoslovaquie Vol. 67. For the crisis over the ex-Emperor's second return see *Survey of International Affairs 1920–1923* (London 1927), 292–98.

44. See for example Doulcet (Budapest) to Paris, 11 January 1922, MAE, Hongrie Vol. 56; Vienne (Budapest) to Paris, 20 June 1927, Tchécoslovaquie Vol. 70.

45. *Ere nouvelle,* 3 September 1920; Fouchet to Paris, 6 November, MAE, Hongrie Vol. 60.

Zsuzsa L. Nagy

Italian National Interests and Hungary in 1918-1919

Hungarian-Italian ties over the centuries still have little-known, scarcely investigated aspects, such as the relationship between the two countries in the eventful crisis year immediately following World War I.[1] The picture provided us by the Hungarian archives, by published sources (from which precisely the Italians seem practically omitted), and by the general literature and contemporary press would be complete only after the disclosure of pertinent materials in Italian, Yugoslav, and other archives. Thus, my article can do no better than approximate the designs, the relations of the respective governments and other official entities.

The Period of the Bourgeois Democratic Revolution

World War I found Hungary and Italy as enemy states, members of two opposite camps. Italy assumed a place among the victorious great powers and, when the Austro-Hungarian Monarchy was forced to lay down its arms, the representatives of the general staff, common to both sides of the Monarchy, signed the armistice agreement proposed by the Italian generals at Padua.

In the Fall of 1918 the Italian government was transformed by way of a temporary solution to a rather chaotic entity; the political tendency which prevailed had as its objective the enhancement of Italy's diplomatic position, including the assumption of an anti-Slav posture, and the achievement of great power status for Italy. Prime Minister Vittorio Orlando and his Foreign Minister, Sydney Sonnino, found support for these goals among the military leaders.[2]

It seemed that the military defeat of the Monarchy and its dissolution could only facilitate such Italian ambitions. One of the specific Italian aims was to take possession of Fiume and, by the same token, to gain influence in the Adriatic and in Balkan affairs—an influence which Italy would have liked to extend to the entire Danube Basin, including Hungary. Italian officials were convinced that Italy, rather than France, deserved those rights in this part of Europe.[3]

Its great power partners, however, not only did not support Italian ambitions, but came up with claims of their own in this area; whereas the Italian claim to Fiume became the source of serious conflicts, of crises, and of the eventual fall of the Italian cabinet. The rivalry between France and Italy affected a number of countries and became one of the heaviest burdens East-Central European nations had to bear.[4]

Italy was most in need of scoring diplomatic victories. The poorest among the great powers, it was here that one would expect, in the aftermath of the war, social tensions, radicalization, a drift towards the left. The Italian government would have liked diplomatic victories in order to channel its internal difficulties, to make its citizens forget the misery of the war with the "fruits of victory." The officials placed the blame for their lack of success on the Anglo-Americans and the French. Mussolini and his circle, who were in the lead in instigating the masses against the allies, as well as being responsible for the attacks against the government, were wont to refer to the great powers as wolves, foxes, jackals.[5]

Italy's weak position, both on the domestic and international fronts, as well as the international ambitions of the Orlando government, made it absolutely necessary to seek partners in the Danube basin. Since it was strictly a matter of achieving power aims, of Realpolitik, we need not be surprised that the tactical maneuvers were full of what appear at first sight as incomprehensible and contradictory measures and statements. The main line of policy, consistently anti-French, prevailed throughout.

With regard to Yugoslavia the Italian objective was to weaken the new state, and thereby to roll back French influence in that area. Italy sought not only to take Fiume from Yugoslavia, but fomented its internal difficulties as well, exacerbating the Yugoslav-Romanian conflict (in the Banat), and preventing its cooperation with the neighboring states in general.[6]

Based on the relationship which evolved in the last years of the war, the Italian military mission in Czechoslovakia, under the command of General Piccione, and including Italian officers in the ranks of the Czechoslovak army, attempted to compete with the French for influence in that country.[7] Its attitude towards the Czechs, however, was not unambiguous. During the dispute over Tešin, for instance, Italy sided with the Poles rather than with the Czechs; Italy also took a clear stand against one of the pet projects of Beneš and his entourage, as well as of the French, i.e., the Czechoslovak-Yugoslav corridor between Austria and Hungary. At the same time it claimed credit for objecting to the corridor with the Hungarians who would have lost further significant territories thereby.[8] It is understandable, therefore, that Czech public opinion, already favorably disposed to the French, seeing the expected leadership of Czechoslovakia in the Danube basin jeopardized by the Italian attitude, did not spare the Italians its attacks. These attacks redoubled when it became clear that Italy was likewise striving to cooperate with Hungary.[9] As a result of this many-faceted Italian diplomacy, the most unlikely combinations of nations seemed possible at the time.[10]

Hungary could not be left out of the Italian projects. In spite of the promises made by the allies, and the latest claims, at the end of 1918 Fiume still remained formally part of Hungary, and it was not possible to predict whether or not the Hungarian government would have a say regarding the fate of the port city. Furthermore, Hungary was important from the Italian point of view both as a sphere of economic and political influence, and as the neighbor of Yugoslavia.

The bourgeois democratic regime which found itself completely isolated, and treated as the regime of a defeated state, without international relations, attached great importance to any step which might lead to the establishment of contact with the allies, or perhaps even to concrete support from one of the great powers. But there were so many obstacles to such prospects that any development in this area seemed beyond the possible. Károlyi and his entourage were known at home during the war as partisans of democratic transformation and of a pro-Entente orientation; on the other hand, they lost their western contacts in the decisive period, during the last two years of the war. The great powers and their lesser allies gave absolutely no credence to Károlyi's pro-Entente politics and viewed the democratic transformation and its possible further evolution with the greatest concern. The oath to the Habsburg king and Jászi's nationalities' policy made a deeper impression abroad than the Hungarian government expected. The fact that the government did not elaborate a foreign policy beyond its generally pro-Entente attitude and its faith in Wilson—an attitude which would have coped with the given realities—constituted a further difficulty.

Thus at the first signs of interest shown by Italy, the Hungarian government reacted favorably, and the settlement of the fate of Hungarian employees and institutions in Fiume provided the occasion for the establishment of legal relations. Hence in December 1918 Jászi sent Lajos Fülep to Fiume as the representative of the Hungarian government.[11] Before his departure Fülep consulted not only with Jászi but also with Dénes Berinkey the under-secretary for internal affairs. Fülep's mission was not precisely defined, but he was given authorization for further, favorable negotiations on behalf of Hungary.[12]

At that time Fiume was occupied by allied troops; the commander of the Italian units and the most prestigious member of the Entente mission was General Francesco Saverio Grazioli who declared to Fülep, at their very first meeting, that the Italians were willing to engage in further negotiations with the Hungarian government, and that, in order to promote a rapprochement, "it might be advisable if Italian troops were dispatched to Budapest."[13]

The background of this proposal was that only *French* troops were stationed in Hungary (in Budapest and Szeged), whereas the Entente committee controlling the Danube was represented at Baja and Szabadka by *English* monitors; Italian participation also appeared advisable because of the model provided by the still promising military mission in Czechoslovakia.[14]

While Fülep was waiting for a reply and further instructions, he also negotiated with Prince Livio Borghese.[15] The Prince confirmed the inclination of his government to establish direct contact; what is more, he proposed to travel to Budapest himself in the near future to meet with Károlyi personally.[16]

Fülep found a connection with Prime Minister Orlando through Riccardo Zanella, who played a leading role in the Fiume council. Orlando approved of the continuation of the negotiations in "appropriate mode and form." Zanella also discussed with Orlando the advisability of sending Italian troops to Budapest, although this was not done at Fülep's suggestion. "It was not because of Bolshevism that he [Orlando] thinks the presence of Italian troops important, but rather—and a company would suffice for the purpose—to establish direct contact between Budapest and Rome. He would think it appropriate, however,"—Fülep reports—"if the President, even if it be in but a private letter to Orlando, should express his desire to that effect." We would derive no disadvantage from this, the Italians emphasized, because nobody would know about it apart from Orlando and Sonnino. In spite of this Fülep added: "On my part I would think it necessary—if indeed this project were to be realized—to combine it with the moves contemplated towards the British and the Americans, in order to avoid even the semblance of a special relationship with the Italians."[17]

Nevertheless, the negotiations broke off at this point. Fülep never received a reply to his reports; he repeatedly urged Károlyi to arrive at a decision, but in vain: "If no quick and meaningful step is taken," he warned, "[Italy] may well abandon any notion of rapprochement, which would be fatal, because so far the Italian government is the only one inclined to support the Hungarian cause at the peace conference. . . ."[18]

But in January 1919 the government had difficulty arriving at unambiguous resolutions for a number of reasons. It had no definite plans for taking advantage of the disagreements among the great powers, and it did not want to permanently commit itself on the side of Italy. The Italian proposal itself (the dispatch of troops) seemed rather worrisome. More importantly, the foreign policy of Károlyi and of the government aimed at winning the United States, and it did not wish to jeopardize this aim by an unduly explicit Italian orientation. Especially not at this time, when two missions under the leadership of Americans happened to be visiting Budapest, and the Hungarian leaders still hoped to bring about in this way decisive changes in Hungary's situation.

Another very significant interfering factor was that the Yugoslav leaders were beginning to take an interest in Hungary at this time. Their none-too-urgent or determined initiative elicited great hopes among Hungarian leaders, and figured heavily when they considered further negotiations with the Italians.

In his last report from Italy, dated January 20, Lajos Fülep, seeing the hesitations of the government and appraising the relation of forces correctly, wrote to Károlyi: "The consequence of our continued hesitation between a Yugoslav and an Italian orientation might be that we shall miss out on both of those possibilities."[19] Although he had received no instructions to that effect he traveled to Rome with the help of General Grazioli. Here, among old friends, he met first of all with Giovanni Amendola, and they attempted to formulate further negotiations with leading political figures together. When it appeared, however, that Budapest not only did not authorize these steps, but regarded them as strictly an individual endeavour and was prepared to disavow them, Fülep decided to return to Budapest.[20]

To drop Fülep, and to interrupt the talks at Fiume or in Rome (in consonance with the hesitating maneuvers of the government) did not imply the complete abandonment of Italian-Hungarian negotiations. On the contrary, these continued in January and February, this time in Vienna. The change of site was intended to avoid publicity. The discretion suited both parties because, as Zanella wrote to Budapest: "the men of the Entente, but especially the French, are watching closely. . . ." Precisely for this reason, while he advocated that the Hungarian press desist from its antagonistic tone in reporting and commenting on news from Italy, he immediately added: "But of course, not in such a manner as to awaken enemy suspicions that some kind of an agreement has been reached between Budapest and Rome. . . ."[21]

The negotiations could be conducted in Vienna for the Hungarian consulate could, without much ado, enter in touch with the Italian mission there under the command of General Roberto Segré. The mission was given ample propaganda material aimed at enhancing the popularity of the bourgeois democratic regime of Hungary abroad. Augusto Bianchieri Chiappori, Sonnino's secretary, was informed of the new Hungarian proposals.[22]

The government requested that Sonnino make it possible to establish direct relations via personal contact. The Hungarian consul in Vienna, Oszkár Charmant, reported to Károlyi on February 3, that "an answer has arrived from Sonnino. He cannot leave Paris now. But he wants to send a representative with whom, he says, we can discuss matters as if we were discussing them with him. The place of the meeting has not yet been determined. I believe Zurich may be the most appropriate place. From there it is possible to travel to Rome, if needed."[23]

All this, however, did not imply an unambiguous preference for Italian friendship. On the contrary; it seems that the interruption of contacts built up by Fülep, and its reconstruction along different lines, was meant to gain time while the Hungarian government was making progress in its contacts with Yugoslavia. The notion that the Yugoslav orientation was not only realistic but more beneficial than the Italian orientation could ever be, became stronger and prevailed in Hungarian foreign policy. The Hungarian government believed that since it had given up Croatia and other southern territories *a priori*, it may reach an agreement with Yugoslavia regarding certain debated areas even before the peace conference handed down its decision. And it saw the basis of further cooperation with Yugoslavia in the fact that the new state needed a "hinterland," whereas Hungary needed an outlet to the sea. Another significant factor was noted by Gyula Szillasy, the Hungarian consul in Bern, in his dispatches which analysed the relations between the great powers lucidly and realistically: in the Danube basin, including Hungary, Szillasy declared, it was the word of France that counted, hence an agreement and cooperation with Yugoslavia, which enjoyed French support, may influence French policy favorable.[24] The arguments of Szillasy found confirmation in the territorial offerings of Yugoslavia, and the whole perspective of cooperation.[25] The modest Italian proposal could not compete with these prospects.

Szilassy, much like Lajos Fülep, warned the Hungarian government about ambiguous experiments which could only end in failure; but, unlike Fülep, he definitely advocated cooperation with Yugoslavia.[26] Károlyi himself accepted this interpretation, and this determined further Italian-Hungarian relations.[27] Accordingly, when Marquis Tacoli arrived in Budapest, apparently in accordance with Sonnino's message, his proposal was accorded a cool reception, even though the notion of sending Italian troops to Budapest had been dropped completely. Tacoli proposed that if Hungary should not be able to hold on to Fiume at the peace conference "it should explicitly advocate that Fiume be attached to Italy." In return the Italians offered to establish a port with separate facilities for the Hungarians, and perhaps the recognition of the Hungarian flag on the high seas. Count Csáky, however, pointed out to the Marquis, that Hungary would prefer to see the area as an international port, for the road leading to it would have to go through Yugoslavia. This road of approach could not be guaranteed by Italy, and thus the port in itself would not be very valuable. According to Csáky, further exchanges of view could be fruitful only if "we could count on the positive support of Italy at the peace conference in certain other matters."[28] Csáky's lukewarm rebuttal of Tacoli's objections to the progress of Yugoslav-Hungarian relations was an indication of the change in the importance attached to the Italian relations. At the beginning of March Tacoli returned to Rome to clarify further possibilities, and then to continue the talks in Budapest.

The increasingly demure attitude of the Hungarian government did not make a very good impression in Rome. Italian leaders expected to find clear approval and immediate results in Hungary. This did not prove to be the case; in fact, the whole affair simply hurt the prestige of Italy vis-à-vis its allies. The Italians blamed the Yugoslavs for the attitude of the Hungarian government and, in order to render the Yugoslav-Hungarian negotiations more problematic, they presented Italian-Hungarian relations as having reached a much more advanced stage.[30]

The right-wing aristocratic opposition to the Hungarian regime wanted to strengthen Italian-Hungarian relations at any price, because it hoped for the dissolution of the regime as a result of the presence of Italian troops. György Szmrecsányi, the governor of the city and province of Pozsony (Bratislava), who had resigned as early as November 4, because he refused to cooperate with the Károlyi regime, asked the Italian mission in Vienna to support his trip to Rome. He argued that "the mutilated country" could have but one serious ally "in face of the Slavic bloc of nations," and that would be Italy. Therefore he proposed that Italy support Hungary in attaining peace terms as favorable as possible and, at the same time, occupy the country militarily to "restore order."[30] He continued his talks until the beginning of March by which time it seemed that Italian officials were even subsidizing his stay in Rome.[31]

His private proposals suited Italian purposes in every regard. Italian leaders had more than once appealed to the French to the effect that Latin nations should stick together in face of the Slavs, and had several times suggested the occupation of Hungary.[32]

Revolution, however, wiped away the bourgeois democratic regime, and the various projects no longer applied.

The Republic of Councils (Soviet Republic)

While the bourgeois democratic regime hardly gained the attention of the Paris peace conference, the proclamation of the Republic of Councils all of a sudden placed Hungary as an important item on its agenda. The proletarian dictatorship in Hungary rendered "Asiatic Bolshevism" a concrete reality in Central Europe; the tide of revolution, so it seemed, was advancing menacingly towards Western Europe. The change in Hungary was an indication that the Hungarian government would refuse to carry out the resolutions of the peace conference, including the establishment of a neutral zone (as per the Vix memorandum).

The mood and atmosphere in Paris seemed particularly favorable to the Italian plans with regard to Hungary. While official Italian policy did not sympathize with the worker state any more than that of the other Great Powers, its representatives understood well that the new situation was favorable to their own position.[33] The British and the Americans regarded the zealous and aggressive French attempts, and the activities of French military leaders as practically the sole cause of the establishment of the Council. The French were primarily blamed for the new situation affecting all of Central Europe.[34]

The French and British representatives left Budapest after March 21, and the Italians strived to fill the vacuum. The Italian military mission remained in spite of the reports that they too would depart,[35] and Prince Borghese, along with his secretary, Prince Pignatelli di Cerchiara, joined the mission. Borghese would have liked to become the official representative of all the allies in Budapest. This plan did not work out, however, partly because of American objections. The Americans were aware that Borghese was guided solely by the special interests of Italy.[36] In spite of this the Prince remained as an unofficial member of the Italian mission for the time being, while informing Orlando that only his family relations detained him in the Hungarian capital.[37]

Borghese and the members of the mission had already established contact with some of the would-be members of the Council even before the proclamation of the Republic of Councils (with Péter Ágoston, Zsigmond Kunfi, etc.) and strived for even closer relations with them from the end of March on.[38] Lacking Italian primary sources, and because of the taciturnity of the memoirs, we know relatively little about the content of the negotiations, especially in the early period of the Republic of Councils. There is no doubt, however, that the Italians attempted to prevent the organization of the proletarian dictatorship through assistance to the centrist and right-wing elements of the administration. Ágoston related somewhat later that the Italians would have liked to orient Hungarian foreign policy in a different direction, and to replace the Soviet alliance with an Italian orientation.[39]

Until the beginning of foreign intervention, however, not many concrete measures were taken beyond the above. At the peace negotiations Orlando and the Italian delegation supported the more moderate policies of the Anglo-Americans against the aggressivity of the French military leaders. At the same time, however, they attempted to use these aggressive plans for their own purposes; as in the debate on Marshal Foch's proposal for the military occupation of Vienna and Budapest for the purpose of stemming the revolutionary tide. At this time the Italian delegation, referring to reports received from their mission, insisted that the occupation troops be Italian rather than French.[40] After the Foch proposal had been rejected, the Italian delegation no longer advocated measures against Hungary. On the contrary, at the end of March, when the Council requested that the peace conference send a diplomatic mission to Budapest, the Italian delegation supported the request, in contrast to Clemenceau's negative attitude. The Hungarian request was relayed to the peace conference by Borghese and, because at the beginning it seemed that the Prince would be included among those accompanying General Smuts, the Italians felt it was important to honor it. At the same time they took advantage of the opportunity to point to the harmful consequences of the French policy.[41] Finally, however, Borghese was left out of the mission; the reports of the visit make no mention of his presence, and are very brief in their account of the activities of the Italian members of the delegation.[42]

Perhaps it is not an exaggeration to assume that Borghese's role as intermediary in Budapest contributed to the fact that Philip M. Brown, the member of the American mission in Vienna delegated to Budapest, who had remained pretty much in the background until then, strived to improve his contacts with members of the Council from the end of March on, and met several times with Béla Kun. From the end of March to the beginning of May, while Brown resided in Hungary, he assumed the leadership among the representatives of the Great Powers. Only the Italians could challenge his primacy.

*   *   *

Foreign intervention created a radically new situation in the domestic and foreign relations of the revolution; its domestic difficulties increased, whereas its relations to the Great Powers necessarily deteriorated still further. The Peace Conference sent no further missions to Budapest, but merely addressed memoranda to the Council. The new situation, however, did not affect Italian-

Hungarian relations negatively, but rendered them more active, more productive for the Hungarian side.

The contradictory attitude of the Italian representatives in Budapest reflected the ambiguity of Italian politics: these representatives maintained relations not only with counter-revolutionary circles; they also initiated and organized those economic measures which were to prove so important to the Council during the blockade.

The catastrophic military situation in late April led both the Italians and the Americans to seek "solutions." At the beginning Borghese suggested to the Council that it negotiate with the Great Powers in return for rescinding or moderating certain measures.[43] This suggestion, however, could not compete with Brown's offers, and Italy's prestige and influence could not be compared with that enjoyed by the United States. Thus, the Council, striving to gain time, negotiated first of all with Brown, keeping Borghese's proposals "in reserve," as it were.

The Italians, however, did not give up, and came up with new sets of proposals. Brown expressed the greatest concern at the negotiations between Béla Kun and other members of the Council with Borghese, and was afraid lest the Italians be the first to find a "solution."[44] His worries were increased by the fact that the roster of the Italian mission to Budapest grew in size at the beginning of May; new officers and employees had arrived from Vienna.[45]

The bolstering of the Italian mission was due, in part, to the expected resignation of the Council, but also to more far-reaching Italian plans. The Italian officers who came to Budapest on instructions from General Segré right away paid a call on Béla Kun and, somewhat belatedly, proposed that, should the Council be reconstituted with more moderate elements, they would guarantee that Budapest would be occupied not by the royal Romanian forces, but by Czechoslovak units under their own command (General Piccione). Of course, Kun's reply was negative, for by the beginning of May the Council had already weathered the crisis.[46]

Lieutenant Colonel Guido Romanelli also arrived in Budapest on May 12 in order to take command of the Italian mission. From that moment its concerns became significantly more active and varied.[47]

The evolution of Italian-Hungarian negotiations was followed with lively interest in Paris and elsewhere. The Czechoslovaks were at least as interested, since they were directly concerned. The press in Prague gave relatively accurate reports of the negotiations, and pointed to their essence in the very headlines ("Is Italy seeking to preserve its back in Hungary?" and "Béla Kun will defend Italian interests in Fiume.").[48]

The Italians proved extraordinarily flexible, and no longer mentioned occupation, since the circumstances had changed. On the other hand, they were well aware that under the blockade the Council was much in need of arms, ammunition, and food, which could not be obtained in legal ways. The Italians offered therefore to fill the gap and to circumvent the blockade. Undoubtedly, the Italian concern was considerably influenced, among other factors, by the so-called Italian crisis which had come about at the end of April at the Peace Conference, and which revolved once more around Fiume and Wilson's rigid rejection of the Italian claim.

As can be seen from the telegram of Kun to Böhm, the Italian mission proposed the signing of commercial agreements and was prepared to place Fiume under the protection of the Council.[49] Brown was convinced that the proposals were prompted by the Italian ambition to occupy Budapest.[50]

Such a military move, however, was never explicitly discussed; the Italians made no demand which might have proved unacceptable to the Council. The acceptance of the advantageous offers seemed natural, even necessary.

While the negotiations were proceeding in Budapest, in Paris Sonnino was insisting, even more forcefully than his French colleague, Pichon, on the strict application of the blockade resolution, and argued that the blockade could be lifted only if the Kun regime collapsed. He also proposed that the pertinent decisions be made widely public.[51] Sonnino could never have reached the same "liberal" stand with regard to the Republic of Councils as Orlando had; differences of opinion frequently arose between the two; still, one is bound to suspect that the actual effect of the proposal changed essentially nothing, yet it appeared to an outsider as a measure to camouflage the shipments.

The mission in Vienna attached special importance to strengthening ties with Hungary. Segré advised Romanelli to study how it "might be possible to take advantage of the unique and advantageous position of our mission in Budapest. We are almost alone here, without competition, and can utilize our influence to build the foundations of our economic penetration."[52] According to their plan they would have shipped to the Council a portion of the goods accumulated in Vienna, in the words of Romanelli, "after the suspension of the blockade."[53] On such a basis, however, precisely because of their awareness of the above-mentioned decision at the peace conference, the members of the Council would have signed no agreement, and would have made no payment. In mid-May, however, at the insistence of Marquis Tacoli, and after negotiations between Count Basselet de la Rosarie and the representatives of the Italian labor unions (Benedetti) on one hand and members of the Council on the other, the parties signed an agreement regarding shipments of goods worth 25 to 35 million crowns. Ostensibly the shipments were of foodstuff, but in actuality consisted of weapons, ammunition, and food. They were followed, in July, by another 20 million crowns worth of textiles and clothing.[54]

The payment of the orders and the shipment of the goods, especially in the case of weapons, was not at all simple, since Hungary was under blockade. The Italians had to overcome not only technical difficulties, but elude the watchful eyes of the allies. The Italian mission in Vienna as well as the Italian sections of the allied economic and aid organizations were quite resourceful in the matter.

The Council attempted to make payments through Vienna, but the Austrian government would not allow it. Thus, the money was taken to the Austrian border under the protection of the Italian mission; at Brück the representatives of General Segré took over.[55]

According to our sources, the bulk of the shipments came from reserves accumulated along the Adriatic, and reached Brück, at the Hungarian border, usually through Vienna. Italian soldiers assured the safety of the ammunition convoys, and they could easily circumvent the none too strict Austrian customs controls.[56] One of the convoys for instance was hooked to the train of the allied relief organization transporting food, clothing, and medicine into Austria. The Italians prevented the American officers of the organization from checking the content of these wagons, and thus the goods reached Vienna safely. From there they were trans-shipped to Brück.[57]

At other times the task was up to the Italian mission in Vienna which, in accordance with an agreement between Austria and Czechoslovakia reached with the help of the allies, was entrusted with the Austrian weapons which were supposed to be forwarded to

Czechoslovakia in exchange for shipments of coal. The Czechoslovakians repeatedly pressed for the remittance of arms, for they were in dire need of them during the counterattack of the Hungarian Red Army in Slovakia. The Austrian government did live up to its obligations, at the price of serious domestic difficulties, and handed the weapons over to the Italian mission. The Czechoslovak government, unaware of all this, waited a while, then delivered a scathing attack against the Austrian government. The latter, knowing itself to be in the right, objected in the same tone. During these debates it became known that the weapons had disappeared at the hands of the Italian mission, and it was feared, in Paris, that the bulk of the weapons had reached Hungary. It was only at the beginning of August, long after the Slovakian campaign, that the Czechoslovak army received some of these weapons.[58]

Though we cannot determine statistically the importance of the Italian shipments of war materials and food, and cannot trace their fate once inside Hungary, their transfer is, nevertheless, an important episode in the relations between the two countries.

The commercial agreements and shipments soon became known, of course. The American mission in Vienna reported them to its own peace delegation, the British to the Supreme Economic Council, the Austrian Foreign Minister to the French mission in Vienna, that is to the council of the Great Powers. These reports were confirmed by the accounts of the British ambassadors to Bucharest and Rome, and were included in the news received by Herbert Hoover, the American head of the Supreme Economic Council, and in the aide mémoire the Romanian government handed to the British ambassador to Bucharest.[59]

None of these objections, however, was as passionate as the reaction in Czechoslovakia. In June several reports claimed that Italians were effectively aiding the Hungarian Red Army; some gave an account of the role played by Italian solders and officers, published the itinerary of the convoys and, in some cases, signaled their arrival.[60]

The successful advance of the Red Army into Czechoslovakia almost caused panic; the papers reported daily on the events in Slovakia, seeking those responsible for the unexpected breakdown. The indignation was directed in part against all the Great Powers. One daily, quoting Klofać, wrote: "Had the Entente Powers not been so soft and merciful, the situation would be entirely different today, and we would not have to shed blood."[61]

The Czech papers did not content themselves with such generalities, but aimed specific attacks at the Italians. They blamed the military defeat largely on the Italian officers,[62] and devoted a whole series of articles to the matter of the Italian shipments to Hungary. It was common knowledge that the Italians had negotiated a deal of several million with the Council, in the framework of which large quantities of rice, lard, etc., had been delivered to the Red Army.[63] According to another daily, the deliveries consisted not of food, but of "weapons and ammunition for the Red Guard."[64] Items appeared in the papers to the effect that an alliance, the object of which was the offensive against Czechoslovakia, had been signed by Italy and the Republic of Councils. The newspapers claimed this was no secret, and believed that the Great Powers were undoubtedly in the know.[65]

Of course, the Czechoslovakian government strongly protested against the measures taken by the Italians. Foreign Minister Beneš sent an extensive memorandum to British Foreign Secretary Arthur Balfour giving details of the shipments.[66]

Our sources, while not sufficiently varied, and while neglecting Italian materials, nevertheless leave no doubt concerning the actual existence of the Italian-Hungarian link. Hence it is rather surprising that the historical literature makes practically no mention of the matter.[67]

Because of the protests and reports the peace conference placed the matter on its agenda several times in the course of June and July. The Italian representatives, however, emphasized that they had no knowledge of the charges and Sonnino ordered a full investigation. Subsequently the Italian general staff headquarters, including General Diaz, categorically denied that the army was involved. The headquarters did not think it impossible, however, that private enterprise had a hand in the shipments. Under the guise of further investigation the Italian delegation succeeded in avoiding the issue for a while.[68] The Italians prepared their report by July 27, and the peace conference placed it on its agenda for August 1. By this time, however, the issue had lost its topicality; with regard to Hungary, the Great Powers were preoccupied with other matters.[69]

In the meantime the British ambassador in Rome brought to the attention of the italian cabinet the harmful effect of the circulating "rumors"; whereas the head of the British mission in Vienna, Cuninghame, strived to convince Prince Borghese of the impossibility of such endeavors. In both places the reply was a categorical denial, what is more, Borghese ascribed the entire rumor-mongering to the French, citing it as another example of their anti-Italian machinations.[70] The French press indeed did take advantage of the opportunity to publish anti-Italian articles from the moment it received notices about the first shipments, openly implicating General Segré; and even Allizé launched a campaign against the Italians.[71] It is strange, however, that in the debates at the peace conference and in the press the names of Romanelli or Borghese, not to mention the other participants, were almost never brought up.

The Italian mission in Vienna, having become the focus of attention and the target of attacks, issued statements several times, and advised Romanelli "to deny the charge in the most categorical manner."[72] Segré and his colleagues denied the charges several times, adding that if there was shipment of some kind, another Great Power must be responsible. At the same time they filed a protest to the effect that the persons who took part in the affair disguised themselves in Italian uniform. All this received extensive commentary in the press from Prague, which resorted to terms that were far from flattering. No one took the Italian denials seriously.[73]

Naturally, the Italians did not accept responsibility for the shipments, whereas the Hungarian government refrained from any declaration whatever. Later on, however, Italian leaders were wont to admit the relationship.[74]

The failure of foreign intervention (for the time being), and the Italian-Hungarian deals were the last straws that prompted the Czechoslovak government to adopt measures against the Italian mission there. Piccione and his officers were replaced by Frenchmen, and thus the Italian prospects in Czechoslovakia vanished. Of course the Italians were not indifferent, and attributed their failure to French interference; Italian papers deplored the end to the friendly relationship with Czechoslovakia. In Prague, however, no tears were shed.[75]

Thus, the relations established with the Republic of Councils did not bring about the desired results for Italy. Antonio Gramsci correctly observed about the venture: "the Italian government was merely following the dictates of 'sacred egoism,' " and Romanelli, "the 'friend' of the Communists, was a faithful servant of the foundry and shipyard capitalists in Milan and Genova who would like to lay their hands on every port on the Adriatic."[76]

Romanelli was dissatisfied with the developments; since there were no rivals, Italy "should have achieved greater success in terms of commercial penetration." But better results could only have come about, he continued, "if our superiors in Rome or Paris would have attributed greater importance to the matter . . . if only they had dealt with it with dispatch and in good faith positively." He felt it was a grave mistake to let Italian primacy fade.[77]

In spite of this they felt that the counter-revolutionary circles were losing their satisfaction with the mission. This made it more difficult to promote their old plan for the forced resignation of the Governing Council.[78]

The Hungarian counter-revolutionaries preferred to seek the support of the Anglo-Americans or the French who enjoyed greater influence and prestige, rather than the Italians who were in touch with the Council and Béla Kun. True, Romanelli and his mission had extensive contacts with the Council's opposition information from them and gave them advice; still, the Italians were unable to compete with the Anglo-Americans.

In June and July when the Peace Conference resorted to diplomatic measures, and eventually to the preparation of decisive military intervention in order to overthrow the Council, the Italian diplomats and military leaders behaved rather passively, and took little part in the passionate debates. Their statements were moderate, but did not prevent the unfolding of the events. In June the attention of the Italian politicians was once again absorbed by domestic matters. Orlando and Sonnino, having fought tooth and nail for the enhancement of Italy's international position and the acquisition of Fiume, could not accept the compromise solution concerning the port, and the cabinet resigned. Its place was taken by Prime Minister Nitti, with Tittoni as Minister of Foreign Affairs.

Nitti and his collaborators were bent on resolving the internal problems exacerbated by the economic and political situation; Nitti entrusted the handling of the Peace Conference almost entirely to Tittoni.[80]

The new administration was compelled to deal with internal matters becaue of the dissatisfaction fanned by nationalism, and also because of the strike movement of the working class and its demonstrations of sympathy on behalf of the Soviet Union and the Republic of Councils.[81]

Hence Hungary was temporarily relegated to the background in

Italian politics. The international position of the Republic worsened significantly by July, and the hegemony of the great powers and their politics made its overthrow inevitable. The fall of Orlando also implied an end to active relations with the Republic of Councils.[82] The Italians now paid closer attention to counter-revolutionary groups.

At the Peace Conference Tittoni himself actively supported the general policy line of "reestablishing order" in Hungary, since he felt that the example provided by the Hungarian dictatorship of the proletariat was more dangerous than that of the Soviet Union.[83] While sharing Clemenceau's unequivocal stand, he pointed out that because of its internal difficulties the Italian government could not contribute troops for the proposed intervention.[84] The Italian workers protested so strongly that Nitti declared, in order to preempt the general strike in preparation: "We will not intervene against the Bolshevik government," what's more, "we will recall most of our troops stationed abroad." He emphasized that "we do not want to interfere in the internal affairs of any country. Therefore I do not think that there is justification for a general strike."[85]

In Paris, Tittoni proposed that the Council be overthrown not by open intervention, but by providing assistance to the counter-revolutionary government at Szeged; thus the action would become an internal Hungarian matter.[86] Tittoni was prepared to send Italian officers to Szeged. There was no need for this, however, because neither the Great Powers, nor their lesser allies, were inclined to collaborate with the Szeged regime, and the French had no desire to see their carefully built relations toppled over by their Italian rivals.

In Vienna, however, the Segré mission and Borghese were actively negotiating with the Social-Democratic leaders. Vittorio Cerruti, who before the war was on the staff of the Italian embassy in Vienna, and became the secretary for political affairs of the Budapest mission from June on, tried to prepare the overthrow of the Council, with the help of Romanelli, in Budapest.[87] Borghese would have liked to form a cabinet under the premiership of Sándor Wekerle, because he felt that the Szeged regime would then be willing to give up their claims, in spite of the fact that four Social-Democratic ministers were to be included in the cabinet.[88]

But the conduct of the negotiations was in the hands of Cunighame, not in those of the Italians. It is true that Cuninghame felt the collaboration of Borghese was important, because he had good personal contacts, and because he felt that due regard must be paid to "the significant Italian interests in Hungary."[89] On the other hand, the French disagreed with the personal proposals of Cuninghame and Borghese, and were convinced that the Italians had no business in Central Europe or in Hungary.[90]

On June 18 Romanelli travelled to Vienna to keep the allied representatives informed of his personal experiences; he had the opportunity to sense Cuninghame's good intentions, as well as the anti-Italian attitude of Allizé and the French mission.[91]

For a short while after the fall of the Republic of Councils the role of the Romanelli mission again became important, since it represented the allies until the arrival of the committee of generals. In the first days Romanelli acted as intermediary beween Budapest and Paris. Borghese was instrumental in bringing about the collaboration of the Social-Democratic leaders and the Bethlen group in view of a coalition government. The Italian mission intervened several times on behalf of arrested politicians during the Romanian occupation, and their presence and experience proved useful at this time for other reasons as well.[92] Italy would have been glad to participate along with Romania in "cleaning up" the Hungarian situation, in the hope of excluding the French.[93]

Later on the Hungarian and Italian governments, dissatisfied with the Paris peace system, found ample basis and reason for the elaboration of closer cooperation, and Hungary once again became a significant target for Italian penetration. But in the 30's the Italy of Mussolini once again clashed with a power greater than itself in this zone—the Germany of Hitler.

Notes

1. So far there are no monographs summarizing all aspects of Italian-Hungarian relations in either language. "Az olasz szocialista munkásmozgalom és az 1919-es magyar szocialista forradalom" [The Italian Socialist Workers' movement and the Hungarian socialist revolution of 1919] by Franco Ferri in A Magyar Tanácsköztársaság történelemi jelentösége [The historical significance of the Hungarian Republic of Councils], és nemzetközi hatása [and its international impact] (Budapest: MSzMP KB Párt örténeti Intézete, 1960), deals primarily with the impact of the Hungarian Republic of Council, without attempting to be exhaustive. Two articles by Antonio Gramsci published in 1919, and edited by Aladár Kiss (Párttörténeti Közlemények, 1962, No. 3) also pertain to the workers' movement. The recollections of Guido Romanelli, Nell'Ungheria di Béla Kun e durante

l'occupazione militare romena. La mia missione, maggio-novembre 1919 (Udine: Doretti, 1964), contains useful observations about the activities of the Italian mission in Budapest; it also deals with Italian political objectives, the relations between the mission and the Council, but especially with the relations established with the Hungarian counter-revolution. It is an interesting supplement to other memoirs and contemporary documents dealing with the Romanian occupation. Giorgio Maria Sangiorgi's *L'Ungheria dalla repubblica di Karolyi alla reggenza di Horthy* (Bologna: Nicolá Zanichelli, 1927) deals with the same period. There is as yet no overall treatment of the relations between the Hungarian governments and the Italian leaders. Yet there are many references to our topic among the monographs, mainly western, dealing with the whole of the period in general terms. Contemporary sources also provide relatively ample information.

2. There remained, however, a significant opposition to this foreign policy. See, for instance, *Dalle case di Giovanni Giolitti: Quarant anni di politica italiana*, III. Dai prodromi della grande guerra al fascismo 1910–1928, ed. Claudio Pavone (Milano: Feltrinelli, 1962). See also, René Albrecht-Carrié, *Italy at the Paris Peace Conference* (New York: 1938), 70–71. This opposition soon became stronger, primarily thanks to Mussolini. Regarding the internal position of the Orlando government and the Fiume issue see Ennio di Nolfo, *Mussolini e la politica estera italiana* (1919–1933) (Padova, 1960). A general treatment of the political situation in Italy can be found in Vittorio Emanuele Orlando, *Memorie* (1915–1919), ed. Rodolfo Mosca (Milano: Rizzoli, 1960) and in Silvio Crespi, *Alla difesa d'Italia in guerra e a Versailles (Diario 1917–1919)* (Milano: Mondadori, 1937).

3. Albrecht-Carrié, 102–103. J. H. Edwards, *David Lloyd George II* (London, 1930), 564. Maxwell H. Macartney and Paul Cremona, *Italy's Foreign Policy 1914–1937* (London, 1938), 121, 196, 198, and 208–209. C. A. Macartney, *Hungary and Her Successors: The Treaty of Trianon and Its Consequences, 1917–1937* (New York, 1937), 316. The most detailed treatment of the Italian-Yugoslav conflict can be found in Ivo J. Lederer, *Yugoslavia at the Paris Peace Conference* (New Haven: Yale University Press, 1963), 77 ff., and in V. E. Orlando, *Memorie*. In 1915 the Entente promised the port to Serbia. At the end of the war, however, it was no longer Serbia, but the newly constituted Yugoslavia, that claimed the promised city, and its claim was strongly backed by France. Italy resorted to the argument, among others, that the Serbia to which the promise had been made, no longer existed, hence its own claim was valid.

4. One of the specialists of the period argues that "perhaps none of the contradictions in the aftermath of the war constituted as serious a danger to European peace as the rivalry between France and Italy." Felix John Vondraček, *The Foreign Policy of Czechoslovakia 1918–1935* (New York: 1937), 100.

5. C. A. Macartney and A. W. Palmer, *Independent Eastern Europe* (London: 1962), 197-198. Di Nolfo, 9, 12.

6. See, among others, a number of documents in I documenti diplomatici italiani Sixth series, 1918-1922, I (Rome: Ministry of Foreign Affairs, 1956) (referred to subsequently as *I documenti*). Also *Papers Relating to the Foreign Relations of the United States. The Paris Peace Conference XII* (Washington, 1967) XII, 475 (henceforth *Papers PPC*), report by A. C. Coolidge dated Februry 27, 1919. Also *Documents on British Foreign Policy, 1919-1939*, First Series (subsequently, *Documents*), VI (London, 1956) 63, report by Rattigan, the British ambassador to Romania, dated July 9, 1919. *Zapisnici sa sednica delegacije Kraljevine SHS na mirovnoj konferenciji u Parizu, 1919-1920*, eds. B. Brizman and B. Hrabak, series III (Grada, Belgrade: Institut drustvenih nauka, 1960). Also see Ivo J. Lederer, *Yugoslavia.* . . .

7. L'udovit Holotik, "Uloha talianskej a francuzskej vojanskej misie na Slovensku r. 1919," *Historicky casopis* (1953), no. 4, and (1954), no. 1.

8. The corridor would have provided Czechoslovakia with an outlet to the sea at the expense of Austria and Hungary. It is characteristic of the attitude of the Italians that while openly rejecting the plan, they advised Beneš confidentially that if Fiume were awarded to Italy, they would support the project. *Archiv Ministerstva zahranicnich veci. Parizsky archiv* (Prague), vol. 43, no. 4710, undated situation report from the conference.

9. This mood is well reflected in the Prague press. The morning edition of *Bohemia*, Nov. 29, 1918, published an article titled "Schwere Genesätze zwischen den Jugoslaven und den Italienern," and in the Jan. 29, 1919, morning issue "Der tschechische Korridor zur Adria. Italienischer Widerstand gegen den französischen Plan." Some of the Italian officers objected to part of the territorial claims of the Prague government in Slovakia (Statni slovensky ustredni archiv, Bratislava, Minister ceskoslovenskej republiky s plnou mocou pre spravu Slovenska, report from March 2, 1919, ref. A-288-815) and expressed their sympathies towards Hungary in other ways as well. (See Archiv Ministerstva, vol. 48, no. 4873.)

10. "Italien für einen Bund zwischen den Deutschen und Ungarn— gegen die Südslaven." Morning issue of *Bohemia*, Feb. 8, 1919, P. S. Wandycz, *France and her Eastern Allies 1919-1925* (Minneapolis, 1962), mentions a project for an Italian-Hungarian-Polish bloc (94). It is worth noting that at the same time the Hungarian government strove for a Yugoslav-Hungarian-Polish bloc. (Hungarian State Archives, *KÜM Res. pol.* (1010), 996.)

11. Lajos Fülep, as a young teacher, spent many years in Italy before the war and had extensive contacts among progressive Italian intellectuals and politicians.

12. He started on his assignment in December 1918 and kept Mihály Károlyi informed by written and oral reports.

13. Hungarian State Archives, *KÜM Res. pol.* (1919), 1132, report of Lajos Fülep.

14. From December 1918 on Italy strove to obtain through official channels, in Paris, that Italian troops be sent to Hungary, while Foch was promoting the French occupation of Vienna and Budapest. *I documenti,* 226, 231, 253, 264, 273, etc.

15. Prince Livio Borghese resided in Budapest; he eventually acted as the political representative of the Italian mission in Budapest. In June he left for Vienna to participate in negotiations with the Social Democratic leaders.

16. Hungarian State Archives, *KÜM Res. pol.* (1919), 1131.

17. Hungarian State Archives, *KÜM Res. pol.* (1919), 1015.

18. *Ibid.*

19. Hungarian State Archives, *KÜM Res. pol.* (1919), 584 (from Count Imre Csáky to the consul in Vienna, Oszkár Charmant, February 6, 1919).

21. Hungarian State Archives, *KÜM Res. pol.* (1919), 1014.

22. Hungarian State Archives, *KÜM Res. pol.* (1919), 584. Regarding the formation of the mission and its task see *I documenti,* 352–353.

23. Hungarian State Archives, *KÜM Res. pol.* (1919), 584. Zanella invited Charmant to Fiume already in his letter of January 22, 1919, adding that from there he could proceed to Rome to negotiate with the head of the cabinet. Hungarian State Archives, *KÜM Res. pol.* (1919), 1014.

24. Hungarian State Archives, *KÜM Res. pol.* (1919), 996; (1919), 1133.

25. The Yugoslav government was disposed to hand over predominantly Hungarian communities along the Dráva River and in the Banat. The Banat had not yet been adjudicated; Yugoslavia and Romania were at odds over the province. The Yugoslavs would have preferred to see the debated territories under the sovereignty of a cooperative Hungarian administration (Hungarian State Archives, *KÜM Res. pol.* (1919), 1133; (1919), 1601.) Romania, which claimed the entire Banat, resented having to share with Yugoslavia. *A History of the Peace Conference of Paris III,* ed. H.W.V. Temperley (London, 1920), 29.

26. Hungarian State Archives, *KÜM Res. pol.* (1919), 996.

7. He wrote to Szilassy: "I particularly agree with Mr. Consul's opinion—and practically all serious politicians share this opinion—that the only purposeful political orientation for us at this time would be the South Slavs." Hungarian State Archives, *KÜM Res. pol.* (1919), 982. A. C. Coolidge also reported to Paris, that the Hungarians were seeking an understanding with Serbia [sic] as against the Romanians. *Papers PPC,* XII, 475, report of February 27, 1919.

28. PI Archivum, papers of the Károlyi trial. Container 2, File 5; strictly confidential report by Count Csáky on March 4, 1919. Marquis Tacoli was the "Hungarian political representative" of the Italian mission in Vienna, followed at this post by Borghese. G. Romanelli, 14.

30. Hungarian State Archives, *KÜM Res. pol.* (1919), 1237. Ivo J. Lederer, 1677-178.

31. *I documenti*, 471-472. Report by Augusto Biancheri Chiappori to Sonnino, dated January 17, 1919.

32. Archiv Ministerstva, Folder 7, Number 731, report to the Foreign Ministry of Czechoslovakia, undated.

33. The military leaders supported the proposal of Szmrecsányi, *I documenti*, 471-472; see the already quoted report. Regarding the Latin bloc and its broader implications see Albrecht-Carrié, 67.

34. Emil Tersen, "Az entent (különösképpen Franciaország) és a Magyar Tanácsköztársaság [the Entente—especially France—and the Hungarian Republic of Councils], 1917-1919," in *A Magyar Tanácsköztársaság. . .*, 164. G. Romanelli, 62 ff.

35. *Organization of American Relief in Europe 1918-1919*, eds. Suda Lorena Bane and Ralph Haswell Lutz (Stanford University Press, 1943), 517, letter by E. Troubridge dated May 26, 1919. *Papers PPC*, I (Washington, 1945), 135, minutes of the session of the American peace delegation, March 27, 1919. H. Nicolson, *Peacemaking 1919* (London, 1934), 297, telegram from Chieherin to Béla Kun dated March 25, 1919, Mrs. Sándor Gábor, *Dokumentomok Szovjetoroszország és a Magyar Tanácsköztársaság kapcsolatairól"* [Documents Regarding the Relations between the Soviet Union and the Hungarian Republic of Councils], *Párttörténeti Közlemények* (1961), no. 1, 211. *Népszava*, March 26, 1919.

36. According to Romanelli the members of the mission were Lt. Col. Murari, Captains Accame and Carbone, eight soldiers, a clerk, etc. Marquis Tacoli was included as the political representative. G. Romanelli, *op. cit.*

27. *Papers PPC*, XII, 424, report by Ph. M. Brown dated March 25, 1919. Franco Ferri, 289. A. Gramsci, 127.

37. G. Romanelli, 28. *Papers PPC*, XII, 418, report by N. Roosevelt dated March 26, 1919.

38. P. Mantoux, *Les délibérations du Conseil des Quatre* (March 24-June 28, 1919) I (Paris: CNRS, 1955), 80; record of March 29, 1919. G. Romanelli, 28, 56-57, 84.

39. P. Mantoux, I, 80. Testimony of Péter Ágoston, PI Archivum, the trials of the People's Commissars, July 14, 1920, 1822-23.

40. *Ibid.*, as well as July 16, 1920, 1907.

41. P. Mantoux, I, 52 ff. Regarding the session of March 27, 1919. *Papers PPC*, XII, 419; report by N. Roosevelt dated March 26, 1919.

42. P. Mantoux, I, 80-83, 98-104. *Papers PPC*, V, 16 ff.

43. H. Nicolson, a member of the mission, gives a detailed account of the journey, but does not even mention the names of the Italian members, 292.

44. Ágoston collection, PI Archivum, Container II, Folder 12. Testimony of Péter Ágoston dated November 19, 1919.

45. Report of May 4, 1919, *Papers PPC*, XII, 460.

46. Report of May 7, 1919, *ibid.*, 459.

47. Reports of May 4 and May 12, 1919, *ibid.*, as well as 460. Regarding Segré's project for the resignation of the Council and the possible entering of Italian troops; also see G. Romanelli, 62–63.

48. G. Romanelli, 10 ff.

49. *Prager Tagblatt*, (evening edition) April 29, 1919, 1.

50. The manuscript collection of Böhm in the PI Archives, 2nd container, file 12 271/5; "Béla Kun soll Italiens Interessen in Fiume schützen," *Prager Tagblatt* (evening edition) April 29, 1919, 1.

51. Report of May 12, 1919, *Papers PPC*, XII, p. 466.

52. *Papers PPC*, IV, p. 694.

53. G. Romanelli, 63.

54. *Ibid.*, 64.

55. Minutes of the meeting of the revolutionary cabinet, dated May 17, 1919, PI Archives; Hungarian State Archives, *KÜM Gazd. pol. oszt.*, bundle 3, A/2, file 23917/1919; G. Romanelli, 63 ff.

56. Minutes of the meeting of the revolutionary council, May 17, 1919, PI Archives; G. Romanelli, 65–66. Romanelli blames Count Basselet de la Rosarie for allowing the Austrian authorities to find out.

57. Memorandum of Beneš, dated June 18, 1919, *Documents*, VI, 69; the report of the Czechoslovak delegation in Zagreb, June 25, 1919, Archiv Ministerstva, bundle 48, no. 4886.

58. *Papers PPC*, X, 372–373.

59. Report by A. C. Goodyear, the head of the Coal Mission, dated September 10, 1919, *Organization of American Relief*, 700; *Papers PPC*, VI, 257; VII, 263–264 (the July 25, 1919, meeting of the Supreme Council of the Great Powers).

60. *Papers PPC*, X, 345, 372–373, 378; XII, 530; *Documents*, VI, 20, 63, 88.

61. Archiv Ministerstva, bundle 48, no. 4880; bundle 72, no. 69823.

62. "Die Ereignisse in der Slovakei," *Der Demokrat* (morning edition), June 4, 1919.

63. *Ibid.*

64. "Die italienisch-ungarische Freundschaft," *Bohemia*, June 29, 1919.

65. "Italien für Sovjetungarn?", *Prager Tagblatt* (evening edition), May 30, 1919.

66. "Ein Gegeimbündnis Ungarns mit Italien?", *Abendblatt* (afternoon edition of *Bohemia*), June 14, 1919.

67. *Documents*, VI, 69–70.

68. Neither does L' Holotik mention in his cited work that this factor may have contributed to the deterioration of the relations between Czechoslovakia and Italy; in fact, he makes no mention of the contacts between Italy and Hungary. Thus the work of Vondraček, already quoted, consti-

tutes an exception, for there is a brief reference to these contacts on page 36.

69. We have no sources pertaining to the control process itself. The Hungarian press, however, eventually did deal with the inspection of the import and export bureau of Trieste on the basis of reports published in the Italian press, as well as with the charges against and arrest of Segré and Romanelli. *Az Ujság*, May 29, 1921, "Ujabb részletek a Segré-Romanelli ügyben" [New details about the Segré-Romanelli affair] and "Segré olasz ezredest szabadon bocsátottak" [The latter title is inaccurate, for Segré had the rank of general.]

70. *Papers PPC*, VII, 478-479; X, 345, 372.

71. *Documents*, VI, 20, 94-95.

72. *Ibid.*, 95; Franco Ferri, 285; A. Gramsci, 127; G. Romanelli, 66.

73. G. Romanelli, 96.

74. "Mobilisierung der Sokolschaft," *Der Demokrat* (evening edition), June 6, 1919; "Die angeblichen italienischen Waffenlieferungen nach Ungarn und Böhmen," *Bohemia*, July 1, 1919; G. Romanelli, 95-96.

75. Franco Ferri, 289-290.

76. L' Holotik, *op. cit.*; "Das Ende der tschechisch-italienischen Freundschaft," *Bohemia*, June 7, 1919. The article quotes at length from the *Corriere della Sera*.

77. Franco Ferri, 285. Quotes from the August 19, 1919, issue of the *Ordine Nuovo*. In 1922 Romanelli was given the red-carpet treatment in Budapest, primarily because of his activities on behalf of the Hungarian counter-revolution. The "grateful Hungarians" rewarded him with a ceremonial sword and his bust sculpted by Alajos Strobl.

78. G. Romanelli, 91.

79. *Ibid.*, 93.

80. Declaration by Prince Livio Borghese in the case of Péter Ágoston, August 27, 1920, PI Archives, A. II, 11/86; testimony by Péter Ágoston, the trial of the commissars, July 16, 1920, PI Archives, p. 1948; Mrs. Sándor Gábor, "The Counter-Revolutionary Attempt of June 24, 1919," *Párttörténeti Közlemények* (1962), no. 2; G. Romanelli, *op. cit.*, especially the chapter dealing with the counter-revolution. As is well known, Romanelli intervened on behalf of the participants of the counter-revolution of June 24. In this connection, and in general, he speaks favorably, and often with high regard, of Béla Kun. See 136-138, 163 ff.

81. Lloyd George, II, 891, 1282; Albrecht-Carrié, 189, 197-199, 233, 235; di Nolfo, 14; V. E. Orlando, 16 ff.

82. Regarding the internal situation in Italy see di Nolfo, chapter I.

83 The contemporaries had a similar view of the situation. See, for instance, "Die italienisch-ungarische Freundschaft," *Bohemia*, June 29, 1919.

84. Session of July 5, 1919, *Papers PPC*, VII, 23.

85. *Ibid.*, 25. At the same time he proposed that the Council be prevented from tracing the confiscated goods, especially hard currency, at all cost. The

Finance Committee was instructed to work out appropriate measures in accordance with this resolution. *Ibid.*, 23, 28.

86. Franco Ferri, 283.

87. Session of July 17, 1919, *Papers PPC*, VII, 177–178.

88. Letter by Cuninghame dated July 1, 1919, *Documents*, VI, 7; G. Romanelli, 175, 245. The Hungarian press later had much to say about Cerruti, because he married a Hungarian woman. See, for instance, the theater column in *Az Ujság*, October 24, 1923.

89. Ágoston collection, diary entry for July 16, 1919, PI Archives.

90. Report by A. Halstead, July 18, 1919, *Papers PPC*, XII.

91. *Iratok az ellenforradalom történetéhez* [Documents regarding the history of the counter-revolution] I (Budapest: 1956) (2nd edition), 108–109. Document HL MNHF reports on the conference of the French mission in Vienna, dated August 2, 1919.

92. G. Romanelli, 217 ff.

93. Ágoston collection, diary entry for August 16, 1919, as well as report by Vilmos Böhm from Vienna dated August 5 1919, PI Archives. Regarding the attitude of the Rumanian occupation forces see the papers of the Bandholtz mission in *Papers PPC*, XII; the reports of the British representatives in *Documents*, VI; also, the last chapters in G. Romanelli, *op. cit.*

94. Memorandum by Troubridge, November 4, 1919, *Documents*, VI, 413–414. Report by Bandholtz, August 28, 1919, *Papers PPC*, XII, 660.

Sandor Taraszovics

American Peace Plans and the Shaping of Hungary's Post-World War I Borders

Wartime American peace plans and policy contributed to the collapse of the Austro-Hungarian Monarchy, and effected the fate of historic Hungary. At the Paris Peace Conference, the American delegation headed by President Woodrow Wilson, favored peace terms which called for a less drastic reduction of the Hungarian Kingdom than the Peace Conference eventually decreed. Although the territorial recommendations of the American plan were not adopted, it had a tempering effect as some of the most extreme claims against Hungary by its neighbors were rejected by the peacemakers.

In the summer of 1914, from the outbreak of hostilities in Europe, President Wilson embraced the idea of peace and offered to mediate in the conflict. The vision of peace and his perceived role in bringing it about seemed to be the force that shaped Wilson's mode of conducting foreign policy before, as well as after, the United States entered the First World War in the spring of 1917. He worked to bring about an end to the war, which he believed, was to be followed by a permanent peace constructed by "new diplomacy" based on "new international norms" and secured by a "League of Nations." The President's dispositions were influenced by the country's isolationist posture as well as by domestic conditions, and also by his close friend and associate, Colonel Edward M. House who, although a neutralist, leaned toward the Allied Powers and was convinced that "an understanding with Britain was an absolute prerequisite for an American peace mission. . . ."[1]

At first, President Wilson used every means at the disposal of a neutral power to offer his good offices to the belligerents. However, "his efforts met with no success. In fact, it increased bitterness, and brought about an extended use of propaganda upon both sides."[2] In 1915, American aloofness and neutrality were sorely tried both by Allied control of the sea lanes (which adversely affected foreign trade), and by the sinking, in May, of the British passenger ship, the *Lusitania*, by a German submarine. Many Americans were among those who lost their lives. This incident, as well as submarine warfare in general, brought the United States close to breaking with the Central Powers. The crisis subsided when the Central Powers pledged in May 1916 to restrict submarine warfare. As American awareness of the war was growing in the Presidential election year of 1916, the President stepped up his peace efforts. On May 27, 1916, Wilson gave a speech in Washington at a rally held by the League to Enforce Peace. He expressed the hope that "peace was close at hand" and implied that the United States was ready to mediate and guarantee it.

The League's rally gave President Wilson the opportunity to state his views regarding the postwar settlement.[3] One of the ideas he espoused was "the right of every people to choose its sovereign affiliation."[4] Wilson also suggested that in order to assure the freedom of the seas and to prevent future wars, "universal association of nations" should be formed.[5] The President hoped in vain that his initiative would be followed by a similar British move. Disappointed, he persuaded himself that the United States should chart an independent course in foreign affairs. Although he had to concentrate on his re-election campaign, he planned, against the advice of Colonel House and Secretary of State Robert Lansing, to launch an independent American peace drive after the election.[6] President Wilson was re-elected in November of 1916, as the man "who kept us out of war," but the peace initiative was temporarily taken out of his hands by the Central Powers.

Emperor Charles, who succeeded to the Habsburg throne on November 21, 1916 (after the death of his uncle, Francis Joseph), inherited a peace plan. It called for a combined statement of war aims and an offer to negotiate. On December 12, 1916, the Central Powers issued separate but similar statements. They proclaimed themselves the victors and professed to be motivated by "the desire to stem the flood of blood and to bring the horrors of war to an end."[7] The Central Alliance invited the Entente governments to enter into peace negotiations. At the same time, Emperor Charles began his long and unsuccessful "search for peace through secret negotiations."[8] When the peace note was issued, President Wilson, as previously indicated, was preparing one of his own and was concerned that the Allied governments might interpret this as a move supporting the initiative of the Central Powers. Nevertheless, on December 18, Secretary of State Lansing relayed President Wilson's appeal to all belligerents calling on them to state their aims. Lansing stressed that the President was not preparing peace, and was not even offering mediation. "He is merely proposing that a sounding be taken in order that we may learn, the neutral nations with the belligerent, how near the haven of peace may be."[9]

On December 19, David Lloyd George, the British Prime Minister, "in full accord with our brave allies," reflected on both of the notes by recalling the words of Abraham Lincoln: "We accepted this war for an object, a worthy object, and the war will end when that object is attained. Under God, I hope it will never end until that time."[10] Then he called for "complete restitution, full reparation, effectual guarantee," adding that, "without reparation, peace is impossible."[11]

The German and the Austro-Hungarian reply to President Wilson, both dated December 26, 1916, stated that their respective governments "now have the honor to propose that representatives of the belligerent Powers convene at an early date at some place on neutral ground."[12]

Then, on January 10, 1917, the Entente governments sent a joint, and somewhat more detailed, note of their war aims to Washington. It called in part for "the restitution of provinces or territories wrested in the past from the Allies by force or against the will of their populations, the liberation of Italians, of Slavs, of Romanians and of Czecho-Slovaks from foreign domination."[13] On January 12, the Foreign Minister of Austria-Hungary, Count Ottokár Czernin, sent a note to Washington that denounced the Entente governments for intending "the annihilation and spoilation of the Austro-Hungarian Monarchy" and indirectly blamed them for the continuation of the war.[14]

Before the joint Allied note and Czernin's retort reached Washington, President Wilson, who wanted to end the war on fair terms, was already preparing his next peace move. On January 3, 1917, he met with House and discussed with him a plan that would spell out "the conditions under which the United States would be willing to join in guaranteeing a peace settlement."[15] On January 22, 1917, the President revealed his plan in an address to the Senate, expressing his belief that the time was near when "a definite discussion of the peace . . . shall end the present war." Wilson felt that the war should be followed not by a balance of power, but a "community of

power; not organized rivalries, but an organized common peace."
And since statesmen on both sides of the "group of nations now ar-
rayed against one another have said . . . that it was not part of the
purpose they had in mind to crush their antagonists," as a guarantee
of future peace and justice, the ending of the war must be a "peace
without victory." He then added:

> Victory would mean peace forced upon the loser, a victor's terms im-
> posed upon the vanquished. It would be accepted in humiliation,
> under duress, at an intolerable sacrifice, and would leave a sting, a
> resentment, a bitter memory upon which terms of peace would rest,
> not permanently, but as upon quicksand. Only a peace between
> equals can last.[16]

The President's address was communicated to all belligerents, but
the anticipated peace negotiations did not take place, for both
groups of belligerents wanted peace with victory. The Entente
governments wanted only American assistance in the war, and the
government of Germany had already decided to resume unrestricted
submarine warfare, beginning February 1, 1917.[17]

As a result of the German decision, the United States broke
diplomatic relations with Germany on February 3, 1917. President
Wilson then made repeated attempts to reach an understanding and
conclude a separate peace with the Monarchy. On February 20,
Wilson received a communique from Lloyd George concerning the
British position regarding the Monarchy which stated that the British
government was ready to receive a formal peace offer from Austria
and that it "did not wish to separate Bohemia and Hungary from the
Habsburg Empire."[18] A reply to the President's overtures to Vienna
was sent on March 13, 1917, in a secret communique. It states in
part:

> Count Czernin repeats that he is disposed to enter upon conversation
> to end the war on condition that it is a question of general peace and
> not a separate peace. It is absolutely out of the question to separate
> Austria-Hungary from her allies the Minister asserts with emphasis.[19]

Meanwhile, President Wilson made one more attempt to keep the
United States out of war. On February 26, 1917, he requested that
Congress pass a resolution of armed neutrality; the motion,

however, was blocked in Congress. In the face of mounting pressure, due especially to the unrestricted German submarine warfare, the President asked Congress to declare war on Germany on April 2, 1917. The Senate voted for war on April 4, the House of Representatives on April 6, and thus, the United States joined the Allies in the war as an Associated Power.

On April 8, diplomatic relations were broken between the United States and Austria-Hungary, but war was not declared on the Dual Monarchy. After some reflection, Wilson stated on June 14 that "the war had been undertaken by the military masters of Germany who happened to be the masters of Austria-Hungary."[20] Wilson believed that the German rulers were responsible for all miseries of the war including the Austro-Hungarian attack on Serbia in 1914 and was still convinced that he could separate the Monarchy from Germany.

In April 1917, British Foreign Secretary Arthur J. Balfour led a delegation to Washington and conferred with President Wilson, Colonel House and Secretary of State Lansing, briefing them on Allied positions, secret treaties and British views on postwar settlement. During a meeting with House on April 28, Balfour suggested a possible territorial settlement for the Danube region. Accordingly, "Austria would cede Bosnia and Herzegovina to Serbia, which would in turn give part of Macedonia to Bulgaria. Rumania would get some Russian territory and part of Transylvania. Three states would be formed from the Austro-Hungarian Empire: Bohemia, Hungary and Austria."[21]

Many others with ideas concerning peace and postwar settlement travelled to Washington, for President Wilson was increasingly considered to be the driving force behind the peace initiatives. For the same reason, various ethnic groups in the United States were organizing and stepping up their efforts to promote the interests of their kindred peoples in Europe. Some of the more successful organizers advocating the break-up of Austria-Hungary were American citizens of Slavonic background who had been born in the Dual Monarchy.[22]

On August 1, 1917, in the midst of persisting rumors that peace was imminent, Pope Benedict XV issued a peace proposal to the rulers of the belligerent peoples. The Pope offered a framework, which he hoped would be accepted as a basis for the termination of hostilities and the foundation of a just and lasting peace. He indicated that "the fundamental point must be that the material force of arms give way to the moral force of right." Regarding territorial questions, the Pope expressed the hope that, "in consideration of the immense advantages of durable peace with disarmament," the belligerents would put "the general good of the great human society" above private interests.[23]

President Wilson could not accept the Pope's peace proposal because he felt it implied that the rulers of Germany would stay in power and as a result the world would remain an armed camp. Before sending his reply, however, which Lansing transmitted to the Pope on August 27, 1917, Wilson consulted with the Allied governments. The final draft emphasized that the United States was not seeking material advantage; it made a distinction between the German people and their government and stated that the wrongs done in the war by the "Imperial German government ought to be repaired, but not at the expense of the sovereignty of any people." Furthermore, the note stated that "the establishment of selfish and exclusive economic leagues are . . . no proper basis . . . for an enduring peace. That must be based upon justice and fairness and common rights of mankind."[24]

The President's reply was received with satisfaction in England and France. Interestingly, the press' reaction in Hungary was also favorable. On September 4, it was reported from Budapest that the evening paper, *Az Est*, regarded Wilson's ideas to be conducive to world peace and acceptable to every friend of peace. For Hungary, the most important consideration was that "America had unconditionally put herself on the side of no annexation."[25]

As peace efforts were intensified, it became obvious that a planning organization was needed in the United States to prepare for an eventual peace conference.[26] A number of individuals came up with the idea at the same time and it was eventually developed by Wilson, House and Lansing. The Secretary of State, although he did not think that the conflict would end soon, requested a concerted study of "the aims and desires of the present belligerents."[27] Unknown to Lansing, President Wilson was also formulating a similar but alternative plan. As a former historian, Wilson considered that "preparing for peace would properly fall within the province of academic scholarship, making use of men trained in the handling of factual evidence."[28] On September 12, 1917, the President asked House to bring together a group of experts which eventually became known as the Inquiry.[29]

Shortly after assembling the core of the Inquiry, House left for Europe as an American representative to the Allied Supreme War Council. During his stay, he tried in vain to persuade the Allies to join the United States in a declaration of war aims, which the Americans hoped would unite the peoples against the Central Powers. The Allies resisted that idea and tried, also in vain, to engage House in "a discussion of the expected territorial spoils following the war."[30] By that time Wilson came to realize that the Allies continued to embrace their original war aims as embodied in the secret treaties.[31] He concluded, therefore, that "America must pursue a definitely independent course."[32]

At that stage, the American peace efforts were faced with a new challenge. On November 8, the leaders of the Russian Bolshevik Revolution issued a declaration in favor of peace, based on the renunciation of conquest by all belligerents and respect for the legitimate desires of peoples to rule themselves. This was similar to Wilson's earlier idea of "peace without victory." But in the heat of war he had already changed his mind and wanted a "victorious peace"[33] which was to lead to a settlement based on his principles, as indicated in his address to Congress on November 4, 1917:

> . . . justice alone at every point and to every nation that the final settlement must affect, our enemies as well as our friends. . . . It is this thought that has been expressed in the formula, "No annexation, no contributions, no punitive indemnities."

Wilson also expressed the necessity to increase American war efforts and to declare a state of belligerency with Austria-Hungary. He was embarrassed by the fact that, although the United States was fighting Germany, it was not at war with Austria-Hungary. At the same time he stated:

> We owe it, however, to ourselves to say that we do not wish in any way to impair or to rearrange the Austro-Hungarian Empire. . . . We only desire to see that their affairs are left in their own hands, in all matters, great or small.[34]

On December 11, 1917, President Wilson proclaimed, on the basis of a joint resolution of Congrss passed four days earlier, that a state of war existed between the United State and the Imperial and Royal

Austro-Hungarian Government.[35] Yet the President continued his efforts to separate the Monarchy from Germany.

Meanwhile, Colonel House returned from Europe in mid-December. After House briefed the President, Wilson asked him to have the Inquiry prepare a comprehensive report which would include propositions concerning various geographical regions. Colonel House presented the report to President Wilson on January 4, and together they began to formulate unilateral American peace objectives. It was hoped that these objectives would impress liberals and socialists in Europe and in the United States when they realized that America wanted to base the peace settlement "on justice rather than on conquest." Wilson and House also hoped to "persuade the Bolshevik leaders in Russia of America's interest in a just settlement, which might serve to prevent Russia's withdrawal from the war."[36]

American war aims and peace terms, which were based to a considerable extent on the Inquiry report, were included in the Fourteen Points, a part of the President's speech delivered to Congress on January 8, 1918.[37] President Wilson considered the last of the Fourteen Points which called for the formation of a League of Nations to be most important. Point Ten which proposed autonomy for the national groups without breaking up the Dual Monarchy was vitally important to Austria-Hungary. It indicated that Wilson agreed with the Inquiry which recommended:

> Towards Austria-Hungary the approach should consist of references to the subjection of the various nationalities, in order to keep that agitation alive, but coupled with it should go repeated assurances that no dismemberment of the Empire is intended.[38]

The Fourteen Points embodied American foreign policy regarding the postwar settlement. Yet the State Department was by-passed in its preparation. As a result, Secretary of State Lansing was very critical of the Fourteen Points. Lansing could not see how the secret treaties of the Allies could be reconciled with the principles of justice declared by Wilson. In Lansing's opinion the intention to maintain Austria-Hungary "was most unwise."[39] Lansing spelled out his views regarding Austria-Hungary and wrote them in his notebook:

> I think that the President will have to abandon this idea and favor the erection of new states out of the imperial territory and require the

separation of Austria and Hungary. This is the only means of ending German power in Europe. Convinced of this, I think we should encourage the erection of a Polish state, a Czech state, and possibly a Ruthenian state. Then would come the union of Croatia, Slovania, Dalmatia, Boznia-Herzegovina, Montenegro, and Serbia under one sovereignty. There should also be considered the annexation of the Roumanians of Transylvania to Roumania and of the Italian provinces to Italy. Finally, to complete the dismemberment, the Austrian Empire and the Kingdom of Hungary could be separated. These independent states would present an insuperable barrier to German ambitions . . . I shall await an opportune time to lay this last question before the President.[40]

The "opportune time" occurred a few months later.

On February 11, 1918, President Wilson supplemented the Fourteen Points with the following Four Principles, which he held essential to a permanent peace:

Principle 1. "Each part of the final settlement must be based on the essential justice of that particular case."

Principle 2. "Peoples and provinces are not to be bartered about from sovereignty to sovereignty as if they were mere chattels and pawns in a game, even the great game, now forever discredited of the Balance of Power," but that

Principle 3. "Every territorial settlement involved in this war must be made in the interest and for the benefit of the population concerned, and not as a part of any mere adjustment or compromise of claims amongst rival states," and

Principle 4. "All well-defined national elements shall be accorded the utmost satisfaction that can be accorded them without introducing new or perpetuating old elements of discord and antagonism."[41]

President Wilson's declarations, especially the Fourteen Points, received world-wide attention. Unfortunately they were accepted by the European belligerent powers as the basis for peace and postwar settlement only after immense additional sufferings, destruction and propaganda campaigns. The Allied Powers held out for victory, which, paradoxically, was possible only with massive American aid as well as increasing military participation. The original German reaction to the Fourteen Points was summed up by General Erich von Ludendorff, on February 5, 1917, during a secret meeting with Count Ottokar Czernin and German Chancellor Georg von Hertling, in his remark: "If Germany makes peace without profit, then Germany has lost the war."[42] Only when faced with imminent defeat in the fall of 1918 were the Central Powers ready to accept the Fourteen Points and the Four Principles without reservation.

On September 15, 1918, the Austro-Hungarian government invited all belligerents to send delegates to a confidential and nonbinding discussion of the basic principles for the conclusion of peace.[43] When that proposal was rejected in Washington, the German government sent President Wilson a note on October 4 concerning an armistice and peace. Three days later, Washington received a second Austro-Hungarian note which offered to conclude with the President of the United States and his Allies an armistice on every front and "to enter immediately upon negotiations for peace for which the Fourteen Points . . . and the Four Principles . . . should serve as a foundation."[44]

Reporting on these notes, Secretary of State Lansing recommended to the President that Germany and Austria-Hungary not be treated alike. "In Germany the population could be convinced that if they adopted a democratic form of government they could escape invasion and total ruin. But Austria-Hungary must give way to new nations."[45] This was clearly at variance with President Wilson's earlier position, but by the fall of 1918, he accepted the idea of the dissolution of the Habsburg Empire. The fundamental change in the President's position was due to complex internal and external developments. It seems, however, that two separate but related diplomatic events in the spring of 1918 were especially influential.

During a speech given in Vienna on April 2, 1918, Czernin attempted a public debate with Wilson over peace aims. He rejected the idea of a separate peace, but restated his readiness for a general peace based on the President's Four Principles stated on February 11, and on the Emperor's proposals. Those proposals were included in a letter secretly communicated to the President on February 20, in which the Emperor adopted the Four Principles and suggested that a general peace could be negotiated if all belligerents would "renounce conquest and annexations."[46] During the speech, Czernin also revealed the secret negotiations with France, implying that they were initiated by Premier Georges Clemenceau. Czernin then blamed the failure to reach peace on the rebellious nationalities and their exile representatives who "ever kindle the expiring war spirit in London, Rome and Paris."[47]

Czernin's speech angered Clemenceau and to show that "Count Czernin lied," he made the so-called "Sixtus letter" public.[48] This letter, wherein the Emperor had expressed a willingness to support France's "just claims in Alsace-Lorraine" in exchange for peace, was sent by Emperor Charles on March 24, 1917 to French President Raymond Poincaré.[49] Czernin apparently had no knowledge of the Sixtus letter and resigned on April 15, 1918. The affair greatly embarrassed Emperor Charles, who was forced to move even closer to Germany.[50] Wilson and Lansing were dismayed over the incident, which destroyed all hopes of separating Vienna from Berlin. "There was always a possibility of something resulting from the evident desire of the Austrian Emperor for peace almost at any price," lamented Lansing.[51]

Almost simultaneously with the Clemenceau-Czernin incident, the "Congress of Oppressed Nationalities of Austria-Hungary" met in Rome. The meeting was organized and orchestrated by Czech exile leader Tomás Masaryk, with the help of two British propagandists, Henry Wickham Steed, and Robert W. Seton-Watson. The idea for such a meeting originated at the time of the Italian defeat at Caporetto on October 24, 1917. It was to demonstrate the "anti-Austrian solidarity of the oppressed peoples of the Habsburg Empire." However, by the time the Rome Congress met, between April 9 and 11, 1918, it also wanted to "convert and firmly commit the Allies, particularly President Wilson, to a strong anti-Austrian policy."[52] It seems that the Rome Congress contributed to a considerable extent to the reversal of American policy toward Austria-Hungary.[53]

The new American policy that accepted the idea of the dissolution of the Austro-Hungarian Monarchy was initiated by an exchange of notes between Wilson and Lansing in May and June of 1918. In a memorandum dated May 29, Lansing wrote to Wilson that the United States should revise its policy related to the nationalities of the Austro-Hungarian Monarchy, which would mean in effect "the dismemberment of the present Austro-Hungarian Empire into its original elements, leaving these independent nationalities to form separate states."[54] Wilson concurred and wrote to Lansing on June 26:

> I agree with you that we can no longer respect or regard the integrity of the artificial Austrian Empire. I doubt that even Hungary is any

more an integral part of it than Bohemia. I have made this judgement
in part upon a very interesting and illuminating conversation I had a
month or two ago with a group of Magyar Americans who spoke
plainly to the point.[55]

The fundamental change in the American position was clearly
reflected four months later in the reply to the Austro-Hungarian
note, which was received in Washington on October 7, 1918. The
ominous letter was written, at the President's request, by Lansing
and dated October 18, 1918. The letter intimated that since the President's principles were announced (on January 8 and February 11),
"the Government of the United States has recognized that a state of
belligerency exists between the Czechoslovaks and the German and
Austro-Hungarian Empires, and that the Czecho-Slovak National
Council is a *de facto* belligerent government . . . It has also recognized in the fullest manner the justice of the nationalistic aspirations
of the Yugo-Slavs for freedom" Therefore the President was "no
longer at liberty to accept mere 'autonomy' of these peoples as a
basis of peace."[56]

The end of hostilities between the Allied and Associated Powers
and Austria-Hungary was signalled by the unconditional armistice
concluded at Padua, Italy on November 3, 1918. It also marked the
end of the Habsburg Monarchy and was a grave turning point for
Hungary. It set in motion or accelerated events and developments
which would lead to the Treaty of Trianon in 1920. During those
two years, Hungary went through the throes of a revolution. Regain-
ing its independence, it became a Republic and was invaded by
Czech, Romanian, Serbian and French troops. The invasion led to
the rise and fall of a Soviet type republic and then to a counter-
revolution, which restored the kingdom under a regent.

Prior to the ending of all hostilities on November 11, 1918, many
in the United States expected that Colonel House would lead the
American team to negotiate peace, and also expected that the Inquiry would play a leading role. Both assumptions were off the
mark. On November 18, President Wilson announced his intention
to lead the American Peace Delegation himself. He was convinced
that only he could impose the new diplomatic order on the world.
Yet as he was leaving for Europe in December, he expressed doubts
about his journey, which he felt "would either be a great success in
history, or a supreme tragedy."[57] As to the organization of the

delegation, the State Department was to be given a leading role and the Inquiry an important, subsidiary role. House was to oversee all political and economic aspects of the delegation's work in Paris, Lansing was in charge of the legal questions, with the President providing the supreme leadership.[58]

The President and his party left for Europe aboard the *George Washington* on December 4, 1918. On December 10, during the crossing, Wilson revealed some of his thoughts about the peace settlement and the League of Nations to the Inquiry and told the members that they "should go only so far in backing the claims of a given power as justice required, and not an inch further." He added: "Tell me what's right and I'll fight for it; give me a guaranteed position."[59] Among the Inquiry members was Archibald C. Coolidge, Professor of East European History at Harvard University, who soon was to be sent to Vienna and Budapest to gather information in the former territories of Austria-Hungary.

President Wilson marshalled all his resources in a singleminded effort to carry out his mission, which started on a high note with his triumphant arrival in France on December 14, 1918. Before the Peace Conference opened in Paris in mid-January, 1919, the President, with his wife at his side, was greeted with enthusiastic popular acclaim not only in France and England, but also (and especially) in Italy. In Rome, he paid a visit to the Pope, whose peace proposal he had rejected earlier; by then he considered the Pope a possible supporter of the League of Nations.

At the time of Wilson's triumphal tour, the newly independent and disarmed Hungary was being invaded from three directions. In the desperate situation, Count Mihály Károlyi, head of the government of the democratic Hungarian Peoples Republic, sought American help and hoped to find President Wilson willing to see to it that Hungary was treated fairly at the coming Peace Conference.[60] The President's attentions, however, were focussed on other matters, primarily the prospects of the League of Nations. But Károlyi's hopes were encouraged somewhat when Professor Coolidge arrived in Budapest from Paris (via Vienna) on January 15, 1919.[61]

During his six days' stay, Coolidge sent several reports to the American Peace Commission in Paris evaluating how he perceived the country's predicament. He interviewed Károlyi (by that time President of the Republic) as well as other officials. He found the Hungarians distressed and in near chaos, united only in their concern for the fate of their country. Coolidge could observe in Budapest the effects of the long war and the unfolding consequences of the foreign invasion. The fact that the invasion and the continued Allied blockade deprived Hungary of most of its vital resources, especially coal, led Coolidge to conclude that "the continuation of these conditions would cripple industry and bring about unemployment, thus increasing the danger of a Bolshevik uprising."[62]

In one of his reports, Coolidge dealt with the complex and sensitive question of the nationalities. He found the Hungarian government ready and willing to transform Hungary into a sort of Switzerland by granting wide autonomy to the various nationalities. The Hungarians expressed to Coolidge their confidence that the great majority of the peoples living in the historical Hungarian state would prefer to remain there rather than be absorbed by their neighbors. They felt, reported Coolidge, that in the name of justice and Wilsonian principles, "these peoples should be given a fair chance to express their wishes."[63]

Coolidge reported to his colleagues in Paris that if the extent of foreign occupation indicated the future boundaries of Hungary, more than three and three quarter million Hungarian citizens would be subjected to alien rule. "To compel what has been since a thousand years a unified country to accept such an arrangement as permanent would be only to condem it to a future of hatred and strife with every probability of violent outbreak before many years have elapsed."[64]

At the time Professor Coolidge stayed in Budapest, Czech troops were in the midst of overrunning and cutting off northern Hungary. He wrote about the Hungarian bitterness towards the Czechs, who proceeded to incorporate the occupied territories without asking the population for their consent, whereas the Hungarian leaders expressed to Coolidge their readiness to "accept the decision of the Slovak people as to whether they wanted autonomy within Hungary or union with Bohemia." The Czechs decided for the Slovaks as they "claimed Bohemia on historical and geographical grounds, Slovakia on the basis of ethnographic, and Magyar-inhabited lands north of the Danube on the basis of economic considerations." The Hungarians, reported Coolidge, regarded the Czech actions as naked imperialism and could not believe that "the Allies and especially America could countenance such a violation of the principles of justice and self-determination."[65] A separate report indicated that

Professor Coolidge was himself convinced by the Hungarian position concerning the unique geographic unity of Hungary, which had assured the viability of the Hungarian state for over ten centuries.[66] In the complete absence of Hungarian representation at the Paris Peace Conference, the Coolidge reports amounted to a presentation of Hungary's case by an American expert.[67] The reports indicated a desirability of upholding the unity of the country, or at least the unity of the Hungarian nation—a nation on the loser's side and in desperate straits, but one with a long past, a nation that trusted its fate to be decided on the basis of the Wilsonian principles of self-determination and free plebiscites with historical, cultural, ethnic, geographic, economic and strategic considerations. But as it was, the Peace Conference took none of these considerations into account.

The Coolidge reports hardly affected the American recommendations; they were too late for that. All but one of Coolidge's reports were dated January 19, 1919, and sent by couriers to Paris where the first concrete and recorded plan for the postwar frontiers of Hungary was just being completed. The plan was part of a comprehensive outline of problems—territorial, political, economic and social—which the Peace Conference was likely to face. It was drafted by the Intelligence Section (composed, for the most part, of former members of the Inquiry) of the American Peace Delegation, in Paris and was dated January 21, 1919.[68]

The frontiers recommended by the plan resembled the eventual territorial settlement of the Treaty of Trianon. Yet in some important details, the plan was not as detrimental to Hungary. One of the most important differences concerned the frontier shared with the new Czecho-Slovak state. The American plan left the island of Csallóköz of the Danube river, with its overwhelmingly Hungarian population, to Hungary. But as the plan pointed out, "(I)n Hungary the recommended frontier runs south of the linguistic border and includes more than 500,000 Magyars."[69] According to the pertinent map of the plan, Ruthenia, with the important Hungarian cities of Ungvár, Munkács and Máramarossziget would have remained part of Hungary, but the text of the report stated: "It is undesirable that the Ruthenians of eastern Hungary should continue under Hungarian rule . . . and a Hungarian wedge be thrust between the Romanians and the Czecho-Slovaks." The report also opposed the idea of uniting Ruthenia with Poland, Galicia or the Ukraine, "which might lead to incorporation within a future Russia . . . it is certainly undesirable that Russia should ever extend across the Carpathians, down the Hungarian plain."[70]

Concerning the borders with Romania, the American plan intended to leave the cities of Arad, Nagyvárad, Nagykároly and Szatmárnémeti within Hungary (see map no. 2). In that way, a broad homogeneously Hungarian populated area would have escaped foreign rule. Significantly, the report pointed out (in case the recommendations were accepted) the necessity to protect another homogeneous Hungarian group in Transylvania, the Székelys. It was suggested that the frontier be carefully defined "so as to do full justice to delicate questions of commercial outlets that affect dense groups of both Romanian and Magyar population."[71]

The Hungarian-Yugoslav frontier proposed by the American report was considerably more favorable to Hungary than the one ultimately laid down by the Treaty of Trianon. The cities of Magyarkanizsa, Szabadka, Topolya and Zenta, together with compact masses of Hungarians, would have been left under the sovereignty of the mother country.

The report pointed out that "the boundaries of proposed Hungary do not follow historic lines, and the new state would have but half the area and population that Hungary had before the war." The reductions were made mostly in order "to satisfy the vital economic needs of neighboring states." The report stressed that:

> Further reduction of Hungary along the lines of Czech and Rumanian claims seems eminently undesirable. It would be unwise to give Rumania the mouth of the Maros. Likewise undesirable is the existence of a corridor between Czecho-Slovakia and Yugo-Slavia, since the region of the corridor is preeminently Magyar in character.[72]

The report recommended that the frontier between Austria and Hungary be left intact. This section of the historical borders of Hungary was the only one not immediately contested by her neighbor upon the termination of the war.

The region's new territorial order was built, however, at Hungary's expense for the most part, and the Peace Conference, in contrast with the U.S. Intelligence section's proposal, accepted most, if not all, of the territorial claims against that country. Interestingly, the first such claim, heard by the Supreme Council of the Principal Allied and Associated Powers on January 31, 1919, set two of the Claimants, Serbs and Romanians, against each other. Both had claims to the Banat, Hungary's rich southern district. The Romanians based their claims to the whole of the Banat on the secret treaty of August 17, 1916, between the Allied Powers and Romania. The Serbs asserted that part of the Banat belonged to them by virtue of the "will of the people." On the second day of the hearing, Ionel Bratianu, the Romanian Prime Minister, stated that he considered the Banat an integral part of the whole of "Transylvania," which Romania demanded on historical as well as ethnic grounds.[73] Vittorio Orlando, the Italian Prime Minister, supported the Romanian claims, by reason that the secret treaty was binding on the Allies. That notion, however, was opposed by Clemenceau, who stated that the Allies' agreement regarding the secret treaty was cancelled by Romania's conclusion of a separate peace with the Central Powers (May 7, 1918). Furthermore, as Lloyd George pointed out, "Rumania was now claiming more than she was entitled to under the secret treaty." At his recommendation, the following resolution was proposed:

> It is agreed that the questions raised in Mr. Bratianu's statement on Roumanian territorial interests in the Peace Settlement shall be referred for examination in the first instance by an expert committee composed of two representatives each of the United States of America, the British Empire, France and Italy. It shall be the duty of the Committee to reduce the questions for decision within the narrowest possible limits, and to make recommendations for a just settlement. The Committee is authorized to consult the representatives of the peoples concerned.[74]

Before the resolution was adopted, President Wilson stated: "The United States of America were not bound by any of the treaties in qustion; they were quite ready to approve a settlement on a basis of facts." And he observed that "the claimants did not always restrict themselves even to the limit set by the Treaties." The President added:

> . . . he was seeking enlightenment, and this would no doubt be afforded by a convincing presentation by the experts. If the resolution proposed by Mr. Lloyd George did not receive acceptance, he would find himself compelled to fight the question merely on the views expressed by the American experts; but he would prefer that these conclusions should be corrected by views of the French, British and Italian experts.[75]

The resolution was adopted and a Committee for the Study of Territorial Questions Relating to Romania was created.

The Czecho-Slovak claims were then presented to the Supreme Council by Eduard Beneš on February 5, 1919. He began by saying that "the Czechs must be prudent, reasonable, and just to their neighbors and they must avoid provoking jealousy and renewed struggles." Then he proceeded to claim for the newly born state the provinces of Bohemia, Moravia, Austrian Silesia and Slovakia. Concerning the latter, which had been an integral part of Hungary since the tenth century, Beneš asserted that "Slovakia had, before the tenth century, formed part of a 'Czecho-Slovak' state when it had been overrun by the Magyars." According to him "the population still considered itself Czech; it wished to belong to the new Czecho-Slovak state."[76] As for the frontier with Hungary, he claimed the river Danube on principle, as well as for economic reasons, so that the landlocked Czecho-Slovak state would have access to the Black Sea. In addition to these claims, Beneš submitted two suggestions for consideration. He informed the Peace Conference that the Ruthenes, eastern neighbors of the Slovaks, who were living in the northeastern part of Hungary, proposed the formation of an autonomous state in close federation with Czecho-Slovakia. The reason for the proposed federation, offered by Beneš, resembled that of the aforementioned recommendation, warning against uniting Ruthenia with the Ukraine or Galicia. He stated that:

> If Eastern Galicia became Russian it would be dangerous to bring Russia south of the Carpathians. If Eastern Galicia became Polish, the Poles themselves would not wish to include this population. It follows, therefore, that this people must either be Hungarian or autonomous. If the latter, they wished to be federated to the Czecho-Slovak state. This would impose a burden on Czecho-Slovakia, but would afford them the advantage of a common frontier with the Roumanians.[77]

The other suggestion, submitted by Beneš, concerned an overland access to the Adriatic Sea by means of a "small corridor" through western Hungary.[78] The idea of the corridor was opposed by the American recommendation. Upon hearing Beneš's presentation, the Supreme Council referred the matter, together with the same stipulations as in the case of the Romanian claims, to a special 'Committee on Czecho-Slovak Questions.'

The Yugoslav territorial claims were presented to the Supreme Council on February 18, 1919. Milenko Vesnić, speaking for his delegation, declared that "his delegation regarded the right of self-determination as inviolable and any treaty disposing of the Yugoslav people without their consent as null and void." Concerning the frontiers that Yugoslavia shared with Romania to the east, he repeated the suggestion made on January 31 during the discussion of the fate of the Banat, that would "allow the population to choose their allegiance." To the north, the Serbs proposed a boundary with Hungary that would include all Croats, Slovenes and Serbs, and would "correspond not only to ethnic, but to geographical realities."[79]

After their presentation, the Supreme Council referred the Yugoslav claims to the committee that was already examining the Romanian claims. With that, the Council heard and referred the three territorial claims against Hungary to special committees "to examine the claims advanced and to formulate recommendations for a just settlement."[80] The recommendations were to help the Principal Allied and Associated Powers make their final decisions regarding the problems; however, as it turned out, the recommendations were accepted as final judgments.

Although the recommendations of the special committees were to affect Hungary vitally, her interests were seldom considered and the Hungarians were never given so much as a hearing. The committees were biased against Hungary by the nature of their tasks, which were to inquire into claims advanced by Hungary's enemies. The committees had to make recommendations for the future frontiers of Czecho-Slovakia, Romania and Yugoslavia, rather than of Hungary.

The Committee on Czecho-Slovak Questions, considering the future of Ruthenia, decided "to advocate in priciple the formation of an autonomous state to include the Ruthenians of Hungary which should be under Czecho-Slovak protection, with guarantees, however, for the freedom of transit across Ruthenian territory between Hungary and Poland, as well as between Rumania and Czecho-Slovakia."[81] The subcommittee of the above committee, which was considering the future boundaries of Czecho-Slovakia, held seven meetings in five weeks, and only the testimony of the Czech representative, Dr. Beneş, was heard.[82]

In drawing up the frontier between Czecho-Slovakia and Hungary, the American and Italian experts of the Committee on

Czecho-Slovak Questions regarded as "a vital consideration to include the smallest possible number of Magyars within Czecho-Slovakia." In the British and French opinion, however, that consideration was secondary to finding the best geographic frontiers for the Czecho-Slovak state. The British and French point of view ultimately prevailed, as it did generally throughout the Peace Conference.[83]

American and French views were at times poles apart. At the first meeting of the Committee for the Study of Romanian Territorial Questions held on February 18, 1919, the members of the committee agreed that "the whole of Rumania's claim to Transylvania should not be allowed." The members proposed different lines for the possible boundaries. The line "proposed by the French was furthest west, giving the largest slice of Hungarian territory to the Rumanians, while the line suggested by the Americans was furthest east," leaving the broad zone of Hungarian-populated regions within Hungary.[84] The differences in the American and French approaches to basic related problems were also indicated by a discussion between André Tardieu, member of the French delegation, and Robert Lansing, Secretary of State. The discussion took place on May 8, 1919, during the proceedings of the Council of Foreign Ministers, which was considering the results of the territorial committees' inquiry. The topic was the future Hungarian-Romanian frontier, and at one point the minutes reported that:

> Mr. Lansing asked why a more accurate ethnic line could not be followed.
>
> Mr. Tardieu explained that it would cut the railway line and suppress continuous communication.
>
> Mr. Lansing asked if anywhere west of the line there could be found a predominantly Romanian population.
>
> M. Tardieu said that this might occur in certain isolated places.
>
> In reply to further questions, M. Tardieu said that some 600,000 Hungarians would remain under Romanian rule, while 25,000 Romanians would remain within Hungary.
>
> Mr. Lansing expressed the view that this distribution did not appear very just; in every case, the decision seemed to have been against the Hungarians.

M. Tardieu said that any other adjustment would have been all in favor of the Hungarians and correspondingly to the detriment of the Romanians.[85]

It should be noted, by that time the Romanians figured prominently in French designs, especially as far as the war against Bolshevism was concerned. In contrast, the Hungarians were considered not only former enemies but current ones as well, after the Károlyi regime gave way to the Communist dictatorship of Béla Kun on March 21, 1919.[86]

The question of the frontier between Austria and Hungary was brought up for the first time on May 8 at the meeting of the Council of Foreign Ministers. During the proceedings, Italian Foreign Minister Baron Sonnino expressed the opinion that their discussion should result in a definition of Hungary's border with Austria. Balfour was of the opinion that the best method of defining the frontiers would be to adopt the results of the inquiry by the territorial committee. In Lansing's view:

> The Council was dealing with a territory which in 1914 had been the domain of Austria and Hungary. It was recognized that this territory was to be dismembered, that Austria and Hungary were to be separate states and that their lands were to be limited by new states, whose frontiers were to be determined. No definition of Austria and Hungary, therefore, appeared necessary. The definition would arise automaticlly as a result of establishing the new states.[87]

Nevertheless, after futher discussion, the Council decided to appoint a commission to collect information regarding possible rectification of the border between Austria and Hungary. No action would have been planned, however, if the question were not raised by the two countries.

The question was raised again at the meeting of the Supreme Council held on May 12, 1919, brought up by President Wilson. He said that the border between Austria and Hungary would have to be defined in the treaty with Austria. Baron Sonnino asked "whether it would not be enough to require Austria to recognize the independence of Hungary, and Hungary that of Austria, without raising the frontier question at all." Reflecting on this, Wilson stated that, according to his information, the Austrians would raise the question. In concluding the discussion, it was decided that "Austria would be required to recognize the frontier of 1867 between Austria and Hungary."[88] Following that decision the Supreme Council adopted the frontiers of postwar Hungary as recommended by the territorial committees. But the question of the frontier between Austria and Hungary was brought to the attention of the Peace Conference once again. In notes submitted between June 2 and 16, 1919, the Austrian Peace Delegation set forth Austria's claim to western Hungary based on geographic, national and economic considerations. They held those territories to be vital to Austria if it was to be a viable state; at the same time they asked that "the right be granted the inhabitants of these territories themselves to decide by a free plebiscite whether or not they wish to be joined German-Austria."[89] Interestingly, the first to protest the Austrian claim at the Peace Conference were the Czechs,who renewed their efforts to secure a corridor through western Hungary. On July 7, 1919, the Supreme Council decided "to ignore the Austrian request for a plebiscite, as well as the Czech protest, and decided to assign western Hungary to Austria without a plebiscite."[90] Hungary protested the decision bitterly and requested that a plebiscite be held in that part of the country but, as in the case of the other contested territories, the request was in vain. The single exception was to be the city of Sopron in western Hungary where the overwhelming majority of the population voted in a plebiscite to remain under Hungarian sovereignty (December 14–16, 1921).

With the decision of July 7, 1919, the Supreme Council of the Principal Allied and Associated Powers completed the dismemberment of historic Hungary. The results did not reflect the Principles of President Wilson nor the American recommendations. Although Wilson expressed readiness to argue the question of territorial settlement on the basis of the recommendations of the American experts, he never actually did so. Decades later, it was observed by an "Inquiry veteran" that "there were considerations of international politics, strategy and common courtesy to our allies which in many, perhaps the majority of cases, prevented President Wilson from following his experts' advise."[91]

As for Wilson's principles, they were compromised at the Peace Conference mostly for the sake of the League of Nations. On May 1, 1919, Lansing noted this when he wrote:

> The feeling is that the principles, which the President laid down in the
> "Fourteen Points" and in his speeches, have been destroyed by com-

promises and concessions, that a victor's peace rather than a just peace is being sought, and cupidity backed by threats of refusal to sign the Convenant controls the situation.[92]

As a result (and quite contrary to the design, wishes and expectations of President Wilson) the postwar settlement was built on quicksand, especially in the Danube region.

Hungary, the country most drastically affected by the decisions of the Peace Conference, was not invited to Paris until December 1, 1919, after its fate was already sealed. The settlement imposed on that country by the victorious powers on June 4, 1920, was devastating in its effects. As demonstrated by subsequent history, it caused incalculable damage to the Danube region, as well as to the rest of Europe.

Notes

1. Inga Floto, *Colonel House In Paris, A Study of American Policy at the Paris Peace Conference 1919* (Aarhus, 1973), 25.

2. Ray Stannard Baker, *The Versailles Treaty and After, An Interpretation of Woodrow Wilson's Work at Paris* (New York, 1914), 9.

3. Laurence Emerson Gelfand, *The Inquiry; American Preparation for Peace, 1917–1919* (New Haven: Yale University Press, 1963), 2.

4. *Ibid.*, 3–4.

5. Victor S. Mamatey, *The United States and East Central Europe, 1914–1918, A Study in Wilsonian Diplomacy and Propaganda* (Port Washington, New York/London: Kennikut Press, 1972, 1957), 41.

6. Floto, *op. cit.*

7. James Brown Scott, *Official Statements of War Aims and Peace Proposals, December 1916 to November 1918* (Washington, 1921), 3.

8. Mamatey, 45.

9. Scott, 15.

10. *Ibid.*, 16.

11. *Ibid.*, 17–18.

12. *Ibid.*, 23.

13. *Ibid.*, 37.

14. *Ibid.*, 43.

15. Mamatey, 48.

16. For the full text, see Scott, 49–55.

17. Scott, 68.

18. Mamatey, 60.

19. *Ibid.*, 62.

20. Quoted by, Jean-Baptiste Duroselle, *From Wilson to Roosevelt,*

Foreign Policy of the United States, 1913–1945 (New York and Evanston, 1968; Boston, 1960; Paris, 1960), 68.

    Ibid., 75–76.

    22. For an extensive work on the topic, see: Joseph P. O'Grady, ed., *The Immigrants' Influence on Wilson's Peace Policies* (University of Kentucky Press, 1967).

    23. For the full text see Department of State. *Papers Relating to the Foreign Relations of the United States. 1917,* I, supplement 2, *The World War,* 2 vols. (Washington: Government Printing Office, 1932), 162–164.

    24. *Papers Relating to the Foreign Relations of the United States. 1917.* 178–179.

    25. *Ibid.,* 191.

    26. Gelfand, 23–24.

    27. *Ibid.,* 25.

    28. *Ibid.,* 33.

    29. See *Ibid.,* XI. Prominent among the members of the Inquiry were Colonel House, Sidney E. Mezes, Isaiah Bowman, David Hunter Miller, Walter Lippman, and James T. Shotwell.

    30. *Ibid.,* 13.

    31. Floto, 264.

    32. Gelfand, 115.

    33. Duroselle, 76.

    34. *Papers Relating to the Foreign Relations of the United States. 1917.* IX–XIX.

    35. *Ibid.,* 459.

    36. Gelfand, 135.

    37. For the full text see Scott, 234–239.

    38. Department of State, *Papers Relating to the Foreign Relations of the United States. 1919. The Paris Peace Conference,* vol. I (Washington: Government Printing Office, 1942), 48. On the margin of the Inquiry report, Wilson wrote the following, which became "Point Ten" of the "Fourteen Points": "The people of Austria-Hungary, whose place among the nations we wish to see safeguarded and assured, should be accorded the freest opportunity of autonomous development."

    39. Gelfand, 151–152.

    40. Cited by Gelfand, 152.

    41. Cited by Harold W. V. Temperley in, *A History of the Peace Conference of Paris,* VI vols. (Oxford, 1969), London, 1920–24, vol. I, 195.

    42. Quoted by *ibid.*

    43. *Ibid.,* 370.

    44. *Ibid.,* 371.

    45. Duroselle, 85.

    46. Mamatey, 226–227.

47. *Ibid.*, 234.

48. *Ibid.*, 235.

49. *Ibid.*, 63–64.

50. *Ibid.*, 235–236.

51. *Ibid.*, 237.

52. *Ibid.*, 234.

53. Temperley, 198.

54. Peter Pastor, *Hungary Between Wilson and Lenin: The Hungarian Revolution of 1918–1919 and the Big Three* (Boulder: East European Quarterly, 1976), 22.

55. *Ibid.*

56. Temperley, 452–453.

57. Quoted by Duroselle, 91. The members of the American Mission to Negotiate Peace were: President Wilson, Colonel M. House, Robert Lansing (Secretary of State), Henry White, and General Tasker H. Bliss.

58. Floto, 85.

59. Quoted by David Hunter Miller, *My Diary at the Conference of Paris*, (New York, 1924), I, 373.

60. Francis Deák, *Hungary at the Paris Peace Conference. The Diplomatic History of the Treaty of Trianon* (New York: Columbia University Press, 1942), 17–18.

61. Professor Coolidge was the head of the so-called Coolidge Mission, which was "appointed by the American Delegation on December 27 and set up headquarters in Vienna." See Arno J. Mayer, *Politics and Diplomacy of Peacemaking. Containment and Counterrevolution at Versailles, 1918–1919* (New York, 1967), 369. Secretary of State Lansing informed Professor A. C. Coolidge in a telegram dated December 26, 1918, that "You are hereby assigned to the American Commission to observe political conditions in Austria-Hungary and neighboring countries." See Department of State, *Papers Relating to the Foreign Relations of the United States. 1919, The Paris Peace Conference*, vol. II, 218.

62. Deák, 16.

63. *Ibid.*, 20.

64. Cited by *ibid.*

65. *Ibid.*, 21.

66. Deák, 362–364.

67. Mayer, *op. cit.*

68. Miller, vol. IV, 209. Document 246. "Outline of Tentative Report and Recommendations Prepared by the Intelligence Section, in Accordance with Instructions, for the President and the Plenipotentiaries January 21, 1919."

69. *Ibid.*, 231.

70. *Ibid.*, 231–232.

71. *Ibid.*, 234.

72. *Ibid.*, 245.

73. According to Bratianu, the Banat had to be considered as whole, "because on ethnical grounds it would be impossible to justify the placing of 580,000 Germans and Magyars under the control of 272,000 Serbs." See Miller, XIV, 146.

74. *Ibid.*, 177–178.

75. *Ibid.*, 180–181.

76. Deák, 34–35.

77. Miller, XIV, 224.

78. Deák, 36.

79. *Ibid.*, 37.

80. *Ibid.*, 38. See also Temperly, 434: "Shortly after the Peace Conference met, two commissions on frontiers were appointed, named respectively the Czechoslovak and the Rumanian, and these in fact determined the fate of Hungary."

81. Cited by *ibid.*, 45.

82. *Ibid.*

83. *Ibid.*

84. *Ibid.*, 47.

85. *Ibid.*, 436.

86. Unlike Károlyi, who pinned his hopes on the Western Democracies and Wilson, Kun turned to the Bolsheviks and Lenin for help.

87. Deák, 434–435.

88. A compromise between Austria and Hungary was reached and the Austro-Hungarian Monarchy was formed in 1867.

89. Miller, XVIII, 496.

90. Deák, 87.

91. Cited by Gelfand, 332.

92. Cited by Floto, 216.

Part III

Hungary and Its Neighbors in the Process of Peacemaking

(See maps at the end of the book)

Peter Pastor

Hungarian Territorial Losses During the Liberal-Democratic Revolution of 1918–1919

Of the 13 clauses and 375 articles in the Treaty of Trianon, none has been considered more catastrophic by the war generation, and more unfair by the succeeding generations, than Clause II, articles 27–35. These defined the new frontiers of Hungary, reducing its imperium to one third of its pre-war size. It doomed millions of Hungarians in the periphery to live under foreign sovereignty.

In 1921 these terms brought into question the viability of Hungary as a nation state. Hungarian public opinion embraced tenaciously the slogan "nem, nem soha!"/No, no, never!/; it became the rallying cry for territorial revisionism. This policy was eagerly adopted by the conservative Horthy regime, which recognized that revisionism helped to buttress an antiquated socio-economic system. As the slogan became synonymous with the Hungarian counter-revolution, few, if any, recalled that it was coined by government propagandists in Mihály Károlyi's revolutionary regime.

The revolution, with its liberal-democratic goals, broke out in the dying days of the Habsburg monarchy. From October 31 to March 20, 1919, the Revolutionary governments weighed options and searched for compromises as an alternative to territorial exactions which roughly overlapped with those that were stipulated in the Treaty of Trianon. The collapse of the Károlyi regime, and the rise of the communist regime of Béla Kun on March 21, 1919, was directly related to the refusal by Dénes Berinkey's liberal-democratic government to accept further territorial amputations spelled out in an Allied *démarche* known as the Vix Ultimatum.

It was the representatives of the counter-revolutionary Horthy regime who, however reluctantly, accepted and signed the punitive peace. This regime represented the interest of those circles which had been primarily responsible for Hungary's support of the war. Yet these groups showed their compatriots no remorse about being involved in a war that had led to Trianon. In a psychological climate receptive to scapegoat-seeking, official circles succeeded in accusing Mihály Károlyi and his supporters of being responsible for the territorial losses.[1]

Mihály Károlyi, then in foreign exile, was judged to be a traitor and his considerable wealth was confiscated. The historians of the era considered him and his government naive and held him responsible for the territorial losses, which was allegedly accepted as early as November 7, 1918.[2] This interpretation has been engraved in the Hungarian collective consciousness to such an extent that even today it finds broad acceptance among them.[3] Due to a similar evaluation found in Francis Deak's *Hungary at the Paris Peace Conference*,[4] this view has also influenced American scholars. Numerous publications of the last two decades, basing their findings on recently opened archival sources in Hungary, France and Britain, have challenged this view, and it is hoped that they will lay the old politically motivated charges to rest.[5]

The roots of the territorial clauses in the Treaty of Trianon could be found in the old adage on the consequence of war—"To the victors belong the spoils." World War I was no exception to this unwritten rule. The Entente powers offered large chunks of Austro-Hungarian territories to Italy (1915) and to Romania (1916) as a reward for joining the alliance in its struggle for victory. It is evident that the harshness of the territorial settlements made by the peace treaties of Brest-Litovsk (1918) and Bucharest (1918) would have been the same had the Central Powers won the war. The victors would have been different but spoils would have existed nevertheless.

Following the Bolshevik revolution of November 1917, Russia and the United States offered a challenge to traditional war aims. The Bolsheviks denounced the goals of the belligerents as being imperialistic. They called for the revolutionary overthrow of the warring regimes by the proletariat and the conclusion of a peace without indemnities or annexations.

President Woodrow Wilson introduced an equally radical program as the United States entered the war on the side of the Allies. He also called for peace without indemnities and annexations. Instead of proletarian revolutions, he called for the establishment of liberal-democratic regimes based on the American model. The right of self-determination for the peoples of the Austro-Hungarian monarchy was also part of this program. Wilson's call was based on a combination of idealism and diplomatic realism.[6] The collapse of the enemy governments, he believed, would force an end to the conflict.

On Wilson's urgings, the Entente abandoned traditional war aims. However, this did not assure the territorial status quo of the Austro-Hungarian empire.[7] Although the Wilsonian solution favored autonomous rights for the various nationalities within the Empire, spokesmen for the Czech and Slovak people, both in the west and in Russia, wanted more than that. They called for the creation of a Czechoslovak state; hence, the end of the Austro-Hungarian monarchy. Their views were influential because western governments relied on emigré specialists. What is more, the formation of volunteer Czechoslovak armies enabled the emigré leaders to make demands on the Allies; they could not be dismissed lightly.[8] The intervention of the Czechoslovak Legion on the side of the Anti-Bolshevik forces in Russia in June 1918 made the Czechoslovak cause even stronger.[9]

The Habsburg Emperor Karl, unable to achieve a separate peace, responded too late to the subversive, yet appealing, ideology originating from the West. Only in October 1918—with his armies on the verge of collapse—did he call for the federalization of Austria. By then the Allies, including the United States, had abandoned their belief that Austria-Hungary's survival was desirable for the sake of international stability.[10]

To assure the decomposition of the realm through revolutions, the Allied leaders had even delayed the execution of a speedy armistice. Thus, when on November 3, 1918, the representatives of Austria-Hungary signed the armistice, the empire no longer existed. Since there was as yet no agreement on the geographical boundaries of the emerging successor states, the Armistice of Padua included purely military clauses, and it was not, therefore, a commitment for a specific type of peace agreement. This was to be worked out at the coming peace conference.[11]

In Hungary, a bloodless revolution brought to power a coalition on October 31 which represented the opposition in and outside of parliament. The head of the revolutionary government was Mihály Károlyi, the leader of the anti-war opposition Károlyi party since 1916. The most important member of the coalition was the Social Democratic party, with no parliamentary representation. The small Radical party rounded out the coalition. Its leader was the sociologist and specialist on the nationalities problems: Oszkár Jászi.

The revolutionary platform called for land and tax reforms and universal suffrage. In essence, it reflected positions held by the coalition members for some time. The platform also overlapped with the liberal-democratic program favored by President Wilson.[12]

For the nationalities of Hungary the government offered self-determination. It assumed that the Croats would secede, but that the others would support the plan of the Minister of Nationalities, Oszkár Jászi. It envisioned the reshaping of Hungary into a confederation, a kind of "Eastern Switzerland," which in turn would be part of a Danubian confederation of states.[13] This project clearly indicated that the leaders of the People's Republic of Hungary expected to preserve the frontiers of the former kingdom.

The ideology buttressing their efforts was Wilsonianism. The Hungarian policy, just as the American one in 1917, was based on idealism and diplomatic realism. The Hungarians were sincere partisans of the Wilsonian program, but they also knew that Hungary lay prostate before the victorious powers. It was incapable of resorting to arms in pursuit of its own interests. Therefore, it was believed that only a Wilsonian peace could extricate Hungary from its unenviable position.

The Hungarian ministers were not alone in their trust of Wilsonianism. A number of American and British officials also hoped that with the guns silent, a new Europe could be constructed,[14] and some type of confederation would replace the defunct Austro-Hungarian empire.[15] It was also believed, however, as Lewis Namier, a British specialist of the Foreign Office noted, that the Allies pledged themselves "to the entire independence of too many of Austria-Hungary's constituent elements to make it practicable."[16] This view reflected a degree of fatalism at a time when firmness by the leadership of the victorious great powers and a belief in confederation could have achieved better results.[17]

The great degree of disorganization among the peacemakers gathering in Paris also contributed to the lack of effectiveness of the Wilsonians.[18] Following the armistices, the threat of bolshevik-type revolutions hung over Europe, diverting the attention of the victorious Allies from the details of the peace terms.[19] Thus, peacemaking, just like warmaking during the previous four years, did not fulfill expectations and did not follow plans set earlier.

In East Central Europe, the intransigence of the Entente's small allies over territorial issues created further complications. Some of these touched Hungary directly. Romania, following the Armistice of Padua, broke the Peace Treaty of Bucharest and re-entered the war against Germany just three days before the armistice at Compiègne was signed. Romania's new declaration of war, however, was used not to further territorial demands against distant Germany, but against neighboring Hungary.

Romania's claims were based on the secret Treaty of Bucharest (1916) in which France and Russia promised Romania a large chunk of Hungary, including Transylvania. These exaggerated war-time promises which the Entente had no intention of fulfilling were also nullified. This was done because Romania had signed a separate peace with the Central Powers.[20]

Due to the anti-bolshevik stance of the Czechoslovak Legion in Russia, the Czechoslovak National Council in Paris was recognized as a government in exile.[21] The emigré government was promised an independent state within "historical boundaries." Although no Czechoslovak state had ever existed before 1918, establishing boundaries for such an entity meant territorial losses for Hungary.[22]

The Entente also had wartime commitments to Serbia on which she intended to cash in. On August 18, 1915, the Entente promised Serbia Fiume and the Banat of Southern Hungry. The same territories were also promised to Italy and Romania—Fiume, to the former, and Banat to the latter.

Under the circumstances, the Károlyi government had assumed a hopeless task when it insisted on the integrity of Hungary's frontiers. It was apparent that most nationality leaders in Hungary were hostile toward the idea of federalism and were enthusiastic about secession instead.[23] Therefore, whether the Allies acted along the principles of Wilsonian self-determination or according to traditional war-time practices, their major task was to redraw the boundaries at Hungary's expense.

Although the Hungarian government's position stated that the nationalities could be persuaded to stay within an integral democratic Hungary, its officials in the cabinet were quite realistic. They believed that territorial concessions were unavoidable. Thus, the avowed insistence on territorial integrity was a maximal position motivated by the desire to secure an advantageous compromise under adverse conditions.

The first occasion to deal with the boundary issue came up during the first week of November. Although the Austro-Hungarian representatives had signed the armistice of Padua in the name of the Hungarians as well, the Commander-in-Chief of the Balkan front, General Louis Franchet d'Esperey, demanded a separate armistice from Budapest.[24] He was still on the offensive against the Germans and the 170,000 troops of General August von Mackensen were still in Transylvania.

An early meeting with Franchet d'Esperey was desirable for the Hungarians. Its purpose would be to secure a favorable demarcation line from this Allied arbiter before the Romanians had a chance to do the same. In conjunction with a mission to the Allied Commander, the government also wanted to send deputies to Romania. The pretext for the latter mission was based on a technicality. Since the Hungarian parliament had never ratified the Peace Treaty of Bucharest, a final settlement between Hungary and Romania was still needed. The Hungarians wanted to make a bilateral deal over territories before Romania's appetite was reawakened.[25] The fall of the Marghiloman cabinet in Jassy and Romania's reentry into the war, made the project superfluous.

The Hungarian cabinet faced the upcoming meeting with Franchet d'Esperey with reservation. Mihály Károlyi, the Prime Minister and Foreign Minister of Hungary, was advised by his colleagues not to take part in the negotiations. It was feared that if the Hungarians were given extremely unfavorable terms, Károlyi would be discredited and his government hopelessly weakened.

The deteriorating economic situation, however, forced the ministers to change their minds. It was concluded that Károlyi's presence was needed as he had a long-established pro-Entente reputation. Therefore, he was expected to prevail upon the Allied commander to lift the economic blockade of Hungary.[26] The considerable debate over the make-up of the mission indicates that neither Károlyi nor the other leaders had illusions about the bleak future facing Hungary.

The final decision to have Károlyi as the leader of the delegation turned out to be a good one. When the Hungarians met Franchet d'Esperey in Belgrade on November 7, it was only Károlyi who was treated with deference, while his entourage, including Jászi, was humiliated.[27] The French general noted in his report to Paris that he thought well of Károlyi, an aristocrat with pro-Entente sympathies, but that he considered his cabinet a bunch of second raters.[28]

Franchet d'Esperey considered the negotiations in line with the changed situation in East Central Europe. Since the Austro-Hungarian Empire had ceased to exist, he believed that the Padua Armistice, signed on the Italian front, needed updating. He considered the terms he was now giving to the Hungarians as an addendum to the armistice, a convention. The agreement was military in nature. It established a line of demarcation only in southern Hungary which put part of Transylvania under French occupation, with the Banat, and part of Baranya under French and Serb occupation.[29]

The Allied occupation of even this limited amount of Hungarian lands led to the insistence by Hungarian negotiators that the convention specify that the demarcation line could in no way be considered as a new political boundary. That was to be settled by the Peace Conference. This stipulation was swiftly accepted by Franchet d'Esperey with the blessing of his superiors in Paris.[30]

The Belgrade meeting indicated success for Károlyi. Franchet d'Esperey, following his government's instructions, did not recognize the Károlyi government *de jure*. Nevertheless, he was sufficiently impressed by it—so much so that he advised Paris that it was in the interest of the Allies to support Károlyi because the latter represented "the party of order."[31]

Fair treatment of the Hungarians was possible only at the cost of leaving some of Hungary's neighbors unsatisfied. Rewards, however, had to be given to the Czechoslovaks for their ongoing intervention in Russia. There was also the price to be paid to Romania if she were expected to do the same.

By the end of November, therefore, the French government, at the urgings of the Czechoslovak foreign minister, Eduard Beneš, broke the terms of the Belgrade Convention in the name of the Allies. It gave the Czechoslovaks a green light to occupy Slovakia without defining its borders. In order to camouflage this unilateral action, the French offered a false explanation. They indicated that Franchet d'Esperey had overstepped his duties at the Belgrade negotiations when he allowed the continuation of Hungarian administration over all territories formerly belonging to the old kingdom. There was also an effort mounted to discredit Károlyi as a "perfidious" leader of an anti-democratic Hungary bent on enslaving the non-Magyar nationalities.[32]

In fact, the Hungarians had attempted to come to an understanding with the nationalities through negotiations. When it was evident that the spokesmen for the Slovaks or the Romanians were unwilling to accept autonomy within Hungary, the cabinet searched for compromise solutions which would be based on the principle of self-determination.[33]

Negotiations were undertaken with Milan Hodža, a representative of the Slovak National Council, and with Iuliu Maniu, a member of the Romanian National Council in Hungary. On December 6, Oszkár Jászi and Minister of War Albert Bartha came to an understanding with Hodža, who also represented the Czechoslovak government. A demarcation line was established in Slovakia which closely followed the ethnic boundaries. Yet Prague, aware that a more favorable line was being prepared in Paris, disavowed the Hodža-Bartha agreement.[34] On December 23, the Allied Supreme Council, dominated by Marshal Ferdinand Foch, transmitted a new demarcation line. This line was similar to the frontier given to the Hungarians at Trianon.[35] It left close to a million Hungrians on the Slovak side.

The shaping of the demarcation line in northern Hungary reflected the apparent French decision favoring, in the words of Foreign Minister Stephen Pichon, a "purely Magyar" Hungary. He further announced that France had no intentions of supporting the principle of self-determination. Instead it favored strong East Central European states which could be the allies of France.[36] Since France was allowed to have primary responsibility for peacemaking in East Central Europe, the case of the Hungarian government became weaker than ever.

Negotiations with the Romanian National Council started on November 13 and 14. Jászi, the head of the Hungarian delegation, offered the abolition of the counties, the old administrative units of Hungary. In their stead, he proposed the creation of national areas which, like the Swiss cantons, would have cultural and administrative autonomy. These cantons were to send representatives to the central government in Budapest. As a temporary solution, he also suggested the transfer of administrative power to the Romanian council, where a Romanian majority existed.

The Romanian National Council, led by Iuliu Maniu, Alexandru Vaida Voevod, Vasile Goldis and Ioan Erdelyi, rejected the offer and demanded full sovereignty for the council. The Hungarian officials returned to Budapest empty-handed.[37] However, Maniu's visit to Budapest at the end of November and his conciliatory manner revived Hungarian hopes for a negotiated settlement.[38]

In response to Maniu's favorable stance, and expecting compromise, the Hungarian government agreed to provide transportation for the Romanians of Transylvania to attend a Popular Assembly sponsored by the Romanian National Council in Alba Iulia. On December 1, this meeting unilaterally decided to unite the twenty-six counties with the kingdom of Romania. Interwar Hungarian historiography branded the Hungarian government's willingness to provide trains to the Romanians as treachery.[39] It is evident, however, that the Hungarian officials acted in good faith and expected positive results.

Oszkár Jászi, as minister of nationalities, recognized that the government could do nothing if the nationalities decided to secede.[40] After the Alba Julia decision, he thought of other alternatives to confederation. He was prepared to consider that in the eventuality that Hungarian villages would come under Romanian control, the national rights of the Hungarian minority would be protected by the Hungarian government.[41] This indicated the consideration of overlapping sovereignty as another compromise solution to the territorial dispute. Put into practice, this concept could have reconciled the self-determination of the Romanians with the needs and expectations of the Hungarians.

Jászi's plan could be considered as the minimum program of the Hungarians. However, the maximum plan—a confederated Hungary—was not jettisoned. The government continued to press for the maximum, fully expecting this position to be challenged and chipped away at the Paris Peace Conference.[42] The weakness of this reasoning was the government's failure to realize that the victors, disregarding traditions, did not intend to invite the defeated to present their case and bargain over details.

The Hungarian government rejected the Alba Iulia decision. According to Jászi, the Romanian leaders could not speak in the name of the majority. The combined Hungarian and Saxon population represented a 57 percent majority in the contested area. Significantly, the Allies also questioned the legitimacy of the Romanian claim on the same basis.[43] The Royal Romanian government's response to the declaration of its co-nationals was guarded at first as it still intended to pursue territorial quests as outlined in the Bucharest Treaty of 1916.[44]

To counterweigh the Romanian National Council in Transylvania, the Hungarian government encouraged the Hungarian

National Council in Transylvania to organize an assembly and to call for continued Hungarian sovereignty over the 26 counties. This tactic was to bring to the attention of the Allies the multi-ethnic character of the region. As another alternative, Budapest reluctantly supported the position of the Székely National Council. Spokesmen for this Hungarian-speaking group with their own distinct cultural traditions favored the formation of a Transylvanian Székely republic.[45]

In addition to these steps, preparations for military resistance were also undertaken. These were necessitated by the march of the Romanian army into Transylvania. The first Romanian troops crossed the Carpathians on November 13. Marosvásárhely (Tirgu Mures) was occupied on December 2, Beszterce (Bistrita) on December 4, and Brasso (Brasov) on December 7. By the middle of the month, the Romanians had reached the Transylvanian segment of the Belgrade demarcation line. By December 24 they surpassed it and occupied Kolozsvár (Cluj-Napoca).[46] In contradiction to the Belgrade Convention, the administration of the occupied areas was taken over by the Romanians.[47]

In northern Hungary, the French government approved the occupation of Slovakia in the name of the Allies. In Transylvania, on the other hand, the expansion of Romanian control was made without Allied sanction but with the support of General Henri Berthelot. Berthelot, as commander of the Allied forces in Romania and in southern Russia, disregarded the orders of his commander-in-chief, Franchet d'Esperey, and gave unqualified support to Romanian expansionist designs.[48]

In response to the Romanian advances, the Hungarian Council of Ministers was forced to decide on appropriate measures. Consideration was given to the resignation of the government and a call was issued to the Entente to govern Hungary. As a result of the continued blockade and territorial losses, Hungary was on the brink of chaos. Passive or active resistance to the absorption of Hungarian lands by Romania was also discussed. Oszkár Jászi proposed that government ministers take personal leadership over a Hungary divided into ten regions. The socialist Minister of Welfare, Zsigmond Kunfi, proposed that, instead of decentralizing, the government should map out a new frontier along solidly ethnic lines. He concluded that this was the price Hungary would have to pay for the lost war.

The cabinet finally decided to issue instructions to the commissioner of the 26 counties, István Apáthy. He was advised to agree to the occupation of Transylvania by Romanian troops acting as Allied representatives. This occupation was already in effect. Apáthy was to insist on Romanian acquiescence to the retention of Hungarian police forces in the occupied areas. These were to be the symbolic representatives of the Hungarian authorities, as sanctioned in the Belgrade convention.[49]

Instead, on December 31, General Berthelot offered Apáthy a new demarcation line. Following negotiations in Kolozsvár, Apáthy accepted the terms on January 3, 1919. The new agreement allowed the Romanians to hold the Nagybánya (Baia Mara)-Kolozsvár-Des (Dej) line. They were to be separated from the Hungarian troops by a 15-kilometer-wide neutral zone. Budapest, however, disavowed the agreement, claiming that Apáthy was not empowered to deal away the more favorable terms of the Belgrade Convention. The Romanians also disregarded the Apáthy-Berthelot agreement as it would have curtailed further expansion.[50]

General Franchet d'Esperey and even Prime Minister and Minister of War Georges Clemenceau were displeased with the unauthorized action of Berthelot. They did, however, accept the agreement *post facto*. Accordingly, Franchet d'Esperey expected that the new demarcation line would put an end to further Romanian expansion.[51]

On January 23, the government of Dénes Berinkey and Mihály Károlyi, who was now the President of the Republic, decided that it had no other choice but resort to armed resistance against Romanian expansion. To stop further Romanian advances, it was decided to dig in along the county lines of Bihar. An offensive was not planned—there were no reserves. The energy crisis caused by the blockade also precluded the transportation of supplies in large quantity.[52]

The Peace Conference, which opened in Paris in mid-January refused to accept the Entente commitments made to Romania in 1916. It also objected to the ongoing Romanian expansion. On January 25, the day after the Alba Iulia decision was enacted in the Romanian parliament, the peacemakers adopted President Wilson's resolution against the use of force for territorial acquisitions.[53] Special committees were set up to resolve the territorial questions. These committees were without either central direction or declared focus other than a resolution of border issues. They did not go about recommending general principles of settlement. They were restricted by the conflicting wishes of the great powers and the demands of the representatives of their small allies.[54] The committees were expected to write their reports in such a way that they could be incorporated directly into the treaty.[55] Since the reports of the committees were due by March 8, the territorial issues concerning Hungary, Czechoslovakia and Romania were decided during the tenure of the Károlyi regime.

Flouting Allied wishes to leave the territorial questions to the Peace Conference, Romanian troops continued to advance. By the end of January they held the Máramarossziget (Sighetul Mamatiei), Zilach (Zalau), Csucsa (Ciucea), Zam (Zam) line. The Romanian occupation of most of Transylvania was complete. Military flare-ups between the Hungarians and the Romanians became frequent and further conflict was imminent.[56]

Franchet d'Esperey, therefore, requested that the peacemakers in Paris establish a neutral zone between the Romanians and the Hungarians. He expected that the Romanians would be told to withdraw to the Apáthy-Berthelot line. Instead, on February 26, the Commission to Study the Territorial Questions Relating to Romania accepted a demarcation line that allowed Romania to occupy a line north of the outlines of historic Transylvania. A neutral zone was established to separate the Hungarian and Romanian troops.

The demarcation lines were drawn upon the advice of the French General Staff. It put strategic railway lines under Romanian control. These additional gains, sanctioned by Paris, intended to assure the success of Marshal Foch's projected grand alliance against Communist Russia. Romania, whose troops were already fighting the Bolsheviks, were natural allies. Hungarian territory was the price for continued Romanian intervention in Russia.[57] Although Foch's plan was soon rejected, the demarcation line assigned to the Romanians was not altered. Subsequently, the Hungarian-Romanian frontier of Trianon closely resembled the Romanian demarcation line as defined on February 26, 1919.

General Franchet d'Esperey was soon instructed to make military preparations for the execution of the decision. The Romanians were informed of the things to come, but the Hungarians were kept in the dark. The Hungarian government remained isolated. It was not recognized by the Allies who claimed that, without a territorial settlement, Budapest represented only a "local government."[58] Consequently, the government also lacked diplomatic accreditation abroad.

As a result of its isolation, which was compounded by a lack of information about the peacemaking spirit in Paris, the Hungarian government could not really formulate policies that would fit the new realities. By February 1919, it was evident that self-determination was *"demodé,"* and that there was no aversion to assigning the Hungarian population in the periphery to the neighboring states.[59]

Charles Seymour, the chief of the Austro-Hungarian division of the American peace commission, recognized this problem. He saw the need to invite the Hungarians to Paris, if not for participation, then for consultation. He expected that in this fashion the Hungarian government could weather the shock which was awaiting it.[60]

The Hungarian government, however, was unable to learn the truth. To curtail further Romanian advances, it was preparing for military resistance. On March 2, Károlyi inspected the troops in Szatmárnémeti and in an address declared:

> If Wilson's principles do not materialize and, instead of a peace based on mutual agreement, a dictated peace demanding territorial dismemberment is offered, I promise you, soldiers, I will never sign such peace terms![61]

The Hungarians were not informed of the February 26 decision of the Peace Conference until the middle of March. Until then, there were only rumors about new demarcation lines.[62] It was during the visit of Halsey E. Yates, the American military attaché to Romania, that the truth was unofficially revealed.

Yates came to Budapest to learn about the position of the government on the border question and to demand 250 locomotives for the Roma ians. It was claimed that these were needed for them to fight against the Bolsheviks. Yates, stationed in Bucharest, was influenced by the Romanian version of the conflict. He considered that some of the American peace commissioners who had visited Hungary and sent favorable reports to Paris were biased in favor of the Hungarians. He intended to get an objective picture for his superiors in Paris and in Washington.[63]

On March 15, Yates met Károlyi. He learned that the Hungarians were reconciled to the loss of the Maros Valley, but intended to resist further Romanian demands by military force. Károlyi argued that additional territorial losses would ruin the country economically. This would cause trouble and discontent and would eventually throw Hungary into the arms of Germany.[64]

Yates told Károlyi that the Hungarians must accept the loss of Slovakia and Transylvania. With this he confirmed the rumors about the new demarcation lines. He warned that, even though the Allies did not have sufficient armies around Hungary to reply to Hungarian intransigence, there were other means at their disposal, such as food blockades and indemnities.[65]

Before leaving Budapest, Yates wired Paris that he "strongly recommended" that the existing lines not be changed until some 100 British and American officers supplied with automobiles could arrive. He also expressed the view that Hungarians could successfully resist the Romanians who could not be resupplied before May 15.[66]

Yates' proposal, however, was not considered. New developments in southern Russia pressed for the transmission of the terms for a neutral zone. By mid-March the French interventionist forces in the area of Odessa were facing the threat of defeat by the Bolsheviks. On March 13, Clemenceau ordered General Berthelot to use Romanian troops to defend the Tiraspol, Razdelnaya, Odessa railway line.[67]

The crisis in Russia gave the Romanians an opportunity to press for the execution of the February 26 decision. On March 14, the Romanian representative in Paris, Victor Antonescu, transmitted to Clemenceau his government's memorandum. In it the Romanians claimed that while Franchet d'Esperey was looking for a suitable French officer to carry out the terms of the Peace Confrence, the Hungarians were stripping Transylvania and spreading Bolshevik propaganda. Clemenceau's response came on the same day. Using almost the exact words of the Antonescu memorandum, Clemenceau referred to the alleged scorched-earth policy of the Hungarians. He ordered Franchet d'Esperey to avoid any further delay and carry out the decision of the Peace Conference.[68]

It is unlikely that Clemenceau bought Antonescu's argument about Bolshevism in Transylvania. However, he was cognizant of the fact that Romanian help in the new crisis in Russia was needed, and that the new demarcation line was the price for continued Romanian participation.

Colonel Yates, following his return to Bucharest on March 17, also saw the need to satisfy the Romanians in order to resolve the Russian problem. He wired to Paris:

The Poles and Rumanians are willing to fight our battles for us but they must be given at once the necessary supplies; and the menaces on their other fronts must be removed by our establishing neutral zones.[69]

Franchet d'Esperey, who would have preferred to blame Romania's military involvement in Transylvania for the fiasco in Russia, had no choice but to order the transmission of the Peace Conference edict to the Hungarians at once. This was done in spite of Franchet d'Esperey's fears that the Hungarian-Romanian clashes above the neutral zone would continue. Furthermore, because of the crisis in Russia, no Allied troops were available to enforce the order in case of resistance.[70]

On March 20, Colonel Vix, in the presence of other Allied representatives, handed the Hungarians the order to withdraw to the new demarcation line. In his instructions, Vix was told to give the Hungarians 48 hours to reply. His directions further stated that in case the Hungarians turned down the ultimatum, no immediate war-like act would be instituted against them. Yet during his meeting with Károlyi and the other leaders, Vix threatened to pack his bags if the government did not acquiesce. This was tantamount to the threat of resumption of war.[71]

Following this meeting, the Council of Ministers and President Károlyi gathered to discuss the required response to the Vix Ultimatum. Károlyi informed the ministers that the *démarche* could not be accepted because it would make the Romanian demarcation line into a frontier, thus depriving Hungary of further territories. In the meantime, French troops in the netural zone would prevent the Hungarians from using force against Romanian territorial expansion. Károlyi gathered that the territorial losses could not be reversed as the Entente intended to use the Serbs, Czechs and Romanians in a war against the Bolsheviks. Since the Peace Conference did not recognize the Wilsonian principles, Hungary needed new internal and external policies. He proposed the creation of a socialist government which could assure better productivity, hence increase the nation's economic strength. It could also gather the support of the international socialist movement. As the only mass party in Hungary, the Social Democratic party could mobilize the workers and, subsequently, the middle classes to resistance. He also proposed that the socialists reach an understanding with the small Communist party, so that Hungary would not be attacked by the Russian Bolsheviks.[72]

The socialists, however, went further than was expected. They fused with the communists. On March 21, following the rejection of the Vix Ultimatum and the resignation of Károlyi and the cabinet, the socialists and the communists established a Soviet Republic. The new government was now dominated by the communist Béla Kun. In alliance with the Russian Bolsheviks, it aimed to undo the dictated frontiers in the north and the south by calling for a war against "Entente imperialism."[73]

The unsuccessful attempts of Károlyi's democratic regime to arrive at some understanding with its adversaries led to its demise. Neither its minimal nor maximal territorial solutions were found to be acceptable by its Czechoslovak and Romanian neighbors. The demarcation lines to which it objected and which it refused to accept became the frontiers that the Allies forced on a right-wing, authoritarian government. For a quarter of a century, the Horthy regime unjustifiably blamed the high price of defeat in war on a government which had actually refused to acquiesce to dictated territorial losses.

Notes

I wish to thank Montclair State College for granting release time for the work on this article.

1. Mária Ormos, "Még egyszer a Vix-jegyzékről" ["Once More about the Vix Memorandum"], *Századok*, vol. 113, no. 2 (1979), 314; Gyula Juhász, *Hungarian Foreign Policy 1919–1945* (Budapest, 1979), p. 39.

2. Zoltán Szende, "Count Michael Károlyi in Belgrade," *Hungarian Quarterly*, vol. 5, no. 3 (1939); Ferenc Nyékhegyi, *A Diaz-fele fegyverszüneti szerződés (a paduai fegyverszünet)* [The Diaz Armistice Treaty (The Armistice of Padua)] (Budapest, 1922); Jenö Horváth, *A trianoni békeszerződés megalkotása és a revizió utja* [The Creation of the Peace Treaty of Trianon and the Course of the Revision] (Budapest, 1939); Jenö László, *Erdély sorsa az uniotól Trianonig* [The Fate of Transylvania from the Union to Trianon] (Budapest, 1940); a recent but similar view in Yves de Daruvar, *The Tragic Fate of Hungary* (Munich, 1974).

3. György Litván, *Magyar gondolat, szabad gondolat* [Hungarian Thought, Free Thought] (Budapest, 1978), pp. 144–145.

4. Francis Deak, *Hungary at the Paris Peace Conference* (New York, 1942, repr. 1972), p. 8; for recent and similar interpretations, see Bennett

Kovrig, *Communism in Hungary* (Stanford, 1979), p. 37; Sándor Szilassy, *Revolutionary Hungary 1918-1921* (Astor Park, Fla., 1971), pp. 26-27.

5. Zsuzsa L Nagy, *A párizsi békekonferencia és Magyarország 1918-1919* [The Peace Conference and Hungary 1918-1919] (Budapest, 1963); Tibor Hajdu, *Károlyi Mihály* (Budapest, 1978); Lajos Ardai, "Angol-Magyar viszony a polgári demokratikus forradalom idején az angol levéltári források tükrében (1918 oktober-1919 március)" [English-Hungarian Relations during the Bourgeois-Democratic Revolution in the Light of English Archival Sources] *Történelmi Szemle*, vol. 18, nos. 2-3 (1975); Peter Pastor, *Hungary between Wilson and Lenin: the Hungarian Revolution of 1918-1919 and the Big Three* (New York, 1976); Mária Ormos, "A belgrádi katonai konvencióról" [About the Belgrade Military Convention], *TSZ*, vol. 22, no. 1 (1979).

6. Inga Floto, *Colonel House in Paris* (Copenhagen, 1973), p. 252; Arno Mayer, *Politics and Diplomacy of Peacemaking* (New York, 1965), p. 16.

7. Wilfried Fest, *Peace or Partition, The Habsburg Monarchy and British Policy 1914-1918* (New York, 1978), pp. 188-189.

8. Kenneth J. Calder, *Britain and the Origins of the New Europe, 1914-1918* (Cambridge, 1976), p. 218.

9. Josef Kalvoda, *Czechoslovakia's Role in Soviet Strategy* (Washington, 1978), p. 17; Fest, *Peace or Partition,* pp. 238-239.

10. Victor S. Mamatey, *The United States and East Central Europe, 1914-1918* (Princeton, 1957), pp. 333-334.

11. Fest, *Peace or Partition,* p. 253; M. L. Dockrill and Zara Steiner, "The Foreign Office at the Paris Peace Conference in 1919," *The International History Review*, vol. 2, no. 1, January 1980, 55.

12. Peter Pastor, "The Hungarian Revolution's Road from Wilsonianism to Leninism, 1918-1919," *East Central Europe*, vol. 3, no. 2, 1976, 211-213.

13. Gabor Vermes, "The Agony of Federalism in Hungary under the Károlyi regime, 1918-1919," *East European Quarterly*, vol. 6, no. 4, 1972, 496; Béla K. Király, "The Danubian Problem in Oszkár Jászi's Political Thought," *The Hungarian Quarterly*, vol. 5, 1965, 127-129.

14. Dockrill and Steiner, "The Foreign Office," p. 56; Zsuzsa L. Nagy, "Összeomlás és kiútkeresés 1918-1919-ben, Jászi Oszkár és a forradalmak" (Collapse and Search for Extrication in 1918-1919, Oszkár Jászi and the Revolutions), *Kritika*, no. 5, May 1978, 3; Charles L. Mee, Jr., *The End of Order: Versailles 1919* (New York, 1980), pp. 103-105.

15. Pastor, *Hungary between Wilson and Lenin,* p. 104.

16. As quoted in, Fest, *Peace or Partition,* p. 58.

17. Charles Seymour, *Letter from the Paris Peace Conference* (New Haven, 1965), p. XXX; Walter A. McDougall, "Political Economy versus National Sovereignty: French Structures for Economic Integration after Versailles," *Journal of Modern History*, vol. 51, no. 1 (March, 1979), p. 11.

18. Dockrill and Steiner, *The Foreign Office*, pp. 67–68.

19. Mayer, *Politics and Diplomacy*, pp. 9–10.

20. Sherman D. Spector, *Rumania at the Paris Peace Conference: A Study of the Diplomacy of Ioan I. C. Brătianu* (New York, 1962), p. 37.

21. Josef Kalvoda, *Czechoslovakia's Role*, p. 15.

22. Zsuzsa L. Nagy, "Magyar határviták a párizsi békekonferencián" [Debates on the Hungarian Frontier Question at the Paris Peace Conference] *TSZ*, vol. 21, no. 3–4 (1978), p. 443.

23. Béla Bellér, "A Magyar Népköztársaság és a Tanácsköztársaság nemzetiségi kulturpolitikája" [The Cultural Politics of the Hungarian People's Republic and of the Soviet Republic toward the Nationalities] *TSZ*, vol. 11, no. 1 (1968), p. 3.

24. Maria Ormos, "A belgrádi katonai konvencióról," p. 26.

25. Budapest, Országos Levéltál [National Archives], *Minisztertanácsi jegyzőkönyvek* [Minutes of the Council of Ministers] K 27 MT jkv. no. 40 (Nov. 4, 1918); no. 41 (Nov. 5, 1918).

26. *Országos Leveltár*, K 27 MT jkv. no. 41 (Nov. 5, 1918).

27. Michael Károlyi, *Memoirs of Michael Károlyi, Faith without Illusion* (London, 1957), pp. 130–137.

28. Jean Bernachot, ed., *Les armées alliées en Orient après l'armistice de 1918, comptes rendus mensuels adressés par le commandant en chef des armées alliées en Orient, à l'état major de l'armée à Paris, de décembre 1918 à octobre 1920* (Paris, 1972), p. 45.

29. Nagy, *A párizsi békekonferencia*, pp. 11–12.

30. Ormos, "A belgrádi katonai konvencióról," p. 29.

31. Bernachot, *Les armées alliées en Orient*, 45.

32. Ormos, "A belgrádi katonai konvencióról," p. 29; Peter Pastor, "The Diplomatic Fiasco of the Modern World's First Woman Ambassador, Róza Bédy-Schwimmer," *EEQ*, vol. 8, no. 3 (1974), 279.

33. Országos Leveltár, K 27 MT jkv. no. 59 (Nov. 29, 1918).

34. Ferenc Boros, *Magyar-csehszlovák kapcsolatok 1918-1921-ben* [Hungarian Czechoslovak Relations in 1918–1921] (Budapest, 1970), pp. 46–47; Országos Leveltár, K 27 MT jkv. no. 58 (Nov. 28, 1918).

35. L. Nagy, "Magyar határviták," p. 444.

36. *Le Temps*, Dec. 31, 1918.

37. Pastor, *Hungary between Wilson and Lenin*, pp. 72–73.

38. Országos Levéltár, K 27 MT jkv. no. 58 (Nov. 28, 1918).

39. László, *Erdély sorsa*, p. 117.

40. Országos Levéltár, K 27 MT jkv. no. 59 (Nov. 29, 1918).

41. Budapest, Országos Levéltár [National Archives], *A Magyarországon élő nemzetek önrendelkezési joga előkészitésével megbizott miniszter* [The Minister in Charge of the Preparation of the Right of Self-determination of the Nations Living in Hungary], K 40, Erdődi Nemzeti Tanács to Jászi and reply (Dec. 3, 1918).

42. Országos Levéltár, K 27 MT jkv. no. 72 (Dec. 28, 1918); no. 58 (Nov. 28, 1918).

43. Spector, *Rumania*, p. 93.

44. Mária Ormos, "Az ukrajnai katonai intervencióról és hatásairól Közép-Európában, 1918 oktober–1919 április" [The Impact of the French Intervention in the Ukraine and in Central Europe] *TSZ*, vol. 20, nos. 3-4 (1977), p. 423, n. 56.

45. Országos Levéltár, K 40, Böhm to Jászi (Dec. 5, 1918); Minutes (Dec. 17, 1918).

46. György Ránki, ed., *Magyarország története, 1918-1919, 1919-1945*, vol. 8 [The History of Hungary, 1918-1919, 1919-1945] (Budapest, 19776), pp. 113-117.

47. Ránki, *Magyarország története*, p. 96.

48. Peter Pastor, "Franco-Rumanian Intervention in Russia and the *Vix Ultimatum*: Background to Hungary's Loss of Transylvania," *The Canadian-American Review of Hungarian Studies*, vol. 1, nos. 1-2 (1974), p. 14. This essay is based on unpublished archival sources from the French Military Archives and the Archives of the Ministry of Foreign Affairs, Paris.

49. Országos Levéltár, K 27 MT jkv. no. 69 (Dec. 18 and 19, 1918); Országos Széchenyi Könyvtár kézirattára [Archives of the National Szechenyi Library], *Apáthy iratok* [Apathy Papers], Quart. Hung. 2455, "Erdély az összeomlás után" [Transylvania after the Collapse].

50. Országos Levéltár, K 27 MT jkv. no. 13 (Jan. 27, 1919); Ormos, "Még egyszer a Vix-jegyzékről," p. 327.

51. Bernachot, *Les armées alliées*, p. 164.

52. Országos Levéltár, K 27 MT jkv. no. 11 (Jan. 21, 1919).

53. Spector, *Rumania*, p. 80.

54. Dockrill and Steiner, "The Foreign Office," p. 66.

55. Dockrill and Steiner, "The Foreign Office," p. 69.

56. Ormos, "Az ukrajnai francia intervencióról," p. 427.

57. Pastor, "Franco-Rumanian Intervention," p. 20; Ormos, "Az ukrajnai katonai intervencióról," pp. 429-430.

58. Pastor, *Hungary between Wilson and Lenin*, p. 83.

59. Sir James Headlam-Morley, *A Memoir of the Paris Peace Conference 1919* (London, 1972), p. 27, 44.

60. Pastor, *Hungary between Wilson and Lenin*, p. 104.

61. Pastor, *Hungary between Wilson and Lenin*, p. 128.

62. Ormos, "Még egyszer a Vix-jegyzékről," p. 331.

63. Washington, National Archives, *War Department General Staff Military Intelligence Division 1917-1941*, MID 220 a 2266-V 174, Report of Yates (March 4, 1919).

64. National Archives, MID 239 2323-354, Yates to Brig. Gen. Churchill (March 15, 1919).

65. Paris, Archives historiques, *Ministère de la Guerre. Etat-Major de*

L'Armée, Campagne Contre Allemagne, Carton 106, dossier 3, Vix to de Lobit (March 16, 1919).

66. National Archives, MID 239 2323-354, Yates to Brig. Gen. Churchill (March 15, 1919).

67. Pastor, "Franco-Rumanian Intervention," p. 20; Ormos, "Az ukrajnai francia intervencióról," pp. 435-436.

68. Pastor, "Franco-Rumanian Intervention," p. 21.

69. National Archives, MID 243 2069-98, Yates to Brig. Gen. Churchill (March 29, 1919).

70. Ormos, "Még egyszer a Vix-jegyzékról," p. 330.

71. Tibor Hajdu, *Március huszonegyedike* [The Twenty-First of March] (Budapest, 1979), pp. 54-57; for the French and Hungarian text of the Vix Ultimatum see György Litván, ed., *Károlyi Mihály levelezése I, 1905-1920* [The Correspondence of Mihály Károlyi I, 1905-1920] (Budapest, 1978), pp. 445-448; for the English version see Deak, *The Paris Peace Conference,* pp. 407-409.

72. Országos Levéltár, K 27 MT jkv. no. 29 (March 20, 1919); part of the minutes in Hajdu, *Március huszonegyedike,* pp. 69-73.

73. Tibor Hajdu, *The Hungarian Soviet Republic* (Budapest, 1979), pp. 28, 34-35.

Josef Kalvoda

The Czechoslovak-Hungarian Dispute

Slovaks living in Upper Hungary, as Slovakia was usually called before World War One, had long-standing grievances against those who held political and economic power in Hungary. The Slovak schools—almost all church-run—were few in number, the administrative language was Hungarian, the economy was controlled by Hungarians and Jews, and the Slovaks were under-represented in the Hungarian parliament.[1] Indeed, the nationality problems and injustices existing in the Habsburg Empire were much more severe in the Hungarian part of the Dual Monarchy. Yet, very few Slovaks expected the dissolution of the Empire when the war started; the most they hoped for was an autonomous existence for their nation that had been a part of Hungary for almost one thousand years.

At the outbreak of the war the Slovak representation in the Hungarian parliament shrunk to one deputy, Ferdiš Juriga; another deputy, Pavel Blaho, was called to military service and the third resigned his mandate.[2] Although Juriga affirmed the loyalty of the Slovaks to the Hungarian government, toward the war's end he and other Slovak leaders began to voice disapproval of the existing conditions in Hungary. Several Slovak leaders living abroad, most notably Milan R. Štefánik, Štefan Osuský and Gustav Košík, cooperated with the Czechs whose aim was the establishment of an independent Czecho-Slovakia.[3]

The Peace of Brest-Litovsk, concluded in March 1918, had some unforeseen consequences. In Austria-Hungary the returning prisoners of war helped to foster popular discontent that was already under way during the last year of the war, and some Czech and Slovak leaders went public rejecting the established political order. In Prague, Karel Kramář, the pre-war leader of the Young Czech party, who was imprisoned in 1915, sentenced to death in 1916 and pardoned by the new Emperor Charles in 1917, became in July 1918 the chairman of the Czech National Committee, promoting the idea of Czechoslovak independence. The May 1918 demonstration in Liptovsky Sv. Mikuláš (Slovakia) produced a pro-Czech resolution that had been inspired by Vavro Šrobár, a pre-war student and follower of Tomáš G. Masaryk, and the leading Slovak advocate of the Czechoslovak orientation.[4]

It may be pointed out that from the beginning those who worked for Czechoslovak independence included Slovakia in the state to be created on the ruins of Austria-Hungary. For Kramář, the leader of the independence movement at home, Slovaks were the closest Slavic kin of the Czechs; he believed that Slovakia was the necessary link between the Czech lands and Russia. The leader of the independence movement abroad, Tomáš G. Masaryk, felt that the Czechs and Slovaks were one nation and that they ought to live in one state.[5]

While the Slovak masses were largely apolitical, the leaders of the Slovak National party and the Slovak People's party did not hold the same view on the future of the Slovaks. Some favored Slovak autonomy within Hungary, while others advocated union with the Czech lands. But when, toward the end of May 1918, the leaders of the Slovak National party met at Turčiansky Sv. Martin (henceforth merely Martin), Father Andrej Hlinka emerged as a spokesman for cooperation with the Czechs. He declared: "We have to state definitely whether we will continue to live with the Hungarians or with the Czechs. We cannot avoid this question; let us say publicly that we are for a Czechoslovak orientation. The thousand-year marriage with the Magyars has not succeeded. We must dissolve it."[6] Yet, for the next few months the political situation in Slovakia remained dormant and only in October did the Slovak leaders formally establish their National Committee.

There were signs of the approaching end of the war and the Habsburg Empire when late in September the Bulgarian front collapsed and on October 2, 1918, the armistice with Bulgaria was concluded. Shortly afterwards the chairman of the Union of Czech deputies in the Vienna parliament announced that the Czecho-Slovak National Council in Paris with Masaryk at its helm, as it was the highest organ of the Czechoslovak armies, was competent to represent the Czechoslovak nation at the Peace Conference. On October 9, 1918, another Czech deputy belonging to the Union declared that the Czechs were leaving the Vienna parliament for good and were severing ties with Austria-Hungary.[7] Then on October 16, Emperor Charles published his manifest announcing federalization of the Cisleithanian part of the Habsburg Empire. The manifest provoked strong negative reaction in Hungary and speeded up the collapse of the Empire from within.[8]

On October 19 the only Slovak representative in the Hungarian parliament, Juriga, read a declaration demanding for the Slovaks the right to decide their own destinies. In particular the declaration denied the right of the Hungarian parliament and the government to speak for the Slovaks. It pointed out that instead of forty Slovak deputies there were only two Slovaks in parliament (in fact, the other deputy was not even present at that time); that the Slovak representatives at the peace conference would have to be selected by their own national assembly or its organ, the Slovak National Council, and that no other person had the right to negotiate and decide on behalf of the Slovak nation. The Slovaks, the declaration said, demand for themselves the right of self-determination, just as they recognize the right to self-determination of the other nationalities in Hungary.[9] The Juriga declaration was the last Slovak word in the Hungarian parliament, indicating that the Slovak leaders decided to part their ways with Hungary.

Juriga's reference to the Slovak National Council reflected the intent of the Slovak leaders to form such a body. Already in mid-September the first steps toward the formation of a Slovak National Council were taken; its purpose was to seek unification of all political segments of the nation in one representative body. On October 30, 1918, in Turčiansky Sv. Martin the Slovak National Council was formally established. Its chairman was Matúš Dula and its secretary Karol A. Medvecký. The Slovak National party, the Slovak People's party and the Slovak Social Democratic party were represented in the Council.[10]

The Slovak leaders who assembled in Martin on October 30 did not know that two days earlier the Czech National Committee in Prague proclaimed Czecho-Slovak independence. They knew, however, that the new Minister of Foreign Affairs of Austria-Hungary, Gyula Andrássy, accepted the Wilsonian peace conditions and recognized the right of the nationalities in Austria-Hungary, more specifically, the right of the Czechs, Slovaks and Southern Slavs, to decide their future destinies.[11] The Slovak National Council, therefore, issued a declaration breaking off the one thousand years' ties with Hungary, proclaiming that "the Slovak nation is a part of the Czechoslovak nation, one with it in language and in the history of its civilization. . . . We also claim for this, the

Czechoslovak nation, the absolute right of self-determination on a basis of complete independence."[12]

The "Martin Declaration," as the document is usually referred to, was a statement of intent; it was neither legally binding nor self-enforcing and it was subject to several interpretations.[13] It was brought to Prague by the Slovak National Council's delegates on November 1, and submitted to the Czech National Committee which was acting now as the provisional government in the Czech lands. In the exile government, proclaimed by Masaryk on October 18, the Slovaks were represented by General Milan R. Štefánik who was Minister of War; he was at this time on his way to the Czechoslovak army in Siberia.[14] Vavro Šrobár became a member of the Prague National Committee; the members of this committee, together with other exile politicians, became the government of Czecho-Slovakia. However, neither the latter nor the Slovak National Council had effective control over Slovakia whose territory had not even been clearly defined. Upper Hungary was under Hungarian administration and the Hungarian government was not prepared to give it up.

As long as the Hungarian authorities had an effective control of Slovakia, the question of jurisdiction of the several revolutionary bodies—the Slovak National Council, the Czech National Committee and the so-called temporary Slovak government consisting of four members led by Vavro Šrobár dispatched from Prague to Slovakia with the task of securing the latter for the new state on November 4—was of little consequence. At the outset of the struggle for Slovakia, the new Hungarian government of Mihály Károlyi had the upper hand; it controlled the administration, police and the armed force present in Slovakia. As early as November 7, 1918, the Hungarian government's delegate came to Prague and notified the Czech National Committee of his government's intention to solve the Slovak issue peacefully, while insisting on the preservation of the integrity of the Hungarian state.[15] Károlyi also sent a telegram to the Slovak National Council in Martin, emphasizing the right of the Slovaks to self-determination and stressing his belief that his government would be able to reach an agreement with the Council. The overtures to both the Czechs and the Slovaks by Károlyi, however, produced negative responses from both.[16] The Czechs notified the Hungarians that "violence of the Hungarians and Jews" will not be tolerated and that Czech military force will be dispatched to Slovakia to protect the Slovaks.[17]

The efforts of the revolutionary government of Károlyi was supported by the highest representative of the Catholic Church in Hungary, Cardinal János Csernoch, archbishop of Ostřihom (Esztergom), who was of Slovak origin and who tried, together with the other Hungarian bishops, to save for Hungary what could be saved. In his instructions to the Slovak clergy, Cardinal Csernoch pointed to the danger for the Slovak people in being attached to the Czechs whom he saw as anti-Church and who, he claimed, would pursue policies of Czechization of the Slovaks. He gave himself as an example of a Slovak who could attain the highest Church position in Hungary and instructed his subordinate clergymen to work for the preservation of the country's integrity.[18] On behalf of the Slovak clergy Father Hlinka responded that they would comply with the decisions of the Slovak National Council. In addition, Father Hlinka stated that he welcomed the establishment of Czecho-Slovakia, since he saw in the latter a new dawn, the fulfillment of the Slovak age-old desires and the shield and protection against the one thousand years of wrongs and injustices.[19]

In a communication of November 5, 1918, the Protestant bishop Sándor Raffay, appealed to the Protestant clergy in Slovakia in a way similar to that of Cardinal Csernoch. Raffay's announcement contained provisions for the preservation of the unity of the Hungarian Protestant church. It promised constitutional protection of religious equality and reciprocity, the maintenance of church-related schools, the increase of subsidies to clergymen, making language concessions and the reestablishment of the Slovak higher gymnasium, among others.[20]

In the early days of November 1918, the Hungarian government did not resist the small Czech armed units entering Slovakia from Moravia. However, the conclusion of the armistice on November 13, 1918, with the French General Louis Félix Franchet d'Espèrey, the commander of the Balkan front, prompted Károlyi to issue a protest against Czech attempts to occupy Slovakia, and he announced his intention to protect Slovakia with armed might.[21] Immediately, Hungarian troops began to attack the Czech military units which were forced to retreat in haste to Moravia. In mid-November the Hungarians placed under arrest the chairman of the Slovak National Council, Matúš Dula and another member of that council. Upon receiving instructions from Budapest, the authority released both the same day.[22]

While the Károlyi government tried to keep the Slovaks within Hungary, the Kramář government in Prague launched its struggle for Slovakia on the diplomatic front with the help of Eduard Beneš, Minister of Foreign Affairs, in Paris, and on the military front by dispatching armed units to that territory. The immediate basis for the Czech claim was the declaration made by representatives of all Slovak parties in Martin on October 30 who wanted their country to become a part of Czechoslovakia. Yet the new liberal government of Count Károlyi secured an armistice agreement with the Allies, signed in Belgrade on November 13, Article 17 of which stated explicitly that all Hungarian territory, with the exception of Croatia and Slavonia, would remain under Hungarian administration and that the Allies would not interfere with the internal administration of the country.[23] Since no provision in the agreement was made for the evacuation of the Slovak-inhabited districts, the Károlyi government understood this to mean that the latter remained part of Hungary. But the Prague government held a different view and sent its representative, Vavro Šrobár, to Slovakia to enforce its authority. Attempting to avoid an open conflict with the Czechs, the Károlyi government proposed the establishment of a Slovak National Council on the condition that the latter recognized Hungarian sovereignty over the disputed area. While the Hungarian government based its claim to Slovakia on Article 17 of the Belgrade armistice, the Czecho-Slovak government contested it on the grounds of Article 3 of the armistice, according to which the Allied powers had the right to occupy all places considered important for the preservation of order.[24]

The principal Czech negotiator in Paris, Beneš, did not like the prospect of having the territorial questions of the new state decided by the Peace Conference. He, therefore, initiated a policy of *faits accomplis* in order to secure the territories claimed by Czecho-Slovakia. This required military occupation of the German-inhabited districts in the borderlands of the historical Czech lands, as well as the whole of Slovakia. In order to accomplish his objectives, Beneš turned to France for help and he received it.

As early as November 9, 1918, Beneš, in his letter to the National Committee in Prague, asked for approval of his plan to bring a French military mission to Prague and "derive from it unusually great political, diplomatic and economic benefits."[25] Upon receiving approval of his proposal to orient the new state on France, Beneš proceeded with the details. The Czecho-Slovak army, formally a part of the French army,[26] was subordinated to the French military command, and the French military officers, dispatched to Czechoslovakia, helped to build the country's armed forces. This was a mutually beneficial arrangement for both countries: the French sought the weakening of Germany and advancing their influence in Central Europe; and the Czechs were able to obtain French consent and assistance in their efforts to occupy the territories claimed by Czecho-Slovakia even *before* the peace conference would discuss the boundary issues.

In his memorandum to the Allies of November 3, Beneš emphasized that while Czecho-Slovakia was an island of peace and order, there was a "danger of Bolshevism in Vienna," and that "the Czechs must occupy militarily Slovakia, because bolshevism threatens Hungary most . . . and it could spread also to Yugoslavia and Italian territories."[27] In the letter of December 16 to the French Prime Minister Clemenceau, requesting the subordination of the Czecho-Slovak army to the Supreme Commander of the French Forces, Marshal Foch, Beneš wrote that the Czech military forces could be used, "should it be necessary, for the maintenance of order and stopping the tide of Bolshevism in the neighbouring countries."[28]

Since the Czech army was built under the supervision of a French mission and was, technically, under the command of Marshal Foch, it was an Allied force and it could participate in carrying out the terms of the armistice which included the right to occupy strategic positions within the Austro-Hungarian territories.[29] Therefore, the occupation of the German-inhabited borderlands of the Czech lands was accomplished during the months of November and December 1918. Yet the annexation of Slovakia was equally important to the Prague government.

Since Slovakia was under Hungarian control, the Slovak leaders who went to Prague to take part in the new government asked the Czechs for help against the Hungarians. On November 15 Prime Minister Kramář tried to pacify the Slovak deputies in the newly established Czecho-Slovak Revolutionary National Assembly in Prague by promising that within two weeks three divisions of Czech troops would be dispatched to Slovakia.[30] It was not practical to implement the promise, for the troops were needed in the Czech lands. The German inhabitants of the borderlands of Bohemia, Moravia and Austrian Silesia proclaimed their own governments and refused to accept the Czech rule; therefore, it was necessary to occupy the borderlands before the convening of the peace conference so that the latter would be confronted with a *fait accompli*.[31] A similar *fait accompli* in the case of Slovakia was much more difficult to accomplish for at least two reasons. First, in contrast to the Czech lands there were no "historical boundaries" in Slovakia. The Slovaks lived largely in mountainous regions of Upper Hungary, an integral part of the old Kingdom. Although it would be relatively easy to determine the northern boundary of Slovakia along the Carpathian mountain ranges, it was difficult to arrive at a border in the south where the Slovaks intermingled with Hungarians and where there was no "natural boundary" between the two nationalities. Second, since occupying of the borderlands of the historical lands had a priority, there were few troops to spare for Slovakia. The first volunteers who entered Slovakia early in November, and the Slovak national guards formed in the revolutionary excitement, were no match for the trained, disciplined, and in some instances combat-experienced Hungarian troops. Czech and Slovak volunteers were easily dispersed by the Hungarian units as soon as the latter received instructions to do so from the Károlyi government. Thus the occupation of Slovakia was a problem that was not resolved by rhetorics in Prague and Budapest, but by the victorious Allied powers, more specifically France.

France had made commitments to Czecho-Slovakia even before the war's end for reasons that cannot be discussed at any length in this essay.[32] In addition, there was a coincidence of interests of the two countries, as mentioned above, and, therefore, the French government gave its Czech ally complete diplomatic support. Beneš, indeed, was able to achieve the change in the terms of the Belgrade armistice when he took up the matter with Marshal Foch, the Supreme Allied Commander. Furthermore, while recognizing and helping Czecho-Slovakia, the French refused to recognize or negotiate with Austria and Hungary.

In contrast to the French government's pursuit of a policy of non-recognition, the Czecho-Slovak government had its representatives and negotiators in both Vienna and Budapest. In the latter city, the Czecho-Slovak representative was Dr. Milan Hodža, who from 1906 to 1910 had been a Slovak deputy in the Hungarian parliament and who knew many Hungarian politicians. He discussed the Slovak situation with the Hungarian Minister of Nationalities, Dr. Oszkár

Jászi.[33] The latter tried to secure Slovakia for Hungary, while Hodža's task was to make Slovakia safe for Czecho-Slovakia. The country was still in the throes of revolution, the situation was uncertain and fluid, and Hodža and Jászi may not have realized that the center of gravity was Paris, not Budapest or Prague, and that the victors would, eventually, make binding decisions.

In the agreement of November 27 that Hodža made with Jászi, the latter was willing to give Slovaks an autonomous status, that is administrative and police powers within Slovakia if that province would remain within the confines of the Hungarian state. The administrative self-government would be vested in the Slovak National Council. The two parties, however, had some doubts about the feasibility of an arrangement by which the Slovaks would have control over schools and internal administration of a territory that would not include Bratislava (Pozsony, Pressburg) and Košice (Kassa, Kaschau).[34] On November 29 the Slovak delegates decided to continue informal discussions only with the consent of the government in Prague. One delegate, Matúš Dula, chairman of the Slovak National Council, was sent to Prague to report directly on the progress of the talks and to give a more detailed explanation of the Hodža memorandum on the November 27 agreement. The Prague government rejected the Hodža report, especially the definition of Slovakia and its more or less ethnic boundary, which was deemed unacceptable for economic and security reasons.

It would seem that both sides were temporizing, attempting to gain advantage by the discussions in Budapest so that they would have a better bargaining position at the peace conference later on. As it happened, time worked for (and of course the French government favored) the Czecho-Slovak cause.

Since the Eastern Front, which reached into Hungry, was under French command and a French officer was the Allied representative in Budapest who was in charge of the execution of the armistice agreement, for all practical purposes Hungary was under French control. Therefore, when the French Ministry of Foreign Affairs approved of the military line of demarcation in northern Hungary that had been agreed upon between Foch and Beneš, the Hungarian troops were required to evacuate the Slovak territory.[35] The boundary drawn by Beneš was delimited by the Danube river up to the mouth of the river Ipel' (Eipel) from which point it was to follow the Ipel' up to the town of Rimavská Sobota (Rimaszombat), then go straight to the river Už (Uh) and along its course up to the Galician boundary.[36] The line resembled the one found on Masaryk's wartime sketches, for it too provided access to the Danube.

The French decision, made without securing the approval of the other Allies, was communicated to the Hungarian government by Lieutenant-Colonel Fernand Vix, French representative in Budapest. On December 3, Vix related to Hodža that the Allies recognized the Czecho-Slovak state and that the latter is entitled to occupy the Slovak territory. At the same time Vix urged the Hungarian government to recall, without delay, its troops from the Slovak territory.[37] The Hungarian government, however, refused to evacuate the "Slovak land," insisting that no such territorial or administrative unit existed and, therefore, the Hungarian troops could not evacuate it. The difficulty with the communication from Paris to Vix and the latter's note to Károlyi was that it did not contain any demarcation line between Slovakia and ·Hungary. Therefore, Hodža hastily agreed with the Hungarian government upon a provisional line—the Danube—Lučenec—Čop.[38]

Acknowledging that the determination of the demarcation line was within the competence of military authorities, Hodža discussed with the Hungarian Minister of War, Albert Bartha, an agreement that was signed on December 6. For Hodža the demarcation line was provisional, while the Hungarians wanted now a definite boundary, realizing that Paris would be more accommodating to the Czechs. From the Slovak point of view the demarcation line of December 6 was highly unfavorable, since it was based on the Hodža-Jaszi agreement of the preceding month. The agreement stipulated that Hungary evacuate most of the indisputably Slovak districts, but leave the districts of southern Slovakia, including the cities of Bratislava and Košice, inside Hungary. The Hodža-made agreement was concluded without the knowledge and approval of the Prague government and was communicated to Vix who forwarded it to Paris.[39]

Realizing their situation, the Hungarian government was satisfied with the agreement and demanded its acceptance as definite. But the Czecho-Slovak government rejected it as unacceptable and demanded a new and more favorable demarcation line that would be in accord with the one contained in the Beneš-Foch agreement made in Paris in November. The French government's main objection to the Hodža-Bartha agreement was that the Czechs did not follow the

French policy of non-recognition when they sent a representative to Budapest to negotiate issues which only the Allies were competent to decide.[40] Beneš, therefore, communicated the French position to the Prague government and the latter immediately dissociated itself from Hodža's negotiations.[41] He also arranged that Marshal Foch communicate to the Hungarian government the line of demarcation as they had agreed on it earlier.[42] Thus, the French note of December 21, 1918, sanctioning Czech occupation of the Czech lands, contained also a description of the demarcation line between Hungary and Slovakia, noting that the Hungarians had already withdrawn behind that line. Thus the French note declared a *fait accompli* in the case of Slovakia's annexation to Czecho-Slovakia.[43]

The French acted alone, without seeking the approval of the Allies, in the matter of changing the terms of the Belgrade armistice and, by doing so, northern Hungary up to the Danube river was incorporated into Czecho-Slovakia. When the Peace Conference came to deal with the Czecho-Slovak boundary issues, the Czech delegation could claim the territory on the basis of self-determination or ethnic rights and insist that the boundary of the new state corresponds to the military demarcation line agreed between Beneš and Marshal Foch in December 1918.

The information about the new demarcation line reached Slovakia shortly before Christmas. On December 24, Hodža gave the Budapest government a note saying that in view of the guidelines issued by the Commander of the Eastern Allied army, the demarcation line must be in accord with "the historical boundary of Slovakia" and that the Slovak territory has to be evacuated up to the boundary line stated by Dr. Beneš in Paris toward the end of November. This boundary line was clearly defined in the note as first following the Danube, than Ipel' up to Rimavská Sobota, then in direct line to the mouth of Uh river to Latorice and then along the Uh river toward the Už pass.[44] The Hungarian government protested against this demarcation line and insisted on the line of December 6 agreement.

Since the Hungarian government was unwilling to evacuate the southern Slovak districts including the cities of Bratislava and Košice, the Czechs used military force. With the borderlands of the Czech lands secured, the Czech troops, including those which had arrived from Italy and France and the Czech and Slovak volunteers, were directed to Slovakia. Commanded by the Italian General Luigi

Piccione, the Czecho-Slovak armed forces entered Bratislava on January 1, 1919, making it possible for the provisional Slovak government, headed by Vavro Šrobár, to move into that city on February 4.[45] Košice was occupied already on December 28, and the so-called National Council of Eastern Slovakia that had proclaimed the establishment of Eastern Slovak Republic in Prešov on December 14, had a very short life. The Czecho-Slovak forces completed the occupation of Slovakia in January 1919. Even the Slovak National Council was disbanded on January 20, 1919, so that there would be no other authority than the Šrobár-led provisional government.[46]

The Hungarian government temporized, hoping to save Slovakia through promises of autonomy and expecting the peace conference to make a more favorable decision than the one made by the French government in December 1918. Yet the Entente powers supported the Czecho-Slovak claims. On March 20, 1919, Vix delivered the Hungarian government another note according to which the Conference of Ambassadors in Paris decided to make a neutral zone whose new demarcation line would go some 50–80 kilometers deeper into Hungary.[47] The note was an ultimatum and the Hungarians were to comply with it within thirty hours. According to Vix, the new demarcation line was to represent also the new political boundary and left no doubt that Hungary lost Slovakia for good. The Prime Minister of Hungary declared that his government cannot accept the conditions contained in the note and, therefore, had to resign. This paved the way for the arrival of the Béla Kun government and the war that followed.

Although the Czecho-Slovak government did not want war with Hungary, the ministry of national defense issued on April 7, 1919, an order to occupy the territories assigned by the Ambassadors' Conference to Czecho-Slovakia. The army, under the command of Generals Piccione (Italian) and Hennoque (French), was to carry out the mission without bloodshed. Due to the Romanian deep penetration into Hungary, a part of the country, adjacent to the territory assigned to Czecho-Slovakia and below the demarcation line, was evacuated by the Hungarian troops. The Czecho-Slovak troops occupied this area, "since anarchy was developing there."[48] In addition, Ruthenia, that was to become a part of Czecho-Slovakia, had to be occupied too. (Its attachment to Czecho-Slovakia brought about the separation of Hungary from Poland and it also linked Czecho-Slovakia with Romania.) Later a controversy developed over the occupation of the territories below the demarcation line and General Piccione was blamed for misjudging the Hungarians' ability to fight back.

Since the Romanians secured their positions in Hungary, the Czecho-Slovak front was the "weakest link" in the "capitalistic encirclement" of the People's (Soviet) Republic of Hungary led by Béla Kun. Although a bolshevik, he emphasized the need to recapture the lost territories, and the Hungarian nationalists supported him in this respect. The Hungarian offensive began on May 20. The Czecho-Slovaks were taken by surprise; at times their retreat became a flight, especially when they ran out of munitions and supplies. The Czecho-Slovaks overextended themselves in April and now they had to abandon one position after another. In June the Hungarians were in control of Košice, where they were welcomed as liberators, and even threatened Bratislava. About two thirds of Slovakia came under their control; in eastern Slovakia they penetrated up to Bardiejov, thus separating the eastern Czecho-Slovak army from the western army and from the Romanian army. The aim of the Béla Kun offensive was the establishment of a junction with the Red Army in the Western Ukraine.[49]

After the occupation of Košice, the short-lived Slovak Soviet Republic, headed by a Czech bolshevik, Antonín Janoušek, was proclaimed. Janoušek attempted to establish contacts with the left-wing Czech Social Democrats and to gain the sympathy of the president of Czecho-Slovakia, Masaryk, but he failed on both counts. The republic collapsed when the Hungarian troops had to leave Košice.[50]

The Czech defeat in May and June brought about a change in the command of the Czecho-Slovak army in Slovakia. General Piccione was succeeded by the French General Maurice Pellé who ordered reorganization of the armed units.[51] With the help of volunteers and fresh troops Pellé was able to start an offensive in the Nitra area on June 7. On that day the Hungarian government received a telegram from the French Prime Minister Clemenceau, demanding immediate cease-fire lest he impose drastic measures on Hungary.[52] Following Kun's conciliatory reply, Pellé stopped the offensive. But since the Hungarians did not cease hostile actions along the whole front, Pellé resumed the offensive. While the Czecho-Slovaks recaptured positions in western Slovakia, the Hungarians pushed toward the Polish border in an attempt to establish a junction with the Red Army. But the latter could not defeat both the Poles and the Romanians and, therefore, was unable to render any effective assistance to the Hungarian army.[53]

On June 13 the Allies at the peace conference decided the definite boundary between Czecho-Slovakia and Hungary and related the decision to Hungary and all the other interested parties, emphasizing that further bloodshed will not help to obtain boundary advantage to any of the states concerned.[54] Defeated on the diplomatic front and unable to win on the military fronts, the Hungarian government, eventually, accepted the Allied ultimatum. Beginning June 30, Slovakia was gradually evacuated. Soon thereafter, the regime of Béla Kun collapsed.

Early in August 1919 Romanian troops occupied Hungary and on August 21 the new Hungarian government issued a decree on national minorities according to which all Hungarian citizens, regardless of their language or ethnic background, were equal. The use of native language by anyone was protected and, in general, the decree contained almost all that the oppressed nationalities in Hungary had demanded in the past.[55]

Once more, before the signing of the Treaty of Trianon that had to determine definitely the boundaries of Hungary with Slovakia, the Hungarian government attempted to formulate its relations toward the nationalities which were lost. After the testimony of Cardinal Csernoch and Admiral Miklós Horthy, the Hungarian government accepted a proposal for Slovak autonomy. (It was not made public at that time.) According to this proposal, Hungary would grant the Slovak nation a broadly based autonomy that would give the latter the possibility of an unlimited cultural development and jurisdiction in all matters which did not directly concern the over-all state interests.[56] Thus, the Slovak-inhabited "Upper Hungary" would be an autonomous, self-governing province consisting, in accordance with the ethnic principle, of all the predominantly Slovak and the immediately neighbouring districts. The definite boundary of Slovakia would be determined by a commission composed of Slovaks and Hungarians after the signing of the peace treaty.[57] The detailed and far-reaching proposal, not published until 1929, came too late. The Peace Conference decided to attach Slovakia to Czechoslovakia.

The signing of the Treaty of Trianon on June 4, 1920 did not end the Czechoslovak-Hungarian dispute. The post-Béla Kun nationalist government of Hungary was headed first by Archduke Joseph and then by Admiral Miklós Horthy who was duly elected Regent (State

Administrator) on March 1, 1920. Law I of 1920 formally reestablished monarchical form of government and made possible for the Habsburgs to press their claim to the Hungarian throne. The Horthy government signed the Treaty of Trianon and the latter was formally ratified by the National Assembly, but the ratification was accompanied by protests against the injustice of the terms imposed on the humiliated nation. Indeed, there were Hungarian minorities in Czechoslovakia, Romania and Yugoslavia representing an *irredenta*. Therefore, to assure the full compliance with the Treaty of Trianon, the Czechoslovak government concluded a treaty of alliance with Yugoslavia on August 14, 1920.[58]

On January 27, 1921, the Czechoslovak Foreign Minister, Beneš, declared that the restoration of ex-Emperor Charles or his son Archduke Joseph of the Habsburg dynasty "would be a real *casus belli* for several of Hungary's neighbors."[59] In discussing the recent history of the Czechoslovak-Hungarian relations he pointed out that after the collapse of the Béla Kun government, when Archduke Joseph took over the government, "it was the Czechoslovak Government in particular which opposed this with the greatest resoluteness and succeeded in rendering his regime impossible." However, it was the Ambassadors' Conference that passed a resolution on Februry 2, 1920, against a return of the Habsburg dynasty. Among other things, the resolution specifically declared that the restoration of the Habsburgs "would be in conflict with the very basis of the peace settlement and would be neither recognized nor tolerated by them."[60]

These declarations notwithstanding, Charles of the House of Habsburg, the last reigning monarch in the former Empire, returned to Hungary on March 27, 1921, in order to assume his royal duties. But the Czechoslovak-Yugoslav alliance helped to frustrate the restoration coup in Budapest.[61]

Charles' claim to the throne was based on the assumption that his act of suspending his reign and renouncing all share in the government did not constitute a formal abdication as both Emperor of Austria and King of Hungary, since under the law of the land, the Act of Abdication, an abdication must be countersigned by the Prime Minister and ratified by both Houses of Parliament. Some leaders in Budapest seized upon the alleged invalidity of the abdication and claimed that the Treaty of Trianon itself was not valid, since Charles still was the legal King of Hungary and he neither signed it nor was he bound by it.[62] When Romania joined

Czechoslovakia and Yugoslavia in objecting to the restoration of the Habsburg monarch in Hungary, and the Conference of Ambassadors (that is, the Great Powers) backed up the three states, Charles had to leave Hungary. Less than three weeks after the event Czechoslovakia and Romania signed a convention of alliance. Later Romania and Yugoslavia signed a similar convention and the formal groundwork of the Little Entente was laid.[63]

In view of the fact that Hungarian minorities lived in Czechoslovakia, Romania and Yugoslavia, and Hungary lost territories to all three of these countries, the Little Entente's purpose was to preserve the peace settlement, especially its territorial provisions. Restoration of Habsburgs would threaten the status quo as established by the Treaty of Trianon, or, as Beneš put it in an article, "the presence of any Habsburg is completely incompatible with the aims of the Little Entente, since his reappearance would mean fight, eventual decomposition and collapse of the new order and, therefore, an inevitable war of all against all."[64]

Shortly after the article appeared in print, Charles made a second return to Budapest in October 1921. This time Czechoslovakia declared mobilization and the Little Entente announced that strong measures would be taken against Hungary. The swift action by the Little Entente, especially the Czechoslovak mobilization, brought about a reproof from the Conference of Ambassadors.[65] The Great Powers' intervention forced the ex-King to leave Hungary the second time.

Yielding to pressures from abroad, the Hungarian National Assembly passed the Habsburg Dethronement Act on November 6, 1921.[66] The action did not imply, however, the Hungarian acceptance of the dismemberment of the thousand year-old-state. Therefore, the Little Entente's avowed purpose was to preserve the peace settlement, though its existence was also justified on several other grounds.[67]

When Hungary agreed to adhere to the Kellogg-Briand Pact of 1928, the Little Entente leaders looked upon it as a step in the right direction and did not pay much attention to the moral reservations the Hungarian government expressed while accepting the principle of renouncing war as an instrument of national policy. In those reservations, reference was made to the injustice of the Trianon settlement for which "the reparation . . . will be secured along peaceful lines."[68]

The Czechoslovak-Hungarian dispute, as any event that has

multiple causes, long lasting consequences and wide-ranging effects on different groups of people, may be seen and analyzed from different points of view. Leaving aside the moral, cultural and other issues involved in the case, the political aspects of the dispute may be summarized as follows: Czechoslovakia was recognized as a victorious power by the Allies and was represented at the Peace Conference, while Hungary was one of the vanquished countries to whom such representation was denied. Territorial claims of the former country were supported by France even before the peace conference dealt with the boundary question.[69] Thus, Czechoslovakia was able to present itself as a state possessing all the attributes of statehood when the conference dealt with the matter. It had a recognized government able to enter into diplomatic relations with other states, it had a population and a defined territory that was under effective control of the government and, above all, it was recognized as an allied country. In contrast to it, Hungary's government was not recognized by France and it had to accept the decisions made in Paris. Rightly or wrongly, the terms of the Treaty of Trianon were justified by the victorious powers on the grounds of self-determination of the Slovaks and the economic and security needs of Czechoslovakia. Hungary's loss was Czechoslovakia's gain.[69]

Notes

1. The best known English language works on Slovakia are: Robert W. Seton-Watson, *A History of the Czechs and Slovaks* (London, 1943); *Racial Problems in Hungary* (London, 1908); *Slovakia Then and Now* (London-Prague, 1931); *The New Slovakia* (Prague, 1924). Also, Jozef Kirchbaum, *Slovakia: Nation at the Crossroads of Central Europe* (New York, 1960); Jozef Lettrich, *History of Modern Slovakia* (New York, 1955); G. L. Oddo, *Slovakia and Its People* (New York, 1960); and Jozeph A. Mikus, *Slovakia. A Political History: 1918-1950* (Milwaukee, 1963).

2. František Bokes, *Dejiny Slovenska a Slovákov* [History of Slovakia and the Slovaks] (Bratislava, 1946), p. 339.

3. In the exile documents and all the documents of the Paris Peace Conference Czechoslovakia's name (and that of Czecho-Slovaks) was hyphenated. When the Czechoslovak Constitution of February 29, 1920, established a unitary and centralistic state, the hyphen was deleted. In this essay the name will be used with and without the hyphen. Among the many books on the Czech and Slovak independence movement abroad one may

mention Karel Pichlík, *Zahraniční odboj 1914–1918 bez legend* [Resistance Abroad, 1914–1918, Without Legends] (Prague, 1968).

4. Bokes, pp. 354–55.

5. For Masaryk's own account of his activities abroad see T. G. Masaryk, *The Making of a State; Memories and Observations, 1914–1918.* An English version arranged and prepared with an introduction by Henry Wickham Steed (New York, 1927). The most extensive works on the independence movement at home are books by Milada Paulová, *Dějiny Maffie, odboj Čechů a Jihoslovanů za světové války, 1914–1918* [History of the Maffie, Resistance of Czechs and Yugoslavs during the World War, 1914–1918] 2 vols. (Prague, 1937); and *Tajný výbor [Maffie] a spolupráce s Jihoslovany v letech 1916–1918* [The Secret Committee [Maffie] and Collaboration with Yugoslavs during the Years 1916–1918] (Prague, 1968).

6. Karol A. Medvecký, *Slovenský prevrat* [Slovak Revolution], 4 vols. (Trnava, 1930–31), III, p. 347.

7. Bokes, p. 359.

8. On the end of the Empire see Oscar Jaszi, *The Dissolution of the Habsburg Monarchy* (Chicago, 1929); and Jan Opočenský, *Konec monarchie rakousko-uherské* [The End of the Austro-Hungarian Monarchy] (Prague, 1928). Space limitations do not allow the citation of all relevant sources.

9. Bokes, pp. 360–61.

10. *Ibid.*, pp. 361–62.

11. *Ibid.*, p. 363; Medvecký, I, p. 347.

12. Text of the Declaration is in Medvecký, III, pp. 364–65.

13. Before the text was published in newspapers, Dr. Milan Hodža made a few changes in it and the original has not been preserved. See Bokes, pp. 364–65; also Mikus, pp. 9–11; Medvecký, I, p. 346.

14. Milan R. Štefánik, a French naturalized citizen and an officer in the French army, was very helpful to Masaryk as was the Czechoslovak army in Siberia. The latter strengthened the Czecho-Slovak position at the peace conference. Štefánik never returned to Slovakia alive; he died when the plane that departed from Rome, carrying him and several Italian officers, crashed near Bratislava on May 4, 1919. See Medvecký, I, pp. 90–104; also Bokes, p. 365.

15. Bokes, pp. 368–69.

16. *Ibid.*, p. 369.

17. *Ibid.*

18. *Ibid.*

19. *Ibid.*

20. *Ibid.*, pp. 370–71.

21. *Ibid.*, p. 371.

22. Many Slovaks had their own understanding of the word "freedom"

and behaved accordingly. Medvecký gives countless examples of looting of Jewish stores and inns. Most of the well-to-do Jews in Slovakia were identified with the Hungarian ruling class and were victimized during the revolutionary time. See Medvecký, III, pp. 3–186.

23. Military Convention Between the Allies and Hungary, signed at Belgrade, November 13, 1918, *Papers Relating to the Foreign Relations of the United States* (FRUS), PPC, 1919 II (Washington, 1942), pp. 183–85. Also Bohdan Krizman, "The Belgrade Armistice 13 November 1918," *The Slavic and East European Review* (48, 1970), pp. 67–87. Text of the document is in *ibid.*, pp. 85–87.

24. Karel Kramář, *Řeči a projevy* [Speeches and Statements]. Edited by František Stašek and J. R. Marek. (Prague, 1935), pp. 22–26; also Vladimír Sís, ed., *Dr. Karel Kramář. Život-dílo-práce. Vůdce národa* [Dr. Karel Kramář. Life-Work-Labor. Leader of the Nation] (Prague, 1936), pp. 203–204.

25. Eduard Beneš, ed., *Světová válka a naše revoluce. Dokumenty* [The World War and Our Revolution. Documents] III (Prague, 1929), p. 509.

26. The Czecho-Slovak army in France was established by a French government decree in December 1917 and the Czecho-Slovak army in Russia, consisting largely of former prisoners of war, was ordered to join the army in France by Masaryk in February 1918. The French government granted Masaryk credits for maintaining and transferring the army from Russia to France. The latter never arrived in France, because in May 1918 it got involved in a conflict with the Bolsheviks. After it occupied the Trans-Siberian Railroad and began to move westward into the Volga region, the Allies recognized the Czecho-Slovak National Council. Similarly as the British recognition of August 8, the United States recognition of September 3, 1918, was based on belligerency of the Czecho-Slovak armies in Russia, Italy and France. By a secret agreement of September 28, 1918, the Czecho-Slovak National Council in Paris gave the French government "the co-operation of its armies for the pursuit of the present war," and the French government made a commitment to support the Council in its efforts to reconstitute an independent Czecho-Slovak state "with borders of its former historical lands," and accorded "to the Czechoslovak nation the right to be represented at the inter-Allied conferences, where questions concerning the interests of Czecho-Slovaks will be discussed." The complete document is in Karel Kramář, *Řeči a projevy*, pp. 89–92.

27. Beneš, III, pp. 496–98.

28. Vladimír Soják, ed., *O československé zahraniční politice v letech 1918–1939* [On Czechoslovak Foreign Policy during the Years 1918–1939] (Prague, 1956), p. 43.

29. The armistice document is in Harry Rudolph Rudin, *Armistice, 1918* (New Haven, 1944), pp. 406–409. See also Supreme War Council, Resolutions,

VIII Session, Fourth Meeting, November 4, 1918, Bliss Papers.

30. Bokes, p. 371.

31. The Czechs had a conflict with the Poles over the Teschen territory; this tied down a considerable number of their troops in the area.

32. See 26 above.

33. Bokes, pp. 372-73.

34. *Ibid.*, pp. 374-76.

35. Eduard Beneš, *Světová válka a náse revoluce* II [World War and Our Revolution] 2 vols. (Prague, 1927-1928), pp. 484-85.

36. *Ibid.*, p. 501.

37. D. Perman, *The Shaping of the Czechoslovak State; Diplomatic History of the Boundaries of Czechoslovakia, 1914-1920* (Leiden, 1962), pp. 92-93.

38. Bokes, p. 375.

39. Perman, p. 93; Bokes, pp. 375-76.

40. Beneš, II, pp. 493-94.

41. Beneš, III, pp. 534-35; Beneš, II, pp. 495-96.

42. Beneš, II, p. 497; Perman, p. 94.

43. Perman, p. 94.

44. Bokes, p. 376.

45. *Ibid.*, p. 380.

46. *Ibid.*, p. 378.

47. *Ibid.*, p. 382. For details see Peter Pastor, "The Vix Mission in Hungary, 1918-1919: A Re-examination." *Slavic Review* (Vol. 29, No. 3, September 1970), pp. 494-97.

48. Bokes, p. 383; Perman, p. 221.

49. Bokes, p. 384. Also V. Kholodkovsky, "Toward the Lenin Centenary: Socialist Community—A Retrospect," *New Times*, no. 30, July 30, 1969.

50. On the Slovak Soviet Republic see Martin Vietor, *Slovenská sovietská republika v r. 1919* [The Slovak Soviet Republic in 1919] (Bratislava, 1955); V. Semyonov, "An Historian Looks Back: The Slovak Republic of Soviets," *New Times*, no. 25, June 25, 1969; chapter two in Josef Kalvoda, *Czechoslovakia's Role in Soviet Strategy* (Washington, D.C., 1978), pp. 21-31.

51. Bokes, p. 384.

52. *Ibid.*

53. *Ibid.*

54. *Ibid.*, pp. 384-85; Perman, pp. 225-26.

55. Bokes, p. 385.

56. *Ibid.*

57. *Ibid.*, p. 385-87.

58. Eduard Beneš, *Problémy nové Evropy a zahraniční politika československá. Projevy a úvahy z r. 1919-1924* [Problems of New Europe

and Czechoslovak Foreign Policy. Statements and Thoughts from Years 1919-1924] (Prague, 1924), pp. 83–90.

59. Ibid., p. 114. The whole speech of January 27, 1921, was published in English. See *The Foreign Policy of Czechoslovakia. Speech of Dr. E. Beneš, Minister of Foreign Affairs, in the House of Deputies, January 27, 1921.* (Prague, 1921), esp. p. 19.

60. *Ibid.*, in Czech, pp. 114–15; in English, p. 20.

61. John O. Crane, *The Little Entente* (New York, 1931), pp. 9–10.

62. *Ibid.*, p. 6.

63. *Ibid.*, p. 10

64. The article appeared in the September 1921 issue of *Revue de Genève,* no. 1; its Czech translation is in Beneš, *Problémy nové Evropy,* pp. 131–40.

65. Crane, pp. 11–12.

66. *Ibid.*, p. 18. The text of the act is on p. 213 (Appendix D).

67. Beneš, *Problémy nové Evropy,* pp. 83–90.

68. Crane, p. 38.

69. The peace conference rejected the Czecho-Slovak claims to Lusatia and the Czechoslovak-Yugoslav corridor that would separate Hungary from Austria. The formation of the corridor was strenuously opposed by the Italian delegation and except France, none of the Allies favored this claim. A complete set of the Czecho-Slovak memoranda presented at the peace conference is in the Hoover War Library, Stanford, California.

Leslie C. Tihany

The Baranya Republic
and The Treaty of Trianon

The Baranya Republic was a short-lived, Soviet-oriented mini-state whose rise and brief existence on occupied Hungarian territory during the peacemaking aftermath of the first World War were tolerated and fostered by the newly-proclaimed Kingdom of Yugoslavia.[1] The political process, which produced antithetic governments within the same national domain, portended similar developments on a global scale after the Second World War. In the chaotic conditions attendant on the restructuring of the lands long ruled by the defeated Habsburg Empire, the separatist government in Baranya temporarily served the national interests of the Yugoslav occupiers as well as the socialist objectives of its Hungarian leaders, but finally foundered on the continental strategy of the victorious Entente powers which aimed to subordinate Middle European territorial appetites to the overriding diplomatic objective of erecting a barrier against the westward expansion of Communism.

As Austria-Hungary entered World War I, Baranya[2] was one of sixty-three Hungarian counties. It was situated in the Danube-Dráva triangle of western Hungary, bordering on the Associated Kingdom of Croatia in the south. In July 1914, the area of Baranya County covered 1,963 square miles and had a population of 299,312.[3] In size, therefore, the prewar county was somewhat smaller than the State of Delaware. Eighty-five percent of the population spoke Hungarian either as a mother tongue (51.3%) or as a second language (33.7%). Speakers of Serbo-Croatian formed 9% of the inhabitants.[4] Because of the rich anthracite mines in the center of the county and the thirty-seven relatively large-size industrial plants around the county seat, Pécs,[5] 52% of the population was engaged in mining industry and related occupations.[6] Pécs had a population of 47,556 during this period, with a labor force of 22,642, of whom 14,897 were manual workers and miners resident in the city and its environs.[7]

In conservative, prewar Hungary, Pécs was known as a "nest of reds."[8] It was the only industrial town in old Hungary with mines in its immediate peripheries. This made for close cooperation between the suburban miners and the urban industrial proletariat. It was perhaps because of this combination of forces that long before the war Pécs had become a stronghold of the trade union and socialist movements in Hungary. The first Hungarian miners' union was established here.[9] Pécs, however, was not only "red" but also "black," in the Stendhalian sense. At the other end of the political spectrum were the powerful and influential clerics. The landed estates of the Roman Catholic Episcopal See and of the Cathedral Chapter covered about 100,000 cadastral *holds* (one Hungarian *hold* equals 1.42 acres). In the center of the city stood a baroque monument to the Holy Trinity, elevating the sculptured image of the Host for all inhabitants, fidel and infidel. In addition to the cathedral, there were also a seminary, a monastery, a convent, a Roman Catholic Law Academy, and a multitutde of churches. In the inner city the street scene was enlivened by a large army of priests, monks and nuns, all wearing their distinctive and characteristic garb. The clerical-socialist polarization probably accounted for the fact that by the time war was declared in July 1914, a "throne and altar" type of patriotic Right was staring a militant, internationally-minded Left in the face.

One of the earliest symptoms of the impending collapse of the Central Powers, a military mutiny and an ensuing firefight between ethnically antagonistic regiments of the multinational Habsburg Empire, took place in Pécs at Whitsuntide 1918. The latent class struggle in the city added to the seriousness of the disaffection in the garrison. News of the mutiny reached the miners in their suburban homes only after its suppression, but on the mistaken assumption that the war was over and a revolution had broken out, they armed themselves, began a march on the city and walked into the arms of the victorious status quo forces. Survivors were freed during the following autumn after the collapse of the old régime and the establishment of the new liberal-democratic government.

Mihály Károlyi (1875–1955), the aristocratic leader of pro-Entente Hungarian liberals, headed the new régime, first as Premier and then as President, from October 31, 1918 until March 20, 1919. The Károlyi government signed a Military Convention amounting to an armistice with the Allies in Belgrade on November 13, under the terms of which Yugoslav forces were allowed to advance into

Hungary and, in accordance with The Hague Regulations, to establish a military government without replacing the existing civil administration in the occupied territories.[10] The Yugoslav Army
crossed the Dráva River into Baranya on November 14, entered Pécs
the same day, but defiantly continued its northward march well beyond the Belgrade Convention line. Four-fifths of the county, including Pécs, were thus detached from the mother country. In exceeding
the territorial provisions of the Belgrade armistice, the Yugoslavs
were motivated by a strategic wish to push their borders as far north
as possible, beyond the southward slope of the Mecsek massif (1,146
feet), and by the dictates of a postwar energy crisis were calling for
possession of the rich Pécs coalmines.

The presence of foreign troops in Baranya was unresistingly recognized by both the conservative Right and the radical Left as a safeguard preventing the opposing ideological camp from gaining the
upper hand in county and city. As long as the Károlyi government
remained in power in Budapest (122 miles to the north as the crow
flies), Right and Left continued their uneasy truce, united in loyalty
to the national capital while under enemy occupation, even though
in the intoxication of victory the Yugoslav forces chose to ignore the
pertinent paragraphs of the Belgrade convention.

The occupiers began establishing a Yugoslav civil administration
and on December 1, 1918, Belgrade officially announced that Yugoslavia would permanently annex all occupied Hungarian areas.[11]
Two days later, in an outburst of Hungarian nationalism transcend-
ing ideological divisions, which took the form of a "People's Resolution," a citizens' assembly in Pécs rejected any change in the territorial status quo under which their city might be wrenched from
Hungary and joined either to Yugoslavia or to any other state structure.[12] As Yugoslav military highhandedness continued and the economic situation deteriorated, a resistance movement came into existence spearheaded by the Socialists and their labor unions in cooperation with the Christian Socialists and the illegal Communist Party.
A general strike, which paralyzed the city from February 21 to
March 13, 1919, was first met with repressive measures on the part
of the occupiers, including the taking of hostages and cavalry
charges in the streets against demonstrators. In Yugoslavia sympathy demonstrations took place, protesting the use of the Royal
Army as Cossacks in Pécs. Increasing pressures at home and in
Baranya finally brought concessions from the Yugoslav military

authorities and constituted a victory for the Socialist workers of Baranya loyal to their homeland. But a week after the end of the strike, President Károlyi and the Berinkey government, unwilling to accept territorial truncations, resigned in Budapest and was replaced by a Hungarian Soviet Republic (HSR) dominated by the communist Béla Kun. The assumption of power by the revolutionary proletariat in the political center was a deathblow to undivided national loyalties in peripheral Baranya. The Right and Left now began to reappraise their positions in the light of class interests: the former at a discreet distance from the territorial integrity ideal of traditional nationalism; the latter fusing with it in a passionate embrace.

Already during the winter of the general strike, there had appeared signs of improving relations between occupying Yugoslav officialdom and the leaders of the Baranya Right, probably in reaction to a leftward drift in the Budapest government. It did not escape notice in Baranya that on January 3, 1919 control over the Salgótarján coalmines in northern Hungary was to be shared between a workers' council and the board of directors.[13] Indeed, the Budapest official gazette announced that by the end of March 1919 all Hungarian mines would be placed under government control as a first step toward nationalization.[14] A land reform law was promulgated on February 16, 1919. The high-minded, idealistic Károlyi began on February 21, 1919 to distribute his own landed property among his incredulous peasants.[15] The provincial Right realized that reunion with the mother country at the end of the Yugoslav occupation would certainly mean the extension of the new Hungarian laws into Baranya. The leftward drift in Budapest appeared to be turning the military demarcation line separating Hungary and Yugoslavia into an ideological boundary between the radicalism of the mother country and conservatism under Yugoslav protection. The Baranya mines and the large estates of the county, including those of the Diocese and the Chapter, were at stake. The changing attitudes of the Right, no doubt motivated by a recognition of the new political realities, could be conjectured from the growing cordiality between the leading clerical circles in Pécs and the top stratum of the occupiers.

The catalytic effect of the Károlyi reforms portended the shape of things to come in Baranya during the ensuing three years. The local political situation began to evolve in the form of three interlocked processes: a tug-of-war between the provincial Right and Left; the governmental metamorphoses in Budapest from bourgeois to proletarian radicalism and then again to ultra-conservatism; and finally victorious Yugoslavia's maneuverings to achieve its maximum territorial aspirations at defeated Hungary's expense. The Entente architects of the new East Central European status quo, however, were more concerned about the Soviet threat from the East than about Yugoslavia's new frontiers. The two problems had to be solved integrally; the new frontiers had to be drawn as functions of the anti-Bolshevik continental grand strategy.

Until this grand strategy of the hegemonial Atlantic powers could prevail over Yugoslav intransigence, occupied Baranya was in a political flux. For the Yugoslavs the basic rule was to side with the opponents of the center. When the Left was in power in Budapest, it was the Baranya Right which turned its back on the center; when the Right took over from the Left in the national capital, it was the Baranya Left which began moving away from the center with Yugoslav backing. The *volte face* of the Yugoslavs occurred abruptly, strictly in response to external events.

The fall of the Károlyi regime and the rise of the Hungarian Soviet Republic on March 21, 1919 had the effect in Baranya of an ideological inhibitor on the Right and of a catalyst speeding up the amalgam of socialism and nationalism for the Left. The interests of the Right required, and its political comportment indicated, that until a return to a rightist political course in unoccupied Hungarian territory, Baranya had better remain under Yugoslav military occupation, at least temporarily detached from the Communist-controlled mother country. As for the left, never before had the Baranya workers and miners been more attached in allegiance to the national government of their country than in the spring and summer of 1919, while the revolutionary proletariat ruled in Budapest.

In the eyes of the Baranya Right the Communists of Béla Kun in power were naturally a greater threat to the socio-economic equilibrium of the county than the bourgeois radicals of Mihály Károlyi. Confirming this assumption, the HSR in Budapest began, before the end of the first week of its existence, to issue a plethora of nationalizing decrees. Between March 20 and April 3, 1919, all Hungarian industrial plants, mines, means of transportation, medium-size and large landed estates as well as educational institutions were declared socialist property. In occupied Baranya all establishment economic interests, both landed and industrial, were at once psychologically affected.

At the other end of the Baranya political spectrum, among the miners and the workers, the amalgam of socialism and nationalism was facilitated by economic factors. Wages were higher in HSR territory than in Pécs and its environs. First a trickle and then a torrent of Pécs-Baranya workers and miners began to flow northward across the line of demarcation into Soviet Hungary. Ten of the Pécs Socialist chiefs transferred their activities to the HSR-controlled parts of neighboring Somogy County. From there they established direct contact with Béla Kun in Budapest.[16] In a letter addressed to Béla Kun and also in personal conversations[17] Gyula Hajdu, the most prominent Baranya Socialist leader in exile, proposed and pressed for the entry of HSR military forces into Yugoslav-occupied Baranya[18]

While the nationalism of the Baranya Left was thus waxing to chauvinism, the economic situation in Pécs was not developing to the liking of the occupiers. A new and disturbing factor entered into the preeminent Yugoslav occupation problem, which was maintaining coal production at a maximum level. After the proclamation of the dictatorship of the proletariat in Budapest, a steady drop in the yield of the coalfields began owing to the northward flight of the Pécs miners to HSR territory.[19] Production was reduced perhaps to as low as one-third of the peacetime yield not only because some of the miners had fled to unoccupied territory, but also because of slowdowns in the shafts by the stay-homes.

All this undoubtedly had an effect on the visibly continuing rapprochement between the Yugoslav occupiers and the Baranya Right, which was paralleled by a growing estrangement between the Serbs and the local Left. Within two weeks of the Hungarian Soviets' coming to power in Budapest, the Yugoslav occupying authorities in Baranya permitted the return to Pécs of its old-regime Mayor Andor Nendtvich, whom they had expelled from their territories on January 30, 1919, during the period of still undivided Right-Left loyalty to the center. Since by late spring the Pécs press had become predominantly leftist military censorship was made more severe.[20] The celebration of May Day, 1919 was banned.

In the course of continuing Serb-Right rapprochement and Serb-Left estrangement in the urban areas, word came to Baranya from the north during the first days of August that the Hungarian Soviets had fallen in Budapest. Hungary, its capital under Romanian occupation, was in a state of anarchy in which counterrevolutionary, anti-Communist, nationalist forces were grouping and regrouping to fill the political vacuum. Once more the signal was given in the center for the peripheral Right and Left to shift positions on nationalist allegiances. For the Baranya Right the disappearance in the center of the leftist inhibitor allowed a return to an old-fashioned, traditional nationalism. Henceforth it was the Right which wanted the Yugoslavs to leave and the Left which was anxious to have them stay. Additionally, the Left was being pushed farther toward its ideological extreme, first, by the political influence of Mihály Károlyi's and Béla Kun's followers fleeing from the White Terror and, second, by the increasing likelihood of Baranya's reincorporation into a counterrevolutionary Hungary.

In the minds of the Paris peacemakers the minor territorial dispute between Hungary and Yugoslavia began to assume a certain relevance to the seemingly westward surge of Bolshevism. The groundwork for the Hungarian peace treaty and for the new, restricted Hungarian frontiers was being laid during an international red scare marked by a Spartacist uprising in Berlin (January 1919), the establishment of the Third or Communist International (Comintern) in Moscow (March 2, 1919), the reality of the Hungarian Soviets (March 21–August 1, 1919), the brief spectacle of a Soviet Republic in Bavaria (April–May 1919), a mutiny at Odessa in the French Black Sea fleet (April 16–22, 1919), the final failure of Allied intervention in revolutionary Russia both via Murmansk-Archangel (October 1919) and, almost simultaneously, in the southern Ukraine. The text of the Hungarian treaty was put in its final shape (January 15–May 4, 1920) in a psychological climate affected by another Spartacist insurrection, this time in the Ruhr (March 1920), by the outbreak of a Polish-Russian war (April 25, 1920), and by impending Red Army landings at Enzeli, on Iran's Caspian coast (May 17, 1920). The need for a East Central European barrier against Communism seemed greater and more urgent than ever. Romania was proving itself staunchly anti-Bolshevik by its war against the Soviets (May 18, 1919–March 2, 1920); the abortive Slovak Soviet republic in Preshov (June 1919) was a thing of the past. Only Yugoslavia, because of its sponsorship of a reportedly "red" regime in Baranya, appeared to be an unsealed spillway in the dam being built against Soviet political and ideological expansion.

Beginning with August 1919 the basic attitude of the Pécs proletarian Left to the occupiers was determined by a recognition of the fact that their presence prevented the eruption of the White Terror. Reacting vehemently to the bloody events, a mass meeting of Pécs Socialist workers on February 26 declared itself in favor of continued Yugoslav occupation of Baranya for the duration of the White Terror in unoccupied territory.[21] The radicalization and leftward shift of the Pécs labor movement was facilitated by another measure of the occupiers. The miners returning from the north were scattered over a twenty-mile radius in the mining area, thus increasing the possibilities of agitation and of forming new clandestine cells. The Yugoslavs turned over the streets of Pécs to the proletarian masses for ideological and political marches and demonstrations. On March 15 they held a protective umbrella over a mass meeting which endorsed the earlier (February 26, 1920) declaration in favor of a continued Yugoslav occupation and ranged the Pécs labor movement on the side of the Comintern, the new international revolutionary organization set up in Moscow the year before (March 2, 1919). On March 21, they saw to the maintenance of order while the workers were commemorating the first anniversary of the fallen Hungarian Soviets. On May 1, 1920, for the first time since the beginning of the occupation, the Yugoslav authorities permitted the celebration of International Labor Day.

The Pécs Right sullenly watched the seeming proletarian dominance of streets and squares. It was confident, however, that soon the conservative prewar establishment would resume its rule in a Pécs reunited with truncated Hungary. It was being whispered that the peace treaty, a preliminary text of which had been handed the Hungarian delegation in Paris on January 15, 1920, would fix the new Yugoslav-Hungarian frontier in a way disappointing to both the occupiers and their left-wing protégés. In Baranya County the new border would run south not only of the military line of demarcation, but also far to the south of the Belgrade Convention boundary, returning Pécs and most of Baranya, including the coal mines, to Hungarian sovereignty.

Either the Right had begun showing too much confidence or the Yugoslav occupying administration started losing its calm, because at the end of 1919 a crackdown on the local right began. Starting on December 11, 1919 and culminating in January of the following year, seventeen former Hungarian military officers had their houses searched and were arrested on charges of conspiracy, espionage, and illegal recruitment of armed forces.[22] When the Interallied Military Commission (IMC) was established in Pécs subsequent to these arrests (May 28, 1920), the Right wishfully and correctly interpreted this event, too, as a portent of an impending Yugoslav evacuation.

A week after the arrival of the IMC in Pécs, news was received from Paris, jubilantly by the Right and mournfully by the Left, that the Hungarian peace treaty had been signed and that the victors had awarded most of Baranya, as far south as Karasica Brook, to Hungary. The Right was ready to accept, although the delineation of the new international frontier entailed a minor loss of Hungarian territory. But the left balked and swore to prevent the entry of Horthy's troops, treaty or no treaty.

All told, the treaty awarded Yugoslavia only 1,193 square kilometers (23.4%) of the total prewar Baranya area of 5,106 square kilometers, containing 34 villages of the Baranyavár, Siklós, and Mohács districts. At the same time it gave her a five year access to the yield of the Pécs mines. Neither Hungary nor Yugoslavia had undue reason to complain about this solution. Hungary gave up less territory in this area than anywhere else along its peripheries, retaining both Pécs and the coalfields. Yugoslavia was satisfied both in its ethnic and economic claims.

But for the time being, this was only on paper. The treaty would not enter into force until after completion of the ratification process, which might yet take months or years. The entry into force would be marked by an exchange of ratifications at the French Ministry of Foreign Affairs. It was only after the deposition of the ratifications that Yugoslavia would be under obligation to withdraw its military forces to the south side of the new international boundary. Would Belgrade comply?

The Yugoslav-controlled leftist press in Pécs opined that the territorial provisions of the Treaty of Trianon need not be considered as final. In its October 13, 1920 number the Pécs Socialist daily *Munkás* (Worker) attributed to a "Yugoslav statesman" the assertion that a separate Baranya Republic could remain an autonomous state under Yugoslav military occupation even after the ratification process of the Treaty of Trianon had been completed.[23] In its October 29 issue, the same paper quoted the Mayor of Pécs, Béla Linder, as disclaiming any connection between the future of Pécs and the ratification of the Treaty of Trianon. The city, Linder commented, would not be returned to Hungary until its working population petitioned for its reincorporation.[24] There was certainly no basis for this statement in the current diplomatic process or in international law.

The occupied status of Baranya thus continued unchanged after the signing of the peace treaty on June 4, 1920. Since the Béla Kun interlude, however, the Hungarian question seemed to have acquired more importance in Paris. The Romanian occupation of Budapest (August-November 1919) was followed by the establishment of a Conference of Allied Diplomatic Representatives and Generals in the Hungarian capital. The Interallied Military Commission (IMC) in Pécs, dominated by the French Major Raoul Dérain, was reporting to the Conference of Ambassadors in Paris through this intermediate body.

Both Hungary and Yugoslavia signed in a revisionist spirit. For fifteen months following the signing, the Yugoslavs continued their effort to cling to their military frontier north of the new treaty line. Ideologically analyzed, the Yugoslavs' attempt in 1920-21 to accomplish this objective was to satisfy their own nationalism while promoting their protégés' socialism. In the East Central Europe of 1920-21 this was a diplomatic impossibility.

In the case of the protégés a choice had to be made between the two ideologies. The left-wing socialist regime in Pécs could continue to exist only in detachment from Horthy Hungary by jettisoning the Hungarian nationalist aim of Baranya's reunification with Hungary in favor of proletarian internationalism.

The eastward Baranya drift began a week after the signing of the Treaty of Trianon. On June 12 the Pécs Social Democratic Party officially changed its name to "Socialist Party in Pécs" (SPP)[25] This was done in order to draw a line between the Social Democratic Party of Hungary which under the leadership of Károly Peyer was willing to compromise with Horthy.

"Our enemies," wrote the Pécs Munkás (Worker), "are the Social Democrats, the social patriots, and the social chauvinists." The Socialist Party in Pécs (SPP) formally declared its adherence to the Comintern in October 1920.[26] At the third Congress of the Comintern, which opened in Moscow on July 22, 1921, the SPP was represented by two invited delegates from Pécs, the chemical industry worker Rudolf Wommert and the miner Richárd Friedl. The two SPP representatives, who had deliberating but not voting rights, submitted a lengthy and detailed report on the Pécs-Baranya situation of the Congress.[27]

The new orientation did not disqualify the Pécs Socialists from Yugoslav backing. In rapid succession, first the defunct (since 1919) Pécs National Council was reestablished on Socialist demand; next, the Council ordered elections for a new municipal governing body of 100 members. The elections took place under Yugoslav supervision on August 29–30, 1920, before the public announcement of the Comintern ties and resulted in an overwhelming Socialist victory. The franchise and the balloting were reportedly less democratic than in a British or French election. The protesting conservative Mayor, Andor Nendtvich, who through some oversight was still sitting behind his desk in his City Hall office, was summarily arrested and deported into unoccupied Hungary.[28] He was replaced by the refugee Béla Linder,[29] briefly Minister of War in the fallen Károlyi regime and then Special Envoy and co-signer of the Belgrade Military Convention. Backed by Belgrade, Linder's immediate objective was a prolongation of the Yugoslav occupation in an autonomous Baranya, for possibly five years, at the end of which a plebiscite should decide the final disposition of the territory.[30]

The experts of the Conference of Ambassadors in Paris correctly analyzed Yugoslav motivation and intentions vis-à-vis Baranya as being primarily centered on coal. For the most part the railroads of Yugoslavia were propelled by Pécs coal. "It is for this reason that the South Slav state has prolonged, *contre tout droit*, the occupation of this region."[31] Accordingly, in order to remove all obstacles to a future evacuation, on December 15, 1920 the Conference of Ambassadors invited the Reparations Commission to take measures that the pertinent provisions of the Treaty of Trianon regarding the exploitation of the Pécs coal mines were applied, implemented, and carried out under its control.[32] It was not until May 7, 1921, however, that the Conference of Ambassadors was able to convey to the Hungarian Government the decision of the Reparations Commission regarding the implementation of the pertinent provisions of the Treaty of Trianon regarding the Pécs mines. The commission had decided, the Hungarians were told, that the Yugoslavs were to be entitled "for the first year, to receive 54% of the net production of the mines in the Pécs basin. . . [and that] this percentage shall be maintained after the first year unless another figure should be adopted."

Bilateral negotiations between Hungary and Yugoslavia (which wanted 60%) on the question of Pécs coal continued unabated in Belgrade nearly until the end of the occupation.[33].

The work of quiet diplomacy was thus not to bear fruit for many months. In the meantime the clash of pro- and counter-evacuation forces continued both nationally and internationally. On December 12, 1920, three days before the Conference of Ambassadors decided to tie up evacuation and coal mines in one package, there was another mass meeting of workers and citizens of Pécs. The assembly noted with satisfaction that most of occupied Baranya was to be returned to Hungary according to the provisions of the peace treaty.

The coal-for-evacuation formula of the Paris experts would prove to be the correct compromise solution for the Baranya problem, but the diplomatic process continued to work very slowly. On July 31, 1920 the Hungarian Foreign Ministry warned Paris that the "Social Democrats in Pécs are planning a *coup d'état* at the beginning of August with the assistance of Yugoslav authorities" and threatened to resort to armed intervention should the *coup* take place.[34] Béla Linder's frequent absences from his mayoral office appeared to substantiate such reports. Linder became a diplomat at large for his Yugoslav-protected Pécs regime. It was no secret that he was trying to negotiate with the occupying power autonomous status for Baranya and to gain the assent of the Little Entente as well as the Great Powers for such a diplomatic *modus vivendi*. Before leaving for Belgrade in November 1920 he did inform the Interallied Military Commission in Pécs that the agenda of his visit to the Yugoslav capital included seeking autonomy for Baranya.[35] Early in January he met with Yugoslav Interior Minister Milorad Drašković in occupied Baja on the Danube, again to discuss Baranya self-rule. Linder was also supported by the ministers of the defunct Károlyi regime who hoped that the establishment of an autonomous Baranya would soon serve as a jumping-off place for a struggle against the Horthy regime.[36] On March 2, 1921 Linder addressed identically worded, lengthy anti-Horthy and anti-Habsburg diatribes, to the Foreign Ministers of Czechoslovakia, Romania, and Yugoslavia, pleading for continued Yugoslav occupation of Baranya until Hungary was once more under a democratic form of government.[37] He continued this para-diplomatic activity probably in ignorance of the fact that on April 27 and May 3, 1921 the Yugoslav Government received two decisive diplomatic communications from the Conference of Ambassadors in Paris. The first of these two communications informed Belgrade that, upon completion of the treaty ratification process, it would be expected to evacuate non-treaty Hungarian territory.[38] The second communication invited the Yugoslav to start preparations for a Baranya evacuation.[39]

Lord Curzon, Foreign Secretary, told the Lords on May 5 that "every measure will be put upon them [the Yugoslavs] by His Majesty's Government to terminate the occupation" of non-treaty Baranya.[40] The British Embassy in Paris suggested to the Conference of Ambassadors in mid-June that (1) the Interallied Military Commission in Pécs supervise and impose an evacuation of all Yugoslav-occupied [non-treaty] Hungarian territory; and that (2) the Allied diplomatic representatives in Belgrade inform the Yugoslav Government of the foregoing, simultaneously requesting an immediate reply to the May 3, 1921 note of the Conference of Ambassadors to the Yugoslav Legation in Paris.[41] In this communication, still unanswered, Belgrade had been invited to declare its intention to evacuate the contested Hungarian areas as soon as the Treaty of Trianon entered into force.

The Conference of Ambassadors was also quite familiar with the diplomatic as well as strategic aspects of the Baranya question in its relationship to the overall policy of Soviet containment. The deliberations of the Conference showed concern not only with a military occupation unjustified by international law but also with the possibility that the occupied area could, under a militantly leftist régime, present a forward base for east-to-west Soviet military movements.[42] The latter assumption was based to a large degree on transmittals of Major Dérain's weekly reports from Pécs. These missives left little doubt in policymaking Entente minds about the ideological affinities and alleged strategic potentialities of the Yugoslav-supported and Comintern-affiliated régime in Baranya. As early as October 31, 1920 Dérain had reported that the new Pécs Municipal Council just established was "an oppressive régime not mitigated by the Yugoslav authorities."[43] In subsequent weekly reports the French Major claimed, however subjectively, that the moving spirit of the Pécs Municipal Council, the Socialist Party in Pécs, "was openly and violently Communist"[44] and that a Communist organization was being completed in the Baranya county seat possibly for a Soviet Russian westward offensive in the spring of 1921.[45] The likelihood of such a military operation made it urgent, Dérain recommended, "to smash without delay this Communist régime."[46] Warnings of such gravity from a trained military observer, supported by Maurice Fouchet, the French High Commissioner in Budapest, could not be taken lightly by the worried and alarmed Allied policymakers on the morrow of the Soviet victory in the Russian Civil War (November 1920), especially in the light of the militantly pro-Soviet sympathies then being demonstrated by British and French labor. In December 1920 the French Chargé d'Affaires in Budapest reported to his government that "the existence of a nest of armed Bolsheviks in Pécs would be [in the event of a Soviet westward offensive] a terrible danger for the civilized world."[47] In February 1921 the Conference of Allied Diplomatic Representatives sitting in Budapest invited Dérain to come up from Pécs and to give a general verbal report on the situation in occupied Baranya. A transcript of Dérain's report and interrogation was prepared and submitted to the Conference of Ambassadors.

In this lengthy document[48] Dérain stated that the heart of the Baranya problem is that contrary to the pertinent provisions of The Hague Regulations and of the Belgrade Military Convention, the occupying Yugoslav power, having expelled most Hungarian civil servants from the local government, installed civilian administrators of its own nationality. These foreign administrators, illegally employed, proceeded "to abuse power, deny justice, arbitrarily requisition property, unjustifiably levy taxes, establish an impermissible electoral system, support Communists in power, allow schools to be set up for Bolshevik propaganda, foment disorder in the area, and endanger the social order of Middle Europe."[49] After making this indictment, Dérain recommended that either the Yugoslav be invited to undertake an immediate evacuation or, short of such a military measure, they should be prevailed upon to "revert to a regular occupation of a purely military character" by removing their irregular, communist-sponsoring civilian administrators.[50]

Showing understandable annoyance, the Ambassadors in Paris now had the French Ministry of Foreign Affairs telegraphically instruct its representative in Belgrade to deliver a *démarche* to the Yugoslav Foreign Office.[51] On July 5, still a new *démarche* was made; July passed; but still there was no movement. Only the treaty ratification process progressed silently and invisibly. Finally, on July 26, 1921 the text of the Treaty of Trianon, bearing its last required ratification, was deposited at the Quai d'Orsay.[52] The treaty was now in force. The Yugoslav Army no longer had the right to remain north of the new international frontier.

News of the completed treaty ratification process reached Pécs while the Baranya Left was trying to adjust to new East Central European political realities. Since late 1920 protecting Yugoslavia had gradually been turning anti-Communist at home. During the November parliamentary elections of that year there were indications that the Belgrade government was not favorably inclined toward giving the proletarian Left a share in legislative power. The Belgrade Government promulgated a decree for the maintenance of law and order, the so-called *Obznana*, which was principally directed against the Communists.[53] On June 28, 1921, a bombing attempt was made by a Communist on the life of Prince Regent Alexander.[54] On July 21 former Minister of Interior Drašković, who had *ex officio* signed the *Obznana*, and then resigned, was assassinated[55] by a member of a terrorist group called "Red Justice." A mass trial of Communists followed. On August 1, reacting to the flareup of terrorism, the *skupshtina* enacted a "Law Concerning the Protection of Public Security and Order in the State."[56] The new statute was used to expel the fifty-eight Communist deputies from the national legislature and to declare the Communist Party illegal in Yugoslavia.[57]

Thus, by the summer of 1921, the Left in Baranya was wedged in between a counterrevolutionary "white" régime in Hungary to the north and an increasingly anti-Communist Yugoslav kingdom to the south. The completion of the treaty ratification process was agitating the Hungarian National Assembly, whose members kept the matter of the delayed evacuation on the parliamentary agenda by frequent interpellations through the spring and summer of 1921.[58] Replying to one such interpolation, Foreign Minister Dr. Gusztáv Gratz promised complete amnesty and no reprisals for acts committed in Baranya during the Yugoslav occupation.[59] The Yugoslavs, in their turn, in order to counteract the adverse reaction among their Baranya protégés of their anti-Communist measures at home, began appealing to the landless peasants of the occupied county with promises of the land distribution in the event of annexation to Yugoslavia.[60]

The Left began to split apart. Three principal leftist factions emerged. A moderate right wing arose, under the leadership of the attorney Gyula Hajdu (who had already played a moderating role at the time of the mutiny in 1918), speaking through the daily *Munkás*

(Worker). This faction considered the Yugoslav occupation as a necessary evil to be endured only as long as the Horthy regime remained in power to the north. An extreme left wing, led by János Polácsi and having the *Pécsi Ujság* (Pécs News) as its press organ, engaged in propaganda for annexation to Yugoslavia at the "spontaneous" request of the Baranya population. In between the two extremes stood the City Hall group of Béla Linder, which was pushing for an autonomous Baranya under the aegis of the League of Nations, protected against external enemies by the Yugoslav Army as a League surrogate.[61] These internal developments strengthened the Linder faction, which sought to reinforce its position by an alliance with the Smallholders Party, representative of the land-hungry but anti-Communist peasants. In an attempt to gain the approval of the Great Powers and the Little Entente, as well as to ward off in advance the possibility of falling victim to Belgrade's incipient anti-Communist measures, the Linder group stressed its lack of Communist ideology and affinity.[62] As proof of their contention, the Linderites pointed to the respect for private property and existence of a multi-party press in Pécs under their rule. They also thought to have solved the foreign political dilemma of whither Baranya. They cast in their lot with Yugoslavia, embracing the already approved formula of a Baranya Republic protected through the Yugoslav Army by the League of Nations.[63] Svetozar Rajić, the Yugoslav Prefect in Pécs, pledged his personal support to this proposed solution of the problem,[64] no doubt because it met with his minimum requirements: an indefinite prolongation of Yugoslav control over most of Baranya.

Action leading to the rise and fall of the Baranya Republic took place on three fronts during the three-week period ending on August 19, 1921: in Pécs itself by the Rajić-manipulated Left; in Belgrade, manifested by Linder's quasi-diplomatic efforts; and in Paris, through regular diplomatic channels between Yugoslavia and the Conference of Ambassadors.

During these three critical weeks the leftist press in Pécs clearly misrepresented Allied intentions by informing its readers that the Allied Supreme Council did not consider a Baranya evacuation timely;[65] that a military intervention by the Little Entente against Hungary was imminent;[66] and that a Yugoslav ultimatum had been delivered in Budapest.[67] Encouraged by such news, the workers of Pécs staged a one-day protest strike on August 12 against evacuation. In a communiqué, also misleading, issued on the following day,

Prefect Rajić stated that "reports of an impending evacuation are without reliable foundation."[68]

It was in this confident spirit that a scheduled trade union conference assembled in Pécs on August 14 to discuss the rising cost of living and to register its disapproval of an evacuation. According to local leftist sources, 15,000 workers and citizens were present[69] (according to the Allied observers: "4,000 Communists").[70] They listened to speeches calling for resistance to Horthy and threatening with destruction of the mines, the factories, and city itself should the Admiral's troops enter it. At least one of the speakers declared that the intent of the mass meeting was "not to set up a dictatorship of the proletariat or to establish communism but merely to maintain an honest democracy."[71] At this point the painter Péter Dobrovits mounted the rostrum unexpectedly. Dobrovits was a Hungarian citizen of Serbian descent who had spent some time in prison for alleged complicity in the mutiny in the spring of 1918, but was set free after the October (Károlyi) revolution of that year. Now he faced the crowd and told them:

> . . . the moment has come to declare to the world that we want to be master of our fate and to proclaim the Hungarian-Serbian Baranya Republic. We will at once inform the Belgrade Government of our decision and will request its approving agreement. Starting with this moment, the fate of Baranya is in the hands of the Executive Committee of the Hungarian-Serbian Baranya Republic . . . Long live the Hungarian-Serbian Baranya Republic[72]

Thunderous approval and a reportedly unanimous show of hands greeted Dobrovits's proclamation. The text of an oath was then read and repeated by the people in the square. Next Dobrovits was chosen by acclamation as President of the new Republic's Executive Committee. Twenty-one members were appointed to this governing body. As the meeting was breaking up, a delegation led by Dobrovits informed Prefect Rajić of what had taken place. The latter noted the information conveyed to him, promised to inform his government at once by courier and, pending instructions from Belgrade, pledged to "support the workers and Dobrovits."[73] By nightfall posters in Hungarian, Serbo-Croatian, and German covered the walls of the occupied city, informing the inhabitants that, in accordance with the people's right to self-determination, the Serbian-Hungarian Baranya Republic had been proclaimed, that the Republic would divide the land among the working peasants, and that it would place itself under the protection of Yugoslavia and the Little Entente.[74] On August 15 the town of Mohács and the villages of Szigetvár, Siklós, Barcs, and Baja declared their adherence to the Baranya Republic. The following day, Dobrovits left for Belgrade at the head of a delegation, formally to place the new mini-state under Yugoslav protection and to obtain permission for the recruitment of a republican army.[75]

The Baranya Republic was proclaimed in Béla Linder's absence. Between August 3 and 19 the Mayor was engaged in shuttle diplomacy between Pécs and the Yugoslav capital. Although the Yugoslav Governments did not seem to be overly optimistic about the future of the Baranya Republic, Linder's reports to his constituents back home were cheerfully confident. He did pass on Premier Nikola Pašić's ominous assurance that, in the event of an evacuation, Yugoslavia would provide asylum for all political refugees from Baranya,[76] but added that "government circles in Belgrade . . . do not consider timely an evacuation of the occupied territories."[77] Both Linder and Rajić saw fit to keep secret the information Linder received in Belgrade on August 9 that there was no way to avoid an evacuation.[78]

Yet, following the events of August 14, the Pécs leftwing press attributed to Linder the statement that "Belgrade government circles have favorably reacted to the proclamation of the Baranya Republic."[79] The press also reported an alleged statement by Pašić to Linder to the effect that "there is no question now of a Baranya evacuation and there will be none possibly for months yet."[80] On August 18 Linder telephoned from Belgrade to say that not only had Pašić assured him that a Baranya evacuation was not on the agenda, but also that the Yugoslav Premier "had agreed to equip and arm republican battalions."[81] On August 19—the day before the Yugoslavs started leaving Pécs—Linder briefly returned to the city and from the balcony of City Hall told a crowd that, although he had brought no orders with him which would assure the maintenance of the occupation, he could state that such orders would not be long delayed.[82]

The French diplomatic sources now available reveal that up to August 15 the Yugoslav Government had not come to a firm determination to withdraw its troops to the new Trianon frontier and that, indeed, between August 16 and 18 it mounted a last-minute diplomatic offensive to prolong the presence of its armed forces in

Baranya. Secret diplomacy succeeded only in postponing the entry of Hungarian troops into the occupied parts by two days (August 18 to August 20) but failed in its larger aspect to prolong the occupation indefinitely, so to save the Baranya Republic.

The Interallied Military Commission (IMC) in Pécs had been designated to oversee the withdrawal of Yugoslav forces from occupied Baranya. When British Colonel F. W. Gosset arrived in Pécs on August 11 to take up his post as Chairman of the IMC, it was assumed both in Paris and in Budapest that the evacuation would start on August 18. However, the Yugoslav Government had still not replied to the Allied *démarche* of June 25. There were other disturbing developments. Belgrade had also ignored an invitation from Paris to appoint a sole military commander for the entire Yugoslav-occupied Hungarian area[83] for a simplified and easily workable liaison with the IMC in Pécs under Colonel Gosset. A new diplomatic roadblock was thrown up on August 16 by Milan Milojević the Yugoslav diplomatic agent in Budapest, who informed the Allied Diplomatic Representatives in the Hungarian capital that his government "feared complications" should Hungarian troops enter occupied Baranya and that consequently Yugoslav evacuation should be postponed until a later date.[84] Milojević also asked for guarantees for his country, including continued use for coal shipments of the main railroad line from Pécs to the Yugoslav frontier via the town of Villány.[85] Then came, on August 18—instead of a Yugoslav reply to the Allied *démarche*—a note from the Yugoslav Legation in Paris to the Conference of Ambassadors, requesting that the evacuation of Baranya be delayed "in view of the events now taking place there."[86] This was an obvious reference to the proclamation of the Baranya Republic on August 14 and a Yugoslav diplomatic followup to Linder's entreaties as well as to Dobrovits's request of August 16 for a Yugoslav protectorate.

The Allied supervisory apparatus was thrown into disarray by these Yugoslav diplomatic moves. In Budapest the Allied Diplomatic Representatives handed Miloyevitch "an energetic note" rejecting his request for a delay in evacuation beyond August 18 and dismissing his demand for guarantees.[87] The note added, apprehensively, that owing to Yugoslav dilatoriness in Baranya, Hungarian evacuation of the Burgenland, awarded to Austria by the Treaty of Trianon, had to be postponed from August 21 to August 23.[88] The Conference of Ambassadors was even more stern. In a note dated August 19 and

addressed to the Yugoslav Legation in Paris, the previous Allied diplomatic *démarche* to Yugoslavia over Baranya was repeated "in the
most pressing manner" and a warning note was added: in the event
of Yugoslav non-compliance with the *démarche*, the Conference of
Ambassadors envisaged "the most serious complications."[89]

Still the Yugoslav were not completely subdued; in fact they were
heartened, because the evacuation target date of August 18 had
passed and their troops were still in Baranya. The Baranya Republic
was getting a reprieve, although it would prove to be only of two
days' duration. But the rank-and-file of the Pécs Left was still
unaware of how close they were to the end. The Yugoslav military,
however, knew. On the evening of August 18 Colonel Gosset in Pécs
called on the Yugoslav Commanding Officer, a Colonel Djoka,
Gjorgjević, and officially informed him that the Allied authorities
had postponed the beginning of the evacuation from August 18 to
August 20.[90]

A long weekend was in the offing. Saturday, August 20 was St.
Stephen's Feast, a traditional Hungarian national holiday, which this
year would be prolonged till Sunday evening. *Munkás* (Worker)
published its last number Saturday morning. The final issue announced the end of the occupation, advised against resistance, and
recommended "quick flight" from Yugoslav-occupied territory.[91] An
exodus of the Left high command and its more immediate followers
began at once. According to a report of Gyula Hajdu the refugees included about 700 miners, approximately 1500 industrial workers,
500 additional manual workers from the rural areas; all told about
2700 men with families. Most of these people stayed in Yugoslavia.
Only 70 Leaders of the Baranya Left continued to Vienna to join the
Hungarian emigres of 1919.[92]

Yugoslav troop withdrawal from the line of demarcation began
early Saturday morning, August 20. It took five days for the Yugoslav Army to complete the evacuation of all occupied Hungarian territory north of the international boundary.

Thus, fifty years after the Paris Commune, the microcosmic
Baranya Republic passed into history unnoticed by the world, yielding without resistance or bloodshed to the forces of a conservative
restoration. As Paris in 1870–1871, so Baranya in 1918–1921 provides an opportunity for the study of subsurface national divisive-
ness along ideological and class lines, rising to dynamic crisis level as
a result of military defeat awaiting diplomatic treatment.

Notes

Abbreviations: In citing the major sources the following abbreviations will be used in footnotes: FFAA (French Foreign Affairs Archives) for the unpublished archival materials microfilmed in the Archives of the Ministère des Affaires Etrangères, Paris; FRH (Foreign Relations of Hungary) for the documents published in Hungary, Ministry for Foreign Affairs, *Papers and Documents Relating to the Foreign Relations of Hungary,* edited by Francis Deák and Dezsö Ujváry, 2 vols. (Budapest, 1939 and 1946); EK (*Emlékkönyv*) for the documents, abstracts, and studies appearing in *A Magyar Tanácsköztársaság Pécsi-Baranyai Emlékkönyve* [The Pécs-Baranya Book of Memories of the Hungarian Soviet Republic] (Pécs, Municipal Council 1960); and *Hajdu* for the memoirs and documents published in Gyula Hajdu, *Harcban Elnyomók és Megszállók Ellen* [Fighting Oppressors and Occupiers] (Pécs, 1957). Less frequently used sources will be cited in full the first time they appear. Diplomatic documents will be cited with names of sending and receiving persons or agencies stated, date given, and place of origin mentioned whenever significant.

1. "Yugoslavia" did not become an official country name until 1929. Between 1918 and 1929 the country now referred to as Yugoslavia was known as the Kingdom of the Serbs, Croats and Slovenes (abbreviated SHS). Before 1918 the central part of the SHS Kingdom had existed as Serbia. During 1918–1921 the occupying forces and authorities were commonly referred to as Serbs in Baranya. In this article the terms Yugoslav and Yugoslavia will be used as most capable of carrying meaning at this writing.

2. The place name *Baranya* (pronounced Ba'ranya) first occurs in writing in 1141. It is probably derived from Slavic *brana*, gate, gateway. See Zoltán Gombocz and János Melich, *Lexicon critico-etymologicum linguae Hungaricae* (Budapest, 1914–1930), vol. I, columns 282–284. Imre Dankó, *Pécs képekben* [Pécs in Pictures] (Pécs, 1957), p. 36 derives the word from a personal name, that of the first *ispán* (province chief) of this region.

3. *Révai Nagy Lexikona* [Révai's Great Lexicon] vol. II (Budapest, 1911), pp. 586–588 (henceforth Révai); *Bolshaya Sovietskaya Encyclopedia*, (Moscow, 1952), IV, p. 228.

4. Révai, II, pp. 586–588.

5. The place name *Pécs* (pronounced Paytch) first occurs in writing in 1093 and is open to etymological speculation. The most likely origin of the word is Old Slavic *pest*, kiln, oven. See Danko, p. 33 and János Kolta, *Pécs* (Budapest, 1967), pp. 16–22.

6. Révai, II, pp. 586–588.

7. Révai, XV (Budapest, 1922), "Pécs."

8. Hajdu (see *Abbreviations*), p. 20.

9. *EK* (see *Abbreviations*), p. 34.

10. On the Hague Regulations (referred to as the Second Hague Convention in the French archival materials) see H. Lauterpacht (ed.) *Oppenheim's International Law* (London and New York, 1944), pp. 335–349. (Henceforth *Lauterpacht*).

11. FFAA, Dérain in Pécs to Allied Diplomatic Representatives in Budapest, February 7, 1921.

12. *Hajdu*, pp. 219–220.

13. Tibor Hajdu, *Az 1918-as magyarországi demokratikus foradalom* [The 1918 Democratic Revolution in Hungary] (Budapest 1968), p. 248.

14. Mme. Mihaly Károlyi, *Együtt a forradalomban* [Together during the Revolution] (Budapest, 1967), p. 299.

15. *Ibid.*, pp. 301, 301, n. `.

16. *Hajdu*, p. 277.

17. *Ibid.*, p. 277.

18. *Ibid.*, p. 286.

19. *EK*, p. 55.

20. *Hajdu*, p. 274.

21. *EK*, p. 63.

22. *EK*, p. 61, *FFAA*, Conference of Allied Diplomatic Representatives, Budapest, Dérain, *Procès Verbal*, February 26, 1921.

23. *EK*, p. 72.

24. *FFAA*, Fouchet in Budapest to Conference of Ambassadors, February 20, 1921.

25. *EK*, p. 191: *FFAA*, Conference of Allied Diplomatic Representatives, Budapest, Dérain, *Procès Verbal*, February 26, 1921.

26. *EK*, p. 72.

27. Hajdu, pp. 390, 4280439; L.C. Tihany, *The Baranya Dispute, 1918–1921* (New York, 1978), pp. 83–94.

28. *FFAA*, Dérain in Pécs to Allied Diplomatic Representatives, Budapest, February 7, 1921; *EK*, p. 68.

29. *Magyar Életrajzi Lexikon* [Hungarian Biographical Lexicon] vol. II: "Linder, Béla" (Budapest, 1969).

30. *FFAA*, Young in Belgrade to Curzon in London, May 16, 1921.

31. *Ibid.*, French Ministry of Foreign Affairs for Conference of Ambassadors to Belgrade and Budapest, December 20, 1920.

32. *FFAA*, French Ministry of Foreign Affairs, for Conference of Ambassadors, to Belgrade and Budapest, December 20, 1920.

33. *FRH*, II, pp. 587, 667.

34. *FRH*, I. p. 530.

35. *FFAA*, Robien in Budapest to Leygues in Paris, Dec. 12, 1920.

36. Great Britain, Public Records Office, C 2341/21; Young in Belgrade to Curzon in London, Jan. 29, 1921; FRH, I, p. 530.

37. *FFAA*, Transmittal from War Ministry (Deuxième Bureau) to President, Council of Ministers, March 17, 1921.

38. *Ibid.*, Conference of Ambassadors to SHS Legation, Paris, April 27, 1921.

39. *Ibid*, May 3, 1921.

40. Great Britain, Parliament, House of Lords: *The Parliamentary Debates* (Official Report), Fifth series, vol. XLV-2, Column 250.

41. *FFAA*, Note from British Embassy, Paris, to Conference of Ambassadors, June 13, 1921.

42. See footnotes 45–47.

43. *FFAA*, Dérain in Pécs to Allied Diplomatic Representatives in Budapest, October 31, 1920.

44. *Ibid.*, February 7, 1921.

45. *Ibid.*

46. *Ibid.*, Conference of Allied Diplomatic Representatives, Budapest: Dérain, Procès Verbal, February 26, 1921.

47. *Ibid.*, Robien in Budapest to Leygues in Paris, December 12, 1920.

48. Full translation in Tihany, *Baranya Dispute* (New York, 1978), pp. 75–82.

49. *Loc. cit.*

50. *Loc. cit.*

51. *FFAA*, Berthelot in Paris for Conference of Ambassadors, to Belgrade, Budapest, Rome, and London, June 25, 1921.

52. For a detailed report on the exchange of ratifications deposition ceremony see *FRH*, II, pp. 55–58.

53. Alex N. Dragnich, *Serbia, Nikola Pašič and Yugoslavia* (New Brunswick, 1974), p. 155.

54. Stephen Graham, *Alexander of Yugoslavia* (New Haven, 1939) pp. 121–122.

55. *Ibid.*, p. 164.

56. Dragnich, p. 164.

57. EK, pp. 80–81.

58. Hungary. *Nemzetgyülés, Napló* (Budapest, 1921–1926) (National Assembly, Parliamentary Record) X, pp. 328–330, 352; XI, pp. 4,7,19–37, 44–46,116,368–371; XII, pp. 84–88, 126,130,335–338, 476–477, 480–481,626.

59. *FFAA*, Fouchet in Budapest to Briand in Paris, March 21, 1921.

60. *EK*, p. 78.

61. *EK*, p. 73.

62. *EK*, pp. 78, 80.

63. *EK*, p. 70.

64. Gyula Hajdu, p. 383.

65. *Ibid.* p. 401.

66. *Ibid.*

67. *Ibid.*

68. *Ibid.*, p. 402.

69. *Ibid.*, pp. 407, 410.

70. *FFAA*, Fouchet in Budapest to Briand in Paris, Aug. 23, 1921.

71. Hajdu, p. 408.

72. *Ibid.*, p. 410

73. *Ibid.*, pp. 410, 411.

74. For a text of the proclamation of the Baranya Republic see Gyula Hajdu, pp. 412–413.

75. *Ibid.*, p. 415.

76. *Ibid.*, 401.

78. *EK*, p. 86; Gyula Hajdu, p. 404.

79. Hajdu, p. 416.

80. *Ibid.*, p. 417

81. *Ibid.*, pp. 417, 418.

82. *Ibid.*, p. 420.

83. *FFAA*, Fouchet in Budapest to Briand in Paris, Aug. 23, 1921.

84. *Ibid.*

85. *Ibid.*

86 *FFAA*, SHS Legation in Paris to Conference of Ambassadors, August 18, 1921.

87. *Ibid.*, Fouchet in Budapest to Briand in Paris, Aug. 23, 1921.

88. *Ibid.*

89. *Ibid.*, Conference of Ambassadors to SHS Legation, Paris August 19, 1921.

90. *Ibid.*

91. Gyula Hajdu, pp. 42–421

92. Full English translation in L.C. Tihany, *The Baranya Dispute, 1918–1921*, pp. 99–102.

93. For a more detailed treatment of the rise and fall of the Baranya Republic see Tihany, *op. cit.*

Thomas Spira

The Sopron (Ödenburg) Plebiscite of December 1921 and the German Nationality Problem

In mid-December of 1921, the citizens of the West Hungarian border town of Sopron and eight surrounding communities[1] voted on whether the area should remain with Hungary, or join the newly created Republic of Austria. The Sopron Plebiscite ranks as a relatively minor incident in postwar history, but it has attracted considerable attention. Not only did the dispute test the authority and prestige of the victorious great powers, it also revealed that some of the area's predominantly German-speaking rural inhabitants had succumbed to German nationalistic fervor by voting for unification with Austria.

Until 1647, when ceded to Hungary by Emperor Ferdinand III, the Burgenland, as the contested area came to be known shortly after World War I, belonged to Austria. The Germans' allegiance was untested until war's end, when the Austro-Hungarian Monarchy disintegrated, and West Hungary's Germans became separated from their brethren in Austria. Burgenland's 1,514 square miles contained nearly 345,000 inhabitants, of whom 75% were Germans and variously called Heinzen, Heanzen, or Swabians (Schwaben). The remainder of the population claimed to be Hungarians, except for a sprinkling of about 10% Croatians and Slovenians scattered throughout the Hungarian and German communities.[2] Responding to Austrian diplomatic pressure, petitions by Austrophile elements in West Hungary, and dismay over Hungary's Marxist government, the Paris Peace Conference reversed its original position to let the territory remain with Hungary. On 20 July 1919, Hungary was ordered to evacuate the larger, predominantly German-inhabited portion of West Hungary. For more than two years, Hungary defied both Austria and the Peace Conference, but finally, it agreed to exchange the region for Sopron and its immediate environs. A compromise agreement, drafted by Italy and signed in Venice on 11

October 1921, called for an internationally supervised plebiscite to determine the destiny of the town and its hinterland.

The plebiscite zone's 80 square miles contained a population of 48,000, of whom 34,000 lived in Sopron, the administrative capital. Unfortunately, the area's heterogeneous ethnic distribution complicated a just settlement. Sopron's German speakers roughly equaled the Magyar population, but in the countryside 9,983 Germans outnumbered the 2,369 Hungarians.[3] To prevent splitting Sopron from its hinterland, the victorious powers decided to let the combined vote determine the disposition of the whole area. Hungary won the plebiscite, conducted between 14–16 December 1921. Austria gained modest majorities in five of the eight rural communities, but Hungary swept Sopron, as the pro-Hungarian vote exceeded the rate of self-professed Hungarians by 29.1%. On 23 December 1921, the Conference of Ambassadors ratified the plebiscite results, and handed the Sopron area to Hungary on 1 January 1922. On 20 February 1922, Austria reluctantly recognized the cession.[4]

Apart from the fact that most West Hungarians in the ceded zone were never consulted as to their national preferences, two other factors complicate judging the Germans' loyalties, even in the plebiscite area. Between Armistice Day and the plebiscite, both Hungary and Austria suffered political upheavals which influenced the allegiance of the Germans. Communism immediately threatened postwar Austria. Fears of bolshevism persisted even under its first chancellor, the Socialist statesman Karl Renner, replaced in June of 1920 by a coalition led by the conservative Michael Mayr. An ultra-conservative government under Johann Schober, dominated by Christian Socials and German Nationalists, assumed power in June of 1921, and remained firmly ensconced even beyond the Burgenland crisis.

Hungary was a political rainbow. Its liberal democratic postwar government, led by Count Mihály Károlyi, led to a Socialist-Communist fusion forged in late March of 1919 by Béla Kun. A counterrevolution overthrew Kun in August, and in November, Admiral Miklós Horthy seized power. His ultra-conservative regime remained firmly entrenched until nearly the end of World War II. These changes bewildered the Germans, most of them unsophisticated and conservative, predominantly Roman Catholic, peasants. Their intelligentsia, especially the influential Magyarized ("Magyarone") administrators, clergymen, and educators, wished to assimilate their people into the prevailing Hungarian ethos.

At war's end, Austria still beckoned as a potential new fatherland to Burgenland's Germans. But its Marxist-tinged Socialist regime offended the predominantly traditionalist Germans. Nonetheless, before Horthy's counterrevolution, Austria might still have attracted their support simply by appearing to be the lesser of two evils.[5] After Kun's demise, but before Mayr, Hungary gained the advantage. However, when conservatism in both capitals eliminated politics as a paramount issue, Hungary became, at best, a doubtful choice for them. The treatment of non-Hungarians would not likely improve without the protective Habsburgs, and the past Hungarian record of accommodating the ethnic minorities was poor. Nonetheless, the Austrians feared that economic and political necessity might bind the Germans to Hungary.[6]

Economic considerations are always powerful in agricultural border regions where markets straddle international boundaries, and West Hungary was no exception. In the Austro-Hungarian pre-plebiscite struggle for German support, both sides issued conflicting and exaggerated claims about their respective commercial importance. On 16 June 1919, Chancellor Renner, and on 22 November 1919, the Provisional National Assembly of German Austria, argued for West Hungary's cession to Austria. They added intellectual, geographic, and ethnic considerations to massive economic arguments. The entire region, they claimed, was indispensable to feeding Vienna, Wiener Neustadt, and Graz. Moreover, these three cities allegedly paid more than Hungarian buyers, who drew upon more diversified domestic sources. Furthermore, West Hungarian farmers could more advantageously exchange their farm products for machinery in Austria than in Hungary. If Burgenland remained Hungarian, Austria's three greatest industrial cities would thus be denied their only food source, whereas Budapest, too distant to draw upon West Hungary's provisions, would not benefit. Indeed, even Hungary's westernmost regions could be conveniently provisioned from elsewhere. The Austrians also claimed that the offspring of petty Burgenland farmers frequently depended on Austrian jobs in industry and mining. For these transient residents, Burgenland's incorporation into Austria was a matter of economic necessity.[7]

Later, when the decision came to apportion Burgenland's western portion to Austria, and allow a plebiscite to decide the fate of Sopron, the Austrians argued that, in Hungarian hands, Sopron would lose its natural hinterland in Austria and wither, while north-south railway traffic would have to be rerouted and cross several international boundaries.[8]

Hungarians in general, and the Hungarian delegation at the Peace Conference in particular, tried to rebut the Austrian arguments. The region allegedly only traded in the food sent to Austria and depended on the great Hungarian Plain, and on Győr's agricultural hinterland. Burgenland's modest industrial production found a ready market in Hungary, but could not compete with Lower Austria's superior and cheaper commodities. Moreover, Burgenland's largely agriculturally oriented factories, notably sugar beet refineries, drew most of their raw materials from Hungary, and almost none from Austria. Burgenland's commerce and light industry would thus decline under Austrian rule. Hungary's other regions would suffer indirectly, and their sacrifices would not alleviate Austria's food shortages in the least. For example, Austria's deficit in wheat flour totaled about seven million tons annually, of which the Burgenland might provide, at most, $\frac{1}{4}$–$\frac{1}{2}$ million tons. Throughout the crisis, Hungary offered to relieve Austrian hunger by establishing an Austro-Hungarian free trade zone, and promised to provision Lower Austria, but only if the Austrians renounced West Hungary. The threat of suspended food deliveries hovered over Austria's industrial cities throughout this period.[9]

The Hungarians won the Sopron plebiscite, and they had Jakob Bleyer and his followers to thank. The Bleyerites barely tolerated Károlyi's government and boycotted the Kun regime's attempts to pacify the Germans. But throughout, they made every effort to persuade their followers to support Hungary's claim for West Hungary, notwithstanding Hungarian harassment of German cultural institutions that occasionally bordered on intolerance.

Bleyer, a man of the people, a devout Roman Catholic of peasant origin from Yugoslav-occupied Bácska, emerged as the most important and influential German leader in postwar Hungary. When the Austro-Hungarian Monarchy collapsed, Bleyer was already known as a leading exponent of German aspirations. In December of 1917, Bleyer, in collaboration with the Roman Catholic cleric Johannes Huber, founded the ultra-conservative daily *Neue Post*, his official publication until it was superseded in January of 1921 by the weekly

Sonntagsblatt. During the war, Bleyer published widely in Hungarian journals, explaining his view of the appropriate German role in Hungarian life. Bleyer claimed that the Hungarians were entitled to assimilate the non-Hungarian intelligentsia. Magyarization of the educated classes was a normal part of urbanization and assimilation through the natural process of acculturation. But German peasant children should not be Magyarized, but rather given a sound, practical Hungarian education in elementary schools that were otherwise purely German. Bleyer believed in the vitality of German rural culture. Even if the Hungarians limited German exclusively to private use, the Germans would survive, provided their ethnic village school system remained vigorous.[10]

As the war wound down, Bleyer clung to his views of 1917. In a *Neue Post* editorial, he attacked Transylvanian Saxon leader Rudolf Brandsch for urging Hungary's Germans to demand full autonomy. Bleyer conceded certain legitimate grievances, but rejected autonomy on patriotic grounds. Restoration of German elementary schools was his only really significant demand, but only in total harmony with the Hungarians.[11] When, on 1 November 1918, Károlyi officially recognized Hungary's first German administrative organization, the *Deutschungarischer Volksrat*, Bleyer announced its program and pledged that all Germans would defend Hungary's integrity, reject autonomy, but demand full national privileges.[12]

Bleyer, however, distrusted Károlyi and his left-wing functionaries. He was apprehensive about the preservation of German traditions in the rural regions of West Hungary. Not surprisingly, only one week after founding the *Volksrat*, Bleyer announced that cultural concessions no longer sufficed; the Germans also deserved all those rights which Károlyi had just granted to Hungary's other minorities.[13] At the same time, however, Bleyer and his collaborators paid lip service to Hungarian unity. Franz Bonitz, a *Volksrat* colleague, urged Germans to "march shoulder to shoulder with Magyardom," while also promoting "a united [German] front . . . both at home and abroad, with respect to our cultural, linguistic, political, and economic aspirations."[14]

Such pressure earned short-term benefits. On 16 November 1918, Germans obtained the right to abolish Hungarian instruction in the first two elementary grades in predominantly German regions. But shortly thereafter, the *Volksrat* insisted on separate German schools, on official German in the courts and the administration of predominantly German areas, and that non-Germans be excluded from German affairs.[15] In order to satisfy these demands, Márton Lovászy, the Minister of Education and Religion, ordered on 21 November 1918 that the educational concessions granted a few days earlier be expanded to include church-run institutions.[16] This was important because nearly 86% of German schools were confessional. The Germans received additional "favors," mostly meaningless, owing to the critical shortage of indigenous teachers.

Signs of German discontent with Károlyi soon appeared. Obviously, the new government had neither the means nor really any strong desire to implement properly the minority policies. Soon complaints filtered into *Volksrat* offices concerning violations of the education ordinance. Throughout Hungary, village and county officials effectively blocked the regime's attempts to provide at least some improvement in the German school system. The Germans also discovered that Count Albert Apponyi's 1907 school law, which forbade non-Hungarian elementary textbooks, was still in effect. So German children were worse off than before. Hungarian instruction shrank, while an effective German education was barred.[17]

The government's inability to enforce its laws rapidly ended Hungarian-German cooperation. On 27 December 1918, Géza Zsombor, the influential editor of the Sopron *Grenzpost*, announced that, failing to gain immediate autonomy, Burgenlanders would proclaim an independent German republic. On 11 January 1919, the *Volksrat* called for German middle schools and academies, and German primary schools on demand even in predominantly Hungarian-speaking areas.[18] On 20 January, Germans in Sopron reiterated Zsombor's autonomy plea and renewed their threat to either proclaim Burgerland's independence, or join Austria.

The government was hard pressed. In deference to the Germans, Károlyi commissioned several of their representatives, notably Peter Jekel, Guido Gündisch, and Otto Herzog, to draft a new statute embodying extraordinary German privileges. The gesture proved futile because a Hungarian, Ödön Berinkey, and Károlyi's State Secretary for German affairs, Heinrich Kalmár, a Hungarian Jew, also participated in its preparation. Conservative Germans objected not only to Kalmár's Judaism, but to the government's alleged impudence in foisting an outsider on them. A similar stigma clung to Berinkey. The Bleyerites admitted only Christian Germans in their affairs. Despite the cabinet's objections that the Germans should not merit special treatment, Law VI of 29 January 1919 granted cultural and political autonomy to Germans in Hungary's predominantly German-speaking areas. This included administration, justice, education, and religion. Although autonomy would be centered in *Deutschwestungarn* (German West Hungary), the Germans acquired a National Assembly (*Deutsche Nationalversammlung*), a German Ministry, district councils (*Gauverwaltungen*), and commissioners.

The Germans remained obdurate. They sensed that these regulations were merely designed to forestall further German defections, mainly in Burgenland, and to lure back secessionists in southern Hungary and Transylvania. Concessions to the Germans of Hungary paradoxically exacerbated the nationality conflict. Bleyer now scorned the new law because he claimed that political autonomy conflicted with his own patriotic views. He believed that the Peace Conference must resolve Burgenland's destiny, and that cultural autonomy was all the Germans ought to accept.[19]

Bleyer's rejection of autonomy was complex. He believed that the Károlyi regime, because of its republican nature and socialist affiliations, was evil, and the autonomy statute unworkable. The Germans also wondered why their cherished goals should have been achieved so easily. Earlier concessions were not carried through and they suspected further treachery. The government would revoke the favorable regulations with a return to stability, leaving the Germans worse off than before. The *Neue Post* accused Károlyi of subverting Germans by sending Social Democratic officials and ideas into their midst. An editorial pilloried the socialist minister of education, Zsigmond Kunfi, for banning religious instruction in the schools, and planning to nationalize education, which would impose government ideological control over German youth. The German press campaign raged intensively, when Bleyer suddenly quit the *Volksrat* and withdrew from contact with the government. On 12 March 1919, the *Neue Post* even hinted at possible secession in Burgenland, because Germans had grown skeptical about the administration of autonomy. Burgenlanders still needed the Austrian market, just as German workers depended on well paying jobs in Austria. The newspaper warned the government not to isolate Austria from Hungary by erecting tariff barriers, or by imposing harsh criteria to obtain border passes.[20]

In the final weeks of Károlyi's reign secessionist activities intensified. Deputations of peasants from Burgenland petitioned Vienna to annex the region. Austrian Foreign Minister Otto Bauer failed to intervene when Austrian agitators infiltrated West Hungary as private individuals. Oscar Charmant, Hungary's envoy in Vienna, reported intensive anti-Hungarian propaganda in Burgenland, with the Vienna-based *Fremdenblatt* being the chief culprit. At the end of March 1919, the Károlyi regime fell for a variety of reasons, including the aggravated Burgenland crisis. Károlyi yielded to the 133-day interlude of Béla Kun's Communist Republic of Councils.

When Kun assumed power on 21 March 1919, only the Ruthenians and West Hungary's Germans remained firmly under Hungarian rule. Bleyer and his supporters went into hiding to plot the overthrow of the Marxist regime. Kun at first ignored the minority situation entirely. Germans were entrusted to radical Social Democrats and Marxists, many of them Hungarians or Hungarian Jews. Soon, however, foreign policy considerations, especially Austrian intrigues in Burgenland, prompted a more pragmatic reappraisal of the German problem in Hungary.

The Communists' ventures into minority politics and diplomacy were dogmatic and amateurish. Kun deemed nationality problems a major nuisance, a bourgeois affectation, and hence just another obstacle to Communism.[21] A Marxist state would not require minority legislation, because the exploitive capitalist system would evaporate. The Germans recognized that Kun had no interest in their ethnic survival, that concessions were meant to court their support to counter Austrian and Allied diplomatic measures detrimental to Hungary's integrity. Indeed, Kun had cause for concern. Although publicly Austria's Social Democrats pledged noninterference in Hungary unless Kun was deposed, their subversions dismayed Hungary's new leaders.[22] Partly, this explains why Kun meant to block German minority rights. He was far more interested in staffing vulnerable West Hungarian border posts with reliable Marxists than with pleasing suspected German nationalists.

The Communists had inherited from Károlyi a slender framework on which to construct a nationality formula that was more suitable than the one they had envisaged at first. They dared not retract even the illusory German gains granted under Károlyi. Almost immediately they established a Hungarian Federal Soviet Republic with two provisional jurisdictions—one for Ruthenia and one for Trans-Danubia (Burgenland). A Commissar attached to the Ministry of German Affairs governed *Deutschwestungarn*, the German region.

A stopgap German autonomy, promulgated on 30 April, seemed attractive, but failed to please the Germans. Although a *Gaurat für Deutschwestungarn* (District Council for West Hungary) functioned as a virtually sovereign body,[23] the government failed to clarify the constitutional status of Germans residing outside *Gaurat* jurisdiction. After prolonged procrastinations, the regime finally limited German autonomy to Burgenland, and blundered again by deferring to the regime's influential and determined Hungarian minority. Bowing to their nationalistic pressures, Kun removed Sopron from the *Gaurat's* jurisdiction. The Germans resented this, because Hungarians comprised only about one-half of Sopron's population.

The Germans resented even more their new leaders and lesser executives, who all turned out to be Hungarian or Hungarian Jewish Marxists. Petty officials, for lack of reliable Marxists, were recruited from the ranks of the former German Ministry and were kept under close surveillance. The Károlyi regime had only recently incurred German disaffection by using non-German higher officials in German-inhabited areas. The Communists committed the same blunder, and suffered the same consequences.

To demonstrate his concern for minority rights, Kun maintained the fiction of a bona fide German cultural association. Bleyer's *Deutscher Volksrat* metamorphosed into the *Deutscher Kulturbund für Ungarn*, but it followed strictly Marxist lines. Heinrich Kalmár, the newly appointed Commissioner, also managed the cultural bureau *Deutsches Volksamt* (German People's Bureau) and its official journal, the *Volksblatt*. The government ordered all authorities to communicate with minority people in their native tongue.[24] This was to assuage non-Hungarians who distrusted this regime even more than previous governments. Kun's biggest mistake was dodging the nationality issue. He repudiated the principle of self-determination of nationalities as a bourgeois concept and hence invalid, in favor of self-determination of the proletariat. Kun's attempts to solve the nationality problem on this basis deepened the growing Hungarian-German gulf, and terminated any further meaningful dialogue. Austria's Socialist regime in particular intensified its efforts to rescue the by now quite willing German Burgenlanders.

The government's ill-considered educational and religious policies dismayed Burgenland's German society. In education, for example, Kun introduced a string of regulations which ultimately might have raised educational standards. Instruction was made more

progressive and humane, and teachers were to be well paid and per-
form educational tasks in the adult community. Promotion into
higher education free of charge was guaranteed to every gifted child,
and plans were laid for an extensive German elementary school
building program in Burgenland and elsewhere.[25] Religion was tied
to education because most German schools were confessional. German peasants cherished religious control over education, a tradition
dating back several centuries. But the Soviet regime published new
school regulations, each more offensive than the last, designed to replace Christian precepts with a Marxist *Weltanschauung* through a
massive teacher reeducation program.[26]

On 23 June 1919, the Kun regime, still soliciting German support,
unveiled its long-heralded final Constitution, with certain favorable
provisions for the minorities. But German public opinion in
Hungary had already spurned Marxism.[27] The confusing directives,
German disaffection bordering on civil war, and a regime of Red
Terror in Burgenland against secessionists, undercut Kun. His regime
fell on 1 August 1919. One of Kun's last official acts was to disap-
prove on 21 July the provision of the Treaty of St. Germain, which
had allocated Burgenland to Austria the previous day. Kun be-
queathed to Gyula Peidl, his Social Democratic successor, an aggravated Burgenland crisis, a German nationality policy in shambles,
and a thoroughly alienated German public in Hungary.

Peidl lasted only five days. Next, István Friedrich, a Károlyi Independence Party renegade, became prime minister through a coup.
His ministry went through three turbulent cabinet changes. Jakob
Bleyer reemerged by having been one of the chief anti-Soviet conspirators in league with Friedrich and other ultra-conservatives. The
two men shared a similar *Weltanschauung*. Both professed pro-
Habsburg sentiments, they hated bolshevism and republicanism, and
they favored moderate concessions for Hungary's German minority.
Bleyer enjoyed such influence at that moment with Hungarians and
Germans alike that he was tendered the choice between two important cabinet posts. On 15 August 1919, Bleyer accepted the portfolio
of Minister of Nationalities in Friedrich's second cabinet.[28]

Several days later, Bleyer issued a position paper. Communism
had injured the Germans by exacerbating nationalistic passions in
Hungary which his ministry would heal. Germans would integrate
themselves into the Hungarian State, but retain their national identity, within linguistic and ethnic boundaries. Bleyer demanded an

effective German elementary school and cultural program, and a modest political action plan. The use of German in all official transactions was essential; but Bleyer remained discreetly silent on autonomy. His New Course intended to convince the Hungarians that the Germans' loyalty for Hungary was sincere, and would restore their somewhat tarnished image.[29]

Bleyer addressed the task of recapturing the allegiance of Hungary's seceded nationalities. It was a convenient way of demonstrating that the Germans were Hungarian patriots. But Bleyer no longer thought in terms of Hungary ruled only by the Hungarians, as he had when Hungary was still part of the Dual Monarchy. Bleyer felt loyalties both to Hungary and to Germandom. While wishing the Hungarians well, he also desired prominence for the Germans. These two contradictory allegiances bred a synthesis of joint Hungarian-German hegemony in Hungary. Bleyer believed that if Germans exceeded the Hungarians as patriots, then cultural and certain political concessions would be forthcoming as rewards. Although neither the seceded Germans nor the Hungarians heeded Bleyer, the Germans of Burgenland and elsewhere in Hungary applauded.[30] Under Bleyer, the German Section performed prodigious paper feats. Bleyer and his aides tried to stem the anti-Hungarian tide sweeping embittered German public opinion. Under State Secretary Georg Steuer, the German Section attempted to reach a modus vivendi of sorts with the Hungarians. They also sought to persuade Burgenland's Germans to remain true to Hungary, to insulate them against pan-German influences, and to safeguard their cultural interests.[31]

The German Section's task of reconciling Germans and Hungarians contained contradictions. If the Germans were to be offered inferior concessions to those they had enjoyed before, then they would reject accommodation. If, on the other hand, they obtained concessions equaling or surpassing those of the radical era, then they would confront an outraged Hungarian public. Bleyer therefore elaborated what he hoped would be a fair compromise. In August, he unveiled a statute that in spirit resembled the Nationality Law of 1868. Its fairness could attract the minorities, whereas its moderation would not offend the Hungarians. By stressing the rights of individuals rather than those of groups, Bleyer sought to balance Hungarian elitism and German ethnic particularism.[32]

Although the Law stopped short of recognizing ethnic groups as corporate structures, it did designate non-Hungarian ethnic groups as national minorities. It thus went beyond the 1868 statute, which merely acknowledged racial (*i.e.*, national or ethnic) distinctions. The new law also established non-Hungarian languages in public life. Unfortunately, many regulations were cumbersome, and the local officials enforcing them were predominantly Hungarians or "reliable" Magyarized individuals. The Law also aroused exaggerated hopes for the establishment of a comprehensive minority education system, from kindergartens to chairs in the universities. But obviously, the largely Magyarized German clergy would insist on pure Hungarian schools, so the provisions had little more than publicity value. Many observers believed that the Nationality Law was a mere maneuver, designed to persuade the minorities that Hungary had shelved her oppressive prewar policies in order to retrieve her lost territories.[33]

Whereas Friedrich apparently had no intentions, or the means, of expediting the Nationality Law, Bleyer and his followers took the statutes very seriously indeed. Their rationale rested on firm ground. Greater Hungary could be restored, but only if the Hungarians propitiated the minorities. Once more, Bleyer and the government faced opposite poles on a fundamental issue. Should Hungary's minorities receive far-reaching cultural and moderate administrative concessions, or should the Law be ignored and the ethnic groups be Magyarized? As on previous occasions, the government maintained that the frontiers of the Hungarian State were sacred, and the domination of the Hungarians exclusive and paramount. The government's intransigence imperiled Bleyer's wish to retain Burgenland. This ambition was no longer visionary. With the conservative Friedrich government ensconced in Budapest, radical Austria's attraction began to fade for both the Entente and many Germans. By now, Burgenland's population was about equally split on the question of secession. The Germans still feared radical Austria, but they also distrusted evasive Hungary. Strangely enough, Hungary did nothing in a practical sense to attract German public opinion.

Hungary's obduracy on the minority issue undercut Bleyer's honeymoon with the Hungarians. At the Ministerial Council on 20 September he complained that his Law was being systematically undermined by Hungarian officials, especially in West Hungary where German functionaries stood accused of pan-German sympathies.

Some of them even wound up behind bars. The government, he argued, ought to have a more equitable ethnic distribution of civil servants in Hungary. The Ministerial Council agreed and promised to act.[34] Little was accomplished, in fact, due partly to a legal technicality. In Hungary, a law remained invalid without an enabling act. As Minister of Nationalities, Bleyer could issue such acts only to a limited degree; for the rest, he had to depend on his various colleagues.[35] But they refused to release these orders. Bleyer observed that, unless the Hungarians improved the condition of their nationalities, those living in the still disputed regions, such as Burgenland, would never believe in Hungary's regard for their ethnic aspirations. These peoples could be persuaded to vote for Hungary in any plebiscite, but only if the government henceforth pursued a benevolent nationality policy, in theory as well as in practice.[36]

Bleyer's pleas fell on deaf ears, partly because Friedrich's was only a caretaker government without broad support. Thus, as Admiral Horthy, soon to become regent of Hungary, rode into Budapest at the head of his troops, the minority problem still rankled, and the Burgenland crisis was as acute as ever. Hungary refused to vacate the area, Austria lacked the strength to seize it, and the Entente temporized, fearing a crisis in an already volatile region.

After Horthy's power seizure, the Burgenland impasse gained instant attention. Hungary's external difficulties defied resolution either through diplomacy or by force. It appeared far more profitable to influence events by applying selective domestic remedies. The Burgenland controversy could be amenable to such an indirect solution. Accordingly, Prime Minister Károly Huszár decided to eliminate what seemed to be a mere technical obstacle to a Hungarian-German entente, by appeasing the Germans. Huszár agreed to activate the Nationality Law through enabling decrees. The first act aimed at the violations in the minority school system, but attempted to please everyone, while hidden caveats and complexities plagued the law's proper application and execution. As in the past, Hungarian or Magyarized officials sabotaged the regulations. The other Ministries took nearly one year to issue their enabling laws, and none brought the Germans closer to their ethnic goals. By the end of 1920, growing Hungarian opposition to concessions left the Hungarian authorities little choice but to interpret the minority legislation in the more conservative spirit of the 1868

Nationality Act.[37] Grievances by non-Hungarian citizens were adjudicated on individual merit, but complaints tendered by minority groups were frowned upon.

Complaints poured into Bleyer's Ministry and to the editorial offices of the *Neue Post*. Most involved abuse of German minority education rights by clerics, teachers, notaries, and intimidation of parents' conferences in rural constituencies. Bleyer frequently petitioned the Minister of Education for corrective measures, but rarely instigated redress of violations.[38] Conservative Hungarian governments apparently had no more intentions of relinquishing Hungarian hegemony than the radicals had. The Germans' oft-repeated slogan that Hungarian patriotism had less to do with proficiency in the Hungarian language than with observing the supranational spirit of St. Stephen, Hungary's medieval Westernizer, found no acceptance in government circles or among the Hungarian public.

Mutual misunderstandings plagued attempts by Bleyer and the government to gain the support of Burgenland's Germans. Notwithstanding the fiasco of the Nationality Law, the government sought to woo Germans with other impressive-sounding programs. The Hungarians even outbid Bleyer, his followers, and his German opponents, by proposing some sort of self-government in Burgenland. Aspirations for German autonomy in the conservative era dated back to 26 August 1919, when a Bleyer antagonist, Dr. Guido Gündisch, demanded political autonomy for Burgenland. Bleyer and the *Neue Post* termed proponents of self-government unpatriotic. Unfortunately, scant communication, if any, existed between Bleyer and the rest of the cabinet, including the Prime Minister, who released an autonomy plan of his own. On 14 February 1920, Huszár proposed a plebiscite for Burgenland. If the Germans remained with Hungary, they would receive self-government. Huszár's offer was ill-timed and counterproductive. Few Burgenlanders believed him, the Austrians scoffed, and Bleyer, who had only recently condemned autonomy in any guise, lost face.

By bungling his autonomy card, Huszár encouraged a spate of German proposals on the status of Burgenland. On 1 August 1920, Huber delivered a speech in Parliament, which reiterated Huszár's earlier demand for a plebiscite, but, like Bleyer, he rejected autonomy. In Huber's view, there had to be a compromise between the two extremes of denying the vote to anyone not fluent in Hungarian, and a Károlyi-type of autonomy plan, which was tantamount to nationalistic agitation.[39] In less than four months' time, Huber changed his mind. On 9 November 1920, supported by his Swabian Christian Social caucus in Parliament, he unveiled an autonomy plan for Burgenland through the *Pester Zeitung*. Austria and Hungary would negotiate a territorial settlement on the basis of an autonomous Burgenland, which would remain an integral part of Hungary. Austria's economic interests would be safeguarded, and in deference to the sensitive strategic position of Vienna, only local militia would be stationed in the demilitarized province. This ill-considered proposal once again revealed the gap between Germans and their government. Apart from the fact that the daily press was not the place for launching a new plan on a sensitive issue during a period of crisis, Huber and his colleagues were private citizens, and hence could not speak for the government. The embarrassed Bleyer, still at the time Minister of Nationalities, failed to sign the manifesto, although he claimed to approve the plan because his trusted friend and collaborator, the diplomat Gustav Gratz, found it acceptable.[40]

Still loyal to Hungary, Bleyer had to resign his portfolio as Minister of Nationalities on 16 December 1920, but he issued a position paper before that on the nationality question. In his view, the recent upheavals had created a new national awareness among Hungary's minorities. Consequently, the government could no longer pacify them with mere bagatelles. The Hungarians would have to decide soon if they really wanted to regain their lost peoples and territories and maintain their grip on those still wavering.[41]

At year's end, in a crisis atmosphere, the new Pál Teleki government resumed Huszár's pacification efforts in Burgenland. The Peace Conference was deliberating on what action to initiate in view of Hungary's refusal to vacate the disputed region, and Hungary's chances of retaining the area were steadily diminishing. On 16 November 1920, Teleki declared in Parliament that Hungary's minorities would be offered cultural and administrative opportunities. The government would establish three levels of ethnic autonomy: communal self-government with unrestricted use of non-Hungarian tongues; this plan would apply anywhere in Hungary where non-Hungarian majorities resided; district (járás) self-government in jurisdictions with sufficient numbers of uni-lingual non-Hungarian communities; and county self-government was to apply wherever non-Hungarians composed a clear majority of the population. The last was to sway Burgenlanders in Hungary's favor. Indeed, this was welcome news to the harassed Germans.[42]

During the first week of 1921, Hungary was ordered to cede Burgenland to Austria forthwith. The Allied Note triggered the last of many major schemes to secure Burgenland for Hungary under the guise of autonomy. The author of this audacious April plan was none other than Bleyer, who had the tacit support of Prime Minister István Bethlen. It followed on the heel of a series of setbacks for both the Hungarians and the pro-Hungarian Germans. A Habsburg restoration attempt by ex-King Charles IV had been only recently averted, leaving Austria more suspicious and resentful than ever about Hungary's aims and purposes. Bleyer's March visit to Germany at Hungary's behest had misfired. Bleyer had sought German support in Burgenland. A delegation composed of Hungary's German parliamentary contingent returned home from Vienna empty-handed after discussing the fate of Burgenland with Mayr. The Chancellor rejected any solution that would have left the region under Hungarian control. Bleyer wanted to indoctrinate and organize Burgenland's Germans for the impending November parliamentary elections. Hopefully, the people would vote for Bleyer's hand-picked pro-Hungarian candidates. Hungarian troops would depart, and be replaced by "reliable" Burgenland detachments. These "civic guards" would prevent Austrian forces from occupying Burgenland, which would then be incorporated into Hungary as a German autonomous region. Although official Hungarian communiqués rejected West Hungarian autonomy, important Hungarians in and out of government supported the scheme.[43]

West Hungarian Germans' support for Hungary was not consistent. Their traditional loyalties gradually eroded in favor of association with fellow Germans in neighboring Austria. The victorious powers arbitrarily transferred most Burgenlanders to Austria, yet most Germans desired to join Austria only during the Károlyi and Kun interludes. Throughout Friedrich's tenure, and especially after Horthy's conservative forces swept into office at the end of 1919, German public opinion shifted sharply toward Hungary. Czechoslovakia's Corridor Plan, which would have created a common Czechoslovak-Yugoslav frontier in the heart of Burgenland, infuriated the Germans. They refused to become either Czech or Yugoslav subjects. The Germans were exasperated with the Hungarians and many distrusted Austrian motives, but they all feared the Czechs, and despised the Yugoslavs. The Hungarian German press publicized Austria's betrayal of Hungary, a wartime comrade-in-arms, hoping to dent the Germans' Austrian preferences.[44]

Sopron's Mayor, Michael Thürner, a vocal German Hungarophile, unceasingly urged his German fellow citizens to spurn Austria and remain true to Hungary. Thürner ventured that, under Austrian rule, West Hungary would atrophy and die. Germans wanted to maintain their ethnic identity, but only in Hungary, and they wished no part of Austria.[45] Thürner apparently struck a responsive chord in the Germans, at least in the more sophisticated "Magyarones" residing in Sopron and other West Hungarian urban centers. This, and fears that the Czech Corridor Plan might be revived despite Allied rejection in March of 1919, united West Hungary's Hungarian and German-speaking inhabitants in righteous indignation against the "godless" Austrian "half-Communist" regime, and its leader, the "anti-Christ" Renner.[46]

Count Kuno Klebelsberg, a Magyarized German of partial Austrian parentage, parliamentary representative of Sopron, and future minister of education and religion under Bethlen, confidently spoke for his constituency, a good half of whom were Germans. The eleven-member German parliamentary contingent issued its own statement defying Austria on 11 February 1920, in a spirit echoing Thürner's earlier sentiments.[47] Several months later, Klebelsberg warned Austria that the Hungarians and Germans would gladly fight Austria for West Hungary.[48]

By early 1921, the hysteria concerning the Corridor Plan had subsided, and the Germans had experienced life in conservative-dominated Hungary over a protracted period. They became far more receptive to Austria. In his dispatches to the Wilhelmstrasse, Count Egon von Fürstenberg, Germany's Minister in Budapest, perhaps exaggerated when he claimed that Hungary's recent ethnic persecutions had engendered a great change of heart among West Hungary's Germans. In his view, Burgenland's parliamentary contingent, though formerly loyal to Hungary, now favored Austria. Even Bleyer had allegedly lost heart and wished to retire. Other sources concurred. The Austrian legation in Budapest, for example, reported that Burgenlanders now hoped for an *Anschluss* with Austria in order to become German citizens. They apparently believed in an imminent German-Austrian fusion.[49]

On the eve of the plebiscite, Hungary's treatment of Burgenland's Germans had indeed deteriorated. German-speaking Hungarians were disturbed by press reports revealing gross neglect in their minority schools. For decades, the Germans of Hungary had enjoyed the highest literacy level in the nation. This hegemony was now clearly in danger. German leaders called on Prime Minister Bethlen, assured him of their loyalty to Hungary, but regretted the frustration and diminished prospects of Hungary's German minority. They demanded the immediate implementation of the existing minority laws, especially in education, administration, and justice, and solicited Bethlen's protection against the arbitrary obstruction of the statutes by local officials. Bethlen blandly reassured the delegation.[50] About the same time, nine German members of Parliament for Western Hungary tendered a memorandum to the Interallied Military Mission in Sopron, protesting West Hungary's unjust cession to Austria.[51]

But the non-Magyarized German intelligentsia remained just as true to the Crown of St. Stephen as their Magyarized brethren, even while deploring the anti-German prejudice and shortsightedness of the Hungarian establishment and public. They hoped that nationalistic passions would eventually subside, and Hungarian-German amity would resume. These unassimilated German leaders welded aggressive ethnic nationalism with Hungarian patriotism. They urged Burgenlanders to remain loyal to Hungary. But they also feared that losing some 300,000 West Hungarian Germans to Austria would weaken the German cause in Hungary. The remaining Germans would be isolated from the German-speaking world, and be submerged in the Hungarian multitude.[52] Hence, partly for patriotic reasons as Hungarians, and partly for the sake of long-range German preservation, a small but decisive majority of Germans in the Sopron area heeded the pleas of their leaders, and in the eleventh hour threw their support behind Hungary.[53]

The Sopron plebiscite demonstrated that, under certain conditions, nationalism may be restrained by countervailing forces. A formidable trinity—the assimilated and the non-assimilated German intelligentsia, and Hungary's conservative government, supported loyally by both German elements, wielded greater influence over the majority of the population than either pro-German sentiments engendered by the war, or Austrian propaganda. These leaders were grounded in the royal-imperial Habsburg tradition, and never flagged in their devotion to that authority. Austria had turned republican, with no hopes of a Habsburg restoration. But Horthy retained the monarchy, and Hungary thereupon became the hope of all royalists.[54] The German intelligentsia in Hungary counseled fidelity to the Crown of St. Stephen as a matter of patriotic regard for the House of Habsburg. Had either Károlyi or Kun remained in power, the German leaders' devotion to the Hungarian State might not have survived their German loyalties. This contest pitted German ethnic nationalism against Habsburg dynastic patriotism. Economic considerations, blown out of proportion by both parties to the dispute, merely obscured the nature of the real struggle.

Notes

1. Actually nine: Ágfalva (Agendorf), Balf (Wolfs), Hárka (Harkau), Fertő-Boz (Holling), Fertő-Rákos (Kroisbach), Kópháza (Kohlenhof), Nagyczenk (Gr. Zinkendorf), Sopron-Bánfalva (Wandorf), and Brennberg, but the last belonged administratively to Sopron, and its vote was included in Sopron's results.

2. Magyar Királyi Központi Statisztikai Hivatal, Magyar statisztikai közlemények. Az 1920. évi népszámlálás (Budapest, 1924), pp. 296–97.

3. 17,318 Germans vs. 15,022 Magyars in 1910; 16,911 Germans vs. 17,166 Magyars in 1920 in Sopron; 9,983 Germans vs. 2,369 Magyars in the rural communities in 1920. Census of 1910, ibid. (Budapest, 1912), pp. 44–45; Andrew F. Burghardt, Borderland. A Historical and Geographical Study of Burgenland, Austria (Madison, Wisc., 1962), p. 155.

4. Sarah Wambaugh, Plebiscites Since the World War I (Washington, D.C., 1933), pp. 291–93; Katalin Soós, Burgenland az európai politikában 1918–1921 (Budapest, 1971), pp. 161–64.

5. Royal Ministry of Foreign Affairs, Hungarian Peace Negotiations I (Budapest, 1921), p. 516ff. Also see Burghardt, Borderland, pp. 176–178. Ludmilla Schlereth, Die politische Entwicklung des Ungarländischen Deutschtums während der Revolution 1918–1919 (Munich, 1939), p. 63, maintains that the Germans remained faithful to Hungary even during the Kun era.

6. For a more thorough coverage, see Thomas Spira, German-Hungarian Relations and the Swabian Problem from Károlyi to Gömbös 1919–1936 (New York, 1977), especially chapters 2 and 4.

7. The Austrian viewpoint was corroborated by Professor A.C. Coolidge's factfinding reports. See Jon D. Berlin, ed., Akten und Dokumente des Aussenamtes (State Department) der USA zur Burgenland-Anschlussfrage 1919–1920 (Eisenstadt, 1977), Doc. 10, January 29, 1919,

p. 42, among others. For a detailed economic account in Austria's favor, see Major Lawrence Martin to A.C. Coolidge, *ibid.*, Doc. 12, February 28, 1919, p. 44ff. Also see Elizabeth de Weiss, "Dispute for the Burgenland in 1919," *Journal of Central European Affairs*, III (1943), p. 157; Wambaugh, *Plebiscites*, I, pp. 274–75: Jon D. Berlin, "The United States and the Burgenland, 1918–1920," *Austrian History Yearbook*, 8 (1972), pp. 39–58.

8. Karl Gottfried Hugelmann, "Deutsch-Österreich und seine Grenzzgebiete," in Karl von Loesch and Max Hildebert Boehm, eds., *Grenzdeutschland seit Versailles* (Berlin, 1930), p. 341. Even a Hungarian observer noted subsequently that Burgenland's population enjoyed far more meaningful economic ties with Austria than with Hungary. See Béla Bellér, *Az ellenforradalom nemzetiségi politikájának kialakulása* (Budapest, 1975), p. 97.

9. *Hungarian Peace Negotiations* I, p. 516ff.; *Pester Zeitung*, January 19, 1921; de Weiss, "Dispute," p. 147; Lajos Reményi, *Külkereskedelempolitika Magyarországon 1919–1924* (Budapest, 1969), p. 76, note 129; pp. 80–1; F.L. Carsten, *Revolution in Central Europe 1918–1919* (Berkeley and Los Angeles, 1972), p. 285; H.W.V. Temperley, ed., *A History of the Peace Conference of Paris*, IV (London, 1921), pp. 383–84. These arguments were proffered by Hungarian Foreign Minister Count Csáky during his first meeting with the Austrians on February 23, 1921. Dezső Ujváry, ed., *Papers and Documents Relating to the Foreign Relations of Hungary*, II (Budapest, 1946), doc. 143, pp. 136–37; Gustav Gratz's statement before the sixth meeting on May 25, 1921, *ibid.* doc. 449, pp. 481–96; the statement of Rudolf Patzenhofer, a sugar refinery owner of Zinkendorf, and Siegfried Spiegel, president of the Sopron Chamber of Commerce, before the third meeting on February 24, 1921, doc. 151, pp. 158–62; Hungarian Minister in Vienna Szilárd Masirevics to Chancellor Schober, note, August 4, 1921, with Memo, "Ödenburg und Umgebung," doc. 678, pp. 686–92.

10. Jakob Bleyer, "A hazai németség kérdéséhez," *Budapesti Szemle* (July 1917), p. 4.

11. Jakob Bleyer, "An die Deutschungarn," *Neue Post* (NP), October 25, 1918.

12. *NP*, November 3, 1918. See Hedwig Schwind, *Jakob Bleyer. Ein Vorkämpfer und Erwecker des ungarländischen Deutschtums* (Munich, 1960), pp. 57–72, on Bleyer's activities in the *Volksrat*.

13. *NP*, November 10, 1918.

14. "Deutschungarn, rasche Organisation!" *ibid.*, November 12, 1918.

15. *Ibid.*, November 16, 19, and 20, 1918.

16. *ibid.*, November 21 and 24, and December 22, 1918.

17. László Koncsek, "A bécsi és Sopron megyei ellenforradalom kapcsolatai 1919-ben," *Soproni Szemle*, 10 (1956), p. 107. Also see C.A. Macartney, *Hungary and her Successors* (London, 1937), p. 50.

18. Johannes Huber, "Was trennt uns von Herrn Brandsch?" *NP*, November 9, 1918. Also see issue of January 11, 1919.

19. The provisions of the law are listed in *Országos Levéltár, Miniszter Tanács*, January 27, 1919, point 67. The *Pester Lloyd*, January 4, 1919 and the *NP*, January 30, 1919, published the full German text. Also see *Budapesti Hirlap*, January 25, 1919, and "Was sagt Professor Bl[eyer]?" *Deutsches Tageblatt*, February 13, 1919.

20. *NP*, January 30, February 1, and March 12, 1919; "Christen, zur Rettung der Kinderseelen," *ibid.*, March 7, 1919.

21. *Pester Lloyd*, April 29, 1919.

22. "Heftige Kämpfe in Westungarn. Eine Denkschrift der Heinzen an den steirischen Landtag," *Reichspost*, June 12, 1919. Austria's Socialist government feared that the Hungarian Marxist regime might instigate a bolshevik revolt in Austria. See Viktor Reimann, *Zu gross für Österreich. Seipel und Bauer im Kampf um die Erste Republik* (Vienna, Frankfurt, and Zurich, 1968), pp.315-24; G. Katalin Soós, "Adalékok a Magyar Tanácsköztársaság és az Osztrák Köztársaság kapcsolatainak történetéhez," *Soproni Szemle*, 13 (1959), pp. 289-304. Also see Otto Bauer's explanation of why Austria deserted Kun. *Die Österreichische Revolution* (Vienna, 1923), pp. 156-57.

23. Law XXVI, paragraph 2, provisional constitution, April 2, 1919, cited in S. Gábor, ed., *A magyar munkásmozgalom válogatott dokumentumai (MMTVD)*, VI (6 vols., Budapest, 1956-69), pp. 100-101; and "A nyugat-magyarországi németek a szovjetállamban," *Soproni Vörös Ujság*, April 30, 1919.

24. *Budapesti Közlöny*, March 24, 1919; Law XLI, April 7, 1919, is listed in B. Halász, I. Kovács, and V. Peschka, eds., *A Magyar Tanácsköztársaság jogalkotása* (Budapest, 1959), p. 86.

25. School nationalization Law XXIV, April 1, 1919, cited in *MMTVD*, VI, p. 73; School order no. 87039, May 5, 1919, "Instruction to Insure the Undisturbed Continuance of Education," cited in K. Petrák and Gy. Milei, eds., *A M.T.K. szociálpolitikája. Válogatott rendeletek, documentumok és cikkek* (Budapest, 1959), pp. 2, 31-35. Also see "Az uj iskola," *Vörös Ujság*, April 3, 1919. Order XCI of the Revolutionary Governing Council, May 14, 1919, is listed in *MMTVD*, VI, p. 482: Order no. 28 of the Commissar of Education, May 12, 1919, is listed in Jenő Pongrácz, ed., *A Forradalmi Kormányzótanács és a népbiztosok rendeletei*, III (5 vols., Budapest, 1919), pp. 21-23, 104-105.

26. Law XXIV, April 1, 1919 is cited in Petrák and Milei, *M.T.K.*, p. 1, and *MMTVD*, VI, p. 73. Vilma Bresztovszky, "A történelem az új iskolában," *Fáklya*, April 29, 1919; Gyula Krúdy, "Új történelmet kell írni," *Magyarország*, April 6, 1919; Zsigmond Kunfi, "A vallás szabad gyakorlása," *Népszava*, April 18, 1919; "A tanítók átképzése," *ibid.*, July 1, 1919. Also see Kun's speech before the National Party Congress, June 12-13,

1919. Béla Kun, *Válogatott írások és beszédek*, H. Vass, I. Friss, and E. Szabó, eds., I (2 vols., Budapest, 1966), p. 107.

27. Halász, *et al.*, *A Magyar Tanácsköztársaság*, p. 71; F. Eckelt, "The Internal Policies of the Hungarian Soviet Republic," Iván Völgyes, ed., *Hungary in Revolution 1918–1919* (Lincoln, Nebr., 1971), p. 101; Katalin Gulya, "Die Westungarische Frage nach dem Ersten Weltkrieg," *Österreichische Osthefte*, 8 (1966), pp. 91–93.

28. "Die Autonomie der Deutschen," *Volksstimme*, August 5, 1919; *Budapesti Közlöny*, August 15, 1919, August 1 and 16, 1919. Law I, paragraph 6, cited in *Budapesti Közlöny*, February 29, 1920, pp. 1–2. On the Peidl and Friedrich regimes, see Béla Bellér, "Az ellenforradalmi rendszer első éveinek nemzetiségi politikája (1919–1922)," *Századok*, 6 (1963), p. 1279ff.

29. "A nemzeti kisebbségek minisztériumának nyilatkozata," *Budapesti Közlöny*, August 17, 1919, p. 6.

30. See Spira, *German-Hungarian Relations*, p. 38; Árpád Török, "Jakob Bleyer als Nationalitätenminister," *Jakob Bleyer als Nationalitätenminister. Denkschrift für Jakob Bleyer* (Berlin and Leipzig, 1934), pp. 40–43, describes Bleyer's attempts at home and abroad to assure Burgenland's incorporation into Hungary.

31. *Országos Levéltár. Miniszterelnökség (OL ME)* 1919, XXII 5768.

32. See text in *Budapesti Közlöny*, November 19, 1919; *NP*, November 23, 1919; *Volksstimme*, November 20, 1919.

33. Spira, *German-Hungarian Relations*, pp. 39–42.

34. *OL ME* 1919, XXII 5440.

35. Paragraph 16 of the Nationality Law made this quite plain. *Budapesti Közlöny*, November 19, 1919.

36. *OL ME* 1920, (XLII) a 8634, meeting of October 2, 1919.

37. Law 209494—1919.B.II. "A nemzeti kisebbségek népoktatásügye," *Budapesti Közlöny*, December 28, 1919; *NP*, January 11, 1920.

38. Hans Eninger, "Die Rechte der nationalen Minderheiten," *NP*, May 4, 1920; *NP*, May 4, 1920; *NP*, January 23, 1920; *Budapesti Közlöny*, January 11, 14, and 23, and November 28, 1920.

39. "Das Treiben der Gruppe Gündisch und Comp.," *NP*, November 25, 1919; "Ein Protest der westungarischen Abgeordneten," *ibid.*, February 5, 1920; "Eine ehrliche Nationalitätenpolitik auf christliche Grundlage," *ibid.*, July 14, 1920; "Die Treue der nationalen Minderheiten zum ungarischen Vaterland," *ibid.*, July 31, 1920; "Die Lösung der Nationalitätenfrage. Protest gegen die Losreitzung Westungarns," *ibid.*, August 1, 1920.

40. *Auswärtiges Amt. Politische Abteilung (AA PA)*, IIb, Pol. 6, Österreich-Ungarn, Bd.I, Fürstenberg to Foreign Ministry, dispatch of 17 January 1921: "Vorschlag zur Lösung der westungarischen Frage," *Pester Zeitung*, November 9, 1920.

41. "Die Verdienste des Ministeriums der nationalen Minderheiten," *NP*, October 23, 1920.

42. "Regierungserklärungen über die Nationalitätenpolitik," and "Altungarische Nationalitätenpolitik," *Pester Zeitung*, November 16, 1920; "Politische Nachrichten," *ibid.*, November 28, 1920.

43. See Spira, *German-Hungarian Relations*, pp. 82–83; Wulf Schmidt-Wulffen, "Das Burgenland und die deutsche Politik 1918–1921," *Österreichische Osthefte*, 5 (1969), pp. 270–287, especially pp. 274–275, discusses German and Hungarian intrigues concerning Burgenland. At the end of August 1921, Hungary did withdraw regular troops from Burgenland, and irregulars under Pál Prónay and Iván Héjjas occupied the region, and on October 4, declared the area to be an independent province called Lajtabánság (Lajta-Banat); however, Bleyer and his associates apparently had no role in this abortive undertaking. See Gyula Juhász, *Magyarország külpolitikája 1919–1945* (Budapest, 1969), pp. 82–83; and a participant's view is found in Paul Szemere and Erich Czech, *Die Memoiren des Grafen Tamás von Erdödy. Habsburgs Weg von Wilhelm zu Briand. Vom Kurier der Sixtus-Briefe zum Königsputschisten* (Zurich, Leipzig, and Vienna, 1931), especially pp. 184–95 and 264–74.

44. See "Das letzte Wort werden wir sagen," *NP*, February 24, 1920; Jacques Hannak, *Karl Renner und seine Zeit* (Vienna, 1965), pp. 387–91.

45. Berlin, *Akten und Dokumente*, pp. 58–65.

46. "Wir bleiben Deutsche, aber in Ungarn," *NP*, January 15, 1920; "Westungarn will bei Ungarn bleiben," *ibid.*, January 20, 1920. Gratz to Somssich, report, January 14, 1920, Ujváry, *Papers and Documents*, I, doc. 75.

47. Also see the statements by Bolgár and Cserny, parliamentary representatives from Sopron and Moson Counties respectively, to Major Lawrence Martin. They claimed that "their German constituents had never expressed the slightest desire to leave Hungary and be united with Austria." Berlin, *Akten und Dokumente*, pp. 55–58.

48. *Országgyülési Napló*, XII (1921), 254th session, August 23, 1921, pp. 616–17.

49. AA PA/IIb. Pol. 6, Österreich-Ungarn, Bd I, January 8, 1921; Viktor Miltschinsky, *Das Verbrechen von Ödenburg* (Vienna, 1922), *passim*, recounts Burgenlanders' resistance to incorporation into Hungary at that time.

50. Nikolaus Degenhardt, "Braucht das Volk Kultur oder nicht?" *Sonntagsblatt*, November 6, 1921; "Selbsthilfe," *ibid.*, October 30, 1921; "Wir halten mit deutscher Treue an dem ungarischen Vaterlande und mit derselben Liebe an unseren Muttersprache," *ibid.*, December 4, 1921.

51. Ujváry, *Papers and Documents*, II, docs. 692, 692A.

52. Johannes Huber, "Ein Mahnruf an die Deutschen Westungarn," *NP*, November 20, 1918.

53. Alternately, the Sopron victory can be attributed partly to Allied vacillations, Magyar terrorism, and Austrian Christian Social diffidence. See Karl R. Stadler, "Fifty Troubled Years: The Story of the Burgenland," *Austrian History Yearbook*, 8 (1972), pp. 59–79, citing p. 75. For additional arguments, see Burghardt, *Borderland*, pp. 185–87.

54. Hannak, *Renner*, p. 391.

Part IV

The Settlement and Its Repercussions

(See maps at the end of the book)

Ivan Sanders

Post-Trianon Searching: The Early Career of László Németh

Hungarian literature was more consciously Western oriented in the early twentieth century than during any other period in its history. The most important periodical of the age was called, significantly, *Nyugat* (West, established in 1908). The Western orientation in literature, which began in the final decades of the nineteenth century and gained momentum in the early years of the twentieth, was symptomatic of the modernizing, liberalizing forces that were making inroads in an essentially traditionalist, backward society. While Hungarian poets and novelists associated with *Nyugat* eagerly responded to modern literary movements such as impressionism and symbolism, enlightened social scientists and political reformers propagated the ideals of new social systems. Budapest became an important culture center during the first two decades of the twentieth century, though much of the impetus for change came from abroad.

When László Németh burst on the literary scene with a prize-winning short story in 1925, most of the early modernists, the founders of *Nyugat*, were still active, but the optimism, the innovative spirit of the pre-war years, was gone. The collapse of the Austro-Hungarian Monarchy, the trauma of successive revolutions and defeats, the loss of about two-thirds of Hungary's territory as a result of the Treaty of Trianon, the installation of an ultra-conservative regime in 1920, left the country reeling and many of its intellectuals despondent and rudderless. The spiritual malaise lasted well into the twenties, and those young writers who were groping for new values, uniquely Hungarian solutions for the nation's problems, raised questions about the Western tradition and about the efficacy of "borrowed" ideologies. László Németh was born in 1901 in the town of Nagybánya, and although he grew up in an urban setting, in Budapest, his father, who was a teacher in a *Gymnasium*, came from a well-to-do family, and the young Németh spent his summers in

Szilasbalhás, a village in Western Hungary. His early interest in foreign culture landscapes notwithstanding, Németh was committed from the beginning of his career to an exploration, a redefinition—in criticism as well as in fiction—of the Hungarian ethos. He extended his horizons only to be able to focus more clearly on a specifically Hungarian reality. His formative experiences in the village, his introduction to a close-knit peasant community had a profound effect on his literary art—his best novels have a rural setting and delve into peasant psyches.

Reflecting the post-war disenchantment with Western ideals, Németh felt that the peasantry was the true repository of traditional national values; in later years he became one of the spiritual mentors of the Hungarian populist movement which rejected many features of Western-oriented urban culture and advocated thoroughgoing reforms whose aim was to upgrade the lives of the notoriously neglected rural masses. As early as 1928 Németh wrote that the peasantry possessed "pre-poetic energies," and was the creative force behind Hungarian culture. There was not one great Hungarian writer, he believed, who was not a disciple of the people. Németh's main criticism of Nyugat was that it produced great personalities but not a coherent cultural tradition. In some ways he had more respect for a previous generation of Hungarian writers who, he felt, may have been less sophisticated, less dazzling as artists, but had stronger convictions.[1] Mihály Babits, the other gret literary figure of the early twentieth century and editor of Nyugat from the late twenties on, attacked Németh bitterly for such views, condemning his "retroactive distortions" as well as his high-handed generalizations about contemporaries.[2]

László Németh drew the ire of most of his fellow writers almost from the beginning of his career. In his very first literary essays he developed the thesis that Hungarian culture reflects the tragic destiny of the Hungarian people. Németh felt that some of the greatest figures of Hungarian literature were prevented by the exigencies of time and place from realizing their true potentials, and their creative efforts were regularly met with incomprehension and indifference. The typical Hungarian literary artist, Németh believed, had always been a lonely, frustrated, tragic individual, crushed by a hostile environment. It was obvious to Németh's foes that the young critic included himself among the ranks of the misunderstood great; at first they chalked up his self-righteous attacks on the state of Hungarian society and culture to youthful arrogance, but as time went on, they had a harder time dealing with his overdeveloped ego and his own extreme sensitivity to criticism. Yet, not even Németh's most vociferous detractors disputed the fact that here was a highly gifted writer, a man of bold conceptions, a tirelessly inquisitive spirit whose writings revealed not only an encyclopedic breadth but a rare ability to combine artistic subjectivity with scientific accuracy. Science was never alien to Németh; he began his career as a scientist, a physician. His life-long attempt to apply, on the one hand, the rigors of the scientific method to humanistic speculation and, on the other, to convey scientific concepts and theories in the suggestive metaphors of the poet can be seen already in his first two papers, one of them a study of Endre Ady's poetry ("Az Ady-vers genézise" [The Genesis of the Ady Poem]) and the other, a scientific study entitled "Új szempontok a status praesens felvételében" (New Perspectives on the Recording of Clinical Data). Németh himself writes in a review of his career: "My aim was to convey, in biological terms and with the help of the then fashionable science of characterology, a budding writer's view of man . . . The other essay, 'The Genesis of the Ady Poem,' traveled the same route but in the opposite direction; it tried to chart the course of a biological entity—Ady's creative character—by following the course of his poetic revolutions."[3] Both of these studies reveal Németh's intense interest in character makeup. It has been pointed out often that Németh's concept of character defines much of his writings. For him character is a unified and largely immutable set of physical, emotional and psychic attributes. One of his favorite words, in fact, is *alkat* which denotes physical structure, body build, as well as character makeup, temperament. To a large extent it is this Gestalt approach to character that accounts for Németh's interest in Greek mythology, in archetypes, in quasi-Nietzschean notions of towering individual excellence, as well as in modern psychological, characterological theories.

Ironically enough, Németh's own *alkat* did not predispose him to his would-be role as social reformer and stern arbiter of literary taste. This is how Gyula Illyés, Németh's great contemporary, describes the twenty-four-year-old winner of *Nyugat's* short story contest: "When the winner appeared before the chairman of the jury, he—as he later told me—thought that the author, whom he hadn't seen before, sent his son to accept the prize money. A slender, fair-haired, girlish-faced young man with the looks of a graduating high school senior stood before him, possessing the modesty of those appealingly well-mannered youths who still blush when they must say or hear anything slightly unusual."[4] Yet, this shy, unassuming young man told Ernő Osvát, the powerful editor of *Nyugat*, that his aim was to become "the organizer of Hungarian intellectual life."[5] The young Németh believed that the age of nationalism, which in many ways created and nurtured the literatures of Eastern Europe, was over by the end of the First World War, and these literatures would lose their direction and purpose if the reawakened national spirit expressed in them did not reflect the changed historical circumstances. It was this renewed national culture that Németh wanted to help bring about. But as Illyés points out in his reminiscence, Osvát wanted to recruit writers, not revolutionaries. To be associated with *Nyugat* naturally appealed to Németh, and contrary to a widespread impression, the rift with the periodical did not come right away. But it did become apparent soon enough that Németh's audacious self-appraisal, his controversial theories about Hungarian culture, his highly personal views of Hungarian writers, and in general his moral strictures and reformist zeal ran counter to *Nyugat*'s esthetics-oriented editorial policy. After the publication of his prize-winning short story about the death of a peasant woman ("Horváthné meghal" [Mrs. Horváth Dies]), Németh tried his hand at a few more peasant stories and a novel, but then he turned to criticism, and during the next few years published a number of important literary essays in the little-known *Protestáns Szemle*, in the neo-conservative *Kelet Népe*, and more significantly, in *Erdélyi Helikon*. (Németh was among the first Budapest-based writers to pay close attention to post-war Transylvanian literary developments, and he continued to survey that scene throughout the thirties.) In most of his early essays, including the one written on the works of the novelist Dezső Szabó, Németh revealed that his literary views and emerging social theories, which were later judged by liberal Hungarian critics to be narrowly ethnocentric and retrograde, could not really be identified with the aggressive chauvinism and mystical racism that gained currency even among serious intellectuals during the interwar years. The ultra-nationalist Dezső Szabó, who swung from extreme left to extreme right without giving up his radical fervor, exerted a considerable influence on the post-World War I generation, including Németh himself. But for Németh race was above all an ethical concept; it did not denote "collective blood ties," but "a spiritual fellowship, a model for human conduct, the gospel of a non-ecclesiastic religion . . . salvation in and through literature."[6] In his essay on Dezső Szabó, Németh ennobles and poeticizes his first idol's nationalism. If anything, the young essayist was challenged, spurred into action, by the post-Trianon gloom. As we shall see, Németh was aware all his life of the extraordinary moral advantages of being an underdog; these early essays already hint at his conviction that adversity brings out the best in an individual, in a nation, and even a siege mentality can do wonders for the national psyche.

In the late twenties and early thirties Németh's brand of creative criticism needed its own forum; it could not conform to the literary-political orientation of any of the existing journals. For a while Németh was on friendly terms with Babits, the new editor of *Nyugat*, who encouraged the young critic to introduce on the pages of the journal the works of talented new writers. But when Németh accused Babits, who administered the prestigious Baumgarten Prize, of using it as a pawn in a literary power struggle, their friendship came to an abrupt end. (In 1930 Németh himself was awarded the Baumgarten Prize, but when Babits's choice was attacked in the press, an offended Németh returned the prize and the substantial money that came with it.) In 1932 Németh decided to go it alone and started his own periodical, *Tanú* (Witness), which he wrote entirely by himself.

During its four years of existence, *Tanú* offered not only a reassessment of modern Hungarian literature and the historical-political circumstances which gave rise to it; its author-publisher took it upon himself to acquaint his readers with the best in recent Western literature. The periodical was to be one man's view of the intellectual currents of his age. Lengthy essays appeared in *Tanú* on Proust, Joyce, Pirandello, Gide, Ortega y Gasset, Freud and others. These erudite and at the same time passionately subjective appraisals won Németh the admiration of even his severest critics. Whatever his subject happened to be—the untamed genius of the ancient Greeks, the glorious wordiness of Shakespeare, the calculated greatness of Goethe, the brilliant dilettantism of Proust—Németh's highly individual point of view, his combative spirit, quickly became manifest. Not only was he often drawn to writers (e.g., Tolstoy, Gide, Proust) who were in some ways kindred spirits, he also tended to reshape them in his own image. When, for example, he writes that for Proust "nature and morality are one," or that the heroine of

Gide's *Porte étroite* "could be happy but she tastes the joy of self-denial," one thinks inevitably of Németh's own notion of heroism (that curious mixture of Nietzschean hauteur and Christian self-effacement), and of Németh's heroes and heroines who exemplify this ideal.[7]

The group of writers, poets and publicists who had the warmest praise for Németh's many-faceted literary activities were the populists. In the mid-thirties the sweeping reforms advocated by this group, their enthusiastic espousal of a constructive kind of ethnocentrism and their rediscovery of peasant cultures caught the imagination of some of Hungary's leading political figures, and for a short while it seemed that as in years past, Hungarian poets and writers would play an active role in shaping their nation's destiny. Many of the populists looked to Németh as the potential ideologist of the movement; but as soon as populism became politicized, Németh had second thoughts—not because he considered himself an ivory-tower intellectual (he always had proposals for political and social reform up his sleeve), but because direct involvement in politics was alien to his temperament. He saw himself primarily as a man of letters and an educator. At a time when liberal democracy in Hungary was an illusion, and the country was fast sliding into the Fascist orbit, Németh wrote of a "Third Hungary," one that would be energized by the latent strengths of the rural masses. In retrospect Németh recognized that "the Third Hungary was closer to a Platonic ideal, which a man not cut out for politics tried to bring down to earth . . . than to a workable political program."[8] Still, at the time there were signs of official recognition. In 1934 Németh was put in charge of the Hungarian Radio's literary programming. Influential members of the cultural establishment were reading *Tanú* and following Németh's career with interest. He became a sought-after lecturer and was one of the founders of the populist periodical *Válasz* (Answer), though after realizing that he couldn't reconcile his own lofty concepts with the more pragmatic reform plans of the populist mainstream, he and the editors of *Válasz* parted ways. During the thirties Németh formulated some of his most important and controversial ideas. They were published in a series of volumes entitled *A minőség forradalma* (The Revolution of Quality, 1940–1943). Influenced by the pessimistic world views of such social critics and philosophers as Spengler, Dilthey and Ortega y Gasset, Németh rejected both capitalism and socialism, believing them to be identical phenomena.

"Both are interested in bringing about, through opposite means, a mass society based on large-scale economic development, mass production," he wrote. "But the profound ill of the world can not be cured by a revolution based on the equal distribution of wealth as conceived by the socialists . . . The real revolution must take place within the individual consciousness." Németh opted for a "third way," quality socialism, a societal order inspired and led by the "latent better ones," who in a self-imposed exile from conventional society set a moral example for the masses. "The revolution of conscience would remain free of violence; moral example would be responsible for its success. An independent societal entity—the intelligentsia—would become the vanguard and try to reshape society in its own image."[9] Németh's ideal was a classless society in which each profession would reach an intellectual level. Under such circumstances class distinctions would disappear, and a truly classless society would emerge.

Németh's ideas were attacked both from the left and the right. The "revolution of quality" was judged to be dangerously elitist and at best naively utopian. And when in a series of essays published under the title *Kisebbségben* (In the Minority, 1942), Németh talked about the "genius" of race and distinguished between "deep" Hungarians (*mélymagyarok*) and "skindeep" Hungarians (*hígmagyarok*),[10] he was called a literary fascist and an out-and-out racist. His views were considered particularly outrageous because their publication coincided with the passage of discriminatory legislation against Hungarian Jews. Ironically, Németh was as concerned about the assimilation of Hungary's Jews as about the *dis*similationist tendencies discernible at this time among Magyarized Germans. But to repeat, terms like race and quality, were charged with ethical significance for Németh. He was neither a professional political scientist nor a trained philosopher; he approached social and political problems as a writer with a strong moralist bent, who tried to reconcile the rationalist world view of a scientist with the idealistic, even messianic impulses of a reformer. In an essay on Németh's ideology, the philosopher Tibor Hanák points out that "quality as a moral ideal cannot be scientifically verified; it cannot be expressed in quantitative language. Quality is 'life,' whereas quantity belongs in the realm of science. Németh tried to bridge the gap between the two on a pedagogical rather than a theoretical plane."[11] Of course he also tried to bridge this gap in his novels and plays. Németh's theories about racial determinants and moral exemplars appear uncompromising and dogmatic when he expounds on them in his essays. But his persistent attraction to self-effacing supermen, secular saints, wronged moral giants make for rich and rewarding fictional works. The theories he advocates so militantly in his essays are much more subtly diffused, and frequently questioned, in these works. The moral fervor of the ideologist is cooled and confounded by the esthetic sensibilities of the artist. In a recently published diary entry Németh himself admits: "It was in my essays that my mission as a writer broke through; my novels and dramas are secondary formations. They aided the process of self-purgation and helped me eliminate unwanted residues. In my novels I fantasized about—and removed—the threats to my psychic integrity . . . I licked my wounds in them."[12] It is important to note, too, that the setting of most of Németh's literary works, including fiction written or completed in the sixties, is post-World War I Hungary. (His last novel, *Irgalom* [Mercy], begun in the Twenties and published in 1965, contains the most elaborate and penetrating portrayal of the post-war scene.) Not only was the ambience of this period most familiar to him, but its problems and hardships as well. Indeed, many of these works can be viewed as a morally aware artist's attempt to fill a spiritual void left by the war and its aftermath. Németh's heroes are defiant idealists who are invariably pitted against worldly and practical-minded antagonists, and struggle valiantly, and often needlessly, pathetically, to save a crass, mean-spirited, conventional world.

Németh began to write his first novel, *Emberi színjáték* (Human Comedy) in 1928. In an autobiographical narrative first published in the Thirties, the author tells us that the model for Zoltán Boda, the novel's hero, was a fellow medical student, a strange, high-strung, impotent boy who dropped out of medical school to become a medicine man in their village. *Emberi színjáték* was meant to be an ironic account of an eccentric boy's quest for martyrdom. Németh's purpose was to show that "sainthood and neurosis are two sides of the same coin."[13] But the hero outwitted the irony. As he was writing this ambitious novel, the young author realized that he was identifying more and more with Zoltán Boda, and found himself smuggling into his hero's life his own dreams and ideals, making him fight for his own causes. Looking back to this period in his life, Németh wrote years later: "I believed I fit into all the roles that a 'normal' person was expected to fit into; I adjusted well to the world. But having reached this peak, I became—the novel attests to it—suspicious of all the wholesomeness and normalcy; didn't it deceive me and shut out forever my better, nobler self, my 'abnormality?' "[14]

Németh's second major novel, *Gyász* (Mourning, 1930), also exemplifies a magnificent obsession; it, too, was intended to be a clinical study of excessive behavior—in this case a peasant widow's defiant grief—that ultimately turned into a tribute to the obsession. In *Gyász* Németh wanted to "unmask the falsity of mourning—the heroic hypocrisy of proud souls like me who know too much about mourning themselves, and don't dare to forget even what they are in fact beginning to forget. The hoarse, bitter laugh of a cousin of mine became the melody, the motto of the novel. The last time I saw her was in the cemetery, at the grave of her son and of her husband who fell in battle. In Zoltán Boda of *Emberi színjáték* I wanted to present an ironic picture of sainthood; the same way in the portrait of Zsófi Kurátor [heroine of *Gyász*] I wished to make pride the object of my irony. But just as sainthood before, pride won out over my irony."[15]

The autobiographical antecedents of Németh's third novel, *Bűn* (*Guilt*, 1936), are even more revealing. Németh married young (he was not yet twenty-five), and his wife, Ella, was a practical, down-to-earth, in many ways conventionally bourgeois woman who bore him six daughters and who—thanks to her ingenuity and perseverence—made it possible for her husband to devote much of his time to writing. As Németh's biographer points out, "*Tanú* as well as Németh's other works may have had a hundred different muses, but they all had one mother: Ella Németh."[16] Her husband was very much attached to her, but because she was easygoing, nonintellectual, an earth mother, the intellectually discriminating and morally squeamish Németh tried often to fight off her powerful and seductive influence. In an unusually frank, posthumously published diary entry the author confesses that despite his love for Ella "my life with her was spent in endless rebellion, dissatisfaction and—dare I say it?—unhappiness."[17] After he stopped publishing *Tanú* and discovered that the populists' reform plans were not taken too seriously by the government, Németh again decided to go it alone. He wanted to establish a community of like-minded individuals, and with this in mind, planned to buy a farm which would become a "tiny island of quality socialism," the first model of a fondly envisaged "Garden Hungary," where the workers would not only be intellectuals but—not so incidentally—Németh's disciples as well. As can be expected, Ella, "the enraged mother," was opposed to this highly impractical venture. Instead of buying a farm she was interested in having a home built for her growing family.[18] The conflict between husband and wife produced *Bűn*, a brooding novel about a simple peasant boy who drifts into the capital and is hired as a laborer by Mrs. Endre Horváth, a wealthy middle-class woman who is having a house built in a fashionable suburb of Budapest. Mrs. Horváth is a materialistic, calculating woman, while her husband, Endre, is a sensitive, anguished intellectual. *Bűn* reveals the huge gap between peasant and bourgeois, and is concerned mainly with Horváth's tragic attempt to bridge the gap, to atone for the guilt he feels in the face of social injustice, by trying to improve the boy's lot. However, the gap proves to be too wide; not only is his wife exasperated by his acts of charity; his gestures are ignored, misunderstood by the lad himself. The novel ends with Horváth's suicide.

After *Tanú* ceased publication in 1936, Németh's career as a publicist seemed to be over. His ideas were attacked, his integrity questioned; more than ever he needed the "cleansing rinse of fiction."[19] He embarked on what he felt would be the most ambitious work of his career: a sweeping novel of education, an encyclopedic fictional treatment of modern Hungarian history, a story, a Proustian dissection of classes, types, intellectual and social currents. It was conceived as a seven-part novel about the momentous struggle for self-realization of one man, Péter Jó. Entitled *Az utolsó kísérlet* (The Last Experiment), this monumental novel was to have been Németh's swan song, his message to posterity: "*The Last Experiment* tried to magnify the dimensions of my own experiment and fall, and provide an encyclopedic synthesis of what before the historic breakup was still intact in my country and its people, and what art—for in art even the vanquished can triumph if he survives—could preserve for more fortunate epochs.[20] Many critics felt that Péter Jó *was* László Németh—and indeed there are quite a number of superficial biographical resemblances between the two, but Péter Jó does not capture the essence of the "Németh character" the way some of his tragic heroines do. The author had to realize that works conceived on a giant scale are not always successful. In attempting to write an all-encompassing novel, Németh described landscapes and milieus he knew little about, and felt compelled to pad his work with too many philosophical mediations. Only the first four volumes of the projected seven-part cycle appeared, the last one in 1941. Németh could not remain a reclusive novelist; too many things were happening around him during these years. He may have felt that he was pushed off the literary scene, but his interest in public affairs, his urge to answer new calls, to respond to new stimuli, was too great. Amazingly enough, in addition to publishing his highly provocative political essays, discussed earlier, Németh found time during this same period to produce a number of important dramas. (In surveying Németh's career, one realizes that his enormous creative abilities were matched only by an almost compulsive need to write—this despite his vows, frequently voiced, never fulfilled, to withdraw into silence. His post-Second World War output is no less formidable than his pre-war production. During the last years of his life, he suffered greatly from the aftereffects of a stroke, but what he found most intolerable was that he could no longer write.)

As a playwright, Németh was also concerned with moral issues—issues that for him took on greater urgency in a fragmented, despondent world. As in his first novels, Németh's early social and historical dramas grew out of his clash with his wife and his family, yet they reflect some of the more profound social ills of his times. The heroes of these plays are driven by an ideal which is irreconcilable with their family's earth-bound needs and desires. The heroes' attempt to abandon society are usually frustrated by a wife or a child. The conflicts are violent and lead invariably to the family's downfall. The names alone of the historical personages that later caught Németh's fancy—Pope Gregory VII, Jan Hus, Galileo, Gandhi, the Austrian Emperor Joseph II, the Hungarian physician Semmelweis—suggest the sense of continuity and consistency in his art. Németh adopted Gregory's motto—"I loved the truth and hated injustice"—for all his historical dramas. The unifying theme of these works is the noble and tragic struggle of individual genius against mass stupidity and intolerance.

From the beginning of his career, László Németh felt he was a writer with a mission. He was indeed a nineteenth-century man in his desire to use literature as a weapon, a means to an end; in believing that a writer can still be teacher, prophet, secular priest. At the same time Németh was also a quientessentially modern writer, whose skepticism and psychological sophistication invariably mocked his own idealism and insistence on moral purity. This is why his characters can be seen either as tragic heroes or egomaniacs, geniuses or misfits. As we said, Németh's novels and plays, despite their revolutionary aims and grand themes, are rather narrow in scope, dealing as they do with conflicts between husband and wife, parent and child. His novels are family novels, his dramas domestic dramas. His few attempts at traditional utopian literature are rather naive and unconvincing. As an artist Németh knew that East Europeans cannot afford to be dreamers. "In this bleak region of history," writes Gyula Gombos in his essay on Németh, "the too beautiful and too perfect always seem frivolous."[21] It was because he wanted to be guided by both faith and reason that the young Németh had trouble fitting into groups or pleasing his various critics. He was too cerebral for the populists, too irrational for the Western-oriented urban writers, too idiosyncratic for the leftists, too heterodox for conservative Christians. Németh the novelist and playwright weighs down his old-fashioned heroes with all kinds of debilitating encumbrances and handicaps; he forever sets traps for them from which they cannot escape, and their greatness lies in the fact that "even with hands and feet tied they keep climbing, grasping."[22] He is irresistably drawn to his doomed heroes, though his attraction to them stems from an identification with the Greek rather than Christian ethos. "Why bother with the damned?" he asks in his brief but seminal essay, "Dráma és legenda" (Drama and Legend). " 'Look at them and keep walking,' says Dante, and with him the entire Christian tradition. But there are other, man- rather than god-centered ages—Ancient Greece, for instance, or the Modern period—that find forbidden pleasure in the self-justifying laments of tormented heroes . . . To bow down and at the same time shake rebelliously the pillars of Eternal Order; to blaspheme God while worshipping Him—this has been the stimulus for great drama ever since Promethius and Sophocles."[23] In his own plays, novels and essays Németh got back at the world. Born out of deep-seated national and personal hurts, they celebrate moral triumphs over physical perdition.

Notes

1. See "A Nyugat elődei," in L.N., *Az én katedrám* (Budapest, 1975), pp. 643–670.

2. "Pajzzsal és dárdával," Mihály Babits, *Könyvről könyvre* (Budapest, 1973), pp. 288–289.

3. "Negyven év," in L.N., *Negyven év—Horváthné meghal—Gyász* (Budapest, 1974), p. 9.

4. "Az Iszony francia kiadásának előszáva," in Gyula Illyés, *Ingyen lakoma* vol. 1 (Budapest, 1964), p. 283.

5. "Íróvá avatnak," in L.N., *Kiadatlan tanulmányok* vol. 1 (Budapest, 1968), p. 64.

6. Miklós Szabolcsi, ed., *A magyar irodalom története* vol. 6 (Budapest, 1966), p. 498.

7. See my review of N.'s *Európai utas* in *Books Abroad* vol. 48 (Autumn 1974), pp. 821–822.

8. "Negyven év," p. 11.

9. See L.N., *A minőség forradalma* vol. 1, pp. 9–21; vol. 4, pp. 10–31, 50–79. (Budapest, 1940).

10. See L.N., *Kisebbségben* vol. 1 (Budapest, 1942), pp. 13–108.

11. Tibor Hanák, "Mennyiség—Minőség," *Új Látóhatár* vol. 22 (Munich, 1971), p. 187.

12. L.N., *Utolsó széttekintés* (Budapest, 1980), p. 160.

13. "Ember és szerep," in L.N., *Homályból homályba* vol. 1 (Budapest, 1977), p. 360.

14. L.N., *Emberi színjáték* vol. 1 (Budapest, 1966), p. 8.

15. "Ember és szerep," pp. 434–435.

16. László Vekerdi, *Németh László—Alkotásai és vallomásai tükrében* (Budapest, 1970), p. 90.

17. L.N., *Utolsó széttekintés*, p. 48.

18. "Negyven év," p. 19.

19. *Ibid.*, p. 22.

20. *Ibid.*

21. Gyula Gombos, "Tanítás a minőségre," *Új Látóhatár* vol. 22 (1971), p. 42.

22. L.N., *Megmentett gondolatok* (Budapest, 1975), p. 642.

23. "Dráma és legenda," in L.N., *Kiadatlan tanulmányok* vol. 1 (Budapest, 1968), p. 601.

Stephen Bela Vardy

Trianon in Interwar Hungarian Historiography

The 19th-century British historian Edward Augustus Freeman (1823–1892) defined history simply as "past politics."[1] Although nowadays we tend to regard history as much more than that, we cannot deny the role of politics therein—not only of past politics, but of current politics as well. And this is true regardless of the specific school of history or orientation one tends to be associated with. Ideally, the discipline of history ought to be detached from party politics and ideological influences of one kind or another. In reality, however, it is generally influenced by numerous outside factors, including the background, the personality and the ideological convictions of the historian himself, as well as by his immediate cultural, economic and political environment.

While these external influences are generally present, their relative influence upon the profession and upon historians does tend to vary from region to region, and from period to period. Not counting instances where historians and their craft are controlled by totalitarian systems and by obligatory ideologies, these outside influences are most acutely felt during periods of national revivals and at times of great national crises. When a nation is in the process of emerging from historical obscurity, it needs the psychological stimuli derived from an allegedly great and glorious past. This also holds true in instances when a nation has been shaken by a major crisis or national catastrophe, and is in need of such stimuli in order to regain its will to live.

One could cite many examples of such phenomena from world history. In Europe such examples are especially plentiful in the history of those small nations in the continent's central and southeastern regions that have emerged or re-emerged from various levels of obscurity in the course of the late eighteenth to the early twentieth century. Some of these nations are still trying to find their places in history through myths and various officially sponsored ideological props that require the mixing of history with generous doses of make-believe and current politics.[2]

Although the Hungarians and Poles were probably the very first among the nations of East Central Europe to become conscious of their nationhood and to go through a complex process of national, cultural and political revival, they too had to pass through various levels of romantic daydreaming, and they too had to witness the intrusion of political-ideological considerations into their historical writings. The most obvious and well-known examples of this phenomenon were the "mirage-chasing" historical works of Ádám Pálóczi-Horváth (1760–1820), István Horvát (1784–1846) and a few others of similar bent during the early nineteenth century, when Hungarian nationalism mingled freely with Romanticism.[3]

This tendency declined and yielded its place to sober, scholarly historical research carried out by detached historians. Had the position of the Hungarian nation not changed in 1918, and had the Hungarian state not been mutilated and the nation dismembered and shaken to its very roots by the Treaty of Trianon, this trend toward scholarly detachment would undoubtedly have continued. But Trianon, which was immediately regarded as one of the greatest, if not the greatest, national catastrophe in the Hungarians' millenial history in the Carpathian Basin, had shaken basically all Hungarians, irrespective of their social standing, economic status, level of learning or political orientation. Certainly, no Hungarian historian who lived through those tragic events could remain unaffected by them. In fact the impact of these events upon the Hungarian mind was so thorough and pervasive that it has rightfully been called an intense "psychological shock."[4]

The historians who labored during and immediately after Hungary's geographical mutilation and who represented a goodly portion of the "conscience of their nation" were probably more affected than anyone else—with the possible exception of the most noted and sensitive poets and other men of letters. The historians were of course used to "living in the past." They had studied, restudied, and even "re-lived" psychologically the ups and downs of their nation's history. The shock-effect of these developments was all the greater as this new disaster came hand in hand with the long sought-after national independence.

The nature and magnitude of Trianon's psychological shock upon contemporary Hungarian historians was best expressed by Gyula Szekfü (1883–1955), the dominant figure of interwar Hungarian historiography and the "father" of the likewise dominant new

Hungarian *Geistesgeschichte* School."[5] Szekfű gave vent to his feelings in the agonizing introduction to his first post-Trianon work, the noted *Három nemzedék* [Three Generations]. "This book had to be written. This book is my personal experience," wrote Szekfű. Then he continued:

> In the midst of those trying events into which the catastrophe of October 1918 [the collapse of Austria-Hungary] had thrust us. . . , I felt . . . that I would never be able to recover my strength and inclination for work until having taken account of the [causes of the] decline that had led us to this disaster. I simply had to confront myself with the forces that have dragged my nation out of a stream of healthy evolution. Thus did I come to write this work, and . . . thus did I redeem my soul.[6]

To Szekfű, the writing of the *Three Generations* constituted a spiritual catharsis through which he was able to release some of the psychological pressures that have accumulated within him. Not every Hungarian historian was able to produce a work of such proportions and such significance. Yet, virtually every historian worthy of the designation has written his own "Trianon book," or at least a "Trianon pamphlet."

Others, particularly amateur historians and other men of letters with less self-discipline than professional historians, lost their direction completely. They began to wander off in the direction of myth-seeking and self-delusion. Some of the most visible manifestations of this trend was the rebirth of the "mirage-chasing" historiography of István Horvát that sought the roots of the Hungarians among the great civilizers of the ancient world (e.g. the Sumerians, Egyptians, Hittites, Etruscans, Indians, etc.), and the rise of a new wave of Turanism that rejected communion with the "faithless" West, and found solace in a hazy Pan-Turanian dream. The latter went so far as to try to purge Hungarian Civilization of its millennial Christian culture and faith, and to replace it with an artificially re-created "pure" Hungarian culture and religion. Szekfű rightfully called this phenomenon a "new paganism" that all civilized Hungarians ought to reject.[7]

Although bitter and dejected about this trend toward self-delusion, Szekfű did not really have to launch a major crusade against this unusual post-Trianon craze. Most Hungarian thinkers rejected this irresponsible toying with the Hungarian past and future. Yet, at the same time, virtually all Hungarian intellectuals, irrespective of their ideological leanings, were extremely bitter about Trianon, and for a while most of them suffered from the so-called "Trianon syndrome." That this was so is best demonstrated by the fact that even such left-leaning cosmopolitan thinkers as Oscar Jászi (1875–1957), associated with the progressive journal *Huszadik Század* [Twentieth Century], and the literary critic and publicist Hugó Ignótus (1869–1949) of the similarly progressive journal *Nyugat* [The West] wrote their own "Trianon books."[8]

Just as their fellow intellectuals in related fields, Hungarian historians of the post-Trianon period also suffered from the Trianon syndrome. This was rather natural, as they were subjected to a diverse number of psychological, ideological, social and political pressures. As catalogued recently by Ferenc Glatz in his book on the relationship between the historian and politics in Hungary, these pressures stemmed from a number of sources.[9] They included: The loss of the familiar "historical stage" which served as the scene of many of the great and sad events of Hungarian history; the loss of much of the written and unwritten sources of this history; the loss of a goodly portion of the educated reading public, who were either cut off by the new borders, or became pauperized and thus unable to buy works of history; and finally the loss of a whole intellectual-ideological "medium," represented by a society and a state on the move—the kind of society Hungary had been before 1914. But Trianon also meant to these historians the end of a relatively secure socio-economic existence, the comfortable way of life that they and their reading public used to know. Thus, from the vantage point of the Hungarian historians, Trianon had turned out to be much more than a major national catastrophe. It was also a personal catastrophe of unusual proportions that undermined both the material and the psychological well-being of historians, and this was bound to affect their relationship to their discipline.

*   *   *

The reaction of the historians and of the historical profession took many forms. Ultimately, however, it resulted in the reorientation of the whole discipline, and in the marshalling of much of the discipline's resources into the service of revisionism.

Already during World War I Hungarian historians were aware

that Hungary's multinational composition, as well as the prospect of defeat, would make the country's mutilation inevitable. This is clearly evident from a series of studies written by respected historians as early as 1916, which tried to prove the Hungarians' sole historical right to the Carpathian Basin.[10] As a matter of fact, arguments based on historical rights became the number one weapon in the arsenal of post-Trianon Hungarian irredentism, which also explains the unusually significant role of historians in the Hungarian campaign for revisionism. Naturally, proponents of revisionism made use of a number of other arguments as well. These included references to historic Hungary's natural geographical and economic unity, to the cultural pre-eminence of the Hungarians in the Carpathian Basin, as well as to the ethnic principles that have been violated by the transfer of 3.5 million Hungarians (one-third of the nation) to the new successor states.[11] The latter argument, however, was much less frequently used, for it could only have resulted in a partial revisionism. Not so the historical argument, which was aimed at restoring the territorial integrity of historic Hungary.

The most popular and most commonly used historical argument was that the Hungarians were the first to establish a lasting and viable state in the area of Greater Hungary; a state which became the bastion of Western Christianity against eastern barbarism, and which was destined to keep the equilibrium between the large Germanic and Slavic worlds. How this was to be done by such a small nation was never discussed. But these views gradually penetrated the whole historical profession, and then began to appear as guinding principles in the works of most historians during the interwar years. Some of these early works were small political pamphlets only inspired by the immediate needs of the moment. Others, however, were serious historical works that came to constitute the very backbone of interwar Hungarian historiography.

Among the numerous early political pamphlets written with the intent to head off the impending catastrophe of Trianon, those put out by the Hungarian Academy and the Hungarian universities were all written by first-rate historians. Thus, the Academy's appeal to the "civilized world" was composed by Dávid Angyal (1857-1947),[12] a noted Professor of Hungarian history at the University of Budapest (1909-1929). Similar appeals by the Universities of Budapest, Pozsony and Debrecen—although not published under the names of the authors—were written by József Holub (1885-1962), Antal Hodinka

(1865–1946) and István Rugonfalvi-Kiss (1881–1957) respectively, all of them significant historians connected with these universities.[13]

The University of Budapest's publication *La Hongrie* (1918)[14] described Hungary's multinational composition in the course of the 12th-14th centuries, pointing out the low proportion of the non-Hungarian nationalities, and then detailed how the number of these nationalities grew through constant immigration during the following period, particularly during the Turkish and the post-Turkish era in Hungarian history. The University of Pozsony's Publication *Pro Hungaria* (1918)[15] concentrated on the Slovak question and tried to demonstrate how Hungarian leniency and liberalism assured their survival as a nationality throughout the centuries. This same work also tried to convince the Slovaks that they had much less to fear from Hungary, a country that had protected and preserved them for a whole millennium than from the projected Czechoslovak state, where they were bound to lose their national identity.

This Hungarian leniency and tolerance was also emphasized by the University of Debrecen's clarion call to "the universities of the civilized world."[16] Like those issued by its sister institutions, this work also tried to gain sympathy for the Hungarians by pointing out that Hungary had always served as Western Civilization's bulwark against the intrusions of the Orient, and that the Hungarians are in effect the victims of their role as the defenders of Christianity. This pamphlet described the Hungarians as a "nation of mediators" and Hungary as a "link" between the East and the West. Historic Hungary was also characterized as a "community of nations" that are bound together by common history, common traditions and common interests.[17]

These four pamphlets produced under the auspices of Hungary's top four scholarly institutions (only the University of Kolozsvár was left out) all contain some of those basic features that will characterize much of the better-quality Hungarian revisionist literature of the interwar period. They were written by historians, they were structured around historical arguments, and they all emphasized the Hungarians' primary historical rights in the Carpathian Basin, as well as Hungary's unique role as the defensive bastion of Western Christianity.

The first historian to tackle the problem of Hungary's dismemberment (or rather, possible dismemberment) from the point of view of historical rights was János Karácsonyi (1858–1929), a Titular Bishop of the Catholic Church and a Professor of Church History at the University of Budapest. He did this as early as 1916 in a book entitled: *A magyar nemzet történeti joga hazánk területéhez a Kárpátoktól le az Adriáig* [The Historical Right of the Hungarian Nation to Our Country's Territory from the Carpathians to the Adriatic].[18] This work appears to have been written as a direct response to Arnold Toynbee's politically motivated work, *The Nationality and the War*, which appeared in 1915.[19] Already at that early stage of the war Toynbee called for the mutilation of the Central Powers and for the dismemberment of Hungary on the basis of ethnic considerations.[20] While trying to apply the principle of national self-determination to Britain's adversaries in the war, however, Toynbee was reluctant to do so in the case of the Entente states and their allies. In the latter case, political and economic considerations seem to have taken precedence over ethnic matters.

Toynbee's work and other similar studies by scholars on the Entente side naturally called for response on the part of Hungarian historians, and Karácsonyi's above cited work was only the first of such responses. Although his study was obviously written with a specific goal in mind, it was not a political tract, but a work of historical scholarship. Karácsonyi based his arguments—as did most subsequent Hungarian scholars—on certain known or presumed facts of history. His main thesis was that the Hungarians, and only they held full historical rights to the territory of Greater Hungary. He pointed out that when they captured the Carpathian Basin in the 9th century, the area was basically a no man's land, with only the fragmentary remains of some of the transitory people who had lived there for shorter or longer periods and then were absorbed by the conquering Hungarians. Thus by the end of the 12th century, in spite of additional settlers invited by Hungary's kings, Hungary was basically populated only by Hungarians. Karácsonyi even denied the presence of the ancestors of the Slovaks in 9th-century Hungary. In his view, the latter had nothing to do with the ephemeral and obscure "Great Moravia." Rather they were latecomers who began to infiltrate Hungary only at the end of the 11th century, and then came in increasing numbers during the Hussite Wars of the 15th century. Moreover, while during the Turkish conquest the Hungarians were decimated, the Slovaks "multiplied happily in their mountains" and thus Slovakized much of Northern Hungary. Although a number of Hungarian scholars did not accept Karácsonyi's view concerning the Slovaks' origins, they all agreed basically that the latter did indeed increase considerably at the expense of the Hungarians.

Karácsonyi also dealt at some length with the Romanians, and true to the generally accepted scholarly view in Hungary and in the West, he too rejected the so-called Daco-Roman origins of the Romanians. He claimed—this time on the basis of generally accepted scholarly foundations—that the latter were likewise newcomers to the area, who began to move into Transylvania from the Balkans only in the late 12th and early 13th century. Prior to that they lived in the mountains of the Balkans, and their language evolved in the vicinity of the Illyrian speaking Albanians.

Unlike the ancestors of the Romanians, the Croats were viewed by Karácsonyi as people who had settled in Croatia before the Hungarian conquest. But Croatia in those days was basically limited to the Adriatic lands, and the area between the Save and the Drave Rivers was solidly Hungarian-inhabited right up to the Turkish period. Karácsonyi also had something to say about the nature of the Hungaro-Croatian union which, he claimed, was based on conquest. Indeed, he asserted that not until the 17th century did Croatian historians begin to talk and write about various alleged conditions to this union (i.e. the *Pacta Conventa* of 1102). From the historical point of view, then, even the rights of the Croatians were thought by Karácsonyi to be based simply on subsequent concessions granted by the Hungarian Crown.

Karácsonyi also devoted some attention to the other nationalities of the Hungarian Kingdom (e.g. Serbians, Ruthenians, Germans, Bulgarians, Vends, Armenians, Albanians, Poles, Jews, Gypsies, etc.), as well as to ethnic groups that had been absorbed centuries earlier (e.g. the Pechenegs, Cumans, Jases, Tartars, Czechs, etc.). He concluded his study by reasserting his belief that only the Hungarians possess full-fledged historical rights to Hungary, and consequently they have the right and duty "to cling to this country, and to view every attack against the integrity of their homeland as treason." By doing so, "all the Hungarian nation does is to defend its millenial rights."[21]

That Karácsonyi's work was generally regarded as a good and effective summary of the Hungarian view of Hungary's history is best demonstrated by the fact that in 1920 it also appeared in a shortened English version.[22] In the following year it was republished in Hungarian,[23] and subsequently it became the number one source for many of the better quality works of Hungarian irredentism. The authors of the latter works also based their arguments almost exclusively on the Hungarians' unique historical rights, and pointed out that Hungary's existing nationality problems are in effect the result of Hungarian generosity in having welcomed national groups in periods when their national existence was threatened. While willing to give credit to the nationalities for their contributions to the Hungarian state, they denied that the latter had the right of separation. In agreement with Karácsonyi, they were unable to perceive the future of the people of the Carpathian Basin in any other way except in a "common Hungarian homeland."[24]

The ever-increasing number of "Trianon books" that followed the appearance of Karácsonyi's pioneering study represented numerous disciplines and rather diverse levels of scholarship. Whether written by historians, economists, geographers or simply publicists, whether evincing a high level of scholarship or simply propaganda, the authors of these works all strove to emphasize the unique historical rights of the Hungarians to the territory of historic Hungary.[25]

As an example, this emphasis is quite evident in the works of the constitutional historian Béla Iványi (1878–1964) of the University of Debrecen, who concentrated on the Slovak question. In his work *Pro Hungaria Superiore* (1919)[26] he tried to buttress Karácsonyi's contention that the Slovaks had nothing to do with the Slavs of Great Moravia, and therefore with the Czechs and the Moravians of the later centuries. In his view the Slovaks were really Wends (Windisch) from the upper Odera region, who began to move across the Northern Carpathians only in the 13th century. As such, they had no pre-conquest historical rights in the Carpathian Basin, as claimed by most of the Slovak national historians.

Similar works, emphasizing the Hungarians' historical rights, were also authored by such "grand old men" of Hungarian historiography as Vilmos Fraknói (1843–1921), Dávid Angyal (1857–1943) and Henrik Marczali (1856–1940), as well as by such younger notables as Sándor Domanovszky (1877–1955), Jenö Horváth (1881–1950), Bálint Hóman (1885–1952), and Gyula Szekfü. Some of these scholars—e.g., Fraknói, Angyal and Horváth—concentrated largely on demonstrating Hungary's innocence in the origins of World War I and on the consequent injustices of the Treaty of Trianon.[27] Marczali devoted his *A béke könyve* [The Book of Peace] (1920)[28] to summarizing the history of the Hungarians in such a way as to make it into "a mission to spread culture and freedom" in the lands of the Hungarian Crown. While discussing Hungary's history in these terms, Marczali also appears to have agreed with the French historian, Louis Eisenmann, who declared that "to preserve themselves, they [the Hungarians] must dominate the whole of Hungary . . . [and then] transform their 'historical' state into a 'national' state."[29] That this situation did not come about in the half century after Eisenmann's statement, according to Marczali, was the result of the fact that social and economic questions in Dualist Hungary were decided on the basis of party and personal considerations, and not on the basis of national interests.

While Marczali concentrated on emphasizing the special mission of the Hungarians in the Carpathian Basin, the younger Sándor Domanovszky, who was the most important exponent of the Hungarian *Kulturgeschichte* School, with a distinct agrarian orientation, returned again to stressing his nation's unique historical rights to the area.[30] His first contribution to this question was a short work entitled *A magyar kérdés történeti szempontból tekintve* [The Hungarian Question from the Historical Perspective] (1920),[31] which was written specifically for the non-Hungarian reader. Domanovszky basically followed the path outlined by Karácsonyi, and began his work by describing the region's ethnic composition in the period between the 9th and the 13th centuries. He claimed that the ethnic fragments found by the Hungarians at the time of their conquest were all assimilated in the course of the next three centuries, along with most of the new settlers of the early Christian period (i.e. the Pechenegs, Cumans, as well as most of the German, Italian French and Spanish burghers of the 11th and 12th centuries). In his view, the nationality blocks along the country's frontier regions came into being later as a result of specific settlement policies of the Hungarian kings, who invited the latter for economic and defensive purposes. The ancestors of the Slovaks, the Ruthenians and the Romanians all came to Hungary in this manner, and then multiplied in their less-exposed mountain regions at the expense of the Hungarians. Domanovszky was also at pains to point out that up to the 17th century there was no nationality question in Hungary. In his view this is quite evident from the fact that the oft-recurring peasant revolts were purely social conflicts, wherein it is impossible to tell the national identities of the combatants. Hungary's nationality problems began to arise only in the 18th century, when the expulsion

of the Turks was followed by a Habsburg-initiated policy to settle
the vacated and depopulated lands with various newcomers. These
included Serbian settlers in Southern Hungary, more Vlach peasants
in Transylvania, and various German and French elements in Trans-
Danubia and the Great Hungarian Plain. Simultaneously with this
settlement policy, the Habsburgs also began to apply the policy of
divide et impera, which gave birth to various separatist movements
among Hungary's ever more numerous national minorities. But these
separatist movements had nothing to do with any real or alleged nationality oppression in Hungary, which, in so far as there was any,
was the product of certain mid- and late-19th-century developments.
Domanovszky closed his study with the conviction that Hungary's
territorial mutilation—carried out to a large degree in violation of
the very principle of self-determination which was used as a pretext
for its dismemberment—could only result in ever more conflict in the
destabilized Danubian lands. In this prognosis Domanovszky was
proved to be correct.[32]

Although one of the most apolitical of interwar Hungary's prominent historians, Domanovszky authored several related studies as
well. Moreover, he also incorporated his views into his short *Die
Geschichte Ungarns* [History of Hungary] (1923),[33] which likewise
reflects his emphasis upon social, as opposed to political, developments in Hungary's millennial history.

The course taken by Karácsonyi, and then by Iványi and
Domanovszky, was also followed by the respected medievalist
Bálint Hóman, whose subsequent involvement in politics and
rightward drift cannot alter the fact that prior to the 1930s he was a
prominent scholar, whose related works are still highly regarded
today.

Hóman's first essay on the subject of Hungarian territorial right
"The Settlement of the Hungarians" (1920),[34] was basically a summary of his views expressed in an earlier work entitled "The Settlement of the Conquering Tribes" (1912).[35] In this work he tried to
reconstruct the general geographical dispersal of the conquering
Hungarian tribes, while at the same time taking account of the
various peoples they may have found in the Carpathian Basin in the
9th century. In his view the latter included the remains of the Avars
and the related Hungarian speaking Székelys (Szeklers) of Eastern
Transylvania, various Slavic tribes (including some of the ancestors
of the Slovaks), as well as various Turko-Bulgarian, Dacian and

Gepidan remains, but no Vlachs (i.e. the ancestors of the Romanians, who still lived in the Balkans). Where Hóman disagreed with
Karácsonyi, Iványi and Domanovszky was the Slovak question,
though he too believed that with a few exceptions, by the late 12th
century most of these pre-Conquest peoples have been assimilated
into the Hungarians, and that by the year 1200 about ninety percent
of Hungary's population was Hungarian speaking and thus largely
homogeneous. Like his fellow historians, Hóman explained
Hungary's subsequent multinational composition in the modern
period by pointing to several waves of new immigrations, particularly during and after the Turkish period.

   Although obviously dejected as was virtually every Hungarian,
Hóman ended his essay of 1920 on a positive note by professing his
faith in the unique destiny of his nation in the lands conquered by
their ancestors: "In the course of the fifteen hundred years that
preceded the Hungarian conquest, about thirty nations have conquered . . . various regions of our country. Yet, none of them was
able to establish a lasting rule. . . . Hungary may be dismembered,
divided and truncated, its political unity may be shattered, but the
country's natural geographical and economic unity, and its people's
cultural unity, which is the product of a long historical evolution,
are indissoluble. For this reason, its political unity is bound to be
restored within a short period by the mighty powers of the laws of
nature and of history."[36]

   These hopeful views enunciated by Hóman in 1920, which may
have been the result of forced optimism, became part of the post-
Trianon Hungarian historiography just as much as the emphasis
upon the Hungarians' historical rights put forth by Karácsonyi four
years earlier. Whether out of true conviction, or simply out of
desperation, professing the natural, and therefore basically indissoluble, geographical, economic and cultural unity of the Lands
of the Hungarian Holy Crown became a guiding principle in much of
interwar Hungarian historiography. It also penetrated the related
works of geographers, economists, and various other men of letters.
And while belief in this principle came to dominate much of contemporary Hungarian historical thinking, the exponents of post-Trianon
Hungary's cultural policy also undertook a conscious effort to
prepare the Hungarian nation for the prophesized reunification of
Greater Hungary and for the position of cultural pre-eminence and

political leadership in that hoped-for reunited "Land of Milk and Honey."[37]

As indicated above, the disorientation and the subsequent reorientation of Hungarian historians and Hungarian historical thinking was a direct result of historic Hungary's dismemberment. The reorientation of the institutional and ideological base of the historical profession, on the other hand, was done consciously and in a premeditated manner by Count Kuno Klebelsberg (1878-1932), Hungary's Minister for Culture during the first half of the interwar period (1922-1931).[38]

Klebelsberg is rightfully held to be the greatest of interwar Hungary's cultural politicians. He was responsible for the total reorganization of the Hungarian educational system from the lowest to the highest level, as well as for the introduction of state support for scientific and scholarly research—a phenomenon that was basically unknown in Hungary prior to World War I.

Before Trianon, i.e. before Klebelsberg's appearance on the Hungarian cultural scene, most historical research was basically the result of individual efforts and initiatives that had been carried on by college and university professors, archivists, librarians, and to a lesser degree by some of the better secondary school teachers. The profession as a whole, however, was under the influence of the Hungarian Academy's Historical Commission, founded in 1854, and the Hungarian Historical Association established thirteen years later (1867). This influence, however, did not mean financial support beyond certain publishing opportunities; these institutions, then were dependent exclusively on foundation money and on private funds. State support was completely absent. This did provide of course an unusual degree of independence for the profession, but it left historians and their organizations dependent upon the good will of well-to-do donors, mostly aristocrats, with all the implications that their support implied.

Klebelsberg was well aware of this system's shortcomings already in the years before Trianon. Thus, when in 1917 he was elected to the presidency of the Hungarian Historical Association (1917-1932), while already serving as State Secretary in the Ministry of Culture, he immediately went to work to elaborate a detailed plan for state support for historical research.[39] This was to include scholarships, research and publication grants, as well as the eventual establishment of a series of state-funded historical research institutes and other centers of Hungarian learning, both at home and abroad.

In line with this policy, as soon as political conditions permitted such measures, Klebelsberg revived the Hungarian Historical Institute in Rome (established by Vilmos Fraknói in 1885), strengthened the Hungarian Institute at the University of Berlin (established in 1916), and—what is much more significant—in 1920 he laid the foundations for the highly influential and prestigious Hungarian Historical Research Institute of Vienna.[40] Although located abroad, the Viennese Institute became perhaps the most significant center for Hungarian historical research. Being close to the important archives of the former imperial city, which held so much of the sources of Hungarian history, the Institute became a magnet for many of the country's noted researchers, and at the same time it also came to serve as the primary post-doctoral training center for the most promising young Hungarian historians.

The foundation of the Hungarian Historical Research Institute of Vienna was soon followed by the establishment of a series of other Hungarian studies centers abroad. These included the Collegium Hungaricums of Vienna, Berlin and Rome, as well as dozens of Hungarian institutes, professorships and lectureships attached to some of the most prominent universities in Europe and the United States.

In 1922 Klebelsberg took several other steps toward increasing the state's financial support for historical and related studies. These steps included the administrative centralization of the country's most important centers of historical research and learning, and the initiation of a series of publication ventures. The aim of the first step was to expedite and coordinate historical research, while the goal of the latter was to make available to researchers the most important sources of modern and recent Hungarian history, and thus, hopefully, present a more balanced view of Hungary's recent past than the one that had been formed and disseminated by the country's critics during the early part of the century. Undoubtedly, this was a political goal; but a goal that in the mind of its author was meant simply to correct a distorted picture, and thus restore truth, justice and a degree of objectivity to the onesided assessment of Hungary's and the Hungarians' recent past. The most important of these publication projects initiated by Klebelsberg was the so-called *Fontes* [Sources] series, which, true to the needs of the times, placed an unusual emphasis upon the sources of the nationality question in 18th and 19th-century Hungary.[41]

While establishing the institutional base of a renewed and reoriented historical profession, Klebelsberg was also at work in formulating the main ideological foundations of interwar Hungarian historiography. Known as neo-nationalism, this ideology switched the attention of the Hungarians from the state to the nation, and from their former political pre-eminence to their current and hoped-for continued cultural pre-eminence in the Carpathian Basin. In a sense, this switch was an unavoidable by-product of the new realities that had constricted Hungarian political control to only a small central section of the former Kingdom of Hungary and placed over one-third of the Hungarian nation under foreign rule.

While emphasizing the significance of the nation over the state, the new ideology of neo-nationalism also stressed the alleged unique state-forming capacities of the Hungarians. Apparently, Klebelsberg was convinced that if the Hungarians are able to retain their cultural pre-eminence in the area, then—in conjunction with their capacity for political leadership—this pre-eminence would ultimately lead to the restoration of historic Hungary's political unity as well. This was the reason behind Klebelsberg's demands for the reorientation of Hungarian nationalism from confrontation to cooperation with the region's other nationalities; even though this cooperation was still to be carried out within the context of restored Hungarian leadership.[42]

The views formulated by Klebelsberg were generally acclaimed and applied by most Hungarian historians. These views certainly came to dominate much of Hungarian historical writing during the 1920s and 1930s, including scholarly works, popular tracts, and of course officially sanctioned textbooks. Even the books written by professional historians such as Sándor Domanovszky, Dezső Szabó, István Miskolczy, and others reflected this orientation.[43] The authors of these textbooks all took pains to emphasize the Hungarians' primary historical rights to the Carpathian Basin, their unique ability for political and cultural leadership, as well as the numerous past sacrifices that they have made in defending Western Christendom against Eastern barbarisms. In this way they played upon the Hungarians' fundamental ties to Christian Central Europe, and contrasted these ties with the Eastern (Orthodox Christian) culture and world view of the majority of their neighbors, including most of the Southern and Eastern Slavs and the Romanians. In effect these textbooks all intimated that Western Christian culture in Central Europe had been basically preserved by the sweat and blood of the Hungarians.[44] (This claim, by the way, was not unique to the Hungarians, for similar contentions were also advanced by most of the peoples of Central and Southeastern Europe.)

In addition to portraying the Hungarians as the primary defenders of Western Christendom, interwar textbooks also stressed the unusual geographical and economic unity of historic Hungary, which they all characterized as being absolute in Europe, and claimed that its forced dismemberment cannot be upheld for a protracted period of time. This was one of the reasons why Hungary's history and geography in interwar Hungarian schools was taught as if Trianon had never taken place.

These views came to characterize interwar Hungarian historiography and were generally accepted and popularized by most professional and non-professional historians of the post-Trianon period. Yet, the scholar who first expressed the essence of these views, and did so most effectively, was Gyula Szekfű, the "father" of the new Hungarian *Geistesgeschichte* School and the most influential historian not only of the interwar years, but perhaps also of 20th-century Hungary in general.

Szekfű first summarized his views on the nature of Hungarian historical evolution in 1917, in his well-known *A Magyar állam életrajza* [The Biography of the Hungarian State],[45] wherein he discussed the history of the Hungarians within the context of the history of "German-Christian" Central Europe, which he regarded as the most important single factor in the development of Hungary. And even though the collapse of Austria-Hungary and the Second Reich in 1918 brought to an end this whole German-Christian Central European configuration, Szekfű continued to stick to this basically defunct idea right into the late 1930s and early 1940s. This is quite evident from most of his writings of the interwar years, including the second edition of the above work (1923), in which he expressed the view that "the Hungarians can hope to escape from their current predicament only by following the well-tread path . . . , i.e. by walking hand in hand with German Central Europe." In Szekfű's view of the 1920s, this was "one of the clear-cut teachings of our [Hungarian] history," that cannot be disregarded without perils and misfortunes to the nation as a whole.[46]

Contrary to many Hungarian historians who held anti-Habsburg views, Szekfű believed that Habsburg-Hungarian relations represented simply the unavoidable common destiny of Germandom and the Hungarian nation. He was so convinced of the benefits of this common destiny that he even bemoaned Hungary's newly won independence that followed World War I. As he put it: "Those of us who amidst the nerve-wracking fever of our collapse were able to preserve our sense of history . . . , were also forced to recognize . . . that our suddenly gained freedom is only the freedom . . . of a hungry winter wolf. Having been freed from the clutches of Central Europe, we stood there alone and friendless. . . . We were a free but also a bloodied and a despoiled small nation. . . . A free prey, free to be robbed, looted and destroyed by anyone who happened to be stronger." Then, as if to drive his point home, Szekfű finished his assessment by pointing to the harsh consequences of this freedom from Central Europe: "And the 'stronger ones' did come . . . , and the borders of our free nation became ever more constricted. . . . Thus did Hungary, freed from its dependence on Central Europe . . . , shrink back by centuries within the span of a few days. As if, together with the war, we also lost our millennial history."[47]

Although anti-Habsburgism continued to pervade a sizable segment of Hungary's educated circles, Szekfű's above analysis of Hungary's dependence on Germanic Central Europe was soon widely accepted. It became one of the important dogmas of interwar Hungarian historical thinking, and then took its place alongside the already discussed emphasis upon the unique historical role and destiny of the Hungarians in the Carpathian Basin.

While appealing in themselves to the dejected Hungarian mind of the early post-Trianon period, these views could not have been made into the dogmas of Hungarian historical thinking without Szekfű's influential multivolumed *Hungarian History* (1928–1934) that he coauthored with Bálint Hóman.[48] This work popularized Szekfű's views—some of them derived from other "Trianon books" by fellow historians—on such a mass scale that they soon came to form the cornerstones of interwar Hungarian historiography. These views penetrated and saturated the works of most professional historians, and then the writings of most popularizers as well. This was true, even though during the 1920s and the early 1930s Szekfű's views fell increasingly under the scrutiny and criticism of a number of the old "National Romantic" historians (e.g. István Rugonfalvi-Kiss, Jenő Csuday, Jenő Zoványi, etc.);[49] while during the late 1930s and early

1940s they were being questioned and attacked by some of the prominent spokesmen of the so-called Populist Movement in Hungary[50] (e.g. Dezső Szabó, László Németh, and the leaders of various youth movements, both in Trianon Hungary and in the lost territories).[51] The latter generally rejected past and future associations with Germanic Central Europe—at least as interpreted by Szekfű—and sought some sort of accomodation with the small peoples of East Central and Southeastern Europe. But as the National Romantics' influence in the profession was very limited, and as the Populists were primarily poets, novelists and publicists who were not taken seriously by professional historians, Szekfű's and his followers' views continued to dominate Hungarian historical thinking right up to 1945, and, to some degree, even beyond.

While the emphasis on the Hungarians' historical rights and destiny in the Carpathian Basin and their overriding desire to remain part of Central Europe became the dominant features of interwar Hungarian historical thinking, Hungarian historians and the whole profession concentrated increasingly on the nationality question, which was rightfully regarded as the primary cause of historic Hungary's dismemberment. This became evident in the Klebelsberg-initiated source publications, among others, especially in the *Fontes* series—a sizable portion of the forty-four volumes published during the interwar years dealt either directly or indirectly with the nationality question and with the development of Hungarian national consciousness.[52]

One of the most important of these volumes was Szekfű's own *Iratok a magyar államnyelv kérdésének történetéhez, 1790–1848* [Documents Concerning the History of the Question of Hungarian State Language, 1790–1848] (1926),[53] which, introduced by a 200-page analytical study, is still viewed today as "one of the most significant works on the history of Hungarian national consciousness."[54] Some of the other related significant works included Gyula Miskolczy's two-volume *The Croatian Question: Its History and Documents in the Age of the Feudal State* (1927–1928), József Thim's three-volume *The History of the Serbian Uprising in Hungary in 1848–1849* (1930–1940), Lajos Steier's two-volume *The Slovak Nationality Question in 1848–1849* (1937),[55] as well as various memoires, diaries, letters and other papers of a number of prominent national leaders whose life and activities were intertwined with the development of nationalism in 19th-century Hungary.[56] The publication of these documents gave a new impetus to the study of nationalism and the whole nationality question in interwar Hungary, and at the same time elevated this study to a far more scholarly level than the polemic political literature that preceded it.

However significant, the publication of the *Fontes* volumes, with their predilection for the nationality question, was only one of several similar undertakings in interwar Hungarian historiography. Much attention was also given to a question that had already been touched by some of the early Trianon-pamphlets, namely: who settled first in the Carpathian Basin? This became a particularly acute historical question in view of the Hungarian-Romanian dispute over Transylvania. Like contemporary Western scholars, Hungarian historians rejected outright the Romanian theory of Daco-Roman-Romanian continuity, and devoted much of their efforts to demonstrating the untenability of these views, which they perceived as being purely politically inspired.[57] But in addition to disproving the Daco-Roman origins of the Romanians, Hungarian scholars also paid considerable attention to the question of the origins of the Hungarian speaking Székelys (Szeklers) of Eastern Transylvania. Although unable to arrive at a scholarly concensus on their origins, most of them viewed the Székelys as Transylvania's "autochtonous" population—the descendants of the related Huns or Avars or both[58]—whose settlement in that province preceded by centuries the presence of the Vlach ancestors of the Romanians. With a very few exceptions (e.g. László Erdélyi, who was generally thought to be eccentric in most of his views),[59] all interwar Hungarian historians prescribed to the view that their own (and their related predecessors') ancestors were the first continued settlers in the Carpathian Basin. This enforced their historical claims to the area—which they believed to be significant in their struggle against Trianon—and also strengthened their national pride.

Dealing with these and similar topics was certainly not an unworthy or unscholarly occupation. But given the general tendencies in Western historical studies toward new approaches (e.g. the sociologically oriented *Annales* School in France, Toynbee's civilizational approach, etc.), these Trianon-inspired undertakings certainly occupied a far greater portion of the Hungarian historians' time and talents than normal circumstances would have warranted. This did not, of course, mean that interwar Hungarian historiography was devoid of all innovations; the fact that it wasn't is best demonstrated by references of Szekfű's *Geistesgeschichte*, Domanovszky's *Kulturgeschichte*, Mályusz's Ethnohistory, and Hajnal's new Universal History Schools.[60] But given their preoccupation with Trianon, the results of their efforts were less, or at least different, than could have been without the burdens of this national tragedy and the resulting national and personal traumas.

The attention given to the above discussed Trianon-inspired topics in Hungarian historical research was parallelled after Trianon by the historians' switch of emphasis from the state to the nation—a phenomenon that was also an important component of Klebelsberg's ideology of Neo-Nationalism. Although increasingly widespread among historians, this tendency came to be expressed on the highest scholarly level in the new Hungarian Ethnohistory School founded by Elemér Mályusz (1898–   ), which can also be viewed as the Hungarian manifestation of the German *Volkstumkunde*, combined with the early influences of Marc Bloch's and Lucien Febvre's sociologically oriented *Annales* School in France. It was this school that introduced the serious study of settlement history in Hungary, while at the same time emphasizing the unique role of the Hungarian "folk spirit" as a driving force behind Hungarian creativity, and thus behind the progress of Hungarian history.[61]

Notwithstanding contemporary political pressures, Mályusz's Ethnohistory School always remained on a strict and high scholarly level, and it had much to offer to interwar Hungarian historiography. Even so, however, the fact that it did become a relatively viable orientation in contemporary Hungarian historical studies was due less to its innate scholarly value, than to its basic tendency to transcend the artificially created political frontiers and thus serve as a scholarly instrument for the study of the ethnic and cultural development of the Hungarian nation without regard to the artificially established political barriers. Moreover, Ethnohistory's emphasis upon the role of the "national or ethnic spirit," as opposed to the role of the "universal spirit" of Szekfű's *Geistesgeschichte* School, also made it more soothing to the battered Hungarian national soul that needed such intellectual medicaments to regain its will to live. For this reason, the Ethnohistory School can also be viewed as a partial by-product of Trianon, or at least as an orientation that suited the nation's post-Trianon needs, and therefore was able to ride on the waves that were produced by the explosion that tore historic Hungary to five different parts.

*   *   *

Interwar Hungarian historiography was under the influence of Trianon throughout the whole period, although its reaction to this national calamity was not the same in the 1920s as it was in the 1930s and early 1940s.

At the beginning the reaction of historians was emotional and somewhat haphazard. Moreover, it was mixed with elements of disbelief, and a kind of uncertain conviction that the harsh terms of Trianon cannot possibly become lasting or permanent. Later, when the hope for a quick return to normalcy faded, historians calmed down and began to organize a more systematic attack against the post-Trianon realities. In line with their goals they redoubled their efforts in the study of certain historical questions (e.g. the settlement of the Carpathian Basin, the origins of the various nationalities in Hungary, etc.), because they felt that the undoing of Trianon depended to a large degree on the appropriate and correct marshalling of historical arguments. Although the inadequacy of their approach should have become rapidly evident, most of them retained their faith in historical arguments throughout the whole period. This was perhaps their most important shortcoming; or at least the shortcoming that preoccupied most of their energies without any real hope of success. Apparently, interwar Hungarian historians were so assured of the significance of historical arguments in deciding current events that they were unable to accept the fact that historical truth or past historical realities carry very little weight in the 20th century.

Nevertheless, interwar Hungarian historiography did register some improvements in a number of areas; and some of these can be attributed directly to Trianon. Not the least of these were Klebelsberg's activities that gave a meaningful impetus to Hungarian historical research, and did so on a high scholarly level. But of at least equal importance were some of the above-mentioned new orientations in Hungarian historical studies, all of which owed at least part of their origin and inspiration to the impact of Trianon upon the Hungarian mind. It should perhaps also be pointed out that by the late 1930s and early 1940s, many Hungarian historians were becoming more realistic about their nation's chances—or rather, lack of chances—for total revision. Moreover, a growing number of them were increasingly alienated by Hitlerite Germany and its heavy-handed involvement in Hungarian and Danubian politics. Thus, driven also by the earlier clarion calls of some of the populist intellectuals, they began to turn more and more toward the idea of some sort of a compromise and cooperation with a number of their lesser neighbors. One of their dreams was partial revision within the context of a resurrected Danubian Confederation that was to have taken the place of the new defunct Habsburg state. This relatively healthy trend was halted only by World War II and by the rise of new national confrontations in the Danubian region. Underneath these confrontations, however, the work of more objective scholars and historians continued almost unabated.

Notes

1. Freeman's exact words were: "History is past politics and politics are present history." Cf. The Encyclopaedia Britannica, 11th ed. (1910), XI, 76–77.

2. This is most evident in current Romanian historiography and its emphasis upon the theory of Daco-Roman-Romanian continuity, which has become a national dogma enforced by the country's political regime. This is examplified among others, by the recent official commemoration of the 2050th anniversary of the alleged foundation of the Romanian State that was in evidence also at the Fifteenth International Congress of Historical Sciences in Bucharest (August 10–17, 1980). For recent assessments on the scholarly value of this theory see M. Dinić, "The Balkans," The Cambridge Medieval History, new ed. (Cambridge: The Cambridge University Press, 1966), VI, 519–565; Aldo Dami, La controverse de la continuité daco-roumaine. Reprinted from Humanitas Ethnica. Ethnos 5 (Wien-Stuttgart: W. Braumüller, 1967); André du Nay, The Early History of the Rumanian Language (Lake Bluff, Ill.: Jupiter Press, 1977).

3. See S. B. Vardy, Modern Hungarian Historiography (Boulder and New York: The East European Quarterly and Columbia University Press, 1976), pp. 32–33; Thomas L. Szendrey, The Ideological and Methodological Foundations of Hungarian Historiography, 1750–1970 (Ph.D. dissertation, St. John's University, Jamaica, New York, 1972), pp. 96–100; and Louis J. Lékai, "Historiography in Hungary, 1790–1848," Journal of Central European Affairs, XIV, 1 (April 1954), pp. 3–18.

4. Ferenc Glatz, Történetíró és politika. Szekfu, Steier, Thim és Miskolczy nemzetröl és államról [The Historian and Politics. Szekfű, Steier, Thim and Miskolczy on the Nature of the State and the Nation] (Budapest: Akadémiai Kiadó, 1980), pp. 15–25. This chapter of Glatz's book had first appeared in a slightly altered form under the title: "Trianon és a magyar

történettudomány" [Trianon and Hungarian historical Sciences], *Történelmi Szemle*, XXI, 2 (1978), pp. 411–421.

5. On Gyula Szekfű and the *Geistesgeschichte* School see Vardy, *Modern Hungarian Historiography*, pp. 62–101; idem, *Hungarian Historiography and the Geistesgeschichte School* (Cleveland: Arpad Academy, 1974); József Szigeti, *A magyar szellemtörténet bírálatához* [A Critique of Hungarian *Geistesgeschichte*] (Budapest: Kossuth Könyvkiadó, 1964); Borbála H. Lukács, *Szellemtörténet és irodalomtudomány* [*Geistesgeschichte* and Literary Scholarship] (Budapest: Akadémiai Kiadó, 1971).

6. Gyula Szekfű, *Három nemzedék. Egy hanyatló kor története* [Three Generations: The History of a Declining Age] (Budapest: Élet Irodalmi és Nyomdai R.T., 1920), p. 4.

7. On this strange phenomenon in the interwar period see Gyula Szekfű, *Három nemzedék és ami utána következik* [Three Generations and What Follows] (Budapest: Királyi Magyar Egyetemi Nyomda, 1934), pp. 480–492; Joseph A. Kessler, *Turanism and Pan-Turanism in Hungary, 1890–1945* (Ph.D. Dissertation; University of California, Berkeley, 1967); S. B. Vardy, *The Ottoman Empire in European Historiography: A Re-Evaluation by Sándor Takáts* (Pittsburgh: Duquesne University Studies in History, 1976), reprinted from *Turkish Review*, II, 9 (1972), pp. 1–16; and idem, *The Image of the Turks in Twentieth-Century Hungarian Historiography* (Pittsburgh: Duquesne University Studies in History, 1980), final version to appear in the proceedings of the Fourth International Congress of Southeast European Studies, August 13–18, 1979, Ankara, Turkey.

8. The two works in question are: Oszkár Jászi, *Magyar Kálvária—magyar feltámadás* (Hungarian Calvary—Hungarian Resurrection) (Vienna, 1920); and Hugó Ignotus, *The Dismemberment of Hungary. Written Especially for American Readers* (Berlin, 1920).

9. Glatz, *Történetíró és politika*, pp. 17–18.

10. See for example László Buza, "A magyar szent korona igényei a volt mellékországokra" [The Hungarian Holy Crown's Claim to the Former Associated Provinces], *Budapesti Szemle*, CLXVII (1916), pp. 397–429; István Györffy, "Magyarország régi balkáni birtokai" [Hungary's Former Balkan Possessions], *Földrajzi Közlemények* LV (1916), pp. 19–37; Stefan Hollósy, "Die Ungarn und die Geschichte Osteuropas," *Kelet Népe*, nos. 7–8 (1916) pp. 63–67; János Karácsonyi's work discussed below.

11. Concerning Hungary's losses as a result of Trianon see C. A. Macartney, *Hungary and Her Successors: The Treaty of Trianon and Its Consequences* (Oxford: Oxford University Press, 1937); and Ladislas Buday, *Dismembered Hungary* (London: Grant Richards Ltd., 1922).

12. Dávid Angyal, *A Magyar Tudományos Akadémia válasza a cseh akadémiának* [The Reply of the Hungarian Academy of Sciences to the

Czech Academy] (Budapest: Hornyánszky, 1920), reprinted from *Akadémiai Értesítö*.

13. On these historians see Vardy, *Modern Hungarian Historiography*, pp. 34-42, 122-127, 139-144; *idem*, "Antal Hodinka," *Hungarian Historical Review* (Buenos Aires), III, 2 (June 1972), pp. 266-274; *idem*, "The Social and Ideological Make-up of Hungarian Historiography in the Age of Dualism, 1867-1918," *Jahrbücher für Geschichte Osteuropas*, Neue Folge, XXIV, 2 (1976), pp. 208-217.

14. József Holub, *La Hongrie. Cartes et nations geographiques, historiques, ethnographique, economiques et intellectuelles* (Budapest, 1918).

15. *Pro Hungaria. Magyarország igazsága. Szózat a békekonferenciához* [For Hungary. Hungary's Justice. An Appeal to the Peace Conference] (Pozsony, 1918).

16. István Rugonfalvi Kiss, *A Debreceni Magyar Tudományegyetem szózata a müvelt világ egyetemeihez* [An Appeal of the Hungarian University of Debrecen to the Universities of the Civilized World] (Debrecen, 1918).

17. On these early "Trianon pamphlets" see also Glatz, *Történtíró és politika*, pp. 15-16.

18. János Karácsonyi, *A magyar nemzet történeti joga hazánk területéhez a Kárpátoktól le az Adriáig* [The Historical Right of the Hungarian Nation to the Territory of our Fatherland from the Carpathians down to the Adriatic Sea] (Nagyvárad: Szent László Nyomda, 1916).

19. Arnold Toynbee, *The Nationality and the War* (London, 1915). Toynbee's work was immediately reviewed by Albert Gárdonyi in the *Századok*, LI, 1 (January 1917), pp. 77-79.

20. Toynbee may have been motivated by his intense Philhellenims and his consequent Turkophobia, which he projected over all of the Central Powers.

21. Quoted by Imre Lukinich in his review of Karácsonyi's work in the *Századok*, LI, 1 (January 1917), pp. 61-65. For a more recent, but much too critical treatment of Karácsonyi's work see Mátyás Unger, *A történelmi tudat alakulása középiskolai történelemtankönyveinkben* [The Development of Historical Consciousness in our History Textbooks for Secondary Schools] (Budapest: Tankönyvkiadó, 1976), pp. 93-95.

22. John Karácsonyi, *The Historical Right of the Hungarian Nation to its Territorial Integrity* (Budapest: Hungarian Territorial Integrity League, 1920).

23. János Karácsonyi, *Történelmi jogunk hazánk területi épségéhez* [Our Historical Right to Our Country's Territorial Integrity] (Budapest: Szent István Társulat, 1921).

24. *Ibid.*, pp. 4-6.

25. These include pamphlets by the Hungarian Territorial Integrity League, published in English, French, Italian and German, as well as an "East

European Problems" series, published simultaneously in London (Low, W. Dawson & Sons), New York (Steiger & Company) and Budapest (Ferdinand Pfeifer). For some of these publications see the bibliographies of the following two works: Count Teleki, *The Evolution of Hungary and its Place in European History* (New York: The Macmillan Company, 1923), pp. 245–312; *La Hongrie dans les relations internationales* (Budapest: Édition de l'Association Hongroise des Affaires Étrangéres pour la Société des Nations, 1935), pp. 354–383.

26. Béla Iványi, *Pro Hungaria Superiore. Felsömagyarországért* [For Upper Hungary] (Debrecen: Debreceni Sz. Kir. Város és a Tiszántúli Ref. Egyházkerület Könyvnyomda Vállalata, 1919). On Iványi see Vardy, *Modern Hungarian Historiography*, pp. 192–193.

27. See for example Wilhelm Fraknói, *Die ungarische Regierung und die Entstehung des Weltkrieges* (Wien, 1919); Dávid Angyal, *Magyarország felelösége a világháborúért* [Hungary's Responsibility for the World War] (Budapest, 1923); Eugene [Jenö] Horváth, *Hungary and Servia: The Fate of Southern Hungary* (Budapest: Hungarian Territorial Integrity League, 1919); idem, *Magyarország felelösége a háborúért* [Hungary's Responsibility for the War] (Budapest, 1926); idem, *A trianoni béke megalkotása* [The Formulation of the Peace Treaty of Trianon] (Budapest, 1924); Horváth's major summary of this whole problem, *A magyar kérdés a XX. században* [The Hungarian Question in the 20th Century], 2 vols. (Budapest: Magyar Tudományos Akadémia, 1939). The two volumes are entitled respectively: *Felelöség a világháborúért és a békeszerzödésekért* [Responsibility for the World War and for the Peace Treaties], and *A trianoni békeszerzödés és a revízió útja* [The Peace Treaty of Trianon and the Path Toward its Revision]. See also Horváth's debate with R. W. Seton-Watson concerning Transylvania: *Transylvania and the History of the Rumanians: A Reply to Professor R. W. Seton-Watson* (Budapest: Sárkány Printing Company, Ltd., 1935). On the above historians see Vardy, *Modern Hungarian Historiography*, pp. 37–53, 139–140, 198–199; Glatz, *Történetíró és politika*, pp. 162–168; Ágnes R. Várkonyi, *A pozitivista Történetszemlélet a magyar történetírásban* [The Positivist View of History in Hungarian Historiography], 2 vols. (Budapest: Akadémiai Kiadó, 1973), I, 217–245.

28. Henrik Marczali, *A béke könyve. A mult tanulsága* [The Book of Peace. Lessons from the Past] (Budapest: Athenaeum, 1920).

29. *Ibid.*, pp. 190, 194. The reference is to Louis Eisenmann, *Le compromis austro-hongrois de 1867. Étude sur le dualisme* (Paris: Société Nouvelle de Libraire et d'Édition, 1904), p. 555.

30. On Domanovszky and the Hungarian *Kulturgeschichte* School see S. B. Vardy "The Birth of the Hungarian *Kulturgeschichte* School," in *Tractata altaica: Denis Sinor Sexagenario optime de rebus altaicis merito dedicata*, eds. W. Heissig, J. R. Krueger, E. J. Oinas, E. Schütz (Wiesbaden: Otto

Harrassowitz, 1976), pp. 675–693, reprinted in *Duquesne University Studies in History* (Pittsburgh, 1976); *idem, Modern Hungarian Historiography*, pp. 161–174; Ferenc Glatz, "Domanovszky Sándor helye a magyar történettudományban" [Sándor Domanovszky's Place in Hungarian Historical Sciences], *Századok*, CXII (1978), pp. 211–234.

31. Sándor Domanovszky, *A magyar kérdés történeti szempontból tekintve* [The Hungarian Questions from a Historical Perspective] (Budapest: Magyarország Területi Egységének Védelmi Ligája, 1920).

32. See also Imre Lukinich's review of Domanovszky's volume in the *Századok*, LV–LVI (1921–1922), pp. 100–101.

33. Alexander Domanovszky, *Die Geschichte Ungarns* (München-Leipzig, 1923). See also his critique of the methods of the Romanian historian Nicolae Iorga: *La méthode historique de M. Nicolas Iorga (A propos du compte rendù)* (Budapest: Université Royale Hongroise, 1938).

34. Bálint Hóman, *A magyarság megtelepülése* [The Settlement of the Hungarians] (Budapest: Szabad Lyceum Kiadványai, 1920), reprinted in Hóman's *Magyar középkor* [Hungarian Middle Ages] (Budapest: Magyar Történelmi Társulat, 1938), pp. 111–127.

35. Bálint Hóman, *A honfoglaló törzsek megtelepedése* [The Settlement of the Conquering Tribes] (Budapest, 1912), reprinted in Hóman's *Magyar középkor*, pp. 63–109.

36. Hóman, *Magyar középkor*, p. 127. Hóman also treated this question in a later study entitled *A magyarok honfoglalása és elhelyezkedése* [The Conquest and the Settlement of the Hungarians] (Budapest: A Magyar Tudományos Akadémia, 1923), reprinted in Hóman's *Magyar Középkor*, pp. 129–189.

37. For a general assessment of Hóman as a historian see László Tóth, *Hóman Bálint a történetíró* [Bálint Hóman, the Historian] (Pécs: Dunántúli Pécsi Egyetemi Könyvkiadó, 1939); Szendrey, *The Ideological*, pp. 319–323, 338–345; Vardy, *Modern Hungarian Historiography*, pp. 79–94.

38. The first Marxist scholar to reassess Klebelsberg's interwar role and to put him into a favorable light was Ferenc Glatz in his study "Historiography, Cultural Policy, and the Organization of Scholarship in Hungary in the 1920's," *Acta Historica Academiae Scientiarum Hungaricae*, XVI (1970), pp. 273–293, which is a somewhat abbreviated version of his "Klebelsberg tudománypolitikai programja és a magyar történettudomány" [Klebelsberg's Program on Scientific Policy and the Hungarian Historical Sciences], *Századok*, CIII (1969), pp. 1176–1200. See also Vardy, *Modern Hungarian Historiography*, pp. 50–61; Szendrey, *The Ideological*, pp. 307–309; and Glatz, *Történetíró és politika*, pp. 20–21.

39. For Klebelsberg's program proposals see his presidential speeches before the Hungarian Historical Association in the appropriate issues of the *Századok*. His most significant speeches between 1917 and 1926 were

reprinted in his *Gróf Klebelsberg Kuno beszédei, cikkei és törvényjavaslatai, 1916-1926* [Count Kuno Klebelsberg's Speeches, Studies, and Parliamentary Bills, 1916-1926] (Budapest: Atheneaum, 1927), pp. 3-73.

40. See Iván Nagy, *Bécs és a magyar tudományosság* [Viennna and Hungarian Scholarly Research] (Budapest, 1928). See also the Institute's yearbooks, which appeared under the title *A Gróf Klebelsberg Kuno Magyar Történetkutató Intézet Évkönyve* [Yearbook of the Count Kuno Klebelsberg Hungarian Historical Research Institute], ed. Dávid Angyal (1931-1935) and Gyula Miskolczy (1936-1941) (Budapest, 1931-1941).

41. On the *Fontes* Series see note 52.

42. On Klebelsberg's neo-nationalism see his own *Neónacionalizmus* (Budapest, 1928). See also Sándor Balogh, "A bethleni konszolidáció és a magyar neónacionalizmus" [The Bethlen Consolidation and Hungarian Neo-Nationalism], *Történelmi Szemle*, V (1962), pp. 426-448; Mihály Mák, "A Magyar neónacionalizmus és terjesztésének főbb módszerei az ellenforradalmi rendszer idején" [The Chief Methods of the Propagation of Hungarian Neo-Nationalism in the Age of the Counterrevolutionary Regime], *Pedagógiai Szemle*, XIII (1963), pp. 441-451; and Vardy, *Modern Hungarian Historiography*, pp. 50-51.

43. For a list of these textbooks see Unger, *A történelmi tudat*, pp. 334-336.

44. On the influence of neo-nationalism in Hungarian history textbooks see *ibid.*, pp. 87-196.

45. Gyula Szekfű, *A magyar állam életrajza* [The Biography of the Hungarian State] (Budapest: Dick Manó Könyvkereskedése, 1917). See also its German version: Julius Szekfű, *Der Staat Ungarn. Eine Geschichtsstudie* (Stuttgart-Berlin: Deutsche Verlags-Anstalt, 1918).

46. Gyula Szekfű, *A magyar állam életrajza*, 2nd ed. (Budapest: Dick Manó Könyvkereskedése, 1923), p. 222.

47. *Ibid.*, pp. 204-205.

48. Bálint Hóman and Gyula Szekfű, *Magyar történet* [Hungarian History], 8 vols. (Budapest: Magyar Királyi Egyetemi Nyomda, 1928-1934).

49. See Vardy, *Modern Hungarian Historiography*, pp. 121-128.

50. *Ibid.*, pp. 129-135.

51. The reference here is primarily to the "Sarló" (Scythe) Movement in former Upper Hungary (Slovakia) and to the "Erdélyi Fiatalok" (Transylvanian Youth) Movement in Romania.

52. For a complete list of the *Fontes* Series and the related *A magyar történettudomány kézikönyve* [The Handbook of Hungarian Historical Sciences], ed. Bálint Hóman (Budapest: Magyar Történelmi Társulat, 1923-1934); see Vardy, *Modern Hungarian Historiography*, pp. 305-309.

53. Gyula Szekfű, *Iratok a magyar államnyelv kérdésének történetéhez, 1790-1848* [Documents Concerning the History of the Question of Magyar

State Language, 1790–1848] (Budapest: Magyar Történelmi Társulat, 1926).

54. Glatz, *Történetíró és politika*, p. 21.

55. Gyula Miskolczy, *A horvát kérdés története és irományai a rendi állam korában* [The Croatian Question. Its History and Documents in the Age of the Feudal State] 2 vols. (Budapest: Magyar Történelmi Társulat, 1927–1928); József Thim, *A magyarországi 1848–49-iki szerb fölkelés története* [The History of the Serbian Uprising in Hungary in 1848–1849] 3 vols. (Budapest: Magyar Történelmi Társulat, 1930–1940); Lajos Steier, *A tót nemzetiségi kérdés 1948–49-ben* [The Slovak Nationality Question in 1848–1849] 2 vols. (Budapest: Magyar Történelmi Társulat, 1937). For a detailed analysis of these works and the views of their authors see Glatz, *Történetíró és politika*, pp. 26–86.

56. See Vardy, *Modern Hungarian Historiography*, pp. 55–58, 305–307.

57. See the works mentioned in note 2, as well as the references listed in respective bibliographies of these titles.

58. Studies on the Huns and on their real or alleged relationship to the Magyars abounded during the interwar period. One of the most scholarly compendiums is *Attila és hunjai* [Attila and his Huns], ed. Gyula Németh (Budapest: Magyar Szemle Társaság, 1940), which was coauthored by half a dozen top scholars, who summarized the generally accepted views on this question. For another significant work that puts much greater emphasis on Magyar-Hun relationship see Béla Szász, *A hunok története. Attila nagykirály* [The History of the Huns. Attila, the Great King] (Budapest: Bartha Miklós Társaság, 1943). This huge volume was intended to be only the first of a projected four-volume work on the Huns and their descendants.

59. On Erdélyi see Vardy, *Modern Hungarian Historiography*, pp. 41–43; *idem*, "Hungarian *Kulturgeschichte* School," pp. 682–685; *idem*, "The Hungarian Economic History School," *Journal of European Economic History*, IV, 1 (Spring 1975), pp. 121–136, with particular attention to pp. 129–130. On Erdélyi's views concerning the origin of the Székelys see his *A tizenkét legkritikusabb kérdés* [The Twelve Most Critical Questions] (Kolozsvár: Szent István Társulat, 1918); *idem*, *A székelyek története* [The History of the Székelys] (Brassó: Erdélyi Naptár Kiadása, 1921); and *idem*, "A székelyeredetkérdés megoldásának sarkpontjai" [Cornerstones of the Solution of the Origins of the Székelys], *Akadémiai Értesítö*, XXXIII (1922), pp. 205–214. The last study was in response to one of Bálint Hóman's studies, *A székelyek eredete* [The Origins of the Székelys] (Budapest: Szabad Lyceum Kiadványai, 1920–1921), which also appeared in German: *Der Ursprung der Siebenbürger Szekler* (Berlin, 1922), reprinted from the *Ungarische Jahrbücher*. For Hóman's response to Erdélyi's attack see Hóman's "Székely eredetkérdéshez" [Concerning the Origins of the Székelys], *Akadémiai Értesítö*, XXXIV (1923), pp. 405–408, reprinted in Hóman, *Magyar középkor*, pp. 61–62.

60. On these historical schools see Vardy, *Modern Hungarian Historiography*, pp. 62–94, 102–120, 161–174, 196–204.

61. *Ibid.*, pp. 102–120; Vardy, "A magyar népiségtörténet atyja, a nyolcvanéves Mályusz Elemér" [The Father of Hungarian Ethnohistory School, the Eighty Year Old Elemér Mályusz], *Új Látóhatár*, XXIX, 3 (1978), pp. 232–237. For a list of Mályusz's publications see *Album Elemér Mályusz* (Burxelles: Les Éditions de la Librarie Encyclopédique, 1976), pp. x111–xx1; István Soós, "Mályusz Elemér müveinek bibliográfiája" [A List of Elemér Mályusz's Works], *Történelmi Szemle*, XXI, 3–4 (1978), pp. 609–621.

Lee Congdon

Trianon and the Emigré Intellectuals

Huddled in rented rooms in Berlin's *Kaiserdamm*, the emigré writer Gyula Háy spoke often to his wife about their homeland's "unfitness for survival as crippled by the Treaty of Trianon—a subject to which every Hungarian inevitably found himself returning over and over again at various levels during those [interwar] years."[1] For Háy and other Hungarian intellectuals living in exile, Trianon presented a dilemma. Although they despised the Horthy government and feared that its obsession with *revanche* might reignite the flames of war, they could not accept with equanimity the terms of the dictated peace. How might treaty revision be effected without having to make common cause with the leaders of "Christian-National'" Hungary? That was the question with which emigrés of every left-wing political persuasion had to wrestle. Refusing to be impaled on either horn of the dilemma, they reformulated the question within a broader East Central European context. What manner of general settlement, they preferred to ask, would satisfy the legitimate claims of all the peoples concerned? With few exceptions, they proposed a Danubian Confederation that would disarm Trianon and necessitate a change of government in Budapest.

* * *

It was Oszkár Jászi who, during the Great War, had resurrected Lajos Kossuth's post-1848 plan for an East Central European Confederation. As Minister of Nationalities in Mihály Károlyi's short-lived government, he had, however, been unsuccessful in his attempts to prevent the non-Hungarian peoples of Hungary from deserting a sinking political ship. After he left Hungary for Vienna in the wake of Béla Kun's assumption of power, Jászi again became the leading spokesman for the confederative plan. But whereas he had formerly addressed his recommendations to Hungary's political leaders, he had now to appeal to the representatives of foreign states. Having learned that the victorious Allies—in particular the French —refused to differentiate between Károlyi and István Tisza,

Hungary's redoubtable pre-war leader, Jászi initially placed his hopes in the successor states, especially Czechoslovakia and Yugoslavia. He adopted, that is, a "Little Entente orientation."

This decision entailed great personal risks, for it exposed Jászi to the charge of treasonable disloyalty to his country. Even some of his friends were uneasy; whatever the régime in Hungary, János Hock preferred its leaders to those who had not scrupled to appropriate Hungarian territory. And in reaction to Jászi's efforts to persuade the Yugoslavs not to return Pécs-Baranya to Horthy's Hungary,[2] Arnold Dániel wrote to his old friend: "On first impression, I regard the entire undertaking as a calamitous idea. One cannot conduct Hungarian politics supported by the greatest enemies of Hungarian concerns."[3] Only recently, Gyula Illyés, one of Hungary's most distinguished men of letters, has taken Jászi to task for allowing himself to be deceived and used by the Little Entente.[4]

Although these criticisms are not without some foundation, Jászi could not envision a viable alternative to a Little Entente orientation. It is true that neither Romania nor Yugoslavia had evinced much interest in a Danubian Confederation, but Jászi knew that the territories lost to Yugoslavia were not for the new state matters of life or death. He knew too that the Serbian intelligentsia tended to be pro-Hungarian if only because it was anti-Croatian.[5] More important, Jászi, Károlyi, and Pál Szende were convinced that Hungary's neighbors, especially the Czechs, would be unwilling to reach a modus vivendi with a right-wing, revisionist Hungarian regime.[6] All the more so because Czechoslovak President Tomáš Masaryk shared many of their sympathies and ideas with respect to social and national questions. In conversations with Károlyi, Masaryk had even expressed interest in the idea of a Danubian Confederation.[7]

The Little Entente orientation was given literary expression by the emigré journal *Tüz* (Fire or Fervor). Edited by Jenö Gömöri, *Tüz* was published first in Pozsony (Bratislava) and later in Vienna. In an effort to enlist the journal in the service of Hungarian-Czechoslovak rapprochement, Gömöri published numerous translations of the work of Czech and Slovak writers.[8] In his programmatic essay,[9] he denied that peace was or even could have been concluded at St. Germain, Trianon, or Neuilly; true peace could be won only with the aid of culture. *Tüz's* purpose, therefore, was to lay the cultural basis for a "United States of Central Europe." This was to be accomplished by building a cultural community first with the Czechs and Slovaks, and later with the Romanians, Serbs, and Croats. Having taken a first step, Gömöri called upon the Czechs and Slovaks to respond in the same spirit of reconciliation.

Despite or perhaps because of the emigrés' expectations, disillusion was not long in coming. The efforts of Béla Linder, mayor of Pécs notwithstanding, the Yugoslav government, under pressure from the Allies, ordered the evacuation of Baranya in August 1921. The preceding fall, Károlyi had been expelled from Czechoslovakia "in friendly fashion," apparently because of Eduard Beneš's suspicions concerning his contacts with the far left, especially with the Czech socialist leader Bohumir Šmeral, who preferred a "United Socialist Europe" to an independent Czechoslovakia.[10] In a letter of 21 March 1922, Jászi told Károlyi that Beneš did not see any "essential difference between Horthy's and the emigration's foreign policy, because he believes that if the emigration returns home, it will not be able to pursue any but a policy of [territorial] integrity."[11] In the same sober mood, Pál Szende observed in 1922 that there were in the successor states politicians and economic groups who sympathized with the Horthy government's methods, particularly vis à vis the working class. "One could say that the Horthy regime owes its existence to the open sympathy of the Entente and the secret sympathy of influential politicians in the successor states."[12]

Finally, and perhaps most important, Jászi could not but observe that the Little Entente countries had failed to keep their promises with regard to the Hungarian minorities living within their frontiers. Already in a 1920 issue of the *Bécsi Magyar Újság* (Hungarian News of Vienna), he had put himself on public record:

The Hungarian democracy can renounce *revanche*, but under no circumstances can it renounce demanding for its separated brethren all of those rights and freedoms that it demanded for the national minorities during the time of Hungarian hegemony.[13]

A year later, he thought it necessary to publish an open letter to General Alexandru Averescu, Minister President of Romania, asking that he ensure the free development of Romania's national minorities.[14]

But although Jászi and his friends came to expect less and less of the Little Entente countries, they continued to believe that the emigration had no choice but to maintain a Western, democratic orientation.[15] With the regularization of the government in Hungary under István Bethlen's able leadership and the failure of the Little Entente orientation, the only avenue left open to Jászi and others of a democratic persuasion was that of informing public opinion in the West concerning Hungary. "In the eyes of Jászi and Co.," the historian Elemér Mályusz wrote in his often scurrilous attack on the emigration, "Western public opinion became a panacea for all ills and the source from which a favourable change of fortune was to come."[16]

Influencing Western opinion was, however, a large order, because few Westerners knew anything about East Central Europe in general, much less about Hungary in particular. The first task, then, was to set contemporary events in historical perspective, to offer Westerners a short course in Hungarian history—political, social, and intellectual. In this effort, Jászi also led the way, publishing German and English translations of his book on the revolutions of 1918-19—*Magyar kálvária magyar feltámadás* (Hungarian Calvary—Hungarian Resurrection).

In his Preface to the English edition, published in 1924 under the less apocalyptic title *Revolution and Counter-Revolution in Hungary*, Jászi identified Great Britain as the only European power to which Hungarian democrats could turn for help in reconstructing their country. They were therefore particularly alarmed to discover that British opinion was "curiously uninformed as to Central European problems."[17] Only such ignorance could explain British support for the Horthy government. By examining the genesis of the Hungarian catastrophe, he hoped to demonstrate that the creation of a stable *Mitteleuropa* depended upon a recognition of Hungary's pivotal importance. At the same time, he emphasized that he would accept no Danubian settlement, however advantageous to Hungary, that ignored the just claims of the successor states.

Jászi's book—part history, part autobiography, part political tract—remains an indispensable source for the study of the democratic and soviet republics. It constitutes, moreover, a forceful indictment of the White Terror that even men of decency seemed willing to tolerate. But in the end, Jászi was more concerned with the future than with the past; in the final chapter, "The Future of Hungary,"[18] he returned to his favorite theme—a Danubian Confederation. He pointed out that war and *revanche* settled nothing; the dismemberment of Hungary only created new irredenta. "In

round numbers, 5,500,000 souls were liberated from the old irredenta, at the price of plunging 4,500,000 into a new one." He concluded, therefore, that the Central European question did not admit
of a territorial solution. What was required was the establishment of
cultural autonomy within the various political territories; only then
would national frontiers lose all significance.[19]

In one of his footnotes, Jászi wrote disapprovingly of the political-
historical sections of Lajos Hatvany's book *Das verwundete Land*
(1921). And yet if Hatvany—a liberal and a man of means—was less
articulate politically than Jászi, he was every bit as eager to educate
and reawaken the conscience of the Allies, in particular the French.
He dedicated his book not to Wilson ("the betrayer of his peace program"), to Clemenceau ("the evil spirit"), or to Lloyd George ("the
cynical mediator and political broker"), but to the pacifist writer Romain Rolland.[20] In essence, the book is a lament that the pacifist intentions of the Károlyi regime were cynically exploited in order to
destroy Hungary. Out of the slough of disillusionment, Hatvany appealed to Rolland to restore his pacifist faith. After providing readers
with a sympathetic portrait of modern Hungarian culture, Hatvany
bitterly attacked the insensitivity and lack of discrimination shown
by the French military authorities in Hungary. When, for example,
Károlyi spoke of "Hungary" as a Frenchman might speak of
"France," General Franchet d'Esperey objected: "Say the land of the
Magyars!" With this remark, Hatvany wrote, Hungary's millennial
unity was destroyed.[21]

Praising Jászi's wartime plan to grant complete cultural autonomy
to the non-Hungarian nationalities, Hatvany appealed to Rolland
and his countrymen for treaty revision. He cited with admiration a
proclamation issued by German officers that renounced *revanche*
but pleaded for peaceful revision of the Treaty of Versailles.[22] It required little imagination for Hatvany's readers to read "Trianon" for
"Versailles."

After Jászi's and Hatvany's books, the most important emigré appeal to the West was Joseph Diner-Dénes's *La Hongrie: Oligarchie,
Nation, Peuple* (1927). Written in the aftermath of a bizarre attempt
by Hungarian civilian and military leaders to circulate 1.5 billion
bogus French francs and thereby disrupt France's economy,[23] the
book expressed the views of the Paris *Világosság* (Clarity) group of
socialists. Headed by Diner-Dénes, this group included Béla Menczer
and Pál Szende, who made regular trips to Paris from Vienna in

order to lecture to the *Collège libre des sciences sociales*. The members of this group hoped to see István Bethlen's regime replaced by a more responsible conservative government capable of opening negotiations with the successor states. Convinced that Hungary's desire for revision was justified, they enlisted Léon Blum in their cause. In his introduction to *La Hongrie*, Blum pointed out that although Budapest was scarcely more distant from Paris than either Rome or Berlin, Hungary remained an enigma for Frenchmen. Proximate in space, it was yet far distant in time, an anachronism in the modern world.[24]

For his part, Diner-Dénes believed the Treaty of Trianon to have been a grievous wrong, but he insisted that one wrong should not be redressed by another. Rather, he recommended a series of *ad hoc* treaties that would link the neighboring states of Central Europe in a common bond. Ultimately, a pan-Europe might be organized on the basis of a further series of treaties.[25]

Convinced that the Hungarian nobility had failed to take advantage of "the psychological moment [1848] to make of Hungary a Switzerland of the East,"[26] Diner-Dénes deplored the Austro-Hungarian *Ausgleich* of 1867 because he believed that it had given currency to the idea that Central Europe would have to choose between the Hungarians and the Slavs. In place of this false dichotomy, he proposed "a formula of friendship: Magyarism and Slavism,"[27] to be inspired and promoted by France. For the Hungarian people, he concluded, "rapprochement with France has always signified liberty, antipathy for France has always signified servitude."[28]

The Western orientation that Diner-Dénes, Jászi, and Hatvany espoused was not, however, accepted by every emigré group. Indeed, the communists regarded these non-communist emigrés as little better than agents of the Little Entente.[29] Much to Jászi's chagrin, Károlyi himself inclined more and more toward an Eastern (Soviet) orientation. As early as the spring of 1920, the ex-President had informed Jászi that he believed an orientation that was exclusively Western to be impossible, in part because he considered the Western governments to be reactionary, in part because he did not want to rely too much on the Czechs.[30] Even more important, however, was Károlyi's growing conviction that the Central European question—indeed the European question in general—could not be resolved without reference to the emerging great powers—the United States and the Soviet Union. Europe, in his view, would have to align itself with one or the other and because Wilson had sorely disappointed him, he was psychologically disposed to cooperate with Lenin. Hence, despite Jászi's warning that in the end he would have to choose between dictatorship and democracy,[31] Károlyi continued to maintain his contacts with the Hungarian communists in exile.[32]

If, however, the Eastern orientation began to disturb the Jászi-Károlyi friendship, it too had as its object a Danubian Confederation, or at least a "Danubian Soviet Republic."[33] László Wessely, a young communist intellectual who lived in France during the 1920s, later recalled that the communists rejected territorial revisions as futile exercises. A Balkan Federation that would include the Central European states was the only proper solution to the nationality question.[34] The question of treaty revision was never, however, answered by the communists with any finality. This was because they were obliged to react to every change in the Comintern line, no matter how inexplicable. In an article entitled "The Hungarian Working Class and Revision" (1929), for example, József Révai denounced the idea of treaty revision as a cynical ruse designed to divert the proletariat from its true, revolutionary mission. A few months later, he published a "self-criticism" entitled "Should the Hungarian Communist Party Fight Against Trianon?" There he argued that it was indeed possible to be both against the "imperialistic" revisionism espoused by the Horthy regime *and* against Trianon.[35] Having begun his career as a nihilist poet of the avantgarde, Révai—like Bertolt Brecht—was able to take such sudden and dramatic reversals in stride.

The vast majority of the emigrés, then, whether they looked to the West or to the East, favored some form of Confederation in East Central Europe. But to say this is to tell only part of the story, for the emigrés did not view the problem of Trianon in isolation. For them, Danubian Confederation was inextricably intertwined with the replacement of the Horthy government by one that was democratic or communist.

*   *   *

Oszkár Jászi was convinced that his plan for a Danubian Confederation could never be realized so long as Horthy was in power. "Only a thoroughgoing democratisation of Hungary," he wrote in *Revolution and Counter-Revolution in Hungary*, "and loyal and intimate relations between this democratised Hungary and the new States, can create such an atmosphere in Central Europe as can cure the gravest evils of the present situation and clear the way for a democratic Confederation of all the small nations which are now tormented by the rigid dogma of national sovereignty."[36]

In *La Hongrie*, Diner-Dénes asked Frenchmen to distinguish between the Hungarian oligarchy (the magnates and gentry) and the Hungarian people; the oligarchy, he maintained, pursued but one goal—the maintenance of its power. In his whirlwind tour of a thousand years of Hungarian history, Diner-Dénes emphasized the oligarchy's domination of Hungarian life, denouncing even Lajos Kossuth as a cynical defender of noble privilege. Fearing revolution, Kossuth and the nobility were willing to reform; the true revolutionaries were those who, like the poet Sándor Petöfi, advocated social revolution.[37] The *Ausgleich* of 1867, Diner-Dénes's bête noire, constituted a self-serving agreement between the Habsburgs and the Hungarian nobility at the expense of the people. By setting Hungarian against Slav in the Hungarian half of the Dual Monarchy, it became an obstacle to Central European peace. Between the Hungarian and Slavic peoples, no opposition existed; but between the Hungarian nobility and the Slavs there was indeed an unbridgeable gulf.[38] If, therefore, Hungary was to take its rightful place in the comity of nations, democratization was necessary. "Authoritarian capitalism," the product of an alliance between modern economic forces and a feudal social structure, would have to give way first to "democratic capitalism" and eventually to "democratic socialism."[39] These views were repeated by members of the Paris *Világosság* group of socialists in such publications as Léon Blum's *Le Populaire, Quotidien*, and *Le Soir*.[40]

In Vienna, the principal leader of the *Világosság* group was Zsigmond Kunfi. A member of both the Károlyi and the Kun governments, Kunfi was a friend of the Austro-Marxists and a regular contributor to *Der Kampf*. For him, social revolution was far more important than treaty revision. In an essay published in 1928,[41] he argued that Hungary had made a mistake in taking up arms after the war; the Kun regime should have accepted the peace terms in order to obtain the breathing space necessary to save the revolution. The conviction that Trianon was an unprecedented disaster was in Kunfi's judgment merely self-deception. The only difference between Trianon, Versailles, St. Germain, and Brest-Litovsk was that

Germany, Austria, and Russia had accepted the treaties in order to gain time to effect and consolidate domestic revolutions. Had Hungary followed suit, Horthy would never have had the opportunity to establish a counter-revolutionary government.

For the communists too, of course, the overturning of the "imperialistic" peace was but a moment in the larger struggle for a world transformed; confederation was possible only among proletarian states. Hence, in their judgment, the principal enemies resided within Hungary's borders, not within those of the successor states. As a party leaflet of 1929 put it: "Down with revisionist humbug! Long live the class struggle! Long live the proletarian revolution!"[42]

*   *   *

In the early 1920s, Vienna was the geographical center of the Hungarian emigration. No longer the capital of an empire, the city was the large head of a truncated body. Thousands of Austrians were starving and out of work, and even those who were able to put food on their tables looked forward to an uncertain future. For the Hungarians too, life was difficult. Poor and with few prospects,[43] they were viewed with suspicion by the Austrian authorities, who might at any time comply with the Hungarian government's request that they be extradited.

What is perhaps worse, they were as homesick as their legendary countryman—Zoltán Kodály's Háry János. "An emigré," the communist writer József Lengyel later wrote of his life in Vienna, "is that person who, living in a foreign country, neither can nor wishes to think of anything but his homeland."[44] This was true of even the most cosmopolitan emigrés, such as the poet-dramatist Béla Balázs: "It is true," Balázs confided to his diary, "that I proclaimed the synthesis of the nations, the European man. . . . It is true that I always felt my deepest metaphysical roots to be beyond *every* race and nation and I knew myself to be a wanderer, solitary. . . . It is true that according to my biological lineage, I am a Jew; thus, there is no more Turanian blood in me than there was in Sándor Petöfi. . . . And yet, what hurts? Why *do I feel* myself to be an exile?"[45]

These restless wanderers passed much of their time in coffee houses, where they critically dissected the Horthy regime and prepared polemical essays. As we have seen, they were in general agreement about the virtues of a Danubian Confederation and about the need for social-political change. As to the precise nature of a new

East Central Europe and the means of creating it, however, they were hopelessly divided. Indeed, if anything, the battles within the emigration were more bitter than those waged against the Horthy government and its apologists. When "bourgeois radicals" (Jászi and his followers), social democrats, and avant-gardists were not exchanging barbs, they were accusing the communists of having made their exile necessary. Lajos Kassák, editor of the avant-garde journal *Ma* (Today), held Béla Kun and György Lukács "responsible for the fact that the revolution came to the bourgeois dead end."[46] In a devastating attack, Pál Szende wrote that "the soviet system had already collapsed internally when Romanian bayonets brought it to an end in July 1919." Communism was, he charged, "a mixture of the messianism and simplicity of primitive Christianity and the intolerance and orthodoxy of Catholicism."[47]

The communists were certainly a match for their opponents, attacking what they regarded as the pusillanimity of the Radicals and social democrats and the nihilistic decadence of the avant-gardists. Yet, they were weakened by a falling-out among themselves. "The Hungarian emigration was deeply split," the Russian revolutionary Victor Serge remembered. "To the opposition within his Party, Béla Kun was a remarkably odious figure. He was the incarnation of intellectual inadequacy, uncertainty of will, and authoritarian corruption."[48] Almost immediately, Lukács and Jenö Landler organized an anti-Kun faction.

The emigration, then, was not merely divided, it was subdivided. And yet, as one reads the various books and journals that propagated emigré points of view, one senses a common spirit—that of Endre Ady. The greatest member of a remarkable generation of Hungarian poets, Ady had summoned his countrymen to national regeneration in the years from 1906, when he published his *Új versek* (New Verses), to his death in 1919.[49] He succeeded, moreover, in forging a spiritual unity out of those who would never have been able to unite on the basis of economic interest, class affinity, or political conviction.[50]

By the mid-1920s, it had become evident that the collapse of the Horthy government was not imminent and the emigrés began to scatter to the far corners of the world. Unable to return to their homeland and increasingly separated from each other, they clung all the more to Ady's memory. Some of the most important studies of Ady's life and work were written by emigrés: Lajos Hatvany's *Ady* világa (Ady's World) (Vienna, 1924); Gyula Földessy's *Újabb Ady-tanulmányok* (Newer Ady Studies) (Berlin, 1927); and György Bölöni's *Az igazi Ady* (The Real Ady) (Paris, 1934). Literally hundreds of Ady's poems were republished in emigré journals of every political stripe and almost every book contained citations from his work. Articles on the poet were legion and German, French, and Russian translations were rushed into print in an effort to suggest something of Ady's poetic vision to a world ignorant of Hungarian.[51]

For the emigrés, the spirit of Ady represented the spirit of peace among the peoples of Danubia. The poet had been born in Érmindszent, a town of Hungarians and Romanians situated at the gateway to Transylvania. He was therefore introduced to Hungary's nationalities problem very early in life. Although his identification with the Hungarians was to be complete, Ady was a friend of the non-Hungarian peoples and a great admirer of Jászi's pioneering study, *A nemzeti államok kialakulása és a nemzetiségi kérdés* (The Evolution of the National States and the Nationality Question) (1912).[52] Even before Jászi had written that the nationalities problem was "democracy's Archimedian point and, as such, the central problem of our existence as a state,"[53] Ady had composed his "Song of the Hungarian Jacobin":

> Why out of a thousand stiffened desires
> Doesn't there arise a solid will?
> Yet Magyar, Wallach, and Slav sorrow
> Remains always the same sorrow. . . . .
>
> Yet our disgrace, our grief and pain
> Are since a thousand years akin
> Why do we not meet, roaring,
> On the barricades of the Spirit?[54]

To be sure, Ady would have been appalled by the Treaty of Trianon, particularly because of the loss of his beloved Transylvania.[55] But only the spirit of mutual respect that Ady urged could lead, as Jászi put it in 1929, to "the kind of confederation of peoples without which the Danubian Basin will remain the battlefield of eternally plundered peoples."[56] In the same year, Jászi wrote to the Romanian leader Iuliu Maniu, reminding him that he had once promised to protect the political and cultural freedoms of the Hungarian minority. He asked that Maniu be guided "by the spirit of my immortal friend Endre Ady," who recognized more clearly than anyone else that the fundamental interests of the Romanians and the Hungarians were identical.[57]

However, it was not only Ady's dedication to the reconciliation of the Danubian peoples that made him a symbol for the emigrés. His democratic, socialist sympathies and apocalyptic visions of a regenerated Hungary resembled, or rather inspired, those of the emigration. For Jászi and the adherents of a Western orientation, Ady was the poet of the October (Károlyi) Revolution, the democratic socialist who received his political education in Paris and who admired Jean Jaurès. For the communists who advocated an Eastern orientation, Ady was the poet of the Soviet (Kun) Revolution,[58] the authentic voice of the armed proletariat. "Ady recognized the decisive significance of the proletariat," György Lukács wrote in 1928, "in the reshaping of Hungary for which he fought throughout his life."[59] Together with Révai, it was Lukács who pioneered the communist co-optation of Ady's legacy.

Just as Ady had forged a spiritual unity out of the disparate members of the "second reform generation"[60] when he was alive, so his spirit united Hungary's emigré intellectuals after his death. As hopes for an imminent return home faded, the emigrés came to rely more and more on the symbolic importance of the poet's life and work. His spirit alone seemed to serve as the guarantor of historical continuity, the bond that would unite their generation of radicals with that which would one day enter the promised land of a new Hungary and a new East Central Europe. "If there is ever a future for Hungary," Jászi could say for all the emigrés, "it can only proceed from the soul of Andrew [Endre] Ady, the truest of Hungarians and the truest of internationalists."[61]

*   *   *

Political exiles are particularly liable to self-deception. In the case of the Hungarian intellectuals, this syndrome comprised several aberrations. From the first, for example, they believed that the Horthy government's days were numbered; the communists even persuaded themselves that world revolution would soon sweep away the last vestige of the old world. Inclined to think that chauvinism was confined to Hungarian ruling classes, they exaggerated the virtues of the peasantry and the working class. This romantic view of the Hungarian people led the emigrés to conclude that Horthy and his lieutenants alone stood in the path of a revolutionary transformation in *Mitteleuropa*. So great was their hatred of the counter-revolutionary leaders, that they often shut their eyes to the self-serving machinations of the leaders of other European states. For that reason, the communists became little more than Soviet agents, while those who favored a Western orientation were either ignored or shamelessly exploited. In a letter he wrote to his ex-wife Anna Lesznai in 1945, Jászi conceded as much. He too, he confessed, had joined the chorus that praised the Czechs extravagantly in the hope that they would act as allies in the struggle for democracy and national autonomy. Too late, he had recognized his mistake; *"mea maxima culpa."*[62]

A penchant for abstractions was also characteristic of emigré thought. Bold in conception and noble in intent, the idea of a Danubian Confederation was, as György Litván has written, "untimely."[63] Easy to defend in abstract argument, it ignored the historical realities and possibilities of the interwar period. And yet, the Hungarian emigrés were undeterred. Alarmed by the advancing shadow of fascism, Pál Szende made an eleventh-hour appeal to East Central Europeans in 1932. Time was running out, he warned; for Hungary and the successor states the formation of an alliance had become an urgent necessity.[64] The tragedy that was soon to overtake East Central Europe testified to the circumstance that nations, like individuals, do not always act in response to a rational calculation of their own interests, much less to the Cassandra cries of intellectuals.

Still, I should not like to conclude on a critical note. Despite their capacity for self-delusion and their commitment to abstract socio-political models, the emigrés were certainly right to keep alive the spirit of Endre Ady. Hungarian to the core of his being, the great poet was also a "European" in the tradition of Nietzsche, Ortega, Camus, Croce, Thomas Mann, and Béla Bartók. If East Central Europeans are ever to effect a reconciliation and to achieve a significant measure of cooperation, they will have to make that tradition their own.

Notes

I am indebted to Fulbright-Hays and the International Research and Exchanges Board (IREX) for the generous grants that made possible my research.

1. Julius Hay, *Born 1900: Memoirs*, trans. by J.A. Underwood (La Salle, Illinois: Open Court, 1975), p. 95.

2. On the Pécs-Baranya question, see Leslie Charles Tihany, *The Baranya Dispute, 1918-1921* (Boulder: East European Quarterly, 1978).

3. The views of Hock and Dániel are cited in György Litván, "*Magyar gondolat—szabad gondolat*" (Budapest: Magvetö Kiadó, 1978), pp. 150-51.

4. Gyula Illyés, "Beatrice apródjai," *Kortárs*, XXI, 9(1977), 1339-64. See also György Száraz, "Válasz Litván Györgynek," *Élet és Irodalom*, (May 3, 1980), pp. 5-6.

5. In this regard, see Béla Menczer's thoughtful remarks in "Menczer Béla Párizsban: Fodor Ilona interjúja," *Valóság*, XVIII, 10 (1975), pp. 43-44.

6. Zsuzsa L. Nagy, "Jászi és a hazai polgári radikálisok kapcsolata a két világháború között," *Történelmi Szemle*, XVII, 4 (1974), 631.

7. Catherine Károlyi, *A Life Together: Memoirs* (London: George Allen & Unwin Ltd, 1966), p. 208.

8. Ilona Illés, "Gömöri Jenö folyóirata, a Tüz" in *Tüz (1921-1923), Diogenes (1923-1927): Repertóriumok* (Budapest: Petöfi Irodalmi Múzeum, 1977), p. 6.

9. Jenö Gömöri, "Induló" in Kálmán Vargha *et al* (eds.), *Program és hivatás* (Budapest: Gondolat Kiadó, 1978), pp. 464-70.

10. Tibor Hajdu, "Károlyi Mihály Prágában," *Valóság*, XV, 9 (1972), 51-57: Josef Korbel, *Twentieth-Century Czechoslovakia* (New York: Columbia University Press, 1977), p. 73.

11. Cited in Litván, "*Magyar gondolat—szabad gondolat*", p. 152.

12. Cited in Ferenc Boros, *Magyar-csehszlovák kapcsolatok 1918-1921-ben* (Budapest: Akadémiai Kiadó, 1970), p. 289.

13. Cited in Litván, "*Magyar gondolat—szabad gondolat*", p. 153.

14. György Litván, "'Tragikai vétség'—avagy idöszerütlen program? Jászi Oszkár és a 'Kisantant-orientáció'," *Élet és Irodalom* (May 3, 1980), p. 5.

15. György Litván, "Documents of a Friendship: From the Correspondence of Michael Károlyi and Oscar Jászi," *East Central Europe*, IV, 2 (1977), 125.

16. Elemér Mályusz, *The Fugitive Bolsheviks* (London: Grant Richards, 1931), p. 170.

17. Oscar Jászi, *Revolution and Counter-Revolution in Hungary* (New York: Howard Fertig, 1969), p. vii.

18. *Ibid.*, pp. 231-36.

19. C.A. Macartney, no admirer of Jászi's, advanced a similar view. See his *Hungary and Her Successors* (London: Oxford University Press, 1937), p. 496.

20. Ludwig Hatvany, *Das verwundete Land* (Leipzig and Wien: E.P. Tal & Co., Verlag, 1921), p. vii.

21. *Ibid.*, p. 428.

22. *Ibid.*, pp. 489-91. Hatvany's views reflected those of the editors of the

Vienna-based emigré journal *Jövö (Future)*: the liberal Márton Lovászy and the moderate socialist Ernö Garami.

23. On this affaire see Andor Klay, "Hungarian Counterfeit Francs: A Case of Post-World War I Political Sabotage," *Slavic Review*, XXXIII, 1 (1974), 107–13.

24. Léon Blum, "Préface" to Joseph Diner-Dénes, *La Hongrie: Oligarchie, Nation, Peuple* (Paris: Marcel Rivière, Éditeur, 1927), pp. II–III.

25. Diner-Dénes, *La Hongrie*, pp. 165–67.

26. *Ibid.*, pp. 122–23. Diner-Dénes praised (p. 124) Kossuth's—and by implication, Jászi's—plan for a Danubian Confederation.

27. *Ibid.*, pp. 118–19.

28. *Ibid.*, p. 170.

29. See for example R., "A Bécsi Magyar Újság és a Jászi-legenda," *Proletár*, (August 25, 1921), p. 13.

30. See Litván, "Documents of a Friendship," 126.

31. *Ibid.*, 127.

32. Tibor Hajdu, "Károlyi Mihály és a KMP kapcsolatáról a húszas években," *Párttörténeti Közlemények*, XXI, 2 (1975), 142–58.

33. See the theses of the Hungarian Communist Party (Moscow, 1924) in László Kövágó, "A magyar kommunista párt nemzetiségpolitikája a Tanácsköztársaság megdöntésétöl a felszabadulásig," *Párttörténeti Közlemények*, XXIII, 2 (1977), 78–79.

34. "Menczer Béla Párizsban," 40–41.

35. Kövágó, "A magyar kommunista párt nemzetiségpolitikája," 82–84.

36. Jászi, *Revolution and Counter-Revolution*, p. ix.

37. Diner-Dénes, *La Hongrie*, pp. 95–98.

38. *Ibid.*, pp. 126–27.

39. *Ibid.*, pp. 163–64.

40. "Menczer Béla Párizsban," 46.

41. Siegmund Kunfi, *Die Neugestaltung der Welt* (Wien: Verlag der Wiener Volksbuchhandlung, 1930), pp. 86–98.

42. Cited in Kövágó, "A magyar kommunista párt nemzetiségpolitikája," 82–83.

43. Peter F. Drucker remembers having Christmas dinner with the Hungarian emigré Karl Polanyi and his family in 1927. Then editor of the distinguished *Österreichische Volkswirt*, Polanyi could offer his guest only old, half-raw potatoes. Mrs. Polanyi (Ilona Duczynska) explained: "Vienna is full of Hungarian refugees . . . and a good many cannot earn an adequate living. Karl has proven his capacity to earn. Therefore it is obviously only logical for him to turn his paycheck over to other Hungarians and then go out and earn what we need." *Adventures of a Bystander* (New York: Harper & Row, Publishers, 1978), pp. 125–26.

44. József Lengyel, *Bécsi portyák* (Budapest: Magvetö Kiadó, 1970), p. 135.

45. "Balázs Béla naplója," ed. by István Gál, *Kritika*, no. 11 (1975), p. 22. Perhaps the most celebrated of all Hungarian national poets, Petöfi was of Slovak descent.

46. Andor Németh, *A szélén behajtva: Válogatott írások* (Budapest: Magvetö Könyvkiadó, 1973), p. 598.

47. Paul Szende, "Die Krise der mitteleuropäischen Revolution," *Archiv für Sozialwissenschaft und Sozialpolitik*, 47 (1920/1921), 365, 367.

48. Victor Serge, *Memoirs of a Revolutionary, 1901–1941*, trans. and ed. by Peter Sedgwick (London: Oxford University Press, 1963), p. 187.

49. On Ady, see my "Endre Ady's Summons to National Regeneration in Hungary, 1900–1919," *Slavic Review*, XXXIII, 2 (1974), 302–22.

50. Oszkár Jászi, "Ady és a magyar jövö," *Huszadik Század* (August 1919), p. 2.

51. See Györgyi Markovits, "Az 'emigráns' Ady," *Irodalomtörténet*, IX, 4 (1977), 1013–24 and József M. Pásztor, "Adalékok az Ady-életmü továbbéléséröl a magyar munkásmozgalomban (1919–1944)," *Párttörténeti Közlemények*, XXIII, 4 (1977), 126–28. Lajos Hatvany pointed out that Ady's closest friends were all living in exile. With them, his spirit would return home. *Ady* (Budapest: Szépirodalmi Könyvkiadó, 1977), pp. 610–11.

52. See Ady's review of the book in Endre Ady, *Költészet és forradalom*, ed. by József Varga (Budapest: Kossuth Könyvkiadó, 1969), pp. 287–90.

53. Oszkár Jászi, *A nemzeti államok kialakulása és a nemzetiségi kérdés* (Budapest: Grill Károly Könyvkiadóvállalata, 1912), p. vii.

54. Jászi made this translation for his study of *The Dissolution of the Habsburg Monarchy*, Phoenix Books (Chicago: The University of Chicago Press, 1961), p. 342. He had used the same lines, in the original, as the motto for *A nemzeti államok*.

55. See Endre Ady, "S ha Erdélyt elveszik?," *Huszadik Század*, XIII (1912), 737–38.

56. Cited in Markovits, "Az 'emigráns' Ady," 1017.

57. Cited in Litván, "'Tragikai vétség'," p. 5.

58. Ady tutored Kun when both were college students; moreover, Kun had acknowledged the poet's influence in his pre-war journalistic articles.

59. Sándor Vajda [György Lukács], "Ady mint program" in Aladár Tamás (ed.), *A 100%* (Budapest: Akadémiai Kiadó, 1977), p. 191. Lukács often used this pseudonym; his authorship is not, however, certain.

60. On this generation, see Zoltán Horváth's pioneering study *Magyar századforduló: A második reformnemzedék története (1896–1914)* (Budapest: Gondolat, 1961).

61. Jászi, *Revolution and Counter-Revolution*, p. 27.

62. Cited in Litván, "'Tragikai vétség'," p. 5.

63. *Ibid.*

64. Paul Szende, "Die Donauföderation," *Der Kampf*, 25, 8/9 (1932), 347.

Agnes Huszar Vardy

Trianon in Transylvanian Hungarian Literature: Sándor Reményik's "Végvári Poems"

In the spring of 1918 a volume of poetry entitled *Fagyöngyök* (Mistletoes) was published in the Transylvanian city of Kolozsvár, containing the collected verse of the young lyricist Sándor Reményik, whose poems, essays and critiques had already appeared in local newspapers and periodicals such as *Ellenzék* (Opposition), *Kolozsvári Hírlap* (Kolozsvár Gazette), *Új Idők* (New Times) and others. The majority of Reményik's poems were poignant manifestations of an especially sensitive spirit: their lyrical beauty, sincerity, strong sense of morality, and distinctly humanistic attitude attracted the attention of the reading public and earned the praise of the critics.[1] One of his poems, "Imádság" (Prayer), is particularly worthy of note, not only for its effective use of imagery and delicate lyrical quality, but because it also embodies Reményik's views regarding the role of the poet in society.[2] In this poem Reményik clearly defines his attitude toward art—an attitude to which he faithfully adhered until the end of his poetical career. "Prayer" expresses Reményik's ardent wish to become a spokesman of his people, to be a transmitter of their pain and suffering. He entreats God to present him with the heavenly gift of the "pure silver of resounding words," with the "hammered gold of ideas" and with the "rustling silk of images," so that each line of his poetry may serve as a symbol of his nation's sorrow. He pleads with the Lord to grant him a "fiery tongue" so that he may penetrate the very essence of his nation's heart. He feels that if God were to grant his wish, even if only for a few short years, his life's mission would be fulfilled, and he would not have lived in vain. Thus, already at the beginning of his literary career, Reményik rejected the *l'art pour l'art* view of literature, and his poetic mission was clearly mapped out: he wished to put his lyrical talents in the service of his nation.

Ironically, a few months after the publication of *Mistletoes*, such an opportunity presented itself, for there arose the need for a poet with a mission as immediate and practical as Reményik's. Following the armistice of November 1918 Romanian troops invaded and occupied Transylvania which had been an eastern bastion of Hungary for a millenium. By December of that same year they demanded that the region be turned over to Romania. The shock of these developments penetrated every segment of Hungarian society. Feelings of apprehension, uncertainty and disbelief became widespread, and when the new political boundaries were finalized by the Treaty of Trianon, Hungary lost one third of her population and two thirds of her territory to the successor states. Consequently, one and a half million Transylvanian Hungarians, along with the nearly two million others whose homeland had been annexed to Austria, Czechoslovakia and Yugoslavia, were cut off from the mainstream of Hungarian society.

The dismemberment of historic Hungary was an immense blow to every Hungarian regardless of where he happened to reside. It was naturally even more difficult for those who suddenly found themselves citizens of a foreign state, and had to adjust to the different political, economic and social milieu of those states. However, no other segment of Hungarian society was touched more than the nation's intellectuals and men of letters, who have traditionally been the "conscience of their nation." Recognizing the new role that was thrust upon them by this unexpected turn of events, most of them expressed the prevailing mood of bitterness and pain; at the same time they tried to alleviate their nation's fears and uncertainties. This was particularly true among the men of letters in the successor states, and especially evident in Transylvania which had the largest number of Hungarians.

Pre-Trianon Transylvania did not nourish a separate Hungarian literary tradition, and with the exception of the flourishing memoir literature of the period of the Turkish occupation of the sixteenth and seventeenth centuries, it did not develop a separate literary culture.[3] Transylvanian Hungarian writers and poets were part of the mainstream of Hungarian literature and their uniqueness lay only in providing local color and a certain degree of regionalism. Nor were there separate Transylvanian Hungarian literary organizations, journals or publications, and not even the reading public was in any way a homogenous entity. Consequently, given the forced separation from the motherland in 1918–1920, Transylvanian Hungarian literature had to be created from scratch, and ironically within the borders of a foreign state. Driven by the conviction that the very survival of the Hungarian minority in Transylvania depended on the existence of a flowering literary culture, virtually everyone with some literary inclination—the talented and the dilettantes—took up the pen with a hitherto unprecendented zeal. In light of the above, literature gained a new significance in Transylvania, while its practitioners, proponents and supporters had a new goal to urge them on toward greater achievements at the expense of great personal sacrifices. Gradually, the less talented and the less hardy disappeared from the scene, while the talented and persevering assumed the additional task of establishing the institutional base for the new Transylvanian literature. Most of these were middle-class, professional people, including doctors, architects, lawyers and priests. They took it upon themselves to organize the literary and cultural life of their people, as well as to create a need for high quality literature that would serve as a unifying force among the Hungarian population. Furthermore, many of them also felt that Transylvania should eventually evolve into a model multinational region, and thus serve as an example for the entire European community. Consequently, this firm belief in the missionary goal of literature dominated the lives of such outstanding personalities as Károly Kós, Sándor Makkai, Aladár Kuncz, Elek Benedek and numerous others without whose untiring organizing and literary activities, Transylvanian Hungarian literature would not have been able to rise to such heights.[4] The 330 newspapers and journals and the approximately fifty book publication series that were established between 1919 and 1926 attest to the flourish of literary activity.[5] Naturally only a relatively small percentage of these proved viable enough to survive for an extended period of time, but those that withstood the vicissitudes of the new political, social and economic environment, served to keep Hungarian literary life alive in Transylvania. The most prominent and influential of the newly established journals were the conservative *Pásztortűz* (Shepherd's Fire) (1920–1944), the socialist-oriented *Napkelet* (The Orient) (1920–1924), the progressive *Erdélyi Helikon* (Transylvanian Helicon) (1928–1944) and the socialist *Korunk* (Our Time) (1926–1940). In spite of the great variation in the basic social, political and ideological orientation of these journals, their goals were identical: aiding the survival of the Hungarian population and the maintenance of Hungarian culture in Transylvania. From among the numerous publication series ventures, only the conservative-oriented *Minerva* and the more progressive *Erdélyi Szépmíves Céh* (Transylvanian Literary Guild) survived until the end of World War II. The literary society that had the most far-reaching influence, and included in its ranks the greatest number of outstanding men of letters, was the *Erdélyi Helikon* (Transylvanian Helicon) which was established in 1926 and functioned until 1944.

In the modern Hungarian tradition, poetry has always played a special role in the dissemination of ideas. Therefore in Transylvania of the post-Trianon period, it was the lyric poets who first began to express the prevailing mood of despair and uncertainty, while at the same time they also attempted to soften the blow and hold up a glimmer of hope for those who were despondent. Of the many scores of "poets" who raised their voices in the midst of this national tragedy, only about twenty succeeded in surviving the initial period. Most of the others turned to poetry only by the force of circumstances, and as such, the majority of them were unable to rise above the patriotic jingoism that reflected much pain and bitterness, but very little of the needed poetic touch. The two major exceptions to this rule were Lajos Áprily and Sándor Reményik, both of whom came to embody the new and unique Transylvanian-Hungarian spirit in Romania during the interwar period.[6] For both of these poets, as well as for the others, "Transylvania" became a mysterious and almost magical word with its own unique significance. It symbolized the tragedy that befell the Hungarian nation with the loss of its ancient land as well as over one and a half million of their fellow co-nationals. The special meaning of the word "Transylvania" is well illustrated, among others, by Áprily's well-known poem "Tetőn" (At the Top), which he fittingly dedicated to Károly Kós, in honor of the latter's efforts on behalf of Hungarian culture and literature in Transylvania.[7] However, during the initial period of turmoil and uncertainty, it was Sándor Reményik who captured most effectively the mood of his compatriots and expressed it with the greatest poetic zeal. For this reason, it was Reményik who enjoyed the widest popularity for the longest period of time. Thus, although under conditions that neither he, nor anyone else expected, Reményik's prayerful wish to become a spokesman for his nation's agony was prophetically realized.

Reményik's poems produced a great sensation both in Transylvania and in Hungary even before his real name became known. Following the publication of his first volume, many of his poems began to appear under the pseudonym of "Végvári" (Frontier Fighter) for political reasons. The enthusiastic fervor of these poems fulfilled a mission during the first period of Romanian occupation, awakening the stunned Hungarian nation on both sides of the border to political realities. The Végvári poems were passed secretly from hand to hand and were eagerly read by all Hungarians. Some were typed, while others were handwritten on scraps of paper and smuggled into Hungary by those who were fleeing from Transylvania. By the fall of 1919 many of these poems appeared in the leading Budapest newspapers under the title Bujdosó Versek (Poems in Hiding) or independently under the name of "Végvári."[8] Soon thereafter they were collected and published in a small volume by the Hungarian Territorial Integrity League, and then in 1921 in an expanded version under the title Végvári Versek (Végvári Poems). Subsequently, several other editions followed. For years to come there was hardly a commemorative festival or patriotic gathering without a few Végvári poems on the program.[9]

It is not the intention of this study to provide a critical analysis of the aesthetic and literary merits of Reményik's Végvári poems. Our purpose is to assess their impact on the Hungarian mind in the immediate post-Trianon period, and to identify the dominant themes that made this impact possible. It cannot be denied that the widespread popularity of these poems was due largely to the sentiments expressed in them. Yet, one has to admit that Reményik's artistic and literary talent also contributed considerably to their success. Their aesthetic value is enhanced by the poet's ability to utilize the special rhythm of language and to create allegories and symbols from simple natural images. And what makes the Végvári poems especially effective and powerful is their sincere tone and lack of affectation.

The Végvári poems are faithful reflections of the mood of wretchedness felt by the "abandoned" Hungarians in Transylvania. Many of them express unfaltering loyalty to Hungary and the Hungarian nation, while others inspire hope for a favorable solution to the nation's predicament. Furthermore, they also encourage an attitude of fortitude and strength in the face of adverse circumstances. The poems reflect a wide range of moods, from anger to defiance, from hopelessness to resolve. But above all, they offer solace. The soft lyricism of Reményik's Mistletoes is replaced in the Végvári poems by a newly-found and profound tone of determination. His resoluteness is illustrated, among others, by the concluding lines of his poem "Átok" (Curse): "Would that God curse this land, if it is taken away from us!"[10] In another poem "Ne legyen tavasz!" (Let there be no more Spring!) he sadly ascertains that "God had died," and that "there is no one and nothing to believe in any more!" His attitude of defiance is attested to by another poem, wherein he reminds the occupying Romanian troops that Hungarians will take note of all the atrocities committed against them, and when the time is ripe "these will be repaid."

Although there is a certain degree of bitterness in a number of Reményik's Végvári poems, this does not hold true for the majority of them, which are neither bitter recriminations, nor promises of revenge, but simply express a sincere concern for the future of his people in Transylvania. Because of the mass flight of the Hungarians, Reményik feared that his narrower homeland would soon be depopulated of Hungarians and consequently lost to Hungary forever. He firmly believed that in spite of the altered political boundaries, Hungarians did have a place in Transylvania, and under no circumstances should they abandon the land that had been their home for over a thousand years. As the Hungarian exodus that began after the Romanian occupation continued unabated, Reményik felt compelled to speak up against it repeatedly. In his "Erdély magyarjaihoz" (To the Hungarians in Transylvania) he calls on Hungarians to pull their resources, face the unknown with courage, and never to give up what is rightfully theirs. He expresses confidence in his nation's ability to surmount these calamitous circumstances and reminds them that although history has not always been kind to them, they have still been able to survive. In his words, "Life is everlasting in us." He admits that "harsh times" are still ahead of them, and he concedes that their suffering and sorrow may become so intense that only their faintly audible heartbeats will reveal the life that is still left in them. But then he consoles them by pointing out that at least "these heartbeats will be Hungarian."

Reményik's lyrical talent and his determination to survive as a Hungarian are aptly demonstrated by another Végvári poem in the same vein, entitled "Eredj ha tudsz!" (Leave if you can!). This poem attracted perhaps the greatest attention and attained the widest popularity among the Hungarian reading public. Besides the skillful use of the sounds and rhythm of language, Reményik uses especially vivid and appropriate imagery as he expresses the innermost yearnings of his soul. He begins with a satirical tone, calling on Transylvanian Hungarians to leave their homeland, "if they can," while at the same time hoping and knowing that most of them won't:

Leave, if you can . . .
Leave, if you think,
That somewhere, anywhere in the world beyond
It will be easier to bear your fate.
Leave . . .
Fly like a swallow, to the south,
Or northward, like a bird of storm,
And from high above in the wide skies
Search for the place
Where you can build a nest.
Leave, if you can.

Leave if you hope
Against hope that homelessness
Is less bitter abroad than at home.
Leave, if you think
That out in the world
Memory will not carve new crosses from
Your soul, from that sensitive
Living tree.

Reményik also reminds his compatriots that "sorrow and homesickness will crucify them on the crosses of memory." He recalls the fate of Kelemen Mikes,—a scribe to the exiled Prince Ferenc Rákóczi II in the early eighteenth century,—who "was unable to live in a captive land" and therefore chose the life of an exile in Turkey on the shores of the Sea of Marmora. Yet, Mikes's heart was never at peace, for it was "torn by the frenzied hordes of memory." Then the poet, almost cynically repeats the refrain: "Go, if you can,/ Toss all your old dreams into the winds,/ Go through jungles, across the sea;/ Offer your two working hands." He shows his own determination not to abandon his homeland as he continues:

Home I shall remain,
Darkly croaking, like a
Winter crow on a dead poplar tree.
I know not yet
Whether I shall ever find a quiet corner
But I shall stay at home.

The next two stanzas contain one of the most effective uses of figurative language which forcefully reflect Reményik's deep conviction that he must stay and fight:

> I'll be a grinding worm in an alien wood,
> I'll be the sediment in an emptied cup,
> I'll be the poison in foreign blood,
> Or a miasma,—fever, a lurking despicable wretch,
> But I shall stay at home!
>
> I want to be the toll of death,
> Which buries men, yet sings to listening ears
> And incites us: to take back what was once ours.
> I want to be the fuse of fire,
> Part of the wick, blazing blood,
> Which secretly crawls for years
> Through ashes in the midst of the night . . .
> Until finally it reaches the powdercask of sorrow,
> And then . . . !

Reményik concludes his poem with a somewhat resigned, yet compelling tone:

> I know not yet
> Whether I shall ever find a quiet corner
> But until *then*,
> Darkly croaking, like a
> Winter crow on a dead poplar tree
> I shall stay at home.

The pervasive earnestness of Reményik's tone, his lively imagination, his use of symbolism, and his ability to create moving images resulted in a number of laudatory critiques of his Végvári poems. These included assessments by such noted poets and literary critics as Dezső Kosztolányi, who asserted that the popularity of the Végvári poems was due not only to their content and message, as often assumed, but also to their demonstrated aesthetic quality.[11] In an article published in 1920 in the progressive Budapest literary journal *Nyugat* (West) Kosztolányi pointed out the unknown poet's sincerity, his keen sense of perception, as well as his unusual ability to portray his innermost emotions and to transmit these feelings to his readers. Kosztolányi was particularly taken by the poem "Leave, if you can," and especially by the lines "darkly croaking, like a winter crow on a dead poplar tree." "After I read these lines," he wrote, "I have become aware of what it is to be one of the millions of Hungarians in Transylvania. Through this uniquely artistic interpretation I experienced fully the profound and distant sorrow that they must have experienced." Kosztolányi referred to the Végvári poems as a "new literary type, sadly timely and agonizing," and he extended a warm if mournful welcome to the "unknown poet" and to his "unfathomable sorrow."

Besides the conviction that Hungarians do have a future in Transylvania, and therefore should not leave their thousand-year-old homeland, many of Reményik's poems also express his fundamental loyalty and attachment to the concept of an undivided Hungarian nation. The editors of the small volume *Végvári Poems* also allude to this strong sense of fidelity to the nation as a whole: "Transylvania, with all its riches, had now become a prey. Only one of its treasures had remained untouched: its loyalty to the (Hungarian) nation."[12] A poem that expresses most emphatically this idea is the "Három szín" (Tricolor). The poet begins by stating that Hungarians are now forbidden to wear their national colors on their lapels. But this does not mean that these colors and what they represent are now lost forever. No, they have simply sunk deeper into the hearts of the people. And even if the lives of Transylvanian Hungarians is "a waste, and the landscape is dipped in blood," and the wearing of the tricolor is forbidden, their heartbeats will always be Hungarian.

> For the tricolor our longing hearts
> Will burn and bleed,
> Let those who have torn them off,
> Tear them from our hearts.

While serving as a catharsis for the poet's and his mutilated nation's pent-up emotions, the Végvári poems raised the consciousness of the nation as a whole and offered hope and consolation to all Hungarians in Transylvania, in the successor states, as well as to those in the mother country. In the poem "Nagy magyar télben picike tüzek," (Tiny Fires in the Great Hungarian Winter), the poet calls on all Hungarians to keep their "tiny fires burning," and then to unite these fires into a giant flame. He admits that there has never before been such a need for unity as today, and if they would only join forces, their combined flames could reach right up to the starry skies and consume everything therein, including the sorrow and misery of the Hungarians.

In another poem, "Szurony erdőben" (Forest of Bayonets), he concludes that the "dark forest (his world) is swarming with the enemy; yet,

> In the depth of the forest
> Faith, Idea and Dreams continue to walk about,
> And they are bound to conquer death.

The poem "Nehéz homályban" (In Dark Shadows) has the same message. It also stresses the importance of joining forces: "No matter how dark the woods may be/ Let's not let go of each other's hands/ We, abandoned, motherless orphans: we Magyars." In the "Új Szövetség" (New Testament) Reményik likewise bewails the fate of his nation, and does so with the "horrible screams of agony." He shouts his pain into the soundless night: "The country exists no more. . . !" Yet, he still concludes his laments with a sign of hope: "At least there are still some Hungarians left."

Another of Reményik's concerns was that the Treaty of Trianon would inevitably give rise to a certain degree of dissent and lack of understanding among the various branches of the dismembered Hungarian nation. He feared that the physical destruction of historic Hungary would be followed by spiritual and ideological disunity. This fear is forcefully expressed in Reményik's address to his fellow poets in rump Hungary: "Némely pesti poétának" (To Some Poets of Pest) where he wonders aloud whether the loss of Transylvania and the other territories of historic Hungary had really caused any pain for the Budapest writers and poets. He wishes "he could gaze into their souls" to see how they pass their time, what they are writing about, and what causes the greatest concern to them. He even explores the possibility that they may already have forgotten their fellow Hungarians in the separated parts of former Hungary, and that they are merely playing around with "colorful words," while their Transylvanian brethren are being "choked to death by the hands of the enemy." The poet wishes that Budapest writers could see the plight of their suffering kin beyond the new frontiers. He refers to Transylvania as Hungary's "dead child," and asks the mother country (impersonated by their fellow poets) to take this child into her lap and bemoan its death like a "wailing Rachel," and to do so with "the strangled verse" of a condemned Transylvanian bard. He wishes they could see the "bloody rags" they are forced to wear "to wrap their beggar bodies," and to witness the work of those "wicked hands that are destroying homes and are tearing holy chains apart." He would also like them to witness the plight of their fleeing brethren, who have been driven from their homes like dogs. They only have time to whisper their final goodbyes to the land that has nurtured them and to the trees that have watched over their lives, and henceforth will shadow only the graves of their ancestors. Reményik ends his plea by proclaiming his powerful desire to scorch these images into the very hearts of his Budapest colleagues, so that they will always carry these images with them, and think and write only about their compatriots in Transylvania.

Further analysis of the themes and general content of the Végvári poems would indubitably add new elements to the nature of the emotional reaction to Trianon, but it would also lead to repetitions. Each of his poems reflects a specific aspect of the emotional and intellectual bewilderment of the Hungarian mind in those fateful days; furthermore, most of them are aesthetically sensitive, generally accurate and, in their impact, very successful reflections. It is not known exactly when the identity of the author of the Végvári poems became known to the public, but we know that as late as 1926, the *Magyar Irodalmi Lexikon* (Hungarian Literary Encyclopedia) lists "Reményik's" and "Végvári's" poetical activities under two separate headings, giving no indication whatsoever that the two were identical and that the Végvári poems were actually composed by the former.

Sándor Reményik continued to write poetry for the next two decades. Altogether he published fourteen volumes of verse until his death at the age of 51 in 1941. Although he was a man of frail physical constitution and deteriorating health, he was extremely active throughout the interwar years. He wrote poetry and took an active part in the shaping of the Hungarian literary and cultural life in Transylvania. He was one of the founding members of the already mentioned journal *Pásztortűz* (Shepherd's Fire), which he edited between 1921 and 1923, and then after 1924 was one of its chief contributors. Naturally, the passage of time, the inevitable consolidation that followed Trianon, and the altered conditions and new challenges gradually directed the poet's attention away from the shock effect of Trianon and from the resulting emotional outbursts that he expressed so succinctly in his Végvári poems. His basic poetic tone, however, did not change, and his popularity as a poet continued unabated. Prevailing circumstances forced him to turn inward and to become more concerned with matters of the spirit.[13] His turning to the spiritual aspects of human existence also had its impact on his appreciation of the beauty of nature. Descriptions of the simple, yet magnanimous quality of the Transylvanian countryside, and the portrayal of the everyday lives of the simple folk around him began to dominate his poetry, which thereby became more profound and universal both in its content and in its form of expression. Gradually Reményik emerged as one of the dominant literary figures and perhaps the most beloved and respected lyric poets in interwar Transylvanian Hungarian literature. Yet, the tragedy of Trianon and its after effects continued to haunt him; they remained one of the underlying forces of his literary art, as demonstrated by so many of his later poems and other writings. The diminishing number of Hungarian schools and churches, mixed marriages between Magyars and non-Magyars and the consequent decline of their numbers, and the slow deterioration of the spoken language among the younger generation are all common themes in his poetry even during the late 1930's and early 1940's.[14] For example, in his poem "Az Ige" (The Word of God), he warns his compatriots not to take the Hungarian language lightly, and to speak it with reverence they would use when speaking to God. He warns them that their native tongue "is their last bastion, a fairy castle and (protective) catacomb."[15] Thus, they should speak it as if they were reciting a prayer, as if they were "bringing gold, frankincense and myrrh," to the Lord of Heavens. In this poem, Reményik also affirms his original belief in the historical mission of poetry as the upholder and promoter of humanistic, ethical, and moral values:

> For he who is a poet, must also be a king,
> A priest, and a prophet; never anything else.

In 1933 one of his devoted admirers asked Reményik in a private letter why he ceased to write more Végvári poems. Reményik felt compelled to answer this question publicly in a poem entitled "Miért hallgatottel Végvári?" (Why Has Veguari Become Silent).[16] He explained that when Végvári's voice broke forth from the depth of the earth, it may have been appropriate for those times. But times had changed. The stake had burned itself out, new challenges had come to the fore, the needs of the people had changed, and a poet's heart could not produce new songs for needs that had been passed up by time. And "to sing without a songless heart" is simply impossible. No, he did not change his views about the injustices of Trianon, for that which has eternal validity cannot be changed, altered or destroyed by earthly misdeeds and sinful human instruments. He was convinced that "what is deeply Hungarian in us" is a force that "no foreign hand can reach" or tamper with. Yet, he also knew that one cannot fight the impossible, but one has to wait for it to pass. In the meantime, however, the nation must live, struggle, procreate and survive. And it must also learn to coexist with others; with the other, and perhaps equally worthy nationalities of their small common homeland, Transylvania. By coming to these conclusions Reményik gradually transformed himself from a rather embittered bard of Trianon's miseries, to a humane troubadour of national coexistence in the much suffered land of Hungarians, Saxons and Romanians:

> It is not our duty to deliver justice.
> Our only duty is to be fair and just.

It was this new view of the world and new view of his role as a poet that forced Reményik to give up his "other self" (Végvári) and to cease being the herald and bemoaner of his nation's sufferings. "From the wild struggle of his life, he fled to God," and entrusted the Lord with the task of dispensing justice to each according to his merits and demerits.[17]

This attitude was not only new with Reményik, but it also conflicted increasingly with the general view of Hungary's political leadership. The latter continued to be intensely nationalistic, and the regime's revisionism was even strengthened by a general tilt to the Right during the 1930's. Moreover, this tilt to the Right was also accompanied by a comparable decrease in the regime's humanitarian content and by the simultaneous increase in its nationalist propaganda. This playing upon national antagonisms and ethnic differences, however, did not sit well with Reményik's new world view. He retained much of his earlier popularity in Hungary, but that popularity continued to rest almost exclusively on his earlier Végvári poems. His new poetry remained either generally unknown, or if known, then largely unappreciated by the reading public that was still being nurtured by the emotional nationalism that had been generated in the immediate pre- and post-Trianon years.

By the mid 1930's Reményik's name became closely connected with his narrower homeland. He wa ; often referred to simply as "the Transylvanian poet," a designation that could hardly have come into being without Trianon. "The Transylvanian Poet"[18] is the title that the editor of the journal *Nyugat* (West), Mihály Babits, had given to his review of one of Reményik's last volumes of poetry *Magasfeszültség* (High Voltage) (1940). Babits pointed out that, in a sense, Reményik of 1940 has returned to the world of his early years. The quiet, meditative and self-searching tone of the *Mistletoes* (1918) has resurfaced in the poems of his last volume. In both collections Reményik bares his soul and the spiritual struggles he has been waging. While it may be impossible for a superficial observer to discern similarities between these lyrical self-searchings and the emotional outbursts and fighting zeal displayed by Reményik in his Végvári poems, they are the products of the same mind and spirit. Babits observed that the whole of Reményik's poetical output originated from the same "mysterious inner compulsion" that moved the poet during his entire life and career. In light of the above, Babits was convinced that Reményik has remained true to himself, and that he expressed in his poetry only those views and emotions that were closest to him at a given time. Finally, as Babits pointed out, the entire spectrum of Reményik's poetical output was the sincere manifestation of "a human being, a Transylvanian, and a Hungarian."

From a hospital bed in Budapest, the seriously ill Reményik thanked Babits for the candid evaluation of his poetical works.[19] Reményik found great comfort in the critic's and fellow poet's understanding of his poetry, and called Babits's concluding statement "a strong consolation to me in the future, if there is still a future for me." Ironically, within less than a year, both poets passed away, Babits being the first to go. Now, forty years later, one cannot help recognizing that, although Reményik's entire poetic career had been shaped and in a way determined by the results of the Treaty of Trianon, at the end he still triumphed over his anger and his bitterness. For this reason it is crucial to see him in his entirety: as a true Hungarian, as a true Transylvanian, and also as a true human being. He should be viewed as a man and as a poet, who like Tennyson's

Ulysses, never ceased "to strive, to seek, to find and not to yield." And Hungarian lyric poetry is the better for it; for without having been Végvári for a few short years, the aesthetic interpretation of Trianon's impact upon the Hungarian soul would also be poorer.

Notes

1. For a general discussion of Sándor Reményik's poetry see the following more important studies: Elemér Jancsó, *Reményik Sándor élete és költészete* [The Life and Poetry of Sándor Reményik] (Kolozsvár, 1942), 44 pp.; István Boross, *A Jánus-arcú költő. Reményik Végvári emlékezete* [The Janus-faced Poet. Reményik's Végvári Poems] (Mezőtúr, 1943), 41 pp.; György Kristóf, *Reményik Sándor* (Kolozsvár, 1944); Joseph Reményi, "Sándor Reményik, Transylvanian Regionalist, 1890–1942 [sic]," in: Joseph Reményi, *Hungarian Writers and Literature* (New Brunswick, N.J.: Rutgers University Press, 1964), pp. 437–443; and László Imre, "Reményik Sándor ulolsó korszaka. Fejezet a magyar humanista, antifasiszta költészet történetéből" [Sándor Reményik's Last Years: A Chapter in the History of Hungarian Humanist, Anti-fascist Poetry] *Irodalomtörténet* vol. 62, no. 2 (1980), pp. 339–352.

2. Cf. *Reményik Sándor összes versei* [The Complete Poems of Sándor Reményik] 2 vols. (Budapest: Révai, 1941) I, p. 43. Today the poems of Reményik are rather difficult to come by. His poetry has not been published in Hungary since 1943, although two collections have appeared in the West: *Eredj, ha tudsz!* [Leave, if you can!] (Köln: Vörösmarty Irodalmi Kör, 1958), 62 pp.; *Reményik Sándor versei* [Sándor Reményik's Poetry] (Lyndhurst, N.J.: Kaláka, 1976), 309 pp. The English translations of Reményik's poems are my own.

3. For a discussion of Transylvanian Hungarian literature see the following: "Magyar irodalom Romániában," [Hungarian Literature in Romania] in Miklós Szabolcsi, ed., *A magyar irodalom története 1919–töl napjainkig* (The History of Hungarian Literature from 1919 to the Present] (Budapest: Adadémiai Kiadó, 1966), pp. 924–1000; "Magyar irodalom Romániában," [Hungarian Literature in Romania] in: Miklós Béládi and György Bodnár, eds., *A magyar irodalom története 1905-tól napjainkig* [The History of Hungarian Literature from 1905 to the Present] (Budapest: Gondolat, 1967), pp. 735–766; Mihály Czine, *Magyar irodalom Romániában* [Hungarian Literature in Romania] (Budapest, 1967) 15 pp. Reprinted from *Jelenkor* vol. 10, no. 12, (1967); Elemér Jancsó, "Az erdélyi magyar lira tizenöt éve," [Fifteen Years of Transylvanian Hungarian Lyric Poetry] in Elemér Jancsó, *Kortársaim* [My Contemporaries] (Bucharest: Kriterion, 1976), pp. 27–97.

4. For an authentic view of the flurry of activity that surrounded the creation of a separate Transylvanian Hungarian literature see: Elemér Jancsó,

Kortársaim and Sándor Huszár, *Beszélgetések kortárs irókkal* [Interviews with Contemporary Authors] (Bukarest: Irodalmi Könyvkiadó, 1969).

5. "Hungarian Literature in Romania," in *The History of Hungarian Literature from 1905 to the Present*, p. 738.

6. Although Áprily left Transylvania in 1929 to settle in Budapest, and later in the vicinity of Visegrád, he continued to live under the spell of his beloved homeland, and often yearned to return.

7. Lajos Áprily, *Megnőtt a csend. Összegyűjtött versek* [Silence Grew. Collected Poems] (Budapest: Szépirodalmi Könyvkiadó, 1972), pp. 92–93.

8. For the reception of the Végvári poems, see "Végvári" in *Magyar Irodalmi Lexikon* [Hungarian Literary Encyclopedia] (Budapest: Studium, 1926), p. 840.

9. The volume *Végvári versek* [Végvári poems] contains those poems that previously appeared in a collection entitled *Segítsetek* [Help] and 38 other poems as well.

10. All subsequent quotations of the Végvári poems are taken from the volume *Végvári Poems*. The English translations are mine.

11. See Dezső Kosztolányi's article "Végvári versei," [The Poems of Végvári] *Nyugat* (1920), pp. 323–324.

12. *Végvári Poems*, p. 5.

13. László Németh believed that the aesthetic quality of Reményik's poetry improved significantly when he abandoned the tone of the Végvári poems. See L. Németh: "Reményik Sándor," in: L. Németh, *Két nemzedék* [Two Generations] (Budapest: Magvető és Szépirodalmi Könyvkiadó, 1970), pp. 202–206.

14. Two of his well-known poems should be mentioned here: "Ha nem lesz többé iskolánk," [When We Won't Have Any More Schools] and "Templom és iskola," [Church and School] in *The Complete Poems of Sándor Reményik*, I, p. 523; II, p. 334. An especially beautiful lyrical poem about mixed marriage is "Elpártolt liliomszál," [Disloyal Lily], *ibid.*, II, p. 336.

15. *The Complete Poems*, I, p. 427.

16. *The Complete Poems*, II, pp. 332–333.

17. *Ibid.*, p. 333.

18. Mihály Babits, "Az erdélyi költő," [The Transylvanian Poet] *Nyugat* (1940), pp. 388–392.

19. Reményik's letter to Babits is reprinted in *Nyugat* (1940), pp. 532–533.

Stephen Fischer-Galati

Trianon and Romania

The dismemberment of Hungary and corollary provisions of the Treaty of Trianon have rankled Hungarians for more than half a century.[1] Redressing the humiliation of Trianon has been a cardinal aim of Hungarian political leaders of the interwar years and, in a more muted form, even of contemporary ones. Crucial to Hungarian revisionism—the most extreme form of expression of Hungarian aspirations—has been the recovery of Transylvania from Romania. Even more moderate exponents of the need for rectification of the injustices inflicted upon historic Hungary at Trianon have, in their determination to keep the Transylvanian question in the forefront of international discussions, focused on actual or alleged abuses of the rights of the Hungarian minority in Transylvania by successive Romanian regimes. And there are good reasons for this preoccupation.

The singling out of Transylvania and of the Romanians as central to Hungarian aspirations is ultimately related to the historic contempt shown by Hungarian ruling classes, and even by many of the non-ruling ones, toward their Romanian counterparts. The Romanians, whether in Transylvania or in the Old Kingdom, have been traditionally viewed as uncivilized, unscrupulous, and inferior to the Hungarians. If Romanian leaders resented Tsar Nicholas's *bon mot* that being a Romanian is "a profession rather than a nationality;" if they expressed outrage at the Germans' concept of the *"Unmensch,"* which embraced the Romanians with other peoples in Southeast Europe, it was the Hungarians' contempt for the Romanians that gave Romanian nationalism the greatest impetus since the late nineteenth century.[2] The "liberation" of Transylvania from Hungarian yoke was the primary goal of Romanian nationalists before Trianon, and conversely, the liberation of that province from the Romanian yoke became the primary goal of Hungarian nationalists after Trianon. Under these circumstances a review of the significance of Trianon for Romania is indeed desirable, particularly because of the continuing importance of the Transylvanian question in the 1980s to nationalists and communists alike.

In the last analysis, the decisions made by the Great Powers with respect to Hungary's dismemberment, and the determination of the Hungarians not to accept their validity, is the root cause of all problems related to Trianon. The Hungarian challenges to the legitimacy of Romanian rule in Transylvania invariably focused on violations by the Romanians of specific provisions of the Treaty of Trianon, particularly those related to the rights and treatment of national minorities.[3] Moreover, as these discriminatory, and thus illegal, practices provided the rationale for the Hungarians' seeking the physical reincorporation of at least those parts of Transylvania in which Hungarians constituted a majority of the population, all Romanian regimes of the interwar years—all committed to the maintenance of Greater Romania—defended their minority policies and rejected all accusations leveled against them as "external interference in domestic affairs." And in these respects, too, little has changed since World War II.

It would be erroneous to assume, however, that Romanian policies in Transylvania were primarily motivated by the need to safeguard the territorial integrity of that province against Hungarian irredentism. And it would also be incorrect to regard the anti-Hungarian policies in Transylvania as a prerequisite for maintaining the spirit of Romanian nationalism at a high pitch during the years when the euphoria of reunification of all Romanian territories into Greater Romania was blunted by the political and socioeconomic realities which faced all Romanians after World War I.[4] It is true that anti-Magyarism was an integral part of Romanian nationalism but it was not necessarily its principal component. It is also true that Hungarian revisionism was unwelcome to Romania's rulers but there was no apprehension over the territorial security of Transylvania. Other problems, some expressly related to Transylvania and others only peripherally so, were more relevant to an analysis of Romanian minority policies than have been suggested by individuals concerned with the Hungarian minority alone.

The primary political issue in postwar Romania was that of consolidation of power by the "unifiers," identified with the political establishment of the Old Kingdom and particularly with Ioan I. C. Brătianu's "Liberals," who entertained the belief that Greater

Romania was their own creation.[5] Brătianu's power base was, however, threatened by the proliferation of political organizations following the territorial expansion of the Old Kingdom and by the Great Powers' lack of confidence in his tactics and policies. His temporary absence from the premiership of Romania, between September 1919 and January 1922, following his resignation over a dispute with the Allies over peace settlements, allowed him to develop political positions designed to discredit his opponents and secure unrestricted power for himself and the Liberals. The main threat to the Liberals' interests was perceived to come from the National Party of Transylvania which, together with the Peasant Party of the Old Kingdom, sought to identify itself with the nationwide interests of the peasantry by advocating acceptance of the popular Transylvanian pattern of agrarian reform as the prototype for the whole Greater Romania.[6] Brătianu, fearful of a likely realignment of political forces, sought and secured the support of all conservative and nationalist forces of the Old Kingdom. In fact, it was the alteration by the Romanian parliament of the Transylvanian pattern of agrarian reform which paved the way for Brătianu's return to power as the protector of the traditional political interests of the creators of Greater Romania.

The anti-Transylvanian aspects of the political struggles of the immediate postwar years clearly transcended the Hungarian question in Transylvania. Whereas the reforms initiated by the Romanian National Party of Transylvania were indeed detrimental to the interests of the Hungarian latifundiaries, they were not adverse to the interests of the rank-and-file of the Hungarian peasantry. Moreover, the reforms were designed to be democratic and nondiscriminatory toward national minorities.[7] As such, they were unacceptable to Brătianu—the self-styled champion and protector of the Romanians' historic interests and guarantor of Romanian supremacy in the Greater Romanian state. Since Brătianu's political philosophy also entailed nonacceptance of "dictates" by the Great Powers in matters related to the rights of minorities and to any form of "external interference in Romania's internal affairs," the rights of the Hungarians in Transylvania became an *ipso facto* issue, but not the main issue, in post-Trianon Romanian politics.

Brătianu's policies toward Transylvania in general and toward national minorities in particular were also affected by external factors not directly related to Trianon. Brătianu was identified as the diagnostician and primary opponent of the "Judeo-Bolshevik conspiracy," both in Romania and abroad, largely because of his actions against Béla Kun's regime and his defiance of the Bolsheviks' demands for restitution of Bessarabia.[8] It was thus incumbent upon the Liberals to protect all Romanians—particularly those of Transylvania and Bessarabia—against Judeo-communists who, by definition, included most Hungarian Jews in Transylvania, most Russian Jews in Bessarabia, and most Jewish, pro-Jewish, or Jewlike intellectuals in all parts of Romania. Jews and communists thus provided a convenient link between internal politics and the primary and most persistent external problem of interwar Romania, that of Soviet revisionism in Bessarabia.

The Bolsheviks' insistence on the return of Bessarabia coupled with Romanian rejection of their demands bode ill for Soviet-Romanian relations.[9] It is not that in the early 1920s the Romanians feared seizure of Bessarabia by force of arms or even by externally-fomented revolutionary actions; yet, Brătianu as well as other Romanian political leaders realized that Soviet revisionism was not to be taken lightly. Whether Romania's rulers were fearful of an actual or potential link between Russian and Hungarian revisionisms is uncertain. But they were aware of the Bolsheviks' anger over Romania's military intervention against Kun's forces which afforded the Russians with the opportunity of branding Romania as the enemy of the "democratic" Hungarian masses. They were also aware of the anti-Romanian sentiments of the Hungarian masses, whether "democratic" or not, and of the Hungarian bourgeoisie and aristocracy who far from looking upon the Romanian armies as "liberators" from Bolshevism viewed the Romanians as rapists and plunderers of Hungarian property, not to mention of Hungarian territories secured by the Treaty of Trianon. Thus, revisionism—of the threatening Soviet variety as well as of the potentially-threatening Hungarian one—became the bugaboo of Romanian foreign policy in the twenties. And, in the process, the groups that could be labeled as supportive of external revisionist forces, specifically Hungarians and Jews, were singled out for discrimination by Brătianu and by other nationalist forces in Romania.

It is fair to say that the ensuing anti-Hungarian and anti-Jewish manifestations were largely based on guilt by association. It is true that there was little love lost between Hungarians and Romanians and between Romanians and Jews in Greater Romania. But it would be difficult to argue that the majority of the Hungarians were revisionists or that most of Romania's Jews were anti-Romanian or pro-Bolshevik. There can be little doubt, however, that most of the Hungarian bourgeoisie, functionaries, expropriated landlords, and intellectuals were anti-Romanian and that many of these educated Hungarians favored the reincorporation of Transylvania into Hungary. And it is also undeniable that most of Transylvania's Jews identified their interests with those of the Hungarians as they considered themselves to be either Hungarian Jews or Jewish Hungarians.[10]

Whether reconciliation of disparate ethnic, socio-economic, and cultural differences could have been achieved within the Romanian body politic under more enlightened rule is a matter of conjecture. The fact is that since 1922, at least, Bucharest made no effort to secure the allegiance of the Hungarians and Jews of Transylvania and, if anything, made a conscious effort to Romanianize Transylvania in a manner detrimental to the interests of most of its inhabitants regardless of their nationality or religion.

The ascendancy of Romanians over Hungarians in Transylvania would have occurred even if political power had been held by the Romanian National Party of Transylvania. The introduction of Romanian as official language, the replacement of Hungarian functionaries, the redistribution of wealth, and similarly radical alterations of previous relationships were prerequisites for the reincorporation of Transylvania into the Greater Romanian body politic. It is possible, but not likely, that the resultant dislocations could have been made less painful had the process of Romanianization been directed by Transylvanians for the benefit of the Romanians of Transylvania but in a spirit of reconciliation toward non-Romanians. But that was not to be since Brătianu and the Liberals were determined to integrate Transylvania into Greater Romania *à la roumaine*. In their dual opposition to both Hungarians and the National Party of Transylvania, the Liberals controlled the process of Romanianization from Bucharest by subordinating it to the central bureaucracy. Although Transylvanian Romanians participated in the transfer of political and economic power they did not direct it. Their displeasure with the arrogance and corruption identified with Brătianu's men became more pronounced as Bucharest continued to direct Transylvanian affairs even after the transfer was completed. As for the

Hungarians, their bitterness toward Romanians was exacerbated by the need to deal with Bucharest-appointed functionaries and to cope with Bucharest methods of governance. Yet, from a Romanian political standpoint, the integration of Transylvania into Greater Romania and subordination of regional to central political interests was essential. Minority rights could be observed to the extent to which they would not affect the interests of the state. Or, in the view of Bucharest, the Hungarians were a potential Trojan Horse because of their presumed allegiance to Hungarian revisionism and, in any event, they and the Jews had to be humiliated because of their historic exploitation of the Romanian masses in Transylvania. Nevertheless, the rights of national minorities were formally respected by the Liberals and by their successors throughout most of the interwar period. Thus, the repeated complaints regarding actual or alleged violations of the provisions of the Treaty of Trianon addressed by the Hungarian government to the League of Nations or to Bucharest were readily refuted by the Romanian government.[11] In fact, such complaints tended to aid Bucharest as they gave credence to the official line that Hungarians, both outside and inside Romania, were revisionists and enemies of Greater Romania and of the Romanians. All the same, relations between the Hungarian minority and the Romanians in Transylvania were correct during the twenties and, if anything, even improved between 1928 and 1933 during the short-lived governance of the National Peasant Party.

Nevertheless, the prognosis for the solution of nationality and political problems in Transylvania was poor by the early 1930s for reasons not necessarily related to Transylvanian affairs. By then the problems of Greater Romania had become a function of major international crises related to the global economy and the corollary alteration of political structures.[12] The economic difficulties facing Romania in the twenties and early thirties were symptomatic of the general economic malaise which facilitated the rise of Mussolini and Hitler and which led to the Great Depression. The Romanian agrarian economy suffered less than the industrialized economies of other European countries in the interwar years, but the peasants' disillusionment with the agrarian reform, and the intellectuals' and students' with the inability of the Liberals and other political organizations to provide remedies for the economic stagnation and unemployment of university graduates and of the intellectual community in general, led to the formulation of Christian populist

ideologies and the organization of extreme right-wing political
groups whose proclaimed mission was to save Romania from Jews
and communists. The virulently anti-Semitic and anti-communist
ideology of the students and intellectuals, who supported Professor
A. C. Cuza's League of National Christian Defense and Corneliu
Zelea Codreanu's Legion of the Archangel Michael, was relatively
ineffectual before the Depression but caused havoc in Romania by
the mid-thirties.[13] Nevertheless, the established political parties, to
counter the impact of Cuza's and Codreanu's appeal to the young,
the unemployed, the intellectuals, and even the disgruntled peasants
and industrial workers, became more and more committed to nationalist formulae in attempting to solve Romania's problems. And
since the problems proved insoluble, the scapegoats were readily
identified as non-Romanian and, presumably, anti-Romanian
elements—the Jews and the Hungarians at home and the Russian
communists and Hungarian revisionists abroad.

It is true that anti-Semitism and anti-Bolshevism ranked higher
with Romanian nationalists than anti-Magyarism, but it is also true
that the spreading of Codreanu's radical ideology into Transylvania
led to a coupling of the anti-Jewish and anti-Hungarian attitudes of
his supporters in that province. In Transylvania the Hungarians and
the Jews, because of their preponderance in urban commercial and
professional activities, were linked as common "exploiters of the
Romanian masses." In Transylvania too the nationality problems
were further aggravated by the presence of the Saxons and the
political significance which that group assumed after the rise of
Hitler in Germany.[14]

The Saxons had received preferential treatment from Romania's
rulers even before the rise of Hitler because of their support of
Bucharest and their sharing of a common antagonism toward
Hungarians and Jews. With Hitler's advent and the corollary
strengthening of the influence, if not yet the power, of the Romanian
extreme right, the Saxons were regarded as a potential link, or at
least contact, with Berlin for those political organizations that were
in power, or seeking power, in Greater Romania. By 1936, as the
first overt expressions of Hungarian revisionism were voiced by
Budapest to its friends in Rome and Berlin, the importance of the
Saxons as a possible counterweight to Hungarian revisionism in
Transylvania and as supporters of Romanian positions in Berlin
became more pronounced. Moreover, as the shift to the right in

Romania in general gained momentum by 1937, the Saxons were used both by Nazi Germany and by pro-Nazi organizations such as Codreanu's Iron Guard as tools in their attempts to fulfill common political goals. It should be noted, however, that even during this period of sharpening of nationality conflicts in Transylvania, violations of the constitutional rights of Hungarians and of their alleged supporters, the Jews, were not legally evident. What was evident was the worsening of the psychological climate, the decline of the levels of toleration by Romanians of Hungarians and Jews. In fact, it was not until 1938 that overt legal violations of minority rights occurred in Greater Romania following the establishment of the first radical right-wing government—that of Goga-Cuza, following the national elections of December 1937.[15] But it should be noted that discriminatory measures against the Hungarians became evident only after the Munich and ensuing crises, which affected Romania's relations with Hungary, with the Soviet Union, with the Axis, and with her traditional allies.

Italian support of Hungarian revisionist claims and Russian reluctance to abandon its own revisionist claims to Bessarabia, so manifest in the 1930s, were taken in stride by Bucharest until German revisionism itself assumed significant proportions. Hitler's support of the Sudeten Germans' demands were perceived as ominous for Czechoslovakia, but the Czechoslovak contacts with Moscow and the Axis' with Budapest were deemed ominous for Romania. The First Vienna Award of 1938 which favored Hungary's claims to Czechoslovakia, caused panic in Bucharest and placed the question of maintenance of the territorial integrity of Greater Romania on the front burner of political activities and concerns. To most Romanian political leaders it was no longer a question of whether territorial revisions were to occur but of how to cut losses.[16]

Reconstruction of the political dynamics of Romania between the fall of 1938 and the fall of 1940, during which period the territorial integrity of the state was the paramount concern of all political forces, remains a difficult and controversial task.[17] It seems fair to say, however, that all political organizations—with the exception of the communists—were united in opposition to any territorial revisionism but aware of the likelihood of Hitler imposing a rectification of Romania's borders with Hungary in the foreseeable future. Few believed that France or England could effectively guarantee Romania's territorial integrity, but most were persuaded that Soviet revisionism could be contained because of Hitler's seemingly implacable hostility toward Stalin's Russia. In fact, the gradual abandonment of the French connection by King Carol II and other astute political leaders was largely based on the assumption that neither France nor Britain could safeguard Romania's integrity and that the French and the British, in their quest for an arrangement with Stalin, would be more likely to support Soviet revisionism against Romania than Hitler ever would.

In line with this general assessment of political realities, Bucharest entered into pourparlers with Budapest and with the Axis powers with a view to ascertaining the extent of likely losses of Transylvanian territory to Hungary. In this process the Romanians sought to exploit the often conflicting German and Italian interests in Eastern Europe in general and with respect to Hungary and Romania in particular. In this process too, Romanian political leaders found it necessary to proclaim their determination to maintain the territorial integrity of Romania and to rally the Romanian masses against revisionists and pro-revisionists, most notably against Jews and communists but also against Hungarians.

The juggling for the survival of Greater Romania and of its political leaders is well known except for one key aspect which affected the ultimate resolution of Hungary's territorial claims in Transylvania. It is clear that the destruction of Greater Romania which occurred in 1940 was not due to Hungarian revisionism as such but to the fatal Hitler-Stalin pact of August 1939. As far as Romania was concerned this unimaginable agreement which rendered all game plans obsolete meant the inevitable loss of Bessarabia to the USSR.

It is uncertain just how many Romanian leaders were aware of the secret clauses of the agreement, but it is certain that many suspected the worst in August 1939. The Soviet occupation of Bessarabia and Northern Bukovina in June 1940 certainly came as no surprise to the communists who had been alerted to the Soviet move; it also failed to surprise political realists whose proverbial mistrust of Russia seemed vindicated by Stalin's action. What did surprise everyone, however, was the realization, soon after the occupation of the Romanian territories, of a connection between Soviet and Hungarian revisionism, which was to affect the ensuing negotiations between Hungary and her Axis partners and the Romanian government in Bucharest.

It has been ascertained by serious researchers of territorial revisionism in Eastern Europe that links between Hungarian and Soviet revisionism antedated June 1940; that, in fact, Moscow was supportive of Hungary's demands throughout the interwar years.[18] Such an interpretation of Russo-Hungarian relations is indeed plausible given the antagonism shared by Moscow and Budapest toward Bucharest following the Romanian military intervention in Hungary before Trianon and the securing of territories deemed Hungarian, and respectively Russian, by Greater Romania after World War I. But pending publication of documented studies of these relations for the interwar years, it seems desirable to limit our observations to actual evidence related only to Russo-Hungarian relations in 1940. In this respect, the evidence is conclusive that Molotov encouraged the Hungarians to push their "legitimate" claims in Transylvania during the summer of 1940 in an obvious effort to lessen Hungary's dependence on the Axis and to so weaken a dismembered Romania as to preclude meaningful revanchist action by Bucharest. It is also clear that Budapest used Moscow's support as leverage in its own dealings with Berlin, Rome, and Bucharest and that the Moscow connection proved to be somewhat counterproductive.[19] Whether Hitler's blueprint for partition of Transylvania would have been more generous to Hungary had it not been for Russia's actions in Romania and overtures to Budapest is uncertain, but it is evident that the Führer was anxious to prevent the total humiliation of Romania and to secure control over Romania's strategic resources, as well as to gain support for Germany's plans against the USSR and for Romania's participation therein by assuming the role of the "honest broker" in matters territorial. Thus, the Second Vienna Award of August 1940 whereby Northern Transylvania was returned to Hungary achieved Hitler's immediate goals but not the long-range ones of the principal parties involved, the Hungarians and the Romanians. The Treaty of Trianon may have been repudiated in 1940, but the fundamental problem of territorial allocations and rights of national minorities in Transylvania remained unsolved. It is thus not surprising that Trianon is still a household word in the vocabulary of international relations some sixty years after the dismemberment of the Austro-Hungarian conglomerate.

In truth, the Vienna Award was unsatisfactory to both Romania and Hungary.[20] The Romanians vowed to recoup the lost territories while the Hungarians thought that they were shortchanged by not receiving all of Transylvania. The treatment of Hungarians in Romanian Tr nsylvania and of Romanians in Hungarian Transylvania was su as to raise animosities among nationalities and governments to historically-unsurpassed levels. Hungarian Jews or Jewish Hungarians suffered more in Hungarian Transylvania than in Romanian territories with the resultant virtual annihilation of that minority, ostensibly protected by the Treaty of Trianon and implementing accords. Only the Saxons benefitted from the repudiation of Trianon. As the protégés of Nazi Germany they enjoyed a privileged status unprecedented since medieval times. But all this was to change in 1945 when Stalin returned Northern Transylvania to Romania.

The repudiation of the Vienna Award was ostensibly based on the illegitimacy of Hitler's actions rather than on acceptance of the validity of Trianon.[21] In fact, Stalin's refusal to return Bessarabia and Northern Bukovina to Romania and Russia's seizure of territories in other parts of East Central Europe were conclusive proof of Stalin's continuing rejection of the legality of previous treaties affecting Eastern Europe. Reconciliation of political differences among nationalities and states concerned with Transylvania was assumed to be inevitable because of the common rejection of fascism and acceptance of the comradely principles inherent to communist doctrine and practice. To demonstrate the validity of this dogma, the equality of rights among coinhabiting nationalities was repeated *ad nauseam* and, during the early years of communist rule, the Romanian leaders extended unusual privileges to "democratic" Hungarians, to antifascist Jews, and even to repentant Saxons. Minority rights were given special attention in the Constitution of 1952 when the Hungarian Autonomous Region was established in the predominantly Hungarian-inhabited part of Transylvania.[22]

But reconciliation and harmony under communism proved to be even more ephemeral than under previous political systems. The harshness of communist rule was unacceptable to most inhabitants of Transylvania. Antagonisms were either papered over or temporarily suppressed but not forgotten. This is not to say that in the late forties and early fifties the Hungarians in Transylvania—or in Budapest for that matter—longed for reincorporation of Transylvania into the Hungarian body politic. It is to say, however, that dissatisfaction with communism in general was nearly all-pervasive among Transylvania's inhabitants and that any change within the extended Soviet empire in East Central Europe would have been welcomed by all nationalities. As it happened, following Stalin's death, limited options became available to the more mobile minorities—the Jews and the Saxons—and by 1956 they appeared to be available also to the Hungarians. And indeed, after the Hungarian Revolution of 1956, the Hungarian question in Transylvania was born again much in the mold of the interwar years, yet within the framework of new internal and external political orders.[23]

The Hungarian Revolution revealed the lack of acceptance of communist rule by Hungarians, whether in Hungary or in Transylvania. The Hungarians in Transylvania did not join the Hungarian revolutionaries but were clearly supportive of the aims of their conationals in Hungary. The anti-communist sentiments of the Hungarians in Transylvania were representative of that of other nationalities in that province but was singled out by the communist Romanian regime for political purposes essentially unrelated to nationality questions. Specifically, the Hungarian Revolution and its reverberations in Transylvania were exploited by Romania's leader Gheorghe Gheorghiu-Dej to secure his own power base which was threatened by Khrushchev's plans to replace the Stalinist Romanian leadership with one of his own choice. As self-styled protector and executor of Romanian national and communist interests, based on "objective Romanian conditions," the self-proclaimed architect of a Romanian road to socialism was able to justify the correctness of his own policies as opposed to the Hungarian ones which led to the threatening Hungarian Revolution. The Romanian road to socialism, after 1956, became increasingly more nationalist as its scope and validity were continually challenged by Khrushchev and his followers in the Kremlin. Thus, first Gheorghiu-Dej and later Nicolae Ceaușescu reverted more and more to traditional Romanian policies on matters related to the rights and privileges of national minorities. And, as pressures from Moscow mounted and a Romanian road to independence within the Soviet bloc emerged more clearly in the 1960s, the Romanian leadership adopted extreme nationalist positions commensurate with claims of execution of historic legacy rooted in the legitimacy of the entire Romanian historic experience since the days of the Dacian warrior Burebista.[24] In the process the Transylvania question, in all its historic aspects, became of paramount concern to Bucharest and, perhaps only to a slightly lesser one, also to Moscow and Budapest.

There are indeed very close similarities between contemporary Romanian positions and policies and those of the interwar years.

The Romanianization of Transylvania and corresponding decline in rights and privileges enjoyed by coinhabiting nationalities—particularly the Hungarians bears striking similarities to the policies of previous Romanian regimes. As in the past, the constitutional rights of the national minorities in Transylvania are being observed *de jure*, but the selective imposition of quotas based on nationality has reduced the one-time virtually unlimited opportunities for employment and political representation enjoyed by Hungarians, Saxons, and Jews. Romanianization has also affected educational and cultural opportunities for members of national minorities again not because of the elimination of schools, theaters, and publications in the languages of the minorities but because of the necessity of integration for possible advancement within the contemporary Romanian order.

The motivations for the adoption of restrictive minority policies, particularly against the Hungarians, are manifold. Apart from the need to pose as the defender of Romania's historic interests and traditions—which by definition entails acceptance of the nationalist historic tradition—Ceaușescu has pursued a Romanian road to communism based on Romanian autarchic principles of long standing, as best expressed in the slogan of the 1920s: "By ourselves." As the implementing policies have been no more successful than those adopted by previous exponents of the same doctrine, Romanian economic conditions today are markedly worse than those of Hungary. Thus, the disaffection of Transylvania's Hungarians with Romanianization is exacerbated by comparisons of their own living standards in Romania with those of their conationals in Hungary. Finally, Soviet exploitation of the disaffection of the Hungarian minority in Transylvania for the express purpose of checking Romanian deviations from policies devised by Moscow and accepted by faithful members of COMECON and the Warsaw Pact has further aggravated the nationality problem in Transylvania.[25]

There is little talk of outright revisionism within the Soviet bloc, although fear of yet another repudiation of the Trianon treaty through a contemporary version of the Vienna Award is apparent in Romania. What tends to contribute to that fear are the activities of interested parties abroad which, in a manner reminiscent of similar attacks during the interwar years, have steadily attacked Romania's policies toward national minorities on the grounds of their violating human rights. And, as in some instances, formulations of classical

Hungarian revisionism with proper reinvocation of the "betrayal" of Trianon are becoming louder and clearer, the specter of actual revisionism has reappeared on the East Central European political arena.

"Plus ça change, plus c'est la même chose" may not be an accurate historic slogan. It is, however, applicable to East Central Europe because the Soviet empire has adopted the essential policies of the Tsarist, Habsburg, and Ottoman empires of yore for the attainment of its goals and because member nations—whether integral components or vassal states of that empire—have not forgotten the lessons of the past.

Notes

1. The text of the Treaty of Trianon will be found in *The Treaties of Peace 1919-1923* Vol. I compiled by Lt.-Col. Lawrence Martin (New York: Carnegie Endowment for International Peace, 1924), pp. 457–648.

2. A succinct study of these issues will be found in Stephen Fischer-Galati, "Romanian Nationalism," in Peter F. Sugar and Ivo J. Lederer, eds. *Nationalism in Eastern Europe* (Seattle: University of Washington Press, 1969), pp. 373–395.

3. R. W. Seton-Watson, *A History of the Roumanians* (Cambridge: Cambridge University Press, 1934), pp. 548–550.

4. The most complete and perceptive analysis of these problems will be found in Henry L. Roberts, *Rumania: Political Problems of an Agrarian State* (New Haven: Yale University Press, 1951), pp. 89 ff.

5. See especially the comprehensive study by Sherman D. Spector, *Rumania at the Paris Peace Conference: A Study of the Diplomacy of Ioan I.C. Brătianu* (New York: Bookman Associates, 1962), pp. 67 ff.

6. Roberts, *Rumania*, pp. 22 ff.

7. *Ibid.*, pp. 36–39.

8. Spector, *Rumania*, pp. 98 ff.

9. Important data will be found in Walter M. Bacon, Jr., *Behind Closed Doors: Secret Papers on the Failure of Romanian-Soviet Negotiations, 1931–1932* (Stanford: Hoover Institution Press, 1979), pp. 3 ff.

10. The most intelligent overview of these problems is by Eugen Weber, "Romania," in Hans Rogger and Eugen Weber, eds. *The European Right: A Historical Profile* (Berkeley: University of California Press, 1966), pp. 501–574.

11. See especially C.A. Macartney, *Hungary and Her Successors: The Treaty of Trianon and Its Consequences 1919-1937* (London: Oxford University Press, 1937), pp. 284 ff.

12. Stephen Fischer-Galati, *Twentieth Century Rumania* (New York: Columbia University Press, 1970), pp. 29 ff.

13. Weber, *Romania*, and the important study by Nicholas M. Nagy-Talavera, *The Green Shirts and the Others* (Stanford: Hoover Institution Press, 1970) are most informative on these topics.

14. See Macartney, *Hungary*, pp. 284 ff. and Hugh Seton-Watson, *Eastern Europe Between the Wars, 1918-1941* (Cambridge: Cambridge University Press, 1945), pp. 277 ff.

15. Roberts, *Rumania*, pp. 206 ff.

16. The essential study is by Béla Vágó, "Le Second Diktat de Vienne: Les Préliminaires," *East European Quarterly*, II:4, 1969, pp. 415-437. See also William O. Oldson, "Romania and the Munich Crisis: August-September 1938," *East European Quarterly*, XI:2, 1977, pp. 177-190.

17. Fischer-Galati, *Twentieth Century Rumania*, pp. 46 ff; Roberts, *Rumania*, pp. 206 ff. See also the interesting contemporary study by Al. Gh. Savu, *Dictatura regală, 1938-1940* (București: Editura Politică, 1970).

18. See Vago, "Le Second Diktat: Les Préliminaires," pp. 415 ff. and especially his "Le Second Diktat de Vienne: Le partage de la Transylvanie," *East European Quarterly*, V:1, 1971, pp. 47-73.

19. *Ibid.* See also Savu, *Dictatura regală*, pp. 407 ff.

20. Seton-Watson, *Eastern Europe*, pp. 303 ff.

21. Ghita Ionescu, *Communism in Rumania 1944-1962* (London: Oxford University Press, 1964), pp. 107 ff.

22. *Ibid*, pp. 217 ff.

23. Stephen Fischer-Galati, "Rumania," in Béla K. Király and Paul Jónás, eds. *The Hungarian Revolution of 1956 in Retrospect* (Boulder, Colorado: East European Quarterly, 1977), pp. 95-101.

24. *Revista de Istorie*, 32:7, 1979, pp. 1215-1233 contains important data on this subject.

25. Robert F. King, *A History of the Romanian Communist Party* (Stanford: Hoover Institution Press, 1980), pp. 128-134.

Yeshayahu Jelinek

The Treaty of Trianon and
Czechoslovakia: Reflections

The Treaty of Trianon was of major importance for the development of the Czechoslovak Republic.[1] It defined the Republic's
borders with Hungary and fixed the fate of several nations and nationalities. This essay will place the problems of borders and nationalities in historical perspective: and discuss their origin before
the First World War, their formation during the years of 1918–1920,
and their lasting impact.

The treaty merely rubberstamped a historical development. The
new Czecho-Slovak state labored to establish facts long before the
Hungarian delegation fixed its signature on the document.

According to Macartney, the Czechoslovak Foreign Minister
Eduard Beneš, in a message to Karel Kramář, the Czechoslovak
Premier, stated the need ". . . to occupy Slovakia *via facti* and create
fait accomplis; we must command the situation . . ."[2] The Slovak
leader Vavro Šrobar put it this way: "The one who first lays hands
on Slovakia would have it for keeps . . ."[3] The new government
strove from the outset to establish itself on Slovakia's territory; the
southern border confronted it with a problem. Hence Hungarian-
Czecho-Slovak military clashes started immediately with the formation of the state. The Czech and Slovak military might was mostly
inferior to the Hungarian, but it sufficed for the politicians to justify
their territorial claims. In the last count, however, the decision of the
Great Powers rather than the fragile *fait accomplis* brought about
the final results. French adroitness and obstinacy was decisive, and
therefore Paris was charged with the deliberate weakening of
Hungary, with the purpose of curtailing its influence in East Central
Europe.[4]

Whether the fate of Hungary is described as punishment, bad luck,
the vindication of the victors, historical justice, or whatever else, for Czecho-Slovakia the treaty meant the fulfillment of a
dream. At an important consultation of Czecho-Slovak (but for all
practical purposes, only Czech) political leaders on 2 January 1919,

the attending parties learned that neither Germans nor Hungarians would be invited to participate in the treaty negotiations. "The conditions will be dictated to them, and it is only up to us to forward our demands."[5] Consequently, Prague coveted large chunks of their hapless neighbour. The contested area contained coal mines, industrial plants, railroads lines and strategic rail terminals, rich agricultural land and vineyards, as well as several hundreds of thousands Hungarians. The politicians attending the consultation were well aware that their demands contradicted the ethnic principle; they relied on the Entente's wish to weaken Hungary. President Thomas G. Masaryk already warned against the creation of a sizeable Hungarian minority within the Czecho-Slovak borders.[6] He would have preferred a border reflecting ethnic realities, one that would have left a smaller number of Hungarians on the Czechoslovak side. In spite of his conviction, however, he approved, when the time came, the incorporation of large Hungarian-populated areas into the new state.

Prague politicians cautioned the Slovaks to be realistic in their demands. One may doubt, however, whether the Slovak public figures possessed a clear enough picture, indeed any picture, of the future southern borders of their country. Enthusiastic but mostly unexperienced, naive and partly ignorant, the Slovaks relied on the judgement of their Czech brethren.

The Czecho-Slovak delegation in Paris included the talented young Slovak lawyer Štefan Osuský and several lesser Slovak consultants. Nonetheless the guiding directives came from Kramář and Beneš. The results of the skillfully managed campaign were quite impressive. To quote Macartney ". . . sympathy with the Magyars must blend with admiration for the skill of the Czechs in negotiating successfully so many finesses and finally making a contract which their cards never seemed to justify."[7]

Because of the obstacle of the ethnic principle, the Czechs were forced to give in several times. While yielding on their most extremist demands, they were able to secure several purely Hungarian districts of economic and strategic importance. The Czech delegates reasoned that a large proportion of Hungarians were distributed over all of Slovakia, and that while they were taking on a large number of Hungarian people, numerous Slovaks would remain in Hungary. Also, the requested space consisted of a compact geographic unit. Some strategic considerations look ludicrous to us in view of contemporary military technology. In practical terms, the assigned regions granted Czechoslovakia a free and easy access to the Danube river, provided military advantages, enabled unhampered rail- and motor-transportation from the South West to the South East, and furnished the mountainous Slovakia with a rich agricultural hinterland. The competent use of proper arguments advanced the Czecho-Slovak cause. The reasoning of historical justice proved to be somehow less convincing.[8]

The politicians alleged—and have done so with scholarly help until today—that a large proportion of the ethnic Slovak population to the south of the Slovak mountains underwent a process of Magyarization.[9] The previously solid Slovak regions lost their ancient homogenous character, and became Magyarized to varying degrees under the pressure of Hungarian national policies.[10]

Beneš was the architect of Czecho-Slovak victory. He enjoyed the full confidence and support of Prague. Yet the Czechs, much more then the Slovaks, understood the pernicious consequences of creating a huge bloc of captive population, potentially hostile to the state of their stay. This internal opposition was different from the aggressive nationalism expressed in the slogan "nem, nem, soha" (no, no, never, i.e. never giving up the claim of a greater Hungary) types. Yet even urban, moderate, and sensible Hungarians, whether living in Czechoslovakia or abroad, could not acquiesce to an arbitrary decision which created a large minority and forced it to live under alien rule. The Czechoslovak-Hungarian border constituted, and still constitutes, a permanent danger, an apple of discord. External enemies of both nations deployed this apple as a convenient tool for winning influence and facilitating intervention. The French were conscious of the advantage which the mutual hostility within the Danubian basin gave their policy-makers and their sympathizers in local capitals.

In a similar fashion the contested borders made Slovak dependence on Prague inevitable, and provided the Czechs with a stick for taming a rebellious Bratislava. Not by mere chance did President Beneš remind the Slovaks repeatedly during the last war of the fate of their southern territories, and of his activities to regain them. This, after the Germano-Italian "Arbitration of Vienna" of 2 November 1938, awarded to Hungary a larger part of the disputed Slovak regions,[11] with its predominantly Hungarian population.

Tensions in Slovakia's southern rim reoccurred periodically. (Let us recall only a few of the more significant dates: 1928, 1938, 1939–1945, 1946–1948, 1956, and the most recent, 1980.) Those of the Czech politicians who understood the problem, and found the negative outweighting the positive, expressed a willingness to revise the borders[12] The leading Czech Communist, Bohumir Šmeral, called for a revision of frontiers as early as 14 June 1921.[13] Naturally, it was easier for a Czech to agree to a revision of Slovak borders than to be challenged over the historic frontiers of his fatherland. It had to be rather entertaining to watch Slovaks, including rabid Czech-mongers and haters of Beneš and his memory, as they piously subscribed to the results of Czech diplomatic dexterity in Paris. In the eyes of many Slovaks, every inch of land obtained in Paris was sacrosanct, a part of the patrimony of the Slovak people, a gift of Providence—a ground drenched by the blood and sweat of Slovakia's children. Such was, the attitude of Gustav Husák and his Communist friends recently, in 1945.[14] While Hungarian nationalists lamented "the amputated, bleeding regions of the fatherland," Slovak patriots sang odes of joy. Orgies of chauvinism are alike. It is not without interest that a few Slovak nationalists, particularly during the existence of the Slovak state, saw Slovakia's allotment not extensive enough, and claimed Hungarian villages with an allegedly ethnic Slovak population as far south as outskirts of Budapest. They resembled, once again, the Hungarian irreden-tists who aspired to regain the *Felvidék* (Upper Hungary, i.e. Slovakia).

Slovakia profited in many ways from the territorial expansion. The narrow mountain strip between Carpathians and Pannonia could hardly provide enough space for economic and social prosperity. The extensive agriculture of the southern lowlands supplied the country with food and with an outlet for redundant labor in the hills.

At Trianon the Great Powers discriminated against Hungary in favor of Czecho-Slovakia. They awarded the Czechoslovak Republic with another prize at Hungary's expense: the Transcarpathian Rus' (Subcarpathian Ukraine). The St. Germain-en-Laye peace treaty with Austria of 10 September 1919 and its minority-rights paragraphs recorded this transfer. Czecho-Slovak personalities coveted this territory long before the end of the war. Masaryk started to negotiate with several Ruthene personalities in the United States early in 1918, and others held similar talks with Ruthene dignitaries in the old country on a later date. Overriding opposition from various corners, Czechoslovaks succeeded in convincing their partners of the advantages of joining the new republic.[15]

The benefits of holding Transcarpathian Rus' were multiple and varied. The country served as a bridge between Czecho-Slovakia and Romania, two states hostile to Hungary. By holding on to it, Czecho-Slovakia prevented territorial contact between Hungary and Poland, something regarded as dangerous to the new state. The annexation of Transcarpathia to Czecho-Slovakia was preceded by thoughts of attaching it to Poland,[16] of making it independent under a United States governor,[17] and by other, even more colorful plans. Some Ruthenes appealed to Prague to cross the Carpathian chain and absorb parts of Western Ukraine.[18] The solution eventually chosen worked well, however. Since there existed prospects, or dangers, of Russia becoming master of Eastern Galicia, the Great Powers saw in attaching the region to Czecho-Slovakia a way of preventing Bolshevik penetration of East Central Europe.[19]

Schools of Russian and of Ukrainian nationalism claimed alternatively the Ruthene population for themselves. Bolshevik troops could easily follow the precedent of the short-lived "West Ukrainian Republic" and try to conquer the strategic region. France in particular dreaded such a possibility, and supported Czechoslovak aspirations.

In addition to political-strategic considerations, the Czech politicians cherished the prospect of economic-commercial benefits. They habitually spoke about "expansion to the East," presumably through Slovakia and Transcarpathian Rus'. Direct connections with Romania promised uninterrupted railway transportation to the Black Sea ports and perhaps to the planned Transcaucasian line to the Middle and Far East. Czech business interests anticipated a significant increase in trade with Russia, and again the Transcarpathia was regarded to be the natural gate to East Slavonic markets.[20] For Hungary, loss of the territory meant a material disadvantage, for it left her bereft of the area of flood control of most of its rivers and deprived the mother country of further tens of thousands of her people.

The Treaty of Trianon solidified Czecho-Slovakia's territorial growth at the expenses of Hungary. It had significant human-national ramifications, too.[21]

In some sense, Trianon could be regarded as a "nation building" instrument. This was true for Hungary, which for the first time in her history became a genuine nation-state, free of the ballast of subservient minority-nationalities. In a lesser degree (and perhaps as an irony of history) one cannot say the same about the other successor states. Neither Czechoslovakia nor Yugoslavia were ever genuine nation-states. Only Romania could assert that distinction, yet even her situation was checkered by the existence of considerable minorities and by the varied and contradictory traditions of the hodge podge of regions composing the Balkanic kingdom.

Slovaks could enjoy the full benefit of the new conditions. Hungarians and Germans living in Slovakia felt a considerable deterioration of status in comparison with the past. Ruthenes were still torn between the multitude schools of national identity. Although the state recognized Jews and Gypsies as independent nationalities, their particular social conditions do not allow us to judge them by general criteria.

Before the war, the development of Slovak national consciousness was curtailed by Hungarian nationalism, and by the social environment in which Slovaks lived. These circumstances slowed down the process of self-determination and hampered the rise of indigenous nationalism. Certain regions of Western and Central Slovakia could boast a rather small, nationally awakened intelligentsia, ecclesiastic (Lutheran and Catholic) and secular; as well as a moderate attention in the broad masses. Eastern Slovakia could not display even such modest achievements.[22] Impoverished and backward, speaking a dialect different from the rest of Slovakia, and worshiping in the Greek rite of Catholicism, the population stayed apart from the majority of the Slovak people. Hungarians utilized the East Slovakian distinctions for further deepening the chasm within the Slovak people. A slight corrective was offered by expatriate emigrants (the region suffered from extensive emigration) who formed their national consciousness in America, and injected the newly gained convictions into the home population.[23] All in all, on the eve of the First World War Slovak nationalism was still underdeveloped and primitive.

During the process of the formation of the republic, the involved parties were aware of Slovakia's condition. Hence Hungarians insisted on a plebiscite to decide the country's future before signing the treaty,[24] while Czechs and Slovak activists resisted the proposal.[25] The deeply religious Slovak people were said to be unable to separate the political angle of the cult of St. Stephen (the *Staatsidee* of the Hungarian state) from the spiritual one, and could be easily influenced in a pro-Hungarian direction, all the more so, if Hungarians were to be in charge of the plebiscite. Also, the vote of many Magyarized Slovaks augured ill for the national cause. Little, wonder, then, that Czecho-Slovak authorities would have nothing to do with the plebiscite.[26] Aware of the realities,[27] and following the *fait accompli* strategy, they refused any sort of democratic decision-making. President Masaryk put it this way:[28]

> The Slovak nation was oppressed to such a degree that it never had an occasion for political thinking, and would not be able to decide its fate. Therefore it is only natural that the opinions of national leaders should be decisive.

The "national leaders" were of course self-appointed political figures without significant public influence and support. They gathered once only, on 30 October 1918 in the city of Turčiansky Sv. Martin in central Slovakia, to vote on and to accept the so-called "Declaration of the Slovak Nation."[29] That document defined Slovaks as a branch of the unified Czechoslovak nation, and for this nation it demanded the right of self-determination. Several members of the gathering, which came to be known as the Slovak National Council, represented political groups and clusters, while others were unaffiliated. The groups were inactive during the war, and represented largely Western and Central Slovakia. The Declaration reached the population in form of leaflets. Local councils occasionally voiced their agreement with it; the populace expressed its approval, it was said, by manifestations of street violence,[30] hardly legal forms of self-determination.

Nevertheless, it would not be easy to argue against Slovakia's joining Bohemia and Moravia in a common state. In an age when self-determination and independence of nations was made into a sacred law, Slovakia's continued existence under Hungarian government made no sense. All the more so as the Hungarians acquired the dubious fame of being inconsiderate and oppressive toward minorities. On the other hand, the Slovaks were not ready for any sort of independent life, and by no means were able to manage their country's existence by themselves. In fact, it was argued that the ones who were interested in returning Slovakia to Hungary's bosom were also the ones who invented and propagated the slogans of Slovakia's autonomy.[31]

The proposals coming from various corners to attach Slovakia to

Poland remained barren. Poles had only limited contacts with Slovaks in the past, partly because of the natural barrier which separated the two nations. Moreover, Poland on the eve of an independent life had no resources to spare and share with Slovakia. Evidently, nobody but the Czechs could offer and advance Slovakia's separation from the Hungarians. But the country's entrance into the Republic did not come about because its national leaders desired it. It was a *via facti* strategy, as well as the Entente's fear of Hungarian Bolsheviks, that toppled the scales in the direction of Czecho-Slovakia. (At the same time, of course, we shouldn't underestimate the value of the wartime preparatory work carried out by Masaryk and his friends, or the importance of other diplomatic, military, and propagandistic activities abroad.)

Several local "republics" stood in the way of Slovakia's self-determination, and they were to be eliminated before further steps could be taken. The most dangerous was the Slovak Soviet Republic founded by Hungarian, Slovak, and Czech Communists in the city of Prešov in 1919; a motley group of Hungarian and pro-Hungarian patriots formed others. Martial law enforced by Czecho-Slovak troops of occupation paved Slovakia's way into Czecho-Slovakia.

An accepted cliché had it that the Czechs and Czechoslovakia saved the Slovak people from national extinction. But this is a deterministic notion; it denies the existence of creative forces within a nation and predicts the future on the basis of narrowly subjective criteria. In an epoch of national awakening among small nations and stirring, even among very small ethnic groups (the Basques, Bretons, and Corsicans are cases in point), it would be presumptuous to presuppose the disappearance of an entire nation. The fable of "Slovak salvation" belongs to the realm of propaganda whose aim was to justify the break-up of Austria-Hungary, the Peace of Trianon, and their outcome.

There is, however, little doubt that Slovak national survival was indeed in serious danger, and that the Hungarian denationalization drive could boast undeniable achievements. Czech public figures, more experienced in public relations and international politics, guided the Slovak attempt to overthrow Hungarian domination. The Czechs based their activity on the thesis of a single "Czechoslovak" nation with a Czech and a Slovak branch. In the coming years this thesis proved to be a failure and a serious blunder because of the threat it posed to Czech-Slovak coexistence. Also the Czechs' patronizing attitude toward the "poor tinkers" was not very helpful in developing a healthy relation between the two groups.

Slovak nationalists, especially the younger ones who did not know Hungarian supremacy, proved themselves to be ungrateful to the Czechs. The uninhibited and loose behavior of the followers of Hlinka's People Party and of the Communist Party, their blind hatred and hostility, called for resolute actions. The essentially derogatory attitude and firm administrative methods of the departed Hungarian aristocratic rulers were apparently more efficient in dealing with some Slovak hot-heads than the conciliatory policies of the democratic Czech peti-bourgeois. Neither was the Czech expansion to the East as altruistic as presented occasionally. Prague reaped political, economic, territorial and psychological benefits from the annexation of Slovakia. Nonetheless, a denial of Czech compassion for their oppressed relatives would be an affront to historical truth. Slovakia needed Czech assistance and, in one way or the other, got it. Trianon contributed definitively to the nation-building of the Slovak people.

The Ruthenes were less close to Czech hearts than were the Slovaks. Abandoned and destitute, the Ruthenes suffered badly from Hungarian denationalization and dreaded continuous Hungarian domination.[32] (Described as *Natio Fidelissima*, the Ruthenes were entitled to a better treatment in Hungarian hands.) The un-Magyarized intelligentsia split over the question of ethnic-national allegiance. Divided into "Russian," "Ukrainian," and "Rusin" factions, the Ruthenes failed to offer a unified action of self defence. The Hungarians exploited the split thoroughly by a "divide and rule" strategy. Later the Czech masters borrowed a few pages from the Hungarian book of recipes.[33] The Ruthene assumption that all Slavonic Greek Catholics of the regions were co-nationals troubled their relations with the Slovaks. These relations suffered even more from the Ruthene claim on a considerable part of the territory that was thought to be Slovak. The others did not sit idle either, and portrayed Ruthenes as renegade Slovaks—at least the ones living in counties claimed by the Slovaks as well.[34] When drawing the borders between Slovakia and Ruthenia, the Czechs favored the Slovak side. Prague also did not honor the promises given to Ruthene dignitaries, and codified in the treaty of St. Germain and in the Czechoslovak constitution, to grant the people of Ruthenia autonomy and self-rule.[35] To summarize, the Ruthenes benefited less from the collapse of St. Stephan's kingdom. Part of the blame goes to the Czechs, the other part to the forever quarrelling Ruthenes. The *Tertium Gaudens* was Moscow, which annexed the country in 1945, and with that finally penetrated into East Central Europe. But quarrels among the Ruthenes, and with the Slovaks, go on happily among immigrants on the American continent.

Hungarians in Czechoslovakia were not beneficiaries of Trianon. On the contrary; as liberal as the Czech leadership might have been toward minorities, liberalism was not prized too highly by Slovak authorities. Hungarians in the country remained a visible symbol of Slovakia's past. They could easily become the whipping boy, the object of Slovak revenge, and the target of their suspicions. The Hungarian leadership too often sailed along winds blowing from Budapest, and these were not exactly friendly winds. Moreover, as the political conditions changed in East Central Europe, the minority moved toward radicalism.

The Hungarians were living in a democratic republic. They had political representation, and social and cultural institutions to satisfy their spiritual-intellectual needs. The state's agencies respected their particularities, at least to a degree. Economically they were better off then many of their co-nationals in Hungary (although their living standards were somewhat below those of the Czech Slovak population). Did the forced separation stimulate an independent ethnic development, a different ethos, a new consciousness? The interwar period was too short a time to observe such changes. Some idiosyncracies did develop, however. At least a portion of the inhabitants was willing to assimilate, and some Magyarized Slovaks did revert to their native culture. A fraction of the minority acquiesced in the given realities, and the various minority rights helped to soothe the pains of others. Again it was the President Masaryk who from the outset labored for a better understanding. Yet, as István Borsody has observed, minority rights were never proved to be a satisfactory substitute for hoped for majority rights.[36]

The intensive propaganda warfare carried on over the heads of the minority by official agencies and private institutions in Hungary and Czechoslovakia, often had little to do with the actual frustration, worries, and joys of the people. Sometimes, though, the Czechoslovak Hungarians did produce ammunition for new battles, and other times intolerant Slovaks were the instigators. How convenient a tool was the ethnic minority itself in the hands of irredentist propaganda. Budapest and Prague spent enormous amounts of money to castigate the other side, in order of course to win sympathy abroad.

This duel kept the atmosphere tense, and decreased the likelihood of a rapprochement. It aided the anti-democratic elements in Hungary, as well as Slovak nationalists and Communists, in their attacks on liberals and in their defense of totalitarian values. The conflict offered the outside Fascist powers opportunities which they did not fail to grasp. Unfortunately, the liberals on both sides were unable to find a common language and to cooperate.

The authorities plainly regarded the Hungarian minority as a hostage; their treatment of that minority depended on the well being of Slovaks in Hungary. The Slovak press started to discuss this unhuman principle as early as 1919.[37] Accordingly, minority rights could be granted or withdrawn on the basis of reciprocity. Hungary counted among her inhabitants Slovaks, who composed solid ethnic islands. However, the Slovaks in Hungary were a fraction of the mass of Hungarians who resided in Czechoslovakia. Their national life it is true, was not sheer pleasure, and complaints were frequent. A system of turning entire minorities into a football of high policies could not be appreciated easily. In the First Republic, the hostage principle was scarcely applied, if ever. But during the Second World War, when Slovakia turned into a *Schutzstaat* of Berlin, and when the Hungarian revisionism reached the pinnacle of achievement and power, there was no limit to the barbarities on either side.

As stated above, Czechoslovak politicians and diplomats alleged in Paris that many of the Hungarian residents of southern Slovakia—northern Hungary were in reality Slovaks, yet they became the victims of Budapest's Magyarization drive. Consequently, one may say, their incorporation into Slovakia would be an act of historical justice. Strangely enough, representatives of the Great Powers swallowed this phony bait, and its impact could occasionally be felt.[38]

Europe is still crowded with denationalized population, and the process of denationalization is still going on. If each nation would demand for itself its lost brothers, international life would turn into perpetual anarchy. In any case, Czechoslovakia promised to honor the rights of minorities, to abstain from challenging their nationality, and to give them schools in their own language.[39] What would not be done by the bourgeois governments of the First Republic, was accomplished by a Communist-led administration of Prague and Bratislava in 1947. The campaign of "Reslovakization" carried out under premiership of the Communist Klement Gottwald was not any tamer than the work of the notorious HAKATA and other dena- tionalization enterprises in modern Europe. The story of Hungarians in Czechoslovakia is a serialised one. New chapters appear at ir- regular intervals, though their appearance is more or less inevitable.

The Germans of Slovakia identified themselves with the Hungarian cause. By 1918 they were on the verge of losing their ethnic identity and becoming loyal Hungarians. The Germans regret- ted Trianon, supported Hungary as long as they could, and once they could not, they defended zealously their own minority rights.[40] In order to decrease the numerical strength of the Hungarians the Republic backed German efforts to preserve a separate German ethnic identity. In the long run the official policies backfired: being nationally conscious yet short of having a faithful and qualified in- telligentsia, Germans of Slovakia imported teachers, administrators, and other professionals from Bohemia and Moravia. The newcomers brought along the political and social convictions prevalent in their milieu and imbued their clients with these ideas. Thus, in the final analysis, the publicly encouraged and supported policies of de- Hungarization assisted in the Nazification of Slovak (and Transcar- pathian) Germans, another unexpected and bizarre result of Trianon.

The Jews do not fit the regular definition of nationality in the terms discussed here (i.e. language, territorial concentration, and a mother country to look after them). They were, however, major beneficiaries of the change in the region after the First World War.

The Slovak population and its leaders accused Jews of pre-war Hungary of a close cooperation with Budapest authorities in the de- nationalization process. František Votruba, a Czech author familiar with Slovak affairs, understood the Jewish dilemma well:[41] "All in- stincts of life preservation led the Slovak Jewry to secure the good will of those in power; above all it needed to liberate itself from con- ditions of illegality and dependence . . . There were few incentives to join the minute and powerless Slovak elite and the masses of ig- norant population devoid of protection of law." What was com- prehended by an objective Votruba could not be and would not be appreciated by the Slovak intelligentsia, and even less by the general population. The hatred of Jews, a heritage of centuries of religious and social indoctrination, frequently sought rational explanation and found it in all sorts of alleged sins. In Slovakia the Jews pursued their traditional professions, innkeeping probably being the best-known among them. This profession, like the others forced on Jews during centuries of persecution was short on high ethic standards. Consequently the innate hatred of Jews got an objective boost. Also the acceptance of Hungarianhood by many Jews, as well as fanatical Magyarization activity of individuals, alienated the nationally conscious Slovak intelligentsia. Finally, Slovak spokesmen attacked Jews for allegedly serving as informers and stool pigeons to the wartime Hungarian authorities. This is another of the notorious defamations of Jews, used by all their adversaries (in our case by Slovaks *and* by Hungarians alike).

When in 1918 the whole of East Central Europe was hit by a wave of anti-Jewish riots, all regions of Czechoslovakia participated in the outrages. Often the wish to rob Jewish—and non-Jewish—property sparked the riots, and even pre-programmed looting was recorded.[42] Czecho-Slovak officials and the press whitewashed the murder and the looting by describing it as a popular revenge for Jewish misconduct in the past and especially during the war. On the other hand, they omitted to mention the social and political unrest that gave impetus to the riots. Czechoslovak troops coming to secure Slovakia and Ruthenia for the new state made the Jews a special target of persecutions, including summary executions on flimsy pretexts. Nevertheless, the authorities were reluctant to extend protection and help.[43] Vavro Šrobár, the Minister for Slovak Affairs in the government of Prague, justified violence and actually made the Jews responsible for it.[44] Even imprisoned Zionist leaders were found to be enemy agents.[45] Hungarian troops, occasionally commanded by Jewish officers and manned by Jewish soldiers, enforced law and order and assisted victims of the disturbances. During the Hungarian Bolshevik invasion Jews again drew the vindictiveness of Czecho-Slovak officials and troops. And again they were between hammer of the Bolsheviks and anvil of their foes. All in all, the new Czechoslovak regime did not augur well for the Jews in Slovakia and Ruthenia. If Jews did nonetheless abandon their pro-Hungarian sentiments and eventually turned into constructive and faithful citizens of the Czechoslovak state it was to a great extent because of the good will shown by President Masaryk and his lieutenants.[46] Protests by Jewish and Zionist organizations from abroad, as well as local Jewish presentations, finally met with a favorable response.

The Republic introduced liberal policies toward the Jews, enabling them to assert their Jewish identity and choose their own representation. The recognition of Jewish nationality was designed also to reduce the number of citizens opting for the German and Hungarian nationality. (Similarly, the Gypsies were given the choice of their own nationality.) In certain municipalities, Jews opting for their own nationality sharply reduced the number of Hungarians (and Germans) and hence put them all outside the bracket required for execution of the minority right as stipulated by the Republic's constitution.

The condition of Jews in the Republic worsened as one moved toward the East. Slovak nationalists in particular refused to recognize the benefits of cooperation with the Jewish population, and made them a convenient scape-goat for the country's ills. In Ruthenia the Czech authorities joined the local Jew-baiters. They tampered with legally granted rights and benefits, and through intimidation pressed the Jews to serve the needs of Czech political parties and of the central government.[47]

Jews of the eastern parts of Czechoslovakia however, reaped major rewards from Trianon. They grew nationally conscious, free of forced national identities. They learned to exercise the legal rights of independent citizens and ceased to be subservient petitioners. The liberal and humane policies accorded to the Jews by the central government made them into convinced believers of Czechoslovak democracy, although Jews were still subject to unfriendliness and discrimination by state agencies. Anti-Semitism did not disappear. In Slovakia Jewish interests paralleled those of the democratic pro-Czechoslovak elements, and Jews offered voluntarily to cooperate with governmental representatives and private institutions. The situation was less ideal in Transcarpathia, though nonetheless better than in the past. Many a Czechoslovak Jew did not regret the treaty of Trianon.

This essay reflected on the territorial and the national changes brought about in East Central Europe by the First World War and the Trianon Peace Treaty. The changes in the lives of millions of human beings who were the silent victims of developments beyond their comprehension, cannot be accurately recorded. It was they who nevertheless tried to make a new life for themselves in a radically altered political, social and psychological environment.

Notes

1. Originally, the name of the state was hyphenated (Czecho-Slovakia). The new constitution, accepted in Summer 1920, stipulated the unhyphenated name (Czechoslovakia).

2. Carlyle A. Macartney, *Hungary and Her Successors* (London, Toronto, New York: Oxford University Press, 1937), p. 106.

3. Quoted by Dagmar Perman, *The Shaping of the Czechoslovak State* (Leiden: E. J. Brill, 1962), p. 78.

4. Stephen Borsody, "Czechoslovakia and Hungary, in Miloslav Rechcigl, Jr., ed., *Czechoslovakia Past and Present* vol. I (The Hague: Mouton, 1968), p. 666.

5. Praměny k ohlasu velké říjnové socialistické revoluce a vzniku ČSR, *Boj o směr vývoje československého statu* vol. I (Prague: Nakladatelství Československé Akademie Vied, 1965), p. 38; document no. 26.

6. *Ibid.* p. 41; document no. 26.

7. Macartney, p. 103.

8. Slovensko, *L'ud* vol. I (Bratislava: Obzor, 1974), pp. 440–51.

9. Praměny: p. 103.

10. Harold W. V. Temperley, ed., *A History of the Peace Conference of Paris* vol. IV (London: Henry Frowde and Hodder & Stoughton, 1921) p. 271; Joseph Chmelař, *National Minorities in Central Europe* (Prague: Orbis, 1937), p. 18.

11. Examples, see at the Balch Institute for Ethnic Studies, Philadelphia, PA, Hurban Papers, box 74–60, Extraordinary meeting of the government, President Beneš's report on his sojourn to the United States, London, June 17, 1943; President Beneš's address: Victory, Before the return home, London, March 28, 1945.

12. U.S. National Archives (Washington, D.C.) 860F.00/1-746, summary no. 377, December 19–25, 1946; 860F.00/9-564, airgram no. A-1254, Jefferson Caffery to the Secretary of State, Paris, September 6, 1946.

13. *Rudé Právo* (Prague), June 14, 1921.

14. Marta Vartiková, "Československá pracovná konferencia KSS v Košiciach ako príos pri tvorbe vládneho programu prvéj vlády Národného Frontu Čechov a Slovákov," *Historický Časopis, XXIII, 2 (1975), pp. 170–200.*

15. Praměny, p. 43; document no. 28; *Národné Noviny* (Pittsburgh), January 23, March 13, and April 24, 1919.

16. New York *Times*, January 2, 1920.

17. *Times*, January 4, 1920.

18. Praměny, p. 79; document no. 54.

19. Praměny, p. 65; document no. 40; pp. 85–86; document no. 60.

20. Praměny, pp. 36–42; document no. 26.

21. In the 1821 census the following number of people reported their nationality as Slovak: 1 967 870; Magyar: 744 621; Ruthene: 461 449; German: 139 880 (in Slovakia only); Jewish 70 522 (in Slovakia only). (Juraj Purgat, *Od Trianonu po Košice* (Bratislava: Epocha; 1970), p. 301.

22. Anton Štefánek *et al.*, ed., *Milan Hodža* (Prague: Českomoravské podniky tiskarské, 1930), pp. 784–87; *NN*, February 20, 1919.

23. *NN*, January 2 and 25, 1919.

24. *Times*, April 14, 1920.

25. Czechoslovak statesmen traditionally disliked plebiscites, because of the inherent dangers in a territory that has national minorities.

26. According to Macartney (p. 103), Oscar Jászi predicted the defeat of Hungarians in the proposed plebiscite. He also favored international supervision of the balloting.

27. Ferdiš Juriga, *Blahozvest' kriesenia Slovenského národa a Slovenskej krajiny* (Trnava: Urbánek a spol., 1937), p. 194; *NN*, August 28, 1919.

28. *NN*, February 20, 1919.

29. Juriga, pp. 81, 82.

30. Štefánek, p. 236; Praměny, p. 21; document no. 11.

31. *NN*, April 3, and June 19, 1919.

32. Praměny, p. 136; document no. 120; *NN*, April 24, 1919.

33. Praměny, pp. 358, 359; document no. 28.

34. *NN*, July 17 and 27, 1919.

35. Praměny, p. 94; document no. 67; pp. 101, 102; document no. 75; pp. 364, 365.

36. Borsody, 670.

37. *NN*, March 27, 1919.

38. Temperley, p. 271; *NN*, April 17, 1919.

39. *NN*, August 28, and September 20, 1919.

40. *NN*, June 5, 1919.

41. Štefánek, p. 281.

42. *NN*, January 2, and 16, 1919. Parents of this writer often recalled the looting in their respective birthplaces, Žarnovica and Prievidza, and the preceding occurrences.

43. The Slovak paper in Pittsburgh *Národné Noviny* (National Press), which regularly charged Jews with Magyarization and with exploitation of the Slovak people, did not hesitate to deny the occurrence of bloody pogroms in Poland and the Ukraine, and described them as Jewish falsehood and propaganda against the Slavonic people (June 5 and 12, 1919).

44. *The Jews of Czechoslovakia* vol. I (New York: Society for History of

Czechoslovak Jews, 1968), pp. 225–27; Prameny, p. 192; document no. 167; NN, August 28, 1919.

45. The Jews, vol. I, pp. 223–25.

46. Jindřich Kohn, "Masaryk a slovenská otázka židovská," in Jozef Rudinský, ed., Slovensko Masarykovi (Prague: Nakladetel'stvo Vojtecha Tilkovského, 1930), pp. 213–18.

47. NN April 24, 1919; Times, March 7, 1920.

Thomas Karfunkel

The Impact of Trianon
on the Jews of Hungary

The Jewish population of pre-Trianon Hungary enjoyed greater legal security, social acceptance and economic well-being than the Jewish communities of other East Central European states. However, anti-Semitism was present and affected, with varying degrees of intensity, all strata of society. It ranged from the cultural snobbery of the aristocracy to the crude popular stereotyping of the lower classes. During the last decades of the Dual Monarchy, to the more traditional, religion-based prejudice was added a politically motivated anti-Semitism that was the product of the reaction to the modernization that was slowly changing the character of society.

The century before World War I witnessed the rapid and fundamental improvement of the condition of the Jews of Hungary. The legislations promulgated, the economic opportunities created, the general absence of anti-Jewish agitation, the enlightened attitude of the ruling circles, all created a propitious atmosphere for growth for the Jewish community. This was noted in neighboring lands.[1] There was a massive migration of Jews into Hungary, primarily from Galicia. The estimated number of Jews in Hungary in 1787 was only 93,000. At the time of the Revolution of 1848, Jews numbered 336,000, by 1869, 542,000, and the census of 1910 showed the presence of 911,227 out of a total population of 18.265,493 in Hungary proper. This was a spectacular increase, an eloquent testimony of Hungary's appeal to the generally persecuted and shunned Jews of East Central Europe.

Numerical increase was accompanied by official acts leading toward legal equality. The Act of Emancipation was granted by the revolutionary government in 1849. In 1867 legal equality between Christian and Jews was promulgated, and in 1895 Judaism was granted the status of a "received religion," a designation that entitled it to governmental support and, ironically, a designation that was withheld from a number of Christian denominations.[2]

There were a number of factors that played a role in producing a favorable climate for Jews in Hungary. The Dual Monarchy was a multinational empire, a hopeless amalgamation of nationalities large and small, with conflicting aims and programs, and with limited appreciation for the accomplishments and aspirations of neighboring groups. The national question, in the Age of Nationalism, was a simmering volcano ready to erupt and jeopardize not only the tranquility of the state, but the state itself. The two nationalities in power, when not preoccupied with their own conflict, were engaged in a perennial balancing act, with a constantly shifting program of concessions and threats vis à vis their minorities, to preserve the status quo. The Census of 1910, the last one held in Austria-Hungary, identified 54.5% of the population of Hungary as Hungarian. This majority status, extremely important for political as well as psychological reasons, was gained with the cooperation of Jews who were not classified as a separate national group and who overwhelmingly opted for Hungarian nationality. Jews constituted only 5% of the population, but it was the difference between a majority or a minority position for the Hungarians. A Hungarian-Jewish alliance was formed.

Jewish self-identification as Hungarians was only partially motivated by the advantages such declaration produced. A large segment of the Jewish community enthusiastically and voluntarily submitted to the process of Magyarization. Jews in Hungary spoke the Hungarian language, championed the Hungarian culture, assimilated, intermarried and energetically supported the objectives of Hungarian nationalism.[3] This process of Jewish acculturation was encouraged and rewarded by the Hungarian establishment. In addition to offering badly needed numerical extension, it also confirmed the claim of Hungarian cultural superiority. It could, and did, serve as an example for the other minorities.

The Hungarian-Jewish alliance was a natural one, based on self-interest. The Hungarian squirearchy was primarily concerned about the perpetuation of its dominant political position, and it appreciated Jewish support. It was also very comfortable with this support, for the Jews could never mature into a threatening partner, with a political program calling for autonomy or separate existence. Simultaneously, the emergence of a Jewish capitalist class, and Jewish economic pursuits in general, received official encouragement. The Hungarian gentry was not overly attracted to these activities and Jewish penetration was preferred to that of any other ethnic group, including, or perhaps especially, that of the German minority.

The Hungarian-Jewish partnership was an effective combination for it blended political authority with economic power. The city of Budapest may be seen as the symbol of this viable and productive alliance. The city was the capital of a large, heterogeneous state ruled over by Hungarians, who controlled all the institutions and instruments of political power. Budapest was also the home of a large Jewish community, comprising almost a quarter of the population. The city and its environments were in the process of being developed into the industrial heartland of the state by a predominantly Jewish entrepreneurial class. Budapest was also the center of a secularized and magyarized Jewish intelligentsia that played a very active role in the cultural life of the nation. It was a city where the social barriers separating Christian and Jew (especially in the upper segments of each group) were lowered, and many Jews completely abandoned their Jewish legacy and embraced a Hungarian identity.[4]

Anti-Semitism, and particularly its more violent and uncontrollable impulses, was frowned upon by the ruling establishment. The ruling circles perceived themselves as a part of the liberal tradition that endorsed the concept of toleration, and sensed that any attack on their junior partners was an attack on the system and on a Hungarian hegemony tenuously maintained. It may be suggested, already at this early point, that the chief component of the Hungarian policy toward Jews was not a very strong philosophical convinction, but rather a pragmatic understanding of national/class interest.

Before Trianon, Jews needed Hungarian assistance to gain legal and social acceptance and economic advancement, but the Hungarians also needed the Jews to maintain their monopoly on political power. C. A. Macartney concludes that

> The talent and industry of the Jewish industrial and financial bourgeoisie was indeed the most powerful prop to the ruling class, which could not otherwise have existed and developed as it did.[5]

Trianon was the watershed in the history of the Jews in Hungary. The pressure of domestic and international events that led to Trianon and its consequences destroyed the Hungarian-Jewish alliance and gradually wiped out all the benefits and advantages that it bestowed on Hungarian Jewry. Trianon-Hungary was a compact and homogeneous state where the dominant nationality, the Hungarians, constituted approximately 90% of the population. The Jewish minority was not needed anymore to maintain a numerical superiority. In addition, Jews were now one of the two significant minorities in Hungary, the other being the Germans.

Trianon-Hungary was the Hungary of Miklós Horthy. The Horthy regime was established by military force after the defeat of the Hungarian Soviet primarily at the hands of a Romanian Interventionist Army. It was an authoritarian system of government, whose authoritarianism was unsuccessfully concealed by a facade of pseudo-parliamentarianism. It was not a totalitarian or fascist dictatorship; some opposition, in Parliament as well as in the Press, was tolerated. Horthy, as Regent, was the symbol and the final authority for a ruling group that was never monolithic in composition or with respect to its political orientation. It was a reactionary regime that moved ideologically further to the Right with the establishment of the Nazi dictatorship and the growth of German influence in international relations.

Anti-Semitism was a basic doctrine of Horthy-Hungary. It appeared consistently, though in a variety of forms and with varying degrees of intensity during the life-span of the regime. Anti-Semitism is usually the product of a number of factors; political, socioeconomic, religious or psychological, and the Hungarian version was no different. However, it is possible to isolate seven primary factors that produced the anti-Semitism of post-Trianon Hungary, and they were: the "Szeged idea"; domestic politicking; the identification of Jews with the dissemination of communist propaganda; the preponderance of Jewish capital in the economic life of the nation; the fear that the Jewish population was growing too rapidly and posed a threat to the character and identity of the nation; the belief that the Jews were an alien and unassimilable minority and the conviction that anti-Jewish acts at home would earn diplomatic support for foreign policy objectives.

The "Szeged idea"

Szeged, a large city in Southern Hungary, was the headquarters of the Horthy-led counter-revolutionary forces. The "Szeged idea" was the philosophical underpinning of a movement that generally stressed action rather than thought. It was a program that envisioned specific and radical changes. It was the original program of the anti-democratic interests that sponsored and carried out the White Terror (Autumn 1919–Summer 1920), and established a dictatorship that ruled the state until the German military occupation in the final phase of World War II. The program, pre-dating the establishment of any fascist system of government, suggested a form of nascent fascism.[6]

Anti-Semitism was a central feature of the Szeged program. It expressed violent opposition to communism, and the Jews were identified as the prime supporters of that doctrine. The program promoted the idea of an exclusionary and racialist Hungarian state where Jews, by definition, could not fit in. It expressed hostility toward the feudal aristocracy that traditionally acted as both the ally and protector of the Jewish capitalist class. It promised jobs in the professions and commerce, where Jews predominated. It was a program appealing to Hungarians and directed against non-Hungarians, and in the long run against Magyarized non-Hungarians as well. There was a call for the radical transformation of Hungarian society, to a very great extent, at the expense of the Jewish community. It was essentially a class-oriented program with benefits offered to the middle classes, and it was also a classic right-radical manifesto, relying on revolutionary rhetoric—it promised fundamental changes, while at the same time making a commitment to preserve tradition. In practical terms little was offered to the urban and rural lower classes. The radical nature of the program was very much evident in the call for the solution of the Jewish problem. The idea was translated into action with promptness by the Order Detachments that conducted a bloody pogrom against the Jews in the countryside while Horthy was still in the process of consolidating his power. The anti-Semitic credentials of the regime were solidly established.

The "Szeged idea" was promoted by a host of officially sanctioned overt and covert organizations. There were patriotic and secret societies, professional organizations, student federations, veterans' groups, irredentist and racist associations. The common feature of all of these formations was the ineligibility of Jews to become members. Some of the associations exercised considerable power. The most potent group was the Hungarian Association of National Defense (*Magyar Országos Véderő Egyesület* or MOVE), organized by officers but including civilians as well. It operated behind the scenes and served as both a pressure group and as a mutual help society. Its success was ensured by the high positions many of its leading members occupied in the regime. In January of 1919 Gyula Gömbös, the future Premier, was elected as the President. Militant anti-Semitism was a central feature of the movement. Gömbös issued anti-Semitic pamphlets with racialist overtones years before that kind of literature became politically fashionable. The civilian inner core of MOVE received the appropriate designation of the Hungarian Scientific Race-Protecting Society (*Magyar Tudományos Fajvédő Egyesület*).[7] The middle class ambitions of the supporters were expressed by attempts to squeeze the Jews out of the professions. In 1920 legislation was enacted, the notorious *numerus clausus*, that restricted the number of Jewish students in higher education to 5%, the approximate percentage of Jews in the total population.

The government did not always pursue policies that were consistent with the spirit of Szeged. The "idea" was often toned down and diluted by successive waves of officials who were forced to govern under the pressures of domestic and international considerations. The *numerus clausus* was not enforced. The degrees earned by Hungarian Jewish students at foreign universities were acknowledged without difficulty by the authorities. But the "Szeged idea" remained, sometimes only as an abstraction, the ideological foundation of the regime.

Domestic politicking

The Szeged movement, from its very beginning, was a coalition of forces. It was an umbrella designation, for under its banners there were different interest groups with different backgrounds and orientations. There was tension and constant jockeying for positions, power struggles between zealous and lukewarm supporters of the (Szeged) program. The latter would pay lip service to the ideals without any strong desire to implement many aspects of it. This, more moderate, wing was more concerned with the establishment of conservative orderliness, and regarded the radical points of the program as sheer rhetoric. The militant wing, on the other hand, consisted of the true believers. There was also a class differentiation between the two groups. The lukewarm supporters of the program were led by representatives of the traditional upper classes, while the militants had a more bourgeois identification. The extreme Szeged orientation had great appeal to the bitter refugees from the successor states, who had comfortable pasts but dim prospects for the future, to the junior officers of the Army who had limited promotional opportunities, to the many jobless diploma-holders, to the struggling Christian commercial interests and to ambitious politicians on the fringes of the establishment. Anti-Semitism was the cutting edge, for it identified and it differentiated. Even so, the Bethlen era (1921–1931) was characterized by the ascendancy of the moderate wing. In the 1920's the Jewish question was downplayed, the Bethlen program was dedicated to consolidation and normalization, and to the gaining of international support. Anti-Semitic acts did not fit into this scheme—the goals of the government would have been jeopardized by them. Militants, like Gömbös, felt betrayed. In 1923 the more resentful Szegedists temporarily seceded from the Government Party and organized an opposition group: the Party of Racial Defence (*Fajvédö Párt*).

Tokenism on the Jewish question indicated indifference to the entire Szeged program. Attacks on the government on the Jewish question by supporters of the regime could mobilize support within the ruling establishment as well as attract popular support against policies and individual policy-makers. It is very much revealing of the ideological atmosphere prevailing in the Horthy establishment that even those individual officials who were not particularly anti-Semitic had to adopt an anti-Semitic posture to disarm potential critics. In the 1920's the government was controlled by "reasonable" anti-Semites. The Bethlenite definition of an anti-Semite as one who hates the Jews more than necessary exposed a mentality that tempered bias with doses of cynicism and pragmatism. The Jewish minority viewed the Bethlen period as an era of relief, a peaceful decade following the brutalities of the White Terror. In the 1930's the more militant Szegedists gained the upper hand and the consequences were inevitably harsh for the Jews.

The Jewish question, freely discussed in Parliament as in the Press, enabled opponents of the regime to agitate and to challenge the legitimacy of the system. Demands for anti-Semitic action served as a generally understood code-word for the dismantling of the existing system and substituting a radically reorganized Hungarian society. Supporters of the New Order indicted the anti-Semitic Horthy regime for not taking drastic action against the Jews. Radical anti-Semitism, therefore, was not only an attack on the Jews, but also on the regime itself. The government tried to outflank the opposition by becoming more militant on the Jewish question. The First Jewish Law passed in 1938 and the Second Jewish Law, enacted a year later, attempted to undercut the growing strength of the Radical-Right opposition. These anti-Jewish measures were denounced as inadequate by political leaders seeking power. Former Premier Béla Imrédy accused the government of not being genuinely anti-Semitic, at the very time anti-Jewish laws were promulgated by it. Ferenc Szálasi and the Arrow Cross movement spotlighted the cordial relationships that continued to exist between leading members of the regime, including the Regent, and Jewish capitalists.

The absence of a radical mass movement of the Left channeled the revolutionary impulses of the lower classes toward extremist right-wing parties, where the call for a radical overhaul of Hungarian society was expressed in politically and legally acceptable anti-Semitic terminology. The Arrow Cross, a violently anti-Semitic party, received massive support from the working classes. Its fanatical anti-Semitic slogans attracted the disenfranchised and the oppressed. In the 1939 election, despite an electoral system that was rigged against it, it gained 31 mandates. The Party did particularly well in industrial centers—in "red" Csepel for example. Indeed "The Arrow Cross performed a function that the socialists were unable to fulfill."[8]

The identification of Jews with the dissemination of communist propaganda

Anti-communism was an ideological mainstay of the Horthy period. Hatred and fear of communism was the catalyst that produced the counter-revolutionary Szeged movement. The anti-communism of the regime, unlike so many of the other postures periodically embraced, had a pure and pristine quality. The short-lived Soviet that pre-dated its coming to power, as well as the looming shadow of the Soviet Union, combined to produce a rigid brand of political intolerance. The Communist Party was driven underground, vigorously and successfully persecuted. Its leadership was either imprisoned or driven into exile. The Party was never able to establish a viable internal apparatus. Its membership in December of 1929 was down to 1,000.[9] The large majority of the population genuinely endorsed this crusading anti-Bolshevism.

The event which imprinted the idea that there was a connection between Jews and communists into the Hungarian mentality was the organization of the Hungarian Soviet in 1919. Jews played a very active role in the communist dictatorship.[10] As a group they made up a very small portion of the Jewish community, and they were all secularized, assimilated and Magyarized, but in the eyes of their opponents they were, first and foremost, Jews. The leader of the Soviet was Béla Kun, a Jew. The terror campaign against the opponents of the Revolution was conducted by Tibor Számueli, a Jew. The Commissar of War and the organizer of the Red Army was Vilmos Böhm, a Jew. Most of the political commissars in the army and most of the judges and prosecutors of the revolutionary courts were Jewish. Leadership roles were played by such future communist (and Jewish) luminaries as Mátyás Rákosi, the post World War II dictator, who served as Deputy Commissar of Commerce, György Lukács, Deputy Commissar of Public Education and József Révai, who was on the staff of the Vörös Újság, the communist newspaper.

The population at large was receptive to a campaign that condemned the entire Jewish community as sympathetic to communism. The spectre of Judeo-Bolshevism, a popular theme in many countries in the turbulent post-war years, was also raised in Hungary. The White Terror was directed against Jews in general, and most of the victims had nothing to do with the Soviet government. Organizations like the Awakening Magyars (Ébredö Magyarok) identified themselves as the champions of Hungarian nationalism in the face of Jewish promoted internationalist communism.

Horthy's anti-Semitism was also shaped by the Kun episode. In the safety of his asylum in authoritarian Portugal, he described his reaction to the communist interlude:

> The atrocities of the Bolsheviks filled the land with horror. The Jews who had long been settled among us were the first to condemn the crimes of their co-religionists, in whose hands the new regime almost exclusively rested.[11]

The Regent was less circumspect in a letter to Hitler written in July of 1940. He wrote ". . . when all decent men were on the front, the Jews engineered a revolution here and made Bolshevism."[12]

The preponderance of Jewish capital in the economic life of the nation

In the interwar period Hungary was still a predominantly agricultural society, and in the absence of any meaningful land reform the economy had a semi-feudal character with large land-holdings controlled by a few noble families, while at the same time there were over one million landless peasants in the land. Industry was developed and concentrated in a few areas, primarily in and around Budapest. The middle class was proportionately small and it included, in addition to the industrial bourgeoisie, the more traditional categories of merchants, professionals and civil servants.

Jews made up a large portion of the middle class. The Jewish community, for historic reasons, was more urbanized than the population at large. In a country where ⅔ of the population was still rural, the majority of the Jews (56%) resided in Budapest and in the ten major cities.[13]

The Treaty of Trianon crippled the economic order. Hungarian manufacturing establishments were deprived of their markets. Hungarian refugees in large numbers fled the successor states. They were generally members of the former ruling circles, property owners, Imperial bureaucrats without an Empire to administer, army officers, teachers and politicians. They played a prominent role in the counter-revolution and were a major pillar of support of the Horthy regime. And now they demanded their rewards, seeking "respectable" and salaried positions in a shrunken, crisis-plagued economy oversaturated with practicing professionals, potential civil servants and people "with an education." The competition was brutal, there were simply not enough "uri" (gentlemanly) positions available to satisfy the expectations. The entrenched Jewish middle class stood in the way of the native bourgeoisie. Anti-Semitism was the outcome of this keen economic rivalry. The Christian Party, supported by the politically moderate Hungarian middle class, and quite powerful in Budapest, generally followed an anti-Semitic orientation that was akin to the anti-Semitism of more right-wing elements.

Hungarian-Jewish economic rivalry was made even more acute by the decision of large numbers of so called Swabians, Hungary's German minority, to Magyarize their names and emphasize the Christian nature of the struggle against the Jews. Public opinion was mobilized against the apparent Jewish domination of the economy.

The statistics of the period confirm the disproportionate role played by Jews in some sectors of the economy. At the same time, Jews were strongly underrepresented in a number of occupational categories where non-Jews were proportionately over-represented.[14] The statistical table reproduced below was slightly edited to eliminate some occupational categories and to include only three denominations. Roman Catholics, Evangelical Christians and Jews numbered 6.612,735 out of a total population of 8.688,319. The picture presented is not altered, however, by the abridgment.

OCCUPATIONAL CATEGORIES ACCORDING TO RELIGION IN 1930[15]

Category	Roman-Catholic	Evangelical	Israelite
Agriculture	2.895.199	299,999	12,976
Industry	1.304,474	107,076	143,687
Commerce & Credit	196,330	19,415	194,211
Military	50,054	4,087	236
Laborer	82,200	8,868	1,718
Domestics	136,890	11,821	2,012
Total Population	5.634.003	534,165	444,567

Roman Catholics formed the largest group in Hungary, approximately ⅔ of the entire population. Evangelical Christians (Lutherans) and Jews were roughly of the same number, and therefore an easy comparison is in order. (Calvinists, the second largest denomination, are not cited.) Note the slight presence of Jews in agriculture, the primary occupation in Hungary, and in the categories of laborers and domestics, the lowest rungs of the socioeconomic order. Jews were (rigidly and arbitrarily) excluded by governmental fiats from military service. The number of Jews in commerce and credit, on the other hand, was spectacularly greater than their percentage in the total population would suggest. This fact enraged the Hungarian population for it underscored the intolerable notion that Jews controlled the country.

Jewish industrialists played a dominant role in the developing industrial life of the nation. The statistical table below vividly illustrates this point. (Numerically small denominations, like the Greek Catholics, are not included in the chart, and therefore only 97% of the population is accounted for.

INDUSTRIAL CORPORATIONS IN 1935[16]

Position	Roman-Catholic	(64.9%)	Reformed	(20.9%)
Owner or Renter	673	33.7%	150	7.6%
Director	789	36.6%	247	11.4%
Technical functionaries	2,517	54.5%	532	11.5%
Commercial functionaries	8,244	45.9%	1,497	8.4%

Position	Evangelical	(6.1%)	Israelite	(5.1%)
Owner or Renter	146	7.4%	1,008	50.9%
Director	197	9.1%	900	41.6%
Technical functionaries	479	10.4%	1,021	22.1%
Commercial functionaries	1,115	6.2%	6,877	38.3%

The numbers in parentheses indicate the percentage of the total population. The low numbers certainly underline the weak development of Hungarian industry. In the most important category of Owner or Renter, Jews, but 1/20th of the population, were an absolute majority. It is important to bear in mind that these numbers speak of Jews from the religious point of view. It will be the contribution of the late 1930's in Hungary's history to introduce the Nazi concept of the racial Jew. A very significant portion of the non-Jewish capitalist class—and in the absence of specific statistics it is necessary to generalize—consisted of converted Jews. Extreme assimilation, including the abandonment of the Jewish faith, was most popular among the most successful and wealthiest segment of the community. Subsequently, to anti-Semites of the Nazi era baptismal rite made no difference.

In Budapest 38.2% of the two-story buildings, 47.2% of the three-story and 57.5% of six or more story structures were owned by Jews.[17]

Even in agriculture where Jews, as indicated above, were underrepresented, Jewish capital made significant inroads. 9.7% of all estates classified as "large" were controlled by Jews.[18] The great Jewish historian of the Holocaust, Jenő Lévai, speculated that about 20–25% of the total wealth of the country was controlled by Jews.[19] There was also great poverty in the Jewish community, a factor that did not lessen a hatred partially produced by the great wealth of some Jews.

The fear that the Jewish population was growing too rapidly and posed a threat to the character and identity of the nation

Anti-Semitism, indeed and all types of racial and ethnic intolerance pays special attention to the numbers game. There is

always concern and anxiety, sometimes articulated and often simmering just beneath the surface, that the host population may be
engulfed by a rapidly growing minority, and the character of the nation may be distorted, damaged, diluted or even destroyed. The feeling is often irrational—the root cause, perhaps, of its existence—because the evidence contradicts it. In Hungary, after
World War I, the Jewish population was actually shrinking not only
in terms of percentage but also in absolute numbers. The statistical
table reproduced below clearly dispels the popular myth that Jewish
growth threatened the Hungarian character of Hungary.

RELIGIONS IN HUNGARY[20]

Religion	1920		1930	
Roman-Catholic	5.105,375	(63.9%)	5.643,003	(64.9%)
Greek-Catholic	175.655	(2.2%)	201.093	(2.3%)
Reformed	1.671,052	(21.0%)	1.813,162	(20.9%)
Evangelical	497,126	(6.2%)	534,165	(6.1%)
Greek-Eastern	50,918	(0.6%)	39,839	(0.5%)
Israelite	473,355	(5.9%)	444,567	(5.1%)
Others	16,721	(0.2%)	21,490	(0.2%)

It is noteworthy that in a ten-year period, while every other group,
with the exception of the small Greek-Eastern denomination, grew,
the Jewish population decreased by about 30,000.

After 1938 Hungary, as an ally of Germany, territorially profited
from both the Western policy of appeasement and the subsequent
establishment of German hegemony in East Central Europe. Some of
the lost territories were regained. The dismemberment of
Czechoslovakia returned the Hungarian inhabited portion of
Slovakia, referred to as Upper Hungary, and Ruthenia. Hungary
also capitalized on the destruction of Yugoslavia and the Bácska
region was reincorporated. Diplomatic support from Berlin compelled Romania to cede about half of Transylvania back to Hungary.
These additions significantly enlarged the total as well as the Jewish
population. In 1942 there were 725,007 Jews in Hungary, 4.9% of
the population, a slight further proportional decrease.[21]

In the late 1930's and 40's anti-Semitic agitation was abetted by the
"visibility" of the Jewish population. In Eastern Hungary and even
more so in the "new territories," Jews tended to be more attached to
Orthodox traditions. There were a great many Hasidic sects. The
general appearance and lifestyle of these Jews; their Oriental caftans,

beards and payes and Yiddish tongue, conspicuously set them apart from the rest of the population (including most of the Jews of Trianon Hungary). There was no fear of economic domination from these Jews, but, there seemed to be so many of them.[22] These Jews, with their large families, concentrated in Ruthenia and some parts of Transylvania, were seen as a direct and physical challenge to the Hungarian nation. In the counties of Bereg, Máramaros and Ugocsa they made up 17.8%, 18.4% and 13.3% of the population.

The "visibility" of Jews was further accentuated by their presence, in disproportionately large numbers, in the urban centers. This was a historic necessity reinforced by the logic of contemporary economics. It was a world-wide phenomenon reflected in all the cities of Hungary. The Hungarian Nazi movements, including the Arrow Cross, by far the most popular, were primarily supported by the radicalized discontented lower classes of the big cities, where the large Jewish communities served as a ready-made ammunition for the propaganda canons of anti-Semitic agitators.

JEWS IN LARGE CITIES[23]

City	Region	Jewish Population	% of Total Population
Budapest	Trianon-Hungary	184,453	15.8%
Miskolc	Trianon-Hungary	10,428	13.5%
Debrecen	Trianon-Hungary	9,142	7.3%
Kassa	Upper-Hungary	10,079	15.0%
Nagyvárad	Transylvania	21,333	22.9%
Szatmárnémeti	Transylvania	12,960	24.9%
Kolozsvár	Transylvania	16,763	15.1%
Ujvidék	Southern-Hungary	3,621	5.9%
Ungvár	Ruthenia	9,576	27.2%

Right-wing publicists inflated these figures. They attacked the reliability of the official statistics and proclaimed that there were far more Jews in Hungary than the actual number recorded by the census takers. It was also emphasized by them that there were many Jews who concealed their true identity and through intermarriage, conversion or the changing of family names, infiltrated into the Hungarian nation without surrendering the characteristics of their race, or that peculiar loyalty and mentality which sets Jews apart from their neighbors. It was declared that these crypto-Jews posed an even greater threat than their more readily identifiable brethren. A typical illustration of this mentality was a pamphlet published by the Arrow Cross Party that differentiated between the racial and the religious Jew, and thus was able to fortify the claim that the Jews were indeed a real and numerical menace to the nation. It is difficult to establish how the numbers were arrived at. However, it is illuminating to note that the allegations were made not only for Hungary, but for other European states as well.

JEWS IN EUROPE[24]

State	Racial Jews	Religious Jews
Hungary	1.300,000	500,000
Romania	3.200,000	1.000,000
Poland	6.100,000	3.500,000
England	1.200,000	300,000
France	2.900,000	725,000

Such allegations reflect the Hungarian racists' notion that anti-Semitism was a defensive measure whose aim was to preserve the Hungarian character of Hungary.

The belief that the Jews were an alien and unassimilable minority

Extreme nationalism was a basic component of the philosophy of the Horthy regime. Generations of schoolchildren were indoctrinated with the injustices of Trianon. Irredentism was the primary foreign policy objective of the government. In the charged emotional atmosphere of the era, all minorities would encounter difficulties. In addition, Hungarians were traditionally very conscious of the fact that they were a small nation, unique and unrelated to the neighboring ethnic groups. The doctrine of integral nationalism was translated into official policies that accentuated the Hungarian character of Hungary. Swabians, despite the presence of a powerful patron-state, were repeatedly victimized by a xenophobic regime.[25] The German minority had to wage an incessant struggle to protect its mother-tongue, school-system and cultural autonomy. Undoubtedly, Hungarian pride suffered in the interwar years as a result of the anti-Hungarian policies pursued by the dominant nationalities of the successor states, former victims of Hungarian intolerance themselves, against their large Hungarian minorities. However, Budapest could not retaliate. The Slovaks, Romanians, Croats and Serbians constituted only 2.4% of Hungary's population.

Hungarian nationalism was very much influenced by the racist theorizing, in vogue after World War I. It employed racist terminology and slogans. The Szeged movement was affiliated with race-protecting leagues. Racists occupied high positions in the government.

Jews were obvious targets and victims of this spirit and policy. It was possible for some of the minorities, like the Germans, to be accepted into the Hungarian nation if certain prerequisites, like family name, knowledge of the Hungarian language, were met.[26] However, Jews always remained Jews. They were perpetual outsiders, an alien minority; they could never become Hungarians. This sentiment was embraced not just by the apostles of marginal hate-groups, nor was it limited only to the leading spokesmen of the reactionary regime—it appealed to many liberal-thinking Hungarians as well. Jews were perceived as a separate nation within the body-politic of the Hungarian nation. They had a different mentality and different characteristics; they posed a permanent danger. In practical terms they were blamed for all the problems and ills of Hungary. On June 6, 1939, Zoltán Meskó, an Arrow Cross deputy, spoke on the floor of Parliament about a housing proposal. In his address he stated that "If we extripate these (unmistaken reference to Jews) from the Hungarian society, then we will not have Social Democracy, or this party or that party; what we will have will be a nation of honest Christian Hungarians."[27]

People in responsible positions echoed, in a more cultured manner, this same sentiment. Premier Imrédy in a celebrated speech in the Upper House on May 20, 1938, spoke about the Jews.

It is undeniable that among the Jews, this racial mentality presents itself rather sharply; therefore the assimilation of Jews is more difficult than that of other elements . . . The other side of the problem is the question of mentality . . . it slowly emerged and in Budapest especially took hold a mentality which in its perception of public, communal and moral problems does not always agree, indeed it frequently sharply differs from, with that Hungarian spirituality (mentality), which we inherited from our forbears and which we want to transmit to our descendants.[28]

It was particularly galling that this "different mentality" was so well entrenched in the cultural and intellectual life of the nation. Jews were very numerous among Hungary's intelligentsia. In 1930 49.2% of the lawyers, 34.4% of the doctors, 45.1% of the private chemists, 31.7% of the journalists, 28.9% of the musicians, 24.7% of the scholars and writers and 24.1% of all the actors were Jewish.[29] These were the numbers after a decade of subtle and direct pressures by the regime on Jewish professionals. In 1930, while practically half of all jurists were Jews, those in governmental service, as judges, prosecutors, administrators, etc., were only 2% Jewish.[30] In the civil service Jewish bureaucrats constituted an insignificant 1.7% of the total number.[31] These "achievements" were not sufficient. Hungarian professionals continued to press for additional measures to ensure the further erosion of the Jewish role in these middle-class occupational categories.

Populist writers, generally of a leftist and reformist orientation, also picked up the theme of the endangerment of Hungarian culture by foreign influence. The Village Explorers (*Falukutatók*) not only revealed the shocking conditions of the Hungarian rural proletariat, the purest essence of the nation, but in their writings they mounted an offensive against the establishment that was responsible for the callous indifference exhibited toward Hungarians and Hungarian values. It was charged that the literary establishment was too attached to a non-Hungarian ethos. The dominant periodical and arbitrator of literary tastes was the *Nyugat* (West), a publication that transmitted Western ideals. The element of anti-Semitism was only implicit. By and large, these Hungarian narodniks were not specifically against Jews, but in their defense of Hungarian culture they identified the Jewish influence as another non-Hungarian factor that had to be eliminated. *Nyugat* for instance, was supported by Jewish financial interests and many of its contributors were Jewish writers.[32]

The conviction that anti-Jewish acts at home will earn diplomatic support for foreign policy ojectives

The primary objective of Hungarian foreign policy, as stated above, was irredentism. To regain the lost territories, Hungary gradually drifted into the orbit of Nazi Germany, another revisionist Power. There were many sharp differences between the totalitarianism of the Third Reich and the authoritarianism of the Horthy regime. However, in order to enlist German support for Hungarian national objectives, the Hungarian government was prepared to ape the German system. There was an element of opportunism in this attitude. Berlin was always suspicious of the ideological purity of the Horthy clique. German-Hungarian relations were made even more complex by the presence, within and on the fringes of the Hungarian regime, of elements that were prepared to identify completely with the Nazi doctrine and objectives. (The Szeged militants constituted one such a group.)

It was the expectation of Germany that Hungary, as a faithful ally, would adopt the anti-Semitism and specifically anti-Jewish measures of the Reich. At the same time, there was concern in Budapest that non-compliance will have negative consequences for Hungary's territorial ambitions. Romania, Slovakia and Croatia were implementing anti-Jewish measures of the Nazi model; Hungary could not afford to do otherwise. The decision to enact the First Jewish Law was made to assure German support in the negotiations over the partition of Czechoslovakia.[33] The Third Jewish Law, passed on August 8, 1941, when Hungary, as an ally of Germany had already declared war on the Soviet Union, was a race-protecting measure that received its inspiration from Nuremberg. With the cooperation of native Nazis, overwhelming pressure was applied by Germany on the Hungarian government to pursue a more and more radical anti-Jewish policy. The anti-Semitism of the Horthy regime was not the anti-Semitism of Adolf Hitler. In the beginning Hungary was prepared to sacrifice the rights and well-being of her Jews to accomplish foreign policy objectives, but as the war progressed and the benefits of being a German ally diminished, her attitude changed. The Horthy regime, especially during the tenure of Premier Miklós Kállay (March, 1942–March, 1944), effectively resisted participation in the Final Solution.[34] The Jews of Budapest escaped deportation to the death camps because of the personal protection extended by the Regent. The mass murder of Hungarian Jewry would take place only after German military occupation of the country.

The anti-Semitism of Horthy-Hungary was a consistent policy. It was an integral part of the ideology of the regime. There were acts of great brutality (the White Terror, the Kamenec-Podolsk massacre of July, 1941), as well as periods of relaxation (1920's), and periods of tension (1930's), but there was always a preoccupation with the "Jewish question." Trianon Hungary was not always a bad place for the Jews, and Jews survived there longer than in Poland, Slovakia or even the Netherlands. The mass destruction of the Jews of Hungary was promoted, supervised and executed by officials of Nazi Germany, but Hungarian anti-Semitism shares in the moral responsibility for the Holocaust.

Notes

1. See Hugh Seton-Watson, *Eastern Europe Between the Wars 1918–1941* (New York, 1967), p. 291.

2. Denominations received official classification. The highest level was that of a "received religion," a less favorable one was that of a "recognized religion," with the right to exercise a degree of self-government, and the lowest level was that of a "non-recognized confession," denominations under police supervision.

3. A unique phenomenon among the Jews of Eastern Europe was the inability of most Magyar Jews, including the religiously observant, to speak Yiddish. See Ivan Sanders, "Tétova vonzalmak" [Tentative Affinities] in *Új Látohatár* (5 Munich, 1975), p. 441.

4. For an illuminating discourse on the subject, see George Barany, "Magyar Jew or Jewish Magyar? Reflections on the Question of Assimilation" in Bela Vago and George L. Mosse, ed. *Jews and Non-Jews in Eastern Europe 1918–1945* (New York, 1974).

5. C. A. Macartney, *October Fifteenth* I (Edinburgh, 1956), p. 20.

6. For such an interpretation see Nicholas M. Nagy-Talavera, *The Green Shirts and the Others* (Stanford, 1970).

7. For a Marxist treatment of the organization see Rudolfné Dosa, *A Move. Egy jellegzetes magyar fasiszta szervezet 1918–1944* [The MOVE. A Characteristic Magyar Fascist Organization 1918–1944] (Budapest, 1972).

8. Istvan Deak, "Hungary" H. Rogger and E. Weber *The European Right* (Berkeley, 1965) p. 397.

9. Bennett Kovrig, *Communism in Hungary. From Kun to Kádár* appendix 2 (Stanford, 1979).

10. Rudolf L. Tökés, *Béla Kun and the Hungarian Soviet Republic* (Stanford, 1967), p. 193.

11. Nicholas Horthy, *Memoirs* (New York, 1957), p. 98.

12. Nicholas Horthy, *The Confidential Papers of Admiral Horthy* ed. M. Szinai and L. Szucs (Budapest, 1965), p. 131.

13. Iván T. Berend and György Ránki, "A magyar társadalom a két világháború között" (Magyar Society Between the Two World Wars") *Új Irás* 10 (1973), p. 100.

14. There is a striking similarity between the roles played by Jews in Hungary and the contemporary roles of Chinese in many Far Eastern countries.

15. *Hungarian Statistical Yearbook* (1935), p. 18.

16. *Ibid.*, p. 136.

17. Alajos Kovács, *A Csonkamagyarországi zsidóság a statisztika tükrében* [The Jews of Dismembered Hungary in a Statistical Mirror] (Budapest, 1938), p. 48.

18. *Ibid.*, pp. 13–Łł.

19. Eugene Lévai, *Black Book on the Martyrdom of Hungarian Jewry.* Edited by Lawrence P. Davis (Zurich, 1948), p. 37.

20. *Hungarian Statistical Yearbook* (1939), p. 18.

21. *Hungarian Statistical Yearbook* (1942), pp. 14–17.

22. A very skeptical Mark Twain reacted to the official census figures in the United States by writing the following disclaimer in the September 1899 issue of *Harper's Magazine* under the title "Concerning the Jews"; "Look at the city of New York; and look at Boston, and Philadelphia . . . how your race swarms in those places!" p. 533.

23. Hungarian Statistical Yearbook (1942), pp. 16–17.

24. Mátyás Matolcsi (comp.), *A Zsidók útja* [The Way of the Jews] (Budapest, 1943) p. 11.

25. For a detailed treatment of the subject see Thomas Spira, *German-Hungarian Relations and the Swabian Problem from Károlyi to Gömbös 1919–1936* (New York, 1977).

26. Gömbös was of German background and Szálasi's non-Magyar ancestry included Armenians. However, when it was revealed, by political opponents, that Imrédy had some Jewish ancestry, he was forced out of office.

27. Hungary. Parliament, Proceedings, I., p. 195.

28. Béla Imrédy, *Múlt és jövő határán* [On the Boundary Between Past and Future] (Budapest, 1938) p. 36.

29. Kovács, pp. 18–19.

30. Berend and Ránki, p. 100.

31. *Ibid.*

32. I am indebted to my good friend Ivan Sanders for his helpful comments on the village explorers.

33. C. A. Macartney "Hungarian Foreign Policy During the Interwar Period, With Special Reference to the Jewish Question" in *Jews and*

Non-Jews in Eastern Europe 1918-1945 (New York, 1974), p. 134.

34. There is extensive primary and secondary literature on this sensitive subject. Helpful sources would include the captured documents of the German Foreign Office, Randolph L. Braham (comp.), *The Destruction of Hungarian Jewry. A Documentary Account*, Jenő Lévai, ed. *Eichman in Hungary. Documents*, the private papers and memoirs, generally self-serving but always revealing of the decision-makers, like Nicholas Kállay, *Hungarian Premier.*

Edward Chaszar

Trianon and the Problem
of National Minorities

The century preceding the outbreak of World War I was characterized by the spreading and intensification of nationalism on the one hand, and by the determined, sometimes ruthless, campaigns for the suppression of national movements on the other. Consequently, at the outbreak of the war the nationality question was one of the major unresolved problems in international relations and one of the most burning domestic issues in multi-national states. In order to satisfy nationalist aspirations at the war's end, the principle of national self-determination was brought to the fore. According to a perceptive observer, the Paris Peace Conference "allowed and sponsored the operation of that principle in a number of cases, chiefly where it worked to the disadvantage of the defeated powers, but admitted other factors as coordinate and, in some cases, overriding elements in the determination of frontiers. The principle of 'one nation, one state' was not realized to the full extent permitted by the ethnographic configuration of Europe, but it was approximated more closely than ever before."[1]

Unfortunately the half-hearted attempt to apply the principle of national self-determination did not eliminate the nationality problem. In fact, by permitting, or contributing to, the creation of new national minorities, it may have aggravated the problem. The case of Hungary serves as a good example.

The victorious Allied and Associated powers dismembered the Austro-Hungarian monarchy by creating a number of so-called "successor states." The idea was to replace the multi-national monarchy with smaller national states, who would jealously guard their newly-won independence and thereby prevent a possible future expansion of Germany into East Central Europe. History was to prove twenty years later that instead of ensuring peace for generations to come, the peacemakers created a settlement that carried within itself the seeds of the Second World War and the Cold War. For the "successor states," were the least capable of checking Nazi aggression. Unwilling to satisfy the aspirations of their inordinately large national minorities, and concerned with preserving their territorial gains, they easily fell prey to Hitler's divide and conquer strategy, offering little significant resistance. Together with the greatly weakened and separated Austria and Hungary, the "successor states" became pawns on the chessboard of Nazi Germany and the Soviet Union.

Beyond doubt the Treaty of Trianon was the most severe of all post-war treaties. Its territorial impositions, disregarding the ethnic or linguistic borders, converted millions of Hungarians into minorities in supposed nation states. Before 1914 Hungary had a territory of 125,600 square miles. This is roughly half the size of Texas, or three times that of the state of Ohio. By the terms of the Treaty Hungary lost 89,700 square miles, or 71.4 percent of her former territory. Of her population of almost 21 million, 63.6 percent, including 3.3 million Hungarians, were detached. The inhabitants of dismembered Hungary numbered only 7.6 million on a territory of 35,900 square miles—the size of the state of Indiana. Romania alone received 39,800 square miles (almost the size of Ohio), more than what was left to Hungary. Czechoslovakia was presented with 23,800 square miles (equal to the size of West Virginia), and Yugoslavia received a similar slice, including Croatia—which for 800 years was associated with Hungary. Even Austria was allotted 1,500 square miles of Western Hungary, a slice of territory slightly larger than Rhode Island.[2]

By comparison, the Treaty of Versailles detached from Germany no more than 13 percent of its territory and 9.5 percent of its population. (The Peace of Frankfurt ending the Franco-Prussian War in 1871, had cost France a mere 2.6 percent of her territory and 4.1 percent of her population.) Having decreed that a multi-national state such as Austria-Hungary was not worthy of having a life of its own, the victors of World War I set up states such as Czechoslovakia, Yugoslavia, and Romania, which were multi-national states not unlike the old Empire.

Thus, the redrawing of the frontiers of the great polyglot empires of Eastern and Central Europe, and the limited reshuffling of populations, did by no means solve the problem of national minorities. The powers, in violation of proclaimed Wilsonian principles, handed over masses of people to alien sovereignties. Inis L. Claude, Jr. estimates the number to have been between 25 and 30 million, and a British authority on the question of national self-determination wrote as follows: "It was ironic that a settlement supposed to have been largely determined by the principle of nationality should have produced a state like Czechoslovakia, with minorities amounting to 34.7 percent of its population, quite apart from the question of the doubtful identity of nationality between Czechs and Slovaks. Poland was not much better off with minorities amounting to 30.4 percent, or Romania, with 25 percent."[3]

Altogether the "successor states" found themselves with 16 million persons belonging to national minorities, out of a total population of 42 million, while Hungary's new borders were far more restricted than the reach of her nationality. With her loss of territory, Hungary surrendered 1,663,576 Hungarians to Romania, 1,066,824 to Czechoslovakia, 571,735 to Yugoslavia, and 26,225 to Austria. Nearly two million of these lived just across the newly created borders, thus forming an integral part of the Hungarian ethnic bloc in the Danubian Basin, but now separated from it. According to Charles Seymour, the American delegate to the Peace Conference, the boundaries of the successor states in many cases did not even "roughly" correspond with ethnic or linguistic lines. In short, national self-determination was denied to the Hungarians.

A great deal was alleged about the treatment of the national minorities in Hungary. However, compared to the situation prevalent in the old Austro-Hungarian monarchy, the lot of the new national minorities was (and continues to be) miserable. "Is it not scandalous"—exclaimed Sir Robert Gower, Member of the House of Commons in Britain some 15 years after the peace settlement—"that a European reconstruction, loudly hailed as one that was going to liberate the national minorities, should have resulted in their persecution, the severity of which is such that there is no parallel to it to be found in the ancient Kingdom of Hungary, where the nationalities had been treated with infinitely more benevolence."[4]

Of the defeated, Hungary was punished the most severely. Furthermore, none of the inhabitants of historic Hungary was given the right to decide his fate. When the Hungarian Peace Delegation was handed the terms of the treaty for signature, the chief of the delegation suggested that in accordance with the principle of self-determination the population affected by the treaty ought to be consulted through plebiscites. "Ask the peoples themselves," exclaimed Count Albert Apponyi to the assembled delegates of the victors; "we will accept their verdict." This, indeed, would have been entirely consistent with the Wilsonian idea of self-determination. The reason for its disregard was revealed bluntly in *La Paix* (Peace) by André Tardieu—who was to become Prime Minister of France twice between the wars—in the following terms: "We had to choose between organizing plebiscites or creating Czechoslovakia."[5]

Perhaps the most important reason why the principle of self-determination was ignored at Trianon was that by the time the peacemakers turned to the treaty with Hungary they were bored with the entire process. In the words of one of the participants: "I am reliably informed that the delegates, and particularly the representatives of the Western Powers, are frightfully bored with the whole Peace Conference . . . Especially since we presented our notes and memoranda they have begun to realize that the Hungarian question should be examined from many angles for which they have neither time nor patience."

On the strength of the argument that Germany had been accorded the right of self-determination with regard to Schleswig-Holstein, Silesia, East Prussia, and the Saarland, the Chief Delegate of the Union of South Africa, General (later Prime Minister) Ian Smuts demanded that in connection with the proposed dismemberment of Hungary plebiscites be held in Transylvania, Slovakia, Ruthenia, and Croatia-Slavonia. At first a lone voice, he was later supported by the other British Dominions, as well as by Japan, Poland, and Italy. The fear of plebiscites, however, prevailed and they were denied. Some years later the Swiss historian and expert on minority affairs, Aldo Dami, wrote: "A plebiscite refused is a plebiscite taken in fact."[6]

The Treaty of Trianon was signed on June 4, 1920. One year later, on June 7, 1921, the Reverend Father Weterle (for many years the protesting voice of Alsace in the German Imperial Parliament) declared in the French National Assembly: "I am profoundly convinced that had plebiscites been held, neither the Serbs nor the Rumanians would have received more than one-third of the votes cast. People have been pushed against their will. There can be no doubt about that."[7] Father Weterle spoke from experience; after all, the Alsatians, although of Germanic origin and language, desired to be French.

The Paris Peace Conference confused the concept of a people's right to self-determination with the principle of defining nationality on the basis of language. The two are by no means identical; an ethnic group may well prefer to belong to a national sovereignty whose majority is linguistically different from its own. The Treaty of Trianon did in fact flout both principles by cutting off large blocs of purely Hungarian inhabited territories and awarding them to Hungary's neighbors for economic or strategic considerations. "The borders drawn at Trianon," asserts Aldo Dami, "excluded from Hungary a first zone of Hungarian territories, plus a second zone inhabited by non-Magyars whose interests were, however, so closely entwined with those of Hungary that there could have been no doubt of their decision, had they been consulted. Hence, the Peace of Trianon is based neither on ethnography nor on popular sentiment, nor even on the interests of the population concerned—which the latter are sure to know best."[8]

The concern with the protection of minorities originated in the religious sphere. Historically, international efforts to protect religious minorities against persecution took the form of *ad hoc* intervention by states on behalf of their co-religionists in other countries. Later practice included guarantees of freedom of religion for inhabitants of territories transferred to other countries by voluntary or forced cession. Occasionally, when religious division was identical with national division, such guarantee protected an entire nationality within a state.

The first express recognition and international guarantee of the rights of national minorities is found in the Final Act of the Congress of Vienna, in which Russia, Prussia, and Austria undertook to respect the nationality of their Polish subjects.[9]

The systematic protection of national minorities did not become a reality until the end of World War I and the establishment of the League of Nations. Even this system was limited in scope and applied only to special cases. A more comprehensive system, one with wider application, has not been established to this day.

As Clemenceau pointed out to Polish Prime Minister Ignacy Paderewski in his oft-quoted letter justifying the imposition of restrictions upon Poland's handling of national minorities, the Allied and Associated Powers felt a solemn obligation to protect those peoples whose future minority status was determined by decree. A plan for the international protection of national minorities appeared to be the only solution, and such a plan evolved out of a multiplicity of conflicting interests and points of view, and utilized an unprecedented set of international machinery: The League of Nations.[10]

The basis of the League of Nations system for the international protection of minorities consisted of a series of treaties, declarations, and conventions whereby particular states accepted provisions relating to the treatment of minority groups and at the same time recognized the League as guarantor.

The international instruments, containing stipulations for the protection of minorities placed under the guarantee of the League of Nations, may be classified as follows:[11]

"Minorities" Treaties signed at Paris during the Peace Conference
Treaty between the Principal Allied and Associated Powers and Poland, signed at Versailles on June 28th, 1919.

Treaty between the Principal Allied and Associated Powers and the Kingdom of Serbs, Croats and Slovenes, signed at St. Germain on September 10th, 1919.

Treaty between the Principal Allied and Associated Powers and Czechoslovakia, signed at St. Germain on September 10th, 1919.

Treaty between the Principal Allied and Associated Powers and Romania, signed at Paris on December 9th, 1919.

Treaty between the Principal Allied and Associated Powers and Greece, signed at Sevres on August 10th, 1920.

Special Chapters inserted in the General Treaties of Peace
Treaty of Peace with Austria, signed at St. Germain-en-Laye on September 10th, 1919 (Part III, Section V, Articles 62 to 69).

Treaty of Peace with Bulgaria, signed at Neuilly-sur-Seine on November 27th, 1919 (Part III, Section IV, Articles 49 to 57).

Treaty of Peace with Hungary, signed at Trianon on June 4th, 1920 (Part III, Section VI, Articles 54 to 60).

Treaty of Peace with Turkey, signed at Lausanne on July 24, 1923 (Part I, Section III, Articles 37 to 45).

Special Chapters inserted in other Treaties
German-Polish Convention on Upper Silesia, dated May 15th, 1922 (Part III).

Convention concerning the Memel Territory, dated May 8th, 1924 (Article II, and Articles 26 and 27 of the Statute annexed to the Convention).

Declarations made before the Council of the League of Nations
Declaration by Albania, dated October 2nd, 1921.

Declaration by Estonia, dated September 17th, 1923.

Declaration by Finland (in respect of the Aaland Islands), dated June 27th, 1921.

Declaration by Latvia, dated July 7th, 1923.

Declaration by Lithuania, dated May 12th, 1922.

Although different in form, all these instruments aimed at safeguarding the rights of "racial, religious or linguistic minorities." And the architects of the system made it clear that they regarded this designation as synonymous with "national minorities."[12]

The rights guaranteed to national minorities in the treaty-bound states fell into two categories: the rights of individuals as such, and the rights of individuals as members of a minority group. The safeguarding of the first category of rights demanded a system of negative equality—protection against discrimination. The second category required, in addition, a regime of "positive equality"—provisions for the equal opportunity of minorities to "preserve and develop their national culture and consciousness."[13] Nevertheless, these were still individual rights, arising out of membership in a minority and facilitating the maintenance and development of group life. Wilson and his fellow architects were too much imbued with the individualist traditions of liberalism to accept the concept of "group rights." The documents mentioned carefully avoided terminology from which it might have been inferred that minorities as corporate units were the "intended beneficiaries of the system."[14] Claude notes only a few exceptions, such as Articles 9 and 10 of the Polish minority Treaty—which could be interpreted as indirectly granting recognition to groups *per se*.

Claude's cautious interpretation of the nature of minority rights is not shared by all. On the contrary, some say that the rights protected by the League were, at least in part, rights accorded to minorities as groups. Thus, André Mandelstam in his *La Protection des Minorités* distinguished between rights of minorities on an individual basis—religious liberty, freedom of using their own language, freedom of education in their own language, freedom of association—and rights of minorities as collective entities—proportional representation in elective bodies, and autonomy.[15]

The League guarantee was collective; the task of enforcing the obligations of the concerned states was assigned to the organization, more specifically to the Council. In addition, although judicial procedures were available through the Permanent Court of International Justice, the guarantee, as established, was basically political in nature. It was part of a larger system designed to facilitate the maintenance of international peace.

In order to discharge its functions as a guarantor, the Council of the League developed certain operating procedures empirically (one

might say "on a trial and error" method), starting with the suggestions contained in the Tittoni Report of 1920, and concluding with
the 1929 report and the recommendations of a special committee
headed by Adatci, the Japanese representative, who served as the
Council's Rapporteur on minority questions.[16]

In its final form the procedure consisted of five successive steps,
namely:

> Acceptance of Petitions (from minorities);
> Communications to the Government concerned for any Observations;
> Communication to the Members of the Council;
> Examination by the Committee of Three (Council Members); and
> Replies to Petitioners

Given the stringent qualifications that had to be met for each successive step, and the half-hearted support the system enjoyed in the
Council, this so-called "petition system" functioned with only
limited success. Its failures and deficiencies were numerous. According to one of its many critics: "It is impossible to maintain that the
minorities obtained an adequate and impartial hearing of their
grievances and demands, or prompt, effective, and reliable measures
of protection . . . The League system was superior to possible alternative arrangements relying exclusively upon internal constitutional
guarantees of minority rights, or resting upon bilateral agreements
unsupported by an international guarantee, or leaving the protection
of minorities dependent upon the unregulated and capricious intervention of kin-states; but it was unable to solve the difficult problem with which it came to grips."[17]

Basically, the League system was unpopular with all those concerned for a variety of reasons. The states with minorities disliked it
because it limited their "sovereign rights." The minorities disliked it,
because it was cumbersome and did not provide the protection
desired. The kin-states were dissatisfied with the system because they
were excluded from it altogether. Moreover, it was a system affecting a few states only, rather than a general one affecting all. This
proved to be very irksome to those who were placed under its obligations, while other nations, though they possessed minorities, were
totally excluded. Czechoslovakia for one was willing to cooperate,
Poland was resentful, and produced, in 1934, a statement that
amounted to a virtual denunciation of minority obligations. On September 13, 1934, Colonel Beck announced to the Assembly of the

League that "pending the introduction of a general and uniform system for the protection of minorities, his Government was compelled to refuse, as from that day, all co-operation with the international organizations in the matter of the supervision of the application by Poland of the system of minority protection."[18]

Following this declaration, the League system of minority protection became increasingly ineffectual, until it was ultimately swept away by the events of World War II.

*   *   *

The problems of national minorities, which the peacemakers left unresolved, continue even today, sixty years after the Treaty of Trianon came into force. Attempts to reduce the scope of the minorities problem by revising the borders drawn in the Treaty have been in vain. The only frontier revisions were those performed by the Axis Powers immediately prior to and during World War II. In the case of Hungary the two Vienna Awards resulted in a new border that followed more closely than before the ethnic or linguistic line. However, these border revisions were declared null and void by the Paris Peace Treaties of 1947. Unlike the treaties of 1919 and 1920, those of 1947 did not even provide for the protection of national minorities.

As a result, hundreds of thousands of Hungarians have been expelled from lands where they were born and where they lived, and millions of others remain oppressed minorities. Their case has been presented repeatedly to the United Nations and other international forums. The U.S. Congress held numerous hearings on the subject. Documents, letters, memoranda smuggled out from Czechoslovakia, Romania, Yugoslavia, and the Soviet Union, tell of wholesale violation of human rights of the national minorities.

Deeply moved by the plight of the oppressed East Central European national minorities, and in possession of overwhelming documentation to plead their case, spokesmen for the American Hungarian community, in observing the sixtieth anniversary of the Treaty of Trianon, called on the President and Congress of the United States to do all that is possible for the protection of human rights and the rights of national or ethnic minorities in Czechoslovakia, Romania, Yugoslavia, as well as in the Soviet Union. "Let the United States continue to be the champion of freedom and human dignity in the world, so as to maintain in high esteem the country and the ideals admired by the oppressed everywhere."[19]

One glimmer of hope for the protection of national minorities on a world-wide basis appeared on the horizon in May, 1978, when the United Nations Commission on Human Rights in Geneva transmitted a number of documents dealing with minority rights to the governments of the member nations. One of the documents was a "Draft Declaration on the Rights of Persons Belonging to National, Ethnic, Religious and Linguistic Minorities," submitted by the government of Yugoslavia for discussion.[20]

It will be years before we know whether the proposal for a declaration on minority rights has sufficient world-wide support to survive the cumbersome and politically motivated procedures of the United Nations system. It if does, it will be only a first step toward creating a more binding international convention. Nevertheless, after a rather long period of neglect, the sentiments of the international community at present appear to be on the side of minorities.

Notes

1. Inis L. Claude, Jr., *National Minorities: An International Problem* (Cambridge: Harvard University Press, 1955), p. 12.

2. For additional comparative data see Yves de Daruvar, *The Tragic Fate of Hungary* (Munich: Nemzetor, 1974), pp. 99–106.

3. Alfred Cobban, *The Nation State and National Self-Determination* (London: Collins, 1969), p. 86.

4. Sir Robert Gower, *La Revision du Traité de Trianon* (Paris, 1937), p. 16, quoted by Daruvar, p. 111.

5. Quoted by Daruvar, p. 92.

6. *Ibid.*

7. Daruvar, p. 93.

8. Aldo Dami, *La Hongrie de Demain* (Paris, 1932), p. 133, quoted by Daruvar, p. 93.

9. For the wording of this undertaking in the original French see C. A. Macartney, *National States and National Minorities*, 2nd ed. (New York: Russell, 1968), p. 160.

10. The text of Clemenceau's letter is reproduced in Oscar I. Janowsky, *Nationalities and National Minorities* (New York: Macmillan, 1945), p. 179-84.

11. Pablo de Azcarate y Florez, *League of Nations and National Minorities* (New York: Carnegie Endowment, 1945), appendix. A complete collection of these instruments is found in League of Nations, *Protection of*

Linguistic, Racial and Religious Minorities by the League of Nations, 1927. I.B.2.

12. Claude, p. 17, referring to *The Public Papers of Woodrow Wilson,* I. 463, 543.

13. Pablo de Azcarate y Florez, p. 82.

14. Claude, p. 19.

15. André Mandelstam, *La Protection des Minorités* (Paris: Hachette, 1925), p. 53–70.

16. Adatci's Report is reproduced in full in the Appendix to Pablo de Azcarate y Florez, *League of Nations and National Minorities* (New York: Carnegie Endowment, 1945). Azcarate was head of the League's Minority Section.

17. Claude, p. 30; and see his Chapter 3, "The Failure of the League Minority System." Detailed criticism is also offered by Macartney, Chapter 10, and by F. P. Walters, *A History of the League of Nations* (London: Oxford University Press, 1965), Chapter 34. The operating procedure is described in detail in the Adatci Report. A good legal analysis of the Minority Treaty obligations is to be found in André Mandelstam, *La Protection des Minorités.*

18. Macartney, p. 503.

19. *U.S. Congressional Record,* Vol. 126, No. 118 (July 28, 1980), p. E 3633.

20. United Nations Document E/CN.4/L.1367/Rev.1. The Draft Declaration was discussed at the 34th Session of the Commission on Human Rights in the spring of 1978. Eventually, after each government reacts in writing, it will reach the General Assembly.

István I. Mócsy

Partition of Hungary and the
Origins of the Refugee Problem

The refugee problem is more than a historical accident, more than a humanitarian issue. In fact, if Heinrich Böll, the German Nobel laureate is correct, the refugee phenomenon is symptomatic of our age. He has written: "When the time comes to seek a name for our century, it will probably be called the Century of Expellees and Prisoners. When people begin trying to add up the worldwide total of these unfortunate people, they will arrive at a number of displaced human beings big enough to populate entire continents."[1] As all such characterizations of an epoch, this is an overstatement. Nevertheless, it does focus attention on a new phenomenon: the systematic dislocation and persecution of civilians in modern states. Not that displacement of civilians is in itself new—in the past peasants, for example, regularly fled from the path of approaching armies; religious persecutions often forced the flight of sizable groups of religious dissenters. But the disturbing regularity of population displacement, the sheer magnitude of the refugee problem, suggests that massive uprooting of civilians is no longer only the occasional and accidental by-product of military or political struggles, but an integral part of the modern system of conflict-resolution. The problem seems to arise either from the contradictory principles upon which modern nation-states are established, or from irreconcilable ideological divisions which often accompany social change. In the first case, the principle of national self-determination may contradict the rights of national minorities, while in the second, the right of the sovereign state to demand ideological conformity from its citizens comes into conflict with the basic rights of individuals.

The subject of this essay is one such group: the Hungarian refugees who, after 1918, fled or were expelled to Hungary from areas awarded in the Treaty of Trianon to the Successor States of Czechoslovakia, Romania and Yugoslavia. These refugees fell victim to the national as well as ideological intolerance of the new regimes. As victims of persecutions, the refugees in Hungary became symbols of the injustices of the Treaty of Trianon; and as a group radicalized by their own misfortunes, they left their mark on Hungary's history as supporters, and often leaders, of the new Radical Right.

The disintegration of the Austro-Hungarian Empire was completed by a two-pronged revolution—a social revolution in Hungary, which in the minority areas was quickly transformed into a national revolution. In the October 1918 revolution the moderate left came to power, the genuine liberals: the Bourgeois Radicals and the Social Democrats. During the previous decades the leaders of these groups were consistent opponents of Hungarian supremacy, and offered a solution to the minority question based on principles of complete equality and democracy and they hoped to achieve their goals through fundamental economic and social reforms. A few years earlier even a more modest program of reform would have satisfied the national minorities, but the conservative Hungarian leaders of the time, defending the political and social predominance of the nobility within the Hungarian nation-state, ruled out democratic reforms. The main reason for conservative opposition was a fear that granting political equality to the minorities would unleash a social and economic revolution which would abolish both the Hungarian character of the state and the dominant role of the traditional ruling classes.[2] In November 1918, however, a policy of reconciliation of all the nationalities of Hungary through prudent political and economic reforms was no longer viable. The same forces which radicalized the Hungarian population, brought to power the moderate left and made meaningful reforms possible, also radicalized the minorities and created for them a more appealing alternative. The First World War brought deprivations and massive suffering to both the military and civilian population, regardless of nationality.[3] These, combined with repressive measures directed against some of the minorities,[4] completed the alienation of a large segment of the non-Hungarian population and accelerated the growth of national consciousness and resistance. The time favored virulent nationalism and national confrontation, and the fate of the country ceased to depend upon the policies of the Hungarian government. The initiative passed to the victorious Western Powers and to their East Central European allies and, to a lesser degree, to some of the well-placed representatives of the national minorities. During the war the Allies committed themselves to certain territorial changes and to a set of general principles that was to be followed during a post-war reorganization of East Central Europe, though this is not to assert that the Great Powers possessed a coherent plan for the region. Short range objectives, the pressures of immediate events, as well as concessions forced by the Successor States were just as influential in shaping the final settlement as the designs of the Great Powers. On one principle the Allies and the Successor States were in agreement: as the end of the war approached, both became determined to satisfy the national ambitions of the former minorities of the Austro-Hungarian Empire, not through mere reform, but through a recognition of the right of minorities to form independent nation-states.[5] The failure to realize the non-viability of the idea of nation-states in a multi-national region led to a reversal of the previous situation. In the territories detached from Hungary, Hungarian supremacy was replaced by Serbian, Czechoslovak or Romanian supremacy, and the formerly dominant Hungarians became an oppressed national minority, whose right to national self-determination was denied. Just as in 1867–68, the minority issue was to be resolved by means of limited legal guarantees, but once again such attempts were doomed to failure. Not surprisingly, reconciliation between the new majorities and minorities became even less likely than during the Dualist Era.[6]

In 1918–1919 the Successor States were little concerned with the establishment of a system that would assure long range cooperation between the small states of the region. They realized that the Western Allies were not in a position to fill the power vacuum left by the military defeat of the Central Powers, and seized upon this unique opportunity to guarantee their security through territorial expansion. The goals of the Successor States were simple: they wished to bring under their control the sought territories immediately and to secure maximum economic and military advantage for themselves, even if in the process a substantial number of presumably hostile minorities had to be incorporated in their states. Without awaiting the final decision of the Paris Peace Conference the Successor States, supported partially by the Great Powers, moved to occupy the demanded territories. Between November 1918 and March 1919 most of these areas were indeed brought under their jurisdiction. At first, Hungarian resistance was only sporadic. But after the establishment of the Hungarian Soviet Republic in March 1919, and until its defeat in August of that year, further encroachment on Hungarian territories was forcefully opposed.[7]

The flight of the Hungarian population from the minority areas paralleled the changing fortunes of their respective regions. Some fled even before the arrival of the occupation forces, while others decided to leave only after repressive measures directed against the Hungarian minority and economic and administrative changes introduced by the new governments directly affected their lives, and made their continued existence in the Successor States precarious or impossible. In all, an estimated 426,000 individuals left the lost territories between 1918 and 1924. Of these, the National Refugee Office (*Országos Menekültügyi Hivatal* or *OMH*) registered about 350,000 individuals. Their distribution according to the country of origin was as follows:

TABLE I

From Territories Ceded to:	Number of Refugees	
	OMH Figures	Estimated Actual Numbers
Czechoslovakia	106,841	147,000
Romania	197,035	222,000
Yugoslavia	44,903	55,000
Austria	1,221	2,000
Total:	350,000	426,000

As a result of the flight of the refugees, the population of Trianon Hungary increased by about 5.3 percent, while the size of the Hungarian population in the Successor States was reduced: by 13.7 percent in Czechoslovakia, by 13.4 percent in Romania, and by 9.5 percent in Yugoslavia.[9] According to the *OMH*, flow of refugees was the heaviest in the last two months of 1918, when about 58,000 arrived in Hungary, and continued at a high rate during the early months of 1919. After a temporary slowdown in refugee arrivals during the four-month existence of the Soviet Republic, the tempo once again picked up and began to decline only during 1921. (Table II.)

TABLE II

Year	Number of Refugees	Year	Number of Refugees
1918	58,784	1922	21,242
1919	110,573	1923	9,041
1920	121,930	1924	2,307
1921	26,123		

In general, the refugees represented the former social and political elite of the lost territories, the past beneficiaries of Hungarian hegemony in the old minority areas of the country. Their livelihood was tied to the continued existence of the Hungarian nation-state, and with its break-up they lost both their political power and economic footing. The largest single group among the refugees were the former state and county officials: judges, prosecutors, court clerks, village notaries, police officers and gendarmes, state pensioners, teachers and professors, officials and workers of the state railroad and other state enterprises. The second largest group consisted of the employees of privately owned Hungarian banks and commercial or industrial enterprises and small business owners or craftsmen. A sizable group of gentry and aristocratic landowners also left the Successor States. Though numerically inferior to the previous groups, this third group was the politically most active and powerful. While the ranks of the Hungarian upper and middle classes were seriously depleted in the lost territories, relatively few peasants chose to leave their homelands. Those who did left mainly for practical economic reasons, in most cases when they found that the new frontiers separated them from their lands.

Out of the 350,000 registered refugees, 160,271 were housewives and other dependents; 86,375 were pupils or university students. The occupation of the remaining 103,254 refugees fit in the following categories:[11]

TABLE III

Occupational Group	Number in Group	Percentage of Total
Public Employees	44,253	42.9%
Commerce and Industry	35,553	34.4
Landowners	10,376	10.0
Gentlemen	8,323	8.1
Professionals	621	0.6
Other	4,128	4.0
Total:	103,254	100.0%

To give up ancestoral estates, to leave homelands rich in cultural and historical traditions and memories is always painful. The decision to depart was made by many Hungarians only after all hopes for a reversal of Hungarian fortunes dimmed, or if economic necessity made it unavoidable. We can identify four causes which at various times influenced individuals or families to leave the old minority areas. First, the fear of physical violence by the occupation armies, or of retribution by the local population for past grievances, real or imagined; second, an ardent Hungarian nationalism which led many people to reject a life under foreign domination; third, loss of economic security; and finally, the inability of many to accept a loss of social status.

For some of the Hungarian officials the terror began with the collapse of the Austro-Hungarian Empire. The disintegration of the armies on the front paralleled the lost of control of population within Hungary. By September 1918 an estimated 400,000 men deserted from the Army[12] and during the last month of the war the pace of desertions accelerated. From the approximately 2.1 million Austro-Hungarian soldiers taken prisoners of war in Russia by the fall of 1918, about 725,000 soldiers were allowed to return. Of these about 152,000 were Hungarian, 94,000 Romanian, 80,000 Croatian, 44,000 Slovakian and 4,000 Serbian.[13] From the fronts soldiers streamed home in great disarray, often in rags and without food supplies. By the end of November 1918 about 700,000 soldiers from Hungary were demobilized and by the end of December their number grew to 1,200,000.[14] Upon hearing the news of the end of the war, the "Green Companies," made up of thousands of army deserters, emerged from their mountain hiding places and joined hands with the returning soldiers, unemployed former prisoners of war and rebellious peasants, and plundered the countryside. Count Tivadar Batthyány, the Hungarian Minister of Interior wrote: "A veritable flood of complaints poured in from every direction that armed groups, small and large, as well as bands of returning soldiers were causing havoc, seizing property, robbing, using force, and even committing murders."[15] In Transylvania returning soldiers, peasants and the hastily formed Romanian National Guards seized entire districts. In every region of the country peasants, both Hungarian and non-Hungarian, attacked, looted and in some cases, burnt down the chateaus and manor houses of the nobility, in the process killing or severely beating some of the overseers who tried in vain to protect their masters' properties. Occasionally landless peasants, fired by the news of an impending land reform, began to divide the nobles' estates among themselves.[16] Great estates were assaulted in northern Hungary, Croatia, Transylvania, Transdanubia and on the Hungarian Plain. For example, some of the Transylvanian estates of the Teleky, Haller, Zichy, Kemény, Hirsch and Bethlen families were attacked and ransacked.[17] The same fate befell the Andrássy chateau at Tiszadob.[18] Not even Mihály Károlyi's estate at Parádfürdő escaped the rage of the peasants.[19] Though peasant attacks were random and disorganized, their pattern was fairly uniform. Disturbances were begun mostly by radicalized and armed peasant soldiers who won over the local population for attacks on the estates.[20] Many of the peasant soldiers arrived in their native villages ready to settle old scores, or to take revenge upon local officials for abusing their families during their absence. Also, because the landlords were absent or were the first to flee, the hatred of the peasants, especially in the minority areas, was vented upon the remaining lesser officials: village notaries, teachers, gendarmes, and even priests, men, that is, who symbolized to them the authority of the old Hungarian state. Since in the minority areas most of the landlords and officials were Hungarian, the social revolution of the peasants in those regions acquired a national character. The notaries and gendarmes were especially harshly treated. According to Oscar Jászi, during the first few days of the revolution alone, one third of the notaries were forced to flee.[21] According to another estimate, about one third of notaries fled from Hungarian villages—one half from Slovak-populated areas and about nine-tenths from Romanian regions.[22] In many villages the notaries were beaten to death or shot; in one instance the deceased notary's body was disinterred and dumped into a ditch.[23] In vain did the notaries protest at their December 5th congress that they were "robbed of their property, vilified," and became the "persecuted martyrs" of the revolution.[24] A main goal of the government was restoration of order, though it was powerless to protect its isolated officials in the villages. Most of the rural gendarmerie stations had to be abandoned and the personnel concentrated in larger towns. On a number of occasions regular military units were called out to restore order. At time aristocrats organized independent military detachments to recapture their estates and to take bloody revenge on the offending peasants.[25] But repressive measures could not permanently reinstate local officials.

Peasant attacks on estates and officials, as well as reactions to them, were part of a social revolution. This is born out by the fact that Romanian and Serbian national guard units were also active in repressing rebellious peasants. What turned the social revolution into a national one, and at the same time sealed the fate of the Hungarian officials and that of the Hungarian middle classes, was the invasion of the country by the Serbian, Czech and Romanian armies. Following the arrival of occupying forces, arrests, murders, and taking of hostages were frequent. News of these incidents spread rapidly and became amplified as they were passed on. Rumors of planned bloody revenges that were to follow the arrival of the Serbian, Romanian or Czech armies were often sufficient to cause many officials, landowners, estate managers, and police officials to seek safety in central Hungary. Some of the desperate officials tried to organize the local population into a military force to resist the invaders, but all such attempts in northern Hungary and most in Transylvania ended in failure. The Hungarian peasantry looked upon these efforts with suspicion and remained passive, while in the urban areas workers and some of the intellectuals were openly hostile to the noble officer recruiters, suspecting, not without justification, that such a force would quickly become a counterrevolutionary army. Moreover, the Hungarian government of Mihály Károlyi, more clearly appreciating the hopeless military position of the country and still clinging to a hope of peaceful, negotiated settlement, discouraged active resistance by the population.[26]

The upper classes and the most exposed champions of Hungarian nationalism left mostly during the chaotic first few months after the armistice. With the establishment of military control by the Successor States, overt acts of violence against the Hungarian population subsided, though they by no means ceased completely. Pressure on the remaining Hungarian minority changed in character; persecution and discrimination became more subtle, systematic and selective, and more a consequence of government policies than of popular hatred. The governments of the Successor States welcomed, actively encouraged, and at times forced the departure of Hungarian families or individuals, partly to reduce the overall size of the Hungarian minority and thereby to strengthen their claims to the seized territories, and, more importantly, to bring about a change in the social composition of the population in the newly acquired territories. Most of the cities in these areas had Hungarian and German majorities, with the Hungarian element dominating. To fully control the new provinces the political influence and economic role of the Hungarian middle classes had to be broken and if possible, Hungarians had to be replaced with newly transplanted, loyal Serbians, Romanians, or Czechs. In each of the Successor States the prime target of continued persecutions was the gentry-dominated middle class, which was the backbone of authority in the old Hungarian state. It was the politically most conscious, best organized, and therefore most dangerous group from whose ranks the potential leaders of a national resistance movement could emerge. This class, however, was particularly vulnerable to attacks because of the excessive dependence of its members upon the old Hungarian state.[27] A continued domination of the administrative hierarchy was inconceivable to the leaders of the new states. Technically, according to the terms of the Belgrade Armistice Agreement of 13 November 1918, the contested areas were to remain an integral part of the Hungarian state until the signing of a peace treaty, even though these areas were under a military occupation. Accordingly, at first, Hungary was ordered to evacuate only its military forces beyond the line of demarcation, but "Civil Administration" was to "remain in the hands of the [Hungarian] Government." Naturally, the laws of Hungary were to continue to be in force. Similarly, "being indispensable to the maintenance of order . . ." the Hungrian police and gendarmerie were to be "retained in the evacuated zone."[28]

The Successor States ignored these provisions and severed the occupied regions' ties with Budapest. Elimination of the Hungarian administrative structure and reform of the educational system was completed even before the signing of the Treaty of Trianon. Serbia acted with the greatest efficiency. The first task of most military commanders was to oust the old Hungarian administration. Often this was not necessary, because many of the old officials fled or were already replaced by the spontaneously formed South Slav Councils even before the arrival of the Serbian Army.[29] The purges conducted in Slovakia and Transylvania were less thorough and more drawn out. In Slovakia, a desperate shortage of qualified replacements slowed down the transition. Then too, the greater concentration of Hungarian population, especially in Transylvania where entire counties were solidly Hungarian, made a complete de-magyarization of the administration impractical. Thus, while the higher posts were taken away from Hungarians, some lower officials were retained. But during various screening procedures many were weeded out as security risks. Others were dismissed on the pretext of reorganization of the administrative structure, or as a result of alleged failure to meet some new standard required of all officials.[30] Such was the language requirement, which made it mandatory for all state officials to learn within a year the new, official Czechslovak, Serbian, or Romanian language.[31] Another device was to demand a loyalty oath from all officials, which confronted every Hungarian employee with a difficult choice of conscience as well as with a practical problem.[32] As Hungarian partriots they could not renounce their loyalty to Hungary and as employees of the old Hungarian state many feared the loss of their pensions if such oath was taken. The Károlyi government, recognizing the dilemma of the Hungarian officials, gave its permission to those in the zone of occupation to take, under compulsion, such oaths, and extended a guarantee of a continued payment of salaries to those who refused.[33] This guarantee tended to encourage the flight of the state employees.

One of the most bitter blows to the Hungarian minorities was the de-magyarization of the educational system in the lost areas. On the other hand, few institutions of old Hungary were as much in need of reform as its school system. To the old subject nationalities of Hungary the most visible sign of their second class status and of their oppression was the disparity between the numbers and quality of the Hungarian and non-Hungarian schools.[34] The reform of the educational system, therefore, was high on the agenda of every one of the Successor States. In practice, however, the Hungarian population's loss of schools did not always represent a gain for the old minorities. In Yugoslavia, the Hungarian educational system was abolished during 1919, and over two-thirds of the more than 1,800 Hungarian teachers were dismissed; the Hungarian schools were reduced to one-sixth of their former capacity.[35] In Czechoslovakia the number of Hungarian schools was reduced from nearly 4,000 to less than 700, and nearly three-fourths of the Hungarian teachers lost their jobs.[36] Out of about 1,600 state-operated schools of Transylvania only 562 were allowed to retain Hungarian as language of instruction.[37] One result of this de-magyarization of the educational institutions in the Successor States was that over two-thirds of the dismissed teachers, some 8,870 left or were expelled from their homelands by 1920.[38] Deprived of educational opportunities for their children, many Hungarian families, especially those of middle class origins, fled or at least sent their children to Hungary to be educated.

Thus, even before the decision of the Western Powers sealed the fate of Hungary and of the Hungarian population of the occupied areas, the Successor States, through forced de-magyarization of the administrative and educational institutions, through seizures of Hungarian, mostly noble, estates, as well as through outright expulsions, achieved a dramatic reduction in the size of the remaining Hungarian minorities. Moreover, the political and economic power of the Hungarian minorities was broken and their social and cultural leadership destroyed. The Hungarian minorities became a socially more homogeneous, overwhelmingly agricultural group, which could be more easily controlled and managed.

The last illusory hope of the Hungarians was a reprieve by the Great Powers during the long delayed peace negotiations. But the ratification of the Treaty of Trianon in June 1920 merely sanctioned the dismemberment of Hungary and the discriminatory and repressive policies of the Successor States. At the Peace Conference the Western Powers rejected every request of the Hungarian delegation for substantive change in the draft treaty.[39] Hungary had to accept the position that in her case, because she was a defeated state, historical rights, economic needs, or ethnic principles did not apply. The collective right to national self-determination of the Hungarian majorities in some of the disputed areas, the right to determine the fate of their region, was denied. The only concession to the transferred Hungarian population was extended to them as individuals, and this concession involved the right to depart. Article 63 of the Treaty of Trianon, the so-called optant clause, stated: "Persons . . . losing their Hungarian nationality . . . shall be entitled within a period of one year from the coming into force of the present Treaty to opt for the nationality of the State in which they possessed rights of citizenship before acquiring such rights in the territory transferred . . ."[40] This clause triggered the last major wave of refugees. Those who up to this point still clung to illusions about the future of their homelands, were forced to face reality. Over 100,000 individuals chose to exercise their right to depart.

From the very beginning, the reception of the refugees in Hungary was mixed. As suffering human beings and as the visible symbols of the nation's tragedy, many of the refugees became beneficiaries of the personal generosity of the more affluent classes. At the same time, the country was in the midst of a social revolution, and refugees as a group were often viewed with suspicion and hostility as representatives of the old ruling and official classes, and as champions of bankrupt conservative politics. The massive influx of refugees also created an intolerable economic burden for Hungary and intensified internal social tensions. With its economy at a standstill, beset by widespread unemployment and shortages of every kind, including food, fuel, and clothing, and without hope of relief from the West due to a continuation of the Allied economic blockade, the government was incapable of satisfying even the minimum needs of the refugees. Moreover, for the Left aid to the refugees was an ideological issue. They could not justify the squandering of the meagre resources of the state on their former class enemies when their own long deprived supporters, the workers and the lower classes, were equally destitute. The same view was taken when the few vacated bureaucratic posts were to be filled or when the even rarer apartments were to be assigned.[42] As a result, refugees had to struggle for even a single room apartment, and thousands were forced to live, often for years, in the same railroad cattle cars (now shunted to the side tracks of the main railroad stations) in which they arrived.[43] The misery of the population was greatest in Budapest. Yet, the demobilized refugee soldiers and officers, the refugee students and officials, naturally flocked to the capital, either to continue their education there or to press the ministries, usually without success, with their demands for aid or jobs.

The refugees left a deep imprint on the post-war history of Hungary; they were heavily involved in the counterrevolution, helped to consolidate the Horthy regime, participated in the establishment of the first fascist groups, and markedly influenced the formulation of the ideology of Hungarian fascism. The reasons for their deep political involvement is not hard to see. The experiences of the refugees—their desperate economic situation and their destroyed political and social roles—primed them for radical action. In an increasingly polarized society the refugees were the most traumatized group who eagerly joined, and often led, the many newly-formed Right wing organizations. Even more than the defeated aristocracy and gentry of inner Hungary, they were prepared to counter the nation's social revolution, and the national revolutions of the former minorities, with a revolution of the Right.

Notes

1. Heinrich Böll, "Hymn to a New Homeland," *Saturday Review* (May 3, 1975).

2. Even the eleventh-hour attempt to grant political equality to all citizens of Hungary was rejected by the conservative leaders. During the February 1918 parliamentary debates on voting rights Count István Tisza declared: "From 1848 until recent times everyone agreed that radical electoral right is the doom of the Hungarian nation, the Hungarian nation-state. . . . It is the enemies of the nation-state who want, desire, demand universal franchise. . . ." *Budapesti Hírlap*, 26 February 1918. On the same subject the leader of the Transylvanian Hungarians Count István Bethlen said: "In Transylvania . . . electoral right is not a question of democracy, nor of conservatism; it is not even a question of class, but a question of survival." *Ibid.*, 2 March 1918.

3. The massive disruption of civilian lives can be illustrated by the size of the military mobilization. Of the 7,264,861 men who were made available for military service in the Monarchy by July 31, 1917, 3,243,323 came from Hungary, representing 72.88 percent of the 18 to 50-year-old male population of the country registered in the 1910 census. Antal Józsa, *Háború, hadifogság, forradalom. Magyar Internacionalista hadifoglyok az 1917-es oroszországi forradalmakban* (Budapest, 1970), p. 36. Proportionately, the contribution of the Hungarians was the highest. The Romanians and Germans were also declared fit for military service at a rate higher (and the Slavs at a rate lower) than their proportion out of the total population. Wilhelm Winkler, *Der Anteil der nichtdeutschen Volksstämme an der öst.-ung. Wehrmacht* (Vienna, 1919), pp. 1–2; cited in *ibid.*, p. 34.

4. The policy of the Hungarian government towards the national minorities during the war needs clarification. The selective harsh treatment of the minorities was not racially motivated, but grew out of the security requirements of the state, and out of attempts to arrest separatist tendencies among some of the nationalities. Accordingly, repressive measures were not uniformly applied, and paralleled the military fortunes of the country. At the outset of the war the policy towards the Slovaks and Croatians, who were considered to be trustworthy, changed but little. However, in areas which came under military jurisdiction as zones of operations, military authorities, at times independently of the government, resorted to bloody repressing. Such was the case particularly along the Serbian frontier, in Serbia itself, as well as in the Ukrainian-populated regions at the time of the Russian invasion of Hungary. Treatment of Romanians changed only after the 1916 Romanian invasion of Transylvania. Though the Romanian population remained generally passive, many Romanians, especially members of the intelligentsia, compromised themselves with the result that tens of thousands fled with the retreating Romanian Army. Thousands of those who remained were subsequently interned and hundreds were charged with treason. For a detailed account of Hungarian policy towards the minorities during the war see József Galántai, *Magyarország az Első Világháborúban, 1914–1918* (Budapest, 1974), especially pp. 175–182, 190–195, 224–225, and 351–352. See also, Zoltán Szász, "Az erdélyi román

polgárság szerepéről 1918 őszén," *Századok* no. 2 (1972), pp. 309–310; Miron Constantinescu *et. al.*, *Unification of the Romanian National State: The Union of Transylvania with Old Romania* (Bucharest, 1971), pp. 100–101.

5. Not until 1918 did the Allies abandon their plans for reorganizing the Austro-Hungarian Empire, allowing "the freest opportunity for autonomous development" among the minorities, in favor of the complete dismemberment of the Empire. But the dissolution of the Empire was already implied in the earlier secret agreements with Serbia and Romania. Alfred D. Low, *The Soviet Hungarian Republic and the Paris Peace Conference* (Philadelphia, 1963), pp. 8–9. For the changing attitudes of the Western Powers towards the future of Austria-Hungary, see Wilfred Fest, *Peace or Partition: The Habsburg Monarchy and British Policy, 1914–1918* (New York, 1978). See also, Kenneth J. Calder, *Britain and the Origins of the New Europe. 1914–1918* (Cambridge, 1976); W. H. Rothwell, *British War Aims and Peace Diplomacy. 1914–1918* (Oxford, 1971).

6. For the text of the minority treaties, see H.W.V. Temperley, ed., *A History of the Peace Conference of Paris* vol. 5: *Economic Reconstruction and Protection of Minorities* (London, 1924), pp. 446–470.

7. See essays by Tihanyi, Pastor and Kalvoda.

8. Baron Emil Petrichevich-Horváth, ed., *Jelentes az Országos Menekültügyi Hivatal négy évi működéséről* (Budapest, 1924), p. 37. Hereinafter cited as *OMH Report*. In estimating the number of refugees, the various post-war censuses and the 1910 Hungarian census were used.

9. As compared to the 1910 census figures.

10. *OMH Report*, p. 37. It seems that most of the estimated 76,000 individuals who escaped registration by the OMH reached inner Hungary during the last months of 1918 or during early 1919. Many of these individuals were already in central Hungary at the time of the occupation of their homelands and simply chose to remain. Others were soldiers and officers returning from the front or released or escaping prisoners of war.

11. *Ibid.*

12. Galántai, *Magyarország az Első Világháborúban*, p. 397.

13. Antal Józsa, *Háború, hadifogság, forradalom: Magyar Internacionalista hadifoglyok az 1917-es oroszországi forradalmakban* (Budapest, 1970), pp. 101–103.

14. József Breit, *A Magyarországi 1918/19 évi forradalmi mozgalom és a vörös háború története* vol. I (Budapest, 1929), p. 37. See also Ervin Liptai, *Vöröskatonák Előre! A magyar Vörös Hadsereg harcai, 1919.* (Budapest, 1969), p. 12.

15. Tivadar Batthyány, *Beszámolóm* vol. I (Budapest, e.n.), p. 294.

16. Zoltán Szász, "Az erdélyi román polgárság, p. 317.

17. *Ibid.*, p. 316.

18. *Vörös Ujság*, February 15, 1919. Article reproduced in László Remete, "Rengj csak, Föld!" (Budapest, 1968), pp. 272–275.

19. Tibor Hajdu, *Károlyi Mihály* (Budapest, 1978), p. 285.

20. Szász, "Az erdélyi román polgárság," p. 317.

21. Oscar Jászi, *Revolution and Counter-Revolution in Hungary* (New York, 1969), p. 61. (Originally published in 1924.)

22. Tibor Hajdu, *Az 1918-as magyarországi polgári demokratikus forradalom* (Budapest, 1968), p. 98.

23. Miklós Kozma, *Az összeomlás: 1918–19* (Budapest, 1934[?]), Journal entries for December 2 and 5, 1918, pp. 51 and 63. See also, Liptai, *Vöröskatonák*, p. 13.

24. János Kende, *Forradalomról forradalomra* (Budapest, 1979), p. 88. See also, Batthyány, *Beszámolom* vol. I., pp. 294, 303. Indeed no other class was treated as harshly during the revolution as notaries. Though some abused their greatly increased powers during the war, most simply carried out state policies. Handling military draft exemptions, forced food requisitions and similar measures inevitably made them many enemies.

25. Szász, "Az erdélyi román polgárság," p. 319. See also Constantinescu *et. al., Unification of the Romanian National State*, p. 248. *Vörös Ujság*, February 15, 1919. György Ránki *et. al., Magyarország története vol 8: 1919–1945* (Budapest, 1976), p. 81. Also, László Kővágó, *A magyarországi délszlávok 1918–1919-ben* (Budapest, 1964), p. 103. Kende, *Forradalomról forradalomra*, p. 63.

26. Only the formation of the Székely Division received official sanction. Its function was to guard the official line of demarcation between the Romanian occupied territories and Hungary, though it also conducted unofficial raids and rescue missions across that line. After the dissolution of the Division in April 1919, a large number of the soldiers became refugees and joined the counterrevolutionary army of Admiral Horthy.

27. The reason for that dependence lies in the decline of the gentry. After 1867 the smaller, less efficient noble estates lost their economic viability and the bankrupt owners joined the ranks of the already sizable class of landless nobles. The state compensated them for their losses by offering them posts befitting their station in a greatly expanded bureaucracy.

28. For the text of the Agreement see Temperley, *History of the Peace Conference of Paris* vol. 4, pp. 509–511.

29. Kővágó, *A magyarországi délszlávok*, pp. 95–96. See also, C. A. Macartney, *Hungary and Her Successors; The Treaty of Trianon and Its Consequences, 1919–1937* (Oxford, 1937), p. 409.

30. In Slovakia, for example, three conditions were set for continued employment of Hungarian officials: first, the taking of a loyalty oath to the new Czechoslovak constitution; second, passing of Czechoslovak language examinations within one year; and, finally, meeting unstated qualifications

for holding a specific office. R. W. Seton-Watson, *Slovakia, Then and Now* (London, 1931), pp. 217, 221.

31. Zsombor Szász, *Erdély Romániában. Népkisebbségi Tanulmány* (Budapest, 1927), pp. 83–84.

32. In vain did the Hungarian government protest to the Western Powers that "the Czecho-Slovak and the Romanian Governments compel the Hungarian officials, professors and teachers—under charge of instant dismissal and expulsion—to take the oath of allegiance to the Czechos-Slovak and Roumanian State[s]" and that this was "a manifest infraction of Article 45 of the Hague Convention." Peace Conference Delegation, *Atrocities Committed by Roumanians and Czechs. Memorandum to the mandatories of the Associated Powers at Budapest regarding the abuses perpetrated by the Powers of occupation in the territories subjected to Czecho-Slovak and Roumanian administration* (n.p., n.d. [1920?]), p. 1. See also, Macartney, *Hungary and Her Successors*, p. 413 and Szász, *Erdély Romániában*, p. 55.

33. According to Batthyány, Károlyi's Minister of Interior, around 8–10 November 1918 he personally issued an order to all state officials authorizing them to take the loyalty oath, but only as a last resort and under duress. Batthyány, *Beszámolóm* vol. I, pp. 298–299. See also, Tibor Hajdu, *Az 1918-as magyarországi polgári demokratikus forradalom*, p. 163. Subsequently, the counterrevolutionary government of Szeged gave similar assurances, though, at the same time, urged the officials to take the oath and remain at their posts. Béla Kelemen, ed., *Adatok a szegedi ellenforradalom és a szegedi kormány történetéhez. (1919). (Naplójegyzetek és okiratok)* (Szeged, 1923), pp. 243, 269.

34. As a negative result of the educational reform of 1907 the number of schools where instruction was offered in the languages of the minorities declined from about 6,000 in 1899 to a little over 3,300 by 1914, representing about 20 percent of the approximately 16,600 schools of the country. These schools offered education in their native tongues to about 35 percent of the minority students. Péter Hanák, ed., *Magyarország története, 1890*–1918 vol. 7/2 (Budapest, 1978), p. 641. Differences in literacy rates between the different ethnic groups are another indication of the inequities of the educational opportunities. In 1910, while 79 percent of the Hungarian and 82 percent of the German population of Hungary were literate, only 65 percent of the Slovaks, 48.5 percent of the Serbs and 36 percent of the Romanians could read and write. Though it should be noted that national discrimination was far from being the only cause of the higher rate of illiteracy among the minorities. Also, low as the literacy rate was for the Romanian population, it was still higher than in the Kingdom of Romania.

35. *A jugoszláviai magyarság helyzete* (Budapest, 1941), p. 14.

36. Jozeph Mikus, *Slovakia: A Political History, 1918–1950* (Milwaukee, 1963), p. 29. Also R. W. Seton-Watson, ed., *Slovakia: Then and Now; A Political Survey* (London, 1931), p. 125.

37. Szász, *Erdély Romániában, pp. 232–233.*

38. László Buday, *Megcsonkitott Magyarország* (Budapest, 1921), p. 260.

39. The unbending attitudes of the Western Powers may be understandable in the case of the original Hungarian proposal for a complete restoration of Hungary's former territories. Less justifiable was the refusal of the Great Powers to consider any modifications in the proposed borders whose aim was to achieve a greater correspondence between the prevailing ethnic and the new political boundaries.

40. Fred L. Israel, ed., *Major Peace Treaties of Modern History, 1648–1967* vol. III (New York, 1967), p. 1888. The optant clause already appeared in the minority treaties signed by all three of the Successor States in 1919.

41. Article 63 of the Treaty of Trianon also guaranteed a right to the optant "to retain their immovable property in the territory of the other State where they had their place of residence before exercising their right to opt." *Ibid.,* p. 1889. This clause became the subject of a major international controversy after the Successor States, and specifically Romania, expropriated Hungarian refugee estates for the purpose of land reform. Hungary sued and won her case, but without a satisfactory compensation for the refugees.

42. Not surprisingly, when the Hungarian Soviet, in a fit of egalitarianism, declared the palaces and townhouses of the aristocracy as well as the spacious apartments of the upper and middle classes underutilized, it was not the refugees but the lower classes of the slums who were allowed to move in.

43. *OMH Report,* p. 38.

William Batkay

Trianon: Cause or Effect—
Hungarian Domestic Politics in the 1920's

As the appearance of this volume attests, the Treaty of Trianon continues to fascinate scholars and writers in a wide variety of disciplines. Even after the passage of 69 years, unanswered, or inadequately answered, questions abound concerning the intellectual, diplomatic, and military background of the treaty, as well as its political, social, and economic consequences for East Central Europe in general and Hungary in particular. The extent and precise nature of the contribution of the treaty to inter-state and inter-ethnic rivalries and tensions, so important a factor in laying the groundwork for World War II, has been an especially attractive object of scholarly concern.

In particular, writers on the period have tended to focus attention on the character and significance of the revisionist foreign policy outlook adopted by successive interwar Hungarian regimes and the destabilizing impact of that policy on international relations in the East Central European area. The goal of integral, that is, complete, revision of the Treaty of Trianon and the devices developed and utilized by Hungarian governments to channel political and societal resources toward its ultimate achievement have furnished the standard framework on which analyses of Hungary in the interwar period have been hung. Few scholars have explored the impact of the Treaty of Trianon on Hungarian domestic politics or the complex interrelationship of Hungarian domestic politics and Hungarian revisionism in foreign policy, especially in the formative period of the 1920's.

This interrelationship cannot merely be deduced from *a priori* assumptions about the Treaty of Trianon and Hungarian foreign policy, but merits, indeed demands, separate investigation. The parameters of this investigation can be established by posing the following question for examination: was the Treaty of Trianon, as some believe, a necessary and sufficient condition for explaining the reactionary and counter-revolutionary character of the political

system erected in Hungary in the 1920's under the aegis of Count
István Bethlen, the architect of post-war consolidation? Or was
obsession with treaty revision itself the product of the reactionary
domestic political goals of the Hungarian political elite?

The thesis that I will develop in answer to these questions is that
the Treaty of Trianon, however central a touchstone it may have
been for Hungarian foreign policy during the interwar decades, in
many respects played only a minimal, at best ancillary, role in
domestic Hungarian political processes during the 1920's. It does not
fully explain those processes nor shed much direct light on them.
Other factors may have been more important, especially the commitment, independent of the question of Trianon, to the restoration
as far as possible of the pre-war social and political system. It is the
character of the political system erected and consolidated by Count
Bethlen in the 1920's that provides a better perspective from which to
examine the foreign policy outlook of his regime vis-à-vis the Treaty
of Trianon.

Let us be clear about the precise character of the issue under consideration. It is one thing to suggest that "this dream of restoring
Hungarian hegemony in Danubian Europe was fundamental to
Bethlen's foreign policy in the 1920's," and that "the goal [of] restoration of a large and powerful Hungary remained constant."[1] It is
scarcely possible to take issue with this judgment, supported as it is
by the amply documented historical record.[2] It is quite another
thing, however, to argue that the Hungarian counter-revolutionary
political system "was itself conditioned and *almost imposed* by the
policy of the World War victors, and by the *consequent* changes in
Hungarian class-structure and outlook."[3] A slightly different version
of this point of view sees the counter-revolution as merely a means to
the end of treaty revision: failure to achieve immediate revision of
the Treaty of Trianon in 1920 led the Hungarian elite to decide that
"domestic consolidation on constitutional, political, cultural, and
economic levels would have to precede an eventual resumption of . . .
efforts to achieve revision."[4] This decision in turn is taken as
evidence of an original commitment by the Hungarian regime "to
subordinate every other consideration to the cause of revisionism."[5]

In contrast to these one-sided views, treaty revision must be seen
as but one element, albeit a highly visible one, in a general program to turn back the political and social clock, as it were, to
the pre-treaty, pre-revolutionary, pre-war period.[6] The essential

dynamics of this process were underway well before the treaty was ratified or even signed, already during the liberal democratic regime of Count Mihály Károlyi in 1918–1919. It was in this early post-war period that the main elements of the Hungarian counter-revolution were organized, primarily for domestic political and social purposes. The separation of Hungary from Austria, implemented by Károlyi, but especially the proclamation of a Hungarian republic in November 1918, generated anxiety and then escalating opposition from several political quarters, of which those on the right are of prime concern to us here. On the one hand, segments of the erstwhile political and social elite, so suddenly and rudely displaced, embarked on a determined campaign of general obstructionism and anti-republican mass agitation in order to overthrow the regime of Károlyi, restore the monarchy, and thus preserve their own political and social status.[7] On the other hand, the regime's mounting economic difficulties elicited an equally hostile, but even cruder, reaction from members of the "frayed white-collar" groups of the middle and lower-middle class, whose socio-economic fortunes had been the most corroded by World War I and its after-effects.[8] Equally opposed to both the reactionary strivings of the propertied strata and the growing strength of proletarian elements, these middle-class groups constituted the bulk of what was to become the right-radical wing of the counter-revolution.[9]

From rather amorphous beginnings these two "tendencies" crystallized into a number of identifiable political parties and direct-action groups to oppose the Károlyi regime in more organized, if not more systematic, fashion. On the conservative right, the politicians created the National Agrarian Laborers' Party (Országos Földmíves Párt) and the Party of National Union (Nemzeti Egyesülés Pártja); on the radical right, military officers, civil servants, and intellectuals formed the ultra-nationalist Hungarian National Defense Force Union (Magyar Országos Véderő Egyesület, or MOVE) and the Union of Awakening Hungarians (Ébredő Magyarok Egyesülete, or EME).[10] These gradually coalesced into a loosely coordinated counter-revolutionary movement after Béla Kun's Communist-Socialist coalition succeeded Károlyi's regime in March 1919.

The counter-revolution found a rallying point in April, when, having removed to the safety of Vienna, Count Bethlen set up an Anti-Bolshevist Committee (ABC) with other aristocratic politicians to coordinate efforts to enlist Entente military help against the new

Soviet Republic in Budapest and to secure funds for a future contingent of counter-revolutionary troops.[11] In a move that was perhaps indicative of the rivalries and competition that were to bedevil the counter-revolutionaries, another Károlyi—Count Gyula—established a second center of anti-Red activity at Szeged in southern Hungary in May 1919, with Gyula Gömbös—head of MOVE, prominent right-radical leader, and future Hungarian prime minister—as liaison with the Vienna group.[12]

Significantly, it was this Szeged government and its right-radical supporters that recruited Admiral Miklós Horthy, future Regent of Hungary, to head a National Army to prosecute the counter-revolutionary cause in the field. This force, however, studiously avoided military engagements with the Red, or indeed, any army, and confined its activities to the unleashing of pogroms against Jews and terroristic reprisals against suspected current or erstwhile supporters of the Reds. These activities, and the ineffectiveness of either of the two civilian groups, soon promoted this force to a position where it exercised what meaningful political power was to be had in Hungary, quite independently of the formal governmental authorities.[13]

Yet a third locus of anti-radical activity was secured in Budapest itself when the Hungarian Soviet government collapsed on August 1, 1919, and its Social Democratic successor was itself ousted in a *coup d'état* led by the conservative politician István Friedrich on August 6. Friedrich's coup marks the real beginning of the counter-revolutionary period in Hungarian political life, for although generally weak and without clear policy goals, the government formed by Friedrich ended the experiments with left-wing politics, laid the foundation for the re-establishment of traditional political life, and permitted the conservative political groups to resume legitimate political activity.[14]

Thus by the time István Bethlen came to power a year and a half later, the counter-revolution had been a going concern for over two years. The division of the movement into a conservative and an extremist camp dominated by the anti-Semitism and crude demagogy of the latter—with which the Horthy-Bethlen system as a whole later became incorrectly identified—was already well established. Whatever impact the Treaty of Trianon came to have on Hungarian foreign policy under Bethlen, the anti-liberal, xenophobic, reactionary character of the movement long preceded it. Hostility to the treaty, and the commitment to revisionism in foreign affairs, were not therefore causes of the Hungarian "retrograde revolution"; if anything, they were a logical outgrowth of and concomitant to it.[15] This point will become clearer when we examine the ideology of the counter-revolution, especially under the Bethlen regime.

The Hungarian counter-revolution in general and Bethlen's regime in particular were not perhaps ideological in a strict sense of the term.[16] Nonetheless, the counter-revolutionaries did develop an outlook, an orientation, that, if never formulated in a coherent, systematic body of doctrines and programs, did gradually assume the character of a unifying ideology.[17] Dubbed the *szegedi gondolat* (Szeged idea), after the southern Hungarian town that was an early hotbed of right-radicalism, this ideology was initially a rather crude pastiche of ideas and affective phases that expressed chiefly the hates and fears of right-radicals like Gyula Gömbös: anti-Bolshevism, anti-Semitism, xenophobia, and hostility to political modernism in any form.[18]

The ideology was at first directed largely at expunging all traces of revolution from the Hungarian body politic and at justifying its adherents' pretension to power. It was thus essentially a pragmatic domestic political work-horse that, already champing at the bit, was later harnessed to the cart of revisionism in foreign affairs. Demagogic and virulently anti-Semitic nationalism was primarily the province of the extreme right, politically useful, certainly, for the more conservative wing of the counter-revolution, but not in the style, nor to the taste, of its largely aristocratic contingent.[19] Still, the extreme nationalism and rigid chauvinism of the *szegedi gondolat* were naturally exacerbated by and came to be focused on the Treaty of Trianon and all that it represented; not even the "gentlemanly" politicians of the old school were disposed to resist its blandishments entirely under those circumstances.

With the appointment of István Bethlen to the premiership in April 1921, and the subsequent launching of the "consolidation period" of the counter-revolution, the *szegedi gondolat* was gradually muted into a less demagogic and less radical "Christian national" orientation. The right-radical component, prominent in the early years, was integrated into a conservative liberalism analagous, if not identical, to that characteristic of the pre-war regimes of the two Tiszas, Kálmán and István.[20] While advocating the goal of territorial revisionism so dear to the hearts of the right radicals, Bethlen and other conservative leaders vigorously opposed the reckless military adventurism of Gömbös and his ilk.[21]

It is vitally important to emphasize here that the "Christian national" orientation embodied notions that were quite independent of the impact of the Treaty of Trianon. Nationalism, anti-Semitism, religiosity, and antipathy to anything even vaguely revolutionary provided a more diffuse and more inclusive set of ideas than did the purely right-radical *szegedi gondolat*, and the central value of nationalism especially served as an indispensable tool of social integration in the interwar period, not only among all factions of the right, but even vis-à-vis the largely discredited left.[22]

Thus the ideology of the Horthy-Bethlen system was developed in the period preceding the overthrow of the Hungarian Soviet Republic in August, 1919, and consequently derived less from the later professed foreign policy goals of the regime than from social and political conditions within Hungary. Toned down and purged of its socially radical elements by Count Bethlen, this ideology was manifestly as much of a reaction to the political and social revolutions effected by the liberal regime of Count Mihály Károlyi and the Communist regime of Béla Kun as to the inequities of the Treaty of Trianon.

It need not be a surprise, however, that the ideology, with its stress on national unity and national interests, proved a most useful rallying point for opposition to foreign influence generally and to the treaty in particular. Indeed, it was precisely in hopes of currying favor with and demonstrating respectability towards the victorious Entente powers that the Bethlen regime suppressed the most demagogic aspects of the *szegedi gondolat*, turning the "Christian national" orientation into a defense for the political and social position of the privileged classes, especially the gentry and "gentroid" bureaucracy.[23] It also served to build and strengthen national consensus on the revisionist foreign policy goals of the Bethlen regime. But the creation of the ideology was occasioned chiefly by domestic political and social developments that were viewed as harmful in themselves by the former ruling groups, especially the gentry and lower-middle class strata.

The body of "Christian National" ideas has justly been called the ideology of the middle class in Hungary.[24] Reflecting at least symbolic recognition of middle class concerns on the part of the traditionalist regime, the ideology played an important role in strengthening the legitimacy of the regime within this class. Since it was the gentry middle class and the lower-level civil servants in the state bureaucracy that were the chief proponents of revisionist nationalism, stress on nationalist goals thus helped secure a strong loyalty to the regime on their part. Since, further, virtually all segments of the political elite also saw revision of the peace treaty, particularly in the direction of recovery of lost territories, as the solution to their economic woes and the balm for their wounded self-esteem, the regime could count on the support of non-right-radicals as well.

It is important, however, to note that the gentry and state bureaucracy saw the cause of their own misfortunes and of those of the entire Hungarian nation not exclusively in the Treaty of Trianon, although that was a highly visible symbol, but in the collapse of the entire system created by Count István Tisza, prime minister from 1913 to 1917, of which system the gentry bureaucrats were the prime beneficiaries. They were more than a little inclined, therefore, to see in Bethlen a successor to Tisza, an identification that Bethlen did nothing to discourage.[25] Following in the footsteps of Tisza's father and model, Kálmán Tisza, prime minister from 1875 to 1890, Bethlen again made the Hungarian state the bulwark of the gentry, via both the symbolically potent "Christian national" ideology and more tangible benefits to the gentry-bureaucrats. Ideologically, political control by the gentry was rationalized by emphasis on traditional concepts of authority, entailing frequent iteration of the importance of what might be termed the leading role of the middle class, of the need to place political direction of the state again into the hands of the "Christian intelligentsia," and so forth.[26]

The tangible benefits, however, were perhaps of greater immediate interest to this group. Economic modernization and consequent social change had already under Kálmán Tisza eroded the position of the landed gentry; the state bureaucracy then became its main professional outlet. The First World War and the social dislocation and economic penury that ensued, aggravated by the Treaty of Trianon, destroyed this new source of gentry security. Bethlen, like Tisza before him, came to the rescue, and vastly expanded the state bureaucracy to accommodate both its now-displaced former incumbents, including legions that had found themselves stranded in the Successor States, and large numbers from the non-gentry lower middle class. The maintenance of the social status and economic security of the civil servants again became a top priority of the regime, and thus an important source of legitimacy for it. To give this group even more of a vested interest in the preservation of the regime, Bethlen gave substance to the ideological posturing by placing the political recruitment process firmly in the hands of the bureaucracy: the holders of top political positions were drawn largely from the major redoubt of the former gentry, the upper levels of the state bureaucracy.[27] The consequent identification of the ideals of the system with the perceived interests of the bulk of the political participants brought a handsome reward to the regime—the unswerving loyalty of its prime beneficiaries.[28]

The independence of the counter-revolutionary political system from the exigencies of the Treaty of Trianon is most clearly apparent in the realm of political processes and institutions. To be sure, these embodied a commitment to integral revision of the treaty;[29] but they also represented institutuional continuity with the pre-war past and thus also served to legitimate the Bethlen regime among its subjects and participants. Independent of its commitment to revision, the Bethlen regime successfully sought to re-establish the major institutional props of the pre-war *pays légal:* the bureaucracy, the cabinet, and the "government party," all under the authority of a strong prime minister.[30]

The state bureaucracy was again made a fief of the descendants of the gentry. But this in itself would have availed them little if the bureaucracy had not been restored to the pre-eminent position in which it had been ensconced by Kálmán Tisza. Here one of the most signal advances of the Bethlen regime over its counter-revolutionary predecessors becomes manifest. From 1919 until Bethlen's accession to the premiership, the bureaucracy, along with the other institutions of government, were in thrall to the depredations of the paramilitary "detachments" and the various extreme rightist secret associations.[31] The government was in fact no government at all, and the administration administered little. By curbing the interference of the military in administrative affairs and the influence of the political parties in the selection of people to the top administrative positions, Bethlen not only restored respect for the authority of the bureaucracy, but also re-established the basic principle of the subordination of the administration to the prime minister, a situation to which the bureaucrats had earlier been quite happily accustomed.[32]

As regards the cabinet, instability was the rule in the period between the fall of Kun and consolidation of Bethlen's position. The prime ministers were, with the notable exception of Count Pal Teleki, prime minister from 1920 to 1921, generally colorless nonentities; Teleki himself was merely ineffectual.[33] In consequence partly of this, partly of other factors, governments tended to be short-lived, their composition highly unstable, and links with the other institutions of the political system feeble.[34] A chaotic and undisciplined multi-party system, whose component parties seemed inspired by no higher ideals than self-aggrandizement, added to the ill-repute of the governments, especially among the military.[35] Aided by the palpable anxiety generated among the political elite by ex-King Charles IV's attempted coup in April, 1921, Bethlen succeeded in dictating the composition of his first cabinet. The traditional pre-eminence of the Hungarian prime minister over his ministerial colleagues was thus re-established, at least tentatively. This tentative superiority became permanent after 1922, with the re-birth of the third element of the pre-war *pays légal*, a voting-majority-based ruling party itself subservient to its leader, the prime minister—i.e., Bethlen.

The significance of the creation of this ruling party, called *Egyseges Part* (Unified Party), is frequently overlooked by Marxist and non-Marxist scholars alike.[36] In fact, it was central to Bethlen's plans for political consolidation, and its creation cannot be explained by reference to "tactical considerations" or the Treaty of Trianon. The party was not indeed even necessary to Bethlen by any ordinary political calculus.[37] Once having secured the enactment of a retrograde voting law in the spring of 1922, he was in a position to secure a perpetual parliamentary majority by electoral manipulation alone.[38] Yet his passionate and unremitting determination to see this party created seems to border on the obsessive. It strains credulity to imagine that this almost Herculean effort, repeatedly frustrated, repeatedly renewed—was aimed solely, or chiefly, or even largely at the Treaty of Trianon. Capping so many of Bethlen's designs, the Unified Party was the keystone to the arch of the reborn system of Tisza's *pays légal*, a sine qua non of Bethlen's consolidation and of the legitimacy and authority of his regime.[39]

Constitutionalism and Parliamentarianism Under Bethlen

Although more or less passing mention is made of them in the literature on interwar Hungarian politics, Hungarian constitutional and parliamentary traditions deserve a more serious place in an examination of Hungarian politics in the 1920's, and even beyond. However powerful the drive to revise the treaty, there were limits beyond which Bethlen, and a large proportion of the political elite, would not go. Some attempt to explain this, again, by reference to tactical or strategic considerations: desire to impress the Entente, curry favor with the League of Nations, win economic concessions from the neighboring states, or what have you.[40] That these considerations played some role in the foreign-directed propaganda—much of it unctuously self-righteous in tone—of the Bethlen regime is undeniable.[41] That they were the most salient factor in the revival of Hungarian constitutionalism and parliamentarianism is at best unlikely.

The parliamentary system had enjoyed enormous prestige under the Dual Monarchy, and its better-known figures were persons of social and political weight and consequence. The election of political parvenus to the first re-constituted single-chamber Assembly occasioned dismay and even ridicule from members of the politically attentive public.[42] The political elite was deeply attached to the idea and ideal of parliamentarianism that even the counterrevolutionary Assembly embodied.[43] To dismiss Hungarian parliamentarianism, as some older Marxist works do, as a sort of public relations gimmick, designed to mask the abject submission of parliament to cabinet, is to be both myopic and insensitive to the operative ideals of Hungarian political life.[44] The gentry, and its bureaucratic offshoot, had long since accepted and absorbed the basic norms of the parliamentary process and, until the collapse of 1918-1919, had never looked beyond them for political gratification. Bethlen's partial restoration of the parliamentary tradition was a concomitant, therefore, to his efforts to return to them what had been theirs—and his—even in the face of a mean and shabby hostility to parliamentary forms and substance on the part of the "frayed white-collar" class and the Horthyite military.[45] Indeed the latter seemed only to increase the resolve of the Bethlenite elite to adhere to a semblance of traditional parliamentarism. Hatred of the Treaty of Trianon and the commitment to its revision do not to this writer appear to have entered seriously into the equation.

Connected with notions of quasi-liberal parliamentarianism were, of course, more general traditions of constitutionalism, to which the gentrified elite also remained quite remarkably loyal and devoted. While it is undoubtedly true that the idea of monarchy and the symbolism of the Holy Crown of St. Stephen had more than a touch of irredentist instrumentalism about them, they also represented a nearly spontaneous revulsion by the "historic classes" against what was viewed as the a-historic and un-Hungarian republicanism, if not worse, of the discredited Karolyi and Kun regimes.[46] Fear and loathing of demagogic dictatorship, not revanchist ardor or tactical flexibility, reinforced the revival of historic constitutionalism and parliamentarianism during the consolidation period.

Domestic Policy in the 1920's

Not only the institutions and processes, but the actual domestic policies, as well, of the Bethlen regime shed light on the theme of our investigation. Although these latter were also conditioned and constrained by Trianon, they reflected a concern with the restoration of pre-war conditions that was independent of the treaty and its impact.

Industrial and commercial policy under Bethlen, almost *malgre lui*, brought about an expansion of urbanization, especially in the Budapest area, and the development of light industry. As a result, by the end of the interwar period Hungary had advanced from being a predominantly agricultural country to being at least a semi-industrialized one. Already in the 1920's this process had resulted in the expansion of employment opportunities for the semi-skilled and for women.[47] But in areas outside of Budapest, at least, this produced no dramatic social change. The proportion of landowners, capitalists (including merchants), and middle strata among the ranks of the largest taxpayers—the so-called *virilistak*—remained both high and stable from the 1880's until the 1940's.[48] Given the professed hatred of the extreme rightists for the economic and social privilege of the "historic classes" and the alleged decisive influence of the former on the character of the Bethlen regime, one would have expected a somewhat different distribution in the 1920's. This avoidance of fundamental change in social or economic policy was sustained by the cooptation of right-radical leaders like Miklos Kozma and Gyula Gombos into positions of political visibility or economic influence, coupled with largely symbolic posturing against the injustices of the Treaty of Trianon. In consequence, these disruptive elements were integrated into the Bethlen system and thus sapped of their potency.[49]

Policy toward the peasantry followed the same pattern. While taking pains publicly to extol the virtues of the peasantry—as did subsequent prime ministers—and to stress the political importance of this class, and especially of its leaders like Istvan Nagyatadi Szabo, Bethlen successfully sabotaged the one major effort at land reform introduced during his tenure as prime minister.[50] In the realm of political relations with the peasantry, Bethlen's regime succeeded in effecting the reduction of the peasantry to its pre-war role of largely passive and accepting spectator of the political process.[51] It accomplished this result by the high-handed introduction in 1922 of an extraordinarily restrictive voting law, one of whose cardinal features was the abolition of the secret ballot in rural districts even for that small proportion of the peasantry permitted to vote.[52] Once again the bogey man of Trianon was invoked in justification of the lack of real social change. Consequently, the integration of the peasantry into Hungarian society had not even begun until the end of the interwar period, long after Bethlen's consolidation had been secured.[53] It is certainly possible to argue that the Hungarian political elite was distracted from domestic economic and social concerns by the perceived evils of the Treaty of Trianon, but this argument rings rather hollow.[54] Revanchism represented not simply neglect of social concerns, but a conscious rationalization of the retrograde, counter-revolutionary character of the consolidation period. In this respect, at least, Trianon was a means, not a cause.

Conclusion

This brief review of the inter-relationship of the Treaty of Trianon and Hungarian politics in the 1920's, especially during the "consolidation period" of the Bethlen regime, has examined the conventional view that the treaty and its consequences were somehow responsible for the development of the characteristic features of the interwar Hungarian political system. Right-radical excesses against Jews, liberals, democrats; social and political oppression, especially of workers and peasants; authoritarian political institutions and processes; in short, the entire counter-revolution, have all been seen as primarily the product, directly or indirectly, of the vindictive Treaty of Trianon, and of Allied policy in general, of which the treaty was, of course, a central part. How far has this view been sustained by the analysis presented here?

This examination of the origins of the counter-revolution and its main institutional features—the ideology of the movement, the perceptions of the gentry-dominated bureaucracy, the chief political institutions of the Bethlen regime, the constitutional and parliamentary traditions of the Hungarian political elite, and the main economic and social policies of the Bethlen regime—has demonstrated that the relationship between Trianon and Hungarian domestic politics was at least more tortuous than commonly assumed. Indeed this essay goes even further—it suggests that the responses by Hungarians to the treaty were in significant part the product of the counter-revolution itself.

The revisionism, military adventurism, xenophobia, and so on, identified by many with the essence of the Hungarian political system of the interwar period, were a logical extension of the counter-revolutionary ethos, which antedated Trianon by two years. Once the political elite, led by Count Bethlen, determined to return Hungary to the domestic *status quo ante*, or at least a close approximation thereof, an unremitting campaign to extend that notion to the realm of international relations was almost a foregone conclusion.

One may well question the wisdom, justice, morality, or common sense of the counter-revolutionary ethos, particularly in light of Hungary's disastrous involvement in World War II, to which it seemed to lead. But to put the blame for the genesis and development of the counter-revolution on the treaty is to distort history. The Hungarian counter-revolution and its leaders must take the responsibility for both its achievements and its better-known failures, without facile appeals to "Trianon." For right-radical, antidemocratic movements, so closely identified with interwar Hungary, were also characteristic of Successor States that benefitted from the treaty or were largely unaffected by it (Poland, Romania, Yugoslavia, especially).[55] It is thus the counter-revolution itself, and the whole complex of social, political, military, economic, and psychological factors that undergirded it, that stand in the dock of history. The Treaty of Trianon cannot be called as a witness for either the prosecution or the defense; it may serve, at best, as an *amicus curiae*.

Notes

1. Thomas Sakmyster, "István Bethlen and Hungarian Foreign Policy, 1921–1931," *Canadian-American Review of Hungarian Studies* 5 (Fall 1978):5, 7.

2. For a comprehensive survey of Hungarian foreign policy in the interwar years, based on the latest available documents, see Gyula Juhász, *Hungarian Foreign Policy, 1919–1945* (Budapest, 1979).

3. Paul Ignotus, *Hungary*, Nations of the Modern World (New York and Washington: 1972), p. 154. Emphasis supplied.

4. Joseph Rothschild, *East Central Europe Between the Two World Wars*, A History of East Central Europe, vol. 9 (Seattle and London: 1974), p. 158. The hope for "instant revision" was apparently supplied by Alexandre Millerand and Maurice Paléologue of France, see essay of Anne Orde.

5. Rothschild, p. 166. A Marxist presentation of this view is provided by László Márkus, "A kormányzati erők a bethleni uralmi koncepció szolgálatában," *Történelmi Szemle* 19 (1970):465–80.

6. At least one recent Marxist appears to share this view of the primacy of domestic reaction over treaty revision: Ferenc Pölöskei, "Bethlen István törekvései az ellenforradalmi rendszer konszolidálására, 1921–1922," *Párttörténeti Közlemények* 20 (1974):53.

7. Erik Molnár, Ervin Pamlényi, and György Székely, eds., *Magyarország története*, 2 vols., 2d ed., rev. and enl. (Budapest, 1967), 2:304, and Michael Karolyi, *Memoirs of Michael Karolyi—Faith Without Illusion*, trans. Catherine Karolyi (New York., 1962), p. 317.

8. The phrase was coined by Max I. Dimont in *Jews, God, and History* (New York: New American Library, A Signet Book, 1962), p. 317.

9. C. A. Macartney, *October Fifteenth—A History of Modern Hungary, 1929–1945*, 2 vols., 2d. ed. (Edinburgh, 1961), 1:27.

10. For a right-radical view of the functioning of these parties and groups, see Dr. Ödön vitéz Málnási, *A magyar nemzet őszinte története* (Budapest, 1927), p. 226. For an analysis of the origins of the two "action groups" and details of their social composition, see Tibor Zinner, "Adatok a szélsőjobboldali egyesületek megalakulásának körülményeihez," *Történelmi Szemle* 22 (1979):562–76. A history of MOVE is provided by Rudolf Dósáné, *A MOVE. Egy jellegzetes magyar fasiszta szervezet. 1918–1944* (Budapest, 1972).

11. For a first-hand account of the creation and functioning of the ABC, see Gusztáv Gratz, *A forradalmak kora: Magyarország története, 1918–1920* (Budapest, 1935), pp. 187–201.

12. The fullest account of the political activity of the Szeged counterrevolutionaries is provided by the one-time interior minister of the Szeged

government, Dr. Béla Kelemen, in *Adatok a szegedi ellenforradalom és a szegedi kormány történetéhez (1919): (Naplójegyzetek és okiratok.)* (Szeged, 1923).

13. A succinct summary of the tactics of the National Army in this period is given in Rothschild, p. 152. Evidence of the political power of Horthy's military forces is provided by the following documents: Hungary. Országos Levéltár (hereafter O.L.). Belügyminisztérium. *A szegedi ellenforradalmi kormány iratai 1919–721*, in Dezső Nemes and Elek Karsai, eds., *Iratok az ellenforradalom történetéhez*, 5 vols. (Budapest, 1953–), vol. 1 (1953): *Az ellenforradalom hatalomrajutása és rémuralma Magyarországon 1919–1921*, ed. Dezső Nemes, p. 135, and O.L. Miniszterelnökség biz. 1919–117, in *ibid.*, p. 137.

14. The generally accepted view of the weakness of the Friedrich government, by a sympathetic observer, is given in Gratz, pp. 248–49. An interesting "revisionist" view, contending that Friedrich's was not the first of the counter-revolutionary governments, but the last of the liberal democratic ones in interwar Hungary, is offered by Eva S. Balogh, "István Friedrich and the Hungarian Coup d'etat of 1919: A Reevaluation," *Slavic Review* 35 (June 1976):269–86.

15. The term "retrograde revolution" is taken from Ignotus, p. 154. Bethlen himself appears to have rejected the view offered here of the relationship between foreign and domestic policy when he stated that the "prerequisite for a correct foreign policy is a correct domestic policy": quoted in Sakmyster, p. 8. But there is no compelling reason to think that this statement reflects anything more than a recognition of the interpenetration of domestic political factors and the conduct of foreign policy generally.

16. In a strict sense, an ideology is a set of political ideas that are overt, systematic, dogmatic, and embodied in a set of institutions: Zbigniew Brzezinski and Samuel P. Huntington, *Political Power: USA/USSR* (New York, 1965), p. 19.

17. It is impossible to find any coherent presentation of the ideology by any spokesman or leader of the counter-revolution, even Bethlen himself. The Bethlen regime never developed a body of "sacred" texts officially and authoritatively interpreted. The ideology of the regime must be adduced, then, from its pattern of practice and its characteristic slogans, found chiefly in the press of the period and in the writing of some publicists. For the more important of these sources, see the exhaustive annotated bibliography in *Magyarország története*, ed., Pál Zsigmond Pach, 19 vols. (Budapest, 1976–), vol. 8: *1918–1919/1919–1945* (1976), ed., György Ránki, Tibor Hajdu, and Loránt Tilkovszky, pp. 1319, 1331–33.

18. This summary of content is from Molnár, Pamlényi, and Székely, p. 384, and István Deák, "Hungary," *The European Right: A Historical Profile*, ed., Hans Rogger and Eugen Weber (Berkeley, 1966), pp. 372, 378.

19. For an understanding of anti-Semitism during this period, see Professor Karfunkel's essay.

20. Oscar Jászi, no friend of the counter-revolution, sums up the character of this shift in *Revolution and Counter-Revolution in Hungary*, trans. E. W. Dickes (London, 1924), p. 158. Whereas Jászi sees this integration of the extreme right as a limitation on its goals and activities, the more dogmatic Marxist writers continue to regard it as a mere smokescreen that allowed the extremists to continue their nefarious activities under government auspices. On this point see, for example, Lajos Serfőző, "A titkos társaságok és a róluk folytatott parlamenti viták, 1922-1924-ben," *Párttörténeti Közlemények* 22 (1976):69-113.

21. Thomas L. Sakmyster, "Army Officers and Foreign Policy in Interwar Hungary, 1918-1941," *Journal of Contemporary History* 10 (January 1975):21-23. Bethlen was less fastidious about other forms of adventurism, especially financial. For one notorious example, which has about it many of the humorous qualities of a Keystone Kops movie, see Andor Klay, "Hungarian Counterfeit Francs: A Case of Post- World War I Political Sabotage," *Slavic Review* 33 (March 1974):107-13.

22. This summary of the main elements of "Christian nationalism" is taken from Ilona Pándi, *Osztályok és Pártok a Bethlen-konszolidáció időszakában* (Budapest, 1966), p. 50. On the integrative role of the ideology, se Andrew C. Janos, "Hungary: 1867-1939—A Study of Social Change and the Political Process" (Ph.D. dissertation, Princeton University, 1961), pp. 120-21, 353. For a discussion of the attraction of the ideology for the moderate left, see William M. Batkay, "The Origin and Role of the Unified Party in Hungary, 1919-1926" (Ph.D. dissertation, Columbia University, 1972), pp. 192-93.

23. The term "gentroid" is distinctively Hungarian. In a narrow sense, it refers to the aping of the mores, fashions, and political style of the former landed gentry by lower-middle class civil servants and others in Hungary in the later period of the Dual Monarchy and during the interwar period. In a broader sense, it implies a sense of spiritual, social, and cultural descent from the landed gentry and largely gentry-staffed bureaucracy of the Tisza era among those later holders of bureaucratic positions that were not of actual gentry origin.

24. Pándi, p. 50; Janos, p. 115.

25. On this point, see the comments of Pál Prónay, a right-radical officer active in the para-military "detachments" in the 1920's, in Pál Prónay, *A határban a Halál kaszál. . . . Fejezetek Prónay Pál feljegyzéseiből*, ed. Agnes Szabó and Ervin Pamlényi (Budapest, 1963), p. 233; see also Bethlen's remarks in a New Year's Day address in 1922, in István Bethlen, *Bethlen István gróf beszédei és írásai* 2 vols. (Budapest, 1933), 1:219.

26. Bethlen, 1:159; 2:57, 160. See also Bethlen's opening speech in the Assembly in April 1921: Bethlen, 1:154-68.

27. Batkay, pp. 111-17, and the sources cited there.

28. Miklós Kozma, a leading right-radical and head of MTI, the Hungarian news agency, in the 1920's, supports this conclusion in a 1924 situation report: ". . . [E]veryone except the extreme right and left wings wants to support Bethlen and his policy" (O.L. Kozma-iratok. 1. cs. Adatgyüjtemény. 1920-1924. Belpolitikai helyzetkép, May 1924, p. 74).

29. Rothschild, pp. 158-59.

30. This application of the French notion of the *pays légal* to Hungary is taken from Janos, p. 264-66.

31. Given Horthy's right-radical sympathies, his election as Regent in the spring of 1920 may have aggravated this situation; it certainly did nothing to alter it. On this point, see Ferenc Pölöskei, "Az államforma és az alkotmányosság kérdései 1919-1920 fordulójan," *Történelmi Szemle* 19 (1976):333. See also Balogh, p. 286, where she notes: "It would be two years before the power of the extreme right could be checked."

32. Bureaucratic acceptance of this subordination is discussed in Miklós Színai and László Szücs, eds., *Bethlen István titkos iratai* (Budapest, 1972), Introduction, p. 16.

33. Gratz, however, notes that Teleki strengthened the office of prime minister by his own personal prestige: Gratz, pp. 332-33.

34. These other factors included Entente pressure for "democratisation" of the Friedrich government in the fall of 1919 and the ignominy of the signing of the Treaty of Trianon by the Simonyi-Semadam government in the summer of 1920.

35. In the spring and summer of 1920 there were threats to dissolve the Assembly by force if the parties did not soon bring some order to their ranks: Dezső Nemes, *Az ellenforradalom története Magyarországon, 1919-1921* (Budapest, 1962), p. 250.

36. There is, for example, no published monograph on the Unified Party in either Hungarian or western scholarly literature. The author's dissertation, cited above, attempts to rectify this lacuna, and will be forthcoming in the East European Monographs series published by the *East European Quarterly*.

37. Samuel Huntington argues, for example, that political leaders "only mobilize and organize masses when they have a real need—ideological or political—to do so. If they are already in power and have no ideological drive to split and remake their societies, they have no reason to make the effort to develop and maintain a strong party" ("Social and Institutional Dynamics of One-Party Systems," *Authoritarian Politics in Modern Society: The Dynamics of Established One-Party Systems*, ed., Samuel P. Huntington and Clement H. Moore [New York, 1970], pp. 14-15).

38. Színai and Szücs, pp. 35-36, and notes 56, 57, 60.

39. See Batkay, where the origin and functions of the Unified Party are analysed in detail.

40. On the appeal of Hungary's constitutional traditions to even hostile foreign observers, see the comments by R. W. Seton-Watson quoted in Ignotus, p. 159.

41. See, for example, Pál Teleki, *The Evolution of Hungary and Its Place in European History* (New York, 1923; reprint ed., Gulf Breeze, Florida, 1975), especially pp. 143–46.

42. See, for example, the comments in the Hungarian newspaper *Budapesti Hirlap*, January 27, 1920, quoted in France. Ministry of War and Foreign Affairs. *Bulletin périodique de la presse hongroise de langue magyare*, no. 39 (March 7, 1920), p. 1.

43. For a discussion of this point, see Janos, p. 352; Színai and Szűcs, Introduction, pp. 25–26, *et passim*.

44. For an example of such myopia, see Dezsó Nemes, Introduction, Nemes and Karsai, *Iratok az ellenforradalom történetéhez*, vol. 2 (1956): *A fasiszta rendszer kiépítése és népnyomor Magyarországon, 1921–1924*, ed. Dezső Nemes and Elek Karsai, p. 29.

45. See note 35. Cf. Horthy's intimidation of the Assembly in March 1920, and the activity of the para-military detachments that preceded it: Prónay, p. 177; Endre Szokoly, . . . *és Gömbös Gyula a kapitány* (Budapest, 1960), p. 96.

46. On the multi-functionality of these symbols, see Macartney, *Hungary: A Short History* (Edinburgh, 1962), p. 214; "Hungary Since 1918," *The Slavonic Review* 7 (March 1929):582–83; Prónay, p. 167; Jászi, p. 159.

47. Anikó Tausz, "Adalékok a magyar ipari munkásság helyzetéhez 1919 és 1929 között," *Történelmi Szemle* 19 (1976):631–59. Tausz argues that despite these improvements, there was no significant change in basic conditions in Hungary, which remained, in her view, among the most backward countries as far as social policy was concerend.

48. These groups constituted 92 percent of the highest taxpayers in Hódmezővásárhely in 1929, for example: Gábor Gyáni, "Hódmezővásárhely legnagyobb adófizetői (1888–1941)," *Történelmi Szemle* 20 (1977):627.

49. At least one author suggests that Bethlen became seriously involved in the government campaign for treaty revision only after he left office: Nandor Dreisziger, "Count István Bethlen's Secret Plan for the Restoration of the Empire of Transylvania," *East European Quarterly* 8 (January 1975):414. On the cooptation of right-radicals, see Macartney, *October Fifteenth*, p. 146; Elek Karsai, *A budai Sándor-palotában történt, 1919–1941*, 2d ed. (Budapest, 1964), pp. 189–90.

50. On the emasculation of land reform, see Rothschild, pp. 159–60.

51. The poor peasants, at any rate, apparently found this state of affairs congenial. The Hungarian poet Gyula Illyés, in his account of his early life among the destitute servants on the great estates, cites as tyical the peasant view that "politics are an affair of the gentry": *People of the Puszta*, trans. G. F. Cushing (Budapest, 1967), p. 147.

52. The provisions of the 1922 electoral law may be found in the minutes of the January 24, 1922, meeting of the Council of Ministers: O.L. Mt. jkv. January 24, 1922 (közig. pol.), in Nemes and Karsai, *A fasiszta rendszer,* p. 257.

53. Joseph Held, "The Interwar Years and Agrarian Change," *The Modernization of Agriculture: Rural Transformation in Hungary, 1848-1975,* East European Monographs, vol. 63 (Boulder, Colorado, 1980), p. 312.

54. Cf. note 5, above.

55. On the right-radical movements in these countries, see, for example, the chapters on Poland, Romania, and Yugoslavia in Rothschild.

Paul Jonas

The Economic Consequences of Trianon

Hungary's economic takeoff[1] occurred between 1867 and 1913. By 1913 the country was firmly on the road of speedy industrialization. Until this time Hungary was steadily reducing the gap which existed between itself and the industrialized centers of Europe.

Much had to be done still. The country was still behind the Western, Central and Northern European states with regard to per capita Gross National Product; life expectancy at birth; adult literacy rate; the distribution of Gross Domestic Product with respect to agriculture, manufacturing, services; private per capita consumption; and other economic success indicators. But a process of structural transformation was under way. The share of industrial production, manufacturing and services increased. Capital- and skill-intensive activities come into their own.

Conventional agriculture, however, still dominated and coexisted with a relatively modern industrial sector which produced and exported, among other products, vehicles, electric bulbs and pharmaceuticals. The role of the state was significant in establishing the socio-economic infrastructure (the legal regulation of economy, the establishment of a satisfactory educational and sanitary system, the development of the road and railway network and a central banking system). The state, however, did not play a significant role in the production of national income and national wealth, leaving relatively free hand for the private sector by using for inducements tax allowances and state subventions.[2]

The Hungarian economic historian Iván T. Berend observed that the economy of Hungary at the end of the 19th century was autarkic, i.e., independent of the world market, since the country was integrated into the Monarchy which consisted of 50 million people and had a common currency. We would like, however, to add that one of the reasons for Hungary's economic success was that if the need had arisen, the country had every possibility to be part of the interdependent European economy. In other words, Hungary was not *pressed* into autarky by protectionist tariff policies or conditions adverse to foreign trade. Independence from the world economy comes about naturally in every large country with regional specialization. In pre-1914 Europe, including East Central Europe, the interference of frontiers and tariffs was at the minimum, and the effect of the so-called "protection duty system" was marginal. In this period, producers could utilize a wide market outside of their large area. About 300 million people lived in Russia, Germany and Austria-Hungary alone. In this area the movement of the factors of production—labor, capital, and technology—was almost totally free. The Monarchy had a common currency, but in fact all the European currencies were maintained at a stable relation to gold and to one another. This situation created an inducement for international cooperation based on specializations. Another necessary prerequisite for a smooth interdependency was that all the trading areas were secure with respect to property and persons. Europe, at this time, was certainly characterized by law and order. This state of affairs had never been experienced before.

The statistics to prove this European interdependence and cooperation are overwhelming. Industrialization needs energy, and the main source of energy, at this time, was coal. Germany was the most active in supplying coal to neighboring states. The output of German coal grew from 30 million tons in 1871 to 190 million in 1913. Since Germany had surplus capital, this flowed to labor-surplus countries such as Hungary where the marginal productivity of capital was much higher. The rate of return for a unit of capital investment, was thus in these countries more profitable than in Germany. It is estimated that from Germany's prewar total foreign investments of about 6.25 billion dollars, around 2.5 billions were invested in Europe's less developed countries such as Austria-Hungary, Romania, Bulgaria, and Turkey. This capital flow was often accompanied by German managers who were the source of technological know-how and various organizational skills. These assets were badly needed in the labor-surplus economies.

Hungary responded favorably to these conditions. From 1867 to 1913, the national income in real terms more than quadrupled. Between 1900 and 1913 the annual rates of growth increased to 3.8 percent per year. If we look at the growth figures for the manufacturing sector, we can observe the country's dramatic takeoff. Starting from a meagre base, industrial development in Hungary rocketed in this period. Between 1867 and 1900 the industrial rate of growth was 6.2 percent, and between 1900 and 1913 it is calculated to be 5.1 percent.[3]

A serious objection to this "golden economic period" of 1867 to 1913 is that economic development generated a considerable maldistribution of wealth and a serious income inequality. Therefore, it is sometimes claimed, this process, from the point of view of the peasants and workers, was a *mirage*.

We propose, however, on the basis of the Kuznets hypothesis,[4] that this period of speedy industrialization occurred because of inequality of the *urban* income distribution. However, using the Hungarian experience, *urban* is stressed since we would like to amend the Kuznets hypothesis by proposing that the unequal distribution of income in the non-urban areas often stabilizes underdevelopment. The reason for that is that the aristocratic or ecclesiastic feudal rich are normally characterized by conspicuous consumption on their estates and during their foreign travels. The significant increments of wealth at the end of the 19th century were controlled, however, by a new class, the urban *nouveau riche*, which preferred the newly acquired power and its consolidation to the pleasures of immediate consumption. Therefore, the significant investments in this period came from the savings of the new urban industrial class, from the *parvenues*, whom the Hungarian landed aristocrats often considered to be without manners, but whose daughters they occasionally married to save their ancestral lands from bankruptcy.[5]

The saving habits of the new industrial class spread. The Hungarian skilled working class was beginning to accumulate money for the education of a son, for the dowry of a daughter, and generally, for the purchase of a durable consumer good.

"The rapid growth of productivity in Hungary (on the eve of the First World War) is striking when compared with other European countries," states I. Katus.[6] This phenomenon may be explained on the basis of the Gerschenkron's hypothesis which refers to the development characteristics in the initial period of industrialization in some European countries; it proposes that these can be explained better if reference is made to the relative backwardness prior to the "great spurt."[7]

Indeed, Hungary started her capital accumulation late and the improvement of her capital productivity even later. (Japan's economic development shows similar characteristics after the Second World War.)

The war of 1914–1918, which set Europe ablaze, halted this development process. The Treaties of Versailles, Saint German, Trianon, Neuilly and Sèvres embodied the results of long and bitter negotiations between the United States, France, England and Italy.

It is proposed by many that these treaties failed to heal the wounds after the war and were not able to reestablish the conditions for normalcy. Moreover, it is assumed that they were directly responsible for a divided, Balkanized, nationalistic Europe; and indirectly for the Great Depression which started off by the collapse of the New York Stock Exchange on October 24, 1929; for the German remilitarization, the birth of Hitler's National Socialist Movement; and ultimately for the Second World War.

A controversy, however, continues among historians as to whether these treaties were just, or too harsh, or not harsh enough.

After the war, on December 4, 1918, President Woodrow Wilson sailed from New York on an army transport, accompanied by Mrs. Wilson and by a whole caravan of savants loaded down with statistics and documents. He left a nation whose sentiments were divided between sharp resentment and apprehensive hope for the best, but he landed on a continent which was prepared to offer him a triumphal reception such as the world had never seen before. The six weeks between his landing at Brest and the opening of the Paris Peace Confrence consisted of a series of processions through England, France and Italy, in which the governments and the people strove to outdo each other in expressing their enthusiasm for the leader of the great and victorious crusade for justice and democracy. Sovereigns spiritual and temporal and heads of governments heaped on him all the honors in their power, and crowds of workingmen stood for hours in the rain to catch a glimpse of him at railroad stations. Even from neutral Holland, divided Ireland and hostile Germany came invitations to the President, and he would probably have been received by those as enthusiastically as by British, French and Italians.

For the war had been ended, Europe thought, on the basis of the ideals of President Wilson. Those ideals had been expressed, however, in vague and general terms, and every government thought that its own war aims coincided with them. Suddenly released from the strain of a long and terrible war, each nation believed that all its troubles were suddenly to be ended by the principles of Woodrow Wilson. Both Yugoslavia and Italy claimed Istria and Fiume, and each felt itself supported by the principles of President Wilson. To Frenchmen those principles meant that Germany must pay for the war forced on France, and to Germans they meant that a ruined France and an uninvaded Germany could start again on the same footing. The autonomy of Austria-Hungary, listed among Wilson's Fourteen Points, gave confidence for Austrians and Hungarians that nothing would change that much.

They contained, among others, the following recommendations: All covenants of peace should be made public and there should be no secret arrangements between nations; the freedom of the seas must be assured and the economic barriers hampering international trade should be eliminated; national armaments must be reduced and budgets should serve primarily peaceful civilian purposes; the concept of the colonial areas should be reevaluated and various sovereignty claims must be given attention; Russia should be left alone to determine her own political development; Alsace-Lorraine should be freed of the burdens of the Prussian occupation; the people of Austria-Hungary, whose place among nations should be safeguarded and assured, must be given the freest opportunity of autonomous development.

President Wilson't Point X dealing with "Autonomy in Austria-Hungary" gave serious hopes to Hungarian politicians for a preparation of a peace settlement that would preserve all or most of Hungary's historic territories. Foreign support, especially from Switzerland, was also indicated for the peace negotiations.[8]

By January 18, 1919, when the Versailles Conference opened, it became obvious, however, that the Wilsonian ideas which had given hope to the world for the reestablishment of the interdependencies of nations and the continuation of the prewar system which had brought peace and prosperity, would not prevail. The enemy: the concept of a *revanchard* policy and nationalism, thought to have been defeated by the Fourteen Points, was still very much alive. President Wilson advocated an American kind of *patriotism*, the love of one's fatherland and its tradition. He had a reverence for the memory of great historical events, a preference for the features peculiar to one's community. However, France's *nationalism* at that time was different from this concept. After so many defeats and humiliations from German military adventures, France felt that the time had come to strike back. The leader of the French radicals, Georges Clemenceau [who had the nicknames *le Tombeur de ministères* and later *le Tigre*], felt that France alone could solve the political, military and economic problems of Europe. To assume this role Clemenceau demanded a huge reparation for his country. Undeniably, France had suffered the most.

Under Clemenceau's influence more and more politicians during the Peace Conference (including some Americans) asked, "Is what Wilson proposes for Europe America's business?"[9]

Leading the French delegation at the Paris Peace Conference, Clemenceau became the main antagonist of Woodrow Wilson.

The person who formulated the most articulate opposition to Clemenceau, basically on economic grounds, was John Maynard Keynes [later Baron Keynes of Tilton], the English economist and monetary expert who in 1919 became principal treasury representative at the Peace Conference but resigned in protest against what he considered the inequitable and unworkable economic provisions of the Treaty. His *Economic Consequences of the Peace*[10] vividly presented his views and won him world fame. Keynes criticized the Treaty from the point of view of classical economics. He contrasted the narrow, autarkic nationalism inherent in the Treaty and the Balkanization of large areas to small dependent mini-states guarded by trade barriers with the relatively free pre-1914 European economy based on stable convertible currencies and low tariffs. He foresaw that German economic weakness and the dissolution of the Monarchy would lead the whole of Europe to ruin.

Keynes believed in an economically integrated Europe and felt that peace treaties should heal wounds and reestablish a system of interdependent economies with maximum free movements of the factors of production. He also favored a coordinated economic policy among nations since he believed in the "we live or die together" concept.

"Paris," wrote Keynes in his sharp critique, "was a nightmare, and everyone there was morbid. . . ." Its atmosphere was "hot and poisoned," its halls "treacherous. . . ." Paris was a "morass." The European statesmen of the Conference were "subtle and dangerous spellbinders," the "subtlest sophisters and the most hypocritical draftsmen"; what inspired them was "debauchery of thought and speech . . . greed, sentiment, prejudice and deception. . . ." Their labors were "empty, arid and intrigue . . . the dreams of designing diplomats . . . the unveracities of politicians . . . the endless controvery and intrigue," were "contorted, miserable, utterly unsatisfactory in all parties." President Wilson was a "blind and deaf Don Quixote," he was "playing blind man's bluff" in the party; he ended in "collapse" and "extraordinary betrayal." The Treaty was clothed with "insincerity," with "an apparatus of self-deception," with "a web of Jesuit exegesis," which were to distinguish it "from all its historical predecessors." Its provisions were "dishonourable . . . ridiculous and injurious . . . abhorrent and detestable"; they revealed "imbecile greed . . . senseless greed overreaching itself"; they represented "oppression and rapine." The Treaty "reduced Germany to servitude," and it refused Germany "even a modicum of prosperity, at least for a generation to come." The Terms of Peace "perpetuated its economic ruin," if it were enforced, "Germany must be kept impoverished and her children starved and crippled." Thus the Peace that would "sow the decay of the whole civilized life of Europe," was "one of the most outrageous acts of a cruel victor in civilized history."

Keynes's basic message was that the politicians of the Conference failed to apprehend "that the most serious of the problems which claimed their attention were not political or territorial but financial and economic and the future lay not in frontiers or sovereignties but in food, coal and transport." Compared to these, other issues such as "territorial adjustment and the balance of power, were unreal and insignificant." Keynes insisted that the Treaty was a betrayal of European and American ideals and was an economic absurdity, an instrument of systematic oppression and murder.

Keynes's study was distributed in the bookstores in the United States in January 1920. Wilson's popularity was already on the wane. The book was used by the President's opponents to accuse him of being unable to stand up for his own ideals, for his country's wishes, of letting himself be terrorized by Clemenceau and hypnotized by Lloyd George. The opposition against Wilson made serious use of Keynes's book and argued that the German Treaty consigns Europe to perpetual famine and chronic revolution and that unless the Treaty is completely revised and rewritten, it must inevitably result in the destruction of the economic system of Europe which will result in turn in the loss of millions of lives and in revolution after revolution, which necessarily follows when people find themselves in the condition to which the people of Europe will be reduced. "The Treaty in its consequences," argued Senator Borah, "is a crime born in blind revenge and insatiable greed."[11]

These words were clearly paraphrasing Keynes's critique. One month later, the Treaty was defeated. The horrors of Versailles became a veritable article of faith. The United States believed that whatever may happen in Europe it was all the fault of the Peace Treaties. The United States repudiated the Versailles Treaty legally from the outset; Great Britain was to abandon it morally in the course of the next twenty years.

In the First World War strategic problems were no longer the exclusive province of the military; on the contrary, strategy had invaded politics and diplomacy and it was primarily the statesman who had to analyze its components. Clemenceau's famous quip that "war is too serious a matter to be left to the military" was echoed widely.

Hungary's role in the 1914–1918 war was an especially thankless one. István Tisza, the prime minister, first thought with many others that the actions against Serbia, where Archduke Franz Ferdinand, an avowed enemy of the Hungarians, was killed, will be only a punitive police action. When he realized that he was wrong he tried to make the best of a bad job. Hungary, and Europe in general, after being bled white by four years of war, was indulging itself in exciting political experiments. Two generations later these experiments seem like the feverish attempts of college freshmen who would try out the various ideologies and systems they were acquainted with during the school year. "Socialism" was introduced in January 11, 1919; than the "dictatorship of the proletariat" has replaced the regime which distributed the lands, and asked them back for state ownership; after sporadic violence mixed with revolutionary rhetorics, anarchy and chaos followed and finally Hungary shifted back to a more moderate "temporary socialist regime" which lasted seven days. Finally, on November 21, 1919, a new "coalition government" was formed which was formally recognized as a *de facto* government by the Allied and Associated Powers. In December 2, 1919, Clemenceau, as President of the Peace Conference, invited the Hungarian Coalition Government to send a delegation to the Peace Treaty. On May 1, 1920, the Hungarian Delegation departed and on June 4, 1920, the Peace Treaty in Versailles at the Palais du Trianon was signed.

The Treaty reduced the territory of Hungary from 325,411 square kilometers (without Croatia 282,870) to 92,833 square kilometers (28 percent, resp. 33 percent), and its population from 20,886,487 (without Croatia 18,264,533) to 7,606,971 (36.6 percent, resp. 41 percent) according to the census of 1910; thereby the density of the population was increased to 81.9 persons per square kilometer.[12]

The territorial and population loss in an economically integrated Europe would have been no great tragedy. With the free movements of the factors of productions, labor and capital, and with the return of convertability among the currencies, the financial officials of the European countries would have worked on developing and increasingly harmonious cooperation. But Europe became isolated and Hungarian balance of payments carried continuous large deficits. Soon the international monetary system was disrupted.

The peacemakers realized that in view of the heavy loss of territory and population, reparation payments could not be immediately expected from Hungary. The amount of the reparation was, however, fixed later, in 1924, at 200 million gold crowns. The amount of compensation payable to Hungary by the Succession States for the so called *biencédés,* i.e., State properties in the territories separated from Hungary, however were never fixed. The idea of such compensation was cancelled in 1930.

The main economic lines of the Treaty of Trianon, which was ratified by Act XXXIII of 1921 and entered on force on July 26, 1921, represented an intellectual idea which was France's and Clemenceau's own. France was bent on the economic subjection of the Central Powers. One should try to understand Clemenceau, even if he takes a different view of the Peace Treaty. France lost 1,251,000 men during the war, in addition 734,000 were crippled, 2,000,000 wounded and 438,000 prisoners martyred in German prisons. She lost 26 percent of her mobilized manpower and 57 percent of her soldiers under 31 years of age—the most productive part of the nation. In addition, a quarter of the productive capital was wiped out, her industrial districts in the north and in the east were systematically destroyed, countless children, women and girls fell into captivity.[13]

Clemenceau wanted to prevent a new war by making sure that Germany and her former allies are kept in poverty.

The American approach was different. Conigsby Dawson from the American Relief Administration took a more understanding view of the fate of Eastern and Central Europe.[14] Dawson came to the American Relief Administration at the end of November 1920 asking how he could serve the cause of humanity and of the United States. As a soldier he had fought heart and soul against armies from several of the countries for which he was pleading. He said: "That I should write in this spirit, pleading for our late enemies, may cause a slight amazement in a public that has read my war books. My reason—I will not say my excuse—is that I have visited our late enemies' need, and in the presence of human agony, animosity ceases. One ceases to wonder how far they are suffering in the outcome of their folly; America can have only a sole aspiration to bind up their wounds—especially the wounds of their children."[15]

Coningsby Dawson felt that the plight of Austria and Hungary was due in large degree to the terms of the Peace Treaty, which cut the natural boundaries and the trade avenues of these nations. "Central Europe wants to work" he said; "it is begging for the chance to work, but it cannot work while it is undernourished. Starvation is caused by the volcanic upheavals of war followed by a political redistribution which has destroyed economic stability and criss-crossed Central Europe with hostile tariff walls in places where the flow of trade was once traditional and amiable."[16]

In the Peace Treaty ideas corresponding to Dawson and formulated most eloquently by John Maynard Keynes were discarded, and the French concept of revenge, i.e., the act of doing harm to another in return for wrong or injury inflicted, was carried out. The Treaty was formulated with the central idea that the former enemies will remain enemies and an allied defense consonant with the security needs of the Allied and Associated Powers should make the Central Powers incapable of resuming hostilities. The punishment was not only addressed to the wrongdoers but to children and future generations. With the exception of the Americans, every delegation presented punitive actions as well as a demand for the total costs of the war.

Hungary, small and isolated, set out on a course which was forced on her and which was crippling her population. Heavy taxation and heavy-handed state intervention were introduced in an attempt to achieve a balanced budget. Every penny was needed.

The Government was authorized by Act IV of 1920 to provide for state expenditure until June 30th, 1920, on the basis of existing taxes and tariffs. These were not yielding enough revenue. So in order to fill state coffers, the production and the sale of sugar was declared a State Monopoly, and the total sale price of this commodity was handed over to the Treasury. The same was done with petrol products. The government also received authorization to fix the price of salt (charged by a governmental Salt Monopoly) and to supplement custom duties by decree.

In accordance with the Act of 1920, a sales tax of 10 percent was levied on luxury commodities and by Act XXXIV duties on transfer of property were imposed.

The first provisional budget was presented to the House for the period February to April 1920. It provided for expenditures of 1.7 billion crowns and for revenues of 800 million crowns, thus leaving a deficit of 900 million crowns.

The government made additional desperate moves; it levied taxes on matches and substitutes, imposed a capital levy on savings and current deposits, introduced additional milling and sales taxes. Then came the severe decision which crippled the Hungarian economy for years to come: Act XLV of 1921, which imposed a capital levy on agricultural land, industrial plant, stocks of goods, raw material and other assets. This capital levy amounted to 6–20 percent of the land and had to be surrendered *in natura*. The capital levy payable by the merchants and commercial corporations amounted to 15–20 percent on the value of goods and materials in stock as well as on the firm's equipment, while industrial enterprises had to pay 10 percent on their total assets. All other assets in the form of commodities were subject to a capital levy of 5–20 percent of their value.

A poor and isolated Hungary did not help European recovery and strength. The continent was composed by countries guarding their "national sovereignty" jealously, and Hungary responded similarly. The pre-war cooperation between governments broke down. The consequence was for Hungary a continuous balance of payment deficit.

TABLE I. Budget and actual results for 1923/24
in 1,000 million paper crowns

Revenues		Expenditures		Balance	
Estimates	*Actual*	*Estimates*	*Actual*	*Estimates*	*Actual*
6,632	5,049	5,225	8,644	+1,298	−3,595

The country had to take additional steps. Act XXXV instructs the Government to reorganize the State Administration and effect reductions in the number of State employees, so as to reduce by 20 percent the corresponding item in the Budget. The Hungarian National Assembly ratifies, by Act of 1924, certain moves concluded by the government in connection with the financial reconstruction of the country. A Central Bank, independent of the Treasury, was founded.

At that time public finances in Hungary were supervised by the authorities of the League of Nations, in particular Commissioner-General Jeremiah Smith, Jr., of Boston and his substitute Royall Tyler. The supervision was exercised by the Commissioner-General until July 1926 when it was terminated upon his own advice.

The actual results for the years 1924/25 and 1925/26 are in million pengő.[17]

TABLE II. Actual figures for Hungarian budgets in million pengős

	1924/25	1925/26
State Administration		
Revenue	747	820.9
Expenditure	635.6	727.1
Surplus	111.4	93.2
State Undertakings		
Revenue	397.2	412.1
Expenditure	424.3	417.3
Deficit	-27.1	-5.2

With the budget of 1925/26 the pigeon was bringing the oil branch to Hungary.

The early post-war period can best be represented with the values of the depreciated crown, which reflected Hungary's relative economic importance in the world market.

TABLE III. Quotation of the Hungarian Crown in Zurich
the value of 100 Crown in Swiss Francs (yearly averages)

1914	99.03	1920	2.34
1915	80.83	1921	1.48
1916	63.06	1922	0.47
1917	45.76	1923	0.089
1918	44.92	1924	0.0093
1919	15.42	1925	0.0073

It is proposed, again, that the value of 100 Hungarian Crowns expressed in Swiss Francs may be a good proxy to represent Hungary's relative economic strength in the international business community. If one analyzes the trends represented in Table III it can be observed that the importance of the Hungarian economy declined continuously from 1914 to 1918. This decline can be attributed to the war expenditures and the use of a productive labor force for nonproductive activities. In 1919 there was a dramatic drop, due to the various discontinuities in administration (the value of 100 Crowns dropped from 44.92 Swiss Francs in 1918 to 2.34 Swiss Francs in 1920).

The decline from 1920 to 1925 (from 2.34 Swiss Francs to 0.0073 Swiss Francs) represents the economic consequences of the Treaty of Trianon.[18]

Historians usually cite a series of incidents which may have started the First World War, but there are serious disagreements about the *real* causes. After two generations the Treaty of Trianon and the post-war Treaties are still under discussion, but it is more and more difficult to reject John Maynard Keynes's arguments according to which nationality and political questions were nearly as important as laws concerning the economies of scale and unhampered trade and economic cooperation.[19]

As we look at Trianon two generations later, burdened as we are with everything that happened these past 60 years, we have to conclude that it contributed to the ills of the world by fragmenting and nationalizing an interdependent Europe. The victors, after the Second World War learned from this dismal experience and with the leadership of the United States tried to heal wounds. Indeed, the former enemies are now among the most reliable partners, both economically and militarily, America has.

Trianon, by breaking down an integrated Central Europe, violated the standards of rationality in human affairs. It proved once more the proposition that anyone who expects rationality in human history reveals his naïveté.

Notes

1. Walt Whitman Rostow, then economic historian at the Massachusetts Institute of Technology, coined the expression and used it first in his *Stages of Economic Growth* (Cambridge, Mass.: M.I.T. Press, 1960). Takeoff is

defined as a stage in a country's economic development when both the technical know-how and the ability to obtain and use the inputs for industrialization are given.

2. *Vide* for the controversy of the role of the state: T. I. Berend and Gy. Ránki, "Az állam szerepe az európai 'periferia' XIX. századi gazdasági fejlodésben." The Role of the State in the 19th Century Economic Development of the European "periphery." *Valóság* 21, no. 3 (Budapest, 1978), pp. 1–11; L. Lengyel, "Kölcsönös társadalmi függőség a XIX századi európai gazdasági fejlődésben." (Socio-Economic Interdependence in the European Economic Development of the 19th Century.) *Valóság* 21, no. 9 (Budapest, 1978), pp. 100–106.

3. *Vide* for data, T. I. Berend and Gy. Ránki, *Underdevelopment and Economic Growth; Studies in Hungarian Social and Economic History* (Budapest: Akadémiai Kiadó, 1979); T. I. Berend and Gy. Ránki, "A gazdasági nekilendülés "emberi" tényezői az elmaradott európai országokban." (Human Factors in the Economic Upswing of Backward European Countries in the 19th Century.) *Közgazdasági Szemle* 25, no. 12 (Budapest, 1978), pp. 1430–44; T. I. Berend, "A Nagy Válság és Közép-Kelet Europa," (The Great Depression and East-Central Europe), *Valóság* 22, no. 11 (Budapest, 1979), pp. 1–10.

4. A more equitable distribution of income has been the often stated objective of developing countries. At the same time economic growth has also been portrayed as a major economic goal. Kuznets and others have questioned whether or not these goals are mutually exclusive and proposed that a more equitable distribution of income will lead to lower rate of savings and thus to lower rate of economic growth. S. Kuznets, "Economic Growth and Income Inequality," *American Economic Review* XLV (March 1955), pp. 1–28; "The Share and Structure of Consumption," *Economic Development and Cultural Change* XI, no. 2 (January 1963), pp. 80–96; "Distribution of Income by Size," *Economic Development and Cultural Change* X, no. 2 (January 1962), pp. 92–124; Paul Jonas and Hyman Sardy, "The Distribution of Income and Their Effect on Economic Growth," *Proceedings, American Statistical Association* (December 1968), pp. 57–73.

5. Count Paul Teleki (1921, repr. 1975), p. 123, in his lectures given at Williams College, stated: "Many of the (Hungarian) nobles lived a peasant life." The eminent geographer, if one examines this statement from a sociological point of view, was probably wrong. Being a "peasant" at this time in Eastern Europe did not mean an individual whose occupation was agricultural work. A peasant was "somebody's peasant." *Vide*, István Bibó, "A magyarságtudomány problémája," (The Problem of Hungarology), *Új Latóhatár* XXXI (München, December 1980), p. 387.

6. I. Katus, "Economic Growth in Hungary During the Age of Dualism (1967–1913). A Quantitative Analysis," in T. I. Berend *et. al.*, *Social-*

Economic Researches on the History of East-Central Europe (Budapest: Akadémiai Kiadó, 1970), pp. 35–70.

7. A. Gerschenkron, "Economic Backwardness in Historical Perspective," in The Progress of Underdeveloped Areas, ed. by Bert F. Hoselitz (Chicago University of Chicago Press, 1962), Economic Backwardness in Historical Perspective (Cambridge, Mass.: Harvard University Press, 1962); "The Early Phases of Industrialization in Russia: Afterthoughts and Counterthoughts," in The Economics of Take-Off into Sustained Growth, ed. W. W. Rostow (New York: St. Martin Press, 1963); "The Discipline and I," Journal of Economic History XXVII (December 1967), pp. 443–59; Paul Jonas and Hyman Sardy, "The Gerschenkron Effect: A Re-Examination," The Review of Economics and Statistics vol. LII, no. 1 (February 1970), pp. 82–86.

8. Béla K. Király, "Paul Teleki, the Theoretician of the Hungarian Revisionism," in Paul Teleki, The Evolution of Hungary and its Place in European History (Albany, New York: Academic International Press, 1921, reprint 1975).

9. Frank Vanderlip, a practical American financier, felt, "If we concentrated our wealth and efforts on America alone and were utterly careless of the fate of the rest of the world, I believe we would lose our soul. I believe that with that loss there could ultimately come a loss of our material advantages." Frank A. Vanderlip, What Next in Europe? (New York: Harcourt, Brace and Company, 1920), p. 46. It is, however, fair to add that West Germany's self-rehabilitation, after the Second World War, was eventually established by the Schuman Plan and by the initiatives of the French statesman—economist Jean Monnet—in a cooperative institution of the European Steel and Coal Community. Germany was reconciled with France by French initiatives, a reconciliation solemnly ratified by President de Gaulle and Chancellor Adenauer in the Cathedral of Reims in July 1962.

10. J. M. Keynes, The Economic Consequences of the Peace (New York: Harcourt, Brace and Howe, 1920), pp. 134–51.

11. Congressional Record, vol. 59, part 3, pp. 2696, et seq.

12. The Census of 1920 gives 86.1 persons per square kilometer.

13. Vide for the data Memorandum of the French Government on the Fixation of the Western Frontier of Germany, February 26, 1919. Quoted by Etienne Mantoux, The Carthaginian Peace (Pittsburgh, Penn.: University of Pittsburgh Press, 1921), p. 21.

14. Conigsby Dawson, It Might Have Happened to You (New York: John Lane Company, 1921).

15. Op. cit., p. 34.

16. Op. cit., p. 42.

17. One gold crown was equal to 17,000 paper crowns or 1.36 pengo in 1924; in 1925, since the pengo was stabilized on the basis of the pound sterling, one gold crown was equal to 14,500 paper crowns or 1.16 pengo.

18. Statistically inclined readers may be interested that it is possible to fit the 1914–1918 data in a power curve which give the result: SF = 105.60 $T^{-0.53}$, where SF stands for Swiss Francs, T for the time period (1914 = 1 . . . . 1918 = 5). The correlation coefficient is a significant r = 0.94.

The data 1920–1925 can be best approximated by the logarithmic curve SF = 14.16 $e^{-1.31T}$ (1920 = 1 . . . . 1925 = 6) with a correlation coefficient r = 0.96 significant at 0.05 level.

19. J. M. Keynes, *The Revision of the Treaty* (New York: Harcourt, Brace and Company, 1922).

Part V

Sixty Years After

(See maps at the end of the book)

Frank Koszorus, Jr.

The Forgotten Legacy of the League of Nations Minority Protection System

Perhaps the most significant legacy of the League of Nations was the protection extended to members of "racial, linguistic and religious" minorities. After reaching that milestone, international concern for the protection of minorities diminished almost to the point of non-existence. Following the demise of the League and at the conclusion of the Second World War, the emphasis shifted from minority protection to the promotion of individual human rights. One commentator wryly observed that it appeared as if "there were fashions in international law just as in neckties" with the fashion of minority protection having been replaced so that "today the well-dressed international lawyer wears 'human rights'."[1]

Conventional wisdom was that the securing of fundamental human rights would make the protecting of minorities' interests superfluous. The standards for the respect of individual human rights, however, have proven to be insufficient to address the unique and complex difficulties faced by minorities. Indeed, the international community is no longer altogether ignoring minority issues. Rather than being a taboo subject, minority protection slowly is resurfacing as a topic of discussion among international lawyers, experts, and even to a limited extent within international organizations.[2]

Although the League of Nations Minority System significantly advanced the concept of minority protection, it had ample precedent to draw upon and, in that sense, represented the apex of what had been an evolving process. For example, the rights of aliens, which is related to group rights, extends back to antiquity.[3] Moreover, among the first direct attempts at minority protection were measures to safeguard religious minorities. These first appeared in the 13th century and grew in importance as a result of the Reformation. By way of example, we might mention the Peace of Augsburg, 1555, the

Pact of Warsaw, 1573, and the Edict of Nantes, 1598.[4] As early as the 17th and 18th centuries, bilateral treaties contained provisions concerning religious minorities. The Treaty of Vienna of 1606 was one of these which guaranteed the right of the Hungarian Protestant minority to exercise its religion in Royal Hungary. By the 19th century, minority protections, including civil and political rights, were enshrined in multilateral treaties and extended to groups other than religious minorities. For instance, the Final Act of the Congress of Vienna was among the first international instruments to embrace national minorities.[5]

The scheme of international protection of minorities in that era was not very satisfactory. Politically motivated powers arbitrarily and unilaterally intervened in the internal affairs of weaker states. Moreover, the scheme lacked the machinery to ensure that minorities would not be maltreated and that they would have the opportunity to communicate their grievances to the "interested" powers.[6]

The 20th century ushered in a new era of minority protection. The League of Nations System for the protection of minorities emerged as a result of the drastic redrawing of frontiers after the First World War, when new states were created or old ones enlarged. In revising the borders, however, the Peace Conference failed fully to apply the principle of national self-determination. Although the Conference reduced the number of minorities, it nevertheless did not solve the nationalities problem, as evidenced by the approximately 30 million individuals who were left or transformed into minorities.[7] For instance, over 3 million Hungarians found themselves under foreign rule as a result of the Treaty of Trianon which drew Hungary's boundary so as to allow the Successor States "to extend their frontiers well beyond the line warranted by ethnography, to meet their economic and, above all, their strategic conveniences."[8]

Even if the framers of the peace treaties would have intended to implement the principle of self-determination, minority problems would still have survived because of the patchwork-quilt pattern of ethnic distribution throughout East-Central Europe. Among the congenital weaknesses of the Paris Peace Conference, therefore, was the application of the theory of the nation state to an area that was not prepared to adapt it because of the national, ethnic, linguistic and religious heterogeneity of the region. Indeed,

[e]xtreme national pride and intolerance did not subside after the establishment of the new nation-states. In fact, rather than settling passions heightened by the Great War, the flaming heat of personal nationalism did not cool with the achievement of political independence; national homogeneity became the ideal rather than national tolerance; the equitable treatment of minorities by the governments of the national states could not be expected; in fact, minorities constituted anomolies and blemishes to be eliminated.[9]

This already volatile situation was further exacerbated by the natural reluctance of the minorities to cooperate with the new states to which they were assigned, and by the revisionist policies of states which viewed the minorities as tools to be used to further their own policies.[10] The potential for international instability, including the threat to the minority states, stemming from the unsolved or newly created minority situations, was recognized by several peacemakers, including Woodrow Wilson who stated on May 31, 1919, at the Peace Conference that,

Nothing . . . is more likely to disturb the peace of the world than the treatment which might in certain circumstances be meted out to the minorities.[11]

It was obvious that tranquility could be assured only if some form of international protection of minorities was erected.

Supporting the official effort to establish a minority protection regime were a number of private organizations. Among them the Jewish organizations were very active and had an impact on the formulation of the evolving system. For instance, the American delegation, including Woodrow Wilson, gave serious consideration to the memorandum of the Committee of Jewish Delegations of May 10, 1919.[12]

While the affected minorities were relatively inactive, the newly created or enlarged states which were to be bound by the minority treaties were opposed to the establishment of a minorities regime. Poland, Romania and Yugoslavia proved to be the most vehement opponents while Czechoslovakia, Bulgaria, and Austria were far less outspoken clearly because of the protection which was to be extended to their co-nationals outside of their borders.[13] In the case of

Hungary, which was left with few minorities but which lost a large number of its co-nationals to the successor states, outright support for the System was reflected by the note of its delegation to the Peace Conference dated February 12, 1920:

> The guarantee concerning the protection of Hungarian minorities entrusted to the League of Nations constitutes for us the most important part of the treaty about to be concluded, and only our trust in the effective realization of this guarantee can make us sign the Treaty of Peace.[14]

As far as the League's Minority System is concerned, it did not establish general principles of international law but rather consisted of treaty and other obligations which only bound a few small states and which were placed under the guarantee of the League. There were five Minorities Treaties concluded between the Allied and Associated Powers and the following new or enlarged states: Poland, Czechoslovakia, Romania, the Serb-Croat-Slovene State, and Greece.[15] Reciprocity dictated that similar minority protection clauses be included in the Peace Treaties concluded with four of the defeated states: Austria, Bulgaria, Hungary, and Turkey.[16] Several other states made unilateral declarations, assuming similar obligations upon being admitted to the League of Nations: Albania on October 2, 1921; Lithuania on May 12, 1922 (including the application of the declaration to the Territory of the Memel which was placed under Lithuanian sovereignty as an autonomous region by the Convention of May 8, 1924, between the Allied and Associated Powers and Lithuania); Latvia on July 7, 1923; Estonia on September 7, 1923, and Iraq on May 30, 1932.[17] Finally, the System applied to special situations such as the Aaland Islands pursuant to the declaration by Finland to the League on June 27, 1921, and the German-Polish Geneva Convention concerning Upper Silesia of May 15, 1922.[18] The System thus initiated by the peacemakers "created a large and continuous Eurasian region stretching from the Aaland Islands down to Iraq, in which the Bill of Rights, being also a common code of protection of minorities . . . came into being."[19]

In the first instance, substantive provisions common to the instruments forming the System first guaranteed rights applicable to all residents, namely, the protection of life, liberty and the free exercise of religion. They also included stipulations concerning the acquisition of nationality. All nationals were further granted the right of equality before the law and equality of civil and political rights; the right to be free from discrimination in public employment, functions, honors or in the exercise of professions and industries irrespective of the individual's race, language or religion; and the right to use any language in private intercourse, at public meetings or before the courts, in religion, in commerce and in the press and publications.

Particularly significant from a minority protection viewpoint were the rights extended to the racial, religious and linguistic minorities, meaning national minorities. They were granted the right to establish at their own expense charitable, religious, social and educational institutions and the right to use their mother tongue and exercise their religion therein.

Moreover, in those towns or districts where a substantial number of minority nationals resided, the state was to provide adequate facilities to ensure that instruction at the primary school level was to be available in the language of the minority. In such areas, public funds were to be equitably apportioned for educational, religious or charitable institutions of the minority. Finally, special provisions were tailored for local conditions, such as Article 11 of the Romanian treaty which provided for the educational and religious autonomy of the Saxons and Székelys (Szeklers) of Transylvania.

The substantive rights enshrined in the minorities' treaties were intended to achieve two objectives. First, the treaties established negative equality of all individuals, namely the right to be free from discrimination on the basis of race, language or religion. Second, members of racial, linguistic and religious minorities were also assured positive equality, namely, the minimum conditions necessary for them to preserve and foster their unique characteristics, language, religion and historical traditions. In the words of the Permanent Court of International Justice:

> The idea underlying the treaties for the protection of minorities is to secure for certain elements incorporated in a state, the population of which differs from them in race, language or religion, the possibility of living peaceably along side that population and cooperating amicably with it, while at the same time preserving the characteristics which distinguish them from the majority, and satisfying the ensuing special needs.[20]

Thus, the basic purpose of the League of Nations Minorities System (and of any system for minorities protection) was to establish an equality between the respective majorities and minorities by permitting the latter to maintain and develop their unique characteristics, and at the same time to assure their freedom from discrimination based on their race, language or religion.

The question raised in connection with the Minorities System was whether it applied to individuals or only to groups. The answer is not perfectly clear. The rights conferred on minorities were certainly in the nature of collective rights, "for no individual is capable of establishing, managing and controlling a fully fledged school by himself and for himself."[21] The System, nevertheless, exhibited an individual bias in that Article 12 of the Polish Treaty—the other minority treaties were patterned after the Polish Treaty—refers to "persons belonging to racial, religious or linguistic minorities"; moreover, states feared that a recognition of minorities as collective entities would derogate their sovereignty.[22]

It is also important to note that while the League System sought to safeguard the rights of minorities, its underlying purpose was political. The peacemakers sought to ensure lasting peace by avoiding ". . . the many interstate frictions and conflicts which had occurred in the past, as a result of the frequent ill-treatment or oppression of national minorities."[23] By promoting amicable relations between majorities and minorities, the peacemakers intended to minimize such interstate tensions and thereby safeguard peace.[24]

The League System, contrary to previous minority regimes, internationalized the rights afforded minorities by virtue of the League's role as guarantor of those rights. By establishing the collective guarantee of an impartial international organization, the weaknesses of earlier regimes, i.e., unilateral intervention by specially interested states, were eliminated.[25] The international guarantee derived from Article 12 of the model Polish Treaty, commonly known as the guarantee clause, which stated, in part:

> Poland agrees that the stipulation in the foregoing Articles, so far as they affect persons belonging to racial, religious or linguistic minorities, constitute obligations of international concern and shall be placed under the guarantee of the League of Nations.

*   *   *

Poland agrees that any Member of the Council of the League of Nations shall have the right to bring to the attention of the Council any infraction of any of these obligations, and that the Council may thereupon take such action and give such direction as it may deem proper and effective in the circumstances.

Poland further agrees that any difference of opinion as to questions of law or fact arising out of these Articles between the Polish Government and any one of the Principal Allied and Associated Powers or any other power, a Member of the Council of the League of Nations, shall be held to be a dispute of an international character under Article 14 of the Covenant of the League of Nations (i.e., a dispute that could be heard and decided by the Permanent Court of International Justice). The Polish Government hereby consents that any such dispute shall, if the other party thereto demands, be referred to the Permanent Court of International Justice.

In addition to placing the substantive provisions of the minorities treaties under the guarantee of the League, the guarantee clause also enumerated the rudimentary procedures to be followed by the organization. By enumerating those procedures, rather than leaving the task of promulgating them to the Council, the guarantee clause initially almost paralyzed the League. Since the responsibility of bringing treaty violations to the attention of the Council devolved on the members of that body, members were thus assigned the difficult task of individually and directly challenging the policies of the minority states. But if this were done, either considerable ill will would have been generated between members and the accused states, or, as would have most likely occurred, members would have refrained from bringing violations to the attention of the Council.[26] The Council quickly remedied this potentially debilitating effect by creating the Minorities Committees in 1920, which "collectivized" the minorities procedure and removed from individual members the onus of being accusers. The report guaranteed that minority issues would be addressed by the League. For this reason, the states bound by the treaty provisions unsuccessfully but strenuously insisted on the "purity of the guarantee clause."[27]

The Council continued to develop the requisite procedures through 1929.[28] These procedures, as finally refined, were triggered by the stated right of any person to submit a petition, which functioned solely as a source of information of minority rights violations.

However, the Council was so adamant on not giving its review the appearance of a judicial proceeding that the petitioners were not only deprived of any rights or standing in the proceeding, but, until 1929, were not even informed of the disposition of their petitions.[29] Eventually, by its resolution of June 13, 1929, the Council decided that petitioners should be informed if their petitions were deemed non-receivable. This failure to notify petitioners about the status of their petitions, except for acknowledgement of receipt, was among the most controversial features of the procedures, particularly before 1929. The criticism was fueled by the discovery that the government concerned was afforded an opportunity to challenge a determination that a petition was receivable.[30]

The petition's receivability was determined by the Minorities Section of the Secretariat.[31] If deemed receivable and if the state in question did not successfully challenge the Minorities Section's determination, the petition was transmitted to the state in question for comment. The petition and the comments by the state, if any, were then transmitted to the Members of the Council and to the Committee of Three (also known as the Minorities Committee), consisting of the President of the Council and two or three other members. The Committee would examine the petition and would either reject it, attempt to resolve the matter by entering into informal negotiations with the state, or decide that the matter should be placed on the Council's agenda.[32]

If the petition was not rejected, the Committee's policy was to engage in friendly negotiations with the state concerned.[33] This practice came under criticism by not only the minorities and their champion states, but also by objective and neutral observers.[34] Distrust regarding such negotiations was exacerbated by the Committee's tendency to accept any agreement on the issues presented.[35] The expediency of negotiations was reinforced, however, by the lack of resolve on the part of the Great Powers to insist on the full implementation of the minority treaties. France was less than committed to minority questions because of its relationship with the Little Entente and Poland; Italy was muted because of its large German minority; and Britain, despite genuine efforts, was ineffective.[36]

Such negotiations were not altogether fruitless, however, particularly when the concerned state sought to avoid the publicity attendant on the matter being considered by the Council. Under these circumstances it would agree to concessions,[37] as did Romania in the matter of Hungarian education in Transylvania, when it modified certain objectionable provisions of a draft law concerning private education.[38]

If the concerned state refused to compromise, the Council could be seized of the matter. Theoretically, the guarantee clause empowered the Council to take any action "it may deem proper and effective." In practice, the Council was governed by its normal procedures, including the rule of unanimity, which severely circumscribed its purported unlimited discretion. The effect of the rule of unanimity required that the state in question participate in the Council's deliberations and concur in its decisions.[39] This rule was the greatest weakness in the League's procedures in general, and as it related to minority questions. It nevertheless reflected reality, since the absence of effective sanctions left no alternative to seeking the concerned state's cooperation, with or without the rule.[40]

The proceedings before the Council actually consisted of two stages. The first stage was investigatory whereby the Council was appraised of all relevant documents and facts. Settlement was still possible if the state adopted a flexible posture, as did Romania in the Hungarian farmers' case in 1925, when it assured the Council that it would "suspend all measures which might affect the *status quo*, as regards the holdings of these farmers" until the Council had formed an opinion on the matter.[41] An indication from the Council that it would interpret the case in favor of the minority in question also promoted settlement. Since compromising at this stage was not equivalent to an admission of wrongdoing (because issues of law would not have been formally determined), the concerned state could still avoid the adverse publicity surrounding formal action by the Council.[42]

If the matter was not remedied at the investigation stage, the Council would proceed to form an opinion and attempt to persuade the state in question to abide by the terms of the applicable treaty.[43] Thus, the Council, as the Minorities Committees, could be compelled to negotiate only by oral pressure and publicity, and skillful negotiations would result in a solution acceptable to the state concerned.[44] In other words, the League's success in blunting minority tensions depended on its commitment, prestige and diplomatic acumen.

The Council in rare instances supervised the implementation of the agreement reached between it and the state concerned. One such instance involved the Hungarian farmers' case in which Romania agreed to pay additional compensation to dispossessed farmers.[45] Post-settlement negotiations were undertaken to ensure the equitable distribution of the 700,000 gold francs to the farmers. Subsequently, the Rapporteur advised the Council of the proposed arrangements whereby the "promised sum had been placed at the disposal" of the farmers,[46] and the Council continued to monitor the matter until a final accounting two years later.[47]

The judicial element of the League System was as significant to the elevation of the concept of minority protection as was the guarantee of the League. By the terms of the minority treaties "difference[s] of opinion as to questions of law or fact" concerning the minority treaty provisions were to be referred to the Permanent Court of International Justice if any Principal Allied or Associated Power or any other power sitting on the Council so requested. This procedure, however, was rarely invoked. Another judicial procedure available to the Council was to seek an advisory opinion from the Permanent Court of International Justice on matters relating to minorities' issues. Although there were few such requests, the advisory opinions rendered by the Court played an important role in defining what was meant by "minorities," in delimiting the scope and nature of their rights, and in persuading obligated states to adopt a more conciliatory attitude, if not to abide by the terms of the treaties. The Council could also enlist the aid of a Committee of Jurists before turning to the Court, as it did in the Székely (Szekler) case.[48] That case involved a petition alleging that certain Romanian agrarian laws discriminatorily expropriated without compensation the property of the descendants of the former Székely Frontier Guards, while they exempted the property of the descendants of two Romanian frontier regiments from similar treatment.

Despite the conceptual advances made by the League System regarding international protection of minorities, the System itself was doomed to failure. The success or failure of the Minorities System was linked to the post-war European order and the prestige of the League. As that order and organization crumbled so did the protection of minorities. The peacemakers were to learn that it was "easier to destroy the Dual Monarchy [old order] than to improve the conditions of Man in Central Europe."[49]

Factors specifically related to the League's Minority System, other than the procedural deficiencies mentioned above, also proved to be damaging and ultimately fatal to the System. Among its primary weaknesses was the limited scope of the obligations. Instead of establishing general norms of international law, the System's purview was restricted to a few small states which resented their seemingly second-class status. This perception was aggravated by the System's exclusion of other states with minority populations, such as Italy, which had embarked on a campaign to denationalize its Austrian and Yugoslav minorities. Even more infuriating to the obligated states was the exclusion of defeated Germany. The ensuing exasperation was reflected by Eduard Beneš, who condemned the inconsistency of having Czechoslovakia internationally bound "while supervision is exercised by states in which the minority problem, though acute, goes unregulated."[50]

As important as the issue of generalization may have been from an international legal perspective, its proponents nevertheless overlooked the origin of the scheme devised by the peacemakers. The Minority System was directly related to the drastic territorial settlements following the War. President Wilson concisely articulated the justification for a minority protection scheme when on May 31, 1919, he responded to Romania's objections by stating,

> But I beg him (Bratianu) to observe that he is overlooking the fact that he is asking for the sanction of the Allied and Associated Powers for great additions of territory . . . and that, therefore, we are entitled to say: 'if we agree to these additions of territory we have a right to insist upon certain guarantees of peace.'[51]

Although the obligated states could have seized the opportunity genuinely to strive to broaden the new international law, their aim was quite the opposite. Their attitude was anything but cooperative and, in fact, the demand for generalization "was nothing more than a code word for outright cancellation of the minorities provisions."[52] This hostility characterized their attitude toward the minorities and the Minorities System and, indeed, the obligated states undermined the System whenever possible. With this goal in mind, they insisted on a strict interpretation of the guarantee clause; used delaying tactics at every stage of a proceeding, which rendered the League's procedures ineffective; prohibited the minorities to invoke the provisions of the treaties in domestic legal proceedings; and judicially did not accept the supremacy of the treaties in their courts.[53]

Equally disruptive of the System was the tendency by the obligated states to equate petitions from minorities with disloyalty. The resulting fear of reprisals inhibited members of minorities from fully exercising their right to bring their grievances to the League's attention, as specifically guaranteed by the System.[54] The continuous effort to vitiate the Minorities System culminated in Poland's virtually unopposed and unilateral repudiation in 1934 when Colonel Beck stated:

> Pending the introduction of a general and uniform system for the protection of minorities, my government is compelled to refuse, as from today, all cooperation with the interntional organization in the matter of the supervision of the application by Poland of the system of minority protection.[55]

This hostility was not justified considering the less than far reaching, yet necessary, provisions of the System. Even Professor R. W. Seton-Watson, who was far from unfriendly towards the minority states, noted in connecion with the Romanian treaty that "only those who are wilfully blind or have assimilationist aims can deny that the treaty contains nothing which runs counter to the paramount interests of state unity and all that is essential for a just settlement of this vexed question."[56]

The minorities also shared in the responsibility for the decline of the System. Instead of adopting a cooperative attitude, some of them agitated conspiratorially with their kindred states against their new states. Orderly political processes were thereby made even more difficult. In addition, many were bitter toward the League and the international order which had transformed them into minorities, often in contradiction to the proclaimed principle of national self-determination. Their bitterness often was reinforced by "their fate [which had] almost everywhere been unfortunate—much more unfortunate, as a general rule, in the new states and transferred territories than in the old states,"[57] and by the League's failure to give them a full, speedy and impartial hearing and the absence of satisfactory remedies.

Some of the Hungarian minorities never fully acquiesced in their new status as minorities under what they considered to be foreign rule, particularly in those transferred territories which were predominantly Hungarian and a homogeneous continuation of ethnic

Hungary. Although genuinely tolerant policies by the new and enlarged states would have contributed to reconciling such minorities,
the treatment meted out to some of them exacerbated their already
restive attitude. It was just a matter of time before they embraced irredentism.

Even more fatal to the League System was that certain minorities
readily became pawns in Hitler's aggressive designs. As Germany
regained its strength, it donned the mantle of the champion of
minorities. It soon became apparent, however, that Germany was
"using the ideology and the instrumentalities of 'Minderheitenschutz'
to undermine and finally blast to pieces the European and international status quo."[58]

Undoubtedly, the League System satisfied neither the interested
nor neutral parties concerned with the general issue of minorities.
That it was less than effective cannot be gainsaid. Nevertheless, the
System does not deserve the harsh judgment passed by some commentators.[59]

From a practical viewpoint, the League System achieved indirect,
modest yet positive successes. Although it is beyond dispute that
most minorities in East Central Europe were maltreated and oppressed, one can merely speculate how they would have fared in the
absence of the Minorities System. The existence of substantive
minority provisions and the international machinery to supervise
their implementation benefited the minorities because "the prospect
of being held responsible before an international body served as a
brake on chauvinist tendencies to oppress minorities."[60] There were
even instances where particular minorities tangibly benefited as a
result of submitting petitions to the League.[61]

Not to be ignored was the League's role in diffusing conflicts arising out of minorities questions. Its mere existence guaranteed that
such tensions would be partially diverted to the League. If left un-
controlled, these conflicts would have further poisoned the already
poisoned atmosphere of the region and could have easily flared into
frequent and serious incidents.[62]

But the most significant contribution of the System was the unparalleled elevation of the concept of minority protection, which
was achieved by internationalizing the guarantees and thereby
theoretically eliminating unilateral state intervention. Had the new
international law of minority protection survived the catastrophe of
the Second World War, it undoubtedly would have served as a core

to be expanded and refined to encompass the varied and complex conditions of minorities throughout the region, if not the world. Just as the law of human rights is ever accumulating, the potential existed for the evolution of minority rights laws which would have complemented and rounded out the protection extended to individuals. Admittedly, the League System was flawed. Yet that imperfect system was far better than the meager standards and machinery for the protection of minorities existing today. A great opportunity was squandered. Indeed, in East Central Europe there are many "who nostalgically view [the League System] a solution—a solution which seems almost an ideal today."[63]

The disintegration of the League unleashed the theretofore checked tendencies of certain states to homogenize their societies by eliminating their minorities. The attempts to "purify" societies ranged from the physical destruction of millions of Jews to the forced expulsions of Hungarians from Czechoslovakia and the severe repression of the Hungarians who were not expelled.

Despite these "solutions," minorities continue to exist in East-Central Europe and their fate makes the necessity for minority protection as acute as ever. Often states which readily acknowledge having minorities will ignore or adamantly deny the reality of the existence of minority problems which, however, are generally present whenever distinctive groups are found in a society.[64] The problems manifest themselves in differing degrees depending on the extent to which a majority is committed to create a culturally and linguistically homogeneous state and on a smaller group's desire and ability to maintain its distinctiveness. Often such minorities lack the requisite political power or are denied the rights which would enable them to preserve fully their unique characteristics, historic traditions, institutions or in drastic cases their very existence.[65] According to one expert, the ensuing attempts to achieve such homogeneity by policies aimed at forcibly assimilating "populations is remarkable both for its brutality and its ineffectiveness. The suppression of a people's language and religion and cultural institutions, the enforcement of severe discrimination against them and the offering of rewards for assimilation have brought about the most bitter suffering on the part of minority peoples for centuries, and it has continued up to the present date in spite of very clear evidence of its fruitlessness."[66]

It was these "problem situations" which, to a limited extent, were addressed by the League of Nations and which today require greater attention by the international community.[67] For instance, the present governments of Romania and Czechoslovakia, with all the instruments of 20th Century totalitarian states at their disposal, have intensified their efforts to discriminate against and forcibly assimilate their Hungarian minorities.[68] These efforts continue without an international organization's braking or at least scrutinizing such nationalities policies (as was done by the League), because international concern today has focused almost exclusively on the protection of individuals as individuals and not also as members of a particular group or community. The United Nations has largely ignored the question of minorities, despite the prefatory language of Resolution 217 (c) adopted by the General Assembly in 1948 which states that the U.N. "cannot remain indifferent to the fate of minorities." Both the U.N. Charter and the Universal Declaration of Human Rights are silent on the minorities issue. While a Subcommission on the Prevention of Discrimination and the Protection of Minorities was created by the Economic and Social Council in 1947, its work has centered on its mandate involving the prevention of discrimination.[69] The fact remains that with the exception of a few weak initiatives, such as Article 27 of the International Covenant on Civil and Political Rights or Article 5 of the Convention Against Discrimination in Education, the United Nations has not undertaken to develop a comprehensive scheme for the protection of minorities.[70] Its glacial pace in addressing minority rights, when the issue is raised, is evident from the lack of progress on the draft declaration on the rights of "national, ethnic, religious and linguistic rights" proposed by Yugoslavia at the thirty-fourth session of the Commission of Human Rights.[71] Three years after Yugoslavia submitted its proposal, one observer expressed his disappointment at the "Sub-Commission's inaction, despite the existence of an open-ended sessional working group, in the draft declaration on the rights of persons belonging to . . . minorities, which had been the subject of much discussion at the Commission's 1980 session."[72]

Not even the post World War II Peace Treaties with Romania, Hungary, Italy, Finland and Bulgaria contain specific minority rights provisions, although they do contain human rights clauses which theoretically offer minorities a modicum of protection. Mention must be made of a few bilateral treaties which came into existence after the War, such as the Treaty of Friendship and Mutual Aid of

March 10, 1947, between Poland and Czechoslovakia regarding their respective minorities. The reach of these treaties is limited, however, in that "of the millions of European members of minorities, only some 450,000 enjoy bilateral protection."[73] The neglect of minority rights law has several root causes. Among the most salient is the conceptual problem presented by the lack of a generally accepted definition of the term "minority."[74] Actually, the term was popularized during the League era; however, because the League was not concerned with a general concept of minority protection, but rather with specific minorities in a handful of states, it did not have to define the term with any precision. That task must be addressed today.

Another obstacle of greater import than the definitional one, at least as it applies to Western States, is rooted in the individualist conception of Western political thought. By emphasizing individualism to the extent that it does, liberal political theory, as developed by Rousseau, Locke and others, lacks an adequate theory of the state. Its centerpiece, the social contract, assumes the existence of an organized society preceding the compact, and since the compact exists between individuals, ethnic and other groups are neither represented by the parties nor do they have a place in society.[75] Thus, Western political thought equates the state with the nation and accepts "as a 'nation' the people living under a particular government without asking why they were living under that government."[76] Consequently, liberal political theory does not address directly the heterogeneity of humankind as it may exist within a state.

Perhaps the greatest obstacle to the adoption of effective minority protection measures is the fear and suspicion engendered by any international scheme for the welfare of distinct groups within a state. The maintenance of heterogeneity and pluralism is regarded by some states as a threat to their unity and stability, and any attempt to remedy the situation is denounced as an interference in their internal affairs in violation of the concept of sovereignty.[77] However, states which discriminate and suppress their minorities may create tensions that truly endanger and undermine their stability. Instead of achieving the desired yet unattainable homogeneity, these oppressive policies may galvanize the groups' resolve to resist such pressures to the point of solidifying their opposition to the state. The ensuing tensions are then subject to exploitation by greater powers as was the case in inter-War Europe.

States expediently point to the difficulties in establishing an international regime for the protection of minorities arising out of the diverse and complex nature of each minority situation. Nevertheless, both the objections of interference in internal affairs and of "complexity" also have been raised in connection with the establishment of the standards for the promotion of and respect for fundamental human rights.[78] Identical arguments have not paralyzed the international community's acceptance of the human rights regime, at least not in theory, even if it has in practice. Neither factors are insurmountable, assuming states are willing to accept a degree of plurality and the establishment of a minorities protection regime.

Despite formidable obstacles and the reluctance of the international community to embrace fully the vexing problem of minorities, it cannot altogether ignore the matter. For instance, the chairman of the U.S. delegation to the Helsinki follow-up conference in Madrid noted in plenary on December 10, 1980, that "the human rights provisions of the Final Act . . . have in many instances not been implemented. . . . We know that the rights of national minorities are often denied."[79]

An even more surprising development occurred in March, 1981, when the United Nations Commission on Human Rights heard a communication, i.e., complaint, filed by the non-governmental International Human Rights Law Group alleging that Japan violated the human rights of its Korean minority by enacting laws which discriminate and deny economic and other cultural benefits to members of the minority. The Commission dismissed the complaint after Japan assured the body that it would take steps to remedy the violations.[80]

Recently commentators have broadly interpreted the existing norms relating to human rights, including nondiscrimination, to embrace the needs of minorities.[81] This exercise does not mitigate the urgency to protect minorities; rather it merely reveals the present void in the law.

In the final analysis, there is an acute need for the development and concretization of comprehensive norms as well as the machinery to implement minority protections. The effort to build a body of international law related to individual human rights is certainly one of the great achievements of twentieth century jurisprudence. However, since individual rights are often secure only if group rights are guaranteed, that body of human rights law is not sufficient by itself to shield humankind from all manifestations of oppression, unless it is supplemented by norms to safeguard the unique characteristics of minorities. Minorities require more than protection from nondiscrimination.[82] True equality cannot exist between a majority and a minority "if the latter [is] deprived of its own institutions, and [is] consequently compelled to renounce that which constitutes the very essence of its being a minority."[83] Anatole France's comment on "the law which, in its majestic equality, forbids rich as well as poor to sleep under bridges or to beg in the streets"[84] aptly applies to the inability of the present human rights law to protect minorities. Ironically, positive equality must be extended to groups to prevent inequality, discrimination and human misery.

The League's experience and accumulated knowledge can be of invaluable assistance in formulating a minorities protection scheme today. Given that minority problems do not necessarily lend themselves to a uniform solution because of each region's unique historical, economic, social and political develpment, a solely generalized approach is not advisable. A bifurcated system would perhaps be the most meaningful solution. First, a universal declaration of the rights of minorities could establish the broad parameters and the considerations common to most, if not all, minorities. Supplementing that declaration, regional protection systems could take into account the factors peculiar and relevant to a particular area and tailor the protections to those circumstances. Whatever the form, however, it can only be hoped that diverse groups will learn to live peaceably with one another and that minorities eventually will be free from the senseless suffering they have to endure solely because of their distinctiveness—a distinctiveness which serves to enrich humankind.

Notes

1. Josef L. Kunz, "The Present Status of the International Law for the Protection of Minorities." *American Journal of International Law* (hereafter cited as *AJIL*) 48 (1954), p. 282.

2. For instance, the United Nations Seminar on Multiethnic Societies (June 1965, Ljubljana, Yugoslavia), declared that, "Integration should never mean the suffocation of the minority concerned . . . all Governments should promote and protect the rights of ethnic, religious, linguistic or national groups not only through the adoption of constitutional and legislative provi-

sions, but also through the promotion of all forms of activities consistent with political, economic and social conditions of the state or country concerned." UN Doc. ST/TAO/HR/23. See also, the United Nations Seminar on the Promotion and Protection of the Human Rights of National, Ethnic and Other Minorities (June-July, 1974, Ohrid, Yugoslavia), UN Doc. ST/TAO/HR/40; Francesca Capotorti, Special Rapporteur of UN Sub-Commission on the Prevention of Discrimination and Protection of Minorities, "Study of the Rights Belonging to Ethnic, Religious and Linguistic Minorities," UN Doc. E/CN.4/Sub.2/384 (1977); Rita E. Hauser, "International Protection of Minorities and the Right of Self-Determination." *Israel Yearbook on Human Rights* I (1971).

3. Helmer Rosting, "Protection of Minorities by the League of Nations." *AJIL* 17 (1923), pp. 641-2.

4. *Ibid.*, pp. 642-43; Inis L. Claude, *National Minorities: An International Problem* (New York: Greenwood Press, 1955), p. 6; C. A. Macartney, *National States and National Minorities* (New York: Russel, 1968), pp. 157-75.

5. Article I of the Final Act provided: "The Polish subjects of the High Contracting Parties shall be given institutions which guarantee the preservation of their nationality and which shall assume such political form as each of the governments to which they are subject shall deem appropriate." Cited in Capotorti, p. 12.

6. Claude, p. 8.

7. *Ibid.*, p. 13; Franjo Tudjman, *Nationalism in Contemporary Europe* (Boulder: East European Monographs, 1981), pp. 28-36.

8. C. A. Macartney and A. W. Palmer, *Independent Eastern Europe: A History* (London: MacMillan, 1966), p. 144. A most comprehensive treatment of the diplomatic history of how the borders of Hungary were drawn is Francis Deak, *Hungary at the Paris Peace Conference: The Diplomatic History of the Treaty of Trianon* (New York: Columbia University Press, 1942). See also, Harold Temperly, "How the Hungarian Frontiers Were Drawn." *Foreign Affairs* 6 (1928), p. 432.

9. Tennent H. Bagley, *International Protection of National Minorities* (Geneva: Georg & Co., 1950), p. 12.

10. *Ibid.*, p. 40.

11. Cited in Adatci Report, League of Nations, *Official Journal, Special Supplement* (hereafter cited as *OISS*) 73 (1929), p. 45.

12. Jacob Robinson, "International Protection of Minorities: A Global View." *Israel Yearbook on Human Rights* I (1971), pp. 65-66; Macartney, *National States*, pp. 212-15.

13. Claude, p. 15.

14. Cited in Adatci Report, p. 80.

15. Versailles Treaty with Poland of June 28, 1919, *AJIL* (Supp.) 13

(1919), p. 423; Saint Germain Treaty with Czechoslovakia of September 10, 1919, *AJIL* (Supp.) 14 (1920), p. 311; Paris Peace Treaty with Romania of December 9, 1919, *ibid.*, p. 324; Saint Germain Treaty with the Serb-Croat-Slovene State of September 10, 1919, *ibid.*, p. 333; and Sevres Treaty with Greece of August 10, 1920, *AJIL* (Supp.) 15 (1921), p. 161.

16. Saint Germain Peace Treaty with Austria of September 10, 1919, *AJIL* (Supp.) 14 (1920), p. 1; Neuilly Peace Treaty with Bulgaria of November 26, 1919, *ibid.*, p. 185; Trianon Peace Treaty with Hungary of June 4, 1920, *AJIL* (Supp.) 15 (1921), p. 1; Lausanne Peace Treaty with Turkey of August 10, 1920, *ibid.*, p. 179.

17. Capotorti, add. 2, p. 9.

18. Adacti Report, p. 43.

19. Robinson, p. 66.

20. Minority schools in Albania, Series A/B, no. 64 (April 6, 1935). *Permanent Court of International Justice* (hereafter cited as *PCIJ*).

21. Yoram Dinstein, "Collective Human Rights of Peoples and Minorities." 25 *International and Comparative Quarterly* (January 1976), p. 115.

22. Claude, p. 19; Capotorti, add. 2, pp. 13–14.

23. P. De Azcarate, *League of Nations and National Minorities: An Experiment*, translated by Eileen E. Brooke (Washington, D.C.: Rumford Press, 1945), p. 14.

24. Bagley, p. 43; Adatci Report, pp. 44–47.

25. See letter by Clemenceau to Paderewski (June 24, 1919) cited in Adatci Report, p. 44; Rodolfo de Nova, "The International Protection of National Minorities and Human Rights." *Howard Law Journal* 11 (1965), p. 278.

26. Azcarate, p. 99.

27. *Ibid.*, p. 112.

28. The Council quickly began to refine the procedures it would follow in dealing with minority issues. The first and most crucial step was its adoption of the Tittoni Report in 1920 which breathed life into the League's Minority System by establishing the right to petition and by creating the Minorities Committee. In the words of the former Director of the Minorities Section of the League, the Report "served as a basis for everything achieved by the League regarding minorities." *Ibid.*, p. 102.

29. Julius Stone, *International Guarantees of Minority Rights: Procedures of the Council of the League of Nations in Theory and Practice* (London: Oxford University Press, 1932), pp. 38–39.

30. Azcarate, p. 104; Capotorti, add. 2, p. 24. The U.N.'s practice in this regard is mixed. Petitioners submitting communications, i.e., complaints alleging violations of human rights, to the Commission on Human Rights or the Sub-Commission on Prevention of Discrimination and Protection of Minorities pursuant to Economic and Social Council Resolution 1503 (XVII)

are not informed about the fate of their communications (the proceeding itself is strictly confidential). On the other hand, the Director General of UNESCO is obligated by Section 14(b)(i) of UNESCO Document EX/Decision 3.3 to "acknowledge receipt of communications [alleging violations of human rights which fall within the competence of UNESCO] and inform the authors thereof of the . . . conditions governing admissability."

31. The criteria of receivability were estabished by the Council's Resolution of September 5, 1923. It provided that the petition to be admissible had to have the protection of minorities in view; could not seek severance of political relations between the minority and the state; could not emanate from an anonymous or unauthenticated source; could not contain violent language; and had to contain facts or information which was not the subject of a recent petition. Resolution reproduced in Stone, appendix III, p. 276.

32. The negotiations were "informal" because the case took on a legal character only when the Council was seized with the matter. *Ibid.*, p. 98.

33. Adatci Report, p. 59.

34. Azcarate, p. 117.

35. *Ibid.*, p. 121.

36. *Ibid.*, pp. 121–22.

37. Stone, p. 107.

38. *OISS* (1926), p. 741.

39. Article 4, paragraph 5, and Article 5, paragraph 1 of the Covenant of the League formed the basis for this "rule." The former provided: "Any Member of the League not represented on the Council shall be invited to send representatives to sit as a Member at any meeting of the Council during considerations of matters specially affecting the interests of that Member of the League." The latter provided: "Except where otherwise expressly provided in this Covenant or by the terms of the present Treaty, decisions at any meetings of the . . . Council shall require agreement of all Members of the League represented at the meeting."

40. Stone, p. 187.

41. *OISS* (1925), p. 891.

42. Stone, pp. 205–06.

43. *Ibid.*, p. 207.

44. Azcarate, p. 118.

45. Stone, pp. 228–31; *OISS* (1925), p. 1348.

46. *OISS* (1926), p. 160.

47. *OISS* (1928), p. 798.

48. *OISS* (1932), pp. 492–93.

49. Wenzel Jaksch, *Europe's Road to Potsdam*, translated and edited by Kurt Glaser (New York: Praeger, 1967), p. 233.

50. *OISS*, spec. supp. 120 (1933), p. 40.

51. Cited in Bagley, p. 75.

52. Robinson, p. 70.

53. Bagley, pp. 127–28; Claude, p. 40; Robinson, p. 70; Jacob Robinson, *Were the Minorities Treaties a Failure?* (New York: Austin Press, Inc., 1943), p. 153; Macartney, *National States*, p. 383.

54. For example, Poland persecuted several of its citizens for submitting petitions to the League. Bagley, p. 121; see also, Macartney, *idem*; Jaksch, p. 235.

55. Cited in Bagley, p. 98.

56. R. W. Seton-Watson, *A History of the Roumanians* (Cambridge University Press, 1934), p. 549.

57. Macartney, *National States*, p. 383.

58. De Nova, p. 281.

59. For instance, Jaksch, pp. 232–38, judges the League's Minority System to have been an abject failure. Compare this view with Macartney's, *National States*, pp. 420–21, which formulates the difficulties which confronted the League in the minority protection area as follows: "The real root of the trouble lies in the philosophy of the national state as it is practiced in central and eastern Europe. So long as the majority nations which have assumed command of the different states persist in their theoretically absurd and practically unattainable endeavor to make of those states the exclusive instruments of their own national ideals and aspirations, so long will the minorities be placed in a position which no system of interntional protection can render tolerable."

60. Robinson, *Were the Treaties a Failure*, p. 261.

61. *Supra*, p. 12, ftn. 45–47.

62. Azcarate, pp. 66–67.

63. Robinson, "Protection of Minorities," p. 90.

64. Kurt Glaser and Stefan T. Possony, *Victims of Politics: The State of Human Rights* (New York: Columbia University Press, 1979), p. 111; Claude, p. 1.

65. Claude, *idem.*, defines the problem as follows: "The problem of national minorities arises out of the conflict between the ideal of the homogeneous national state and the reality of ethnic heterogeneity."

66. Bagley, p. 21.

67. An irony of the modern perception of the problem confronting groups, such as ethnic groups, is identified by Glaser and Possony, p. 208, who state that "it is a peculiar tendency of our times that the world community will witness without much emotion large-scale suppression if it is defined in an ethnic ideological context, but will condemn with passion a far milder case of suppression which is defined as racism." Indeed, "ethnic, religious, and language quarrels can also erupt into violence. In recent years they have cost more human lives than fighting between races." *Idem.*, p. 161.

68. The Romanian government's pressures against its Hungarian minority

include: closing Hungarian-language educational institutions and eliminating Hungarian universities; dissolving compact Hungarian communities; suppressing Hungarian (and other minority) languages; confiscating archives of Hungarian churches; curtailing human contacts and cultural exchanges with Hungarians outside of Romania; and persecuting or condemning outspoken individuals to labor camps or psychiatric hospitals. See, Amnesty International, *Romania* (U.S., 1978); Tufton Beamish and Guy Hadley, *The Kremlin's Dilemma: The Struggle for Human Rights in Eastern Europe* (London: Collins & Harville, 1979); Committee for Human Rights in Rumania, *Rumania's Violations of Helsinki Final Act Provisions Protecting the Rights of National, Religious and Linguistic Minorities* (New York, 1980); Statement of Frank Koszorus, Jr., attorney, "The Interntional Human Rights Law Group," *Hearings on Waiver of Freedom of Immigration Requirement to the Socialist Republic of Romania and the Hungarian People's Republic before the Subcomm. on Trade of the Committee on Ways and Means*, 97th Cong., 1st Sess. (Washington, D.C., 1980), p. 258; George Schöpflin, *The Hungarians of Rumania*, Minority Rights Group, report no. 37 (1978); Richard F. Staar, *The Communist Regimes in Eastern Europe*, 2nd ed. (Stanford: Hoover Institution Publication, 1975). Regarding the situation of the Hungarian minority in Czechoslovakia, see, *Report of the Committee for the Protection of Rights of the Hungarian Minority in Czechoslovakia, Prepared for the Participants of the Czech Civil Rights Movement* (Czechoslovakia: November 1979) (mimeographed); *Report of the Committee for the Protection of the Rights of the Hungarian Minority in Czechoslovakia* (Czechoslovakia: February 1980) (mimeographed); Report to the Congress of the United States by the Commission on Security and Cooperation in Europe, "Implementation of the Final Act of the Conference on Security and Cooperation in Europe: Findings and Recommendations Five Years After Helsinki," 96th Cong., 2nd Sess. (August 1, 1980), p. 333.

69. For an excellent review of the origins and work of the Sub-Commission, see John P. Humphrey, "The U.N. Subcommission on the Prevention of Discrimination and the Protection of Minorities," *AJIL* 62 (1968), p. 869.

70. Article 27 of the International Covenant on Civil and Political Rights provides: "In those states in which ethnic, religious or linguistic minorities exist, persons belonging to such minorities shall not be denied the right, in community with other members of their group, to enjoy their own culture, to profess and practice their own religion, or to use their own language." Article 5, 1(c) of the Convention Against Discrimination in Education provides: "It is essential to recognize the rights of members of national minorities to carry on their own educational activities, including the maintenance of schools and, depending on the educational policy of each state, the use or teaching of their own language. . . ."

71. E/CN.4/L.1367/Rev.1. See E/CN.4/Sub.2/L.754 for the revised and consolidated text of the draft declaration submitted on July 2, 1980.

72. Hurst Hannum, "The Thirty-Third Session of the U.N. Sub-Commission on Prevention of Discrimination and Protection of Minorities," *AJIL* 75 (1981), p. 178.

73. Robinson, *Interntional Protection of Minorities*, p. 86.

74. Glaser and Possony, p. 105, define a minority as a ". . . group or category of persons within a specific political unit who are differentiated from a dominant group through one or more cultural or somatic factors such as lifestyle, language, religion, geneology, physical characteristics, nationality, ethnicity, or historicity and who because of this differentiation are subjected to discrimination, disqualifications, limitations, inequalities, or disabilities in respect of opportunities, power, status, and prestige." Compare also, Dinstein, p. 112, ". . . the test for the existence of a minority entitled to protection under international law is not always numerical. Perhaps we can think of a minority in the sense that such a group plays a minor role in the affairs of the country," with Capotorti, E/CN.4/Sub.2/384/Add.1, p. 10, who, in connection with the study on Article 27 of the International Covenant on Civil and Political Rights, states, that ". . . an ethnic, religious or linguistic minority is a group numerically smaller than the rest of the population of the state to which it belongs and possessing cultural, physical or historical characteristics, a religion or language different from those of the rest of the population."

75. Vernon Van Dyke, "The Individual, the State, and Ethnic Communities in Political Theory." *World Politics* XXIX (April 1977), pp. 346–49; Vernon Van Dyke, "Human Rights and the Rights of Groups." *American Journal of Political Science* XVII (November 1974), p. 726.

76. Glaser and Possony, p. 115.

77. Capotorti, E/CN.4/Sub.2/384, pp. 4–5. An unarticulated yet undoubtedly real concern to many states is the right of self-detrmination as that right may apply to groups within their boundaries.

78. *Idem.*

79. Statement by Judge Bell at phase one plenary session of the Madrid meeting of the Conference on Security and Cooperation in Europe on December 10, 1980, p. 2.

80. "Japan Promises to Increase Rights of Korean Minority," *The Law Group Docket* I (Spring, 1981), p. 4.

81. For example, see Myres S. McDougal, Harold D. Lasswell and Lung-Chu Chen, "Freedom From Discrimination in Choice of Language and International Human Rights," *Southern Illinois University Law Journal* 1 (1976), pp. 151–74; see also Capotorti, E/CN.4/Sub.2/384/add.5 who concludes his study on Article 27 of the International Covenant on Civil and Political Rights by stating: "In order to give effect to the rights set forth in Article 27

of the Covenant, active and sustained measures are required from states. A purely passive attitude on their part would render these rights ineffective."

82. The inability of the principle of nondiscrimination, at least as that principle has been developed by the UN, fully to protect minorities is identified by Glaser and Possony, p. 25, as follows: "The principle of nondiscrimination must be concerned mainly with discriminatory treatment of groups. There is no way to prevent discrimination in relationships between individuals, all of whom discriminate between kin and stranger, friend and foe, persons they like and dislike, people with whom they enter into professional relationships and people they marry or jilt. . . . The distinctions and discriminations which are to be eliminated are those between groups, such as races and religions, men and women, or persons who speak different languages. Yet *the various rights proposed to eliminate discriminatory treatment refer mainly to treatment given to individuals, while problems related to group treatment are rarely taken up.*" (Emphasis added.)

83. Minority Schools in Albania, PCIJ Series A/B, no. 64 (April 6, 1935), p. 17.

84. Cited in Bagley, p. 41; Glaser and Possony, p. 330, provide an example from the interwar period of the neglected truism that individual rights can often be fully protected only if group rights are protected by describing the situation in Czechoslovakia where ". . . all citizens were theoretically granted equal access to the public service on the basis of individual abilities. But a law passed in 1923 required all state employees to be proficient in the 'Czechoslovak language' even if employed in German speaking districts. The result was wholesale dismissal of public servants belonging to the German and Magyar ethnic groups, who had been included in the Czecho-Slovak state against their will in the first place. Apologists for the first Czecho-Slovak Republic have pointed out, quite correctly, that all citizens enjoyed equal *individual* rights. But they were denied the *group right* to participate in public functions in their own languages." (Emphasis included.) This situation was exacerbated by laws whereby ". . . members of the non-Czech nationalities were prevented from seeking a restructuring of the state permitting them further political expression. To create an artificial 'majority,' the myth of a 'Czechoslovak nation' became a theme of official propaganda, and the hyphen in Czecho-Slovakia, which had been retained until the Slovaks were firmly incorporated in the new state, was quietly dropped by the Prague government and later by most commentators. To the dismay of the Slovaks, the 'Czechoslovak language' turned out in many instances to be the Czech language used by Czech officials and teachers assigned to Slovakia." *Ibid.,* p. 353. See also, Tudjman, p. 31. But *cf.* with Macartney, *National States,* p. 414, who concludes with respect to inter-war Czechoslovakia that, "In her attitude towards her minorities Czechoslovakia has in many respects set an example to most of the Treaty States."

Michael Sozan

Hungarian Minorities and
Minority Boundary Maintenance in Burgenland

"Mi nem vagyunk se igazi nimetek, se igazi magyarok, mi őriek vagyunk."

(We are neither real Germans nor real Hungarians. We are of the Őrség.)

—A peasant man of Alsóőr, Austria.

The extent of ethnic cultural maintenance in lands once part of Hungary is difficult to measure. Official census records by the host countries are unreliable sources for scientific inquiry.[1] The reasons for this are largely political. In the perception of the governments involved, Hungarian revisionist claims to the detached territories continue to kindle ethnic hostility. It is therefore in the interest of the host countries to keep figures on Hungarians as low as possible. One way of underenumerating a given ethnic group is to define nationality in ambiguous terms; another is to place an undesirable ethnic group in a socially or economically disadvantageous position. In the latter case (used both in Czechoslovakia and in Romania) the government hopes that in the succeeding census people will claim to be members of the ruling nationality. The criteria of ethnicity include language usage, self-declaration, residence, or a combination of these. There are serious problems with any such census techniques, even in relatively pluralistic/egalitarian Austria,[2] let alone such countries as Czechoslovakia and Romania.

The above described situation requires that the quantification of ethnic maintenance be approached with the utmost caution. If we are to gain meaningful results, qualitative approaches, such as in-depth types of community studies, must replace the strictly demographic type of investigation. One such approach is the community-based, participant-observation technique utilized by anthropologists among tribals and peasants. A central focus of cultural anthropological investigations has been the exploration of the "normative picture," the question of how people view themselves and their ethnic strength. Yet, here too, we must be careful. Some scholars maintain that if people think they are assimilating, their self-perception should be accepted as a rule. In the Hungarian language village, Unterwart (Alsóőr), where I conducted fieldwork between 1973 and 1976, I found that people exaggerated the degree of their assimilation into Austrian society.[3] By exaggerating, they made normative statements of how things ought to be. This, in itself, is very revealing of benign Austrian ethnic policies. However, subsequent investigations indicated that in spite of their self-perception they were far from adopting German culture.

The visibility factor has a powerful influence on self-perception (or self-deception), especially among the rural population, which is, by most signs, rapidly shrinking in East Central Europe. Because the Hungarian element in Burgenland has been traditionally rural, and entire villages of Hungarian origin are disappearing, the conclusion drawn by some observers is that Hungarian ethnicity is in real danger of extinction.[4] Since at this time reliable scientific evidence on the fate of the Hungarians in Hungary's neighboring nations is totally lacking, attempts to assess their evolution, such as the present one, must be repeated many times before ethnic trends can be properly evaluated.

The decision to award Western Hungary to Austria by the Paris conferees in 1919 was received in Hungary and by the Hungarian negotiators with special dismay. This area of 3,900 square kilometers comprised one of Hungary's most ancient and tenaciously defended regions. It was given to Hungary's most faithful ally, a country, one might say, for which Hungary went to war. No wonder that Hungarians at that time could not reconcile themselves to, nor emotionally or intellectually accept, such a decision. They felt that even the Austrians had betrayed them in their final agony.

Historically, Western Hungary was established as a military border zone during the 10th century by the Árpád Dynasty as a buffer zone against the Holy Roman Empire. It has never been a peaceful land.[5] During the Middle Ages the region was often occupied by Austrian kings and turned into fiefdoms. Although the 150-year-long Ottoman occupation of Hungary had a lasting effect on the Hungarians of Western Hungary (especially the Ottoman campaigns against Austria in the 1530s), the Bocskay (1604) and Rákóczi (1703–11) Insurrections took an even heavier toll among the

Hungarian ethnic group, which until the 16th century was numerically superior to the others. The ensuing demographic vacuum was filled during the 18th century by German and Slavic-speaking groups.

By the middle of the 19th century today's Burgenland was a colorful mosaic of multi-ethnic land with a decisive German demographic superiority. The region was now drawn well into the orbit of Vienna, Lower Austria and Styria. During the 300 years of Habsburg rule in Hungary, the monarchs considered the region to be more German (Austrian) than Hungarian. Cultural, commercial, and social ties were strengthened between individuals and institutions in the border regions, resulting in a high degree of Germanization.

After the establishment of the Dual Monarchy in 1867, the Hungarian government reversed the process of Germanization. Hungary began to reestablish its supremacy by instituting far-reaching politico-administrative and educational measures. Germans and Croatians of Western Hungary offered no resistance to Magyarization. In fact, a strong "Hungarian vogue" swept through the region. Many Germans and Slavs Magyarized their names, dressed in the Hungarian style, and joined associations for the study of Hungarian culture.

But the above are not the only reasons why Burgenland's ethnographic makeup and its man-made environment still look typically Hungarian, even to Austrian writers. Both its material and non-material culture has drawn heavily upon "inland Hungary." Settlement patterns, dwelling structures, techniques of land cultivation and animal husbandry, costumes, kinship and family structure, folk customs—almost all manifestations of rural life—bear the strong impress of Hungary.[6] In spite of the fact that Western Hungary was geographically close to technologically more advanced Austria, innovations came from Central Hungary. The fact is most technological innovations arrived decades after they were introduced in Central Transdunabia. Such was the case with the use of the iron plow, the three-field system, special cultigens, and many other agricultural tools and techniques.

Thus, Hungarian cultural influence upon Germans and Slavs was profound prior to 1921. This is partially due to the mediating and organizing roles of the great Hungarian estates, whose owners and managers were predominantly Hungarian. Although Croatian peasant culture underwent a higher degree of assimilation into Hungarian cultural patterns than did the German, the German "minority" did not lag too far behind in the degree of its adaptation to the Hungarian configuration. Due to a high degree of village propinquity and commercialism, interaction among ethnic groups was intense throughout historical times.

During the past sixty years, earlier ethnic processes were reversed in favor of German influence. The most marked form of change occurred in the region's demographic makeup.[7] In 1920 Burgenland had a total population of 294,849, of which 221,185 were Germans, 44,753 were Croatians, and 24,867 were Hungarians. In 1971, of the total population of 272,119, there were 241,254 Germans, 24,526 Croatians, and 5,673 Hungarians. Both the absolute and relative losses of the minority ethnic groups were devastating. While in 1920 the Hungarians comprised 9.5 percent of Burgenland's population, in 1971 they comprised a mere 2.8 percent. The Hungarians therefore suffered a 77 percent loss of their ethnic strength. The Croatians had only a 45 percent decline during this time. It is not the purpose of the present essay to investigate the causes of this unparalleled demographic crisis, but these can be generally summed up under the following heading: emigration to the New World, rural-to-urban migration, and assimilation into Austrian society.[8]

The demographic pressure emanating from German numerical superiority ruptured many Hungarian communities in Burgenland. Today there are only four Hungarian communities extant in Burgenland. These are: Alsóőr/Unterwart, the "Upper Section" (*Felszeg*) of Felsőőr/Oberwart, Őrisziget/Siget in der Wart, and Középpulya/Mittelpullendorf. In the present essay the anthropological convention of using the local vernacular name of the village will be followed. Alsóőr, Felsőőr and Őrisziget comprise the Hungarian language island in Southern Burgenland, referred to in Hungarian as the Őrség. Felsőpulya is located approximately 45 kilometers from the Őrség, while the villages of the Őrség neighbor one another.

Contouring the right bank of the Pinka creek, Alsóőr is one of the earliest settlements in Historical Hungary.[9] Today it has a population of 845 Hungarian speakers (1973 statistics).[10] Most of the population is bilingual. Seventy-two inhabitants of the village are Gypsies, many of whom are trilingual (Hungarian-German-Romani). Although only 27.7 percent of its people farm, Alsóőr is considered an agricultural village by both outsiders and natives. The rest of the population—28.1 percent "retired peasants," 36.6 percent blue collars and 5.9 percent white collars—are also deeply enmeshed in the network of reciprocal obligations to farming. To be an *ugyis alsóőri* (native of Alsóőr) means to be Hungarian, Catholic, and to a varying extent a *paraszt* (peasant). It is little wonder that the Hungarians of Burgenland are more or less synonymous with "peasant."

Today, peasant life is under heavy attack from many sides; therefore it should not be surprising that young people are trying to escape from their parents' profession (who also urge them to leave)—and logically—from Hungarian ethnicity. However, the cost of escaping one's ethnicity is high. The individual must leave the community altogether, which requires total extrication from a multitude of unpaid obligations, which one or one's ancestors have accumulated. Few people are willing to leave debts behind, and everyone wants to return with honor. Therefore, the village has been holding onto its population fairly successfully, which is borne out by statistical evidence (see footnote 10).

Since the agriculturists comprise the heart of the village, and are under the greatest pressure to change, they deserve our closest attention. The agricultural essence of Alsóőr finds best expression in the behavior of the landholding class—an ideologically homogeneous but economically heterogeneous core group of villagers. Conservative in economic and political matters and forming a single political party, these peasants are least susceptible to the many subtle forces of urbanization and Germanization. They control political decision-making by dominating the village government; they set and maintain rules of social behavior, adhere most closely to linguistic and religious standards, and keep a highly visible profile in the daily life of the village. Three strata of this class may be distinguished: rich peasant, middle peasant, and small peasant.[11] The first two strata comprise the *alapvagyonos*, or "people with basic property," and the third make up the *szegény paraszt*, or poor peasant stratum. All practice intensive agriculture, fatten cattle and pigs for the market, and sell milk and grain. In a narrower, more technical sense, agriculturists in Alsóőr may be termed farmers, but because of their strong community orientation and traditionalism, the more appropriate anthropological term used for such producers is 'peasants' (see Wolf, 1966).

The survival of an ethnic minority is predicated upon many

conditions, some of which are "given" by the major culture, while others must be generated by the group from within. Favorable "given" conditions are seldom adequate for ethnic maintenance. If it is to survive, the minority group must cultivate a psycho-social feeling of "we" as opposed to "them." The case of the Hungarians in Burgenland demonstrates that this opposition does not necessarily rest on antagonism or inter-ethnic tension. However, it does mobilize forces and mechanisms which have evolved during the Middle Ages within the ethnic group itself and through contact with others. Many of these practices are symbolic in nature, but symbols often have greater importance for group identity than, say, forms of violence. When symbolic identification is coupled with practical actions for group cohesion, ethnic boundary maintenance is most likely ensured. The following segment will examine four such mechanisms. These are highly interrelated practices, some having greater symbolic than practical values.

For the natives of Alsóőr these "mechanisms" are taken for granted; they are integral parts of daily life in the village, and their mere listing, let along separation, would no doubt sound peculiar to the natives.

Family and kin. The primary social institution in Alsóőr (as in the other Hungarian villages) has remained intact throughout the past few turbulent decades of European social change. It is based on the patrilocal residential rule of marriage, which requires the wife to move to the house of the husband's parents. Until a few years ago a strong stigma was attached to husbands who moved to their bride's home of birth. The head of the family is the most productive male, who nowadays shares many of his previous decision-making powers with his wife. Most husbands are still the primary wage-earners. Twenty percent of the families are "extended" or "joint" families (with more than one nuclear family living together), where decision-making is even more diffuse than in the single nuclear families, due primarily to diverse sources of income. The average family consists of 4.7 individuals, a sharp decrease since the 1920's when it was 6.3.

The hold of the domestic unit upon the individual is profound. In everyday life and throughout the entire life cycle the family sets the limits of one's social actions. Mate selection, the choosing of fictive kin (*komaság* or god-parentage), friends, social, economic and political alliances, are chosen with one's family traditions in mind. Even in families where the family is not a unit of production, members spend as much time together as possible. For example, men working in neighboring towns a few kilometers away often eat lunch at home and commuting workers to Vienna return every weekend. Family obligations are numerous, ranging from agricultural tasks, in which white collar members also participate, to repaying a debt of building someone's house. One of the fundamental matters that must be solved with final family approval (in some cases with action initiated by the family) is mate selection. One's choice of mate is vigorously debated by all members of one's family and kin, long before relationships get "serious enough." The vast majority of parents prefer their children to marry within the Hungarian ethnic group. For today's East Central European standards, a remarkably high degree of village endogamy is practiced in Alsóór. Approximately half the marriages are contracted within the village, and more than two thirds are ethno-endogamous. Almost all ethno-exogamous marriages are contracted by village women. Such women usually move out of Alsóór. "Foreigners" moving into the village by marriage quickly learn Hungarian and assimilate into the culture of the Örség. Austro-Germans or Croatian brides and grooms must learn Hungarian or face social isolation and a good measure of ostracism.

Some families consider ethno-exogamous or village-exogamous marriages desirable for their children: "We have been marrying within the village for much too long. We must refresh our blood." Austro-Germans are more desirable as mates than Croatians because they are perceived as wealthier and more modern, and therefore more capable of raising the economic standard of the family. Since girls are increasingly attracted to non-peasant life styles, their preference for non-peasant foreigners is especially noteworthy. Such a person is free of the many long-accumulated obligations which are characteristic of a young adult of Alsóór. One significant condition of this outward-orientation is education. There is a direct correlation between education and exogamy. The better educated or skilled a person is, the greater the likelihood of his marrying out of the village and his ethnicity.

Although intergenerational differences have increased substantially in the past sixty years, respect for elders is still strong. This is another insurance against breaking ethnic boundaries. As one of my informants put it: "My wish for a Hungarian son-in-law is respected by my daughter." At the same time, this father admitted that a

German son-in-law would not be rejected. He added: "If she insists on marrying a *vidiki* (foreigner) so be it. But I know her. She will think about us when choosing a mate."

In addition to family-centrism, village norms dictate adherence to kinship rules, forms of address, and inheritance practices. The Hungarian kinship system is termed bilateral or cognatic, which means that approximately equal importance is attributed to one's mother's and father's relatives in both reckoning kin and in one's obligations toward them. Although the "inland" Hungarian pattern has a slight (and at times strong) patrilineal bias, the bilateral pattern of the Őrség is strictly adhered to. When inquiring about someone's descent, both mother's and father's family trees are traced, and even specific houses in which ancestors were born are identified. In sharp contrast to the pattern of the Őrség, the German and the Slavic models used by neighboring villagers are patrilineal. This means that the role of one's *agnates* (male relatives in the male line) is paramount in agricultural and social cooperation. The Hungarian model, in which one may rely on relatives on either side of the family, allows for greater flexibility and facilitates a higher degree of cooperation as well as indebtedness.

Relationships within the family are warm and intimate. The closest and most affectionate ties can be found among mothers and daughters, followed by grandparent-grandchild relationships. Since fathers are expected to be strict disciplinarians, they must project a stern and outwardly less emotional attitude toward their children. Affection between father and child is restricted to infancy and special occasions, such as confirmation, engagement and wedding.

Warm relationships between grandparents and grandchildren extend beyond the marriage of grandchildren. If they live apart from one another, the grandchildren visit grandparents at least every other day. Grandparents and parents reciprocate by "helping out" (*kisegitis*) with infants, cooking and agricultural tasks. Naturally, the more urbanized, or less agricultural a family is, the less cooperation is needed with the elderly, and the more ritualistic the interfamilial relationships become. Although intergenerational cooperation and interdependence have diminished drastically in the past sixty years, young people do not weaken their ties with their elders. On the contrary, non-economic intergenerational relationships are much more intimate than half a century ago. Freer from work than before, the elderly spend many hours around their children and grandchildren, recounting and thereby transmitting their experiences to eager listeners. Most young people can give colorful descriptions of old customs, agricultural practices, names of objects and places.[12] *Rules of land tenure and inheritance.* Ethnic erosion in the peripheral regions of historical Hungary (and sometimes in Central Hungary) was almost always accompanied by the alienation of arable land. This has been the case in Transylvania and in Southern and Northern Hungary, where ethnically homogeneous Hungarian villages were gradually mixed with Romanians, Serbs, Germans and Slovaks. At times, large demographic vacuums were left as a result of prolonged warfare. Such was the case following the Ottoman Turkish occupation of Central Hungary (1526–1686). The Habsburg rulers were quick to settle foreigners in these depopulated areas. Large numbers of Germans, Slavs and Romanians wedged themselves within the Hungarian population. This process has not stopped today in the areas once part of Hungary.

The process by which a village becomes, let us say, Romanian, is through the alienation of arable land. Interestingly, this process has seldom been violent. Characteristically a certain ethnic group "invites" members of another into a community, usually for a given economic advantage such as labor opportunities, cash, or other valuables. Thus, even when land is not donated outright by a monarch or a landlord, a village community can easily justify the presence of a strange ethnic group. Newcomers may also find entrance to a village through marriage, or by taking over a given trade or skill. The latter was in fact the case of Felsőőr, where the entire central section of the town was settled by German merchants, specialists, and government officials. The number of Germans in Felsőőr grew dramatically during the past sixty years. Hungarians today comprise barely more than one fourth of the town (a complete reversal of the demographic distribution of sixty years ago).

Until the latter part of the 19th century, Western Hungarian communities practiced three forms of land tenure. The township was divided into three sections. The first was owned by the village and referred to as the "commons," the second by the descendants of the original settlers, and called "arrow lands" (named after the method of "drawing arrows" for rotating plots), and the third was owned privately by individuals. Until the middle of the 19th century no more than one-third of the township's land was privately owned. Private plots were tiny, often too small to turn around in with a harrow, and such family estates were not valuable enough to attract outsiders.[13] By the end of the 19th century the commons were reduced by two-thirds and the arrow lands were distributed for private ownership. These lands were now subject to trading and selling, frequently to outsiders. Most of the buyers were from the neighboring Hungarian villages. They tended to be the highest bidders, since they wanted to achieve contiguity in their land holdings. The threat of foreign buyers was further minimized by the continuing practice of the Hungarian inheritance system. This practice is termed partible ideology, which assumes that all children receive equal portions of the family property regardless of age, sex and order of birth. As far as it can be ascertained from the rather poorly documented cases of the past, and from the memory culture of the elderly, unequal inheritance, such as primogeniture or ultimogeniture, was not and is not in practice in the Örség.[14]

While it is true that a strict adherence to both forms of inheritance practices, partible and impartible, will help maintain ethnic boundaries, by keeping the land within the ownership of the residents and by making it possible to pass it down to consanguineal (blood) kin successors; nonetheless, impartible inheritance, such as primogeniture, expels the nonrecipient from successful agricultural competition and denies him an opportunity to form a family within the village. When land and job opportunities are scarce, heirs not receiving a share in the family's property must leave the village. For an ethnic island such as the Örség, impartible inheritance would have accelerated assimilation into the major culture.

Within partible ideology the recipients of the divided estates face a set of conditions which are in sharp contrast to the conditions of the undivided inheritance system. Heirs receive only a portion of their elder's estate, which as in the case of Alsóór, is too small to operate successfully. They know that a land share under a certain size and soil quality is not viable as an independent farm operation. The minimum land size for unsupported subsistence operations prior to World War II was 5 *holds* (1 *hold* = 1.4 acres), and today a viable estate must exceed 10 *holds*. Yesterday's rich peasant is the middle-to-poor-peasant of today, and poor peasants have gone into other professions.

The natural process of estate fragmentation following the inheritance is thus a potential threat to economic equilibrium. Inheritors who once lived under the roof of a farm house that was in full operation are faced with the prospect of total or partial inoperability. If the elders' property was large enough or the number of heirs few enough to safeguard viability (as in the case of most rich peasants), the new owner's estate and his socioeconomic position within the village could have remained the same as those of his elders. If, however, the holding of the elders was small to begin with, as was frequent among small and medium peasants, or the number of heirs greater than the rules of viability would demand, the heirs were faced with important decisions. They had to either convert their inherited shares to other forms of wealth (i.e., house, forest, money) and seek employment outside, or look for marriage partners whose inheritance complemented theirs and thereby formed a viable holding. Theoretically, succeeding generations in this process could slide downward on the social ladder, but due to the highly disparate number of inheritors (or family size), it was always possible to keep the standing of one's family of origin by marrying a person with the "right amount of land." It was—and still is—possible for one to "marry up," thereby gaining more land than he brought into the marriage. Many conditions influenced the chances of upward mobility, such as the prestige of the family, the reputation of the individual, his diligence and shrewdness, and the potential network of consanguineal, affinal and neighborhood allies he could utilize for running a farm operation. It is true that peasant social structure in the past was rigid and the above justifications had to be made quite clear to both parties before someone moved up on the social scale, but in the cases investigated, a large percentage of marriages combined estates of unequal wealth. On the basis of the testimony of the elderly and the cadastral records, it appears that the ideal was always to match marriage partners according to their inherited wealth. Today this consideration is largely ignored because agriculturists are desperate for brides.

At present approximately half the marriages are exogamous. By far the overwhelming majority of exogamous marriges are contracted by workers, peasant-workers and members of the white collar class. Peasants, for the reasons mentioned below, would rather marry their children down than out to Austrian or Croatian villages.

Land tenure in Alsóor can be likened to the movement of an accordion. Successive generations disperse holdings through inheritance and consolidate them through marriage. The longevity of fragmented land tenure in a single generation varies considerably.

Since land division occurs after the reading of the will, already-married children who have invested labor in their parents' estate abruptly become independent. The choice is theirs to make whether to continue farming by setting up an independent operation or remaining at home with the elders. This will largely depend on the size of their share. Parents prefer to keep a son at home to care for them. A daughter-in-law obeys (*szuofogad*) better than a son-in-law who may be more disagreeable because of his highly disadvantageous position in the matrilocal marriage. In the Orség matrilocal marriage was referred to as *firhomenis*, and it carried a stigma similar to those in other regions of Transdunabia. The *firhoment* male had difficulties with his wife's *agnates*, neighbors, and the traditional allies of the farmstead of his wife's family. This situation changed significantly after the 1950's, because fewer men are now willing to be farmers.

In 1973 the largest category of viable landholdings was that of middle peasant. This group is significant not just as a statistical category. It is made up of the most conscientious, vocal and active farmers, and has the most successful operations in terms of energy investment and returns. The average middle peasant family has 2.2 children, which for purposes of land division means an almost even split of the estate. Thus, a 20-*hold*-estate would split into two estates of 10 *holds* each after inheritance. With 10 *holds*, the heirs can declare independence and attempt to manage the new holding. Until the 1950's there was strong competition among siblings for the farmstead which also included a somewhat larger share of the arable land, received in return for supporting the elders. (For practical purposes, the concept of lateral partible ideology remained only an ideal.) In Alsóőr parents were supported by their favorite child. The other heir then tried his luck in accordance with the spirit and rules of capitalistic competition, which required the pursuit of two distinct but interrelated goals. His first goal was to increase his landholding by the aforementioned process of endogamous marrige, and the second was to maneuver carefully for land consolidation. Thus, an attempt was made not only to expand holdings but also to create estate contiguity. The cultivation of widely scattered fields has been costly especially since the sudden rise of fuel costs in 1974. The best time for the consolidation of the estate is when husband and wife combine their inheritance. This intricate mission of diplomacy requires locating and convincing one's field-neighbors to trade, sell or rent their plots. All strata are equally affected by the problems of the scattered field system; they, too, need consolidation. Marrying out of the village effectively puts a stop to such a mission. People are not sympathetic to the cause of field consolidation when it is needed for a mixed marrige. "Hungarian hospitality" has its limits. Middle and poor peasants naturally need additional land after division more than rich agriculturists do. Therefore, the smaller the land holding, the greater the need for marrying within the village. This rule, of course, loses its operational value with the bottom strata of landholders, or with families with too many children.

A new goal of the not-yet-competitive heir is to mechanize his farmstead. Two alternatives are available in this area. One is to seek outside employment and leave the wife in charge of the farm. The other—less workable for Hungarians in Austria—is to marry someone from the outside possessing cash inheritance. In the latter case, which similar to that of rich peasants (see below), the problem of the *vidiki* (foreign) wife may present some obstacles in the smooth operation of the farm. Therefore, the most reasonable and widely practiced route taken by peasants wishing to be competitive will again be village endogamy. It is from the middle peasant stratum that worker-peasants emerge. They now comprise a sizable portion of Alsóőr's agricultural class.

Among the rich and the few upper-middle peasants (altogether about 20 percent of the agricultural class), there is no great need to increase holdings. In this well-to-do range marriageable people can look outside the village for a mate. Of the 196 farmsteads there are approximately 30 "fully equipped" rich farming operations which could, in theory allow for exogamous marriages without seriously endangering viability. But there are tasks requiring manual labor for which farmhands must be hired. These part-time farm laborers are usually workers' wives and retired peasants. It is the rich peasant who relies most heavily upon the labor resources of the village. More than the middle or poor peasant, the rich peasant needs to build a network of continuously available farm help to ensure the functioning of a large operation. This necessity ultimately binds together rich and poor, young, middle aged and old, in sharp contrast with past practices when cooperation reflected the divisions between the various economic strata.

In selecting a partner the rich peasant must consider his wife's personal attributes. Will she be a good partner-manager, and will she be able to deal with workers in a shrinking labor market? Can she organize and mobilize farm hands when the need arises? The farmer's wife works alongside laborers in the fields as well as on the farmstead. A German-speaking wife, no matter how efficient, will not be able to partake in conversations carried on in Hungarian during work. She will be looked upon as "the boss" or as an outsider, and will create a sterner atmosphere. Farm laborers will feel ill at ease with her. Rich peasants, like other agriculturists, want a wife from the village.

Based on the aforementioned findings, it may be concluded that village endogamy is practiced by the three land-owning strata of Alsóor for reasons other than simply to prevent ethnic pollution or to maintain the ethnic boundary between Hungarians and German-speaking Austrians. Endogamy is simply profitable and it also happens to fit into centuries-old norms. Marrying out is a luxury one cannot afford if he wants to remain a peasant. For those who want to escape the peasant lifestyle and assimilate into Austrian society, exogamous marriage is necessary. Almost all the exogamous marriages are made by members of the worker and white collar classes.

Poor peasants want to marry in the village to acquire land without cost, and to gain cooperation from their wife's relatives and friends. The middle peasant who wants to move up on the social scale needs a wife who brings more to the estate and who manages it while earning wages in industry—wages that can be used to purchase more land and machinery. The rich peasant who can afford to marry out does not do it because he relies heavily on agricultural labor which comes from the village. His wife would not fit in with his labor crews. Unlike his predecessors, the rich peasant today cooperates with various strata and age groups, bringing them closer together than they were ever before. For all three strata, consanguineal and affinal kin, friends as well as neighbors are very important, even in the age of mechanized agriculture. Their effort to acquire mates reflects their desire to improve farm operation. Theirs is a valiant struggle, taking place at a time when farming and being a peasant are low in prestige in East Central Europe.

Political control. Although Burgenland was awarded to Austria at the Paris peace treaties in 1919, it was not until 1921 that total political control was handed over to the new regime. Hungarian volunteer fighting units operated for two years in almost the entire region; stormy plebiscites were held in certain areas (i.e., in the city of Sopron, and in some South Burgenland villages); and diplomatic maneuvers to retain the region continued. But in the end the Hungarian defenses collapsed and the regional government fled to Hungary.[15]

On November 21, 1921, three hundred Austrian infantrymen marched into Alsóőr on the Lower Mill Road and camped on the Main Square in front of the Catholic church.[16] According to eyewitnesses there was no resistance from the population and the "invaders" showed a substantial measure of good will. Peasants invited soldiers for lunch, officers exchanged political ideas with their hosts. The transition of power was orderly, and people were satisfied that no blood was shed. This mutual respect characterized relationships between Austrians and Hungarians in Burgenland until the annexation of Austria by the Third Reich in 1938. Initially, Hitler's political attitude toward minorities in Austria was one of tolerance, but later, secret plans to relocate them during the invasion of the Soviet Union in the newly acquired territories leaked out and caused much consternation among the population. The deportation of Jews and Gypsies was a grim reminder of what might happen to Hungarians and Croatians as well. But other than the ban on the teaching of minority languages, the villagers felt no recriminations. Their political system remained intact while economically the village enjoyed considerable prosperity, primarily because of mechanization and the annulment of outstanding farm debts.

The post World War II Austrian political model provides for a parliamentary democracy with a multi-party system that guarantees loyal opposition. In contrast to its eastern neighbors, Austria has been willing to insure total freedom of political action for the local community. Within this system the political actor's self-perception as a free agent of socio-political power serves as a fundamental political motivating force. Village communities (as well as larger ethnic organizations) can initiate action to insure ethnic boundary maintenance, and can react to potential threats against survival. They may, in addition, form political parties, which is forbidden in a Communist country.

The village government (the Council, or *Gemeinderat*) in Austria is established by proportional representation, which in turn is based on political strength shown at national elections. The duration of service of the elected officers is five years. The head of the Council is the *bíró* (mayor), who must be elected by the Council from the victorious party. The Council supervises and carries out laws and ordinances, oversees practices of land tenure, and is in charge of general safety, traffic, public utilities, entertainment, education (theater, museums, libraries), public housing, funeral parlors, the commons, the village inn, and village-owned apartments. It also adjudicates minor disputes unworthy of court action. Although the official language of the government is German, it is seldom used. People usually mix German with Hungarian when "doing official business" at the *községháza* (townhall). In spite of the two councilmen of Eisenzicken (monolingual Germans), the combined councils of the two villages hold meetings in the Hungarian language.

There are two political parties operating in the community. Almost all agriculturists, conservative workers and the white collar class favor the *Österreichische Volks Partei* (ÖVP, commonly referred to as Blacks), while liberal workers and most white collars sympathize with the *Sozialistische Partei Österreichs* (SPÖ, called Reds). The primary reason for such a high degree of correlation between occupational groups and parties is the difference between the philosophies of the two parties. The ÖVP considers itself to be a "progressive party of the center . . . a party of progress and no experiments." In essence, the Blacks believe in balanced budgets, moderate social progams, and a powerful central government. They favor private enterprise and—a crucial factor in Austrian politics—believe in maintaining a hard line against Communism.

Most mayors run on the Black ticket, and all attempts to break this line of continuity have thus far failed miserably. The primary prerequisites for village leadership are prestige, wealth, and descent. With the exception of one mayor, all have come from families of farmers, and have been of noble descent. Only after being satisfied with these preconditions do people inquire into the candidate's leadership qualities. Let us briefly examine the concept of noble descent.

The entire western border region of historic Hungary was settled by military garrison communities between the 10th and 11th centuries. The guards, called *örök*, received privileges from the kings, which were later to be broadened into territorial nobility. The latter prevented the powerful fiefs of the Middle Ages from taking over their lands. In addition to territorial enclosure, the noble status of the őrök ensured that the line of demarcation between them and the non-noble or serf population would remain well defined, who were German and Croatian in Western Hungary. These petty noblemen continued to look upon themselves as different even after the emancipation of serfs and the erasing of noble privileges in 1848. To do this was not an easy task, since by the middle of the 19th century almost a third of the village population was of common birth. These agilisek (literally, non-noble newcomers), who settled in the Őrség for the first time in the 17th century, were allowed to form separate village councils paralleling those of the noblemen, which were responsible for the welfare of the agilisek. The tension between the two distinct political organizations within a single village was great. The agilisek wanted more from the village commons, and the noblemen wanted to exclude them from every form of economic benefit the village offered. Following the social revolution of 1848, only one village council could operate within a community. The result was that for more than a half century the agilisek and their descendants were excluded from the new village councils. This continued discrimination has modern-day implications, especially in regard to the election of mayor.[17]

Since an open insistence on noble descent is strictly prohibited by contemporary Austrian law, it can only be maintained as an unspoken norm. Under no circumstances would a villager admit the existence of this central value to an outsider. The villagers themselves rarely discuss the issue, and when the outsider inquires about it, they show some measure of embarrassment. It took many months of close association with the people, and a thorough familiarity with village norms and attitudes before the issue of nobility was raised by a non-nobleman. But even non-noblemen are reluctant to elect or support a commoner as a mayor. They refer to them as "drifters" (gyütt-ment). An exception was made when in 1971, in the absence of a noble candidate, a compromise candidate was chosen in the person of a non-nobleman. But in the next election people "regretted" their decision, and once again they elected a man of noble descent.

The party of opposition, the SPÖ, eliminated its earlier extremist elements under the leadership of Austria's Chancellor, Bruno Kreisky. This party favors a more equitable distribution of wealth, and supports social legislation. It is a party of the working man and does not champion peasant causes (e.g., it campaigns for the lowering of agricultural prices).

The growing number of blue collar workers in the village contributed to the rising popularity of the SPÖ. Membership in Alsóőr increased from a handful of voters in 1951 to almost half the electorate in 1971. There is every likelihood that the SPÖ's prestige will further increase, but it is unlikely that Black control over village politics will be relinquished in the near future.

Village politicking is strongly interwoven with local customs. The pub (kocsma) is the focal point of such activity. The most important days for such discussion are Sundays; certain evenings are also designated for party meetings. In addition, there are several village-based organizations (i.e., the Glee Club, the Volunteer Fire Association, and the Water Service Association), which offer ample time for the expression of political thought. The least formal, and most *ad hoc* political forums are the familiar East Central European street-bench-talks. The number of participants at "bench-talks" is less than five, which allows for lengthy face-to-face dialogues in the evening. Nonetheless, the kocsma's social environment remains the most appropriate forum for testing one's political strength. One's popularity is measured by the number of people accompanying him, and the degree of agreement with his opinions and pronouncements.

As we have noted, in addition to the covert prerequisite of descent, the would-be candidate's personal attirubtes of leadership are also considered crucial. First, "people must listen to him . . . they must accept his advice." Inquiries about the kind of advice one might seek resulted in an unequivocal answer: "advice regarding farming." Thus, a leader is expected to be an authority on such problems as crop usage, crop rotation, fertilizer, machines, the utilization of day-laborers, marketing, and any other topics related to agriculture.

Secondly, a leader has to be a respected person within the community. He and his family must exhibit a high moral and religious standard. He should be a good family man (preferably a grandfather), and should not be a drunkard (riszeges). Women are not interested in political leadership.

Thirdly, to qualify for leadership, a person must be smart (eszes), bordering shrewdness. A cunning person (ravasz), however, has no chances in political competition. People feel that such persons would swindle the community, embezzle funds and practice favoritism.

Finally, a good leader is a good adjudicator of disputes. He must keep in mind the needs of the community, and balance traditional norms with modern attitudes—a most challenging task for today's leaders. People in Alsóőr find this quality to be one most lacking in present-day leaders. Many informants complained about recent cases of corruption and nepotism in local politics. The typical political leader is still a wealthy farmer. The Hungarian proverb: "dogs bark but money talks" is often heard. There is a belief that only industrious and wise people can become wealthy. Of course, there is plenty of evidence to the contrary, but when it comes to electing leaders, exceptions are ignored. Poor people are poor, local belief has it, because they are lazy, dumb, or inherited "bad blood" (a fajdban van, literally: it is in one's race). Therefore poor people cannot be good advisors.

Village polity in Alsóor today has been successful in maintaining a working relationship between the two parties. The equilibrium is strong enough to sustain itself for the time being, if the larger political process in Austria remains intact. Even if there should be a sudden German or Croatian influx into the village (which is quite unlikely, given Alsóor's limited carrying capacity), the newcomers would encounter enormous opposition from the natives, who join political forces when they perceive an outside threat.

Additional factors of ethnic maintenance. There are several additional mechanisms for cultural survival whose detailed examination must be deferred to another occasion. At this time a very brief analysis must suffice. One of these mechanisms is language maintenance by Hungarians in Burgenland. This issue has been the topic of research by two Hungarian-born linguists, Samu Imre and Susan Gal. Imre is a native of Felsőőr, whose highly pedantic analyses of the öri dialect and the process of Germanization[18] identified linguistic retention, form, and admixture with German. He also made some profound observations about the problems of the assimilation of the young people of the Őrség.[19] Gal is an anthropological linguist who conducted fieldwork in Felsoor in 1974. She concluded in her highly scholarly work that linguistic erosion is first accompanied by bilingualism, and a gradual dropping of Hungarian. Language shift is the outcome of the process of urbanization, and the simultaneous erosion of peasant prestige.[20] Both scholars are pessimistic about the future of Hungarians in Felsőőr.

The examined evidence indicates, however, that in Alsóőr and Őrisziget, in spite of the great advantage of the German language in the fields of education and mass communication, Hungarian linguistic maintenance has not failed completely. The language of communication in these villages is still Hungarian in every sphere of interpersonal communication. One sign of bilingual limitation is the performance of Alsóőr's highschool children in Felsőőr's German educational institutions. There, teachers complain about Hungarian students who "cannot express themselves in German either verbally or in writing." Indeed, very few people in Alsóőr use German at home, and most middle-aged and elderly people are quite uncomfortable with it. During the second part of the fieldwork (two years following the first), this author noticed a substantial increase in Hungarian language usage among those youths who previously attempted to become German monolinguals. There was very little enthusiasm for becoming a German monolingual. The most obvious reason for this "remagyarization" is to be found in the improvement of Austro-Hungarian political relations. The stigmatization of Hungarians as "Communists" has all but vanished. Today Hungary is "a nice place to visit," where consumer prices are lower, and where rural Austrians enjoy a considerable amount of prestige. The people of the Őrség are the greatest beneficiaries of this international tourism, for they speak Hungarian and can "feel at home" in Hungary.

In the past six years a broadly-based cultural and athletic program was initiated by the two ministries of culture. Professional and amateur performers and clubs visit the Őrség from Hungary, and the Austrian-Hungarians reciprocate. These contacts have helped to rejuvenate peasant culture in the Őrség. Among those that survived are traditional rites of passage (baptismal, confirmation, wedding and funeral ceremonies), some calendrical rites (St. Nicholas, lucázás, the May-tree, and others), and various devotions to saints. More than fifty individuals go on an annual pilgrimage to Mariazell in Styria from the village, where they are received with special attention by Hungarian priests from Vienna. There they may sing ancient Hungarian religious hymns and the Hungarian national anthem.

There are examples of peasant traditions, such as folk medicine, folksongs, folk poetry and theatrical plays, which have remained in the forefront of village culture in Alsóor.[21] Plays are staged by the school principal or priest, while chorus performances are given by the Glee Club. These events are attended by the entire village.

Finally, since the 1960's, when crossing the Hungarian border became easier for Austrians, the Hungarians of Burgenland have established or rekindled ties with their ethnic relatives. Today both governments use the Hungarians of the Őrség to demonstrate their good will towards each other, and to eradicate the last vestiges of the Cold War. During the 1970's an increasing number of Hungarian workers and technocrats gained employment with Austrian firms contracted by the Hungarian government. These "ambassadors" offer a counter-example to young people wishing to assimilate into Austrian society. The message is clear: it is worthwhile to remain Hungarian.

During the past sixty years the Hungarians of Burgenland under-went dramatic demographic, economic and cultural changes. Already a small minority in 1921 their number shrank rapidly, not because of discriminatory state policies, but as a result of emigration and voluntary assimilation into the German world. One of the most intriguing and ancient ethnographic and linguistic units in Hungary, this westernmost enclave of rural people has been reduced to three villages in Southern Burgenland. Their techniques of ethnic survival emanate from a successful socio-economic adaptation to the Austrian state, which, in return, has guaranteed their minority status. Four of these mechanisms were examined here. Three of them (the family and kinship system, land tenure and inheritance prac-tices, language and folk custom maintenance) are autogenerative devices invented in earlier centuries. They are central to maintaining a clear line of ethnic demarcation between the Hungarians and other Austrians. Without a stable family, partible inheritance, linguistic maintenance, and a strong feeling of "we, the örök," the Hungarians in Austria would now be indistinguishable from the German popula-tion.

Two external conditions, the Austrian political system and relatively unrestrained travel to Hungary, have added to the success of ethnic maintenance. These favorable factors allow the individual to play the role of a free political actor, and to gain prestige by being Austria's "ambassador" to Hungary.

As long as conservative village politicians allow the youth to par-ticipate in the village polity, where they can feel effective and rele-vant, and as long as there is advantge to being a member of a minor-ity group, assimilation will be retarded.

The Austrian example demonstates how Hungarians may benefit in a host of countries that decided to embark on a policy of ethnic tolerance directed toward a people who sixty years ago represented the ruling ethnic group in the Carpathian Basin, a part of which is the land now called Burgenland.

Notes

1. For inconsistencies in Romanian census data, consult B. Satmarescu, "The Changing Demographic Structure of the Population of Transylvania." *East European Quarterly* 8 (1975):425–39; Michael Sozan, "Reply" to Romanian Research Group, "On Transylvanian Ethnicity." *Current Anthropology* 20 (1978):140–48.

2. The Austrian Census Bureau used the term *Umgangssprache* (colloquial language) for assessing ethnic minority population.

3. Anthropological fieldwork was financed by the International Research and Exchanges Board (New York).

4. For a comprehensive appraisal of Hungarians in Austria, see István Szépfalusi, *Lássátok, halljátok egymást!* [See and hear each other!] (Bern: Az Europai Protestáns Magyar Szabadegyetem, 1980); Ernő Deák, "Burgenland: a magyarság helyzete a századfordulótól napjainkig" [Burgenland: the situation of Hungrians since the turn of the century]. *Katolikus Szemle* 31 (1979):254–65.

5. For scholary assessments of the importance of the Western Hungarian frontier, see Andrew Burghardt, *Borderland* (Madison: University of Wisconsin Press, 1962), pp. 57–161; Hansgerd Göckenjan, *Hilfsvölker im mittelalterlichen Ungarn* (Wiesbaden: Franz Steiner, 1972), pp. 1–22; Alfred Schmeller, *Das Burgenland* (Salzburg: St. Peter, 1974), pp. 9–39; Ladislaus Triber, ed., *Die Obere Wart* (Oberwart: Tyrolia, 1977), pp. 77–257; Harald Prickler, *Burgen und Schlösser im Burgenland* (Wien: Birken Verlag), pp. 5–11.

6. Burgenland's traditional material culture as reflected in agricultural implements found in Alsóor during the 1950s and 1960s, are thoroughly analyzed by Károly Gaál, *Zum Bäuerlichen Gerätebestand im 19. und 20. Jahrhundert* (Wien: Herman Böhlaus, 1969), pp. 1–29.

7. See *Österreichischen Statistischen Zentralamt* (Wien, 1951, 1961, 1971).

8. Consult Deák, pp. 257–59.

9. Consult Márton Kovács, *A felsőőri magyar népsziget* [The Hungarian ethnic island of Felsőőr]. (Budapest: Sylvester, 1942), pp. 11–29; Ernö Wallner, "A felsoorvidéki magyarság települése" [The settlement pattern of the region of Felsőőr]. *Földrajzi Közlemények* 54 (1926):1–5.

10. The following figures express Alsóor's demographic trend: 1910: 1464; 1951: 989; 1961: 916; 1971: 847 (Peter Csoknyai, "Statistische Daten" in

Ladislaus Triber ed., *Die Obere Wart* (Oberwart: Tyrolia, 1977), p. 302.

11. Socioeconomic differentiation of Alsóor's households utilizing land size as an index of status:[a]

peasants	before 1945[b]	after 1945[c]
"rich"	10-20 holds[d] (4%)	20-100 holds (16%)
"middle"	5-9 holds (30%)	10-19 holds (24%)
"poor"	0-4 holds (66%)	0-9 holds (60%)
	total: 100%	total: 100%

a. The terms "rich," "middle," and "poor" are of local usage and the size of the land associated with them is computed from the responses of 45 informants.
b. Percentages for 1925 are from Wallner, p. 19.
c. Percentages for after 1945 are from the village records, gathered by Josef Bertha, Notary.
d. One *hold* equals 1.4 acres.

12. I visited the local ethnographic museum on many occasions, accompanied by teenagers who could easily identify several hundred implements by name, which were long out of use. They are also familiar with most field names in Alsóör and with the Hungarian names of villages and towns in Southern Burgenland.

13. As can be readily understood, there were many people who owned larger tracts and sold them at a high profit to outsiders, or set up their son-in-laws in fragmented estates. Such deals can be found in the earliest commercial transaction documents dating from the 17th century.

14. One of my more knowledgeable elderly informants, S.J., gave the following account of the late 19th century: "Every child received an equal portion of land and everything else when the father reached the age of immobility. Some fathers favored one of the children. This child received better or more land. Often the children divided the wealth after the death of their father with much bickering. The person who was chosen to take care of the elderly received more than others."

15. For a representative Austrian interpretation, see Richard Berczeller and Norbert Leser, *Mit Österreich verbunden* (Vienna and Munich: Jugend und Volk Verlagsgesellschaft, 1975), 368-74, and for a Hungarian one, see Katalin Sós, *Burgenland az europai politikában* [Burgenland in European politics]. (Budapest: Akadémiai Kiadó, 1971), pp. 135-60.

16. Karl Seper, *Unterwarter Heimatbuch* (Graz: Druck Leykam AG, 1976), p. 58.

17. The "noble clans" (*nemesi törzsek*) are well known to the villagers, and they are distinguished from the non-noble clans (*nem nemes törzsek*) on the basis of the *Book of Clans* (*Törzskönyv*) kept in the Notary's office for anyone's inspection.

18. Samu Imre, *A felsőöri földmüvelés* [Agriculture in Felsőör]

(Debrecen: Dolgozatok a M. Kir. Ferenc József Tudományegyetem Magyar Nyelvtudományi Intézetéből, 3, 1941); *Német kölcsönszók a felsőőri magyarság nyelvében* [German loan words in the Hungarian dialect of Felsőőr] (Kolozsvár: Dolgozatok a M. Kir. Ferenc József Tudományegyetem Magyar Nyelvtudományi Intézetéből, 13, 1943); *A felsőőri nyelvjárás* [The dialect of Felsőőr] (Budapest: Akadémiai Kiadó, 1971).

19. Imre Samu, "Ausztriai (burgenlandi) magyar szórványok." [Scattered Hungarians in Austria (Burgenland)], *Népi Kultúra-Népi Társadalom 7* (1973), pp. 126–30.

20. Gal's conclusions are the following:

Conversational language-switching, while being a step in language change, is, at the same time, also an instrument of the social change that language shift reflects. In conversational language-switching, the opposing values and differential prestige of the peasant and urban ways of life are symbolically juxtaposed; the social contrast is thereby implicitly equated with some interpersonal contrast in the immediate conversation. For instance, when in the midst of a disagreement conducted in Hungarian, one speaker switches to German, the effect is to imply that the German statement should win in the interpersonal conflict just as the way of life it symbolizes dominates in the social sphere (Gal, Susan, *Language Shift* (New York: Academic Press, 1979), p. 174.

21. Károly Gaál, *Spinnstubenlieder* (Münich: Schnell und Steiner, 1966), pp. 11–32.

Andrew Ludanyi

The Hungarians of Transylvania

The objective of the present study is to provide a capsule presentation, an overview, of the fate of the Hungarians in Transylvania since the Treaty of Trianon. The fate of the Hungarians in Transylvania deserves our attention since their fate is closely intertwined with the rest of East Central Europe. Ethnic animosities in this area have been the cause of a number of major conflicts. Because the Hungarians compose the largest minority population in the area, their treatment affects the international relations of most states in Eastern Europe, but particularly that of the USSR, Romania, Yugoslavia, Czechoslovakia and Hungary.[1]

Transylvania includes the territory that lies east of present-day Hungary and Yugoslavia and west and north of the former provinces of Moldavia and Wallachia (the latter is divided into Muntenia and Oltenia today) which had composed the "old" kingdom of Romania prior to World War I. (See maps for the geographic location and limits of Transylvania.) Transylvania (including the Crisana, Maramures and part of the Banat) is 39,903 square miles (102,787 square kilometers) in size. In the present study all of the above area will be referred to as Transylvania, since in the popular mind "historical Transylvania" has been grouped together with the Crisana (Partium) the Banat and the Maramures (Máramaros) by the Hungarians as the territory lost to Romania through the Treaty of Trianon following World War I and by the Romanians as the new areas acquired on the "other" (i.e., western and northern) side of the Carpathian mountain range. The name Transylvania itself means "land beyond the forest." This is the name by which the area is known internationally, while the Hungarians call it "Erdély" (wooded land), the Romanians call it "Ardeal" and the Transylvanian Saxons refer to it as "Siebenbürgen." (In the future, when reference is made to specific areas in Transylvania, the present

The paper was presented at the twelfth national convention of the American Association for the Advancement of Slavic Studies, in Philadelphia, on November 8, 1980.

Romanian name will be given first, followed by the Hungarian name enclosed in parentheses.)

The treatment of ethnic minorities in Transylvania has a long and varied history. To understand the present Communist Romanian approach to this problem, it will be necessary to examine this background. We will do just that by tracing the development of nationality conflicts to the eve of Communist ascendancy.

The area of Transylvania has been settled since time immemorial. We cannot determine the ethnic or linguistic affiliations of these earliest inhabitants, but we do have archaeological evidence which points to human habitation in this area at least by 150,000 B.C. Archaeological evidence also points to a number of succeeding forms of human existence from the stone age, through the bronze age and iron age, right down to the present computer age.

The earliest archaeologically identifiable peoples who inhabit this area are the Scythians, the Celts, and the Thracians, in roughly this order. The control of any of these peoples over the area must have been somewhat tenuous. At any rate, the emergence of a rudimentary Dacian political system extended its sway over the area of present-day Transylvania in the 1st century B.C. A Dacian political community continued to exist until the Roman empire conquered the area in 106 A.D. Roman rule over it collapsed under the pressure of the *Völkerwanderung* in 271 A.D. What followed was a succession of conquering peoples, none of which held sway over the area for too long. Goths, Vandals, Huns, Gepids, Longobards and Avars followed one another as overlords. Only the Avars seemed to hold the region for a significant length of time. After their defeat by Charlemagne, the area fell under Bulgarian control, until the Hungarians appeared on the scene in 896 A.D.

From 896 A.D. Transylvania's destiny was linked to the medieval Hungarian state until a little after the battle of Mohács, more specifically, until the fall of Buda in 1541. Then Ottoman Turkish (1541–1594, 1610–1698) and Austrian Habsburg (1594–1610, 1699–1867) forces invaded the Carpathian Basin. Under their respective dominance Transylvania led a more or less independent existence, under Hungarian leaders, who acknowledged the "guardianship," alternately, of the Ottoman Empire and that of the Habsburgs.[2] Between 1867 and 1918 Hungary regained control over the region. However, in 1918, the Romanians obtained it with Entente support, and ruled it until 1940. Then Hungary regained the northern two-fifths of Transylvania briefly until the end of the war. After the collapse of Hungary in the war, Romania gained, through Allied intercession, possession of all of Transylvania.

During Transylvania's long and colorful past, its demography underwent great changes.[3] In particular, the Turkish occupation of Hungary, followed by Austrian hegemony, drastically altered its ethnic composition. While at the end of the 15th century the Carpathian Basin was overwhelmingly Hungarian (75–80 percent), by the end of the 18th, the Hungarians composed less than 50 percent of the population.[4] This radical change was a result of the phenomenal decimation of the Hungarian population during the struggle against the Turks, as well as of the subsequent Habsburg policy of colonizing the depopulated and war-devastated areas with non-Hungarians.[5] The non-Hungarian composition of certain areas of the country was also enhanced by a less systematic and artificial process: the great influx of refugees from Turkish oppression. Most of these refugees settled in Transylvania and Southern Hungary (i.e., the present Vojvodina).

Following the Turkish retreat from East Central Europe, the most far-reaching changes in demographic structure were to be found in Transylvania and Southern Hungary.[6] In Transylvania the Romanians now composed a greater segment of the population than all three of the historic "nations" combined.[7] To this day the Romanians have maintained and increased their numerical majority in the area. Yet, this is only part of the story. For while Romanians compose the overall majority, many geographic subdivisions of Transylvania are in turn overwhelmingly or significantly Hungarian or German. This is the case in the border strip adjacent to present-day Hungary and the Székely districts in the eastern corner of the province.[8]

For the evaluation of the recent ethnic composition of Transylvania, a number of census results are available. While each one of these statistical sources is biased in one way or another, it is possible to get a fairly good idea of the present ethnic composition of Transylvania by referring to all of them. Table I presents the population of Romania and Transylvania according to the census results of the last 70 years.

What the data of Table I fails to show is the geographical distribution of the various nationalities. To find out where the Hungarians or Germans are strongest, it is necessary to examine the area's population statistics on the regional, or county level. An examination

TABLE I. * The Population of Romania and Transylvania According to Nationality (in thousands)

Nationality	1910	1920	1930	1948	1956	1966	1977
Transylvania							
Romanians	2,830	2,930	3,208	3,752	4,081	4,559	—
Hungarians	1,664	1,306	1,353	1,482	1,616	1,597	—
Germans	565	539	544	331	372	372	—
Jews	182	181	178	30	30	14	—
Others	201	337	444	197	170	178	—
Total	5,260	5,112	5,549	5,792	6,232	6,720	—
Romania							
Romanians	10,524	13,186	11,360	13,598	15,081	16,746	19,002
Hungarians	1,823	1,362	1,553	1,500	1,654	1,620	1,706
Germans	829	593	636	344	395	383	358
Jews	820	873	260	139	34	43	22
Ukrainians	1,032	576	45	38	68	55	54
Bulgarians	340	261	64	14	13	11	—
Turks	222	174	43	29	35	18	—
Slovaks & Czechs	25	32	42	35	25	32	—
Yugoslavs	66	53	47	45	43	44	41
Tatars	32	35	—	—	—	22	—
Gypsies	—	—	90	53	67	64	—
Others	126	133	141	78	74	65	—
Total	15,723	17,641	14,281	15,873	17,489	19,103	21,559

*Based on table in Appendix B of *Transylvania: The Roots of Ethnic Conflict* to be published by Kent State University Press in 1983.

of this sort reveals that the western parts of the Crisana, Banat, and Maramures have a heavy Hungarian population. As has already been noted, this makes the Romanian border strip adjacent to Hungary, predominantly Hungarian in population.[9]

Other areas where the non-Romanian elements are strong are the cities, the old "Saxon" and the more recent Swabian settlements, and the compact Hungarian Székely area in the eastern corner of Transylvania. Until recently, the Jewish settlements in the Maramures were also significant. But there are numerous other settlements of Jews, Germans and Hungarians scattered throughout the whole of Transylvania. In the western Banat, besides Germans and Hungarians there are also many Serbs. In general, the Hungarians and Germans inhabit the river valleys and the lowlands, while the Romanians compose the bulk of the population in the mountainous areas, and the Jews form an important segment of some urban populations.[10]

Since World War II, some changes have taken place in the ranks of the non-Romanian ethnic groups, particularly among the Germans and the Jews.[11] These changes were due to the dislocations of the war, including deportations, territorial transfers and exterminations. The net result of these changes has been that only the Hungarians remain as a strong minority (although they too have been weakened), and the predominant role of the Romanians further increased.

The Hungarians of Transylvania did not suffer deportation, extermination or encouraged emigration; the stagnation of their population figures requires some other explanation. Is it due to forced or voluntary assimilation, to low birthrate or to falsification of census results? The aggressive nationalism of most Romanian administrations since 1918–20 would seem to suggest that all of the above have been contributing factors. At least one significant study on the population profile of Transylvania has made the claim that the Hungarians are not reported accurately in the Romanian census. According to Satmarescu's study of 1975,[12] the actual number of Hungarians in Transylvania is definitely over two million, and is perhaps closer to 2.3 million than to the 1.6 million indicated in the official statistics. Whatever the case may be, the present study will focus on this minority, and reflect on nationalities policies as they have emerged under the Romanian version of "proletarian internationalism."

On the basis of the foregoing, we can give the following profile of the Hungarians of Transylvania. They are first of all a large minority of over two million, who constitute 25–38 percent of the population in Transylvania and anywhere from 7–9.5 percent of Romania's total population. They live throughout Transylvania and constitute the major part of the population along the Western border strip and in the Székely counties. They differ from the Romanian majority not only linguistically (Uralic vs. Latin-Slavic) but also culturally and religiously (they are Roman Catholic, Calvinist or Unitarian as opposed to Romanian Orthodox). More recently social-economic differentiation has become more and more apparent, with Hungarians occupying the lower strata in the Transylvanian class system. This is a complete reversal of roles, since prior to 1918 the Hungarians were in a more advantageous position economically. This reversal of roles is also apparent when one considers the nationality of persons in significant policy-making positions both in the CPR and in government administration on both the local and national levels.

Recent history and the communist ascendancy in Romania can, in part, explain the present fate of this significant European minority. The rise of nationalism in the early part of the 19th century is probably the source of the conflicts that are again becoming all too apparent. In the early 19th century, the Hungarians felt threatened by the large number of non-Hungarians in their domain and they began to sponsor programs that would make Transylvania, as well as all of Hungary, more Hungarian. The South Slavs and the Romanians reacted violently to this policy. When the Hungarians sought to throw off the yoke of Habsburg absolutism in 1848–49, most Serbs, Croats and Romanians sided with the latter. This confirmed Magyarizers' belief that Vienna had been successful in playing the game of divide and conquer.[13] It inspired them to redouble their effort to assimilate the national minorities. What many of these individuals failed to realize was that the minorities by this time also had a taste of the nationalism inspired by the French Revolution.[14] This was particularly true for the Serbs of southern Hungary and the Romanians of Transylvania.[15]

Since Hungary was unsuccessful in its war for independence, it was placed under direct Austrian administration in 1849. However, in 1867 Austria and Hungary buried their differences and the nationalities had to seek a *modus vivendi* with the Hungarians.[16] This paved the way to Magyarization. Among some nationality groups it met with little or no resistance.[17] But among the Romanians, Serbs and Croats, the policy provoked resistance.[18] The national consciousness of these ethnic groups had already "crossed the Rubicon." Many of them could no longer look on themselves as "Hungarians of Romanian or Slavic ancestry." At any rate, the First World War interfered with the realization of the dream of a Hungarian nation-state within historic boundaries. The Austro-Hungarian defeat brought about the collapse and disintegration of the empire.[19] The disintegration, supposedly a consequence of putting into practice the principles of self-determination, actually resulted in the emergence of a totally fragmented East Central Europe. The Treaty of Trianon legalized the subsequent political chaos.[20] The fragments, the new nation-states, provided the setting for the next twenty years of Europe's confused and heated political history.

Transylvania became the object of dispute between Romanians and Hungarians. This phase of European and Romanian-Hungarian history reflects best the bourgeois nationalism so frequently denounced by today's Communist ideologues. According to them, this was the age when nationalism pushed into the background all ideas of social reform, and diverted the attention of all to narrow and nationalist aims.

The ensuing twenty years did, indeed, see a no-holds-barred struggle of nationalisms. The foreign policy of Hungary was carried on in direct response to the injustice of the Treaty of Trianon.[21] All Hungarians hoped for the day when this detested treaty would be revised. Revisionism became, in effect, the heartfelt desire of a nation.[22] This was opposed by no less fervently held Romanian policies, which had as their guiding star the rigid preservation of the *status quo*.[23] The formation of the Little and the Balkan Entente are but two manifestations attesting to the attempts of Romania and other satisfied powers to perpetuate the existing state of affairs.[24]

In the greatly enlarged post-World War I Romania, the position of the Hungarians underwent a drastic change. From a position of most favored they were pushed into the position of least favored. Their treatment was, of course, tied directly to both domestic and foreign policy developments.

As part of France's defense structure of the *status quo*, the enlarged Romania was placed in direct opposition to Hungary and Bulgaria. This opposition did not have to be encouraged since Romania had gained territories at the expense of both Hungary and Bulgaria. The latter countries desired a revision of these gains. In the face of such desires Romania looked to France and other satisfied countries, like Czechoslovakia and Yugoslavia, for assistance.

Events in Transylvania became entangled with world events as Europe moved into World War II. As power relationships altered, political changes gained momentum in East Central Europe. Hungary saw in these changes an opportunity to regain Transylvania. With the collapse of the Little Entente, Romania found itself isolated between unfriendly Bulgaria, Hungary and the USSR. From each of these countries it had gained extensive territories after World War I. These countries demanded a restoration of their territories by Romania. Following the outbreak of World War II the USSR confronted it with a demand for the Bukovina and Bessarabia, while Bulgaria demanded Dobruja, and Hungary wanted the return of Transylvania.[25] The cessions of Bukovina, Bessarabia and Dobruja went relatively smoothly.[26] The cession of the former two to the USSR, however, drove Romania into the arms of Germany.[27] It sought German support against the demands for Transylvania. By 1940, war was threatening between Hungary and Romania over this question.[28] This, Hitler wanted to prevent at all cost, since he was just preparing to launch the attack on the USSR. Moreover, for this attack he needed access to the Romanian oil fields as well as peace between his lesser allies. He asked Romania and Hungary to solve their problems peacefully by negotiating their differences.[29] When these talks broke down, Hungary threatened military action in spite of Hitler. At this point, King Carol II of Romania asked for an arbitral decision from the Axis powers.[30] The result of that decision was the Second Vienna Award.

Although this Award was a compromise, neither Romania nor Hungary was completely satisfied. Hitler used these dissatisfactions to urge the two countries on to greater efforts in the war against the USSR. He dangled before their eyes the prospect of the loss or gain of more territory according to their performance in the war.[31] This tactic was by no means used only by Hitler. Stalin, in particular, had approached the Hungarians on more than one occasion before and during the war, to convince them that cooperation would mean territorial gains later.[32] The Allies, too, were aware of the bargaining importance of Transylvania's future. They succeeded in approaching Romania with the promise of this territory.[33]

Romania did, in fact, switch sides as the armies of Germany were pressed back on every front. The defection came on August 23, 1944, after the Allies promised to give Transylvania "or the greater part thereof" to the Romanians.[34] However, this also required that they join the Allies in expanding the war against the still active German and Hungarian forces. This, too, was done. Thus, Romania gained the support of the Allies, which was to mean so much at the Conference table following World War II.

In the immediate post-war period, the Hungarians in Transylvania fared much better than their co-nationals in Yugoslavia or Czechoslovakia. This was due, in large part, to post-war Soviet policies. To be more specific, the Soviet occupation had different consequences for the various countries within its expanded empire. Two factors, in particular, determined the varying nature of the Soviet occupation. These were the former enemy status of conquered Hungary and occupied Romania, and their non-Slavic ethnic composition. It's true that the Peace Treaties transferred Transylvania *in toto* to Romania in return for its belated support of the Allies,[35] but the Soviet Union did not give something for nothing. Besides the reward for past defection, which was now past history and useless to the Soviets, Stalin seemed to have seen the transfer of northern Transylvania as an avenue toward the rapid communization of Romania.

The attitude of Soviet occupation authorities in Transylvania seemed to support the contention that the transfer was more than mere gratitude for Romania's defection. For one thing, the Red Army held on to northern Transylvania and administered it until the spring of 1945, when the Groza government came to power.[36] This reduced the number of atrocities that took place, since the Soviet troops defended the Hungarian inhabitants of the area against the revenge-seeking Romanians. The Soviets were motivated not so much by compassion as by their desire to utilize the Hungarian ethnic element to hasten the incorporation of Romania into the Soviet sphere.[37] The Hungarians had little choice but to acquiesce to such Soviet pressures.[38]

Thus, the national minorities were skillfully utilized by Stalin to weaken the anti-Communist forces in Romania and to enable his puppets to seize power.[39] Using the policy of *divide et impera*, playing nationality against nationality, Stalin attained his aim. His success was due in no small measure to the nearsighted and narrow revenge-seeking attitude of some democratic Romanian leaders. It was their hate and intolerance that drove the Hungarians in desperation to support Groza, whose "proletarian internationalism," they believed, would defend them against the excesses of "bourgeois nationalism."

Communist ascendancy in Romania resulted in a complete reformulation of the nationalities question on the basis of Marxist-Leninist nationalities theory.[40] This changed ideological context provided Romania with new guidelines for the treatment of its Hungarian and other minorities. Henceforth, the ethnic minorities of Romania were guaranteed an existence which was national in form, but socialist in content.

Until Stalin's death, satellite leaders simply mimicked Soviet nationalities policies as well as constitutional forms.[41] However, as de-Stalinization unfolded within the bloc, the Soviet pattern was remolded to fit the national peculiarities of each state. This process affected both the ideological and the constitutional context of nationality policies in Romania.

The Communists in Romania immediately applied the national form and socialist content of Soviet nationality policy. As in the Soviet Union, the reason for adopting this policy in Romania was closely tied to considerations of power seizure and power consolidation. The policy attempted to popularize the Communist Party among the country's national minorities. It entailed the guaranteed right to use their language in public discourse, in education and in their relations with the government. It also guaranteed equality with the Romanians in political, social and economic relations. In fact, in the Sacuesc (Székely) districts it even provided for autonomy in line with the Soviet example.[42]

The development of the national cultures of the respective minorities is also guaranteed. This right of nationality groups is sanctioned as long as it is provided with a socialist content. To this end, the constitution provides the national minorities with the guarantee of "the free use of their own language, tuition of all categories in their own language, and books, newspapers, and theatres in their own language."[43] It also obligates the Romanian state to ensure "the development of the culture of the Romanian people and of . . . the national minorities . . ."[44] While these guarantees are supposed to apply throughout Transylvania (throughout Romania for that matter), they have been applied in practice mainly in the Mures-Hungarian Autonomous Region (prior to 1960 called Hungarian Autonomous Region and since January 1968 called Harghita and Covasna counties).[45] See map at the end of the book.

Parallel to these cultural rights, the Hungarians are also guaranteed equal treatment before the law irrespective of "nationality or race."[46] This is underscored by the stipulation that judicial procedure "in the regions and districts inhabited by a population of another nationality than Romanian, the use of the mother tongue of that population is assured."[47] Those unfamiliar with the language of the judicial proceedings are guaranteed an interpretation and a summary in their own language.[48]

Romania's legal definition of the place of minorities is anything but clear. Nonetheless, certain tendencies are apparent in its constitutional development. The constitutional metamorphosis represents a more thorough integration of the Hungarians into the life of the country as a whole. It also represents a diminution of their ability to defend their cultural heritage by referring to constitutional guarantees. The Socialist Constitution of 1965, provides them with no autonomy and negligible self-government. It places them within the framework of a unitary and indivisible state, which provides them with some generalized guarantees of nationality rights. These rights, in turn, are counterbalanced by restrictions and obligations that make the original guarantees almost meaningless.

The evolution of constitutional law in the direction of less tolerance, followed closely those international and domestic events which reinforced Romanian nationalism. On the international front we already noted that the events of 1956–58 were particularly critical. On the domestic scene the most important developments concerned the changing nationality profile of the Romanian communist party leaders and the party rank and file. The most dramatic development having long-range effects on the position of Transylvania's Hungarian inhabitants was the rapid growth of the CPR following the seizure of power.

The rapid growth of the Party, particularly in the years up to 1948, drastically altered its ethnic make-up. This growth relegated the ethnic minority Party members, who in the past composed the bulk of the CPR, into a secondary position as Party ranks were swelled by ethnic Romanians who had seen the handwriting on the wall.[49]

The rapid post-war growth of the Party was the first major step toward its Romanization. After 1948, however, the CPR stabilized its membership and carried out purges among elements which it regarded as unhealthy. Even these purges, however, caused the greatest damage not in the ranks of the newly-recruited ethnic Romanians, but in the ranks of the veteran ethnic minority Communists.[50] Thus, both the growth and the purges of the Party contributed to the strengthening of the ethnic Romanian sectors of the CPR. The most recent increases in Party membership have even further accentuated this trend.[51] At present, the regime's search for popularity among the masses has allowed it to lower its standards for membership. This has enabled many to join who are ignorant of, if not hostile to, the tenets of proletarian internationalism and to the traditional policies of minority tolerance which had prevailed prior to this growth in Party membership.

The examination of the fate of the Hungarians in Transylvania provides an opportunity to reflect on the nature of present-day Romania's actual objectives relative to the largest minority within their state jurisdiction. On a theoretical level we can project minority policies on a continuum from most tolerant to least tolerant. At the intolerant end of the spectrum is the policy of physical extinction or genocide (e.g., Hitler's "final solution"). Close on its heels would be a policy that excludes, by expulsion or deportation, unwanted peoples (e.g., Germans from East Prussia following World War II and Chinese from Vietnam in the wake of the war in Cambodia). Another form of exclusion would be to isolate the minority within society and reduce to a minimum its contact with the rest of society (e.g., Jewish ghettos, apartheid in South Africa). Still another way to treat minorities is to extinguish them culturally through a policy of acculturation or assimilation (e.g., Russification, Magyarization, Romanization), which seeks to absorb the minority into the national community in such a way that the minority will abandon its own identity for the identity of the majority nationality. A fourth alternative is to fuse or integrate the minority with the majority, to create a union that is more than its component parts (e.g., U.S.A., Canada). The fifth or most tolerant alternative is to assert that unity and diversity can complement one another. In the latter instance unity is assured by providing security for diversity (e.g., Switzerland), implying active state support for both minority and majority interests.

Romanian policies toward the Hungarians of Transylvania were initially guided by the spirit of proletarian internationalism imposed by Stalin. It envisaged a relationship between Romanians and Hungarians which would not necessitate the abandonment of their respective national cultures. It demanded only that the two peoples live together within one state as co-inhabiting nationalities, struggling shoulder to shoulder to defeat the forces of reaction and inaugurate the new socialist millenium. This definition of the place of the Transylvanian Hungarians made them partners of the majority nationality.[52] They were given every opportunity to preserve their cultural identity, as long as they supported the process of Socialist transformation and the Soviet Union's hegemonial interests. These opportunities were spelled out both in the country's ideological commitments and its constitutional objectives. Until October 1956, these opportunities were also put into practice. Schools, publications, policies relating to the Hungarian Autonomous Region reflected the integrationist approach.

Changes in Romania's internal and external political relations have turned it away from the integrationist solution. In the years between 1952–1967, the CPR lost its cosmopolitan character and became, both in membership and leadership, primarily an ethnic Romanian organization. This ethnic Romanization of the Party paralleled the period of de-Stalinization in the bloc, which loosened Soviet hegemonial controls. The Hungarian Revolt of 1956 led to unrest among the Hungarians in Transylvania. This made the Hungarians suspect in the eyes of both Romanian and Soviet policymakers. Romanian efforts to help quell this unrest, as well as the Hungarian revolution itself, increased Soviet confidence in Romania's dependability to such an extent that in 1958 all Soviet troops were removed from the country. This military withdrawal gave Romanian leaders more control over their internal policies. By the beginning of the 1960's they also gained more control over their foreign relations as the Soviet Union became more and more embroiled in its ideological and political dispute with China.

By 1963, Romanian policies began to reflect openly the country's more nationalist orientation both internally and in the international arena. Defiance of COMECON integration efforts was one evidence of this new Romanian nationalism on the international front. Internally, the shift to an assimilationist nationality policy became its most concrete expression. The reduction of Hungarian educational and cultural opportunities, as well as their symbolic self-government in the Mures-Hungarian Autonomous Region, reflected the new Romanian socialist patriotism on the domestic front. Only at the end of 1968, following the Czechoslovak crisis, did Romanian assimilationist policies slacken in momentum. Thus, Romanian nationality policy can be summarized as integrationist from 1945 to 1958,[53] and assimilationist since the withdrawal of Soviet troops. Briefly, from 1968 to 1972, it returned to an integrationist posture. However, since 1973, the policies in Transylvania have again become assimilationist.

In the context of this brief study it is impossible to assess the entire spectrum of discrimination which currently weighs on the Hungarians of Transylvania. Other assessments are available, including the classic study by Robert R. King, on *Minorities Under Communism* (1973),[54] and the recent collection of personal testimonies published under the title, *Witnesses to Cultural Genocide: Reports on Rumania's Minority Policies* (1980).[55] Instead of attempting to portray the whole range of shortcomings in Romanian nationality policies, I will focus only on the area of education for this is the most critical area. A brief summary of developments regarding minority educational opportunities will give a taste of the treatment of the Hungarians, and enable us to categorize prevailing minority policies in Transylvania.

Although much of the information on this sensitive area has been available for some time, the Helsinki Final Act (1975) and the debate concerning human rights has flushed out a number of significant testimonies on the question, including the 1977 summer revelations of Károly Király, a former high-ranking Hungarian member of the Romanian Communist Party.

As we noted above, the fate of the Hungarians from 1945 to 1953–56 was—in terms of minority-majority relations—in many ways better or equal to the fate of their co-nationals in Yugoslavia or Czechoslovakia. The Hungarian Revolution of 1956, however, changed all this.

Using the revolution and the parallel disturbances in Transylvania as a pretext, the Romanian Ministry of Education initiated and is now actively pursuing educational policies which are designed to reduce and eventually eradicate all forms of national particularism and isolationism.[56] These policies were to achieve their goal by stressing socialist content rather than national form in education.[57] While the national form was hedged in and carefully limited, the new designs to de-emphasize national form entailed curbs on the presentation, and reduction in the content, of curricula. In content, more emphasis fell on Romanian subjects and less stress on those which are of more particular relevance to national minorities. The most outstanding feature of minority education in Transylvania has been the appearance of parallelization. Though parallelization has always played a part in the educational process, it has become particularly important since 1956.[58] Parallelization means the setting-up of Romanian language classes parallel with the existing minority language classes. This is done even in areas where there is only one Romanian student to attend them. The primary purpose is to induce minority students to leave their own schools and classes to attend the schools and classes of the majority nationality. This policy reduces, in the long-run, the existence of the nationality schools. What happens is that one minority school after another is closed because there are supposedly not enough pupils to attend them.[59] Until 1973, the law required a minimum of 15 minority students per grade to justify classes in the minority language at that level in any school district. Since then the minimum has been raised to 25 students.

Thus, the parallel schools and sections were set up to absorb the students of the minority schools, after they have been pressured into deserting the latter.[60]

As the national minority schools lose students to the parallel Romanian institutions, the government closes the former and replaces them by nationality sections, which are then attached to the formerly parallel Romanian institutions. In this way the parallel Romanian schools become the only schools for the minority as well as the majority.

This policy has steadily reduced the number of independent educational institutions of the nationalities—increasing the nationality sections attached to the Romanian institutions.[61] Parallelization is then followed by the progressive curtailment and reduction of the nationality section, until it too becomes indistinguishable from the rest of the new parent school either in curriculum or in staff.[62] Decree/Law 278 of 1973 has accelerated this discriminatory policy even further by requiring that there must be a minimum of 25 students per grade on the elementry level and 36 students per grade on the high school level to maintain or establish instruction in the language of any minority in any given school system.[63]

The result of these policies has been to reduce Hungarian educational opportunities by 50 percent between 1956 and 1978. As Table II indicates, the proportion of those allowed to be educated

TABLE II.

Preschool Education	1955/1956	1974/1975	1977/1978
All Students	275,433	770,016	837,884
In Hungarian Classes	38,669	52,765	52,580
% in Hungarian Classes	14.4%	6.8%	6.3%
Primary and Secondary Education			
All Students	1,603,025	2,882,109	3,145,046
In Hungarian Classes	152,234	160,939	170,945
% in Hungarian Classes	9.5%	5.6%	5.4%
High School of General Culture			
All Students	129,135	344,585	813,732
In Hungarian Classes	10,370	19,050	29,028
% in Hungarian Classes	8.0%	5.5%	3.5%
Vocational Education			
All Students	123,920	615,876	
In Hungarian Classes	7,585	8,974	N/A
% in Hungarian Classes	6.1%	1.5%	

in Hungarian has dropped overall from 14.4 percent in 1956 to 6.3 percent in 1978. In primary education the drop in this same period was from 9.5 percent to 5.4 percent, while in high schools it dropped from 8.0 percent to 3.5 percent and in vocational schools from 6.1 percent to less than 1.5 percent already as of 1974–75. (The chart at the end of the book presents this reduction in a more graphic fashion.)[64] In a political system where everything follows a plan, this dramatic shift cannot be explained away with reference to student choice.

Parallelization has also affected universities and higher institutions. In fact, it is on the level of higher education that this policy most clearly reveals the attempt to Romanianize and to assimilate.[65] During the period of "proletarian internationalism,"[66] the Hungarian minority had its own independent Bolyai University at Cluj (Kolozsvár), its Medical and Pharmaceutical Institute in Tîrgu-Mures (Marosvásárhely), its István Szentgyörgyi School for the Dramatic Arts in Tîrgu-Mures, the Hungarian Teacher's College in the same city, and a Hungarian section in the Petru Groza Agricultural Institute and at the Gh. Dima Conservatory, also at Cluj.[67] Since 1959, these have been parallelized. The Bolyai University was the first to meet this fate, when in 1959, it merged with the parallel Romanian Babes University.[68] This was followed by the reduction (i.e., absorption) of the Hungarian section of both the Petru Groza Agricultural Institute and the Hungarian Medical-Pharmaceutical Institute at Tîrgu Mures in 1962.[69] Since that date all higher education for Hungarians is to be received at Romanian institutions, and at the few remaining Hungarian sections, which still maintain a precarious existence within such Romanian facilities.[70]

The Romanizing effects of parallelization on the highest levels can be seen in the academic publishing activity of the Babes-Bolyai University. Before the Babes and the Bolyai Universities were merged, in 1958, their learned journals were published in Romanian and Hungarian respectively.[71] After the merger, the academic publications still appeared in both languages, but now the Romanian and Hungarian studies appeared together rather than in separate journals. In most cases each of these studies was followed by a brief summary of its contents in the other language.[72] However, with the passage of time (less than seven years) the Hungarian language studies have been completely eliminated.[73]

As a perusal of these studies indicates, Hungarian scholars now publish their studies mainly in Romanian.[74] This tendency is not a natural process. It is a consequence of both faculty and editorial pressure.[75]

Perhaps an even more telling indicator is the format of these academic journals. In the years immediately after the merger, the journals were truly bilingual in appearance as well as content. The table of contents in each journal listed the articles according to the language in which they were written. The Hungarian article listings were even followed by Romanian translations.[76] Titles, in tables of contents, for example, appeared in both languages. At first even the name of the place (Cluj-Kolozsvár) of publication, was provided in both languages. But this was not to last. By 1959, the place of publication was listed only in Romanian.[77] In some journals even the bilingual designation for contents (*Sumar-Tartalom*) was replaced with the Romanian *Sumar*.[78] While this may seem trivial, it indicates how the national form was being eliminated in the university life of the Transylvanian Hungarians.

A substantive analysis of these articles also indicates that the socialist content of higher learning fits more and more into a national

TABLE III. Population Changes of Eight Cities in Romania, 1966–1977[26]

Cities	1966			1977			1966–1977
	Total Population	Hungarian Population	Hungarians as % of Total	Total Population	Hungarian Population	Hungarians as % of Total	% Decrease of Hungarians
Kolozsvár (Cluj-Napoca)	185,700	76,900	41.41	262,000	85,400	32.59	-8.82
Temesvár (Timişoara)	174,200	31,000	17.79	282,700	36,200	12.80	-4.99
Brassó (Braşov)	163,300	27,800	17.02	262,000	34,000	12.97	-4.05
Arad (Arad)	126,000	31,000	24.60	195,400	34,300	17.55	-7.05
Nagyvárad (Oradea)	122,500	63,000	51.42	161,700	75,700	41.66	-9.76
Marosvásárhely (Tirgu Mures)	86,500	60,200	69.59	152,600	81,800	53.60	-15.99
Szatmár (Satu Mare)	68,200	34,500	50.58	103,600	47,600	45.94	-4.64
Nagybánya (Bai Mare)	62,700	20,600	32.85	117,600	25,200	21.42	-11.43

Romanian, rather than an international Communist mold. This, of course, is discernable only in studies which fall within the scope of the Social Sciences. A comparison of the pre-merger Hungarian language journal with its post-1958 successors reveals that the earlier studies were often concerned with local Transylvanian problems and Hungarian cultural matters,[79] while later studies have been concerned more with the problems, culture and history of Romania as a whole.[80]

An even more menacing feature of Romanian educational policy has been the steady decrease in the training of minority-nationality teachers. While reliable data on this trend are available only up to about 1957, some later sources indicate that this process has since been accelerated, so that today the minority teachers' program has been reduced drastically.[81] The appointment, in 1976, of a Romanian as Rector of the Hungarian Teacher's College has already had detrimental consequences. Since this appointment, existing courses in Hungarian language and literature, Hungarian music and Romanian-Hungarian literature have been eliminated from the program.[82]

There is no doubt that through these methods the Romanian administration has reduced the opportunities of the nationalities to foster their respective cultures. In this way Romania has reverted to a policy similar to that of the inter-war Romanian bourgeois nationalists. Yet, it has done this under the pretext of eliminating national particularism and isolationism, two handmaidens of nationalist reaction. Gheorghe Gheorghiu-Dej, Ceaușescu and others have deemed this struggle as a means to further proletarian internationalism and socialist patriotism. But as the emphasis is placed increasingly on socialist patriotism rather than on proletarian internationalism, the pattern of nationalism emerges quite clearly.[83] The educational policies have in fact not only Romanized the national form of minority education; they have also, to a great degree, put a Romanian imprint on the socialist content.

One is made to wonder: what are the prospects for the Hungarians of Transylvania? Unlike the Saxons and the Jews, they do not have the option or the desire to emigrate from their homeland. Can they withstand the assimilationist pressures of both official and unofficial Romanian policy? Probably. Their historical sense of common destiny and their national solidarity is enhanced by the current discriminatory policies of the Romanian administration. At the same time, their numerical strength, and their awareness of being East Central Europe's largest minority will enable them to survive, to maintain themselves and perhaps even to become stronger.

For a while after the Warsaw Pact invasion of Czechoslovakia in 1968, it looked almost as if the Ceauşescu regime would come to some accommodation with the Transylvanian Hungarians and satisfy their basic concerns. The temporary reduction in assimilationist policies from 1968 to 1972 gave some indication that relations between minority and majority can be improved. However, the reversion to an aggressive assimilationist policy since then suggests that Ceauşescu is more interested in playing on the nationalist sentiments of the majority, to draw attention away from the country's economic problems, than to improve relations with the Hungarians. If this pressure continues, it can only lead to a further deterioration in the relations between Romanians and Hungarians. This is not just a domestic affair, it also has important international ramifications. If the fate of the Transylvanian Hungarians again becomes a volatile international issue, the Romanian nationalists, with Ceauşescu at their head, can blame only themselves and their intolerant assimilationist policies.

Notes

1. The fact that these nationalities are at odds now—a fact denied by most Communists—and were in the recent past does not mean that this has always been the case. On the contrary, before the rise of modern nationalism, harmony rather than discord characterized relations among the peoples of Transylvania and the Vojvodina. Indeed, both areas encourage harmony and cooperation because of the interdependent geography within the Carpathian Basin. For some consideration of this question see: Paul Teleki, "Transylvania's Situation in Hungary and in Europe," in Louis Craig Cornish, *Transylvania, The Land Beyond the Forest* appendix V (Philadelphia: Dorrance and Company, Inc., 1947), p. 244; C. A. Macartney, *Hungary and Her Successors* (London: Oxford University Press, 1937), pp. 7-9.

2. The dates given here are not above dispute. However, they do provide a simplified chronology of the power shifts in the Carpathian Basin.

3. Stefan T. Possony, "Political and Military Geography of Central, Balkan, and Eastern Europe," *The Annals* no. 232 (March 1944), pp. 3-4, states that: "Differential birth rates have been of extreme importance during the whole course of central and eastern European history, as they are the fundamental cause of the incessant change in the power position of nations.

We know little about vital statistics of former times, but it is certain that some eastern European peoples, such as the Poles, the Czechs, and the Hungarians, once had a 'larger' population than today, comparatively speaking."

4. Nicholas Kallay, *Hungarian Premier* (New York: Columbia University Press, 1954), p. 56; C. A. Macartney, *Hungary and Her Successors*, pp. 9–10; Francis S. Wagner, "Szechenyi and the Nationality Problem in the Habsburg Empire," *Journal of Central European Affairs* XX (Oct., 1960), p. 294; footnote 17. Peter F. Sugar, "The Rise of Nationalism in the Habsburg Empire," *Austrian History Yearbook* III, Part 1 (1967), p. 112, maintains that in 1787 the proportion of the Magyars was as low as 29 percent.

5. C. A. Macartney and A. W. Palmer, *Independent Eastern Europe* (London: Macmillan and Co., Ltd., 1962), p. 3; C. A. Macartney, *National States and National Minorities* (London: Oxford University Press, 1934), p. 89.

6. Macartney, *Hungary and Her Successors*, pp. 9–12, indicates these changes. On p. 9, he states: "The Turks not only made havoc of Hungary's civilization; but the brunt of their attack and subsequent occupation fell full upon the unprotected central plains which were the stronghold of the Magyar population, the German, Slavonic, and Roumanian areas of the periphery escaping far more lightly. They thus altered the balance of the population . . . to the disadvantage of the Magyars."

7. The historic "nationalities" of Transylvania were the Magyars, Saxons, and Székelys (a people akin to the Magyars who occupy the eastern corner of the area).

8. Macartney, *National States and National Minorities*, pp. 521–26; Macartney, *Hungary and Her Successors*, pp. 353–54.

9. Pro-Romanian writers blur this fact by using only absolute figures for entire regions. They almost never break down the statistics to the "plasa" level (interwar administrative equivalent of the "judet" or county). See for example Roucek, *Contemporary Roumania and Her Problems*, pp. 186–97; Clark, *Racial Aspects of Romania's Case*, p. 19; Pavel Pavel, *Transylvania at the Peace Conference of Paris* (London: Love and Malcomson Ltd., 1945), pp. 5–6; Alfred Malaschofsky, *Rumanien* (Berlin: Junker and Dunnhaupt Verlag, 1943), pp. 35–39. Only in *Roumania at the Peace Conference: Paris 1946* (Switzerland: Romanian Government Publication, 1946), pp. 76–78, are the statistics broken down to the "plasa" level. However, in this case two misleading factors are emphasized: (1) that the Magyars only have a relative majority (plurality) in the border strip, and (2) that the other nationality groups living there would not favor Magyar rule. The latter contention ignores the fact that many of these "nationalities" are Magyarized Swabians and Jews who consider themselves to be Magyars regardless of how the Romanians classify them.

10. Dragomir, *The Ethnical Minorities of Transylvania,* p. 40; Macartney, *National States and National Minorities,* pp. 521–26.

11. Regarding the classification of Jews in the census of 1910, 1930, and 1956, it must be noted that the latter two place them in an ethnic category. This was not the case in the census of 1910. According to this early census a Jew could designate—on the basis of preference—what nationality he belonged to; only on religious grounds was he differentiated in statistics. The Romanians have placed the Jews in a separate category in order to weaken the statistics of the Magyars, for in the past the Jews have on most occasions opted for that nationality.

12. G. D. Satmarescu, "The Changing Demographic Structure of the Population of Transylvania," *East European Quarterly* VIII (Jan., 1975), pp. 432–33.

13. Wagner, "Szechenyi and the Nationality Problem in the Habsburg Empire," p. 309.

14. *Ibid.,* pp. 289, 307, 309.

15. *Ibid.,* Rustem Vambery, "Nationalism in Hungary," *The Annals,* no. 232 (March, 1944), p. 78.

16. Robert Lee Wolff, *The Balkans in Our Time* (Cambridge, Mass.: Harvard University Press, 1956), pp. 76–77; Oscar Jaszi, *The Dissolution of the Habsburg Monarchy* (Chicago: The University of Chicago Press, 1929), pp. 90–99, 108–18.

17. Macartney, *Hungary and Her Successors,* pp. 18ff.

18. C. A. Macartney, *October Fifteenth: A History of Modern Hungary, 1929–1945* vol 1 (2nd ed.; Edinburgh: The Edinburgh University Press, 1961), p. 8.

19. For a description of this disintegration consult Jaszi, *The Dissolution of the Habsburg Monarchy,* part V and VI, pp. 271–429; Zeman, *The Breakup of the Habsburg Empire 1914–1918.*

20. Macartney, *October Fifteenth,* I, 4, 5, 21, provides a brief but concise summary of the losses suffered by Hungary as a result of this treaty.

21. R. G. Waldeck, *Athene Palace* (New York: Robert M. McBride and Company, 1942), p. 135; Vambery, "Nationalism in Hungary," p. 81; Macartney, *October Fifteenth,* I, 5.

22. Grigore Gafencu, *Last Days of Europe,* trans. E. Fletcher-Allen (New Haven: Yale University Press, 1948), pp. 156, 163, 167–68; and John O. Crane, *The Little Entente* (New York: The Macmillan Company, 1931), p. 6, describe this from a pro-Romanian perspective. Robert Gower, *The Hungarian Minorities in the Succession States* (London: Richards, 1937), p. 21, defends the Hungarians. He maintains that the ". . . difference between the situation of the Hungarian minorities and that of other minorities is this: the Hungarian minorities are firmly convinced that their present situation is due to the errors of a misguided and ill-conducted Peace Conference, whereas the

other minorities owe their existence to circumstances such as neither human foresight can avoid nor human skill control."

23. Emil Ciurea, "The Background," *Captive Rumania* ed. Alexandre Cretzianu (New York: Frederick A. Praeger, Inc., 1956), pp. 9–10; Roucek, *Contemporary Roumainia and Her Problems*, p. 214; Macartney, *Independent Eastern Europe*, pp. 265–71; Waldeck, *Athene Palace*, pp. 21–22.

24. Gower, *The Hungarian Minorities in the Succession States*, p. 18; Crane, *The Little Entente*, pp. 6–7; Temperley, "How the Hungarian Frontiers Were Drawn," p. 434.

25. Clark, *Racial Aspects of Romania's Case*, p. 1; Macartney, *October Fifteenth*, I, 387–89, 318–24, 429–30.

26. Alexander Cretzianu, "The Soviet Ultimatum to Roumania (26 June 1940)," *Journal of Central European Affairs*, IX (Jan., 1950), 396–403.

27. Kallay, *Hungarian Premier*, pp. 58–61; Waldeck, *Athene Palace*, pp., 27, 37, 113, 124–25. Grigore Gafencu, *Prelude to the Russian Campaign*, trans. E. Fletcher-Allen (London: Frederick Muller, Ltd., 1945), pp. 52, 64.

28. Macartney, *October Fifteenth*, I, 389; Markham, *Rumania Under the Soviet Yoke*, pp. 114, 124–25; Macartney, *Independent Eastern Europe*, pp. 419–20.

29. *Ibid.*, pp. 421–22; Waldeck, *Athene Palace*, p. 131; Kallay, *Hungarian Premier*, p. 59.

30. A. C. Leiss and Raymond Dennett, eds., *European Peace Treaties After World War II* (Worcester, Mass.: The Commonwealth Press, 1954), p. 102; Macartney, *October Fifteenth*, II, p. 351.

31. As some have observed, the objective of the Second Vienna Award was not to divide and conquer, but to bring about peace in the rear of Hitler's armies. On the other hand, this does not mean that Transylvania did not remain a potential reward to the state which performed its wartime duties better. See Macartney, *October Fifteenth*, II, pp. 253, 319; Kallay, *Hungarian Premier*, p. 64. For a Communist Hungarian interpretation see Miklós Horváth, *A. 2. Magyar Hadsereg Megsemmisülése A Donnál* (Budapest: Zrinyi Kiadó, 1959), pp. 9–10. For a Romanian view see Pavel, *Transylvania at the Peace Conference of Paris*, p. 37. That war achievements were considered important is also illuminated from another angle by Waldeck, *Athene Palace*, pp. 355–56. Compensation given on the eastern front (Bessarabia, Bukovina, Transnistria) is here regarded as partial payment from Hitler for losses sustained in the West (Northern Transylvania and Dobruja).

32. Kallay, *Hungarian Premier*, p. 58, footnote 27; Macartney, *October Fifteenth*, II, p. 405. However, Stalin did not forget the Romanians either. For his approaches in this direction, see Alexander Cretzianu, "The Rumanian Armistice Negotiations: Cairo, 1944," *Journal of Central European Affairs*, XI (Oct., 1951), p. 251.

33. Emil Ciurea, "The Background," *Captive Rumania*, ed. Alexandre Cretzianu (New York: Frederick A. Praeger, Inc., 1956), pp. 18–19; Markham, *Rumania Under the Soviet Yoke*, p. 173; Macartney, *October Fifteenth*, II, pp. 191–92, 204–05, 216.

34. Leiss, *European Peace Treaties After World War II*, pp. 101–102, 299.

35. *Ibid.*, pp. 101–102.

36. Hugh Seton-Watson, "The Danubian Satellites," *International Affairs*, XXII (April, 1946), p. 250; Schieder, *The Expulsion of the German Population from Hungary and Rumania*, III, p. 85.

37. Hugh Seton-Watson, *From Lenin to Khrushchev* (Paperback Edition; New York: Frederick A. Praeger, Inc., 1962), pp. 256–57, gives a brief discussion of Czech versus Slovak animosities which were utilized by the Soviet Union and the local Communists. In a similar way, the Soviets also used Romanian-Hungarian discord in Transylvania.

38. Markham, *Rumania Under the Soviet Yoke*, pp. 215–17, blames the Hungarians for the success of Communism in Romania. He fails to mention, however, that the Hungarians had acquiesced to Soviet pressures only because the bourgeois Romanian leaders (i.e., Iuliu Maniu, Ilie Lazar and their "democratic" followers) were bent on revenge against the "disloyal" national minorities who had turned toward Hungary during 1940–1944. The Hungarians had no alternative left but to support the Soviet-backed Petru Groza, who had promised tolerance and respect for the national minorities. See Seton-Watson, "The Danubian Satellites," p. 247; Schieder, *The Expulsion of the German Population from Hungary and Rumania*, III, pp. 84–85.

39. Markham, *Rumania Under the Soviet Yoke*, pp. 230, 249.

40. The "nationalities theory" and "policy" which has been taken over from the practice and experience of the Soviet Union, has been variously designated. Recently, the designation "Marxist-Leninist" has become more and more popular. In Yugoslavia this is the most commonly used. In Romania, on the other hand, the designation is simply "Leninist." Prior to de-Stalinization, in Romania this policy was always referred to as "Leninist-Stalinist." In Yugoslavia this was also the designation until the Tito-Stalin split of 1948.

41. Boris Levitski, "Coexistence within the Bloc," *Survey*, no. 42 (June, 1962), pp. 28–29, 33–34. A good example of such mimicry is I. Nistor, "Example of the Soviet Union is a Guiding Light," under heading "Rumania," *The Current Digest of the Soviet Press*, IV (Feb. 7, 1953), p. 18. The original article appeared in the December 27, 1953, issue of *Izvestia*, p. 3.

42. *Ibid.*, p. 18, points out, however, that for Lenin (and Stalin, we may add) such "rights" were really secondary. Lenin was ". . . cool, indifferent, even hostile to the national state and to nationality. But, in general, the proletariat and the Party have the solemn obligation to support the national liberation movement because democracy and socialism demand it."

43. "Constitution of the Rumanian People's Republic 1952," in *Constitutions of Nations*, ed. Amos J. Peaslee (2nd ed., Hague, Netherlands: Martinus Nijhoff, 1956), art. 82, p. 250; "Draft Constitution of the Socialist Republic of Romania 11/A supplement to *Documents, Articles and Information on Romania* (Bucharest: "Agerpress," 1965), art. 22, p. 9.

44. *Ibid.*, art. 17, p. 242; Randolph L. Braham, "The Rumanian Constitution of 1952,"*Journal of Central European Affairs*, XVIII (July, 1958), p. 176.

45. "Constitution of 1952," in Peaslee. See, Preamble, p. 239; arts. 58, 82, pp. 247, 250. Later documents skirt the question of local "autonomy." In this they are reverting to the position of the earliest post-war Constitution. See *Constitution of 1948*, arts. 75–85, p. 20. For the territorial alterations of the Magyar Autonomous Region, see: Gyula Miklós, "A Román Népköztársaságban 1950 óta végrehajtott közigazgatási-gazdasági körzetbeosztások néhány tapasztalata," *Földrajzi Közlemények*, IX [LXXXV] (1961), pp. 307–25; Ceauşescu, "Exposition on the Improvement of the Administrative Organization of the Territory of the Socialist Republic of Romania," pp. 1–31.

46. *Short Document on Rumania*, p. 4; "Constitution of 1952," art. 81, p. 249; "Draft Constitution of 1965," arts. 17, 102, pp. 7, 30.

47. *Ibid.*, art. 102, p. 30; "Constitution of 1952," art. 68, p. 248.

48. *Ibid.*, "Draft Constitution of 1965," art. 102, p. 30.

49. Stephen Fischer-Galati, ed., *Romania* (New York: Frederick A. Praeger, Inc., 1956), pp. 69–71; Ghita Ionescu, *Communism in Rumania 1944–1962* (London: Oxford University Press, 1964), pp. 204–208.

50. This is verified by the fact that in December 1955, 79.2 percent of the members were ethnic Romanians in the CPR. By 1968, 88.43 percent were ethnic Romanians. Compare *ibid.*, p. 243, with "Report by Nicolae Ceauşescu on Organizational Measures for the Steady Strengthening of the Moral-Political Unity of the Working People," *Documents, Articles and Information on Romania*, no. 27 (Oct. 28, 1968), p. 30.

51. Randolph L. Braham, "Rumania: Onto the Separate Path," *Problems of Communism*, XIII (May-June, 1964), pp. 16–17, footnote 5.

52. That Stalin was thinking along these lines is also indicated by his abortive plan to have Romania and Hungary "federated." See Milovan Djilas, *Conversations with Stalin*, trans. Michael B. Petrovich (New York: Harcourt, Brace and World, Inc., 1962), pp. 177–78.

53. In the area of education, however, the turn toward assimilationist policies was evident already in the 1956–57 academic year.

54. Robert R. King, *Minorities under Communism* (Boston: Harvard University Press, 1973).

55. Committee for Human Rights in Rumania, *Witnesses to Cultural Genocide: Reports on Rumania's Minority Policies* (New York: 1980).

56. Randolph Braham, *Education in the Rumanian People's Republic*

(U.S. Dept. H.E.W.; Washington, D.C.: U.S. Government Printing Office, 1963), pp. 78–79; George Bailey, "Trouble Over Transylvania," *The Reporter* (November 19, 1964), p. 26; Stephen Fischer-Galati, "Rumania" in *East Central Europe and the World*, ed. Stephen D. Kertesz (Notre Dame, Ind.: University of Notre Dame Press, 1962), pp. 158–166. Actually, even one year prior to the revolution there were some hints of a turn toward more nationalistic policies. Along this line see László Bányai, "Tizéves a Bolyai Tudományegyetem," in *A Kolozsvári Bolyai Tudományegyetem (1945–1955)* (Cluj: Állami Tanügyi és Pedagogiai Könyvkiadó, 1956), pp. 5–13.

57. *Ibid.*, László Bányai, "Forum: irodalomtanitás és hazafias nevelés," *Igaz Szó*, VII (Feb., 1959), pp. 236–242.

58. "The Hungarian Minority Problem in Rumania," p. 76; Skilling, "Two Orthodox Satellites," p. 388; Tamás Schreiber, "A Magyar Kisebbség Helyzete Romániában," *Irodalmi Ujság* (July 15, 1961).

59. In contradiction to the above contention it is possible to show that the total number of minority students in 4-year schools increased to 131,773 in 1956-57 from 127,634 in 1955-56. Yet in this same space of time the number of minority schools decreased from 1,416 to 1,343 in these same 4-year schools. This pattern is also apparent on the higher levels of education. See Braham, *Education in the Rumanian People's Republic*, p. 65, table 13. While the decreases of the years prior to the above seem more natural, the decrease in later years certainly does not. Now the decrease of minority schools is followed by the decrease of minority students rather than the other way around.

60. These pressures are of various kinds, some direct and some indirect. See in this regard "The Hungarian Minority Problem in Rumania," p. 76; Schreiber, "A magyar kisebbség helyzete Romániában." F. K., "Románia Szüntesse Meg az Erdélyi Magyarok Üldözését," *Katolikus Magyarok Vasárnapja*, 71 (June 21, 1964), p. 1.

61. *Ibid.*, Schreiber, "A Magyar Kisebbség Helyzete Romániában"; "Levél Erdélyből," *Irodalmi Ujság* (Aug. 1, 1964).

62. "Levél Erdélyből," *Irodalmi Ujság*; Schreiber, "A magyar kisebbség helyzete Romániában"; F. K., "Románia Szüntesse Meg Az Erdélyi Magyarok Üldözését!"

63. "Statement by the Committee for Human Rights in Rumania" before the Subcommittee on International Trade of the Committee on Finance, United States Senate, at hearings on continuing Most-Favored-Nation Tariff Treatment of Imports from Rumania, July 19, 1979, p. 17.

64. *Ibid.*, p. 16.

65. Higher education demonstrates this trend best because (1) it has been totally "Romanized," (2) it has affected the leading strata (i.e., intelligentsia) of the Transylvanian Hungarians, and (3) it has been least possible to camouflage or hide from world scrutiny the absorption of these important

institutions. In this regard see Bailey, "Trouble Over Transylvania," pp. 26-27; David Binder, "Rumania's Minorities Pressed by Nationalist Drive," *New York Times* (July 14, 1964), p. 4; J. F. Brown, "The Age-Old Question of Transylvania," *The World Today*, XIX (Nov., 1963), pp. 503-504.

66. Seton-Watson, *The East European Revolution* (New York: Frederick A. Praeger, 1951), p. 341, notes that this early policy was by no means whole-heartedly and enthusiastically supported. He maintains that: "This liberal nationality policy was not carried through without strong opposition, not only from the Rumanian nationalist followers of Maniu but also from a part of the Rumanian Party itself, led by the former Minister of Justice Lucretiu Patrascanu. The removal of Patrascanu from his office and his disgrace within the party were certainly to some extent due to his 'incorrect' attitude on the national question."

67. "Cluj Regiune" according to *Faclia*, Feb. 6, 1958, in "Comprehensive Regiune Summaries," *Weekly Summary of the Rumanian Provincial Press 4-9 Feb. 1958* (JPRS/Washington, D.C.: April 22, 1958), p. 3.

68. Brown, "The Age-Old Question of Transylvania"; Braham, *Education in the Rumanian People's Republic*, pp. 78-79; Bailey, "Trouble Over Transylvania," pp. 26-27. It was in connection with this "parallelization" that three Hungarian professors committed suicide. One of them, Szabédi László, was a famous Communist poet and intellectual of the Hungarian minority. See in this regard "The Hungarian Minority Problem in Rumania," p. 76.

69. *Ibid.*, Bailey, "Trouble Over Transylvania," p. 27.

70. Besides this formal pattern of "integration" there is also an informal trend along similar lines which is stressed and fostered by the Romanian regime. The most recent example of this policy has been the sharing of rooms in student hostels and dormitories by Romanians and Hungarians. The pretext for this is that the Hungarian students will more easily learn Romanian if they share rooms with Romanian students. See "The Hungarian Minority Problem in Rumania." This policy received its inception soon after the Hungarian Revolution of 1956. A. Rosca, "The Party Organizations and the Patriotic Education of the Youth," *Lupta de Clasa* (Nov., 1957), pp. 87-96 in *Selected Translations from East European Political Journals and Papers* (JPRS/Washington, D.C.: Feb. 28, 1958), p. 126.

71. Compare *Buletinul: Universitatilor V. "Babes" Si "Bolyai,"* vol. I, Nr. 1-2 (1957), and V. *Bábes és Bolyai Egyetemek Közleményei*, I, év., 1-2 sz. (1956).

72. *Ibid.*, *Buletinul: Universitatilor V. "Babes" Si "Bolyai,"* vol. I, Nr. 1-2 (1957).

73. In 1956-57 it was still possible to find scholarly works in Hungarian. In V. *Bábes és Bolyai Egyetemek Közleményei*, I év., 1-2 sz. (1956), there are

fourteen Hungarian language studies and five Romanian language studies followed by the Hungarian summaries of seven Romanian studies. By 1960 it is evident that Hungarian language studies decline in numbers. *In Studia: Universitatis Babes-Bolyai* Series 1, Fasciculus 2, Anul 5 (1960), there are 26 items, articles and studies of which only one appears in Hungarian, while 21 of the contributors are Hungarian. By 1965 the situation is even worse. *Studia: Universitatis Babes-Bolyai* (Series Philosophia et Oeconomica, Anul X, 1965), contains seventeen items, articles and studies of which none appear in Hungarian in spite of the fact that five of the contributors are Hungarian.

74. *Ibid.*

75. That such faculty and editorial pressure exists is hard to substantiate. This contention is based on the observations of two scholars, a Pole and an American, who spent extended periods of time doing research at the Babes-Bolyai University in Cluj (Kolozsvár) during 1967 and 1968 respectively. Both maintained, in personal conversations with this student, that the pressure was evident in the language used by the Hungarian faculty members. They never speak to one another in Hungarian, if even one Romanian faculty member is present.

76. *V. Bábes és Bolyai Egyetemek Közleményei*, I ev., 1–2 sz. (1956).

77. Compare *ibid.*, and *Studia: Universitatis Babes-Bolyai*, Series 1, Fasciculus 1, Anul 4 (1959).

78. *Studia: Universitatis Babes-Bolyai*, Series 1, Fasciculus 1, Anul 5 (1960); *Studia: Universitatis Babes-Bolyai*, Series 3, Fasciculus 1, Anul 4 (1959); *Studia: Universitatis Babes-Bolyai*, Series Psychologia Paedagogia, Anul 9 (1964).

79. *A Kolozsvári Bolyai Tudományosegyetem (1945–1955)* (Cluj, Transylvania: Állami Tanügyi és Pedagógiai Könyvkiadó, 1956), contains some of these studies. Also representative are: Emil Petrovici, "A Román öris, Oriş, Orşia, Oraşa, Oraşani, Oraşeni Magyar Varjas," pp. 223–26, Attila T. Szabó, "A Gyermekló és rokonsága," pp. 235–251, and Mózes Gálffy and Gyula Márton, "A Bolyai-Egyetem Magyar Nyelvészeti Tanszékének nyelvjáráskutató Tevékenysége a Magyar Autonom Tartományban," pp. 253–279, in *V. Bábes és Bolyai Egyetemek Közleményei*, I, ev., 1–2, sz. (1956).

80. Some examples are: A. Bodor, "Adalékok a helyi elem fennmaradásának kérdéséhez a romaikori Dáciában: A Liber és a Libera Kultusz," *Studia: Universitatis Babes-Bolyai*, Series 4, Fasciculus 1 (1960), pp. 25–58; Zoltán Farkas, "Állam, nemzet es szuverénitás a szocializmusban," *Studia: Universitatis Babes-Bolyai*, Series Philosophia, Anul XI (1966), pp. 19–27.

81. Pál Nagy, "Huszonnyolc uj tanitó," *Igaz Szó*, VIII (Aug., 1960), p. 243, mentions that 28 students graduated from the Józsa Béla Pedagogic Institute in 1960. This is already indicative of significant cutbacks in the

area of teacher education only two years after the merger of the Bolyai and Babes universities.

82. "Statement by the Committee for Human Rights in Rumania," p. 23.

83. V. A. Varga, "The Fundamental Laws and Characteristics of the Great October Socialist Revolution," *Probleme Economice* (Oct., 1957), pp. 8-10, in *Selected Translations from East European Political Journals and Newspapers* (JPRS/Washington, D.C.: March 7, 1958), pp. 138-39; Bányai, "Forum: irodalomtanitás és hazafias nevelés," pp. 236-242; Rosca, "The Party Organization and the Patriotic Education of the Youth," pp. 115-126.

Károly Nagy

A Contemporary Analysis of Trianon's Aftermath: Gyula Illyés' *Spirit and Violence*

"Trianon to us bears the meaning of a human slaughterhouse: it is there that every third Hungarian was crushed into subsistence under foreign rule; it is there that the territories of our native language were torn to pieces."[1] The writer who uttered these words on the eve of the sixtieth anniversary of the concluding of the Trianon peace treaty has been called the Grand Old Man of Hungarian letters. He is also referred to sometimes as perhaps the last of the national poets—"national" in the sense that he has taken it upon himself to voice his people's, his nation's, vital concerns. The role of advocate, prophet, crusader, intellectual leader—while it usually took considerable courage to assume—became an honorable burden in a country which often faced domestic and foreign tyranny, enslavement, even virtual extinction during its thousand-year history.

Gyula Illyés was born in 1902 and became one of the most significant writers of his time in Hungary and, as translations of his works reach an ever-growing number of readers everywhere, he will be known in other parts of the world as well. As Alain Bosquet, the French writer said: "Only three or four living poets have been able to identify themselves totally with the soul of the century . . . Their genius burns in the Hungarian poet Gyula Illyés . . . In his poems we find the charm, the fire, the grave thoughts and feelings underlying the need to embrace the world and transform it through the Word."[2]

Gyula Illyés has voiced his concern about the human rights of Hungarians everywhere, has stood up for their freedom to preserve their cultural heritage, to maintain as ethnic minorities their schools, churches, and literary forums. This has often resulted in his being called a "nationalist" by various official and other critics. Illyés has repeatedly rejected this label and showed it to be a malicious and deliberately misleading reversal of truth.

It is a fateful deception to call 'nationalists' those who try to repel or reduce nationalistic oppression, instead of identifying as nationalists those who actually practice and intensify nationalistic discrimination.[3] To call 'nationalism' the cries of those who suffer from oppression, and not the oppressor, provides ammunition for the real nationalists whose intentions border on genocide! The almost alarmingly accelerating efforts of many ethnic groups to become independent is an unexpected symptom of our century. So is the startling orgy of nationalism. To call the essence of these two processes the same, however, is to mistake cause for effect. The two are: water and fire, mutually exclusive, in the deepest war with each other.[4] I am not a nationalist . . . Nationalists violate rights, patriots protect rights. I want equal rights for all people, including the Hungarian people.[5]

The changed demographic situation and the oppression of the Hungarian minorities in the territories annexed to Czechoslovakia, the Soviet Union, Romania, and Yugoslavia in 1921 were taboo subjects, forbidden to be publicly discussed after World War II in East-Central Europe. The political leaders of Hungary, as well as of her neighbors to the North, East, and South, ruled in the name of socialism, internationalism, and communism—ideologies which deemphasize national consciousness and national identification. During those years, Hungary, Czechoslovakia, and Romania came under Soviet domination and the Soviet Union condoned not only the Trianon borders but also the disenfranchisement of the minorities. Oppression of minorities, after all, was a traditional policy in Stalin's totalitarian state. Only in the late 60's after a period of political relaxation had set in in Hungary did it become again possible to raise questions publicly about some of these previously forbidden issues. One of the issues was the survival of the Hungarian minorities beyond Hungary's borders. The official and unofficial censors yielded very grudgingly, and very slowly. By the end of the seventies there seemed to be only three taboo subjects left: the revolution of 1956, the single (communist) party's autocratic rule, and the presence of the Soviet military occupying forces (referred to officially as "friendly troops stationed temporarily on our country's territory"). In today's Hungary, beside these forbidden topics, there are writings which are "tolerated" and, of course, works which are supported by the authorities. These three official reaction patterns are said to have created three categories of literary works—the three "T" 's (in Hungarian "tiltott [forbidden], "türt" [tolerated], and "támogatott" [supported]).

Thus, it took courage to refer in the 1960's and 1970's to the problem of the Hungarian minorities who live in Hungary's neighboring countries. At the time Illyés started talking in public about the fact that there were 15 or 16 million Hungarians in the world and one full third of them live outside of Hungary, even these demographic data were unmentionable. It was perhaps partly Illyés' enormous prestige and brave persistence, and also the continued flexibility of the ruling regime, that enabled this topic to move into the "tolerated" sphere. But not always, and not quite.

A few years ago Illyés—at the insistence and with the support of his friends—put together a collection of twenty pieces of his writings on this subject matter, including an introduction, a poem, some essays, letters, lectures and interviews, a majority of them previously published. The book came to 280 pages and was published by *Magvető* publishing company in Budapest in 1978, bearing the title of one of the newly written essays: *Szellem és erőszak* (Spirit and Violence).

The book never left the publishing company's warehouse. It cannot be obtained in any bookstore, it cannot be read in any library, it is not mentioned anywhere. It was ordered from the "tolerated," back to the "forbidden" category. One optimistic note: the book was not destroyed, it is still waiting to be released. Another hopeful sign: Illyés was not intimidated by the banning of his book. Indeed, the opposite occurred: in the three years since then, his efforts to bring this issue to the public's attention increased. A good example is a TV interview he gave in February 1980, the text of which was published in the May 1980 issue of *Alföld,* one of the best regional literary journals of Hungary. In the interview Illyés states:

> Hungarians are in a tragic situation: there are fifteen million Hungarians in the world, but only ten million live within the present borders of their country. The rest live beyond these borders, and many of them are deprived of the opportunity to maintain their language, and are being discriminated against in other ways as well. If we are not concerned with them, we commit not national treason, but ethical treason—treason against our brothers and sisters, against a people.[6]

One of the earliest pieces in *Szellem és erőszak* is a 1963 interview Illyés gave to a French newspaper: *L'Express.*[7] In it Illyés called chauvinistic intolerance what took place in the annexed territories after Trianon.

L'Express: You have travelled in Eastern countries and have recently visited some Western countries as well. What really caught your attention in these countries?

Gyula Illyés: Perhaps the disturbing remnants of chauvinism. When I was young, we thought that as a result of the French revolution and the works of the very logical 19th century thinkers, internationalism would become the new world order. But eventually we had to give up this hope!

First, there were the nationalistic explosions of the 20's, then came Hitlerism. Hitler is dead, Nazism is annihilated, but intolerance, chauvinism, racism, separatism, language disputes keep stirring up the world. Not even the most thoroughgoing social changes could solve these problems. There is a province in Romania: Transylvania, which for centuries was the real birthplace of Hungarian civilization and literature. In this province they have recently closed the only university which served the more than two million Hungarians living there. The position of Hungarian writers and intellectuals there is very precarious.[8]

Elsewhere he characterizes the patterns of oppression practiced by Hungary's neighbors against the Hungarian minorities as cultural intolerance, deprivation, subjugation into a sort of proletarian existence, a system of *apartheid.*

Nationalistic intolerance cloaks itself in forms of intolerance against native languages. This has happened even in countries which took some steps toward socialism in their economic structure.[9]

Our language seems to be under some kind of a death sentence beyond our borders. Let me state this clearly: consciously or unconsciously efforts are made to bring about the disappearance of our language, which would cause untold suffering to millions of innocent people.[10]

Of the fifteen million Hungarians, only ten million live in the State of Hungary. Every third Hungarian inherits, on account of his native language, a socially disadvantaged life, a kind of proletarian fate.[11]

The native language of Hungarians is not Germanic or Slavic, or Latin; it is related, in Europe, only to the languages of the distant Finns and Estonians. Therefore, every third Hungarian, who may not know or find it hard to learn the completely different majority language, has to contend with a multitude of difficulties. This fact has not been sufficiently recognized up to now. The basic cause of these difficulties is that humanism, even that which is advocated by socialism, has remained ineffective in many parts of the world against unexpectedly

widespread nationalistic hostilities, especially the intolerances that tor-
ment the life of minorities in our century.[12]

I was humiliated in Czechoslovakia. They told me not to talk in my
native language. They rebuked the lady in my company, my wife,
with the same words, and I had no way to protect her. Thus, they let
me know, and more than once, that I was not welcome there. Since
this happened in a city and in a province where virtually everybody
spoke the same language as we did, that is: Hungarian, I had to conclude that they would like everybody in that region to leave his home.
This puzzled me because there were signs and posters everywhere on
the streets proclaiming the sacred slogans of the highest stage of
humanism: socialism. But then: these proclamations were not written
in the population's native language.[13]

The largest national minority of Europe is Hungarian. According to
factual, verifiable data this minority does not have universities or
other higher educational institutions, and soon will not have high
schools either where the language of instruction would be Hungarian.
Their few remaining high schools are being turned into vocational-
technical schools, where the language of instruction is the "official
language," which is other than Hungarian. The result is that a minority youth can't learn a trade in his own language; therefore, he can't
become a skilled worker or a machine operator. He can only aspire to
unskilled day-laborers' jobs.

In the Hungarian minorities' elementary schools the children have to
learn lies in their own language about their ancestors who, their textbooks tell them, were barbarian invaders, inferior savages. Twenty
percent of the Hungarian children do not learn the alphabet in their
own language. This is partly because some parents do not want to
send their children to Hungarian schools—who would not want to
save his children from an almost apartheid way of life?

If, after having received their diplomas, young Hungarian professionals still insist on using their mother tongue, they are often assigned
to jobs far away from any Hungarian community. Many of the professionals who are assigned to work in Hungarian towns, on the other
hand, are people who do not speak or understand the local population's language.

Hungarian intellectuals are disappearing from entire regions. Every
function of Hungrian culture, art, and education is discontinued in an
increasing number of traditionally Hungarian towns and cities.[14]

In Czechoslovakia and in Romania there are officially encouraged
and recognized scientists, linguists, historians and others who
keep turning out hundreds of publications whose theme is that

Hungarians were wandering barbarians before they invaded those regions where the native ancestors of Czechoslovakians and Romanians had already established their superior cultures. This historical falsification serves as the basis for discrimination against Hungarians, forcing them to assimilate or to leave their homeland. Illyés calls this pattern "pathology," "a nightmare," and the issue of "who was here first" completely irrelevant.

> Historians wrote volumes about the question: which of the contemporary populations of the Danubian basin arrived here first? They would have had to write less if that which is clear today would have been clearer earlier: it does not matter who was here first because it does not change the deep psychological reasons for intolerance. Nobody should be able to drive out anybody from this region, from his native village, on the basis of having settled there first. If this were a valid reason, then Americans might have to leave the States, I imagine, as long as one American Indian would insist on expelling them![15]

Some people attempt to justify the deprivation of the Hungarian minorities of their human rights and of their opportunities to maintain their language and culture in Czechoslovakia, in the Soviet Union, and in Romania by pointing out that Hungarians have also oppressed their minorities when they had ruled the multi-national regions of Central Europe.

Illyés notes this reasoning, but finds it to be an insufficient explanation and calls for a responsible and substantial exposition and discussion of this issue, including a comparison of the historical and the present practices of minority oppression in Central Europe.

> The reason our native Hungarian language upsets some people who live around us—the reason that a ring of hostility surrounding us has been glowing with increasing heat for the past half century—is that there was a time when it was the Hungarians who insulted these people. At the end of the past century Hungarians closed the national schools and cultural organizations of their minorities, continuing the oppression which these people had suffered for centuries.
>
> I find this reasoning inadequate. It is not the root cause. If it were, then we could overcome the hurt with apologies, compensations and reparations. But in my opinion, the causes of the present problems go much deeper.[16]

Some people blame Hungarians for past practices of forced assimilation and language intolerance against other nationalities. If these people want to be objective, they have to admit that such practices could be cited only for about a fifty-year period from the Compromise of 1867 to the years of 1917-1918. Prior to that it was we, Hungarians, who were forced to assimilate by the Austrians. Let us compare those fifty years with the laws and practices suppressing the Hungarian minorities during the last sixty years! Yes, let us mutually discuss these questions. I hope that this might happen because in no other way can we reach understanding that is in the national and international interest of every nation in the Danubian Basin. The question of minorities is a pressing world problem, which we have to try to understand and, eventually, solve.[17]

Illyés also calls attention to the fact that it is a time-honored Hungarian historical tradition to foster brotherhood and cooperation with the nations of the Danubian Basin, bearing in mind their shared fate, and interdependence. He cites László Teleki and Wesselényi, leaders who fought for the equal rights of national minorities, living on Hungarian territory. He also mentions many of the most significant modern Hungarian writers, poets, and musicians—Jókai, Tömörkényi, Mikszáth, Ady, László Németh,[18] Móricz, Babits, Bartók and Kodály—who all turned with understanding toward the nations around them and were all truly interested in making the idea of brotherhood in the Danubian Basin a well defined program.

We might call to mind the utterances of some of the men mentioned by Illyés, which express their views on equality and interdependence.

- Miklós Wesselényi, the politician, wrote in his *Szózat a magyar és szláv nemzet ügyében* (An appeal in the Matter of Hungarians and Slavic Nationals) published in Hungarian in Leipzig in 1843, and in German in 1844: "It is not necessary for the non-Hungarian nationals to forget their native languages. This should not be seen as a goal. Legislation must be immediately promulgated which would prohibit any office or person to curtail the personal or public use of the nationals' native language, or which would force them to use the Hungarian language." (P. 318.)
- Endre Ady, one of the greatest Hungarian poets at the beginning of the twentieth century, wrote in his poem: *The Song of the Hungarian Jacobins.*

Hungarian, Rumanian, Slavic trouble
will always be the same trouble.
Our disgrace and our grief
has been the same for a millenium . . .
When will we finally unite,
We, oppressed, crushed
Hungarians and non-Hungarians? . . .
    Why can't a thousand numb desires
finally become one strong will? . . .
Tomorrow we can have everything if we want,
if we dare.

- Béla Bartók wrote in a letter to Octavian Beu, a Romanian musicologist in 1931: "I am a Hungarian musician. My works use Hungarian, Romanian and Slovak folk musical sources, thus my music can be seen as representing the idea of integration. My guiding thought, of which I have been conscious ever since I have found my own voice as a composer, is that different people should become brothers in spite of wars and feuds."

"This is what we tried to transmit to the generations following ours," Illyés asserts. "We made them believe that if they will reach out, their hands will be grasped by brotherly hands. That if they look not just towards Paris, but also toward Pozsony, Bucharest and Belgrade, they would receive encouraging signals. I am ashamed to say that we were turned down."[19] "It is not the first time that I had to describe this painful experience. We did not receive similar brotherly attention. We were waiting for an Ady or a Bartók to appear on the other side. We hoped that if such a person existed he would have kind words for us."[20]

I do not recommend that we compare how much of their literature we translated into Hungarian, and how much of our literature they translated into their languages. We, in Hungary, are not the only ones who are aware of them and who translate their works. The periodicals of the millions of Hungarians living beyond our borders also provide us with ample interpretations and commentaries on their literature. This is simply not the case on the other sides—we know much more about our neighbors than they know about us.[21]

What does Gyula Illyés think of the future implications of the minorities problem sixty years after the Trianon peace treaty? What can they mean to millions of Hungarians? As a writer and as a moral man, he feels that he and his peers must act courageously on behalf of human rights.

> How do we, humanists, have to behave so that our actions may be useful in countering barbaric forces of mass oppression, policies aimed at depriving people of their human rights because of their national origin and native language?
>
> We have to start pounding on the closed prison doors and pound unceasingly!
>
> We have to create a well-disciplined movement that will not only deliver resounding blows on their doors but will finally break them down.
>
> If I expect it to be natural that my community be a kind of protective sanctuary for me, do I not also have to defend my community's rights? When at the same time they are universal human rights? There can be no disagreement about this. But should we intellectuals take it upon ourselves to pound on those doors with our own tools: words, thoughts and reason? Is it our responsibility to do battle for these rights? It certainly is . . . And what happens when people don't speak up against rules which forbid their neighbors to speak in their own language in their own town? Eventually, even they will be forced to leave that town. And later they will be forced to abandon other areas of human existence. Finally they will be forced to give up life itself.[22]

Illyés has offered bold examples in the past few years on how to use words, thoughts, and reason to "pound on those doors" of intolerance, of un-reason, of inhumanity. One such courageous act was to submit his *Spirit and Violence* for publication. He knew that its words and thoughts would be considered dangerous by the dogmatic elements in the ruling structure. He also attempted to enlist the support of the international news media to help expose the discriminatory, nationalistic policies aimed against Hungarian minorities. In an interview he gave to the Stockholm newspaper *Svenska Dagbladet* Illyés pointed out that continued oppression could even lead to another world war.

> Imagine that all the road signs where you live were written in a foreign language. Imagine that your public officials and policemen could not utter a single sentence in your language. In Romania, this problem becomes doubly severe, because many Romanian peasants learn to believe the official propaganda and view the Hungarians as

inferior creatures, second-class citizens. This is happening in territories where Hungarians had lived for centuries. It is happening in Transylvania, which had traditionally been a country of tolerance and intellectual freedom.

Nationalism is a horrible poison. Was it not precisely the problem of national minorities in Europe which provoked the two world wars? And, as long as national hostilities exist, as long as national minorities are being discriminated against in Europe, I am not so certain that these circumstances could not once more become an important factor leading to the outbreak of a new world war.[23]

Immediately after his book was banned, Illyés took an even riskier step: he wrote an introduction to a book which was published in West Germany. The manuscript, along with the introduction, was smuggled out of Hungary, after the original manuscript had been smuggled in to Budapest from Czechoslovakia. The book is a 320-page historical study by Kálmán Janics about Czechoslovakia's persecution, disenfranchisement and partial deportation of its Hungarian minority population between 1945 and 1948.[24] In the introduction Illyés writes:

Even the newest historical developments seem to work against the national minorities. Industrialization centralizes; it creates and expands cities. And the cities are assimilation centers where the majority language, the official state language, prevails. It is relatively easy for the oppressive forces to break up the homogenous ethnic regions of the minorities by building factories and purposively directing the relocation patterns of their new worker populations.[25]

Illyés' observations of this modern method of forced assimilation are borne out by current demographic data. In Romania, for example, by 1977 only one of the eight largest, traditionally Hungarian cities had a Hungarian majority. The fastest population shifts occurred in the past decade.[26] The multitude of laws and regulations, which restrict or prohibit the maintenance of minority institutions and practices, results in a shift from majority to minority status in these cities, which in turn forces the Hungarian population to give up its language and culture. It is estimated by a demographer that about 20–25 percent of Hungarian children do not currently have the opportunity to learn to read and write in their own language.

In the introduction to the book about Czechoslovakia's Hungarian minority, Illyés comes to hard conclusions about the future of minority rights:

> Prospects for the future are dim, but the lessons of the past bring some truths into sharp focus. If a 'majority' society is incapable of providing equal opportunities to its 'minorities,' then it is unworthy to govern them. Mankind itself has to protect these minorities, to protect itself from the recurrence of barbarism on the troublesome road toward civilization. The symptoms of barbarism reveal themselves most alarmingly in our behavior toward the weak, the defenseless.[27]

Illyés turned 79 years old on the sixtieth anniversary of the Trianon treaty. He is ailing. His admonition to young writers, at a two-day meeting on May 18 and 19 at Lakitelek in Hungary, to take up the issue of human rights and the cause of the Hungarian minorities could be taken almost as his spiritual last will.

The issue of nationhood, and that of national minorities, became the foremost issue of the twentieth century. The plight of Hungarians beyond our borders has become a world problem because it is a question of universal human concern. Here is your challenge: either you, too, take responsibility for doing something about this problem, or you will pass on without having made your mark as a generation of writers on the literature and history of our nation.[28]

Notes

1. Illyés, Gyula: "Írói gondok" [The Writer's Concerns], *Tiszatáj* (September 1980), p. 5.
2. Kabdebo, Thomas and Paul Tábori, ed.: *A tribute to Gyula Illyés* (Washington: Occidental Press, 1968).
3. Illyés, Gyula: "Írói gondok" [The Writers Concerns], *Új Tükör* (February 17, 1980), p. 9.
4. Illyés, Gyula: "Bevezető" [Introduction], in Kálmán Janics, *A hontalanság évei, a szlovákiai magyar kisebbség a második világháború után 1945-1948,* [The Years of Homelessness; The Hungarian Minority in Slovakia After the Second World War, 1945-1948] (Munich: Europai Protestáns Magyar Szabadegyetem, 1979), p. 19.
5. Illyés, Gyula: "Utódaink nemcsak testünkből származnak—szellemünkből is" [Our Offsprings Generate Not Only From Our Bodies, But Also From Our Spirit], *Alföld* (May 1980), p. 75.

6. *Ibid.*, p. 73.

7. Illyés, Gyula: *Szellem és erőszak* [Spirit and Violence], Magveto (Budapest, 1978), p. 12-20.

8. *Ibid.*, p. 18-19.

9. *Szellem és erőszak*, p. 91-92.

10. *Szellem és erőszak*, p. 71.

11. *Szellem és erőszak*, p. 214.

12. *Szellem és erőszak*, p. 254-255.

13. *Szellem és erőszak*, p. 36.

14. *Szellem és erőszak*, p. 256, 257, 258.

15. *Szellem és erőszak*, p. 56.

16. *Szellem és erőszak*, p. 44.

17. *Szellem és erőszak*, p. 272-273.

18. *Szellem és erőszak*, p. 271-272.

19. *Szellem és erőszak*, p. 72-73.

20. *Szellem és erőszak*, p. 91.

21. *Szellem és erőszak*, p. 93.

22. *Szellem és erőszak*, p. 175, 176, 180, 190-191.

23. "Diktarprotest med politikst eko" [Protest of a Poet With a Political Echo], *Svenska Dagbladet* (Stockholm), May 12, 1978.

24. Janics, Kálmán.

25. Janics, Kalman, p. 17.

26. Semlyén, István: *Hétmilliárd lélek*, [Seven Billion Souls] Kriterion (Bucharest, 1980).

27. Janics, Kálmán, p. 19.

28. Illyés, Gyula: "Lehet még nemzedék?" [Can There Yet Be a Generation?], *Forrás*, Kecskemét, XI, 9 (September, 1979), pp. 117-118.

George Schöpflin

Trianon Two Generations After

Two generations after the Treaty of Trianon, Hungarian society continues to be haunted by its provisions. In a very real sense, Hungary has yet to come to terms with the loss of empire. The establishment of an independent state of Hungary, achieved at the Paris Peace Settlement, has not proved sufficient compensation for the loss of people and territory at Trianon. The loss of empire was the first of the three caesuras of 20th century Hungarian history and despite the enormous changes resulting from all three—the other two having been the collapse of 1944-45 and the revolution of 1956—the effects of Trianon continue to influence Hungarian perceptions in a variety of ways, above all where Hungary's neighbours are concerned.

The specificity of the Hungarian problem lies in the fact that it was not merely territory that was lost, but a substantial proportion of the ethnically Hungarian population. Territorial losses, where the territory concerned does not involve the loss of co-nationals, can be comparatively easily absorbed, but where the territory in question remains inhabited by co-nationals, the problem lives on the consciousness of the nation that has suffered. In the case of Hungarian national consciousness, the matter has been exacerbated by the loss of Transylvania, because Transylvania has been perceived as having made the vital contribution to the continuity of Hungarian statehood and the survival of the Hungarian nation. Thus at some level, Transylvania has come to form an integral part of the area perceived by the nation as its ideal homeland, without which the nation state is felt to be truncated. This complex of factors has weighed heavily on Hungarian political consciousness and on political behaviour. It has contributed significantly to what István Bibó diagnosed as the 'cul-de-sac of Hungarian history.'[1]

The second caesura brought with it one major change. The myth of the Crownlands of St. Stephen[2] was effectively destroyed with the destruction of the political class that had deployed it as an instrument of legitimation in the interwar period. The experience of 1938-45, the reannexation of Hungarian-inhabited territories from the successor states, was regarded after the end of World War II as closing this particular chapter. The reannexations had been purchased at too high a price—the involvement of Hungary in the Second World War and the physical and human losses that resulted. This change in perceptions did not, however, mean that the sense of community with the Hngarian minorities had evaporated; rather, the concept of integral revisionism was jettisoned, especially after the vain attempts to salvage a minimum at the 1947 peace negotiations had failed.[3]

The second caesura brought with it another important political innovation—a strengthening of the Danubian component in Hungarian national consciousness.[4] The impulse towards the establishment of a Danubian confederation, which, its protagonists hoped, would resolve most or all of the intertwined question of minorities and irredenta, had had some antecedents in Hungarian thinking. Indeed, Kossuth had favoured it, albeit only after he had lost political power. But after 1945, an influential section of the intelligentsia hoped to be able to create new bonds with Hungary's neighbours, to effect a nation-to-nation reconciliation, and in this way, to outflank the provisions of Trianon. Ideally, a Danubian confederation would have provided a framework within which the minorities in the successor states could retain sufficient links with the Hungarian state to unite them into a relatively heterogeneous cultural community, while safeguarding their separate political loyalties, i.e., to the successor states.

The Danubian idea resurfaced in 1956, at the next caesura when it was put forward as a means of reassuring the successor states that Hungary had no irredentist demands to make. There was a fairly clear undercurrent of thought in Czechoslovakia and Romania that the Hungarian revolution would rapidly turn to nationalism and that demands for territorial revision would not be far away thereafter;[5] even the Yugoslavs were influenced by this equation. It was to settle this complex of doubts, presumably, that the radio station controlled by the Borsod county workers' council proclaimed: 'Our country should be a member of the Danubian confederation as planned by Lajos Kossuth,' an idea Imre Nagy advocated prior to the revolution.[6] The general mood in 1956, according to the various statements made at the time, was that Hungary sought friendly relations with its neighbours and that territorial revision was not on the agenda.

The Danubian idea made another appearance in the 1960's, when Kádár's government began to float the idea of Danubian cooperation.[7] Four states would be involved—Hungary, Yugoslavia, Austria and Czechoslovakia—and the Hungarians envisaged a very loose form of cooperation, not much more than regular consultation on matters of mutual interest, but under the symbolic umbrella of the Danubian idea. The plan came to nothing. The Austrians were enthusiastic, the Yugoslav and Czechoslovak governments ignored it. But as far as Hungary was concerned, the project was intended to serve two longer term purposes. First, it would help to place Hungary on the international map and might even produce solid economic benefits. Over and above that one could sense in the proposal the reactivation of the circumventing of Trianon, of finding a way to establish links with the minorities without offending the sensibilities of the successor states. The plan suffered from defects—neither of the two relevant successor states (Czechoslovakia and Yugoslavia) had any interest in it and it sought patently to isolate Romania, which by this stage was already embarked on its strategy of substituting Romanian nationalism for Marxism as the ideology of the state.

In the 1970's, the Hungarian government tried another tack. If multilateral cooperation was a non-starter, then bilateral means might work. This was the principle behind the series of agreements signed between Hungary, Czechoslovakia, Yugoslavia and Romania, respectively, to the effect that the minorities in Hungary and the Hungarian minorities in the other states formed bridges.[8] By creating an internationally recognized framework, the Hungarian state presumably hoped to establish a *locus standi* for itself vis-à-vis the minorities. It was not a great success, though it did represent a step forward. As far as Yugoslavia was concerned, the agreement worked adequately but then the position of the Hungarian minority there was incomparably better than in the other two countries. Romania had to be dragged kicking and screaming to the conference table and in practice, there is precious little reality to the minorities forming a bridge between the two states. Indeed, on closer examination, the idea that a Romanian minority of 25,000 in Hungary was in any way comparable to a Hungarian minority of 2 million in Romania was absurd.

At the popular level, perceptions of the successor states in Hungary were very largely dependent on how they were thought to be treating their Hungarian minority. This resulted in one of the most remarkable distortions of political evaluation that Eastern Europe had witnessed since 1945. Whereas for world opinion, the Dubček reform program in Czechoslovakia was viewed in terms of democratization, institutional change, ideological renewal and the like, Hungarian opinion concentrated exclusively—though obviously there were some individual exceptions to this—on how the minority in Slovakia would fare.[9] Hungarian history had once again gone down a cul-de-sac. It is fair to say, however, that the equipment taken there was lighter. Despite the legacy of Trianon, there was no particular enthusiasm in Hungary that Hungarian military units had participated in the occupation of Slovakia and were for the most part stationed in the areas inhabited by Hungarians. Rather, the response was to ignore the entire event.

Perceptions of Romania, however, did not rest quite so lightly on Hungarian consciousness. Even in the 1960's, there was mounting concern at every level of Hungarian opinion at what it suspected was happening to the Hungarians of Transylvania. For a variety of reasons, it would seem, the loss of Transylvania left much deeper scars than the loss of the Hungarian-inhabited parts of Slovakia or Yugoslavia. The myth value of Transylvania, its symbolic function as the ideal homeland, has already been mentioned. The purely demographic factor of there being two million Hungarians in Romania as against 600,000 in Slovakia was another. The Czechoslovak government likewise contributed to this complex of perceptions, in that access to Slovakia was generally open to Hungarians, and there was no attempt made to prevent Hungarians travelling there. The Romanian authorities, on the other hand, made it evident that they greatly disliked the attention paid by Hungarians to Transylvania and the decision to ban foreign travellers from staying in private houses was widely seen by Hungarians as directed specifically at them.[10] That view was only reinforced by the requirement imposed in the summer of 1979 that foreign tourists would have to pay for petrol in hard currency.

The popular attitude towards Romanians was further demonstrated by two attitude surveys. The first of these was carried out by Radio Free Europe's Audience Research Department and was devoted to a measurement of Hungarian autostereotypes and heterostereotypes; Romanians were included among the latter.[11] This survey suggested the existence of very deep-seated feelings of antagonism and cultural superiority vis-à-vis Romanians. The Romanians scored next to nothing on attributes like 'courage,' 'generosity,' 'love of peace' and 'hard work,' while they scored high on 'cruelty,' 'conceit,' 'laziness,' 'backwardness' and 'a tendency to dominate.' This remarkably negative heterostereotype was directly attributable to the failure of Hungarian society to come to terms with the loss of Transylvania, a process made much more difficult by the policies of the Romanian government and, equally, of the Hungarian government.

This last refers to the policy of the Hungarian authorities for much of the 1960's and 1970's, of pretending that Transylvania was not an issue as far as Hungarian opinion was concerned.[12] It led to the state of affairs where over one-fifth of secondary pupils could fail to give an adequate answer to the question, 'What language is spoken by the Szekelys?' As Gyula Illyés pointed out, that answer should have been automatic. In essence, because of the tergiversations of official policy—for example, on whether the capital of Transylvania should be referred to as 'Cluj' or 'Kolozsvár'—a sense of uneasiness has arisen on this topic, with the result that distorted perceptions continue to be reproduced in each generation. In the late 1970's, there was an appreciable change in this connection, and Transylvania ceased to be quite the taboo topic that it had been. This was partly attributable to the bilateral declaration of 1977; it also derived from the official policy of increasing reliance on an unstated Hungarian nationalism as a source of legitimacy. The speech made at the Helsinki summit by János Kádár was an important milestone here, for he referred in overtly rhetorical terms to the losses of people and territory suffered by the Hungarian nation after 1918, something which was automatically interpreted as a hint about Transylvania.[13] In the second half of the decade, the silence about Transylvania ended, although this did not signify an open debate. Rather it was the customary method of allusive, tangential debates and articles, in which the polemics with Romanian historians about Daco-Roman continuity were probably the most pointed. Confusion in this area was demonstrated by an audience survey in Hungary carried out under the aegis of the Mass Communications Institute.[14] This survey

returned a fairly high number of respondents who believed that
Romania had been on the victorious side in the Second World War
(which was technically correct, of course, as far as the end of the war
was concerned). The results of this survey were made all the more
remarkable by the fact that it had been carried out immediately after
Hungarian television had shown a documentary series on World
War II. To be sure, some of the confusion must be attributed to ignorance, but the deeper perceptions about the Transylvanian question must also have played a role.

In all, Trianon and its results continue to haunt Hungarian opinion, both the intelligentsia and through the mediation of the intelligentsia, the broader public too. The most obvious explanation
for this is the continued existence of a very significant number of
Hungarians in the successor states and the perception in Hungary
that these co-nationals, by reason of having been detached from the
Hungarian state, suffer various disabilities in consequence. Thus in
this way, the romantic integralist view of Hungarian nationhood has
become fused with questions of minority rights and it has become
next to impossible for the two to be disentangled. By the same token,
Hungarian society has been unable to adjust to the 'loss of empire'
suffered after 1918 and the sense of loss has changed but not
diminished over time. Here again this is self-evidently attributable to
the continued existence of an ethnically, culturally and, in the eyes of
the Hungarians of Hungary, politically Hungarian population in the
successor states. Short of radical changes in the policies of the latter,
there seemed little likelihood of Hungarian perceptions being
modified in this respect.

Notes

1. István Bibó, 'Eltorzult magyar alkat, zsákutcás magyar történelem,'
Harmadik Út, (London: Magyar Könyves Céh, 1960).

2. A clear assessment of the myth of the Crownlands of St. Stephen may
be found in Walter Kolarz, *Myths and Realities in Eastern Europe* (London:
Lindsay Drummond, 1946), pp. 86–98.

3. On Hungary's experience at the Paris Peace negotiations, see Stephen
Borsody, *The Triumph of Tyranny* (New York: 1960).

4. Among other works produced in this vein and which were clearly
didactic in purpose were Elemér Radisics, *A Dunatáj*, 3 vols. (Budapest:
Gergely R.R.-T., 1946-47); István Borsody, *Magyar-Szlovák kiegyezés*

(Budapest: Officina, n.d.); László Szenczei, *Magyar-Román kérdés* (Budapest: Officina, n.d.).

5. Evidence for Czechoslovakia comes from the interview given by Gyula Lőrinc in *Új Szó,* 28 March 1968; in Romania, the Hungarian events had even more direct repercussions, in the form of demonstrations in several Transylvanian towns, *Magyar Hiradó* (Vienna), January 1, 1978.

6. Borsod radio is quoted by Vilmos Juhász, 'A forradalom követelései,' in Gyula Borbándi and József Molnár, eds., *Tanulmányok a magyar forradalomról* (Munich: Auróra, 1966), p. 492; Imre Nagy, *On Communism: In Defence of the New Course* (London: Thames & Hudson, 1957), pp. 239–244.

7. A very detailed analysis of the question of Hungary and the Danube Valley, with a lengthy assessment of the cooperation project of the 1960's, is by Charles András, "Neighbors on the Danube: New Variations of an Old Theme of Regional Cooperation," *Radio Free Europe Research* (Munich: RFE, 1967).

8. The agreements with Yugoslavia and Czechoslovakia were apparently reached without too much difficulty and the Hungarian-Yugoslav agreement is regularly held up as a model of good relations. Romania was much more difficult to persuade to attend at the negotiating table and Ceauşescu's reluctance was hardly disguised. Hence it cannot be excluded that some Soviet pressure was involved, especially as the signing of the agreement (1977) coincided with a period of Romanian accommodation to Soviet pressures in other areas.

9. Rudolf L. Tőkés, 'Hungarian Intellectuals' Reaction to the Invasion of Czechoslovakia,' in (eds.) E. J. Czerwinski and Jaroslaw Piekalkiewicz, *The Soviet Invasion of Czechoslovakia: Its Effects on Eastern Europe* (London, New York: Praeger, 1972), pp. 139–157 at p. 148.

10. George Schöpflin, *The Hungarians of Rumania,* Minority Rights Group Report no. 37 (London: 1978), p. 15, for details.

11. APOR, *The Hungarian Self-Image and the Hungarian Image of Americans, Russians, Germans, Rumanians and Chinese* (Munich: Radio Free Europe, 1970).

12. Gyula Illyés, 'A *Magyar Nyelvőr* ünnepére,' *Népszabadság,* 16 January 1972 and Lajos Für, 'Milyen nyelven beszélnek a székelyek?,' *Tiszatáj,* 26:8 (August 1972), pp. 57–66 contain powerful indictments of the shortsightedness of official Hungarian information policy on Transylvania, the crux of which is that the absence of information on what is an integral part of the Hungarian identity, i.e., Transylvania, has created confusion and distortions of perceptions of national identity.

13. *Népszabadság,* August 1, 1975. Kádár had already begun to prepare Hungarian opinion for changes in this area by his comments at the 11th

Congress of the Hungarian party, where he expressed the hope that Hungarians outside Hungary would enjoy rights as far-reaching as the non-Hungarians in Hungary; he reiterated this at the 12th Congress in 1980. *Népszabadság*, December 10, 1980, carried a report summarizing the views of the Hungarian delegate to the Madrid follow-up conference on European security. This contained possibly the harshest attack made by an official Hungarian spokesman on Romania since the communist takeover and as good as accused the Romanian authorities of oppression of the Hungarian minority.

14. Mária Dankánics, 'Különböző korú munkások tudati képe a II. világháborúról,' *Szociológia*, 3–4 (1976), pp. 494–501.

Biographical Index

Adatci, Baron
Japanese representative in the Council of the League of Nations. Rapporteur on minority questions.

Ady, Endre (1877–1919)
Hungarian poet and journalist.

Ágoston, Péter (1874–1925)
Socialist publicist, state secretary for internal affairs during the Károlyi regime, 1919, and Assistant Commissar of Foreign Affairs of the Hungarian Soviet Republic.

Alexander I (1884–1934)
Regent, 1918–1921, then King of the Serbs, Croats, and Slovenes, 1921–1929. King of Yugoslavia, 1929–1934.

Allizé, Henry (1860–1930)
Head of the French military mission in Vienna, 1918–1919.

Amendola, Giovanni (1886–1926)
Italian publicist and politician. Cabinet minister in the Nitti, Bonomi and Facta governments, 1919–1921.

Alpári, Gyula (1882–1944)
Hungarian communist leader and an associate of Béla Kun.

Angyal, Dávid (1857–1943)
Liberal historian, representative of the Positivist School in interwar Hungary.

Antonescu, Ion (1882–1946)
Romanian chief of state and dictator.

Antonescu, Victor
Romanian envoy to France, 1919.

Apáthy, István (1863–1922)
Biologist, political leader of the Hungarians in Transylvania and briefly commissioner of Transylvania during the Karolyi regime, December, 1918.

Apponyi, Albert Count (1846–1933)
Politician and statesman. Minister of Education, 1906–1910, and 1917–1918. President of the Hungarian peace delegation. Chief representative of Hungary to the League of Nations, 1923–1931.

Aprily, Lajos (1887–1967)
Poet, translator.

Asquith, Herbert Henry (1852-1928)
    Prime minister of Great Britain, 1908-1916.
Athelstan-Johnston, Wilfred (1876-1939)
    British Acting High Commissioner and Chargé d'Affaires in Hungary,
    1920-1921.
Avarescu, Alexandru (1859-1938)
    Military officer, three-time Minister President of Romania.
Babeş, Victor (1854-1924)
    Scientist and educator; the Romanian Babeş University in Cluj was
    named after him.
Babits, Mihály (1883-1941)
    Hungarian poet, an editor of the progressive journal *Nyugat* (West).
Bajcsy-Zsilinszky, Endre (1886-1944)
    Publicist and politician, leader of the Hungarian anti-fascist resistance.
Balázs, Béla (1884-1949)
    Poet, dramatist, and film theorist.
Balfour, Arthur J. (1848-1930)
    British Secretary of State for Foreign Affairs, 1916-1919.
Bartha, Albert (1877-1960)
    Minister of War in the Károlyi cabinet, November 9, 1918-December 12,
    1918.
Bartók, Béla (1881-1945)
    Hungarian composer and ethnographer.
Batthyány, Tivadar Count (1859-1931)
    Politician, Minister of Interior of the Károlyi government, 1918.
Bauer, Otto (1882-1938)
    Socialist theoretician and politician, leader of the II. International and of
    the Austrian Social Democratic Party. Minister of Foreign Affairs,
    November 1918-July 1919.
Benárd, Ágost (1880-   )
    Christian-Socialist politician. Minister of Welfare, 1920-1921. Signatory
    to the Trianon Peace Treaty.
Benedek, Elek (1859-1929)
    Hungarian writer, publicist.
Benedict XV (1854-1922)
    Pope, 1914-1922.
Beneš, Eduard (1884-1948)
    Foreign Minister, later President of Czechoslovakia.
Berinkey, Dénes (1871-1948)
    Minister of Justice in the Károlyi cabinet (1918); Prime Minister, January
    11, 1919-March 21, 1919.
Berthelot, Henri-Mathias (1861-1931)
    French general, reorganized the Romanian army in 1917; commander of
    the Allied forces in Romania and Southern Russia, 1918-1919.

Berthelot, Philippe (1866–1934)
  Secretary-General, French Ministry of Foreign Affairs, 1920–1921, and
  1925–1932.
Bethlen, István Count (1874–1947)
  Member of Hungarian peace delegation, 1920; Prime Minister of
  Hungary, 1921–1931.
Beveridge, William H. (1879–1963)
  Secretary of British Ministry of Food, 1919.
Blaho, Pavel (1867–1927)
  Slovak deputy in the Hungarian parliament, later deputy in the
  Czechoslovak parliament.
Bleyer, Jakob (1874–1933)
  Literary historian and university professor. Leader of the German
  minorities in Hungary. Minister of nationalities in various cabinets from
  August 1919–December 1920.
Bliss, Tasker Howard (1853–1930)
  Soldier, scholar, diplomat; American military representative on the
  Supreme War Council.
Blum, Léon (1872–1950)
  French socialist and premier, 1936–1937, 1938.
Böhm, Vilmos (1880–1948)
  Socialist leader, Minister of War of the Berinkey Government, Com-
  missar of War of the Kun regime.
Bolgár, Elek (1883–1955)
  Lawyer and historian. Ambassador to Austria during the Hungarian
  Soviet Republic, then a member of the Foreign Affairs Commissariat.
Bölöni, György (1882–1959)
  Hungarian writer and critic.
Bolyai, János (1802–1860)
  One of the founders of non-Euclidian geometry; the Hungarian Bolyai
  University in Cluj was named after him (since 1953, Babeş-Bolyai Univer-
  sity).
Bonitz, Frantz (1868–1936)
  Head of the press bureau of the prime minister, 1920. Leader of the Ger-
  man nationalities in Hungary.
Borah, William Edgar (1865–1940)
  U.S. Senator, 1907–1940; Chairman of the Senate Committee on Foreign
  Relations, 1924–1940.
Borghese, Livio Prince
  Italian diplomat and representative in Budapest, March to June, 1919.
Brandsch, Rudolf
  Transylvanian Saxon leader in Hungary, later in Romania.
Brătianu, Ioan I.C. (1864–1927)
  Romanian political leader, head of the National Liberal Party.

Briand, Aristide (1862–1932)
French Prime Minister, 1921–1922, 1925–1926; Foreign Minister, 1921–1922, 1925–1930.

Brown, Philip Marshall (1875–1966)
Professor of International Law, 1915–1929, Princeton University; a member of the Coolidge mission in Vienna.

Burrows, Ronald M. (1867–1920)
British scholar, co-editor of The New Europe.

Cambon, Paul (1843–1924)
French diplomat, ambassador to London, 1898–1920.

Carol II (1893–1953)
King of Romania, 1930–1940.

Ceausescu, Nicolae (b. 1918)
Communist party Secretary of Romania since 1965. President of Romania.

Cecil, Lord Edgar A. (1864–1960)
British Assistant Secretary of State for Foreign Affairs, 1918–1919.

Charles (1887–1922)
Emperor of Austria, King of Hungary, 1916–1918.

Charles-Roux, François (1879–1961)
Counsellor, French Embassy, Rome, 1916–1925.

Charmant, Oszkár (1860–1925)
Attorney of the Károlyi family. Representative of the Károlyi government in Vienna, 1918–1919.

Churchill, Winston Leonard Spencer (1874–1965)
British politician and statesman. Minister of Munitions, July 1917; Secretary of War, January 1919–1921.

Claude, Jr., Inis L. (b. 1922)
American scholar, author.

Clemenceau, Georges (1841–1929)
French politician and statesman; Prime Minister and Minister of War (1917–1920); President of the Paris Peace Conference, 1919.

Clément-Simon, Gustave (1833–1937)
French diplomat, Minister plenipotentiary in Prague in 1918 and in Belgrade in 1921.

Clerk, George R. (1874–1951)
Head of Allied Mission in Hungary, 1919.

Coandă, General Constantin
Premier of Romania.

Codreanu, Corneliu Zelea (1899–1933)
Romanian political leader of the Iron Guard.

Cook, Joseph (1860–1947)
Australian Minister for the Navy, 1917–1920.

Coolidge, Archibald Cary (1866–1928)
American scholar, member of the American delegation to the Peace Conference, 1919.

Couget, Joseph
  French Minister to Czechoslovakia, 1920–1926.
Crowe, Eyre (1864–1925)
  Assistant Under-Secretary of State for Foreign Affairs, 1912–1920.
Csáky, Imre Count (1882–1961)
  Austro-Hungarian diplomat; Head of the Political Department of Károlyi's Ministry of Foreign Affairs, 1918–1919; Minister of Foreign Affairs, 1920.
Csáky, István Count (1894–1941)
  Secretary of the Hungarian peace delegation, 1920.
Csernoch, János (1852–1927)
  Cardinal of Esztergom, 1913–1927; Primate of Hungary, 1914–1927.
Csuday, Jenő (1852–1938)
  Catholic priest, historian, follower of the National Romantic School.
Cunninghame, Thomas Montgomery, Sir (1877–   )
  Head of the British Military Mission in Vienna, 1918–1919.
Curzon, Lord George N. (1859–1925)
  British Secretary of State for Foreign Affairs, 1919–1924.
Cuza, A. C. (1857–1940)
  Romanian politician; head of the League of National Christian Defense.
Czernin, Ottokar Count (1872–1932)
  Austro-Hungarian ambassador to Bucharest, then Minister of Foreign Affairs, 1916–1918.
Dami, Aldo (b. 1898)
  Swiss historian, expert on minority affairs.
Dániel, Arnold (1878–1968)
  Radical, sociologist, economist.
Dawson, Coningsby (1883–1959)
  American economist.
Deák, Ferenc (1803–1876)
  Hungarian statesman, framer of the Compromise of 1867.
Derby, Earl of (1865–1948)
  British Ambassador to France, 1918–1920.
Dérain, Raoul
  French major, head of the Interallied Military Commission in Pécs, 1919.
Deshanel, Paul (1855–1922)
  President of the French Republic, January-September, 1920.
Diner-Dénes, József (1857–1937)
  Socialist publicist, journalist and critic.
Dobrovits, Péter
  Painter; President of the stillborn Baranya Republic.
Domanovszky, Sándor (1877–1955)
  Historian, university professor, representative of the Hungarian *Kulturgeschichte* School of interwar Hungary.

Drašković, Milorad (1873–1921)
Yugoslav statesman, Minister of Interior, 1920.

Drasche-Lázár, Alfréd (1875–1949)
Head of the Prime Ministry's news bureau, 1914–1918; government official during the Károlyi regime, 1918–1919. Special envoy and minister; signatory to the Treaty of Trianon.

Duczynska, Ilona (1897–1978)
Left-wing socialist and radical publicist/historian.

Dula, Matúš (1846–1926)
Slovak nationalist politician, in 1918 the President of the Slovak National Council.

Erdélyi, Ioan
Leader of the Romanians in pre-war Hungary; member of the Romanian National Committee.

Erdélyi, László (1868–1947)
A historian-priest of the Benedictine Order, medievalist at the University of Szeged.

Földessy, Gyula (1874–1964)
Literary critic and historian.

Foch, Ferdinand (1851–1929)
French marshal, chief of the French General Staff, Commander-in-Chief of the Allied forces, 1918.

Fouchet, Maurice
French High Commissioner in Hungary, 1920–1921.

Fraknói, Vilmos (Wilhelm)
Historian, titular bishop of the Catholic Church, and early representative of the Positivist School in Hungary.

Franchet d'Esperey, Louis Félix (1856–1942)
General, later Marshal of France; commander of the Allied Army of the Orient, 1918–1919.

Franz Ferdinand, Archduke (1863–1914)
Heir to the Austro-Hungarian Monarchy. Assassinated in Sarajevo, Bosnia, June 28, 1914.

Freeman, Edward August (1832–1892)
British historian, representative of the political-historical orientation.

Friedl, Richard
Comintern delegate from Pécs.

Friedrich, István (1883–1959)
Hungarian politician. Prime Minister, 1919; Minister of War, 1919–1920.

Fülep, Lajos (1885–1970)
Philosopher, art historian, esthete. Lived in Italy, 1907–1914. Because of Italian contacts, was sent on diplomatic missions to Fiume by Count Mihály Károlyi, 1918–1919.

Fürstenberg, Egon von
German Minister in Budapest.

Garami, Ernő (1876–1935)
Editor and moderate socialist leader.

Gheorghiu-Dej, Gheorghe (1908–1965)
Romanian Communist Party secretary, 1944–1965; Prime Minister, 1954–1955; Head of State, 1961–1965.

Gjorgjevic, Djoka
Colonel in the Yugoslav army.

Glatz, Ferenc (b. 1941)
Historian, head of the Historiographical Section of the Institute of History, Hungarian Academy of Sciences.

Goldis, Vasile (1861–1934)
Romanian political leader from Arad.

Gömbös, Gyula (1886–1936)
Prime Minister of Hungary, 1932–1936.

Gömöri, Jenő (1890–1968)
Poet and editor.

Goode, William (1875–1944)
British representative on the Supreme Economic Council at the Paris Peace Conference.

Gosset, F. W. (1876–1931)
British colonel, head of the Inter-Allied Military Commission in Pécs, 1921.

Gottwald, Klement (1896–1953)
Czech communist politician; leader of the Communist Party of Czechoslovakia, 1919–1923; third president of Czechoslovakia, 1948–1953.

Gower, Sir Robert (1880–1953)
Member of the House of Commons, jurist and author.

Gramsci, Antonio (1891–1937)
Italian communist activist and thinker.

Grátz, Gusztáv (1875–1946)
Hungarian statesman and historian.

Grazioli, Francesca Saverio (1869–1951)
Italian general, commander of the Inter-Allied troops occupying Fiume, 1919.

Grey, Sir Edward (1862–1933)
British statesman; Foreign Secretary, 1905–1916.

Groza, Petru (1884–1958)
Founder of the Ploughmen's Front and Prime Minister of Romania between 1945–1952; also President of the Presidium of the Grand National Assembly, 1952–1958.

Gündisch, Guido
A leader of the German nationalities in Hungary.

Hajdu, Gyula (1886-1973)
Lawyer, leader of the Pécs labor movement.

Hajnal, István (1898-1956)
Historian, university professor and the originator of a new sociological-technological orientation in Hungarian historiography.

Halmos, Károly
Hungarian lawyer.

Hatvany, Lajos (1880-1961)
Writer and critic, Ady scholar; in 1918 a member of the Hungarian National Council and an envoy to the Belgrade armistice negotiations.

Hay, Gyula (1900-1975)
Marxist dramatist.

Hennocque, Edmond
French General.

Herczeg, Ferenc (1863-1954)
Writer, journalist, politician; President of the Revisionist League.

Hertling, Georg (Friedrich), Graf von (1843-1919)
Conservative German statesman and thinker; German Chancellor, November 1917-September 1918.

Hitler, Adolf (1889-1945)
German Chancellor, 1933, and dictator of the Nazi state, 1934-1945.

Hlinka, Andrej (1864-1938)
Slovak Roman Catholic priest and nationalities leader, following the Trianon treaty, demanded autonomous rights for the Slovaks in Czechoslovakia.

Hock, János (1859-1936)
Catholic priest, President of the Hungarian National Council, 1918-1919.

Hodinka, Antal (1865-1946)
Historian and a significant Slavic specialist at the University of Pécs.

Hodža, Milan (1878-1944)
Slovak politician in pre-war Hungary, Czecho-Slovak representative in Hungary, December 1918; Prime Minister of Czechoslovakia, 1936-1938.

Hohler, Thomas B. (1871-1946)
British High Commissioner in Budapest, 1919-1920; Minister, 1921-1924.

Holub, József (1885-1962)
Constitutional historian at the University of Pécs and one of the younger representatives of interwar Hungarian positivism.

Hóman, Bálint (1885-1952)
Medievalist, Hungarian Minister of Culture; later became involved in rightist politics.

Hoover, Herbert Clark (1874-1964)
U.S. President, 1929-1932; active in international food relief organizations following the armistices of 1918.

Horthy, Miklós (1868-1957)
Regent of Hungary, 1920-1944.

Horvát, István (1785-1846)
Self-taught literary scholar and historian in the period of Hungarian Romanticism and national revival.

Horváth, Jenő (1881-1950)
Diplomatic historian, studied the origins and results of World War I.

House, Colonel Edward Mandell (1853-1938)
Leader of the *Inquiry*, a close advisor of President Wilson.

Huszár, Károly (1882-1941)
Politician, Minister of Education and Religion in the Friedrich cabinets, August 1919-November 1919; Prime Minister, November 1919-March 1920.

Huber, Johannes
German nationalities leader in Hungary.

Husák, Gustav (b. 1913)
Slovak communist politician, the seventh president of Czechoslovakia, 1975- .

Ignotus (Veigelsberg), Hugó (1869-1949)
Literary critic, poet; one of the founders of the journal *Nyugat* (West).

Illyés, Gyula (b. 1902)
Poet, dramatist, essayist.

Inverforth, Lord (1865-1955)
British Minister of Munitions (1919-1921).

Imrédy, Béla (1831-1946)
Pro-fascist politician; Prime Minister of Hungary, 1938-1939.

Ionescu, Take (1858-1922)
Romanian Foreign Minister, 1920-1921.

Iványi, Béla (1878-1964)
Constitutional historian at the University of Debrecen and later at the University of Szeged.

Janics, Kálmán (b. 1913)
Hungarian medical doctor and sociologist in Czechoslovakia.

Janoušek, Antonín (1877-1941)
Czech communist, head of the short-lived Slovak Soviet Republic.

Jászi, Oszkár (1857-1957)
Sociologist, political writer, and Minister of Nationalities in the Károlyi cabinet, 1918.

Jaurès, Jean (1858-1914)
French socialist leader and historian.

Joffre, Joseph (1852-1931)
French marshal, Commander-in-Chief of the French forces, 1914-1916.

Jókai, Mór (1825-1904)
Hungarian romantic writer.

Joseph August, Archduke (1872-1962)
(József Habsburg) *Homo regius* of King Charles in Hungary, October 1918; reclaimed this title in August 1919 and appointed the Friedrich

government. Resigned from his position on Entente pressure on August 25, 1919. Was active supporter of the Horthy regime.

Juriga, Ferdiš (1874–   )
Catholic priest, Slovak deputy in the Hungarian parliament, later in the Czechoslovak parliament.

Kállay, Miklós (1887–1967)
Conservative politician; Minister of Agriculture in the Gömbös government, 1932–1935; Prime Minister, 1942–1944.

Kalmár, Heinrich (1873–1937)
Socialist leader in Pozsony and editor of Westungarische Volksstimme. State Secretary in the German Nationalities Ministry during the Károlyi regime; Commissar of German Affairs during the Soviet Republic.

Kánya, Kálmán (1869–1945)
Politician and diplomat. Permanent Foreign Secretary, 1920–1925.

Karácsonyi, János (1858–1929)
Medievalist and church historian; titular bishop of the Catholic Church in Hungary.

Károlyi, Gyula Count (1886–1947)
Conservative politician, Minister of Foreign Affairs, 1930–1931; Prime Minister, 1931–1932.

Károlyi, Mihály Count (1875–1955)
Hungarian politician and statesman, leader of the October Revolution (1918).

Kassák, Lajos (1887–1967)
Poet and artist, leader of the Hungarian avant-garde.

Keynes, John Maynard (1883–1955)
Economist and philosopher, principal representative of the Treasury on the British Delegation at Paris; Member of the Supreme Economic Council.

Király, Károly (b. 1931)
Former member of the Romanian Communist Party Central Committee and Vice President of the Hungarian Nationality Council in Romania.

Klebesberg, Kunó Count (1875–1932)
Hungarian politician and government official, 1914–1930.

Klofáč, Václav (1886–1942)
Pre-World War I leader of the Czech National Social Party, Czechoslovakia's first Minister of National Defense and leader of the Czechoslovak National Socialist Party.

Kodály, Zoltán (1882–1967)
Composer, pedagogue.

Korányi, Frigyes Baron (1869–1935)
Hungarian economist and Finance Minister, 1919–1920.

Kós, Károly (1883–1977)
Poet, writer, architect and painter.

Košík, Gustav
American Slovak working for Czechoslovak independence.

Kossuth, Ferenc (1841-1914)
Son of Lajos Kossuth. Returned to Hungary in 1894, following father's death, and became a leader of the opposition Independence Party.

Kossuth, Lajos (1802-1894)
Leader of the 1848-1849 Hungarian Revolution.

Kosztolányi, Dezső (1885-1936)
Poet, writer, publicist.

Kozma, Miklós (1884-1941)
Hungarian counter-revolutionary politician; head of MTI, the Hungarian news agency; Minister of Interior, 1935-1937; Commissioner of Sub-Carpathia, 1940-1941.

Kramář, Karel (1860-1937)
Czech politician, first prime minister of Czechoslovakia, 1918-1920.

Kun, Béla (1886-1939)
Leader of the Hungarian Soviet Republic (1919).

Kuncz, Aladár (1886-1931)
Writer, publisher. Following World War I, cultural leader of the Hungarians in Romania.

Kunfi, Zsigmond (1879-1929)
Socialist leader and political writer; member of the governments of Károlyi and Kun regimes (1918-1919).

Kuznetz, Simon (b. 1901)
Russian born American economist; Nobel Memorial Prize winner in 1971.

Láng, Boldizsár Baron (1877-1943)
Chief of military cabinet to Miklós Horthy, 1920.

Lansdowne, Henry Petty-Fitzmaurice Lord (1845-1927)
British statesman; minister without portfolio in the Asquith government, 1915-1916.

Lansing, Robert (1868-1928)
American politician, Secretary of State of President Wilson, 1915-1920.

Landler, Jenő (1875-1928)
Left-wing socialist, later communist; leader of communist opposition to Béla Kun.

Laroche, Jules (1873-   )
Assistant Political Director, French Ministry of Foreign Affairs.

Leeper, Alexander W.A. (1887-1935)
Member of the British Delegation at the Paris Peace Conference.

Lefèvre-Pontalis, Hubert
French Minister to Austria, 1920-1924.

Lengyel, József (1896-1975)
Writer, poet.

Lenin, Vladimir Ilyich (1870-1924)
Russian communist revolutionary.

Lesznai, Anna (1885-1966)
Poet and artist, wife of Oszkár Jászi, 1913-1920.

Lincoln, Abraham (1809-1865)
President of the United States, 1860-1865.

Linder, Béla (1856-1962)
Lt. Colonel, Staff officer in the Austro-Hungarian Army; briefly Minister of Defense in the Károlyi cabinet and Mayor of Serb-occupied Pécs, 1920-1921.

Lloyd George, David (1863-1945)
British Prime Minister, 1916-1922.

Lobit, Paul-Joseph-Jean-Hector de,
French general, Commander of the Allied "Army of Hungary," March, 1919.

Loucheur, Louis (1872-1931)
French Minister of Reconstruction, 1919-1920; Minister of Liberated Territory, 1921-1922.

Lovászy, Márton (1864-1927)
Politician and journalist; member of the Károlyi cabinet.

Ludendorff, Erich von (1865-1937)
Chief of Staff of the 8th army in 1914, adjutant to Field Marshal Paul von Hindenburg. Commander of German land force, 1916-1918.

Lukács, György (1885-1971)
Marxist philosopher and literary critic.

Mackensen, August von (1849-1945)
German general, commander of the German forces in Romania, 1917-1918.

Macartney, Carlile Aylmer (1895-1978)
British historian of the Danubian region, a critic of the Treaty of Trianon.

Makkai, Sándor (1890-1951)
Calvinist bishop of Transylvania; college professor and writer. Active in the Romanian Senate for minorities rights. Left Romania in 1936.

Mályusz, Elemér (b. 1898)
Medievalist and founder of the Hungarian Ethnohistory School.

Mandelshtam, Andrei (1869-1949)
Jurist, author, director of the Department of Legal Affairs of the Foreign Ministry of Imperial Russia.

Maniu, Iuliu (1873-1953)
Politician, before 1918 a member of the Hungarian Parliament; leader of the Romanian National Peasant Party and Minister President of Romania, 1928-1930, and 1932-1933.

Marczali, Henrik (1856-1940)
The best known Hungarian historian of the Positivist School.

Marghiloman, Alexandru (1854-1925)
Conservative premier of Romania, 1918.

Masaryk, Tomáš Garrigue (1850-1937)
Chief founder and first President of Czechoslovakia

Mayr, Michael (1864-1922)
Austrian Chancellor, 1920-1921.

Medvecký, Karol Anton (1875-1937)
Catholic priest, secretary of the Slovak National Council, labor member of the Slovak provisional government and a deputy in the Czechoslovak parliament.

Menczer, Béla (b. 1902)
Writer and historian.

Meskó, Zoltán (1883-1963)
Rightwing politician, parliamentary deputy and participant in the Arrow Cross movement. Founder and leader of the Hungarian National Socialist Party in 1933.

Milojević, Milan
Yugoslav diplomat.

Mikes, Kelemen (1680-1761)
Writer, advisor and companion to Ferenc Rákóczi II in his Turkish exile.

Mikszáth, Kálmán (1847-1910)
Hungarian writer.

Millerand, Alexandre (1859-1943)
French Prime Minister, 1920; President of France, 1920-1924; President of the Council of Ambassadors of the Peace Conference.

Miskolczy, Gyula (1892-1961)
Hungarian historian, one of the younger exponents of the *Geistesgeschichte* School, and a specialist in Croatian affairs.

Miskolczy, István (1881-1937)
A Catholic historian-priest, member of the Piarist Order in Hungary.

Móricz, Zsigmond (1879-1942)
Hungarian writer and publicist.

Mussolini, Benito (1883-1945)
Italian fascist dictator, 1922-1943.

Namier, Lewis B. (1888-1960)
Temporary Clerk in the Foreign Office (1918-1920); during the war, member of the Intelligence Bureau and the P.I.D.

Napoleon, Bonaparte (1796-1821)
French Emperor.

Németh, Andor (1891-1953)
Writer, critic, editor.

Németh, László (1901-1975)
Hungarian novelist, dramatist and essayist.

Nendtvich, Andor
    Mayor of Pécs.
Newton, Lord Thomas Wodehouse Legh (1857–1942)
    British statesman.
Nicolson, Harold G. (1886–1968)
    British diplomat and author; Secretary in the Foreign Office, 1918–1920.
Ninčič, Momčilo (1876–1949)
    Foreign Minister of Yugoslavia, 1921–1926.
Nitti, Francesco Saverio (1868–1953)
    Italian liberal politician; Prime Minister, 1919–1920.
Nivelle, Robert Georges (1856–1924)
    French general; Commander in Chief of the French forces in the North
    and North-east, 1916–1917.
Northcliffe, Alfred Charles William Harmsworth, 1st Viscount (1865–1922)
    British newspaper publisher and founder of popular modern journal-
    ism. Director of the Department of Enemy Propaganda during World
    War I.
Orlando, Vittorio Emanuele (1860–1952)
    Italian statesman; Prime Minister, 1917–1919.
Osuský, Štefan (1889–1973)
    Slovak supporter of Tomáš G. Masaryk during World War I. Secretary
    General of the Czecho-Slovak delegation at the Paris Peace Conference.
    Later, Ambassador to France.
Padarewski, Igancy (1860–1941)
    Polish Prime Minister, 1919–1921.
Palacký, František (1798–1876)
    Czech historian; a leader of the Czech national awakening.
Palmerston, Henry John Temple Lord (1784–1865)
    British statesman; Foreign Secretary, 1830–1841, 1846–1851; Home Sec-
    retary and Prime Minister, 1852–1855.
Paléologue, Maurice (1859–1944)
    Secretary-General; French Ministry of Foreign Affairs, 1920.
Palóczi-Horváth, Ádám (1760–1820)
    Poet and a self-proclaimed "historian" of the early Romantic period in
    Hungary.
Panafieu, Hector de
    French Minister to Poland, 1919.
Pašić, Nikola (1846–1926)
    Yugoslav statesman.
Paul-Boncour, Joseph (1873–1972)
    Socialist labor leader and politician; Minister of Foreign Affairs, 1933 and
    1938.
Pellé, Maurice (1863–1924)
    French general, commander of the French military mission in Czecho-
    slovakia, 1919–1920.

Petőfi, Sándor (1823–1849)
Poet and social radical; killed in the 1848–1849 Revolution.

Piccione, Luigi
Italian general, commander of the Czechoslovak forces occupying Slovakia in 1919.

Pilsudski, Jozef (1867–1935)
Polish soldier and statesman.

Polácsi, János
Teacher, union leader and Socialist Party activist in Pécs. Expelled from the party in November, 1920, for favoring Yugoslav annexation of the county of Baranya.

Polányi, Karl (1886–1964)
First president of the Galileo Circle; Radical Party member; later world-famous economic historian.

Pichon, Stephen (1857–1933)
Minister of Foreign Affairs in the Clemenceau cabinet.

Poincaré, Raymond (1860–1934)
President of France, 1914–1920 and Prime Minister, 1922–1924.

Popovici, Aurel C. (1863–1917)
Romanian nationalities leader and publicist in Hungary.

Popovics, Sándor (1862–1935)
Financier, Governor of the Austrian-Hungarian Bank, 1909–1919; Minister of Finance, February 1918–October 1918; Financial specialist of the Hungarian Peace Delegation in Neuilly, 1920.

Prešan, General Constantin
Commander in Chief of the Romanian army in Hungary, 1919.

Radič, Stepan (1871–1928)
Croatian political leader.

Raffay, Sándor (1866–1947)
Protestant bishop and theologian.

Rajić, Svetozar
Serb administrator.

Rákóczi, Ferenc II (1676–1735)
Prince of Transylvania and leader of the unsuccessful Hungarian War of Liberation, 1703–1711.

Rákosi, Jenő (1842–1929)
Writer, publicist and nationalist politician; active proponent of magyarization.

Rákosi, Mátyás (1892–1971)
A commissar of the Kun regime; a prisoner of the Horthy regime during the interwar years; Stalinist dictator after World War II.

Rakovskii, Khristian (1873–1941)
Comintern leader; Bulgarian by birth, Romanian by nationality; Soviet ambassador designate to Hungary, 1918; ambassador to England, to France in the 1920's.

Reményik, Sándor (1890-1941)
Hungarian poet, editor of a literary journal.
Renner, Karl (1870-1950)
Socialist politician; first Chancellor of the Republic of Austria.
Révai, József (1898-1959)
Hungarian writer and communist party theoretician.
Rolland, Romain (1866-1944)
French writer.
Romanelli, Guido (1876- ?)
Italian general, leader of the Italian military mission to Hungary, 1919.
Roosevelt, Nicholas (1893-1982)
Member of the Coolidge Mission in Hungary.
Rostow, Walt W. (b. 1916)
American economic historian and government official.
Rothmere, Harold Sidney Harmsworth Lord (1868-1940)
Conservative British politician and publisher. Publicly criticised the terms of the Peace Treaty of Trianon following 1927.
Roux, Charles
French ambassador to Romania.
Rugonfalvi-Kiss, István (1881-1957)
A traditionalist historian of the National Romantic School at the University of Debrecen.
Saint-Aulaire, Charles conte de (1866-1954)
French diplomat, ambassador to Romania, 1916-1920; Spain, 1920, and Great Britain, 1921-1924.
Sapieha, Prince Eustacy Kajetan (1881-1963)
Polish Foreign Minister, 1920-1921.
Schober, Johann (1874-1932)
Austrian Chancellor, 1921-1922.
Scialoja, Vittorio (1856-1933)
Italian Senator and Minister of Foreign Affairs, November 1919-June 1920 in the Nitti cabinet.
Serényi, Sándor
Hungarian Politburo member.
Serge, Victor (1890-1947)
Writer, international anarchist of Russian background.
Seton-Watson, Robert W. (1879-1951)
British scholar, founder and editor of *The New Europe*.
Seymour, Charles (1885-1963)
Scholar, American member of the Territorial Commission for Romania.
Sforza, Carlo Count (1873-1952)
Italian liberal politician; Prime Minister, 1920-1921.
Simonyi-Semadam, Sándor (1864-1946)
Hungarian Prime Minister, March 1920-July 1920.

Sixtus, Robert Borbon Count of Parma (1886–1934)
Brother-in-law of Emperor Karl, go-between during the period of secret peace feelers between Austria-Hungary and France.

Šmeral, Bohumir (1880–1941)
Left-wing socialist; founder of the Czechoslovak Communist Party, 1919–1929.

Smith, Walter Bedell (1895–1961)
American soldier and statesman. Delegate to the Paris Peace Conference of 1947; Ambassador to Moscow, 1946–1949; Director of the CIA, 1950–1952; Undersecretary of State, 1953–1954.

Smuts, Jan Christian (1870–1950)
South African politician and general, and minister in the Lloyd George cabinet. In April, 1919, he was sent to Hungary by the Peace Conference to negotiate with Béla Kun.

Somssich, József Count (1864–1941)
Diplomat; Minister of Foreign Affairs in the Friedrich and Huszár cabinets, 1919–1920; Ambassador to the Vatican, 1920–1924.

Sonnino, Giorgio Sidney (1847–1922)
Minister of Foreign Affairs in the Orlando cabinet.

Šrobár, Vavro (1876–1950)
Slovak politician, minister plenipotentiary for Slovak affairs, 1918–1920.

Stalin, Iosif Visarionovich (1879–1953)
Soviet dictator.

Steed, Henry Wickham (1871–1956)
British publicist of The Times, famous for his anti-Austro-Hungarian sentiments.

Štefánik, Milan R. (1880–1919)
Minister of War of the first Czechoslovak government.

Steier, Lajos (1885–1938)
Journalist, self-trained historian and a noted authority on the Slovak Question in Hungary.

Szabó, Dezső (1879–1945)
Novelist, essayist, important ideologist of the Hungarian Populist Movement.

Szabó, Dezső (1882–1962)
Historian and professor at the University of Debrecen and one of the younger members of the interwar Hungarian Positivist School.

Szabó, Imre (b. 1912)
Scientist, member of the Hungarian Academy of Sciences.

Szabó, István Negyatádi (1863–1924)
Hungarian agrarian political leader, Minister of Agriculture in various governments, 1919–1924.

Szálasi, Ferenc (1897–1946)
Leader of the fascist Arrow Cross Party; Nazi puppet dictator, 1944–1945; executed for war crimes.

Szamuely, Tibor (1890-1919)
Deputy People's Commissar of War in the Hungarian Soviet of 1919.

Szekfű, Gyula (1883-1955)
Interwar Hungary's most influential historian and a founder of the Hungarian *Geistesgeschichte* school.

Szende, Pál (1879-1934)
Radical, sociologist, historian, Minister of Finance in the Berinkey Government, 1919.

Szentgyörgyi, István (1842-1931)
Hungarian dramatist; School for the Dramatic Arts in Tirgu Mures was named after him.

Szerényi, Sándor

Szilassy, Gyula (1870- ?)
Professional Austro-Hungarian diplomat; Hungarian envoy to Switzerland, February to April, 1919.

Szmrecsányi, György (1876-1932)
Government official (*főispán*) Pozsony and Pozsony county, 1917-1918.

Sztójay, Döme (1883-1946)
Military man and diplomat with pro-Nazi sympathies; Prime minister of Hungary, March 1944-October 1944; executed for war crimes.

Tahy, László (1881-1940)
Hungarian diplomat and politician; Ambassador to Prague, 1920-1922.

Tardieu, André (1876-1945)
Politician; President of the Territorial Commission for Romania of the Paris Peace Conference; Prime Minister in 1929, 1930, and 1932.

Teleki, László (1811-1861)
Politician, writer, revolutionary, favored a liberal nationalities policy.

Teleki, Pál Count (1879-1941)
Noted geographer; conservative politician; Hungary's Foreign Minister, 1920-1921; Prime Minister, 1920-1921 and 1938-1941.

Tennyson, Alfred Lord (1809-1892)
English poet.

Thim, József (1864-1959)
Physician and self-trained historian, Hungary's most important authority on the Serbian Question.

Thurner, Michael
Mayor of Sopron.

Tisza, István (1861-1918)
Leading politician and statesman; Prime Minister of Hungary, 1903-1905 and 1913-1917.

Tisza, Kálmán (1830-1902)
Hungarian political leader; Prime Minister, 1875-1890.

Tittoni, Tomasso (1855–1931)
Italian Foreign Minister, 1919.

Tömörkényi, István (1866–1917)
Writer, anthropologist and antiquarian.

Toynbee, Arnold J. (1889–1975)
English historian whose *A Study of History* analyzes the rise and fall of human civilizations.

Troubridge, Sir Ernest (1862–1926)
British admiral, commanding on the Danube, 1919.

Tyrrell, William G. (1866–1947)
Assistant Under-Secretary of State for Foreign Affairs, 1918–1925.

Ullman, György Baron (1857–1925)
President of the Hungarian Credit Bank, 1909–1925.

Vaida Voevod, Alexandru (1872–1950)
Member of pre-war Hungarian Parliament; a leader of the Romanians in Hungary; member of the Romanian National Committee; Prime Minister of Romania, 1919.

Vesnić, Milenko (1862–1921)
Yugoslav statesman; representative of Yugoslavia to the Peace Conference, 1919–1920.

Vix, Fernand (1872– ?)
Lieutenant-Colonel, head of the Allied Military Mission in Hungary, 1918–1919.

Wekerle, Sándor (1848–1921)
Economist; Prime Minister of Hungary, 1906–1910, 1917–1918.

Wesselényi, Miklós Baron (1796–1850)
Political writer and member of the reform generation.

Wessely, László (1904–1978)
Communist writer, journalist translator.

Weterle, Rev. Father
For many years the protesting voice of Alsace in the German Imperial Parliament, later deputy in the French National Assembly.

William II (1859–1941)
German Emperor and King of Prussia, 1888–1918.

Wilson, Woodrow (1856–1924)
President of the United States, 1913–1921.

Wommert, Rudolf
Comintern delegate from Pécs.

Wrangel, Pietr Baron (1878–1928)
Commander of the Russian White armies, 1920.

Yates, Halsey E.
American military attaché to Bucharest, 1919.

Zanella, Ricardo
Member of the Fiume city council.

Zoványi, Jenő (1865–1958)
 Progressive Protestant church historian, known for his strong anti-Habsburg and anti-*Geistesgeschichte* views.

Zsombor, Géza
 Swabian leader and publicist in Western Hungary.

Gazetteer

The list below contains place names which appear in the texts or on the maps of this collection. The left column is in Hungarian, the right column contains their form in the other languages of the successor states.

Legend: Cz = Czecho-Slovak   G = German   R = Romanian   Russ = Russian
　　　　Uk = Ukrainian   Y = Serbo-Croat

Alsóőr	G. Unterwart
Arad	R. Arad
Bácska	Y. Bačka
Bánffyhunyad	R. Huedin
Bártfa	Cz. Bardiejov
	G. Bartfeld
Bega r.	R. Bega r.
Belényes	R. Beiuş
Bethlen	R. Betlen
Beszterce	R. Bistrite
	Cz. Bistríta
Besztercebánya	Cz. Baňská Bystrica
Borgó Pass	R. Borgo
Borszék	R. Borsec
Brasso	R. Braşov
	G. Kronstadt
Breznóbánya	Cz. Brezno nad Hronom
Csernova	Cz. Černova
Csallóköz	Cz. Žitný ostrov
	G. Grosse Schütt
Csap	Cz. Čop
	Russ. Chop
Csíkszerda	R. Miercurea Ciuc
Csucsa	R. Ciucea
Dés	R. Dej
Déva	Y. Deva
Dráva r.	Y. Drava
	G. Drau
Erdély	R. Ardeal
	G. Siebenburgen

Érsekujvár	Cz. Nové Zámky
Eperjes	Cz. Prešov
Eszék	Y. Osjek
Esztergom	Cz. Ostřihom
Felsőőr	G. Oberwart
Fiume	Y. Rijeka
Garam r.	Cz. Hron
Gölniczbánya	Cz. Gelnica
Gyergyószentmiklós	R. Gheorgheni
Gyulafehérvár	R. Alba Iulia
Hernád r.	Cz. Hornad
Holics	Cz. Holič
Homonna	Cz. Humenné
Ipoly r.	Cz. Ipel
	G. Eipel
Ipolyság	Cz. Ipel'ské Šahy
Karánsebes	R. Caransebeş
Kassa	Cz. Košice
	G. Kaschau
Késmárk	Cz. Kežmarok
Kolozsvár	R. Cluj-Napoca
	G. Klausenburg
Komárom	Cz. Komárno
	G. Komorn
Körmöczbánya	Cz. Kremnica
Kőrös r.	R. Crisul
Korpona	Cz. Krupina
Középpulya	G. Mittelpullendorf
Latorca r.	Cz. Latorice
Léva	Cz. Levice
Lipótvár	Cz. Leopoldov
	G. Leopoldstadt
Lippa	Cz. Lipova
Liptószentmiklós	Cz. Liptovský Sväty Mikuláš
Lőcse	Cz. Levoča
Losonc	Cz. Lučenec
Lugos	R. Lugoj
Máramarossziget	R. Sighetul Marmaţiei
Maros r.	R. Mureş
Marosvásárhely	R. Tirgu-Mureş
Munkács	Russ. Mukachevo
Nagybánya	R. Baia Mare
Nagybecskerek	Y. Veliki Bečkerek
Nagykároly	R. Carei
Nagyrőce	Cz. Revúca

Nagyszeben	R. Sibiu
	G. Hermannstadt
Nagyszombat	Cz. Trnava
Nagyvárad	R. Oradea
	G. Grosswardein
Naszód	R. Năsaud
Nyitra	Cz. Nitra
Nyitra r.	Cz. Nitra
Olt r.	R. Oltul
Őrisziget	G. Siget in der Wart
Pécs	G. Fünfkirchen
Pöstény	Cz. Piest'any
Pozsony	Cz. Bratislava
	G. Pressburg
Radna (Máriaradna)	R. Radna
Radna Pass	R. Rodna
Raho	R. Rachov
Rimaszombat	Cz. Rimovská Sobota
Ruttka	Cz. Vrútky
Soborsin	R. Săvîrşin
Selmecbánya	Cz. Baňská Št'avnica
Sepsiszentgyörgy	R. Sfîntu Georghe
Sopron	G. Oedenburg
Szamos r.	R. Someşul
Szabadka	Y. Subotica
	G. Mariatheresiopol
Szalard	R. Salard
Szamosújvár	R. Cherla
Szatmárnémeti	R. Satu-Mare
Szászváros	R. Orăstie
Székelyudvarhely	R. Odorheiu-Secuiesc
Szilágycseh	R. Cehul-Silvaniei
Temes	R. Timiş
Temesvár	R. Timişoara
Tisza r.	G. Theiss
Topolya	Y. Topolje
Trencsén	Cz. Trenčin
Turóczszentmárton	Cz. Turčiansky Svätý Martin
Újvidék	Y. Novi Sad
	G. Neusatz
Ung r.	Cz. Už
	G. Uh
Ungvár	Uk. Užhorod
	Rus. Uzhgorod
Uzsok Pass	Cz. Už Pass

Vaskoh	R. Vaşcău
Verecke Pass	Cz. Veretsk
Zám	R. Zam
Zimony	Y. Zemun
Zilah	R. Zalău
Zimony	Y. Zimun
Zombor	Y. Sombor
Zolyom	Cz. Zvolen
Zsolna	Cz. Žilina

List of Maps and Charts

1. Ethnic Hungarian Population of the Kingdom of Hungary in 1910 and of Partitioned Hungary After 1920
2. American Boundary Recommendations and the Trianon Borders of Hungary
3. Transylvania and Southeastern Europe
4. The Vix and Other Demarcation Lines
5. Opportunities for Hungarian Language Education at the Elementary and High School Level in Romania

ETHNIC HUNGARIAN POPULATION OF THE KINGDOM OF HUNGARY IN 1910 AND OF PARTITIONED HUNGARY AFTER 1920

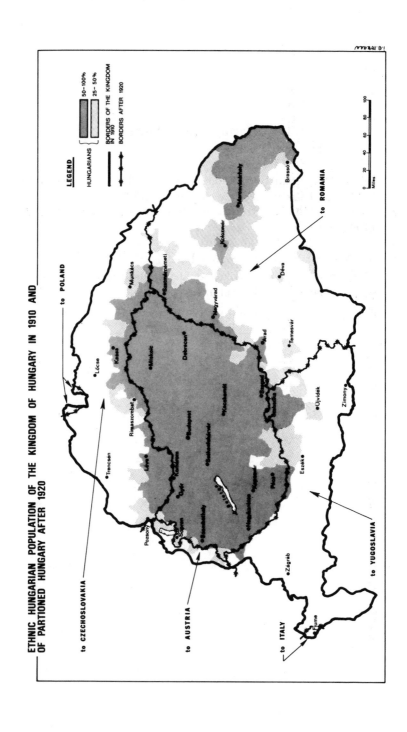

LEGEND

HUNGARIANS
- 50-100%
- 25-50%

— BORDERS OF THE KINGDOM IN 1910
—+—+— BORDERS AFTER 1920

to POLAND

to CZECHOSLOVAKIA

to AUSTRIA

to ITALY

to YUGOSLAVIA

to ROMÁNIA

Miles
0 20 40 60 80 100

AMERICAN BOUNDARY RECOMMENDATIONS AND THE TRIANON BORDERS OF HUNGARY

LEGEND

— — — PRE-WAR BORDERS OF HUNGARY (1914).

—○—○— AMERICAN BOUNDARY RECOMMENDATIONS.

▬▬▬ TRIANON TREATY BORDERS (JUNE 4, 1920).
(borderline omitted where it coincides with
the American boundary recommendations -
○—○— rim omitted where borders do not
concern post-war Hungary proper).

RUTHENIA

TRANSYLVANIA

BÁNÁT

Adriatic Sea

Ungvár
Munkács
Máramarossziget
Kassa
Szatmárnémeti
Nagykároly
Nagyvárad
Szamos
Kolozsvár
Nagyszeben
Debrecen
Körös
Maros
Arad
Temesvár
Béga
Rimaszombat
Szeged
Szabadka
Zenta
Topolya
Pozsony
Komárom
Vác
Budapest
Duna
Pécs
Dráva
Száva
Zágráb
Fiume

Miles
0 20 40 60 80 100

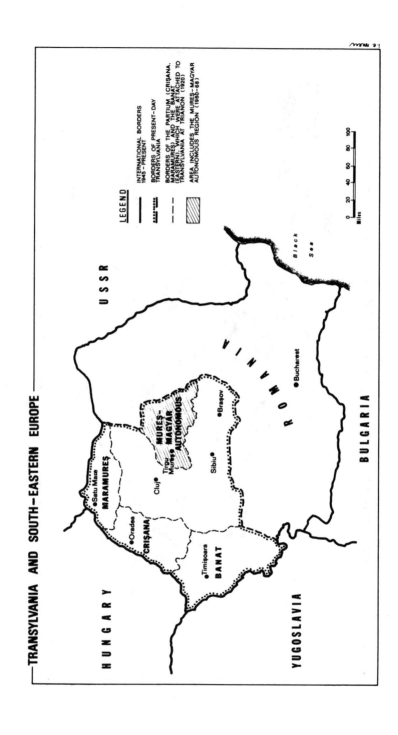

TRANSYLVANIA AND SOUTH-EASTERN EUROPE

LEGEND

INTERNATIONAL BORDERS
1945 – PRESENT

BORDERS OF PRESENT-DAY
TRANSYLVANIA

BORDERS OF THE PARTIUM (CRISANA,
MARAMURES), AND THE BANAT
(EASTERN), WHICH WERE ATTACHED TO
TRANSYLVANIA AT TRIANON (1920)

AREA INCLUDES THE MURES – MAGYAR
AUTONOMOUS REGION (1960–68)

Miles
0   20   40   60   80   100

USSR

Black
Sea

HUNGARY

Satu Mare

MARAMURES

Oradea

CRISANA

Timișoara

BANAT

Cluj

Tirgu
Mures

MURES–
MAGYAR
AUTONOMOUS

Sibiu

Brașov

ROMANIA

Bucharest

YUGOSLAVIA

BULGARIA

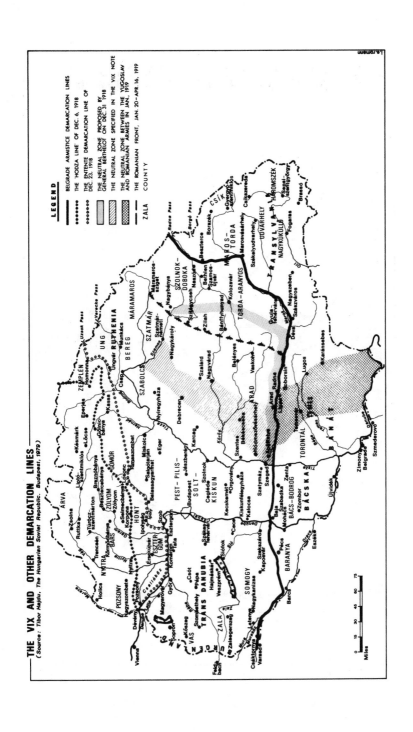

THE VIX AND OTHER DEMARCATION LINES

(Source: Tibor Hajdu, The Hungarian Soviet Republic. Budapest, 1979)

LEGEND

●●●●●● BELGRADE ARMISTICE DEMARCATION LINES

●●●●●● THE "HODZA LINE" OF DEC. 6, 1918

●●●●●● THE ENTENTE DEMARCATION LINE OF DEC. 23, 1918

▨ THE NEUTRAL ZONE PROPOSED BY GENERAL BERTHELOT ON DEC. 31, 1918

▨ THE NEUTRAL ZONE SPECIFIED IN THE VIX NOTE

▨ THE NEUTRAL ZONE BETWEEN THE YUGOSLAV AND ROMANIAN ARMIES IN JAN., 1919

— · — THE ROMANIAN FRONT, JAN. 20-APR. 16, 1919

ZALA COUNTY

OPPORTUNITIES FOR HUNGARIAN LANGUAGE EDUCATION AT THE ELEMENTARY AND HIGH SCHOOL LEVELS IN ROMANIA*

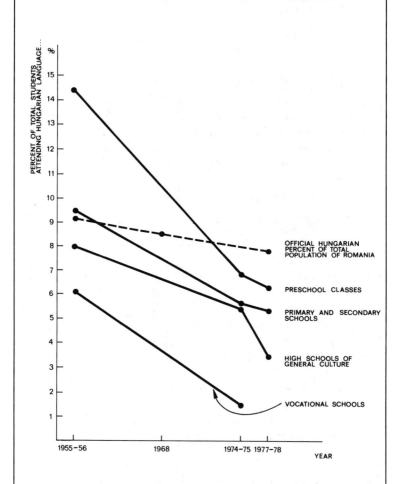

PERCENT OF TOTAL STUDENTS ATTENDING HUNGARIAN LANGUAGE...

%

OFFICIAL HUNGARIAN PERCENT OF TOTAL POPULATION OF ROMANIA

PRESCHOOL CLASSES

PRIMARY AND SECONDARY SCHOOLS

HIGH SCHOOLS OF GENERAL CULTURE

VOCATIONAL SCHOOLS

1955–56   1968   1974–75 1977–78

YEAR

*Sources:

The Hungarian Nationality in Romania. (Bucharest, Romania: Meridiane Publishing House, 1976) pp. 8, 15-17.

A Living Reality in Romania Today: Full Harmony and Equality Between the Romanian People and the Coinhabiting Nationalities. (Bucharest, Romania, 1978) p. 15.

List of Contributors to Trianon

Magda Ádám—Senior Research Fellow, Hungarian Academy of Sciences, Institute of History, Budapest

William M. Batkay—Assistant Professor of Political Science, Montclair State College, New Jersey

Iván T. Berend—Professor and Chairman of the Department of Economic History, University of Economics, Budapest

Stephen Borsody—Professor Emeritus of History, Chatham College

Edward Chaszar—Professor of Political Science, Indiana University of Pennsylvania

Lee Congdon—Associate Professor of History, James Madison University, Harrisonburg, Virginia

Stephen Fischer-Galati—Professor of History, University of Colorado

Yeshayahu Jelinek—Senior Lecturer, Ben-Gurion Research Institute, Sdeh Boker, Israel

Paul Jonas—Professor of Economics, University of New Mexico

Josef Kalvoda—Professor of History, Saint Joseph College, West Hartford, Connecticut

Thomas Karfunkel—Professor of History, New York City Technical College of CUNY

Stephen D. Kertesz—Committee on International Relations, University of Notre Dame

Béla K. Király—Professor of History, Brooklyn College and the Graduate School and University Center, CUNY; Director, Program on Society in Change

Frank Koszorus, Jr.—Practices law in Washington, D.C.; *Pro Bono* Associate, International Human Rights Law Group

Andrew Ludanyi—Associate Professor, Political Science, Ohio Northern University

István I. Mócsy—Assistant Professor of History, The University of Santa Clara, California

Károly Nagy—Professor of Sociology, Middlesex County Community College, New Jersey

Zsuzsa L. Nagy—Senior Research Fellow, Hungarian Academy of Sciences, Institute of History, Budapest

Anne W. Orde—Lecturer in Modern History, University of Durham, Great Britain

Mária Ormos—Senior Research Fellow, Hungarian Academy of Sciences, Institute of History, Budapest

Peter Pastor—Professor of History, Montclair State College, New Jersey

György Ránki—Deputy Director, Hungarian Academy of Sciences, Institute of History, Budapest; Director, Hungarian Chair, University of Indiana

Thomas L. Sakmyster—Associate Professor of History, University of Cincinnati

Ivan Sanders—Professor of English, Suffolk Community College, New York

George Schöpflin—Lecturer in East European Politics, London School of Economics, Great Britain

Hugh Seton-Watson—Professor of Russian History, School of Slavonic and East European Studies, University of London

Michael Sozan—Associate Professor of Sociology-Anthropology, Slippery Rock State College, Pennsylvania

Thomas Spira—Professor of History; Editor, *Canadian Review of Studies in Nationalism,* University of Prince Edward Island

Sandor Taraszovics—President, Committee for Danubian Research, Washington, D.C.

Leslie C. Tihany—Distinguished Service Professor Emeritus, Northern Kentucky University; Adjunct Professor of History, University of Cincinnati

Agnes Huszar Vardy—Associate Professor, Department of Humanities, Robert Morris College, Pittsburgh

Stephen Bela Vardy—Professor of History; Duquesne University

Károly Vigh—Doctoral Candidate, Hungarian National Museum Budapest